Marriage, Family, and Intimate Relations

Marriage, Family, and Intimate Relations

Ronald G. Stover
South Dakota State University

Christine A. Hope
College of Charleston

Harcourt Brace College Publishers

Fort Worth   Philadelphia   San Diego   New York   Orlando   Austin   San Antonio
Toronto   Montreal   London   Sydney   Tokyo

Publisher Ted Buchholz
Acquisitions Editor Chris Klein
Senior Developmental Editor Meera Dash
Project Editor Nancy Lombardi
Production Manager Erin Gregg
Book Designer David A. Day
Photo/Permissions Editor Mark Brelsford

Address for Editorial Correspondence: Harcourt Brace & Company, 301 Commerce Street, Suite 3700, Fort Worth, TX 76102.

Address for Orders: Harcourt Brace & Company, 6277 Sea Harbor Drive, Orlando, FL 32887. 1-800-782-4479, or 1-800-433-0001 (in Florida).

Cover art: Ron Taylor Crouch, *Reunion,* 1991. Oil on canvas. Collection of the artist. Photograph by Leo Wesson.

Photo credits and permissions appear on pages PC-1–PC-2 which constitute a continuation of the copyright page.

ISBN: 0-03-031263-9

Library of Congress Catalog Card Number: 91-78062

Printed in the United States of America

345678901 039 98765432

To the memory of
Pauline Wright Stover —
a widow who raised two sons alone,
a kind, gentle, and loving single mother —
and to
Clifford and Dolores Hope,
who continue to teach their six adult children
about family life, justice, equality, and humility
through the examples
they set.

Teachers of marriage and family and related courses have special challenges arising from the diversity of students who typically enroll in such courses. Because these courses tend to be classified as "service" courses, few instructors can make safe academic and personal assumptions about the students sitting before them on the first day of class. The classes might include some students with no experience in college-level social science courses, some who are taking the course as part of a social science major, some first-semester freshmen, some last-semester seniors, and students with a variety of academic skills. Nor can the instructor make easy assumptions about the students' relationships and living arrangements. The current class of one of the authors, for example, includes married students with small children, cohabiting students, students living with one or both parents or a parent and a stepparent, and students living with roommates in dorms and apartments. Students also come from a variety of socioeconomic, racial, ethnic, and religious backgrounds and range in age from late teen to senior citizen.

Despite their diversity, these students share an intense curiosity about the course's subject matter. They come to class with questions and opinions. Their questions, curiosity, and willingness to apply class material to personal life offer definite advantages to instructors of marriage and family courses.

In writing *Marriage, Family, and Intimate Relations,* we faced both challenges and advantages. We sought to anticipate students' questions, direct and enhance their curiosity, and communicate the value of social science applied to this particular area of human social life. We have written this book not only to present the most recent interdisciplinary research in easy terms, but also to show students how that research can help them better understand past, present, and future relationships.

Themes, Scope, and Sequence

Thirty-three years of full-time teaching have led us to conclude that our book should have three major themes: intimate relationships, choice, and change. Given the fact that today's students live in a variety of family and nonfamily arrangements, it would be restrictive to limit our book to "marriage" or to "marriage and family." We use the term "intimate relationships" to include marital and family relationships but also close sexual and nonsexual relationships outside the context of marriage and family. Thus, this is not just a "marriage" book, not just a "family" book, and not just a book on sexuality and sexual relationships; rather, it is a book about all types of intimacy.

Many of the questions students ask about intimate relationships are questions about choices and the consequences of those choices: What should I look for in choosing a marriage partner? Why did my parents choose to divorce? What causes some people to choose homosexual relationships over heterosexual ones? Are children hurt when both parents choose to work outside the home? Social science can help students understand the choices they have made thus far, make them aware of and appreciative of options they might never have considered, and point out the consequences of various choices. We see *Marriage, Family, and Intimate Relations* as a vehicle for communicating a wide range of fascinating social science information about choices in relationships, marriages, and families to a college audience.

The themes of choice and change are closely interrelated in that social change shapes the choices available. Many students come to the course with a vague belief that "families are really different than they used to be" without knowing when change occurred, what has changed, and what has not. Changes in the nature of intimate relationships, marriages, and families are ongoing, influenced by large-scale changes in the economy and society. It is often difficult to see that family change is a constant throughout history, not simply a phenomenon of the past twenty years. To breathe life and ease into the study of change in marriages and families, we use the concept of the birth cohort, a group of people born within a given range of years. The first chapter of the text introduces four twentieth-century birth cohorts known as New Century, Depression, Baby Boom, and Baby Bust. Subsequent chapters compare the attitudes and behaviors of the people of these four different generations. The cohort is a valuable teaching tool, but we also hope that students will enjoy comparing their own generations with others.

Marriage, Family, and Intimate Relations consists of fifteen chapters. The text is comprehensive enough to cover the critical issues but short enough to manage within a single quarter or semester. Wherever possible, we have incorporated information about racial, ethnic, and religious differences and similarities into all chapters rather than "ghettoizing" them in separate chapters. We applied the same principle to relationship aggression. Rather than a separate chapter on family dysfunction and violence, we integrate the material. For example, we discuss dating violence in the dating chapter, spouse abuse in the chapter on communication and conflict, and child abuse in the parent-child chapter.

Most of the chapters end with an "Alternative Choice" or "Alternative Situation" section that describes a position currently occupied by a minority of the population. Examples include staying single, adopting a child, and sharing household work equally. By discussing such nontraditional choices in the context of an appropriate chapter rather than lumping them into an "alternatives" chapter, we hope to convey that these are legitimate choices, not deviant ways of life.

Pedagogical Features

Most college teachers expect students to do much of their learning outside of class. We have designed our book to encourage active out-of-class learning. Several features "hook" students into the chapter, help them follow the chapter once they have begun to read, aid them in remembering the major concepts and research findings, and reinforce the impact of choice and change on intimate relationships. Every chapter has all or most of the following features:

1. A chapter outline provides an overview of the chapter.
2. "What Do You Think?" questions ask students to give their opinions about topics they will read about in the chapter. These questions help students think about their opinions, often make them aware of alternatives, and compel them to review their opinions in a social science context. For questions that come from sociological surveys, we include survey results in the chapter, allowing students to compare their answers with those of a national sample.
3. A compelling literary selection, vignette, or news item at the beginning of the chapter encapsulates one or more of the concerns of the chapter.
4. **Cohort Comparisons** are featured in nine of the chapters. These sections compare the experiences of the four twentieth-century birth cohorts introduced in Chapter 1. For example, Chapter 9 on "Dividing Marital Work" has a Cohort Comparison section about the differences in participation of women in the labor force. The Cohort Comparisons show how groups of people responded to historical and technological changes, and encourage students of all ages to think about people of other generations.
5. **Personal Applications**, in fourteen chapters, allow students to quiz themselves about an aspect of their intimate relationships or offer practical information related to the chapter. For example, Chapter 14 on the "End of A Marriage" has a Personal Application that suggests ways of helping children cope with the divorce of their parents.

6. Major concepts appear in bold typeface with definitions in the text, and a glossary in the margin facilitates review of these concepts.
7. Tables and figures summarize quantitative information and illustrate historical change.
8. A chapter summary succinctly reviews the main ideas of the chapter.

All chapters address the themes of intimate relationships, choices, and change intrinsically as well as explicitly in the pedagogy. The ''What Do You Think?'' questions, Personal Applications, and in-text Alternative Choice sections reinforce the element of choice in intimate relationships. The Cohort Comparisons and sections dealing with social change illuminate the importance of change.

Ancillaries

A number of multimedia materials are available to help students and teachers use the textbook more effectively.

1. **Study Guide.** A student study guide, created by the textbook authors, will help students recognize and learn the book's major concepts and findings and aid them in preparing for exams. For each chapter of the text, the study guide provides an overview, learning objectives (repeated in the instructor's manual and referenced from the test bank), a vocabulary review, and practice test questions.
2. **Instructor's Manual.** The instructor's manual describes some of the methods and supplements we have found helpful in making our own courses relevant and rewarding for students. The manual includes a sample syllabus for the course, chapter outlines, teaching objectives (from the study guide), methods of using special features of the textbook, lecture ideas, and recommendations for in-class activities such as debates, oral presentations, videos, and surveys. The instructor's manual also provides a list of books and periodical articles to help in lecture preparation or to assign as supplementary reading.
3. **Test Bank.** A test bank, created by Pamela Chaney-Land of Cincinnati Technical College, features approximately 1,125 multiple-choice, true-false, and short-answer questions. The questions involve recalling material, applying knowledge, and reading figures from the textbook. The questions are grouped by learning objectives listed in the instructor's manual and in the study guide.

4. **Computerized Test Bank and Gradebook Software.** Available in IBM, Macintosh, and Apple formats, the testing software, ExaMaster™, allows you to create tests using few keystrokes, guided by easy-to-follow screen prompts. ExaMaster™ offers three easy-to-use options for test creation:

   a. EasyTest lets you create an entire test from a single screen in a few easy steps. You can select questions from the database or, using your own parameters, let EasyTest randomly select the questions for you.

   b. FullTest lets you use the whole range of available options:
   - select questions as you preview them on the screen
   - edit existing questions or add your own questions
   - add or edit graphics in the MS-DOS version
   - link related questions, instructions, and graphics
   - randomly select questions using a wider range of criteria
   - create your own criteria on two open keys
   - block specific questions from random selection
   - print up to 99 different versions of the same test along with answer sheets

   c. RequesTest is an option available to those who do not have access to a computer. When you call 1 (800) 447-9457, software specialists will compile questions according to your criteria and either mail or fax you a test within 48 hours!

      Included with ExaMaster™ is ExamRecord, a gradebook program that allows you to record, curve, graph, and print out grades. ExamRecord takes raw scores and converts them into grades using your criteria. You can see the distribution of the grades in a bar graph or on a plotted curve.

      If questions arise, the Software Support Hotline is available Monday through Friday, 9 A.M.–4 P.M. (Central Time) at 1 (800) 447-9457.

5. **Overhead Teaching Transparencies.** A set of 50 full-color acetates enhances classroom lectures. The transparencies illustrate such topics as male and female differences, comparisons of family income, households headed by women, the U.S. divorce rate, spending habits of single men and women, and age distribution in the U.S. population.

6. **Video Programs.** Selected video programs from the Dallas County Community College District telecourse will be available to instructors, based on the HBJ video policy. These half-hour videotapes encourage students to tap into their sociological imaginations. The programs include ''Social Class,'' ''Family,'' ''Social Change,'' and other titles.

Acknowledgments

Large projects require help from many quarters. As we are teaching, we are taught. Over the years, our students have contributed to this book in numerous ways. Their responses to the material we presented in class influenced some of our choices of topics, guided us in selecting visual aids, kept our ''What Do You Think?'' exercises relevant and strong, and undoubtedly helped the book in other ways.

The carefully considered reactions and thoughtful suggestions of instructors who reviewed the prospectus, every chapter, and the final draft of the book helped reduce the weaknesses and develop the strengths of the text. These reviewers were: Richard Barasch, Rancho Santiago College; Carol Carroll, Middle Tennessee State University; Pamela Chaney-Land, Cincinnati Technical College; Peter Chroman, College of San Mateo; Mary Beth Collins, Central Piedmont Community College; John Engel, University of Hawaii; Carol Gardner, Indiana University, Indianapolis; Mary Louise Glen, University of Toledo; Daniel McDonald, Marquette University; Charles Petranek, University of Southern Indiana; Richard Phillips, Kalamazoo Valley Community College; William Pooler, Syracuse University; Nasim Rao, Belleville Area College; Ellen Rosengarten, Sinclair Community College; Jack Sattel, Normandale Community College; Metaleen Thomas, Caldwell Community College; John York, Sam Houston State University; and Andrea Zabel, Midland College.

Our editors also obtained information about marriage, family, and intimate relationship courses for us through surveys and conversations held at conventions and on campuses. We gained particular insight from Richard Barasch, Rancho Santiago College; Suzanne Brandon, College of St. Catherine; Ben B. Bruggen, College of Lake County; Pamela Chaney-Land, Cincinnati Technical College; Peter Chroman, College of San Mateo; Robert E. Clark, Midwestern State University; James E. Floyd, Macon College; Nancy Greenwood, Purdue University; Dianne Kochenburg, Mission College; Larry Peterson, Memphis State University; Jack Sattel, Normandale Community College; Jean Giles-Sims, Texas Christian University; Monica A. Seff, University of Texas, Arlington; Sylvia Stalnaker, Southwest Texas State University; Kenrick S. Thompson, Northern Michigan University; and J. Allen Williams, Jr., University of Nebraska.

We received invaluable help from the staff at Holt, Rinehart and Winston, and later at Harcourt Brace Jovanovich. Senior developmental editor Meera K. Dash and project editor Nancy Lombardi deserve special thanks. They taught us the many elements necessary to produce a good book and handled our frequent fumbles with patience, good humor, and understanding.

Closer to home, we received guidance and encouragement, particularly in the early stages, from experienced sociologist textbook author and colleague, George E. Dickinson, College of Charleston. Jack Seitz of Wofford College voluntarily and consistently provided newspaper clippings on children's issues. C. L. Abercrombie, also of Wofford College, contributed to the project in many ways; the most tangible of these involved steering a 1946 Taylorcraft through cloudy skies so that our original prospectus could be delivered to the appropriate editor. Penny Stover assisted in many aspects of the book's preparation. She coordinated the permissions, checked figures and references, and offered valuable suggestions as we read through our final draft. Thank you, Penny.

Since we are both full-time teachers and perform the usual service, administrative, and research obligations associated with academic life, the immense amount of time dedicated to this text was often taken from our own intimate relationships. We wish to acknowledge the sacrifices our loved ones made to accommodate our need to spend time on "the book." Perhaps now that the book is nearing its final stages, we can make up for the lost hours, missed family gatherings, and late birthday cards. We will certainly try.

R.G.S.
C.A.H.

Contents in Brief

CONTENTS

DATING AND PREMARITAL SEX

CHAPTER 4

CHAPTER 5 | COHABITATION

CHAPTER 6 | THE DECISION TO MARRY

CHAPTER 9 | THE TASKS OF MARRIAGE: DIVIDING MARITAL WORK

CHAPTER 10 | THE TASKS OF MARRIAGE: MANAGING MONEY IN A CHANGING ECONOMY

CHAPTER 13 | MARRIAGES AND FAMILIES IN THE MIDDLE AND
             LATER YEARS

CHAPTER 14 | THE END OF A MARRIAGE

REMARRIAGE AND STEPFAMILIES | CHAPTER 15

FEATURES

Marriage, Family,
and Intimate Relations

CHAPTER 1

INTIMATE RELATIONSHIPS, CHOICES, AND CHANGES

For each of the following items, please circle the response that best represents your opinion.

1. When there are children in the family, parents should stay together even if they don't get along.

   Strongly Agree   Agree   Don't Know
   Disagree   Strongly Disagree

2. Do you feel almost all married couples who can *ought* to have children?

   Yes   It Depends   No

3. Most of the important decisions in the life of the family should be made by the man of the house.

   Strongly Agree   Agree   Don't Know
   Disagree   Strongly Disagree

4. If a man and woman have sex relations before marriage, do you think it is:

   Always Wrong   Almost Always Wrong
   Wrong Only Sometimes   Not Wrong at All

5. What is your opinion about a married person having sexual relations with someone other than the marriage partner?

   Always Wrong   Almost Always Wrong
   Wrong Only Sometimes   Not Wrong at All

Otto (widowed, remarried, divorced, remarried again) and his wife Maxine (widowed, remarried) live on a Maryland farm with the four youngest children from Otto's first marriage and the two children, now adopted by Otto, from Maxine's first marriage. They raise most of their own food and are nearly economically self-sufficient (Howard, 1978).

In Glassboro, New Jersey, ten college students share a house in a neighborhood zoned for family housing. The ten maintain a common checking account and share meals and household chores (Sullivan, 1990).

Angela, a secretary, lives with her nine-year-old son Buzzy in a Long Island apartment complex. Angela never married Buzzy's father, who departed when Buzzy was two (Howard, 1978).

Lauren, a school speech pathologist, and Blair, a school social worker, have been involved in a relationship for seven years. They currently share a suburban home with Lauren's two teenage children from a previous marriage. The children visit their father on weekends (Blumstein & Schwartz, 1983).

Millie and her brother Mortimer, both in their eighties, share a modest home in a small town. Millie never married and spent most of her adult life living with a variety of female roommates, all of whom are now deceased. Mortimer moved in with Millie after his wife died two years ago.

Henry, a department store executive, and Gene, a free-lance illustrator, share a spacious duplex. Henry and Gene have lived together as a gay couple for thirty-eight years (Blumstein & Schwartz, 1983).

Oscar, a truck driver, and his wife Gloria share a four-room inner-city apartment with seven other people—their own four youngest children, their son's girlfriend and her child, and a family friend, who is staying with Oscar and Gloria until she makes peace with her own family. There will soon be two more people in the apartment—one of the daughters and the son's girlfriend are both pregnant (Valentine, 1978).

Keith and Karen, married for sixteen years, live in a luxury apartment complex in Atlanta. Both have time-consuming jobs in the television industry and lead active professional and social lives. They have no children and plan to have none.

INTIMATE RELATIONSHIPS, MARRIAGES, AND FAMILIES

In each of the cases introducing this chapter, two or more people share living space, resources, and some degree of emotional affection. Each grouping is the result of a series of choices made over a period of time—to follow heterosexual or homosexual orientations, to marry or not to, to have children or to avoid having children, to move out or to stay put. Some, but not all, of these household groupings would have been extremely rare one hundred years ago or even thirty years ago; some are becoming more common with each passing year. Although each of the household groups described has some family-like characteristics, none perfectly matches the most prevalent standard family image: a husband and wife in their first marriage living with their dependent children.

This text deals with marriages, families, and other types of intimate relationships in the United States today. It describes the kinds of choices people make in deciding whether, when, and how to live with others in shared households and the consequences that follow the choices. You will learn how people seek, develop, sustain, and break close ties with others and how the patterns of seeking, developing, sustaining, and breaking up have changed over the course of U.S. history. You will also discover how age, gender, social class, race, and ethnic background shape peoples' choices.

Chapter 1 introduces the major themes of the text. First, we will define a few of the core concepts used throughout the text—intimate relationship, marriage, family, and household—and explain how they are connected to one another. The people presented in the introductory vignettes will serve as examples in illustrating some of these concepts.

1 Intimate Relationships, Choices, and Changes

Next, we will look at the issue of choice, discussing the freedom to make intimate relationship choices and the recent expansion of such choices as well as the responsibility and limits involved in choice-making. The next major section of the chapter deals with social change. Here we will describe some of the major changes in U.S. family life over the last 300 years and the factors shaping these changes. The final part of the social change section focuses on twentieth century changes by introducing the cohort comparison method of analysis.

What Is an Intimate Relationship?

Intimate relationship
a sharing, emotionally and physically close, committed tie between two people.

An **intimate relationship** is a sharing, emotionally and physically close, committed tie between two people. People who are intimate with one another typically share living quarters or at least spend a great deal of time with one another. Their possessions—money, furniture, stereo

Does this scene match your image of a family?

systems, tools, dishes—are often so commingled that it is impossible to say what belongs to whom. More importantly, intimacy involves a sharing and uncovering of selves. The word "intimate" is derived from the Latin word *intimus*, meaning "inner" or "inmost" (Perlman & Fehr, 1987). People who are intimate tell one another their private thoughts, dreams, insecurities, and triumphs; they *know* a great deal about one another. Lillian Rubin (1983), in a book about intimate relationships between men and women, expressed it like this:

> Intimacy is some kind of reciprocal expression of feeling and thought, not out of fear or dependent need, but out of a wish to know another's inner life and to be able to share one's own (p. 90).

Intimacy also involves physical closeness and affection. Intimate partners kiss, hug, hold hands, caress, or otherwise show physical affection for one another. They are comfortable doing so; the physical closeness between them is mutual and noncoercive. Often, a part of the physical closeness is sexual in nature. However, a relationship can be intimate without being sexual, and many sexual relationships are not intimate ones.

An intimate relationship is a committed relationship. The people involved in it intend to stay close for a long period of time, trust one another, are willing to make sacrifices and help each other, and feel that their relationship is special and exclusive (Kersten & Kersten, 1988; Perlman & Fehr, 1987). Intimate partners are committed to one another's well-being. One partner knows what the other needs and is willing to use his or her own resources to help obtain it. To borrow writer Francine Klagsburn's (1985) words from her book *Married People: Staying Together in the Age of Divorce,*

> ... such a commitment requires an expansion of self, an ability to feel what someone else feels, know what someone else needs and put oneself out, when necessary, to satisfy the other person's feelings and needs (p. 21).

In recent years, both researchers and the general public have directed most of their attention toward the emotional closeness and communicative aspects of intimacy and away from the commitment aspect (Cancian, 1987; Veroff, Douvan, & Kulka, 1981). To measure intimacy, social scientists ask individuals involved in relationships questions about how much time they spend together, how often they disagree and how they resolve their conflicts, whether and how they are physically affectionate, and how often they share their fears and dreams with one another, among other things. The following Personal Application provides an example of one intimacy scale researchers use.

Personal Application

Miller Social Intimacy Scale

	Very Rarely			Some of the Time			Almost Always		
1. When you have leisure time how often do you choose to spend it with him/her alone?	1	2	3	4	5	6	7	8	9	10
2. How often do you keep very personal information to yourself and do not share it with him/her?	1	2	3	4	5	6	7	8	9	10
3. How often do you show him/her affection?	1	2	3	4	5	6	7	8	9	10
4. How often do you confide very personal information to him/her?	1	2	3	4	5	6	7	8	9	10
5. How often are you able to understand his/her feelings?	1	2	3	4	5	6	7	8	9	10
6. How often do you feel close to him/her?	1	2	3	4	5	6	7	8	9	10

	Not Much			A Little			A Great Deal		
7. How much do you like to spend time alone with him/her?	1	2	3	4	5	6	7	8	9	10
8. How much do you feel like being encouraging and supportive to him/her when he/she is unhappy?	1	2	3	4	5	6	7	8	9	10
9. How close do you feel to him/her most of the time?	1	2	3	4	5	6	7	8	9	10
10. How important is it to you to listen to his/her very personal disclosures?	1	2	3	4	5	6	7	8	9	10
11. How satisfying is your relationship with him/her?	1	2	3	4	5	6	7	8	9	10
12. How affectionate do you feel towards him/her?	1	2	3	4	5	6	7	8	9	10
13. How important is it to you that he/she understands your feelings?	1	2	3	4	5	6	7	8	9	10
14. How much damage is caused by a typical disagreement in your relationship with him/her?	1	2	3	4	5	6	7	8	9	10
15. How important is it to you that he/she be encouraging and supportive to you when you are unhappy?	1	2	3	4	5	6	7	8	9	10
16. How important is it to you that he/she show you affection?	1	2	3	4	5	6	7	8	9	10
17. How important is your relationship with him/her in your life?	1	2	3	4	5	6	7	8	9	10

Source: Miller & Lefcourt, 1982, p. 516.

Marriage and Intimate Relationships: What's the Connection?

What is the connection between marriages and intimate relationships? Are all marriages also intimate relationships? Is marriage the only form an intimate relationship can take?

It is probably accurate to say that when most people in the contemporary United States think about "marriage" in the *ideal* sense, they think of the characteristics of intimate relationships we have described. It is also probably correct to say that marriage is the most common type of intimate relationship in the United States today. However, "marriage" and "intimate relationship" do not have identical meanings.

Marriage is a legally and socially recognized union between at least two adults involving certain obligations and privileges. In the United States, a legal marriage can involve only two people—one man and one woman—and a person can be involved in only one marriage at a time. Each state has additional requirements a couple must meet before their marriage can be recognized. In the introductory vignettes, Otto and Maxine (the economically self-sufficient remarried couple), Oscar and Gloria (the husband and wife sharing their small living space with their large family), and Keith and Karen (the television professionals with no children) all meet the definition of marriage.

> **Marriage**
> a legally and socially recognized union between at least two adults involving certain obligations and privileges.

Although many couples who marry do meet "intimate relationship" criteria, no couple has to prove intimacy in order to marry or stay married. Some couples choose to marry in order to have their already established intimate relationship recognized by others and to gain the advantages of marriage. Others marry before they are truly intimate but develop an intimate relationship during the course of their marriage. Still other couples lose the intimacy they had at the beginning of marriage but still remain married. Some marry and stay married without ever developing an intimate relationship in all respects. For example, quite a few wives, although sexually involved with and committed to their husbands, continue to share their innermost secrets and concerns with their same-sex friends rather than with their spouses (Thompson & Walker, 1989, p. 846). Thus, not all marriages are intimate relationships in every sense.

Nor are all intimate relationships marriages. Some male-female couples who are dating, engaged, or living together (such as suburban housemates Lauren and Blair in the introductory examples) meet the criteria of intimacy but are not married. In addition, some gay couples, like Henry and Gene—the men in the introductory vignette who have been together for thirty-eight years—also meet the intimate relationship criteria of sharing, physical closeness, and commitment but cannot be legally married.

Although most same-sex nonhomosexual friendships lack the physical closeness and long-term commitment of true intimate relationships, there are certainly some that approach it. For example, the relationship between the elderly, never-married woman quoted below and the female roommate she has lived with for sixty-one years is certainly an intimate one in most respects:

> We've seen three continents together, lost our parents together, pooled our money and assets for more than fifty years, and shared every friend each of us has ever had. I rely on her in every imaginable way. But, happily, that's a two-way street, so it works out fine. God knows we've had our spats, but none that we could not resolve with a bit of trying (Simon, 1987, p. 102).

In discussing intimate relationships, we will place major emphasis on marriage, the most commonly experienced intimate relationship in the United States today. However, we will also discuss nonmarital intimate arrangements, such as dating, cohabitation, and homosexual unions in various places throughout the text.

Families and Intimacy

Is intimacy restricted to couple relationships? Are other types of relationships, particularly those between people biologically related, also intimate relationships? In short, what part does intimacy play in family relationships other than marriage?

Most marriages and some nonmarital intimate relationships eventually result in the birth or adoption of children; these children are typically cared for by at least one of the adults who brought them into the family. Especially during the years when children are growing up, they share living space, possessions, and resources with their parents. In many cases, parents and their children also show physical affection for one another and share secrets and thoughts. The parent-child bond also implies a good deal of commitment, especially on the part of the parent.

Does this mean that parent-child relationships are intimate ones? The relationship between parent and dependent child cannot be thought of as completely intimate, in the sense in which we have used the term, because much of the giving is one-way; the parent may well listen to the child's secrets, anticipate the child's needs, and be committed to caring for the child but the child, especially when young, is not in a position to return the care. As parent and child both grow older, the amount of reciprocal sharing of self *might* increase, but the physical contact and day-to-day sharing of possessions usually declines. Thus, although the typical parent-child relationship contains different elements of an intimate relationship at different times, it is not usually intimate in the same sense that marriage is.

There is a good deal of culture-to-culture and family-to-family variation in the nature of the parent-child relationship, however, and some parents develop a more intimate relationship with an adult child

Although intimacy occurs most often between people of about the same age, some grandparent-grandchild relationships develop intimate qualities as well.

than they have with their spouse or partner. Much the same can be said for other blood relationships: sibling-sibling, grandparent-grandchild, cousin-cousin, and so forth. These types of ties are emphasized more in some cultures and in some families than in others and, in some cases, develop into intimate relationships. By and large, however, intimacy is more optional in these types of relationships than it is in marriage. While marriages often break up when a couple loses or fails to achieve intimacy, blood relationships persist whether they are intimate or not.

What Is a Family?

Although we use the term "family" in the preceding paragraphs, we have not yet provided a definition. You will see as you read on that the question "What is a family?" has become controversial. In doing research, federal government agencies such as the Bureau of the Census and most family researchers use a definition of family that places major emphasis on legal relationships: "A **family** is a group of people related by blood, marriage, or adoption." The definition is fairly clear-cut and can be easily applied across cultures. It covers, but is not restricted to,

Family
a group of people related by blood, marriage, or adoption.

two of the most common meanings of "family" in everyday language: the parent-child care-giving unit (as when a young married couple is asked "When are you going to start your family?") and "family" as a larger, multi-generational kin network (as in "I'm attending a family reunion this weekend" or "My family has been in the United States for fifty years"). To show how researchers use this definition to distinguish between family and nonfamily groupings and to illustrate some of the diversity in family types in the contemporary United States, we return to our beginning-of-chapter vignettes.

Family Households

Each of the groups described in the opening examples can be classified as either a family household or a nonfamily household. But what is a household? The Bureau of the Census, source of many of the statistics used in this text, defines a **household** as "any separate living unit occupied by one or more persons" (Wetzel, 1990, p. 5). Six of the households described at the beginning of the chapter—those headed by Otto, Angela, Lauren, Millie, Oscar, and Keith—are family households by Census Bureau standards. As previously noted, to be a **family household**, a living unit must contain at least two people related by marriage, blood, or adoption (Wetzel, 1990).

The category "family household" incorporates quite a lot of diversity. The Census Bureau divides family households into "married couple family households" and "other family households" and further divides married couple households according to the presence or absence of children under eighteen years old. Sociologists make further subdivisions.

Keith and Karen, the married couple who have no childen and desire none, belong to the most common type of family household *and* to the most common household type overall in the United States today—a married couple family household with no children under eighteen. Other types of married couples classified in this way include couples whose youngest child is over eighteen, couples who expect to have children someday but are currently childless, and the involuntarily childless.

Two of the other households described at the beginning of the chapter—those headed by the remarried farm couple Otto and Maxine and by inner-city apartment-dwellers Oscar and Gloria—qualify as married couple family households with children under eighteen, the second most common type of U.S. household. They are family households both because they contain a married couple *and* because they contain parents and children related by blood or adoption. Because Otto and Maxine brought children from previous marriages into their current marriage, their family can also be called a **stepfamily**.

Household
any separate living unit occupied by one or more persons.

Family household
any living unit containing at least two people related by blood, marriage, or adoption.

Stepfamily
a family household composed of a married couple and at least one of their children from a previous marriage.

Oscar and Gloria's nine-person household illustrates another variation in family households. In contrast to the other family households, Oscar and Gloria's is an extended family as opposed to a nuclear family. The basic meaning of the term **nuclear family** is the mother-father-children unit. Parts of such units (for example, elderly Millie and her brother Mortimer, single mother Angela and her son Buzzy, and married couples like Keith and Karen) are also considered nuclear families. Nuclear families contain one generation or two adjacent ones. An **extended family** includes either additional generations *or* more than one related nuclear unit *or* both. Oscar and Gloria's extended family household contains both a third generation (their grandson) and an additional related nuclear unit (their grandson and his mother). Nuclear family households have predominated in the United States throughout its history. Low income families like Oscar's, as well as newly arrived immigrant families from less industrialized countries, however, have long found that the combined economic and emotional resources of an extended family household are a better way of adapting to their situation than is the nuclear family household.

> **Nuclear family**
> the two-generation mother-father-children unit or some part thereof.

> **Extended family**
> a family unit consisting of three or more generations *or* of more than one related nuclear unit *or* of both.

The household headed by unmarried mother Angela, the household composed of unmarried couple Lauren and Blair and Lauren's children, and Millie and Mortimer's household are also family households. Because none of them contains a married couple, each is classified as an "other family household." In each case, a blood relationship (sibling for Millie and Mortimer, parent-child in the other two cases) makes the household a family household. Although "other family households" come in a variety of shapes and sizes, most households classified in this way are composed of a never-married or divorced mother and one or more dependent children (Wetzel, 1990).

The Lauren-Blair household deserves a few additional comments. Note first that if Lauren's children moved out and Lauren and Blair continued to live together unmarried, their household would no longer be considered a family household by Census Bureau definitions. Secondly, Lauren's children actually belong to two nuclear family units—themselves plus their mother *and* themselves plus their father. This arrangement, a parent-child family located in more than one household, is known as a **binuclear family**. Like the nuclear and extended family distinctions, the binuclear family distinction is made by social scientists but not by the Census Bureau.

> **Binuclear family**
> a group of parents and children who used to live together but now live separately, due to divorce or separation.

Nonfamily Households

Nonfamily households are living units containing one person (never-married, separated, divorced, or widowed) living alone or several people who are unrelated to one another (Wetzel, 1990). In the examples at the

> **Nonfamily household**
> any living unit containing one person living alone or composed of several unrelated people.

beginning of the chapter, the gay couple and the ten students sharing a house provide two examples of multiperson nonfamily households. Neither of these cases involves a legally recognized blood, marriage, or adoptive relationship. Other examples of multiperson nonfamily households include unmarried male-female couples or lesbian couples living together without children at home, and landlady-boarder arrangements.

Although the proportion of multiperson nonfamily households is increasing, most nonfamily households continue to be one-person households composed of never-married, separated, divorced, or widowed individuals living alone. As illustrated by Figure 1–1, one-person households are about five times as common as multiperson nonfamily households and, in 1990, made up about 24 percent of *all* U.S. households (Wetzel, 1990). Figure 1–1 also presents a summary picture of the prevalence of various types of family households in the United

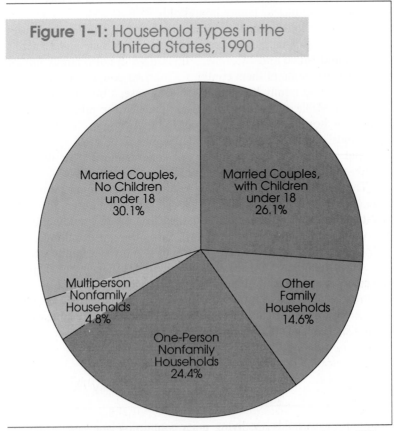

Figure 1–1: Household Types in the United States, 1990

Married Couples, No Children under 18 30.1%

Married Couples, with Children under 18 26.1%

Multiperson Nonfamily Households 4.8%

Other Family Households 14.6%

One-Person Nonfamily Households 24.4%

Although most households in the United States are still family households, more than one out of four contains either a person living alone or nonrelated people living together.

Source: Data from Waldrop & Exter, 1990, p. 27. © American Demographics, January 1990. Used with permission.

States and should help you place the opening examples into a larger context.

Changing Definitions of Family

Perhaps because of the modern interest and emphasis on emotional intimacy in relationships and the increasing number of "family-like" households, some citizens, judges, and local governments are beginning to question the formal, rather legalistic research definition of "family" introduced earlier. There are several indications of this questioning attitude. For example, one 1989 nationwide survey asked people to choose between the Census Bureau definition of the family (Definition A) and a definition emphasizing feelings (Definition B):

> **Definition A:** "A family is a group of people related by blood, marriage, or adoption."
>
> **Definition B:** "A family is a group of people who love and care for each other."

Three out of four people surveyed selected Definition B, a definition that ignored legal relationships and focused on how people felt about and treated one another (Seligmann, 1990, p. 38). Using Definition B, *all* or *none* of the households described at the beginning of the chapter could be considered families, depending on how loving and caring their relationships are.

Defining the term "family" is more than a theoretical exercise. Membership in a family may entitle one to an array of benefits such as coverage under a spouse's or parent's health insurance, paid sick leave to care for an ailing family member, the privilege of living in neighborhoods zoned for families, and reduced rates at recreational facilities. Individuals living in intimate, but nonfamily, relationships do not typically qualify for these benefits.

In recent years, some judges have expanded the definition of family for certain limited policy purposes. For example, a 1989 case tried by the New York Court of Appeals declared that, for purposes of passing on the rights to a rent-controlled apartment after death, a long-term homosexual partner should be treated as a surviving spouse. One judge in the case wrote, "We conclude that the term family . . . should not be rigidly restricted to those people who have formalized their relationship by obtaining, for instance, a marriage certificate" (Associated Press, 1989, p. A4; Glaberson, 1989; Gutis, 1989). In a second case, the ten college students described earlier were brought to court for violating a zoning ordinance stating that only families could live in the neighborhood. The presiding judge declared that the students' sharing behavior made them the "functional equivalent" of a traditional family and allowed them to stay (Sullivan, 1990). As we shall see in Chapter 5, such "family-like" nonfamily households are still *not* treated as families for most legal and policy purposes. However, these court cases and the shift in public opinion may eventually result in erasing many family-nonfamily distinctions.

By deciding to marry, this couple has already made a number of important choices. Many more lie ahead.

THE IMPORTANCE OF CHOICE

Intimate relationships, especially those in modern societies, are *chosen* relationships. Individual partners choose to become involved with one another, choose how to communicate and how much to self-disclose, choose whether and how to express physical affection, and choose their level of commitment. During a typical lifetime of seventy or more years, the average person will make many, many intimate relationship choices.

Although many of the choices made within intimate relationships are very private ones, most are affected by factors other than the immediate situation of the two people involved. Consider, for example, a boy and a girl contemplating a first kiss. They are much more likely to kiss if they live in a culture that considers kissing an appropriate display of affection early in the relationship rather than in one that considers mouth-to-mouth kissing obscene. Kissing is also more likely in a culture that allows young people to go out on their own, without chaperones. The couple's decision to kiss or not to kiss is probably also affected by what their friends think and by their age—what was "gross" one year may be highly desirable a year later. Finally, how each of them thinks about the "first kiss" is shaped by their upbringing; for example, the boy may think of the kiss as a first step to further sexual intimacy and the girl may consider it the ultimate peak of the relationship. The point is this: people seldom make intimate relationship choices based *only* on their own personal feelings and desires. The "outside factors" affecting choice-making are what social scientists mean when they refer to "social context."

Freedom and Expansion of Choice

The social context prevailing in the contemporary United States offers considerable freedom of choice and presents an increasing array of possibilities. The racial and ethnic diversity and the positive values attached to innovation, individualism, and equality in the United States make it a place in which people have a great deal of choice in their personal relationships. After all, a racially, religiously, and ethnically diverse society presents people with more alternative possibilities than a society in which everyone shares a similar background. A society valuing innovation is less likely to punish people for trying new things than a society valuing tradition. A society placing a premium on individualism is more likely to allow individuals to pursue happiness in their own ways than a society stressing responsibility to the group. In societies emphasizing equality, no one category of people makes decisions for others.

Events of the late twentieth century have worked to expand freedom of choice to more individuals and to increase the number of choices to be made. Equality between men and women, whites and racial minority groups, older generations and younger ones, increased during the 1960s, 1970s, and 1980s. These changes mean that more people have choices that were once limited to only a few (Modell, 1989). The choices themselves have also increased.

Attitude Change and Expanded Choice

Today there is greater societal tolerance for choices once frowned upon. Consider the What Do You Think? questions you answered at the beginning of the chapter. Researchers who have asked people to respond to questions like these see some interesting changes over the last twenty-five or thirty years.

Tables 1–1, 1–2, 1–3, 1–4, and 1–5 show these patterns of change. The first three tables are arranged similarly. Each repeats the statement or question people (in this case, the same set of mothers interviewed first in 1962 and reinterviewed in subsequent years) were asked to respond to and what proportion *disagreed* with the statement in various years from 1962 to 1985. To see how opinions changed over the years,

Table 1–1 Opinions on Parents Staying Together

When there are children in the family, parents should stay together even if they don't get along.

% of Mothers Disagreeing or Strongly Disagreeing			
1962	1977	1980	1985
51.0	80.4	82.1	82.3

Table 1–2 Opinions on Family Decision Making

Most of the important decisions in the life of the family should be made by the man of the house.

% of Mothers Disagreeing or Strongly Disagreeing			
1962	1977	1980	1985
32.3	67.6	71.2	77.7

Table 1–3 Opinions on Having Children

Do you feel almost all married couples who can *ought* to have children?

% of Mothers Saying No		
1962	1980	1985
6.8	53.6	52.1

Source for Tables 1–1, 1–2, and 1–3: Thornton, 1989. Copyrighted (1989) by the National Council on Family Relations, 3989 Central Ave. N.E., Suite #550, Minneapolis, MN 55421. Reprinted by permission.

Table 1–4 Opinions on Premarital Sex

If a man and woman have sex relations before marriage, do you think it is Always Wrong, Almost Always Wrong, Wrong Only Sometimes, or Not Wrong at All?

	% Answering Always Wrong or Almost Always Wrong		
	1965	1975	1986
Women under 30	69	21.5	21.9
Women 30 or over	81.1	56.7	45.4
Men under 30	64.8	15	14
Men 30 or over	61.7	42.2	33.9

Table 1–5 Opinions on Extramarital Sex

What is your opinion about a married person having sexual relations with someone other than the marriage partner?

	% Answering Always Wrong or Almost Always Wrong		
	1965	1976	1985
Women under 30	93.9	74.1	88.3
Women 30 or over	96.2	88.2	90.5
Men under 30	90.7	76	84.3
Men 30 or over	92.1	83.1	84.2

Source for Tables 1–4 and 1–5: Thorton, 1989. Copyrighted (1989) by the National Council on Family Relations, 3989 Central Ave. N.E., Suite #550, Minneapolis, MN 55421. Reprinted by permission.

simply read across the page. As you can see in Table 1–1, in 1962, barely half of the mothers disagreed with the idea that parents should stay together for the sake of the children; by 1985, over 80 percent disagreed. This indicates an increasing tolerance for divorce over time. Tables 1–2 and 1–3 also show increasing tolerance, with most of the change occurring between the early 1960s and the late 1970s.

Tables 1–4 and 1–5 are a little more complex. Note that each reports results according to the age and sex of the respondents (the labels down the side of the tables) and according to the year of the interview (the labels across the top of the tables). To see how people of a certain age and sex felt about each issue in a given year, find where the age-sex category and the year intersect on the table. For example, Table 1–4 shows that 15 percent of the men under thirty felt that sexual relations before marriage were always or almost always wrong in 1975. To make comparisons across years, read across the table. To make comparisons between people in different age-sex categories in a given year, read down the page. Table 1–4 shows that all age-sex groups became less disapproving of premarital sex between 1965 and 1986 but that, in every year, older people more often disapproved than younger ones and women disapproved more often than men. Using these table-reading guidelines for Table 1–5, what do you see?

The tables taken together show that individuals in the 1980s had more leeway (that is, risked less public disapproval) in their choices about whether to stay together in the face of marital problems, about who should make family decisions, about whether to have children, and about whether to engage in premarital sex than did people in the 1960s. Researchers find similar opinion changes when they ask people about the acceptability of not marrying, living together unmarried before or instead of marriage, women working outside the home, and men sharing housework (Thornton, 1989).

Technology and Expanded Choice

The development and spread of modern technology have also added to the variety of intimate relationship choices. For instance, advances in electronic technology have given people better access to information about the available alternatives. People cannot really make choices when they do not know what the alternatives are. In the past, most people discovered the alternatives available to them by observing what those around them did or, occasionally, through reading. Today, however, people in the most remote areas of the country can hear about parents who allow their teenagers to be sexually active in the family home, gay couples who adopt children, couples who divorce after forty years of marriage, and many other choices in intimate relationships. Learning about these possible alternatives is as simple as renting a video or just tuning into a TV talk show.

New technology can also make certain choices easier to implement than they were in the past. One good example is the development of reliable methods of birth control. Married couples who wanted to restrict their family size forty or fifty years ago had to either limit their sexual activity or depend on unreliable methods such as douching or withdrawal. In short, carrying out their choice to limit family size probably resulted in more tension and anxiety than does carrying out such a choice today.

Technology—in particular, better knowledge about basic health care and medical technology—has also increased choices by increasing the length of time most people live. People who live longer have more choices to make. For example, more parents than ever before have to make choices about how to interact with offspring who are middle-aged or older. A forty-year-old parent might feel justified in questioning the dating behavior of a fifteen-year-old child but what if the parent is sixty-five and the child is once divorced and forty years old? At the same time, more middle-aged people have to make choices about how close to remain to very elderly grandparents and how to care for ailing parents.

Technology can also work in curious ways to reduce choice, or at least to make some choices riskier. Many people today feel limited in their choices of sexual partners (who and how many) because of the danger of sexually transmitted diseases. Technology contributes to the spread of such diseases by making it possible to travel easily between distant points. Many of the early AIDS cases in the United States and Canada originated with a single individual—a gay international airline steward who travelled regularly between Europe, Los Angeles, and New York and had approximately 250 different sexual partners each year between 1979 and 1981 (Shannon, Pyle, & Bashur, 1990, pp. 118, 160). Once introduced, the spread of AIDS within the United States followed the modern interstate highway system (Shannon, Pyle, & Bashur, 1990, Chapter 6). In this case, transportation methods, combined with the choices of a fairly small number of individuals and a dangerous virus, resulted in affecting the options of people throughout the world.

The Responsibility and Limits of Choice

The other side of freedom of choice is the responsibility of making informed choices. Each decision made about intimate relationships precludes certain others and determines what future choices lie ahead—for instance, if you and your partner decide to have a child, you will have to make choices about how to have the child, whether to breastfeed or bottle-feed, who should provide most of the daytime care, which values to emphasize, what type of discipline to use, and on and on. Once the child is born, you cannot change your minds about parenthood; your choice is now your responsibility. Note that refusing to make a choice, simply "drifting into" dates, intimacy, marriage, or parenthood does not relieve you of the responsibilities involved in the choice. To make things even more complicated, the choices you make affect not only you but also a variety of others. Parents, grandparents, children, and sometimes others in the kin group or community might benefit or suffer from your choices.

One purpose of this book is to put you in a better position to make responsible, well-informed choices. Throughout, we describe alternative choices and trace the probable consequences of each. Our information comes from the most recent social scientific studies. Sometimes such research will confirm what you already believe or have heard from friends and relatives, sometimes it will challenge or contradict what you now believe. We cannot and will not tell you what to choose; our objective is to make you aware of the full range of choices available as well as their consequences.

Another aspect of learning about intimate relationship choices and their consequences is recognition of the limits of choice. Along with the freedoms it affords, the United States, like all other societies, places limits on peoples' choices. Within any society, people who make personal relationship choices that go against the law or established custom risk disapproval and sometimes more formal punishment. Laws in the United States regarding sexual relationships, marriage, and family follow, for the most part, the guidelines set by the Protestant, Anglo-Saxon, white heterosexual male tradition. This means that, although many racial and ethnic family traditions are present in the United States, only some of them are real choices if one wishes to stay within the law.

This book presents several historical examples of this; there are contemporary examples as well. For example, Hmong tribesmen from Vietnam frequently form extended family self-help networks of 50–150 people who live near one another and share resources. When Hmong families immigrated to the United States after the U.S.–Vietnamese war in the middle 1970s, the U.S. Immigration and Naturalization Service had a policy of "scattering" Indochinese refugees around the United States so that only eight Hmong family members were allowed to immigrate together. In order to enter the United States, the Hmong had to give up (at least temporarily) a type of family grouping that provided security and familiarity for them in order to conform to U.S. policy (Cerhan, 1990; Westermeyer, 1987).

Another constraint on making choices is personal resources. Generally, people with more resources—education, money, influential connections, interpersonal skills, and personal attractiveness—have more ways of finding out and implementing their choices than do people with fewer resources. For example, an infertile husband and wife with money and the interpersonal skills to deal with medical specialists and lawyers probably have a better chance of obtaining the baby they want than an infertile couple with less money and fewer skills. This does not necessarily mean that the resource-rich have an easier time making choices or that they make wiser choices; it does mean that they usually have more options.

SOCIAL CHANGE AND INTIMATE RELATIONSHIPS

Everyone who has ever been involved in an intimate relationship knows that such relationships fluctuate from time to time and that the two people involved might modify their attitudes and behavior towards one another. In other words, intimate relationships change. Some of these fluctuations can be reliably predicted throughout an individual's life. We will trace such predictable changes by using a life-cycle approach; initially discussing childhood training about intimate relationships, moving to events, such as dating, that typically occur first in adolescence, describing early marriage and the parenthood years, and then discussing marriage after the children are grown. Many people depart from this typical pattern in some way or another; their choices are also a part of the book.

This book also deals with social change, a type of change that differs from life-cycle-related change and is also distinct from the unpredictable up-and-down changes in individual intimate relationships. The term **social change** refers to fluctuations and modifications occurring in the larger groups, institutions, and societies to which individuals belong. Social change is large-scale change. Compare these situations:

> **Social change**
> large scale fluctuations and modifications occurring in larger groups, institutions, and societies.

- You have a big fight in public with your partner and the two of you refuse to speak to one another for a week. This is a change in your relationship but *not* a social change.
- A country's divorce rate increases from one out of every five marriages to one out of every three marriages. This *is* a social change.
- A married couple has their first child and finds that they must readjust their entire daily routine. This is certainly a change in their intimate relationship but *not* a social change.
- The number of children the average U.S. woman gives birth to drops from 3 to 2 over a ten-year time span. This *is* a social change.

What is the connection between choice and social change? From the examples you have just read, you might infer that the choices of individual couples *contribute* to social change—many more individual couples must decide to divorce for the divorce rate to increase and many more individual couples must decide to stop at two children for the average number of children per woman to drop. In both of these instances, however, individual couples were probably responding, in some way or another, to some other social change—perhaps to changing ideas about what marriage should be like or to a change in the cost of living. Thus, there is a two-way connection between social changes outside of intimate units and choices made within them.

Families and Long-Term Social Change

Although the social changes of the late twentieth century have affected families in many ways, U.S. families in other centuries also experienced a good deal of social change. Knowing something about the long-term social changes in family relationships is important. Once you learn about these long term social changes, you will be able to see that many of the changes in family life and intimate relationships that people worry about today are simply the continuation and culmination of changes that began hundreds of years ago. Family historians Steven Mintz and Susan Kellogg (1988) put it like this:

> Ours is not the first generation of Americans to worry about a loosening of family bonds or to complain that parents are growing more selfish and irresponsible or that children are becoming more defiant of adult authority.... The history of American family life suggests that we need not be disturbed by change in and of itself, because change—and not stability—has been the norm (p. 243).

Family historians typically identify three broad changes in family life over the course of U.S. history (Hareven, 1988; Mintz & Kellogg, 1988; Shorter, 1975). These changes are:

1. Family households have moved from being predominantly economic units to being predominantly emotional, intimate units.
2. Family households have moved from being large and rather public to being small and very private.
3. Family households have moved from having a patriarchal authority pattern to having an egalitarian authority pattern.

Traditional family
an economically based, large, public, patriarchal family type.

Modern family
an intimate, small, private, egalitarian family type.

The economically based, large, public, patriarchal family type is often called the **traditional family**; intimacy, smallness, privacy, and egalitarianism are the characteristics of the **modern family**.

The shift from traditional family characteristics to modern family characteristics has been underway for almost 300 years. However, not all U.S. families today are intimate, private, or egalitarian. In general, these changes affected urban, Anglo-Saxon, Protestant, middle class families first and most completely (Hareven, 1988). This group seldom, if ever, made up the majority of the U.S. population. The adaptations these white, middle class, urban dwellers made to economic and demo-

Economic changes frequently bring about changes in family life. How do you think this farm auction will affect the lives of the former farm owners?

graphic change were not necessarily ideal or even the most adaptive but their patterns are important because *this group made the laws and set the standards that ultimately affected everyone else living in the country.* Family laws, family policies, and family images to which every racial and ethnic group in the United States must respond in one way or another are derived from the family experiences of this white, Anglo-Saxon group. In addition, the economic and demographic factors that changed these families also eventually affected African-American and Native American families, non-Anglo-Saxon immigrant families, lower-income families, and rural families.

We will describe each of the broad social transformations—moves toward intimacy, privacy, and egalitarianism—in turn. As we do so, we will identify the even larger social changes which made the shift to modern family characteristics both possible and probable. Our approach here will be to trace the very broad outlines of social changes in family life. At the same time, we will briefly note how the changes affected different ethnic groups in different ways.

The Move to Intimacy

Today, most people marry because they are in love. They expect continuing intimacy with their spouse, have children in hopes of achieving even more emotional closeness, and often divorce when the intimacy fades. In short, the family home or something like it is where people look to fulfill their needs for emotional closeness.

Contrast this situation to that existing some 250 years ago in the United States. In the mid-1700s, some husbands and wives were emotionally close to one another and some parents lavished affection on their children. But they chose a mate, married, stayed married, and had children for reasons of economic survival, not as a way to find intimacy. The marriage was a work unit and its success was based on how successfully husband, wife, and their eventual children worked together. In short, home was a workplace. A husband, wife, or child might find intimacy at home but was probably more likely to find it among friends of the same age and sex (Mintz & Kellogg, 1988).

The transformation of the family home from workplace to emotional haven occurred primarily as the result of larger economic changes. Beginning in the late eighteenth century, the United States moved from being a preindustrial economy based on agriculture to being an industrial society based on turning raw materials into manufactured goods. This industrialization process brought about many changes. The one that most affected families was the separation of work and home (Laslett, 1978). When the transition from mostly agriculture to mostly manufacturing is made, one or more family members must leave the family home each day to work in separate locations. Individual family members are still involved in the larger economy but they are involved as individuals, not as a family unit. Industrial family households, no longer as important as economic production units, focus more on being emotional units, providing the love and understanding their members need after working all day in an often impersonal world. Historian Barbara Laslett (1978) writes:

> ... the idea of the private family and the home as a personal sanctuary grew throughout the nineteenth century. Family life began to be characterized as an oasis, a retreat, a haven from the uncertainties, immoralities, and strains of life in a rapidly changing society.... Insecurities in public roles and disappointments in the occupational sphere ... reinforced a belief in the family as the only place where meaningful relationships are possible (pp. 484–85).

Demographic changes

social changes specifically concerned with population: birth rates, death rates, life expectancy, migration.

Industrialization also brings about **demographic changes**, social changes specifically concerned with population such as changes in birth and death rates, life expectancy, and migration. Death rates decline and life expectancy rises because of better nutrition, sanitation, and medical technology; birth rates drop because children become more expensive (Kain, 1990). Figure 1–2 traces changes in U.S. life expectancy since 1900, the earliest date for which comprehensive figures are available. Note that the vertical axis of Figure 1–2 is life expectancy at birth, the number of years a person born that year could expect to live given the

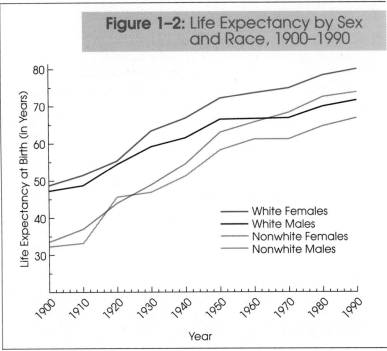

Figure 1–2: Life Expectancy by Sex and Race, 1900–1990

Life expectancy for both white and nonwhite males and females increased between 1900 and 1990. For example, a nonwhite female born in 1900 could expect to live about 35 years; her 1990 counterpart can expect to live until age 76. (Data for 1990 are estimates.)

Source: Data from U.S. Bureau of the Census (1975) Series B, pp. 107–115 for years prior to 1970; since 1970, U.S. Bureau of the Census (1990) p. 72.

prevailing conditions. The horizontal axis represents time, starting with 1900 and going to 1990. Each of the four lines represents a different sex and racial category. By following the lines, you should be able to see that life expectancy for both white and nonwhite males and females increased between 1900 and 1990. For most years in the past and even more so today, females live longer than males. And, although the gap has decreased in recent years, whites still live longer than nonwhites of the same sex.

Figure 1–3, (on page 26) documenting changes in U.S. fertility rates, is set up in much the same way. The vertical axis indicates average births per woman and the horizontal axis represents the passage of time. Note both the overall trend and the differences between blacks and whites.

Both rising life expectancy and falling fertility rates have the effect of encouraging family intimacy. Husbands and wives who can reasonably expect to live long lives have more years and more reason to pay attention to the emotional aspects of their relationship. And parents with only a few children have more time and energy to devote to each child, increasing the chances that a close emotional relationship will develop (Wells, 1985; Uhlenberg, 1980).

Not all families in the United States emphasize intimacy over economic survival. This is perhaps particularly true of new immigrants

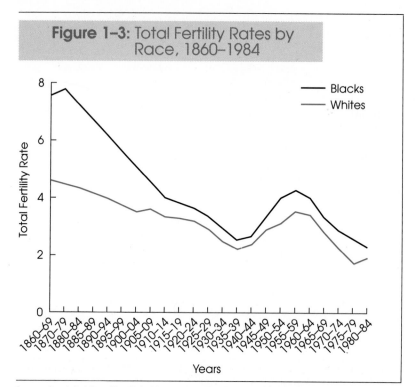

Figure 1–3: Total Fertility Rates by Race, 1860–1984

With the exception of the Baby Boom period (1946–1964), total fertility rates have declined steadily since 1860. In the 1860s, the average black woman gave birth to seven or eight children and the average white woman to four or five; by the 1980s, both black and white women averaged about two children.

Source: Reprinted from *The Color Line and the Quality of Life in America,* by Reynolds Farley and Walter Allen © 1987, Russell Sage Foundation. Used with the permission of the Russell Sage Foundation, p. 19.

coming to the United States from nations where traditional family characteristics prevail. Consider the Mui family, described by journalist Samuel Freedman (1990) in his book *Small Victories.* The Mui family, composed of husband, wife, and three children, arrived in New York City's Chinatown from rural China in 1980. Once in New York, the parents worked seventy-two hours a week and the grade-school-aged children twenty hours a week in a garment factory owned by a cousin. This family was very much an economically-based unit; given the length of their work week and the poor conditions of their workplace, it is difficult to imagine that they had much time or energy for emotional closeness.

The Move to Privacy

As noted, one of the effects of industrialization was to separate peoples' home lives from their work lives. As these two parts of life became more separate, families became less public and more private. They have done so in two ways: families perform fewer public services than they used to *and* the public pays less attention to what happens inside families than it once did (Hareven, 1988).

Besides raising crops and animals and producing clothing and furniture, the eighteenth century preindustrial family also performed such public services as teaching children to work, read, and write, taking care of the sick and frail, and functioning as a miniature church and government by enforcing both moral and civil rules. These "functions," as sociologists usually call them, were gradually transferred outside the home to more specialized institutions during the nineteenth and twentieth centuries as part of the overall industrialization process (Hareven, 1988). Families became increasingly dependent on outside institutions to meet their needs but had less influence over how the institutions did so. In short, families, although not necessarily all individual family members, withdrew from public life.

Concurrently, the public withdrew from the family. In preindustrial times, the local governing body might decide that a family should take in and provide for a widow with no children or that a rebellious teenage son should be placed in another family or that an adulterous wife should be subjected to public humiliation (Mintz & Kellogg, 1988). In other words, what went on inside families was everybody's business! Beginning in the early 1800s, the idea that families should be left to make their own decisions and handle their own problems began to take hold. Families became more private. They performed fewer functions and did so with less public scrutiny.

Family privacy is easier to attain, of course, when the family household is small and consists only of family members (Wells, 1985). A trend toward decreasing household size is another long term change. Although most U.S. family households have always been nuclear rather than extended, eighteenth- and nineteenth-century families were much more likely than late twentieth-century families to contain nonfamily members—servants, boarders, children from other families—as household members (Hareven, 1988; Laslett, 1978). The departure of such nonfamily members from most households plus dropping birth rates help explain the overall decreases in average household size shown in Figure 1–4 (on page 28). In summarizing the overall increase in family and personal privacy, family historian Robert Wells (1985) writes:

> A rough rule of thumb to describe the change is that in the eighteenth century there were approximately two people for every room in a typical American house. By the second half of the twentieth century, this ratio has changed so that there are approximately two rooms per person (p. 55).

For a number of reasons, most black families have not become private and small to the extent that most white families have in the United States. In general, urban dwellers and higher income groups are

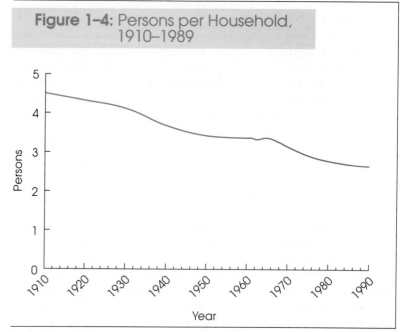

Figure 1–4: Persons per Household, 1910–1989

Source: Wetzel, 1990, p. 6.

The number of persons living in the average household dropped steadily during the twentieth century, reflecting an increase in the proportion of people living alone and a decrease in fertility rates.

the first to be affected by lower fertility rates and increased life expectancy. Blacks, with a long history of living in rural areas and subsisting on low incomes, have long had higher fertility rates and lower life expectancy than whites. Look again at Figures 1–2 and 1–3 to confirm this.

Black households tend to be larger than white households because blacks have more children, but also because they are more often extended family households. Blacks brought a tradition of strong extended family ties with them from Africa and such ties helped their families survive through slavery and afterwards. Today, black families are more likely than white ones to have nonfamily members or extended family members sharing a household at least part of the time. Such large households often lack privacy (Staples, 1988).

The Move to Egalitarianism

Patriarchal authority system

a system of family authority in which older people have authority over younger ones and men have authority over women.

The Europeans who settled in the United States and established the laws and customs governing family life brought with them a patriarchal system of family authority. In a **patriarchal authority system**, older people have authority over younger ones and men have authority over women. The oldest male in a completely patriarchal system chooses his children's marriage partners, their occupations, and their place of residence. The parent-child relationship is a very formal one. Similarly, a patriarchal husband-wife relationship is one in which the husband controls the wife's property, decides which household work she does and how she does it, and makes all family decisions. In the most patriarchal households, the wife and children are treated as employees or servants (Shorter, 1975).

Over time, families in the United States have moved towards more equalized patterns of family authority. An **egalitarian authority system** is a system of family authority in which males and females have equal authority and younger family members have some input. In an egalitarian husband-wife relationship, husbands and wives have equal influence over family decision making and share or split control over money and property. In an egalitarian parent-child relationship, children are allowed to express their opinions about some family decisions, interact informally with parents, and make their own decisions about marriage and adult work.

Patriarchal authority is easier to maintain when the oldest male generation controls all access to economic opportunity. If the only way a young man can make a living is through farming and if his father controls the only available land, then that father can exercise considerable authority over his son. You should be able to see that this type of authority, particularly over adult children, breaks down fairly quickly in an industrializing society because fathers no longer control most of the jobs. Patriarchal authority of older generations over younger ones was further weakened as early as the 1700s in the United States due to ample opportunities for geographical mobility. Sons who did not want to wait around to inherit their father's land and daughters who did not want to marry the man their parents selected could move to a new part of the country (Mintz & Kellogg, 1988).

Patriarchal authority of men over women in U.S. families diminished less rapidly. On a formal, legal level, such authority lasted well into the twentieth century and continues to some extent today. The separation of work and home that occurred as part of industrialization *emphasized* patriarchal authority to some extent by making women (who were supposed to stay home) economically dependent on men (who were supposed to leave the home to work). However, on a more informal basis, U.S. patriarchal authority, even in the early days, tended to be of a more moderate variety than that found in Europe and Asia (Mintz & Kellogg, 1988). Furthermore, increases in intimacy generally mean increases in egalitarianism as well. It is difficult, after all, for two people to be truly intimate in an emotional sense when one has considerably more power than the other (Shorter, 1975). In recent years, the contributions women make to household income have further decreased male authority and increased the feelings of equality between husbands and wives (Blumstein & Schwartz, 1983).

Racial minorities and recent immigrants are, in some respects, more modern than middle-class white families when it comes to the

Egalitarian authority system

a system of family authority in which men and women have equal authority and younger family members have some input.

patriarchy-egalitarianism dimension. Black families had little chance to develop a strong patriarchal tradition in the United States because most arrived as slaves and lived for many years in a situation in which the slaveowner was the patriarch. After slavery, both black wives and black husbands often had to work outside the home to survive economically. Husband-wife egalitarianism is more common when both spouses bring in income. Thus, most blacks had egalitarian marriages before most whites did, and black marriages today are more egalitarian than white ones (Staples, 1988).

The Mui family, the recent Chinese immigrants introduced earlier, illustrate that economic survival in a new land often demands increased egalitarianism between parents and children. While the Mui family retained patriarchal ideals for the parent-child relationship, they found it difficult to put these ideals into full practice. Like many poor immigrant parents before them, the Mui parents, illiterate in Chinese and with no knowledge of English, had to rely on their children to accomplish basic family tasks:

> See Wai [the son] served, in many ways, as his parents' portal to the outside world, writing their letters to relatives in China, addressing their Christmas cards to friends in New York, translating the words of cashiers and traffic cops. When a utility bill claimed the Muis owed $800, See Wai battled the company down to the correct figure of $300 (Freedman, 1990, p. 204).

In this family, for some purposes at least, the younger generation made decisions for the older one—not exactly egalitarianism, but not traditional patriarchy either.

Social Change in Action: Four U.S. Birth Cohorts

Cohort
any group of people who experience something at the same time.

Birth cohort
all the people born in a single year or block of years.

One way to see the effects of social change on a more personal level is to make comparisons between different cohort groups. A **cohort** is "any group of people who experience something at the same time" (Kain, 1990, p. 23). For example, your high school graduation class is a cohort. The type of cohort most often used in studying social change is the **birth cohort**, all the people born in a single year or block of years. Members of the same birth cohort experience important historical events and major social changes at about the same age and family stage and often respond to them in similar ways. For example, members of the 1973 birth cohort were ten when Michael Jackson recorded his most famous album, thirteen when the space shuttle *Challenger* exploded, and high school students during the Persian Gulf Conflict of 1991.

The other side of this is that the same historical event "hits" different birth cohorts at different points in their lives and often affects

Members of the New Century birth cohort reached young adulthood just as the Great Depression of the 1930s began.

Members of the Depression birth cohort reached young adulthood during the 1950s, when this photograph was taken.

Baby Boom cohort members reached young adulthood— and sometimes parenthood—during the 1970s.

Members of the Baby Bust cohort reached young adulthood during the early 1990s.

them in different ways. Thus, Michael Jackson made a big impact on many people who were in late childhood or early adolescence in 1983 but was barely noticed by those who were middle-aged or elderly or babies at the time. The widespread introduction of the automobile during the 1920s probably made little impact on people in their seventies (the 1850s birth cohort) at the time, but it greatly changed the courting habits and the number of potential mates for those just entering their late teens and early twenties (the birth cohorts of 1900–1910).

Comparing different birth cohorts is an excellent way to see social change in action (Ryder, 1965). As you will see throughout this book, different birth cohorts have made different choices about when to have first sexual intercourse, when and whether to marry and divorce, how many children to have and when to have them, and how to spend their money. At the same time, comparing members of the same birth cohort to one another (for example, comparing native-born 1973 birth cohort members to foreign-born 1973 birth cohort members) is a good way to learn about social diversity (Kain, 1990; Ryder, 1965). Because both social change and social diversity are important, we make both types of comparison.

Cohort Comparison boxes throughout the book compare four twentieth-century birth cohorts:

The New Century Cohort (born from 1910 to 1914)
The Depression Cohort (born from 1930 to 1934)
The Baby Boom Cohort (born from 1950 to 1954)
The Baby Bust Cohort (born from 1970 to 1974)

In the remainder of this chapter, we will focus on describing the most important economic changes and historical events that coincided with each cohort's childhood, early adulthood, and middle age. Figure 1–5 (on page 34) provides a summary of this information.

The New Century Cohort

Members of the 1910–1914, New Century cohort were born during the last phases of the industrialization of the United States. In 1920, ten years after the first members of this cohort were born, the United States, for the first time, had more urban residents than rural ones—the usual indicator that a society is industrialized. Many of the babies born between 1910 and 1914 were born to large farm families; others were the children of the newly arrived immigrants, mostly from Eastern and Southern Europe, and grew up in big city tenements. The schooling these New Century babies received depended largely on where they lived and the income of their parents. Most cities and states had compulsory school attendance laws by the time the New Century babies

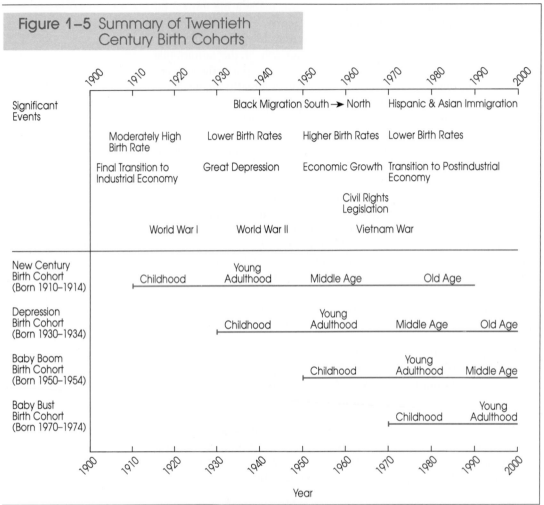

Figure 1–5 Summary of Twentieth Century Birth Cohorts

One way to read Figure 1-5 is to select a year and read down to see what was happening in which life stage of each birth cohort. For example, in 1950, after World War II and before major Civil Rights legislation, blacks were moving from South to North, birth rates were higher, and the economy was growing. New Century cohort members experienced these events in early middle age. Another way to read the figure is to select a birth cohort group and read from left to right, noting what events cohort members lived through and at what age. For example, the Baby Bust cohort experienced neither World War and were babies during the Vietnam War.

were school-aged; but those children, especially black children, who grew up on poor southern farms may not have had a school available at all. About half the whites in this birth cohort but less than 25 percent of the blacks finished high school (Farley & Allen, 1987, p. 194). This cohort reached their late teens and early twenties, the age at which

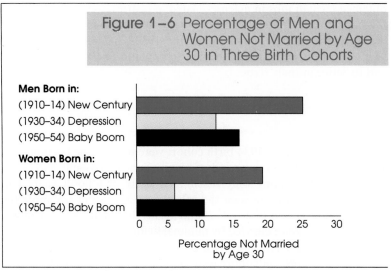

Figure 1–6 Percentage of Men and Women Not Married by Age 30 in Three Birth Cohorts

Men Born in:
(1910–14) New Century
(1930–34) Depression
(1950–54) Baby Boom

Women Born in:
(1910–14) New Century
(1930–34) Depression
(1950–54) Baby Boom

Percentage Not Married by Age 30

Each birth cohort shows a different pattern in terms of how many remained unmarried at age 30. Twenty-five percent of the men and almost 20 percent of the women born during the New Century cohort had never been married by age 30. Only about 10 percent of the Depression cohort remained unmarried at age 30.

Source: Calculated from figures given in Schoen *et al.* (1985), p. 22, Table 3.

people typically make decisions about work, marriage, and parenthood, during a worldwide, long-lasting economic depression. Figures 1–6 and 1–7 show how the economic depression affected the New Century cohort's decisions about marriage. By the time they reached their thirties, World War II had opened up new jobs. Both men and women

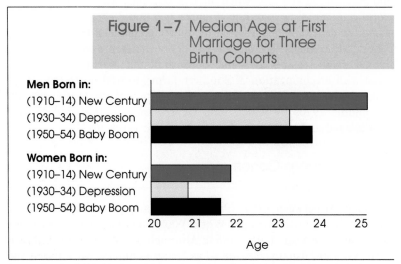

Figure 1–7 Median Age at First Marriage for Three Birth Cohorts

Men Born in:
(1910–14) New Century
(1930–34) Depression
(1950–54) Baby Boom

Women Born in:
(1910–14) New Century
(1930–34) Depression
(1950–54) Baby Boom

Age

The median age at first marriage means the age at which one-half the members of the cohort were married and one-half were not. (Data for New Century men are approximate.)

Source: Cherlin (1981) *Marriage, Divorce, Remarriage.* Cambridge: Harvard University Press, p. 9 and Sweet & Bumpass (1987) *American Families and Households.* New York: Russell Sage Foundation, p. 17.

obtained civilian jobs in defense-related industries; some of the men in this cohort were drafted into the military. Due to policy changes made during the economic depression of the 1930s, members of the New Century cohort were among the first to pay into Social Security funds and to retire in their sixties.

The Depression Cohort

Members of the 1930–1934 birth cohort were born at the beginning of the Great Depression, a period of massive unemployment and widespread poverty, ending only when their early childhood years had passed. These conditions kept the cohort rather small in size (note the 1930s fertility rates in Figure 1–3) and meant that many of its members had childhoods characterized by minimal living standards, sporadically employed and constantly worried parents, and frequent moves. Members of the Depression cohort were more likely to be born into small families, live in towns and cities, and go to school than were members of the New Century cohort. Slightly more than 70 percent of the whites in the cohort received at least a high school education (Farley & Allen, 1987, p. 194). The educational attainment of Depression cohort blacks and Hispanics was lower than that of their white counterparts but greater than that of blacks and Hispanics born twenty years earlier (Bean & Tienda, 1987, p. 242; Farley & Allen, 1987, p. 194). Depression cohort members were young adolescents or preteens during the years of World War II and made their decisions about work, marriage, and parenthood at a time when the U.S. economy was dominant in the world and rapidly expanding. Figures 1–6 and 1–7 show how these economic developments affected the marriage plans of the Depression cohort. Many black, Southern members of the Depression cohort, attracted by increasing economic opportunity in Northern cities and faced with mechanization of Southern farms, moved north (Muller & Espenshade, 1985). The period of economic prosperity continued until the middle 1970s by which time Depression cohort members were middle-aged and usually fairly secure in their positions.

The Baby Boom Cohort

People born between 1950–1954 were the early part of a "boom" (or increase) in the birth rate after World War II that lasted for a period of about eighteen years (1946–1964). Although all people born between 1946–1964 are usually referred to as "baby boomers," we will use the term in our cohort comparisons to refer specifically to those born between 1950 and 1954. The very large 1950–1954 cohort began its life during a period of great national optimism. Most of them grew up in families with several brothers and sisters. Many of the white cohort members grew up in the new suburban areas surrounding major cities (Mintz & Kellogg, 1988) while many black cohort members spent at least part of their childhood in northern cities, having moved there from the rural South (Muller & Espenshade, 1985). Most families in all racial groups saw improvements in their standard of living during the 1950s and 1960s (Mintz & Kellogg, 1988; Levy, 1987). The Baby Boomers received more education on average than previous cohorts, nearly 90 percent of the whites, almost 75 percent of the blacks, and over 50 percent of the Hispanics have at least a high school diploma (Bean & Tienda, 1987, p. 242; Farley & Allen, 1987, p. 194). They attended college in greater numbers than any previous generation and, while there, some became involved in the social movements (anti-war, Black Power, Sexual Revolution) of the time. Those members of the cohort who did not attend college may well have been involved in the controversial war in Vietnam. These Baby Boomers entered the labor force during the 1970s, a time of increased international competition and higher prices. This, plus the great numbers of people in the cohort entering the labor market at about the same time, made the competition more intense and progress less certain than it had been for their parents. At the same time, the Civil Rights Movement of the 1960s and the Women's Movement of the 1970s opened up more educational and workplace opportunities for racial minority and women Baby Boomers. All these events taken together influenced many Baby Boomers to delay marriage, a fact illustrated in Figures 1–6 and 1–7.

The Baby Bust Cohort

Members of the 1970–1974 Baby Bust Cohort, as their name indicates, were born during a period of declining birth rates. Typically born into small families during a time of rapidly increasing divorce rates, members of this cohort were more likely than prior twentieth-century cohorts to experience family instability. Proportionately more Baby Busters than Baby Boomers grew up in families that were very well off financially. However, a higher proportion of them also spent at least part of their childhood in poverty or near poverty (Sidel, 1986). The Baby Bust cohort is probably the most ethnically diverse cohort of any of those we are considering. During the 1970s and 1980s, large numbers of Latin Americans and Asians, some of them with children born between 1970 and 1974, immigrated to the United States (Muller & Espenshade, 1985). Born after the major Civil Rights Movement and during the beginning stages of the Women's Movement, the Baby Busters are perhaps the first cohort to expect equal treatment of blacks and whites and of men and women. If the Baby Busters follow the pattern of the late 1960s cohort immediately preceding them, they will end up with somewhat *less* education than the Baby Boomers had (Waldrop & Exter, 1990). The Baby Busters are not included in Figures 1–6 and 1–7 because they have not yet reached the relevant ages.

Summary

Intimate relationships are two-person relationships characterized by emotional and physical closeness, sharing of possessions and selves, and commitment. Marriage is the most usual intimate relationship but not all marriages are intimate and not all intimate relationships are marriages. Intimate relationships can also develop between unmarried heterosexual or homosexual couples and between some family members. The usual research definitions of terms such as marriage and family emphasize the legal relationships of people sharing the same residence. However, increasing numbers of people today live in family-like, emotionally close relationships with people to whom they have no legal relationship. To them, and to many of those involved in legally defined marriages and families, emotional closeness or intimacy is the crucial measure of whether or not a "family" exists.

Intimate relationships always involve choices. Although the choices are made by individuals, they are shaped by cultural and social factors outside the relationship. The freedom to make choices also implies the responsibility of making them wisely and of living with the consequences. Laws often reflect the preferences of one particular group in society, thus limiting the choices of other groups. People with more resources generally have more choices. Despite the constraints, peoples' choices in intimate relationships are greater today than in the past because of more tolerant attitudes, modern technology, and longer life expectancy.

Choices in intimate relationships change as the society does. Economic and demographic changes have affected families throughout the history of the United States. Three major transformations have occurred in U.S. families over time: a move from being economically based to being emotionally based; a move from being large, public units to being small, private ones; and a move from patriarchal to egalitarian authority patterns. Because of differing migration and economic experiences, different ethnic groups have experienced these changes in different ways. U.S. families have continued to change throughout the twentieth century. One way to demonstrate the changes is to compare people born in different birth cohorts. Throughout the text, we will be comparing the New Century (born 1910–1914), Depression (born 1930–1934), Baby Boom (born 1950–1954), and Baby Bust (born 1970–1974) birth cohorts.

CHAPTER 2

BECOMING FEMALE OR MALE

Check the answer that best matches your opinion.

1. It is more important for a *girl* than for a boy to be interested in *art* (like drawing or painting).
   — 1. Yes, it is more important for a girl.
   — 2. Yes, it is somewhat more important for a girl.
   — 3. No, it is not more important for a girl.
2. It is more important for a *boy* than for a girl to be good at *sports*.
   — 1. Yes, it is more important for a boy.
   — 2. Yes, it is somewhat more important for a boy.
   — 3. No, it is not more important for a boy.
3. It is more important for a *girl* than for a boy to like *music*.
   — 1. Yes, it is more important for a girl.
   — 2. Yes, it is somewhat more important for a girl.
   — 3. No, it is not more important for a girl.
4. It is more important for a *boy* than for a girl to be able to *drive a car*.
   — 1. Yes, it is more important for a boy.
   — 2. Yes, it is somewhat more important for a boy.
   — 3. No, it is not more important for a boy.
5. It is more important for a *girl* than for a boy to be *quiet* and *not call attention to herself*.
   — 1. Yes, it is more important for a girl.
   — 2. Yes, it is somewhat more important for a girl.
   — 3. No, it is not more important for a girl.
6. It is more important for a *boy* than for a girl to be a *leader*.
   — 1. Yes, it is more important for a boy.
   — 2. Yes, it is somewhat more important for a boy.
   — 3. No, it is not more important for a boy.
7. It is more important for a *girl* than for a boy to be *cheerful* and *good-natured*.
   — 1. Yes, it is more important for a girl.
   — 2. Yes, it is somewhat more important for a girl.
   — 3. No, it is not more important for a girl.
8. It is more important for a *boy* than for a girl to *stick by his decisions*.
   — 1. Yes, it is more important for a boy.
   — 2. Yes, it is somewhat more important for a boy.
   — 3. No, it is not more important for a boy.

9. If you are a boy, please answer this:
Almost every boy sometimes feels it is hard or difficult to be a boy. How often do you feel this way?
   — 4. I often feel this way.
   — 3. I sometimes feel this way.
   — 2. I rarely feel this way.
   — 1. I almost never or never feel this way.

9. If you are a girl, please answer this:
Almost every girl sometimes feels it is hard or difficult to be a girl. How often do you feel this way?
   — 4. I often feel this way.
   — 3. I sometimes feel this way.
   — 2. I rarely feel this way.
   — 1. I almost never or never feel this way.

10. Suppose you could be born over again. If you could have your wish, would you rather be born a boy or a girl?
    — 1. I would definitely rather be born a boy.
    — 2. I would probably rather be born a boy.
    — 3. I would probably rather be born a girl.
    — 4. I would definitely rather be born a girl.
    Scoring for item 10 1: definitely be other sex, 2: probably be other sex, 3: probably be own sex, 4: definitely be own sex.
    Please check — boy
    — girl
11. Role of boy or girl.
    Boys generally have an easier time of it than girls.
    — 1. Yes, boys definitely have an easier time of it.
    — 2. Yes, boys have a somewhat easier time of it.
    — 3. No, girls have a somewhat easier time of it.
    — 4. No, girls definitely have an easier time of it.
12. A girl has a more interesting life than a boy.
    — 4. Yes, a girl definitely has a more interesting life.
    — 3. Yes, a girl usually has a more interesting life.
    — 2. No, a boy usually has a more interesting life.
    — 1. No, a boy definitely has a more interesting life.
13. Girls have to worry about more things than boys do.
    — 1. Yes, girls definitely have to worry about more things.
    — 2. Yes, girls probably have to worry about more things.
    — 3. No, boys probably have to worry about more things.
    — 4. No, boys definitely have to worry about more things.
14. It is harder for a boy than for a girl to make a success of life.
    — 4. Yes, definitely harder for a boy.
    — 3. Yes, somewhat harder for a boy.
    — 2. No, somewhat harder for a girl.
    — 1. No, definitely harder for a girl.
15. Some people feel boys have the advantage in social life and dating because, for one reason, a boy can ask out a girl he would like to get to know better. Other people feel it is easier for a girl because, for example, she doesn't have to do the asking and risk being refused. What do you think?
    — 1. The boy has the advantage in social life.
    — 2. The boy has somewhat of an advantage.
    — 3. The girl has somewhat of an advantage.
    — 4. The girl has the advantage.

WHAT DO YOU THINK?

Source: Lewin & Tragos, 1987, pp. 132–35.

I tried to believe my parents when they told me I was a boy, but I could find no objective proof for such an assertion. Each morning during the summer, as I cuddled up in the quiet of a corner with a book, my mother would push me out the back door and into the yard. And throughout the day as my blood was let as if I were a patient of 17th-century medicine, I thought of the girls sitting in the shade of porches, playing with their dolls, toy refrigerators, and stoves.

There was the life, I thought! No constant pressure to prove oneself. No necessity always to be competing.

Through no fault of my own I reached adolescence. While the pressure to prove myself on the athletic field lessened, the overall situation got worse—because now I had to prove myself with girls. Just how I was supposed to go about doing this was beyond me, especially because, at the age of 14, I was four foot nine and weighed 78 pounds. (I think there may have been one 10-year-old girl in the neighborhood smaller than I.)

It was the boy who had to ask the girl for the date, a frightening enough prospect until it occurred to me that she might say NO! That meant risking my ego, which was about as substantial as a toilet-paper raincoat in the African rainy season. But I had to thrust that ego forward to be judged, accepted, or rejected by some girl. It wasn't fair! Who was she to sit back like a queen with the power to create joy by her consent or destruction by her denial? It wasn't fair—but that's the way it was.

Now, of course, I know that it was as difficult being a girl as it was a boy, if not more so. While I stood paralyzed at one end of a dance floor trying to find the courage to ask a girl for a dance, most of the girls waited in terror at the other, afraid that no one, not even I, would ask them. And while I resented having to ask a girl for a date, wasn't it horrible to be the one who waited for the phone to ring?

No, it wasn't easy for any of us, girls and boys, as we forced our beautiful free-flowing child-selves into those narrow, constricting cubicles labeled female and male. (Reprinted by permission of the author. Copyright 1973 by Julius Lester.)

Julius Lester's commentary clearly points out that being a boy, striving to meet the expectations that mothers, male peers, and girls hold forth, is often difficult. Boys are not the only ones with the problem: girls too are constrained and frustrated by others' expectations of how they should behave. Lester sees growing into manhood as inevitable ("Through no fault of my own I reached adolescence") but views the process of becoming masculine (or feminine) as distinctly unnatural (". . . we forced our beautiful free-flowing child-selves into those narrow, constricting cubicles labeled female and male").

Lester wrote his sad tale of boyhood frustrations in 1973, depicting a 1950s childhood. Have expectations about boys and girls changed since then? Would he have an easier time growing up male today? Where do expectations about boy and girl behavior come from, and to what extent are they linked to the biological differences between males and females? How much do males and females differ from one another in behavior, feelings, abilities, and personal traits? To the extent that they differ, why?

These questions and others like them are basic to any study of intimate relationships, marriages, and families. People involved in such relationships are involved not simply as human beings but as female or male human beings. Their awareness of themselves as male or female shapes their own behavior within the relationship; their awareness of their partner as male or female shapes their expectations of him or her.

Every chapter in this book deals with the issues of male-female differences and similarities and with how they affect intimate relationships. Chapter 2 sets the stage for these later discussions. First, we consider a few of the observable differences between men and women and assess the extent to which these differences are biologically based. Then we discuss how culture contributes to male-female differences by describing gender-related expectations prevailing in the United States today and how they have changed over time. The final, and major, part of the chapter details how children learn to be male or female and whether such training has changed in recent years.

MALE AND FEMALE DIFFERENCES AND SIMILARITIES

A casual glance around your classroom will likely reveal a number of differences between men and women. Here are some of the differences you might observe: more of the men probably enter the room holding their books against the side of one leg with their arm straight and extended downwards, more of the women hold their books close to their upper body with an arm bent at the elbow; the women are likely to sit in their desks with legs together with knees or feet crossed, men can be seen in a variety of sprawling postures, often with legs apart; you may notice as well that more women than men have "decorated" themselves with makeup and jewelry, and that they wear a wider variety of clothing than the men do. Figure 2–1 illustrates some other body posture differences. What accounts for these apparent differences?

Physical Characteristics

Males and females differ physically from one another in four major respects:

2 Becoming
Female or Male

1. Genetically, they have a different combination of chromosomes on the chromosome pair that determines biological sex.
2. Their bodies are affected by proportionately different amounts of certain hormones.
3. Their internal reproductive organs are different.
4. Their external reproductive organs are different.

Figure 2–1: Female or Male?

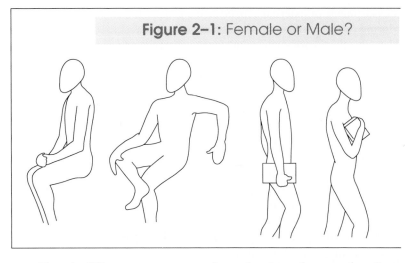

Although the artist has given no anatomical clues, you can probably determine whether each of the individuals is male or female by looking at the way each stands or sits. Males and females learn different body postures as part of socialization into a particular culture.

Genetic differences are present from the time of conception. In a normal conception, the female parent contributes an X chromosome and the male parent contributes either an X or a Y chromosome to the chromosome pair that determines biological sex. An XX combination typically sets off a series of events resulting in a female child; an XY combination usually produces a male child.

While the XX or XY combination starts a human organism on the way to becoming male or female, the action of hormones determines whether it will develop male or female organs. **Hormones** are chemicals that act as signals from one part of the body to another. For our purposes, hormones can be classified into two major groupings—androgens and estrogens. Both males and females produce both types of hormones. However, male bodies produce proportionately more **androgens**, sex hormones that contribute to the development of typically male features (like the growth of body hair) and females produce proportionately more **estrogens**, sex hormones that aid in the development of typically female features (like the development of rounded breasts).

Hormonal effects first show up in the fetus about seven weeks after conception. For the first six weeks after conception, future females and future males are identical except for the difference in sex chromosomes; in fact, both possess the rudimentary internal ducts of both sexes. About seven weeks after conception, the Y chromosome causes the secretion of the androgen testosterone. This event causes the male internal organs to enlarge and grow; other chemical processes induce the rudimentary female organs to shrink. Meanwhile, fetuses with XX chromosomes do not release testosterone and do not develop male organs. The relative lack of androgens in female fetuses causes the development of female internal organs beginning at about the twelfth week of prenatal development and leads to the shrinking of the incipient male organs. The

> **Hormones**
> chemicals that act as signals from one part of the body to another.
>
> **Androgens**
> sex hormones that contribute to the development of typically male features.
>
> **Estrogens**
> sex hormones that aid in the development of typically female features.

development of external reproductive organs follows some time later, during the fourth month of pregnancy (Archer & Lloyd, 1985). We will describe the various male and female internal and external reproductive organs in Chapter 3.

Hormones become important again in the early teenage years or slightly before. At that time, the bodies of young girls produce more estrogens and the bodies of young boys produce more androgens. The increased production of estrogen in girls' bodies sets into motion the female reproductive cycle (described in Chapter 3) and induces breast growth, broadening of the hips, development of a subcutaneous layer of fat, and the appearance of darker body hair under the arms, on the legs, and in the genital area. Increased production of androgens in boys' bodies has parallel effects: their external and internal sexual organs mature and become reproductively capable. Meanwhile, their muscle mass increases, their shoulders broaden, their voices deepen, and body hair appears under their arms, on their faces, genital areas, arms and legs, and (perhaps) chest, back, and toes. Thus, people who used to look like boys and girls look like men and women after undergoing the hormonally induced changes associated with adolescence.

Most of the internal and external physical differences between males and females are directly associated with the different parts they play in reproduction, and many appearance differences not directly related to reproduction (for example, different amounts of body hair) are side effects of reproduction-related hormones. In terms of external appear-

In a given group, most men are taller and larger than women. The differences are not always obvious.

ance, as many variations occur within each sex as occur between them. For example, adult men can weigh 90 pounds or 300 pounds, can be very hairy or virtually hairless, or can be very muscular or very non-muscular. Similar variations occur among adult women. *On average*, men are taller, heavier, and hairier than women, but some individual women are taller, heavier, and hairier than some individual men.

Although male-female reproductive differences are important and male-female appearance differences make human life more interesting, *in most ways, male bodies and female bodies are alike.* Brains, stomachs, hearts, lungs, eyes, and ears (to mention only a few examples) work in the same way in both male and female bodies. Both females and males have to eat, sleep, and protect themselves from heat, cold, rain, and sun. In short, similarities outweigh differences even on a physical level.

Psychological Characteristics

Do the biological differences in males and females lead to differences in their mental abilities, their predominant personality traits, or their level of motivation? Many people believe that men are naturally more competitive, aggressive, ambitious, and analytical than women are, and that women are naturally more sociable, gullible, emotional, and sensitive than men. Is this, in fact, the case? Research on this topic has been done for many decades and, by now, has reached voluminous proportions. A 1974 summary of studies on this issue, for example, identified literally thousands of articles and books, all of which dealt with the question of innate male-female differences in abilities, personality traits, and behavior (Maccoby & Jacklin, 1974).

What does this research show? Marie Richmond-Abbott (1983) summarizes the findings in this way:

1. There is no evidence that males and females differ in overall intelligence or in analytic ability.
2. The evidence suggests that females have achievement motivation equivalent to that of males (although perhaps directed at different goals) and that females seem to be as persistent as males in attaining their goals.
3. There is little evidence that females are innately more sociable than males.
4. Females are no more innately passive nor suggestible than males are.

There are some documented differences as well, but only a few. First, males are more aggressive than females. The two sexes also differ in terms of some mental abilities: females have slightly greater verbal ability than males, while males show slightly better mathematical and visual-spatial abilities (Richmond-Abbott, 1983). The documented differences are small ones and, as with physical appearance differences, they are stated in terms of group averages and say nothing about the abilities or behavior of any particular male or female (Richmond-Abbott, 1983). Thus, the average male score on a standardized math test is usually a little higher than the average female score on the same test but some individual females score much higher than some individual males.

Basing their conclusions on the available research, experts in the area of sex-based psychological differences have reached consensus on two general conclusions. First, there are very few biologically based differences in the competencies, intellectual abilities, or psychological traits between the two sexes. Second, the biologically based differences that do exist are minor and are probably artificially accentuated by the social environment in which males and females find themselves (Kain, 1990; Anderson, 1988; Giele, 1988; Richmond-Abbott, 1983).

MALES, FEMALES, AND CULTURE

We will be documenting differences, similarities, and changes in male and female social behavior—communication patterns, feelings about sexuality, work roles within the family, and so forth—throughout the book. As you might guess from your own observations, we will indeed uncover a great many social behavior differences. The question is "Why so many differences?"

Specifically, if males and females are not really all that different in intelligence, capabilities, or motivation, why are there so many differences in male and female social behavior? Why do more women prefer movies about relationships and more men prefer action-adventure movies? Why do more men like to talk about things and more women like to talk about people? Why do women take care of children more often than men? Why are more men in order-giving jobs and more women in order-taking jobs? And, why, if women and men are not innately different in abilities, do occupational patterns such as those in Table 2–1 appear, with women concentrated in people-care occupations and men in object-manipulation occupations?

Social scientists—from anthropologists to psychologists to sociologists—concerned with such questions agree that the two most important explanations for male-female differences in social behavior are culture and socialization. This major section deals with the culture side of the explanation; the next section takes up socialization explanations.

Table 2–1 Percent of Women in Selected Occupations, 1989	
Occupation	Percent Female Workers
Electrical Engineer	8.5
Registered Nurse	94.2
Automobile Mechanic	0.7
Child Care Worker	96.3

Source: U.S. Bureau of the Census (1991) pp. 395–97.

Culture and Gender Roles

One major reason that males and females show different social behavior has to do with culture. **Culture** refers to the set of knowledge, beliefs, attitudes, and guidelines for behavior commonly held by people who share a common territory, history, and language. Every culture develops and lays out a set of blueprints providing guidance for how its people are expected to act. Some of the "blueprints" are quite rigid, while others allow a considerable amount of flexibility. Some are formally written into the law, but more are informal in nature.

There are many sets of guidelines within every culture. But the guidelines most important for our discussion are the ones that lay out the expectations for male and female behavior. These guidelines about how females and males are supposed to act, think, and feel are collectively known as **gender roles**. Gender roles define what is considered "masculine" (appropriate for boys and men) and "feminine" (appropriate for girls and women) in a given society. Different cultures define different gender roles: some specify very different behavior for females and males; others do not make a great many distinctions. And, because gender roles are created by human beings within a culture, they are always subject to change.

A few cultures include gender role options other than just masculine or feminine. For example, in India people recognize a "third sex" and define a corresponding third gender role (Nanda, 1990). Third sex individuals, who belong to a special religious sect known as hijras, are individuals born with ambiguous-looking genitalia (probably because of unusual prenatal hormone production) or are males whose male organs fail to function. They undergo the removal of their penis, testicles, and scrotum and take up a specialized gender role in their society. Nanda (1990) describes the hijra gender role like this: "Hijras, *as neither men nor women*, function as an institutionalized *third gender role*. Their

Culture
the set of knowledge, beliefs, attitudes, and rules of behavior commonly held by people who share a common territory, history, and language.

Gender roles
cultural guidelines for how females and males are supposed to act, think, and feel.

ambiguous sexual nature accounts for their traditional occupation, that of performing after the birth of a child, at weddings, and at temple festivals" (p. xv; emphasis added).

The gender roles of any particular culture range from being very specific ("Women should remove body hair from underarms and legs; men should remove only facial hair") to being very general ("Be a man" or "Act like a lady"). Within intimate relationships, gender roles influence how females express emotions versus how males do, what sexual intercourse means to women versus what it means to men, what each expects to gain from living together without marrying, and the importance of work and family to women versus men. Gender roles provide guidance to parents as they rear their girl and boy children and to young adults as they plan their future choices. Gender roles will be discussed throughout the book. Here, we focus on describing the tra-

In India, people recognize a "third sex" in a group known as the hijras, *and define a corresponding gender role.*

ditional gender role script for males and the traditional gender role script for females in the twentieth-century United States. Since the traditional scripts are currently a matter of controversy, we also focus on the extent to which gender roles are changing.

Traditional Male Gender Roles

The gender roles that people in the United States think of as being "traditional," the traits they see as being "masculine" and "feminine" are not particularly ancient. As you will learn in Chapter 9, the separation of women and men into distinctive spheres of life and the development of very different, almost totally opposite, guidelines for male and female behavior were fully elaborated only during the nineteenth century (Filene, 1986; Bernard, 1981; Welter, 1966). They stayed in force, although with some changes and fluctuations, until the late 1970s. Many of them remain influential in the 1990s. What are these guidelines?

A 1970s exploration of the prevailing male gender role in the United States identified four major themes. Robert Brannon (1976), the author of the exploration, asserted that despite all the variations and fads in what men did, thought, and said, they were expected to avoid "sissy stuff," become "big wheels," present themselves as "sturdy oaks," and be aggressive.

No Sissy Stuff: The Stigma of Anything Vaguely Feminine   The rule specifying that men avoid "sissy stuff" was a negative one: to be a real man, a male must not do what women do. "Real" men, according to the guidelines, avoided anything feminine, because to do something feminine calls into question a male's manhood. Thus, men were not to cook (unless they were cooking outside on the grill) or do housework, were to do as little child care as possible (although they could help if their wives needed assistance periodically), and were advised not to be concerned with fashion, clothes, and color coordination. Such activities were associated with femininity and were to be avoided. Little boys, as future men, were expected to reject dolls as suitable playthings and to protest being dressed up in formal clothing (Brannon, 1976).

The Big Wheel: Success, Status, and the Need to Be Looked up To
To be considered a real man under traditional gender role guidelines, a male had to be successful at something. Occupational success was the most usual measure of manhood. Men who could not achieve occupational success could still be considered "real men" if they succeeded at something else—outdrinking friends, driving the fastest car, or dating the prettiest (or most) women. Men who failed to outcompete other men in something were considered losers and less than real men (Brannon, 1976).

Jessie Bernard (1981), in her analysis of the traditional male gender role in the United States, suggests more restrictive criteria for true success. According to her, occupational success was the principal criteria the culture used to evaluate masculinity: "To be a man one had to be not only a provider but a *good* provider. Success in the good-provider role came in time to define masculinity itself" (Bernard, 1981, p. 4). Success as a father, husband or member of the community was virtually irrelevant if a man was not also successful occupationally and economically.

The Sturdy Oak: A Manly Air of Toughness, Confidence, and Self-Reliance   According to traditional gender role guidelines, a real man stood up for himself, his family, and his principles and was prepared to endure the costs of his actions. Confident in his abilities, he felt he could handle himself in difficult situations. Although he might feel emotions, such as love, fear, or tenderness, he kept them under control (as the old saying goes, he was careful "not to wear them on his sleeve") or expressed them in a masculine way (Brannon, 1976).

The stories told about many of our male cultural heroes—George Washington, the defenders of the Alamo, Martin Luther King, Jr.—are framed to emphasize the virtues of tough, confident, enduring men. Thus, men like Captain Edward Smith of the Titanic, who placed the welfare of his passengers above his own welfare and ordered "Women and children first!" into the lifeboats, are admired and remembered, and men like Captain Yiannis Avranas, who in the summer of 1991 boarded a lifeboat and abandoned 225 passengers on his sinking cruise ship Oceanos, are harshly criticized (Lord, 1991).

Give 'em Hell: The Aura of Aggression, Violence, and Daring   Finally, the traditional gender role script for men included the expectation that men would be aggressive, daring, and capable of violence: "To be seen as a 'real man' . . . , there should be at least a hint of untamed primitive force beneath a civilized exterior" (Brannon, 1976, p. 33). Thus, for years, male movie heroes often have been extremely violent as well as sturdy and nonemotional. And pain-inflicting male sports such as boxing, football, and hockey have long been popular.

Traditional Female Gender Roles

A comparable set of cultural guidelines described the gender roles associated with true femininity. These guidelines can be summarized in the form of three lessons impressed upon young women growing up prior to the early 1970s: accommodation, inferiority to men, and domesticity (Weitzman, 1984).

Accommodation   The gender role ideal for women was to be accommodating to the needs and wants of others. This meant that women were to be nurturing, cooperative, sweet, expressive, not too intelligent, and fairly passive. Whereas men were expected to take a stand based on individual principles and remain true to it, women were expected to ascertain what those around them felt, needed, and wanted before deciding what to do and to leave the big issues to men.

These expectations were incorporated in the ways women were trained to use language. In an intriguing article entitled "Talking Like a Lady," Robin Lakoff (1979) noted that, traditionally, women were encouraged to talk about relatively minor topics, such as precise discriminations of color and changes in fashion, and leave the important issues of power and money to men (thus explaining why many elderly widows have so little information about their families' financial situation when their husbands die). Further, people encouraged women to express strong emotions in a sweeter, more "lady-like" way than men. Women were expected to fuss, complain, whimper, or cry when confronted with situations about which men could (and should, according to the rules) yell, shout, and swear. Finally, adults trained future women to communicate in a less assertive way than men. Women more frequently use what Lakoff calls a "tag question"—a sentence that is a cross between an assertion and a question that is used to give information in a non-assertive way. Imagine a young woman who, having fixed dinner, asks her husband "Dinner will be ready at 6:00, OK?" From an objective standpoint, this question makes no sense; he does not know when dinner will be ready, she does. But from the standpoint of the accommodation rule, the question makes sense. The use of the tag question allows the young woman to do two things: inform her husband in a non-assertive way that dinner is ready and to *hint*—not order—that he should be ready for dinner at 6:00.

Inferiority to Men   The second lesson that young women growing up prior to the 1970s were expected to accept (or to at least pretend that they accepted) was that they were less capable and less important than men, especially men their age or older and from the same or a higher social class. In a classic gender role study, Mirra Komarovsky (1946) asked female seniors in an elite women's college about the way they interacted with males. Many of the written replies indicate these women were aware of (but not happy with) the inferiority lesson. One fresh-man had written to her brother about a delightful date and was sur-prised at his response:

> "For heaven's sake," came the reply, "when will you grow up? Don't you know that a boy likes to think he is better than a girl? Give him a little competition (in ping-pong), sure, but miss a few serves in the end. Should you join the Debate Club? By all means, but don't practice too much on the boys." Believe me, I was stunned by this letter, but then I saw that he was right. To be a success in the dorms one must date, to date one must not win too many ping-pong games. At first, I resented this bitterly. But now I am more or less used to it and live in hope of one day meeting a man who is my superior so that I may be my natural self (p. 186).

Another senior wrote about a work situation:

> I was once at a work camp. The girls did the same work as the boys. If some girls worked better, the boys resented it fiercely. The director told one capable girl to slow down to keep peace in the group (p. 188).

Domesticity   The third traditional gender role lesson outlined a fe-male's major goal and purpose in life: to be a full-time wife and mother. The strongly held expectation was, that except under unusual circum-stances, women should marry and should have children. Furthermore, they should expect to devote their major energies to nurturing and making a home for their husband and their children. Women who failed to (or chose not to) find a husband and bear children were less than complete women, considered "unnatural" or "masculine" (Veroff, Douvan, & Kulka, 1981).

Getting married was the feminine way of demonstrating that one had grown up—that one was no longer a girl but a woman. The timing of the transition, however, varied depending on individual circum-stances. The critical time for lower- and working-class girls, for example, was the end of high school. Their senior year represented the "terminal year"—their last year of high school and their last year "to find a husband" (Weitzman, 1984). Middle-class girls could postpone their terminal year by going to college (or maybe even to graduate or pro-fessional school). But they too eventually faced it. As Weitzman (1984) notes: "But whenever it (the terminal year) comes, it brings the same pressures to marry and settle down—to find a husband, to buy a home, to have children—and to fulfill one's role as 'a woman'" (p. 193).

In one sense, the traditional gender roles just described for men and women were merely suggestions: many individual males and females disagreed with one or more of the gender guidelines and chose their own ways of being male and female. Others accepted the suggestions but found them impossible to fulfill given their own personality traits or circumstances. However, in another sense, the traditional gender roles were also much more than suggestions to individuals. *They also formed the basis for the allocation of opportunities and rewards.* A few examples should make this last point clear. In each case, traditional gender roles operated to open opportunities to some and close them to others.

Example 1   Until 1976, women could not enter the national military academies, regardless of their personal qualifications and desires. The academies stressed masculine values and offered opportunities felt to be very suitable for men but not at all suitable for women, given the prevailing gender roles.

Example 2   The expectation that men would be providers and that women would be full-time wives and mothers led many employers to pay men much higher salaries than women doing the same or comparable work. These unequal pay patterns held regardless of the family situation of the individuals involved: bachelors with no one to support but themselves frequently made higher salaries than single mothers with several children.

Example 3   In most junior high and high schools, only girls could take home economics and only boys could enroll in shop and woodworking classes, reflecting and reinforcing the traditional gender roles. Schools often had a full program of interschool athletic competition for boys, in line with expectations that boys should be competitive and achievement oriented. When athletic programs for girls existed, they were often intramural or very poorly funded.

Variations in Traditional Gender Roles

The traditional gender roles we have just described represent guidelines as defined and disseminated by white, Protestant, middle-class families. As noted in Chapter 1, the views of this group are important since they make the laws and shape the contours of popular culture. During the years when these traditional guidelines were most prevalent, the United States contained many males and females who were not white, Protestant, or middle class. Ethnic, racial, social class, and religious diversity is even more characteristic of the United States in the 1990s. Did the traditional gender roles hold for nonwhite, nonmiddle-class groups as well?

For the most part, the differences between white, middle-class gender role expectations and those of other groups are variations of degree rather than being completely different expectations. For example, different subcultural groups within the United States emphasize different parts of the traditional male gender role previously described. Working-class and rural people put somewhat more emphasis on the Sturdy Oak and aggressiveness dimensions of the male gender role, while urban, middle-class people focus on the Big Wheel dimension (Brannon, 1976). Being a successful breadwinner is somewhat important to men in all groups, but is an especially important dimension of manhood for Hispanics (Horowitz, 1983) and African Americans (Taylor *et al.*, 1990; Vega, 1990). As a final male example, the Sturdy Oak and aggressiveness dimensions are antithetical to Jewish cultural traditions, which encourage emotional expressiveness and intellectual, rather than physical, approaches to problems. However, because of their culture's emphasis on academic and occupational achievement, Jewish men are very familiar with the Big Wheel dimension of masculinity (Kimmel, 1989).

Some subcultural groups within the United States—the working class and Chicanos, for example—tend to think of males and females as having more differences than other subcultures do. They therefore emphasize the importance of making clear separations between boys and girls and between men and women. Thus, lower- and working-class families have traditionally been less accepting of behavior not conforming to strict gender roles. For example, they tend to be uncomfortable with a daughter's desire to excel in school rather than going on dates or a son's tendency to cry when frustrated (Weitzman, 1984). Similarly, Chicano families expect teenage boys to show their independence while simultaneously expecting teenage girls to stick close to home and go out only under supervision (Horowitz, 1983). Not surprisingly, the domestic role of wife and mother receives special emphasis in all these groups (Weitzman, 1984; Horowitz, 1983).

The wife-mother gender role expectation has long created special problems for many nonmiddle class and racial minority group families, however. Given the realities of discrimination and low paying jobs, few men could afford to be the sole income-earners in their families. As a result, they continued to hold to the *ideal* of a stay-at-home wife and mother but simultaneously acknowledged that women might sometimes have to work outside the home. The results of such compromises between ideals and reality are illustrated well by research on black women. On the one hand, researchers have found black women to be strong, assertive, independent, and self-sufficient and to value these qualities. On the other hand, black women also embrace the same traditionally feminine attributes as white women: they want to be tender, sensitive, gentle, and compassionate (Anderson, 1988; Weitzman, 1984). Attempting to explain the apparent conflict in these two very different characterizations of black women, Weitzman (1984) suggests that they are not contradictory at all. Rather, they reflect the particular circumstances in which black women find themselves. First, since they are raised in the United States and exposed to the same kinds of popular culture influences as are white women, they hold many traditional "feminine" values. But, because black men face considerable difficulties finding and holding jobs with high enough incomes to support a family, black women have been unable to count on marriage or on men for their economic security. They learn early in life that they have to take care of themselves. Since work is an important avenue to economic security, and since education is an important avenue to a good job, both work and education (typically "masculine" values) have long been highly valued by black women (Weitzman, 1984).

Changes in Traditional Gender Roles

As we pointed out in Chapter 1, people in the United States changed their attitudes about many family-related issues during the late 1970s and early 1980s. Many changed their behavior as well. What effect did these changes have on traditional gender roles?

Both sexes, but especially women, have more choices and flexibility today than they did twenty-five or thirty years ago. The traditional gender roles have not disappeared: being married and having children are still very important goals for women, and being married, having children, and providing for their families are still very important goals for men (Taylor *et al.*, 1990; Vega, 1990; Weitzman, 1984; Thornton, Alwin, & Camburn, 1983). In a sense, gender-related family roles have been added to rather than eliminated or reversed. As you will learn in Chapter 9, there are growing expectations that married mothers should help provide for the family and that married fathers should take an active part in caring for their children (LaRossa, 1988).

Many, but not all, of the opportunities once blocked because of the strong influence of traditional gender roles are now open to both sexes. Thus, both boys and girls are now allowed to enroll in home economics and shop and to participate in interschool athletics. Women can now enter and graduate from the national military academies. In academic year 1989–1990, for the first time ever, a woman cadet became First Captain of the Corps of Cadets at West Point (*U.S. News & World Report*, 1989, pp. 26–27). Although legally prohibited by federal law from being given a combat assignment, women have led (in one case) troops into combat and been killed in military action. In addition, women have entered many other occupational fields once considered suitable only for men. With these types of changes, the traditional gender role instructions to women to be passive and to downplay their intelligence and competency have undoubtedly weakened.

Although a few observers believe that the family provider role for men has decreased in importance to be partially replaced by a free-wheeling playboy guideline (Ehrenreich, 1983), most commentators believe that traditional male gender roles have undergone much less change than traditional female gender roles (England & Swoboda, 1988). Males are still encouraged to avoid the appearance of being associated with feminine things and marketers help them in this regard. Boys, for example, do not play with "dolls" (that would be too girlish) but rather with doll-like toys called G.I. Joe, GoBots, or Masters of the Universe. And, when men buy a fragrance to wear, they do not purchase a perfume (which is associated with femininity), but rather a cologne with a masculine name such as Brut, Iron, or English Leather.

The male gender role specification about aggressiveness seems, if anything, more important than ever. Consider, for example, some of

Bill Orr, husband of Kay Orr, Nebraska's first woman governor, is an example of a man who has overcome traditional gender roles.

the most popular male sports. North American professional hockey (played under U.S. rules designed to facilitate a certain amount of fighting) is characterized by fights, while Olympic hockey (played under international rules designed to prevent fights) is not. Professional boxing, football, and wrestling are all very popular sports and all contain violence as a (or *the*) core part of the action. And popular movies, such as the Rocky or Terminator series, are filled with male violence and aggression.

As noted in Chapter 1, attitudes related to certain aspects of gender roles—authority in the household, parenthood, and premarital sexual activity—have greatly changed since the 1960s and early 1970s (Thornton, 1989; Giele, 1988; McBroom, 1987). Nonetheless, people still tend to believe that certain personality traits characterize males, and other, quite different, traits characterize females. One study of college students in 1988, for example, found that they were just as likely to think about males and females in stereotypical terms as students in 1972 were (Bergen & Williams, 1991). As you will see throughout this book, much has changed in the realm of gender roles but much has remained the same.

SOCIALIZATION: LEARNING TO BE MASCULINE OR FEMININE

Every culture provides some guidelines for how to be masculine or feminine, but babies are not born knowing these guidelines (or anything else about the culture they have entered). The process through which new members of a culture learn its language, values, beliefs, and behavioral expectations is known as **socialization**. We are particularly concerned with learning about maleness and femaleness, masculinity and femininity. The topic is an important one, because early learning affects later life. The lessons boys and girls learn about masculinity and femininity shape their own behavior and their expectations of the opposite sex throughout life; the disparate socialization of girls and boys undoubtedly explains some of the differences in adult male and female behavior.

> **Socialization**
> the process through which new members of a culture learn its language, values, beliefs, and behavioral expectations.

What Do They Have to Learn?

Socialization into maleness or femaleness involves at least four elements.

1. Learning one's sex—whether one is a male or a female.
2. Identifying psychologically with one sex or the other, developing a **sexual identity**.

> **Sexual identity**
> the psychological identification of an individual as either male or female.

3. Learning the gender roles set forth by the culture in which one lives.
4. Integrating certain of those gender roles into one's own personality, thus developing a **gender identity**.

Biological Sex and Gender Roles

You might note that both one's sex and the gender role guidelines are decided upon by others. "Male" and "female" are labels that other people assign to one at birth (or in this era of ultrasound technology, even before birth) based on the appearance of certain external organs. Being able to identify each person as male or female is so important in U.S. society (as well as in most others) that babies who are born with ambiguous-looking external organs or who are born with the reproductive organs of both sexes are "assigned" to one sex or the other. Appropriate surgery and hormonal therapy is then instituted to make sure their external appearance will conform to their societally assigned sex (Gagnon & Henderson, 1980; Money & Ehrhardt, 1975). Children still have to learn which sex they have been assigned, but the assignment has been done by others.

A similar situation exists with respect to learning gender roles. Gender roles, although subject to change and to subcultural variation, are created by others, not by the child. The child has to learn what the guidelines are, but someone else has written them.

Sexual Identity and Gender Identity

Establishing a sexual identity and a gender identity are both psychological processes occurring within a child's mind. An individual with a male sexual identity *thinks* and *feels* like a biological male. Most of the time sex and sexual identity correspond: people thought of as females by others also identify themselves that way, and people thought of as males also identify themselves as male. However, an individual's biological, assigned sex and sexual identity may be inconsistent. The case of Jan Morris, the reporter who accompanied Sir Edmund Hillary on his historic climb of Mount Everest, illustrates this possibility (Gagnon & Henderson, 1975). Jan Morris (known as James before her sex change operation) lived much of her life as a psychological female "locked" in a male's body; "I was three or perhaps four years old when I realized that I had been born into the wrong body, and should really be a girl. I remember the moment well, and it is the earliest memory of my life" (quoted in Gagnon & Henderson, 1975, p. 3). At age 46, James Morrison, conventional male, successful writer, husband, and father of five, underwent the ordeal of a sex change operation. Afterward, her sex and her sexual identity matched for the first time.

Gender identity
the extent to which an individual has learned and incorporated the behaviors and expectations associated with a gender role into his or her own personality.

Similarly, gender identity refers to the extent to which an individual has incorporated into his or her own personality the behaviors and expectations associated with one or both gender roles. Note that there is a good deal of individual choice here. Two girls might be exposed to the same lessons about female gender roles but establish quite different gender identities. For example, one might incorporate all elements of traditional femininity into her idea of who she is ("I am nurturant, sweet, soft-spoken, and not as smart as boys, and I plan to be a wife and mother someday") while the other thinks of herself as having a "masculine" personality ("I like sports, am very ambitious and competitive, and hope to be an aeronautical engineer some day"). Both girls are biologically female, both have a female sexual identity, and both know about the gender roles regarding femininity. They differ only in gender identity: the first thinks of herself as a feminine female and the second as a masculine female. The Personal Application that follows provides a way for you to assess your own gender identity.

Personal Application

Gender Identity Assessment

How would you describe your personality traits to someone else? Do you identify with and incorporate mostly "feminine" traits? mostly "masculine" traits? traits associated with neither masculinity nor femininity? traits associated with both? This exercise will help you think about your gender identity. First, check those attributes on the list that you think apply to you. Then, read the instructions for interpreting your choices.

I would describe myself as:

___	1. strong	___	19. tough
___	2. sensitive	___	20. submissive
___	3. intellectual	___	21. funny
___	4. aggressive	___	22. muscular
___	5. dainty	___	23. emotional
___	6. nice	___	24. determined
___	7. authoritative	___	25. handsome
___	8. delicate	___	26. quiet
___	9. kind	___	27. good-natured
___	10. dominant	___	28. hardworking
___	11. weak	___	29. frail
___	12. friendly	___	30. loving
___	13. breadwinner	___	31. hard
___	14. soft	___	32. pretty
___	15. generous	___	33. content
___	16. big	___	34. powerful
___	17. nurturing	___	35. housekeeper
___	18. sexy	___	36. polite

Now, mark each attribute with an "a," "b," or "c," starting with the first attribute (#1), then moving to the second (#2), etc. "Strong" will be marked "a," "sensitive" will be marked "b," and "intellectual" will be marked "c." Now, start over with "aggressive"; it will be marked "a," "dainty" will be marked "b," and "nice" will be marked "c." Continue this pattern for all 36 attributes. You will end up with 12 attributes marked "a," 12 marked "b," and 12 marked "c." The attributes marked "a" were listed by students in the authors' classes as typically associated with "masculinity," those marked "b" were typically associated with "femininity." Those marked "c" were considered neutral.

1. How many typically "masculine" ("a") attributes did you check? How many typically "feminine" ("b") ones? Did you check an equal number of both, or did you have more of one than the other?
2. If you are involved in an intimate relationship, you might want to have your partner do an assessment like this. Is your partner's personality very different from yours? If it is, is that a problem or an advantage?
3. What about your parents (and perhaps grandparents), what are their personalities like? Are you different from your parents? Are your parents different from your grandparents? Do you see evidence of change in your own family (from your grandparents to your parents to you) in terms of masculinity and femininity in males and females?
4. If you had total control over the personality of your current or future children, which of the attributes on the list would you want your daughter(s) to have? your son(s)?

Just as there is no logical necessity for consistency between sex and sexual identity or between gender role and gender identity, neither does logic demand consistency among all four elements. One of the most intriguing examples of potential inconsistency among the four is found among the Nandi of Kenya. In this society, women have the option of adopting a masculine gender role by *taking a wife and becoming a husband* (Oboler, 1980). The advantages for doing so are clear once one understands Nandi culture. First, Nandi culture allows polygyny, a marriage system characterized by one husband and more than one wife. Second, Nandi women, with very few exceptions, do not have the right to own property. Third, inheritance is from father to son; when a Nandi male dies, all his wealth is divided evenly among his wives and it is passed through the wives to their sons. A woman who has no son has no claim to "her" portion of her husband's wealth; her wealth will be divided among her husband's other wives to be passed on to their sons.

To exert any control over the wealth, a Nandi wife must have a son. While some "sonless" Nandi women adopt sons, many avoid this strategy because of its expense and because the children who are available for adoption are often sickly or in other ways undesirable.

A second option, one many Nandi women prefer, is to take the wealth she would have spent adopting a male child and use it to purchase a wife *for herself*. Having purchased a wife, the Nandi woman acts as a husband towards her new wife *although she is still married to her own husband* and expects her new wife to treat her as a husband. As one Nandi female husband stated: "No, I don't (carry things on my head). That is a woman's duty and nothing to do with me. I became a man and I am a man and that is all. Why should I assume women's work anymore?" (quoted in Oboler, 1980, p. 69)

To produce sons, the Nandi female husband allows her wife to have male lovers. While these male lovers can have sex with the female husband's wife, they do not have any claim to any child created by the sexual relationship. All of the children of the female husband's wife belong to the female husband. In this way, a "sonless" Nandi female is able to have a male child who can then inherit her portion of her husband's wealth. To put this example into the context of our discussion, these Nandi women are female (their *sex* is female), have the *sexual identity* of female (they know that biologically they are female), play masculine *gender roles* (they perform the duties of a husband to their wife), and have a masculine *gender identity* (they consider themselves to be a man when interacting with their wife).

How Do They Learn?

The process of learning one's sex, establishing a sexual identity, learning the gender roles associated with one's sex, and developing one's own gender identity is a complex one. Experts argue about exactly how it occurs (Fagot & Leinbach, 1989; Maccoby, 1966). They agree, however, that the process depends, at least initially, on the child picking up clues from others about sex and gender differences. As it turns out, others are very generous about giving out such clues. Most often the clues correspond closely to traditional beliefs about masculinity and femininity.

Clues

As noted, the first label a new baby is likely to be given by others is a label indicating biological sex; all new babies are quickly labeled as either "boys" or "girls." The label is important because it gives parents, grandparents, friends, and strangers a well-known and convenient way of deciding how to respond to the infant. Research indicates that the label *does* make a difference; boy babies and girl babies are thought of and treated differently from the beginning of their lives. In one study, researchers interviewed parents within twenty-four hours of their baby's birth and asked them to describe their babies as they would to a relative or friend and to rate their babies on a variety of measures. Both mothers and fathers rated daughters as softer, finer featured, littler, prettier, and more inattentive than sons. Meanwhile, doctors who evaluated these same infants on a variety of objective measures (for example, birth length and weight, respiration, heart rates, and reflexes) determined there were no significant differences between the boys and the girls. In other words, within hours of the birth of their children, parents already were "seeing" objectively nonexistent differences based only on knowledge of their baby's biological sex (Rubin, Provenzano, & Luria, 1974).

People with no personal relationship to a baby show similar patterns. Condry and Condry (1976) videotaped a nine-month-old infant responding to a variety of stimuli and showed the video to several college student audiences. The college students described the actions of the infants in stereotypical ways. In one especially illustrative situation, a jack-in-the-box popped up in front of the infant. The infant responded by crying. When the college students were told the infant was a girl named Lisa, they were likely to say she was frightened. But when they were told it was a boy named David, they said he was angry. The video remained the same; only the sexual designation of the infant had been changed. But that change was enough to affect how strangers interpreted the baby's behavior.

Different interpretations of behavior lead to different responses. Take the case of Lisa, David, and the jack-in-the-box, for example. Would you not treat a child differently if you thought she were frightened (probably picking her up to comfort her) than if you thought he were angry (perhaps you would give the jack-in-the-box a fake punch)? Would you not be more likely to play vigorously with an infant you believed to be sturdy and strong (as infant boys are often perceived) and to smile and coo at one you believed to be pretty and little (as infant girls are often perceived)?

The differential assessment and treatment boys and girls receive as infants do not have an immediate effect on their self-identification and behavior. Infants act pretty much alike regardless of sex and are mentally incapable of thinking in categories such as "male" and "female." Exposure to differential treatment and clues about masculinity and femininity continues beyond infancy, however. Parents, relatives, and friends act out their ideas about what girls and boys should be like in their choices of clothing, toys, and room decorations. Consider this summary of a study of the contents of the rooms of preschool boys and girls: "The contents of the boys' rooms were more varied and contained more toy animals, vehicles, and live animals, whereas girls' rooms contained more dolls, dollhouses, floral wallpaper, fabrics, and lace" (Archer & Lloyd, 1985, p. 260).

Children pick up additional hints about maleness and femaleness by observing children and adults of both sexes, by reading about them in books, and by watching male and female characters on television. Children's television presents a particularly exaggerated view of traditional gender roles:

> Contemporary shows are either essentially all-male, like "Garfield," or are organized on what I call the Smurfette principle: a group of male buddies will be accented by a lone female, stereotypically defined. In the worst cartoons... the female is usually a little sister type, a bunny in a pink dress and hair ribbons who tags along with the adventurous bears and badgers (Pollitt, 1991, p. 22).

Developing Gender Categories and a Sexual Identity

Using clues provided by their social environment, most children begin to label themselves as "boy" or "girl" and to become aware that boys and girls belong to different categories sometime between their second and third birthdays (Fagot & Leinbach, 1989). The ability to use labels does not necessarily mean that they are firmly committed to a male or female sexual identity: some research indicates that until about age five or six, children believe that sex can be changed (for example, that a girl could become a boy by cutting her hair or that boys can grow up to be mommies) (Archer & Lloyd, 1985; Kohlberg, 1966). Once established, however, sexual identity—the firm psychological conviction that one is male or female—does not change. Thus, by the age of five or six (and perhaps somewhat before), children are well aware that there are two sexes and that they will belong to one of them for the rest of their lives.

Children learn the gender role guidelines of their culture at about the same time that they learn to separate people into male and female categories and often before they have clearly established their own sexual identity. By the age of three or four, children use the same descriptions of males and females that older children and adults do. These characterizations reflect the traditional gender roles described earlier and correspond closely to mass media depictions. Consider the following examples.

When preschool children are shown videos of babies labeled as male or female and then asked questions about the babies, they answer in much the same way as adults. In one study, children between the ages of three and five watched videos of a boy and a girl infant. For one set of children, the infants were labeled correctly; for a second set, the labels were reversed. Researchers asked both sets of children to describe each infant using a predetermined set of adjectives. The children more often described the baby they believed to be a boy as big (versus little for infants labeled as a girl), fast (versus slow for girls), strong (versus weak for girls), loud (versus quiet for girls), and hard (versus soft for girls). The children, apparently, had already learned to pay more attention to the label than to the baby's actual behavior (Haugh, Hoffman, & Cowan, 1980).

Young children's ideas about gender-appropriate occupations also tend to follow traditional gender role guidelines. Gettys and Cann (1981) asked three groups of children (ages two to three, four to five, and six to seven) to assign one of 10 occupations to either a male or a female doll, dressed as much alike as possible. Boys and girls responded in similar ways but the child's age did make a difference, with younger children giving less stereotyped responses. As illustrated in Figure 2–2, 78 percent of the two to three year olds and more than 96 percent of the four to five year olds and the six-to-seven-year-old students assigned the occupation "construction worker" to a male doll. Meanwhile, 56 percent of the two to three year olds, 16 percent of the three to four year olds, and only three percent of the six-to-seven-year-old students assigned the occupation "librarian" to a male doll. The differential responses by children according to age in this study illus-

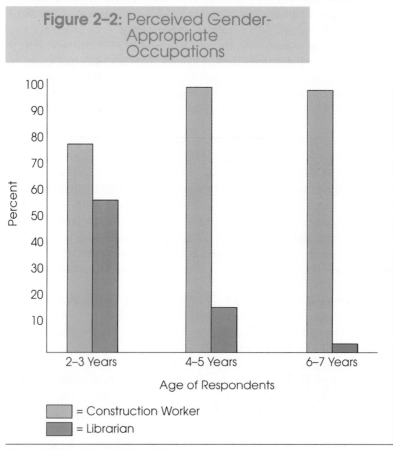

Figure 2–2: Perceived Gender-Appropriate Occupations

Percent

Age of Respondents

☐ = Construction Worker
■ = Librarian

As they approach school age, children become more stereotyped in their thinking about which occupations are appropriate for men and women. The bars show the proportion of children assigning the occupation to a male (as opposed to a female) doll. By age 6–7, almost all the children designated the construction worker role to the male doll, while only 3 percent assigned the librarian role to the male doll.

Source: Gettys and Cann, 1981, p. 304.

trate just how quickly children absorb gender role information once they learn the labels.

Developing a Gender Identity

As noted previously, however, people can know about gender roles and even think about them in traditional ways without necessarily using them as strict guidelines for their own behavior. Thus, the question of *how* boys and girls develop their own unique gender identity remains. There are two major points of view on the issue: social learning theory and cognitive development theory.

Social Learning Theory   **Social learning theory** states that the reaction of others to a child's behavior is the key to explaining gender identity formation (Mischel, 1966). Children observe both sexes and try out the behaviors of both. They continue those behaviors for which they are rewarded (by attention, praise, encouragement, and so forth) and abandon those for which they are punished (by scolding, teasing, physical punishment, or lack of attention). Thus, a boy who is praised in his attempts to lift heavy objects but shoved outside when he expresses an interest in playing "tea party" with his sister will probably continue to practice the "masculine" things and give up on the "feminine."

Social learning theory receives strong support from case studies of children whose biological sex is not entirely clear, where assigned sex and actual sex do not correspond in all ways. Perhaps the best-known case concerns an identical male twin whose penis was destroyed in a medical accident when he was seven months old (Money & Ehrhardt, 1975). A plastic surgeon advised the parents to reassign the child as a girl rather than to deal with the issue of raising a male child without a penis. Over the next several years, the physical transformation was accomplished through surgery and hormonal therapy. The parents, employing reinforcement techniques used by many parents to insure gender role conformity, trained their genetically male child to adopt a female sexual identity and a feminine gender identity. Two social scientists studying the case reported:

> The first items of change were clothes and hairdo. The mother reported: "I started dressing her not in dresses but, you know, in little pink slacks and frilly blouses . . . and letting her hair grow." A year and six months later, the mother wrote that she had made a special effort at keeping her girl in dresses, almost exclusively, changing any item of clothes into something that was clearly feminine. "I even made all her nightwear into granny gowns and she wears bracelets and hair ribbons." The effects of emphasizing feminine clothing became clearly noticeable in the girl's attitude toward clothes and hairdo another

Social learning theory a theory of socialization stating that the reaction of others to a child's behavior is the key to explaining gender identity formation.

year later, when she was observed to have a clear preference for dresses over slacks and to take pride in her long hair.

Related to being dressed nicely is the sense of neatness. The mother stated that her daughter by four and a half years of age was much neater than her brother, and in contrast with him, disliked to be dirty; "She likes for me to wipe her face. She doesn't like to be dirty, and yet my son is quite different. I can't wash his face for anything . . . . She seems to be daintier. Maybe it's because I encouraged it." Elsewhere in the recorded interview, the mother said: One thing that really amazes me is that she is so feminine. I've never seen a little girl so neat and tidy as she can be when she wants to be . . . (Money & Ehrhardt, 1975, pp. 47–48).

Cognitive Development Theory   While social learning stresses the importance of outside reinforcement and rewards, **cognitive development theory** posits that children form a strong, internal image of themselves first (a sexual identity) as a natural stage of mental development, and then select behavior appropriate to that identity (Kohlberg, 1966). The rewards are internal rather than external; the individual feels rewarded when he or she successfully performs behavior consistent with his or her sexual identity. A cognitive development theorist would note, correctly, that sex reassignment and differential reinforcement of gender-appropriate behaviors do not work after a child already has a firm sexual identity.

The same basic processes at work during early childhood continue to shape gender behavior in later childhood and adolescence. Peer group reactions to "inappropriate" gender behavior become more influential as children grow older. Some observers feel that the pressure to conform to one's traditional gender role intensifies during adolescence, a period in which peer groups are especially important and parents often begin to apply different rules to girls and boys. As the "Alternative Choice" section points out, however, not everyone chooses to conform.

> **Cognitive development theory** a theory of socialization stating that children form a strong, internal image of themselves first (a sexual identity), and then select behavior appropriate to that identity.

Changes in Socialization

To what extent has the socialization of boy and girl children changed since the 1970s? One clear change is that both boys and girls are able to see women (including their own mothers) doing many more kinds of work today than could their counterparts twenty-five years ago. And their mothers and fathers can purchase, if they so choose, identical colorful outfits for boys and girls, toys designed to be gender-neutral, and childrearing books such as Pogrebin's *Growing up Free* (1981) that give advice about how to rear well-adjusted children while avoiding the rigidity of traditional gender roles.

Children's books have changed as well, at least up to a point. A comparison of children's readers in 1972 to children's readers in 1989, for example, found that the 1989 readers featured many more girls and women than the 1972 readers, showed women in a larger variety of occupations, and portrayed girls being brave and boys crying slightly more often than the 1972 books (Purcell & Stewart, 1990). Figure 2–3 presents some of the information from this study. Picture books for children also show some changes. A study of Caldecott Award winners (the Caldecott is given to the most distinguished picture book of the year) done in 1972 noted that these prize-winning books seldom featured females at all while males starred and were portrayed as active, adventurous, and independent (Weitzman *et al.*, 1972). Picture book studies done in the early 1980s showed an increase in the number of

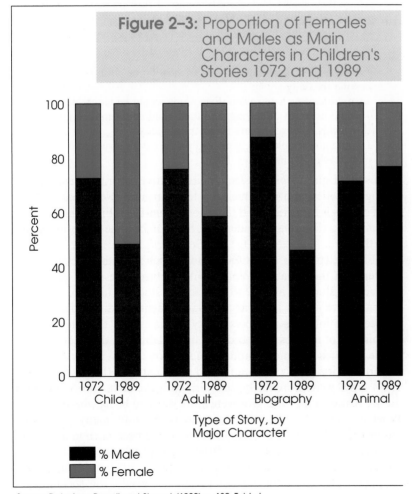

Figure 2–3: Proportion of Females and Males as Main Characters in Children's Stories 1972 and 1989

The proportion of female main characters in stories found in children's readers greatly increased between 1972 to 1989. Only animal main characters remained overwhelmingly male.

Source: Data from Purcell and Stewart (1990) p. 180, Table I.

females portrayed and somewhat less stereotyping of behavior (Davis, 1984; Kolbe & LaVoie, 1981). Another change in books is the availability of books that are explicitly nonsexist, designed to counteract traditional stereotypes (Davis, 1984).

Despite these changes, children continue to think in terms of traditional gender roles, perhaps because so many other things have not changed. Compare the following sets of quotes. In the first set, boys are giving their views about what women are like; in the second, they are commenting on how their life would change if they were turned into girls.

> [Women are] . . . indecisive; they are afraid of many things; they make a fuss over things, they get tired a lot; they very often need someone to help them; . . . they don't know what to do in an emergency, they cannot do dangerous things; . . . they are scared of getting wet or getting an electric shock; . . . they are not very intelligent; . . . Women do things like cooking and washing and sewing because that is all they can do (Hartley, 1959, p. 462).

> Instead of wrestling with my friends, I'd be sitting around discussing the daily gossip.
> I would have to hate snakes. Everything would be miserable.
> I would use a lot of makeup and look good and beautiful, knowing that few people would care for my personality.
> I would not be able to help my dad fix the car and truck and his two motorcycles (Baumgartner, 1983).

Both sets of quotes picture females as inactive, restricted, engaged in boring activities, and not much fun to be around. Note that the first set of quotes is from 1959 and the second from 1983. From the perspective of boys, the female gender role has not become more attractive with time.

Finally, consider an attitude study which used the questions you answered in the What Do You Think? feature. The study compared high school students in 1982 to high school students in 1956. The 1982 students were just as likely as the 1956 students to distinguish clearly between the interests and personality of males and the interests and personality of females and to do so in a traditional direction (for example, they felt it is more important for a boy to be a leader and more important for a girl to be cheerful and good-natured) (Lewin & Tragos, 1987). Boys were more likely than girls to make distinctions, but both did so. However, in 1982, girls were more satisfied being who they were. When compared to the girls from the 1956 study, many fewer girls answering in 1982 said that they wish they had been born male (Lewin & Tragos, 1987). The authors of the study concluded that "the self-image of girls had improved" (Lewin & Tragos, 1987, p. 125). Perhaps the finding also shows that, at least for females, gender role socialization leaves open more possibilities than in the past.

Alternative Choice

Androgyny
label for a personality combining the positive attributes of both feminine and masculine personalities.

Androgyny and Beyond

One possibility more recognized today than in the past is the possibility of androgyny. **Androgyny** is the term used to describe a type of personality that combines the positive aspects of both masculinity and femininity. Pursuing the idea that a person might be feminine in some ways and masculine in others, Sandra Bem and her colleagues (1977, 1976, 1975, 1974) argued that the assumption that masculinity and femininity were opposite ends of a continuum had obscured the possibility that some people might be " . . . *both* masculine and feminine, *both* assertive and yielding, *both* instrumental and expressive—depending on the situational appropriateness of these various behaviors . . . " (1974, p. 155). They developed a technique called the BSRI—the Bem Sex Role Inventory—to determine whether a person had a feminine, masculine, or androgynous personality.

Some people choose an androgynous way of life in which there are few differences in how females and males act or dress.

Using the BSRI, Bem found most of the university students she surveyed had gender role identities consistent with their sex; 54 percent of the females had feminine or "near feminine" (i.e., scores on the BSRI that were close to feminine scores) personalities, and 55 percent of the males had masculine or "near masculine" personalities (Bem, 1974). However, about one third of the students (34 percent of the males and 27 percent of the females) were androgynous. Eleven percent of the males and 20 percent of the females had personalities inconsistent with their sex.

Subsequent research on androgynous personalities found that androgynous individuals are more adaptable (Bem, 1975) and competitive (Alagna, 1982). Androgynous fathers are more loving and responsive to, but less demanding of, their children than masculine fathers (Baumrind, 1982). Scores on the BSRI also are related to dating behavior (DeLucia, 1987). All students engaged in some cross-gender type behavior, but students scoring high on masculinity tended to engage in masculine dating activities (for example, opening the door, making reservations, paying, deciding when and where to go out to eat, and verbally expressing sexual desires) and students scoring high on femininity tended to engage in feminine dating activities (for example, sensing the other's disturbance about something, giving in to the other's wishes, watching the other participate in activities outside the relationship, avoiding decision-making, and nonverbally letting the other know they would like to have sex). Androgynous students were less restricted in their dating activities; both male and female androgynous students felt free to engage in either masculine or feminine dating behaviors (DeLucia, 1987).

While the enthusiasm for androgyny as a social science concept has faded (Giele, 1988), it still communicates a very powerful idea—that feminine and masculine attributes are not opposites (Weitzman, 1984). Rather, both are sets of attributes that can be combined in one individual; an individual can be both masculine and feminine in a given situation (for example, be both independent and nurturant when addressing a problem), or be masculine in one situation and feminine in another.

Summary

Males and females differ physically in genetic makeup, hormones, internal reproductive organs, and external reproductive organs. Several appearance differences are derived from these physical differences. The physical differences are important mostly insofar as they contribute to male and female roles in reproduction. Other than their reproductive roles, males and females have few innate differences.

In most respects, the intellectual, psychological, and emotional variations within each sex are greater than the differences between them.

If innate biological differences cannot explain the observed behavioral differences between males and females, what can? "Culture" and "socialization" are the answers social scientists give most often. Every culture provides gender roles, guidelines for how males and females are expected to act. Traditional U.S. gender roles for men include avoiding femininity, being successful (especially in providing for one's family), being sturdy and steadfast, and being aggressive. Traditional female gender roles emphasize accommodation, inferiority to men, and importance of being a wife and mother. Different racial, ethnic, religious, and social class groups within the United States emphasize different facets of these general gender roles. Current gender role expectations are in a state of flux, due in part to the widespread entry of women into the labor force. The expectations for women's behavior have broadened to include many behaviors formerly restricted to men, while those for men have changed only marginally.

Socialization, the process of learning one's culture, also helps to explain why men and women behave differently. Through socialization, boys and girls learn which sex they are, establish a sexual identity, learn the gender roles of their culture, and choose which gender expectations to incorporate as their own gender identity. The distinctions made between boys and girls during infancy and childhood, observation of others, and popular culture give children clues about sex and gender. Children are typically very aware of traditional gender roles, are able to accurately label males and females, and are secure in their sexual identity by about age six. Which particular gender roles they adopt for themselves depend on reinforcement from others, according to social learning theorists, and on consistency with internally developed self-image, according to cognitive development theorists. Some aspects of socialization—especially the availability of nonsexist materials and changes in how often girls appear in books, and how they are portrayed—have changed, but many remain unchanged. Boys, especially, continue to think about sex and gender in terms of traditional gender role guidelines.

Androgyny, a personality type combining the most positive aspects of both masculine and feminine gender roles, presents an alternative to rigid traditional gender roles. Androgynous individuals can be both masculine and feminine, or masculine in one situation and feminine in another.

CHAPTER 3

SEX AND CONTRACEPTION

Sexually active couples in the United States use many techniques and products to avoid unwanted pregnancy. Some of these are listed below. Rank them according to their effectiveness in preventing pregnancy, listing the most effective as "1," the second most effective as "2," and so forth. If you know nothing about some of the techniques or products listed, take a guess or leave the ranking space blank. You can check your answers by using Table 3–1 or Figure 3–6.

Technique or Product	Effectiveness Ranking
Birth control pills	_____
Condom	_____
Diaphragm with cream or jelly	_____
Female sterilization	_____
IUD	_____
Male sterilization	_____
Rhythm	_____
Vaginal foam	_____
Withdrawal	_____

In 1988, Sandra Caron and Rosemarie Bertran, instructors of a human sexuality class at a large university in the United States, published a list of questions their students frequently asked. Here are some of the questions:

Body Functions/Parts
What exactly is a virgin? Can guys be virgins, too?
Is being a virgin the same thing as being frigid?
What's the purpose of menstruation?
Does it hurt when a guy has an erection?
I don't get anything out of having my breasts touched—is there something wrong?
Is it normal for a man, on occasion, not to be able to get an erection while being stimulated?
What is the most sensitive part of the penis?
How and where do you locate a woman's clitoris?
What is oral sex?
Do men really enjoy giving oral sex, or do they do it to please their partner?

Pregnancy/Birth Control
Can you get pregnant before/during/after your period?
When is the best (safest) time for a woman to have sex without the worry of pregnancy?
How long does the penis have to stay in the woman's vagina to let the sperm out?
Can you get pregnant the first time you have sex with someone?
What is a rubber? How do you put it on?
What is the safest form of birth control?
What is a diaphragm? What does it look like?
How soon after conception does a woman know if she is pregnant?
How do you use the Pill? How does it work?

Orgasm/Ejaculation
Why do guys reach orgasm after 30 seconds? Is it my fault?
Why do girls hold off having an orgasm longer than guys?
Can a man become sterile from an ultra-active sex life?
Is it true that men must have ejaculations fairly regularly for physical reasons?
Is it possible to become sexually aroused and/or have an orgasm while under the influence of alcohol?
Is there such a thing as multiple orgasms?
I think I have had an orgasm, but I am not sure. How do I know?

Intercourse
Can a guy's penis be too big for a girl?
Do my parents still have sex? I find it hard to believe.
Does the average girl think about sex as much as the average guy, or do guys just verbalize thoughts more?

How come I'm always horny or thinking about sex?
During sex, how can I tell if the man is ejaculating if he doesn't tell me?
Is it unusual that I don't always need sex?

Reprinted with permission from Caron, S. and Bertran, R.: "What college students want to know about sex,"
Medical Aspects of Human Sexuality (1988) 22(4):20–25.

These questions from college students indicate that they are simultaneously curious, fascinated, and ambivalent about male and female bodies, the varieties of sex, sexual feelings, and sexual risks. Sex is a pervasive but sensitive theme in contemporary U.S. culture. Sexuality is on constant display, dominating soap operas, commercials, novels, movies, and many types of popular music. But legal attempts to *control* sex are equally pervasive. State and local laws define appropriate and inappropriate ways of displaying sexuality, expressing sexual affection, and having sex, while also specifying appropriate and inappropriate sexual partners. Local school boards debate how much teenagers should know about sex and when and where they should learn it. Given the cultural fascination, ambivalence, and confusion about sex, it is not surprising that college students have so many questions.

Chapter 3 seeks to answer some of these questions about sex. We will use the terms **sex** and **sexual behavior** to refer to all activities associated with the expression of sexual feelings of one person for another.

> **Sex** or **sexual behavior**
> activities associated with the expression of sexual feelings; includes holding hands, embracing, kissing, necking, petting, oral stimulation of genitals, and intercourse.

The brain is the most important sexual organ. The attitudes and values of the couple, and the guidelines provided by the society in which they live affect the expression of sex in an intimate relationship.

**Sexual intercourse
or coitus**

the insertion of
the penis into the
vagina.

These activities can include, but are not necessarily limited to, holding hands, embracing, kissing, necking, petting, oral stimulation of the genitals, and intercourse. The term **sexual intercourse** or **coitus** will refer only to the penetration of a female's vagina by a male's penis. Although much of sex research and much of this chapter deals with sexual intercourse, coitus actually represents only a small part of all sexual behavior.

This chapter focuses on the biological aspects of sex. Biology is not all there is to sex; later chapters will deal with the psychological, social, historical, and legal aspects of sexual behavior and discuss how sex fits into marriage and other intimate relationships. We start with the biology of sex because of the lack of general knowledge and abundance of curiosity about it. The chapter begins by describing male and female sexual organs and explaining how they function to produce both babies and pleasure. Next we describe what happens to human bodies when they are sexually aroused and detail the stages of human sexual response. Then we discuss some of the physical and psychological problems that interfere with the pleasurable aspects of sex, leaving discussion of reproductive sexual problems to Chapter 11. Sex, though pleasurable, is also risky. The final sections of the chapter deal with how to minimize the risks of unwanted pregnancy and with sexually transmitted diseases.

HUMAN SEXUAL ANATOMY

Our discussion of the biological aspects of sex begins with a description of the sexual anatomy of male and female bodies. Men and women use their sexual organs both to conceive children and to achieve pleasure. We will describe the female reproductive organs and menstrual cycle first, then describe the male reproductive organs, and finally focus on the organs involved in sexual pleasure. Our reproductive-pleasure distinction is made for the sake of convenience. As you will learn, some sexual organs, like some sexual behaviors, contribute to both reproduction and pleasure.

3 Sex and
Contraception

Female Reproductive Organs

Five parts of a woman's anatomy are crucially important to reproduction: the ovaries, the fallopian tubes, the uterus with its endometrium lining, the cervix, and the vagina. Figure 3–1 (on page 80) shows the locations of these organs. Note that in the female body, these reproductive organs are close to, but distinct from, the excretory organs—bladder, urethra, and anus.

Females are born with two **ovaries**. At maturity, the ovaries are about the size and shape of unshelled almonds and lie on either side of the uterus. The ovaries are egg containers and egg releasers. Inside each ovary are tiny sacks called **follicles** that surround the immature eggs. At birth, a female has as many as 400,000 immature eggs. During a woman's reproductive years, one, or occasionally more, of these eggs mature under hormonal influence each month and are then released by one ovary. The two ovaries alternate in releasing a mature egg; one releases an egg one month, and the other the next. If one of the ovaries

Ovaries
the two female organs that contain immature eggs and release mature eggs.

Follicles
sacks inside the ovaries that surround the immature eggs.

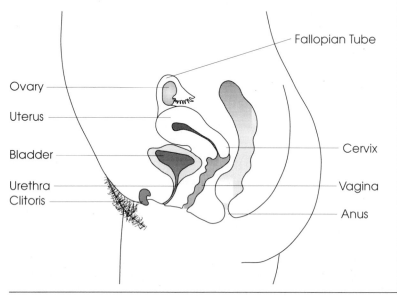

Figure 3–1: Female Reproductive and Sexual Organs (side view)

The five primary female reproductive organs are the ovaries, fallopian tubes, uterus, cervix, and vagina. The vagina and clitoris are sexual pleasure organs.

Fallopian tube
a tiny vessel leading from each ovary to the uterus; the site of fertilization.

Fertilization
the union of a woman's egg and a man's sperm.

Uterus
the female organ that protects and nourishes the developing fetus.

Endometrium
the inner lining of the uterus; the part of the uterus that provides a nutrient-enriched environment for the fertilized egg.

Cervix
the lower part of the uterus, located next to the vagina.

Vagina
the female organ into which the penis is inserted during intercourse and through which the infant passes during childbirth.

is damaged or destroyed, the remaining ovary will take over and release an egg every month.

Once the egg is released from the ovary, it begins to migrate toward the **fallopian tube**, a tiny vessel leading from the ovary to the uterus. Tiny hairlike structures (or cilia) inside the fallopian tube create a gentle current in the fallopian tube fluid; this current slowly sweeps the egg into and then down through the tube. **Fertilization**, the union of a woman's egg and a man's sperm, generally takes place deep inside the fallopian tube, at the end closest to the ovaries (Rome, 1984).

A fertilized egg continues its slow movement down the fallopian tube and into the **uterus**, the organ that protects and nourishes the developing fetus. In the uterus, the egg attaches itself to the **endometrium**, the blood-engorged lining that provides the egg with a nutrient-rich environment, and begins to develop. Approximately nine months later, this same fertilized egg—now grown into a "cute little bundle of joy"—will force itself through the **cervix**, the very narrow lower part of the uterus, through the vagina, and into the outside world.

The **vagina**, a very flexible, barrel-shaped organ about three to four inches long, marks the last stage of the journey of the fertilized egg (now developed into a baby) out of a woman's body but also the first stage of the whole reproductive process (Hyde, 1990, p. 700). The vagina is the insertion point for the penis during intercourse and receives the **semen**, the combination of sperm and alkaline fluid a male ejaculates during orgasm. After insertion into the vagina, the viable sperm in the semen quickly begin their search for the mature egg that may be waiting for them in one of the two fallopian tubes.

The Menstrual Cycle

If you have followed our discussion so far, you should have a basic idea of how each of the female reproductive organs contributes to the reproductive process. Another way of understanding this process is to focus on the **menstrual cycle**, the series of hormonal changes that prepare a woman's body for possible pregnancy during each month of her reproductive years.

There are four phases in the menstrual cycle: the follicular phase, ovulation, the luteal phase, and menstruation. The length of the menstrual cycle varies from woman to woman and from cycle to cycle. Some women have 20-day cycles while others have cycles lasting 40 days. And the same woman might have a 32-day cycle one month and a 27-day cycle the next. Stress, illness, nutrition, and changes in routine can affect the release of hormones and thus the length of the cycle. The average cycle is about 28 days, and we will assume a 28-day cycle for the purposes of our explanation. Keep in mind, though, that actual cycle length is highly variable.

Because the first day of the menstruation is the most identifiable day in the cycle, we identify it as Day 1. However, the first phase of the cycle, and our discussion, begins with Day 5. Day 5 marks the start of the **follicular phase**. First, the level of **FSH** (follicle-stimulating hormone) rises and triggers the maturation of one egg (or occasionally more) inside its follicles. This egg moves to the surface of the ovary. Second, high levels of estrogen stimulate the endometrium to begin thickening and producing substances that will nourish the fertilized egg. The follicular phase, lasting from the end of the woman's menstrual period until ovulation, is the most variable stage of the cycle. In a 28-day cycle, the follicular phase extends from Day 5 until Day 13; in a 44-day cycle, this phase would extend from Day 5 until Day 29.

The second phase of the menstrual cycle is **ovulation**. In this short phase (Day 14 of a 28-day cycle), a surge in two hormones, LH (lutenizing hormone) and FSH, stimulate the ovary to release its mature egg, which then begins its journey into and through the fallopian tube. The egg can be fertilized for about the first 12 to 24 hours after ovulation (Hyde, 1990). Because of variations in cycle lengths, however, it is difficult to know the exact timing of these 12 to 24 hours. Women who

---

Semen
the fluid the male expels during orgasm; it contains sperm and alkaline fluid from several organs.

Menstrual cycle
the series of hormonal changes that prepare a woman's body for possible pregnancy during each month of her reproductive years.

Follicular phase
the first stage of the menstrual cycle, during which one or more eggs begin to mature and the endometrium begins to prepare for a fertilized egg.

FSH
the follicle-stimulating hormone that triggers the maturation of one or more eggs inside their follicles.

Ovulation
the second stage of the menstrual cycle, when the egg is released from the follicle.

Luteal phase
the third phase in the menstrual cycle, during which progesterone stimulates the endometrium to produce nutrients and the implantation of the fertilized egg (if present) occurs.

Menstruation
the fourth phase in the menstrual cycle, during which the endometrium lining is shed if implantation of the fertilized egg has not occurred.

Testes
male sex organ, located in the scrotum, that manufactures sperm and male hormones.

Scrotum
the sack, below the penis, containing the testes.

Seminiferous tubules
the set of coiled tubes in the testes that manufacture sperm.

Epididymis
the set of coiled tubes in the testes where the sperm mature.

Interstitial cells
the tissues in the testes that produce male sex hormones.

have consistent 28-day cycles are most likely to conceive between Day 12 and Day 16 (Byer, Shainberg, & Jones, 1988). At other times during the cycle, they are relatively "safe" in terms of avoiding pregnancy.

The third phase, the **luteal phase**, is the most predictable of the phases. It lasts fourteen days (plus or minus a day or two)—from ovulation to menstruation. During these fourteen days (Days 15–28 in a 28-day cycle), the egg-releasing follicle continues to make hormones that affect the woman's cycle. For 10 to 12 days, it produces progesterone, a hormone that stimulates the endometrium to produce nourishing substances for the fertilized egg. If a fertilized egg is not implanted in the endometrium during that time, the production of progesterone drops, and the final stage of the cycle begins.

The final stage is **menstruation**, the shedding of the endometrium lining. Menstruation occurs only if no fertilized egg has been implanted. The menstrual period, lasting two to six days, is set off by a sharp fall in estrogen and progesterone levels. The menstrual fluid released during one menstrual period totals about two ounces and consists of both blood from the endometrium and of degenerated cells and mucus from the cervix and vagina. A new lining starts forming immediately. The fall in estrogen levels triggers the production of FSH, which in turn stimulates the maturation of a new egg and the beginning of a new menstrual cycle.

Male Reproductive Organs

Males also have a number of specialized reproductive organs. These are pictured in Figure 3–2. The **testes** (sometimes called the testicles), the male organs analogous to the female's ovaries, produce the male sex cells (sperm) necessary for reproduction. Suspended in a sack (called the **scrotum**) below the penis, the testes consist of three separate sets of tissue. The first set—consisting of about 1000 long coiled tubes called the **semi-inferous tubules**—manufacture sperm. As millions of immature sperm are produced, they are moved to the second set of tissue found in the testes. Called the **epididymis**, this tissue is one long tube (about 20 feet) that acts as the storage unit for maturing sperm. The final set of tissues in the testes is the **interstitial cells**, producers of male sex hormones.

The pathway that moves the sperm out of the testes is called the **vas deferens**. Consisting of two tiny tubes leading from the testes, the vas deferens traces a winding path out of the top of the male's scrotum, over the pubic bone, beside the urinary bladder, through the prostate and to the urethra. Once the two vas deferens connect with the **urethra**—the tube leading out of the male's penis and through which

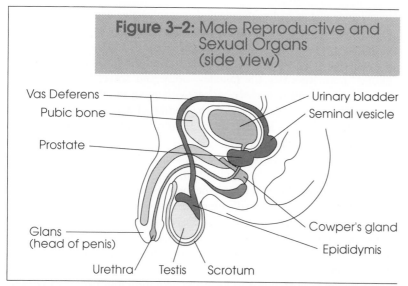

Figure 3–2: Male Reproductive and Sexual Organs (side view)

Vas Deferens
Pubic bone
Prostate
Urinary bladder
Seminal vesicle
Cowper's gland
Epididymis
Glans (head of penis)
Urethra   Testis   Scrotum

Sperm are manufactured in the male's testes, are carried through the vas deferens to the urethra, and leave the male's body when he ejaculates. The penis is the center of male sexual pleasure and also serves as a reproductive and excretory organ.

Vas deferens
the pair of tubes leading from the testes to the urethra that carry sperm.

Urethra
the tube in both males and females through which the bladder is emptied; in males, it is also part of the pathway for the sperm to exit the body.

Seminal vesicles
a pair of male organs next to the bladder that add fluid to the semen.

Prostate
the male organ located below the bladder where the two vas deferens join; it adds alkaline fluid to semen, and its spasms during orgasm push semen through the urethra.

Cowper's glands
a pair of glands located below the prostate that add alkaline fluid to the semen.

Penis
the cylindrically shaped male sex organ.

the male urinates or ejaculates—inside the prostate, a complete path has been established for the sperm to move out of the male's body.

As the sperm journey through the male's body, they are assisted by the seminal vesicles, the prostate, and the Cowper's glands. The **seminal vesicles** are two small organs adjacent to the bladder that produce a fluid which adds to the volume of the semen. The **prostate**, an organ about the size and shape of a chestnut, lies just below the bladder. Within the prostate, the two vas deferens join to form the urethra. The prostate is important for two reasons. First, it adds an alkaline fluid to the semen that helps neutralize the damaging acidic environment of both the urethra and the vagina. Second, its contractions during orgasm provide muscle power to push the semen through and out of the urethra. The third set of organs important to the journey of the sperm is the **Cowper's glands**. These tiny glands, located just below the prostate, add an alkaline fluid to the ejaculate.

Once in the urethra, the sperm have a clear path out of the male's body. The sperm, numbering about 300,000,000, are expelled during orgasm by the involuntary contractions of the epididymis, the vas deferens, the prostate gland, and the urethra. Once inside the vagina, the sperm, stimulated into action by the secretions of the prostate and the seminal vesicles, begin their search for the egg.

The single most important male reproductive organ is the **penis**, a cylindrically shaped external organ vitally important in both sexual and excretory functioning. The penis is the organ through which the male participates in reproduction; the insertion of the penis into the vagina allows sperm to enter the female's body and travel to the fallopian tube. The penis, more densely packed with nerve endings than any other part of the male's body, is also the center of sexual stimulation and pleasure for the male. Finally, the penis allows males to eliminate bodily wastes through urination.

For intercourse to occur, the penis must be at least partially erect. Erection results from the swelling of the three sets of spongy tissue within the penis. When the male becomes sexually excited, the spongy tissues become engorged with blood because more blood flows in than flows out. The average **flaccid** (unaroused, not erect) penis is somewhere between 2.5 and 4 inches long. An average erect penis is about six inches long, although some as long as 13 inches have been measured (Hyde, 1990, p. 58).

Flaccid
not erect, used to describe the penis.

The penis is designed to keep the urination and procreation functions separate and distinct. The male can urinate only when the penis is not fully erect. When it is erect, the opening connecting the bladder to the urethra is closed and the pathway from the testicles through the urethra is unobstructed.

Sexual Pleasure Organs

Several bodily organs play an important part in the pleasure aspect of sex for women. Of these, the **clitoris** is the most important. In many ways, the clitoris and the penis are alike. Both develop from similar tissue before birth, have a shaft and a glans, become erect due to engorgement of blood, are packed with nerve endings, and are more sensitive to erotic stimulation than any other part of the body. But unlike the penis, the clitoris has no other function; it is solely an organ of sexual pleasure (Fisher, 1983).

Clitoris
small, highly sensitive female sexual organ located above the vaginal entrance.

A second female sexual pleasure organ is the vagina. When unaroused, the walls of the vagina lie against each other, but when aroused they expand like an inflated balloon to accommodate the penis. While the vagina does have a generous supply of nerve endings (making it sensitive to erotic stimulation), these nerve endings are concentrated in the lower one-third of the vagina. The inner two-thirds have virtually no nerve endings and are not very sensitive to stimulation. Thus, women may not be stimulated by penetration of a very long penis into the far reaches of the vagina.

The breasts also play a significant part in erotic response. Consisting of twenty clusters of mammary glands, breasts are designed to produce milk for a nursing infant. However, the nipples, or breast tips, are richly supplied with nerve endings and are thus very sensitive to stimulation. When the breasts and nipples are touched provocatively, the nipples respond by becoming erect. Writing about breast sensitivity, Hyde (1990) notes that small breasts have the same number of nerve endings as large breasts: "It follows that small breasts are actually more erotically sensitive per square inch than large ones . . ." (p. 53).

Some men report enjoying having many parts of their bodies— breasts, nipples, and testicles—caressed but the male organ most sensitive to sexual stimulation is the penis. While the entire penis is sensitive to stimulation, the **glans** (the head) and the **corona** (the raised ridge separating the glans from the shaft of the penis) are by far the most sexually excitable regions of a man's body (Hyde, 1990).

> **Glans**
> the head of the penis.

> **Corona**
> the raised ridge on the penis separating the glans from the shaft of the penis.

HUMAN SEXUAL RESPONSE

To this point, we have described male and female reproductive and pleasure-oriented body parts. But how do the parts work together? Actual scientific knowledge about what happens when human bodies are sexually aroused is rather recent. Gynecologist-obstetrician William Masters and his co-researcher, Virginia Johnson, were the first to describe in great detail what they called "human sexual response" (Gagnon & Henderson, 1975, pp. 28–29; Masters & Johnson, 1966). **Human sexual response** is the pattern of biologically based reactions that the human body experiences as it goes from being sexually aroused, to orgasm, to "afterglow." To gather their information about human sexual response, Masters and Johnson (1966) watched, filmed, and measured individuals' physiological responses during all kinds of sexual activities. They supplemented these laboratory-gathered observations by intensively interviewing their subjects.

> **Human sexual response**
> the pattern of biologically based reactions that the human body experiences while being sexually aroused.

The particular stimulus that "triggers" sexual arousal and the response cycle Masters and Johnson described varies from person to person and from situation to situation. Young people's bodies can be triggered by stimuli as diverse as dreams, the sight of a "sexy" body, the smell of cologne or perfume, erotic pictures or sounds, mental imagery, or physical stimulation. Older people, though, frequently need direct physical contact to set off the response cycle (Brecher, 1984).

In many ways, the most important sexual organ—at least in terms of sexual arousal—is the brain for it is the brain that helps us decide what is sexy or erotic. Anthropologist Martha Ward discovered the importance of the brain in determining what is sexually desirable when she studied the Pohnpeians of the Pacific. Writing to her colleagues in the United States, she compared what the Pohnpeians thought was sexy with what Americans thought was sexy.

They (the Pohnpeians) expect women to eat a lot, gain weight, keep weight on after each pregnancy, and stay on the large size of pleasantly plump . . . . Men are compared to brown doves, a bird which eats a bite of fruit, leaves it and goes to another, always to nibble sparingly. . . . So the men are noticeably thinner. Men who eat too much are subject to ridicule and the women who are rotund, Rubenesque, roly-poly are objects of sexual interest. (1989, p. 46)

Regardless of the source of stimulation individuals in the Masters and Johnson laboratory showed remarkably consistent patterns of sexual response once they were sexually aroused (Masters & Johnson, 1966). That is, those who masturbated to orgasm showed the same cycle of response as those who had intercourse with a partner; couples who used different positions in intercourse had similar responses; and those with a same sex partner experienced the same response cycle as those with a partner of the opposite sex.

What exactly is this response cycle? Masters and Johnson (1966) simplified their discussion of the complex human sexual response cycle by dividing it into four phases: excitement, plateau, orgasm, and resolution. We will describe the basic characteristics of each phase, noting when the male and female responses differ substantially. Figures 3–3 and 3–4 (on pages 87–88) present a visual representation of the four phases of the cycle.

Excitement

Excitement
the first phase of the sexual response cycle

Vasocongestion
the accumulation of blood in the veins and arteries of the pelvic area during the excitement phase of the sexual response cycle.

The **excitement** phase is the first and potentially longest of the four phases, lasting from several minutes to several hours. In this phase of sexual response, the clitoris or penis swells, blood pressure increases, heart rate speeds up, blood starts to accumulate in the veins and arteries in the pelvic region (a process called **vasocongestion**), breasts swell, and nipples become erect. Some people, more often females than males, experience a sexual flush over their upper abdomen and the chest. The flush, resembling a measles rash, may also appear in later phases of the response cycle.

The vagina and the uterus react in specific ways during this first phase. Ten to thirty seconds after arousal begins, a lubricating fluid appears on the walls of the vagina. Quickly thereafter, the upper two-thirds of the vagina expands dramatically to accommodate the entrance of the penis. At about the same time, the uterus shifts position, making a larger opening in the cervix, which allows an easier entrance for sperm. In the male, the skin of the scrotum thickens and the scrotum is pulled up close to the body. As the scrotum moves close to the body, the testes are elevated.

Although males and females have similar physiological responses in the excitement phase, males are more likely to be aware that they are

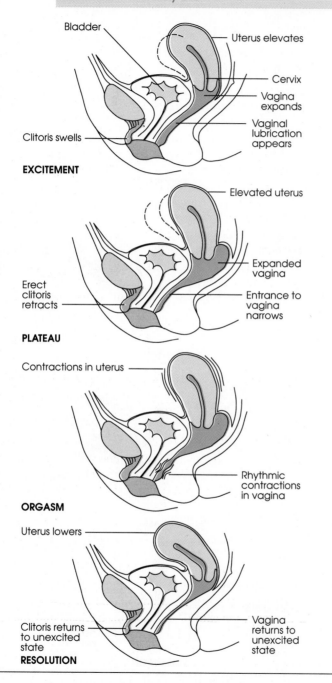

Figure 3–3: Changes during the Female Sexual Response Cycle

Bladder

Uterus elevates

Cervix

Vagina expands

Vaginal lubrication appears

Clitoris swells

EXCITEMENT

Elevated uterus

Erect clitoris retracts

Expanded vagina

Entrance to vagina narrows

PLATEAU

Contractions in uterus

Rhythmic contractions in vagina

ORGASM

Uterus lowers

Clitoris returns to unexcited state

Vagina returns to unexcited state

RESOLUTION

Note how the female reproductive and sexual organs change in size, position, and movement during the four stages of the sexual response cycle.

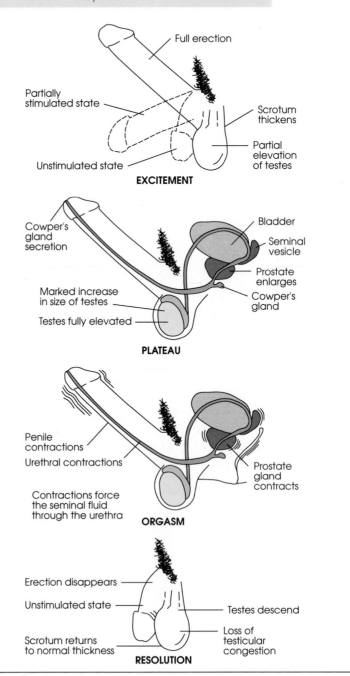

Figure 3–4: Changes during the Male Sexual Response Cycle

Full erection

Partially stimulated state

Scrotum thickens

Partial elevation of testes

Unstimulated state

EXCITEMENT

Cowper's gland secretion

Bladder

Seminal vesicle

Prostate enlarges

Cowper's gland

Marked increase in size of testes

Testes fully elevated

PLATEAU

Penile contractions

Urethral contractions

Prostate gland contracts

Contractions force the seminal fluid through the urethra

ORGASM

Erection disappears

Unstimulated state

Testes descend

Loss of testicular congestion

Scrotum returns to normal thickness

RESOLUTION

Note how the penis, testes, and prostate gland change and move during the four stages of the sexual response cycle.

excited and to recognize its signs. At least that is what psychologist Julia Heiman and her colleagues found in their research done in the 1970s (Heiman, LoPiccolo, & LoPiccolo, 1976; Heiman, 1975). These researchers exposed male and female college students to a variety of sexual stimuli, asked them which stimuli aroused them, and measured their physiological responses by using two specially designed devices—a penile strain gauge (fitted around the base of the male's penis) and a photoplethysmograph (a tampon-like electrical device inserted just inside the entrance of the female's vagina).

Both males and females responded physiologically to openly erotic material, especially if it portrayed the female as the one initiating the sexual activity, and neither sex was turned on physiologically by expressions of love and affection. However, while few males were unaware of their arousal, many females were unaware they had been aroused. Exploring this difference in a subsequent phase of the experiment, the researchers instructed female subjects to pay particular attention to the changes in their body as they observed the erotic material. After receiving these instructions, females were just as likely as males to report being aroused. Heiman (1975) believes that these findings indicate that males and females receive differential socialization in respect to sex: males are encouraged to pay attention to the signs of arousal in their own bodies, females are not.

Plateau

The **plateau** phase, in many ways a continuation of the excitement phase, lasts only a few minutes. Vasocongestion is at a peak and the rate of breathing, pulse rate, and blood pressure continue to rise.

The clitoris, by now fully erect, withdraws up into the body. The outer one third of the vagina swells, reducing the entrance to the vagina. The net effect of this reduction may be a noticeable increase in the vagina's grip on the penis.

The penis is now completely erect. The testes, engorged with blood, are as much as 50 percent larger than normal. During this phase, a few drops of fluid, probably from the Cowper's glands and occasionally containing viable sperm, may appear at the tip of the penis. Given the right circumstances, these sperm can enter the vagina, travel through the cervix, the uterus, the fallopian tube, and fertilize an egg. Fertilization, then, can occur in the absence of ejaculation.

Orgasm

The orgasmic phase is the shortest and most intense phase of the sexual response cycle. The **orgasm** itself is a set of muscle spasms occurring

Plateau
the second stage of the sexual response cycle.

Orgasm
the set of intense sensations and rhythmic muscle contractions that occur at the height of the sexual response cycle.

about eight-tenths of a second apart and lasting a total of less than 10 seconds. These muscle spasms are accompanied by sharp increases in pulse rate, blood pressure, and breathing rate. Muscle tension is at its peak. During the orgasm, the total attention of the individual is concentrated on the pelvic region where the sensation of the orgasm is centered.

The muscle spasms in female orgasm occur in the outer third of the vagina. There may be as few as three or four or as many as a dozen spasms. The uterus also contracts rhythmically and other muscles, such as those in the anus, might also contract.

The male orgasm occurs in two stages. During the first, the semen is forced into a bulb at the base of the urethra. In the second, the prostate gland, urethral bulb, and penis contract and force the semen out. This second stage is called **ejaculation**.

Ejaculation
the expulsion of semen from the penis during orgasm.

The strength of orgasms varies greatly, from mild to extraordinarily powerful. Orgasm strength is apparently related to the amount of blood that has accumulated in the pelvic region: the more blood, the more powerful the orgasm (Fisher, 1983).

The subjective experience of an orgasm—what one actually feels—seems to be very comparable for men and women. In one study, researchers asked college students to give written descriptions of what an orgasm felt like. The expert panel of medical students, obstetrician-gynecologists, and clinical psychologists who read the descriptions could not reliably determine which of the descriptions were written by men and which were written by women (Vance & Wagner, 1976). Apparently both sexes experienced similar sensations during orgasm.

Resolution

Resolution
the final stage in the sexual response cycle.

In the **resolution** phase, the body returns to a physiologically unaroused state. The changes associated with the excitement and plateau phase are reversed: breast swelling is reduced, the clitoris or penis returns to its normal size, the sexual flush disappears, the uterus returns to its normal position, the vagina shrinks, the testes shrink and descend, the scrotum thins, the blood pressure and heart rate decline, and the breathing rate slows down.

Masters and Johnson (1966) discovered that the female's body could be restimulated to orgasm during resolution. Depending on the circumstances, some females were capable of multiple orgasms in rapid succession, with second and subsequent orgasms sometimes more powerful than the first.

>   ... Masters and Johnson found that women in masturbation
> might have 5 to 20 orgasms. In some cases, they quit only when

physically exhausted. When using a vibrator, less effort is required, and some women were capable of having 50 orgasms. (Hyde, 1990, p. 206)

According to Masters and Johnson (1966), a major difference between males and females in the resolution phase is that males experience a refractory period after orgasm. The **refractory period** is the time following orgasm during which the male cannot be restimulated. The length of the refractory period depends on the male's age, his general physical health, his drug and alcohol usage, and the amount of sex he has had recently. The older he is, the worse shape he is in, the more drugs or alcohol he has used, and the more sex he has had recently, the longer his refractory period will be. Some men have a refractory period of a few minutes; others cannot be restimulated for twenty-four hours.

Despite Masters and Johnson's laboratory findings, others (Dunn & Trost, 1989; Kinsey, Pomeroy, & Martin, 1948) have suggested that some males may be capable of experiencing multiple orgasms without a refractory period. Dunn and Trost (1989) found some men who could have an orgasm, with or without ejaculation, remain erect, have another orgasm, remain erect, and so forth. In the interim between orgasms, the men either did not experience a refractory period or had such a short one they were, in effect, multi-orgasmic. This study was an exploratory one and its authors have no way of estimating how many multi-orgasmic men there are.

> **Refractory period** the period of time after orgasm when a male cannot be sexually stimulated.

SEXUAL PROBLEMS

The human sexual response cycle is a complex phenomenon, incorporating both physical and psychological components. If sexual organs are not in working order or if psychological factors make it difficult to become sexually aroused, individuals may be unable to achieve sexual pleasure. Since contemporary U.S. culture stresses sexual performance and emphasizes the importance of pleasurable sex in couple relationships, failure to achieve sexual pleasure is seen as problematic. Many individuals, even those deeply in love, are troubled by sexual problems at some time during their lives.

The most common sexual problems for females are inhibited sexual desire, dyspareunia, and anorgasmia (Hatcher *et al.*, 1990; Hyde, 1990). Males with sexual problems are most often troubled by inhibited sexual desire, impotence, premature ejaculation, or ejaculatory delay (Hatcher *et al.*, 1990). Some males also experience dyspareunia (Hyde, 1990).

Inhibited Sexual Desire

Inhibited sexual
desire (ISD)
lack of sexual desire.

Many men and women today identify lack of interest in sex as their major sexual problem. Sexual therapists use the term **Inhibited Sexual Desire (ISD)** to refer to this lack of sexual interest or desire. During the 1980s, ISD was the most frequent sexual complaint of those seeking sexual therapy (Spector & Carey, 1990; Peterson, 1989; Gelman *et al.*, 1987). Surveys of nonclinical populations—those not seeking therapy—find much the same thing. One such survey found that about one in three women and about one in six men complained of lack of sexual desire (Frank, Anderson, & Rubinstein, 1978).

In some cases, physical factors contribute to ISD. Hormonal imbalances, health problems, the use of birth control pills, and drug use have all been shown to be associated with lack of sexual desire (Hatcher *et al.*, 1990; Hyde, 1990). In other cases, social or psychological circumstances result in sexual disinterest (Hatcher *et al.*, 1990; Hyde, 1990; Stuart, Hammond, & Pett, 1987). For example, individuals who are tired, overworked, depressed, or under a great deal of stress are often just not interested in sex. Those in an unsatisfying marriage can feel the same way. Stuart, Hammond, and Pett (1987) found that the most important differences between their sample of ISD women and a control group of non-ISD women was the quality of their marital relationship; "ISD (inhibited sexual desire) women reported significantly greater dissatisfaction with nearly every reported relationship issue" (pp. 102–103).

Dyspareunia

Dyspareunia
painful intercourse.

Vaginismus
a painful spasm of
the outer third of
the vagina and
an involuntary
tightening of
vaginal muscles,
making penetration
by the penis
extremely painful.

For some women and a few men, sexual intercourse hurts. The condition of feeling pain during intercourse is known as **dyspareunia**. For men, the pain is felt in the penis; for women it is felt in the vagina, around the vaginal entrance and clitoris, or deep in the pelvis (Hyde, 1990). Men with prostate problems, infections, or allergic reactions to contraceptive douches, jellies, creams, or foams may experience painful intercourse. So might women who have allergic reactions to the contraceptives used, whose vaginas are not fully lubricated because of insufficient stimulation, who suffer from a urinary infection, or whose vagina or pelvic region has been injured (for example, through rape or childbirth). Women who have gone through menopause might also experience dyspareunia as the walls of the vagina become thinner and more susceptible to tearing, vaginal lubrication lessens, and the vagina itself becomes more inelastic.

Sometimes painful intercourse for women is the result of **vaginismus**, a painful spasm of the outer third of the vagina and an involuntary tightening of vaginal muscles that makes penetration by the penis extremely painful (Hyde, 1990; Sanford, Hawley, & McGee, 1984). In some cases, the contraction is so severe the entrance to the vagina is closed and intercourse is impossible. Vaginismus also can result from painful intercourse associated with other causes (Fulton, 1988). Vaginismus may occur in both young women who have never been able to have intercourse and in sexually active women who have experienced a severe trauma such as rape (Hatcher *et al.*, 1990; Sanford, Hawley, & McGee, 1984).

Anorgasmia

Anorgasmia is the inability to have an orgasm. The problem, fairly common among women but rare among men, is classified by therapists as a "female sexual dysfunction" (Hatcher *et al.*, 1990; Hyde, 1990). Sex experts estimate that 5 to 10 percent of all women over 25 have not yet learned how to have an orgasm and that another 20 percent have orgasms only sporadically (Hatcher *et al.*, 1990, p. 20; Hyde, 1990, p. 521; Spector & Carey, 1990). One small-scale study of women in stable relationships came up with similar results: 9 percent of the respondents had never reached orgasm and 18 percent reported situational difficulties (Spector & Carey, 1990, p. 399).

> **Anorgasmia**
> inability to have an orgasm.

The ability to reach orgasm is often a matter of learning and practice. Some women never learned to have orgasms because the subculture or religion in which they grew up heavily discouraged masturbation or other forms of sexual experimentation. Others simply lacked the opportunity to practice (alone or with a partner) in a private, supportive atmosphere. Lack of factual knowledge about sexuality or the absence of a warm, responsive, sensuous female role model can also inhibit learning about orgasm. Finally, having a partner who ejaculates prematurely or who has erectile difficulties can get in the way of learning to be orgasmic (Hatcher *et al.*, 1990, pp. 20–21).

The loss of the ability to be orgasmic is often associated with some physical problem or emotional upheaval. For example, alcoholism, depression, grief, illness, or estrogen deprivation due to menopause can all interfere with female orgasmic ability (Hatcher *et al.*, 1990).

Impotence

Impotence or **erectile difficulty** is the inability to have an erection or to maintain one long enough to have intercourse (Hatcher *et al.*, 1990). There are no accurate statistics for the prevalence of impotence but results of two different studies suggest that as many as one out of every ten men has some type of impotence problem (McFalls, 1990).

> **Impotence** or **erectile difficulty**
> the inability to achieve or maintain an erection.

Impotence can be either transient (temporary) or permanent. Much transient impotence is drug-related. Certain prescription tranquilizers, antidepressants, and antihypertensives are associated with impotence in men. Addiction to heroin usually leads to impotence as can heavy, long-term use of cocaine and marijuana (Butler & Lewis, 1986). Widely used drugs, such as tobacco and alcohol, also have negative effects on sexual functioning. Smoking can constrict blood vessels and interfere with the flow of blood into the penis. And alcohol use contributes to a variety of male sexual problems.

> Even a few drinks before sex can affect a man's sexual perfor-
> mance, especially as men reach their forties. Erections may be less
> firm and ejaculation more difficult. . . . Up to 80% of men who drink
> heavily are believed to have serious sexual side effects, including im-
> potence, sterility, or loss of sexual desire. Many of the effects of
> moderate to heavy drinking may be reversible if drinking stops in
> time. However, heavy drinking over a long period irreversibly destroys
> testicular cells, leaving men with shrunken testicles. Both sexual desire
> and sexual capacity can be damaged. . . . Total sterility as well as
> impotence can result. (Butler & Lewis, 1986, p. 105)

Illness, stress, and fatigue can also lead to transient impotence (Butler & Lewis, 1986).

Permanent impotence is considered infrequent, especially among young males. McFalls (1979) found that the rate of permanent impotence varied directly with age; the older the males, the higher the rate of permanent impotence. According to McFalls' estimates, about 1 percent of males in their twenties and about 4 percent of males in their forties were afflicted.

In an early study of sexual functioning, Kinsey's team (1948) found that while very few males younger than 35 suffered from permanent impotence, as many as four in ten of those over 65 did. Further, their data indicated that the rate of impotence continued to rise. However, the sample included very few men over age 65, so these findings, reproduced in Figure 3–5, should be interpreted with caution. Among the factors leading to permanent impotence are excessive drug and alcohol use, damage to the prostate, and damage to the lower part of the spinal cord where the erection reflex center is located (Hyde, 1990; Butler & Lewis, 1986).

Premature ejaculation
the inability of a male to control the ejaculatory reflex.

Premature Ejaculation

Premature ejaculation is the inability of a male to control the ejaculatory reflex (Sanford, Hawley, & McGee, 1984). Premature ejaculation is considered a sexual dysfunction if the male has an orgasm without

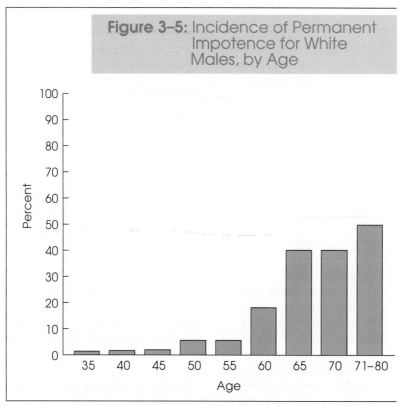

Figure 3–5: Incidence of Permanent Impotence for White Males, by Age

This graph shows the proportion of males who are permanently unable to have or maintain an erection at each age. Although the study is several decades old, it still provides one of the most complete sets of estimates for impotence. However, the small number of males aged 70 and older makes estimates for them unreliable.

Source: Kinsey, Pomeroy, and Martin, 1948, p. 236. Reprinted by permission of The Kinsey Institute for Research in Sex, Gender, and Reproduction, Inc.

any sense of control "too quickly" after initiating intercourse (Hatcher *et al.*, 1990). Premature ejaculation is almost always psychologically based, especially for males who have never learned to control the timing of their orgasm. For those males who at one time could control the timing of their orgasm but who have lost that control, physical factors—disease or neurological damage—may be involved (Hyde, 1990). An estimated 36 to 38 percent of males experience premature ejaculation (Spector & Carey, 1990) with those under 25 most often affected (Hatcher *et al.*, 1990).

Ejaculatory Delay

Ejaculatory delay (sometimes called ejaculatory incompetence) is the inability of a male to have an orgasm while having intercourse. Men suffering from this problem are able to have an orgasm by masturbating or through other types of stimulation but cannot have one during sexual intercourse. While ejaculatory delay can be caused by diseases

Ejaculatory delay or ejaculatory incompetence the inability of a male to have an orgasm while having intercourse.

that attack the nervous system, by Parkinson's disease, or by diabetes, it most often has a psychological origin (Hyde, 1990). Males who suffer anxiety about their sexual performance, have developed a masturbation pattern they cannot duplicate with a partner, or receive insufficient stimulation from intercourse may be unable to have an orgasm during sexual intercourse (Hatcher *et el.*, 1990).

Treating Sexual Problems

As noted, any number of physical, psychological, and social conditions can contribute to sexual problems. Sex is not separate from the rest of life, but very much affected by it. The treatment of sexual problems varies with their cause. Medical doctors, particularly those with some training in treating sexual disorders, should be consulted first to determine if the sexual problem is physical in nature. Some sexual dysfunctions can be treated with medication. For example, vaginal dryness in postmenopausal women can be relieved by the use of lubricants or with hormone replacement therapy (Barrow, 1989, p. 255; Roff & Atherton, 1989, p. 73) and a new drug that "makes the brain horny and increases sexual appetite" (*Discover*, 1988, p. 10; *Science Impact*, 1988a, p. 2) may soon be available to help those with unusual difficulty in achieving arousal, erection, and orgasm.

Sex therapists, particularly those recommended by the American Association of Sex Educators, Counselors, and Therapists, can help with a variety of sexual problems. A therapist might suggest practice exercises to help premature ejaculators and anorgasmic women, recommend new ways of showing sexual affection to those unable to have intercourse, or help a couple analyze the cause of their sexual difficulties. If sexual problems are a symptom of deeper relationship problems, a marriage counselor might be helpful. Finally, as might be predicted, some sexual problems are associated with certain stages of the family life cycle and generally are relieved with the passage of time. These will be noted throughout the book.

CONTRACEPTION

In certain periods of U.S. history, only sexual activities that could result in reproduction were encouraged; non-intercourse forms of sexual behavior and sexual intercourse intended solely for pleasure were prohibited or discouraged. This is no longer the case. True, during a limited number of years, most married couples look to sexual intercourse to bring them children as well as pleasure. But the major impetus behind most sexual activity in the United States today is pleasure. This creates somewhat of a dilemma. Although most sexually active, reproductively capable couples do not undertake sexual intercourse for reproductive purposes, there is a very high probability that their actions will result in reproduction unless they take special measures. Without these special measures, nine out of ten sexually active, fertile women can expect to become pregnant within one year (Trussell & Kost, 1987, p. 271). The dilemma is poignantly illustrated by a letter to Ann Landers from a woman in the top 10 percent of her college class who married and dropped out of school because of pregnancy.

> We slept together for almost a year without giving a single thought to birth control. I became pregnant. . . . I was lucky for 10 months and now I'm wearing maternity clothes and wondering if I will ever return to college and have the career I've always yearned for. (Landers, 1985, p. 3b. Permission granted by Ann Landers and Creators Syndicate.)

The "special measures" sexually active couples take to prevent or lessen the probability of pregnancy are known collectively as **contraception** (literally, "against conception"). According to current estimates, over 90 percent of all U.S. women at risk for unintended pregnancy (that is, those who are sexually active, not sterile, and do not want children) use some form of contraception (Forrest & Fordyce, 1988, p. 117). What contraceptive methods do modern couples use? How effective are these methods? What are the patterns of contraceptive use?

> Contraception strategies used to prevent or interrupt pregnancy.

Contraceptive Methods

Contraceptive methods can be classified into five categories:

1. those that depend on self-observation and self-control.
2. those that create a barrier between sperm and egg.
3. those that involve hormonal intervention.
4. those that involve surgical intervention.
5. those that interrupt the reproductive process after conception has occurred.

Table 3–1 (on pages 99–101) lists the particular contraceptive methods falling under each classification, gives a brief description of how each method prevents conception or interrupts pregnancy, and

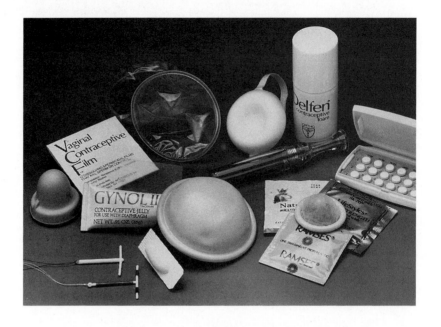

People who are sexually active have a variety of contraceptive methods available. Pictured in the top photo (clockwise from the right side) are birth control pills, condoms, a diaphragm with contraceptive jelly, a vaginal suppository; IUDs, a cervical cap with spermicide, a female condom, a sponge, and vaginal foam with an applicator. Norplant is shown in the bottom photo.

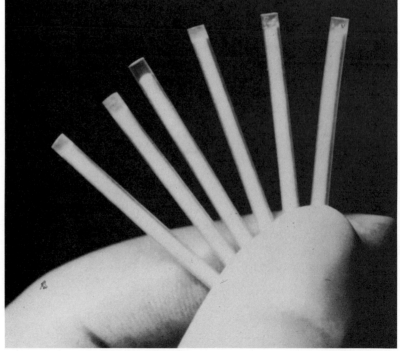

Table 3–1 Contraceptive Methods

Method	How It Works	Effectiveness Rating	Lowest Expected Failure Rate, %[a,b]	Typical Failure Rate %[a,c]	Yearly Costs[d]	Advantages	Disadvantages
Unprotected Intercourse	Chance	Poor	85	85	None		
SELF-CONTROL METHODS							
Withdrawal	Male withdraws penis from female's vagina prior to ejaculation	Poor to fair	4	18	None	No cost; accepted by Roman Catholic Church	Requires high motivation
Rhythm	Couple avoids penis-vagina contact during female's fertile period after making careful observations of her cycle	Poor to fair	1–9	20	None	No cost; accepted by Roman Catholic Church	Requires high motivation, prolonged abstinence, not all women can use
BARRIER METHODS							
Condom	Rubber sheath placed over penis so that semen cannot enter vagina	Good	2	12	$75	Easy to use, protection from STDs, availability	Interference with coitus, continual expense
Diaphragm with Spermicide	Rubber cup, fitted over cervix, holds spermicidal cream or jelly which kills sperm trying to enter	Poor to fair	6	18	$175	Remains in place up to 12 hours; no side effects	Must be fitted by physician; aesthetic objections
Cervical Cap with Spermicide	Miniature diaphragm with a tall dome; creates airtight seal around cervical opening, preventing sperm passage	Poor to fair	6	18	—	Can remain in place up to 48 hours; no side effects	Must be fitted by physician
Vaginal Foam and Suppositories	Spermicidal foam inserted into vagina keeps sperm from entering cervix and kills them	Poor to fair	3	21	$75	Easy to use; availability	Messy

a. Trussell et al., 1990, p. 52.
b. Among couples who initiate use of a method (not necessarily for the first time) and who use it *perfectly* (consistently and correctly), Trussell *et al.*'s (1990) best guess of the percentage expected to experience an accidental pregnancy during the first year if they do not stop for any other reason.
c. Among *typical* couples who initiate use of a method (not necessarily for the first time), the percentage who experience an accidental pregnancy during the first year if they do not stop use for any other reason.
d. Based on 150 acts of intercourse. Costs vary greatly. Use for comparison only.
e. Every five years.
f. Since procedure is permanent, have to pay only once.
g. Information on female condom from Seligman, 1992.

Sources: Seligman, 1992; Findlay, 1990; Hyde, 1990; Trussell et al., 1990; Carr, 1989; Associated Press, 1988; Lamanna and Riedmann, 1988; Bell, 1984.

(continued)

Table 3-1 (continued)

Method	How It Works	Effective-ness Rating	Lowest Expected Failure Rate, %[a,b]	Typical Failure Rate %[a,c]	Yearly Costs[d]	Advantages	Disadvantages
Sponge	Doughnut-shaped, polyurethane sponge, presaturated with spermicide, placed at cervical entrance forms barrier over cervix and con-tinually releases spermicide	Very poor to fair	6–9	18–28	$250	Easy to use; availability	Continual expense
Female Condoms; NOT YET AVAILABLE: FDA approval expected by end of 1992[g]	Seven-inch-long trans-parent plastic bag with flexible ring inside closed upper end (which sur-rounds cervix) and another flexible ring at open bottom end (which stays outside woman's body and keeps condom in place)	Poor to fair	—	15	$350	Easy to use; protection from STDs; availability; no side effects; reported to be more pleasurable than condoms	Unusual appearance; interference with coitus; continual expense
HORMONAL METHODS							
Combined Hormone Birth Control Pills	Female body is hor-monally "tricked" so that ovary is prevented from releasing monthly egg	Excellent	0.1	3	$300	Highly effective; not used at time of coitus; improved menstrual cycles	Cost; possible side effects; must be taken daily
Progestin only Birth Control Pills	same	Excellent	0.5	3	same	same	same
Norplant	Tiny rods implanted under female's skin release hormones which prevent ovulation. Works for 5-year period	Excellent	.04	.04	$500[e]	Highly effective; automatic; semi-permanent; reversible	Some side effects; no STD protection
SURGICAL METHODS							
Male Sterilization	Each vas deferens is cut and tied so that sperm can no longer be carried from testes to penis	Excellent	0.1	0.15	$350[f]	Permanent and highly effective	Permanent; possible psychological effects
Female Sterilization	Fallopian tubes are cut and tied or otherwise blocked, so eggs cannot make entire journey to uterus	Excellent	0.2	0.4	$1000–$1200[f]	Permanent and highly effective	Permanent; expense

Table 3–1 (continued)

Method	How It Works	Effectiveness Rating	Lowest Expected Failure Rate, %[a,b]	Typical Failure Rate %[a,c]	Yearly Costs[d]	Advantages	Disadvantages
AFTER-CONCEPTION METHODS							
Inter-uterine Device (IUD)	Changes uterus in such a way that fertilized egg cannot implant	Excellent	0.8–2.0	3	$175 (1 yr.) $350 (3–4 yrs.)	Requires no memory or motivation	Side effects; may be expelled
Abortion	Fetus is sucked or otherwise removed from uterus	Excellent	0	0	$400	Available when other methods fail	Expense; moral or psychological unacceptability

lists some advantages and disadvantages of each. In addition, the table provides estimates of costs and effectiveness.

The effectiveness rating in the table is based on failure rates. "Failure" in the case of contraception is pregnancy. The failure rate for each particular method is calculated by determining the number of women out of every 100 using that method who become pregnant during the course of one year. For example, if 100 couples use condoms as their birth control method and 12 women from these couples get pregnant during the year, the failure rate for condoms is 12 percent. Table 3–1 lists two different failure rates: the lowest expected failure rate and the typical failure rate. The **lowest expected failure rate** is the lowest pregnancy rate expected among couples who use a method consistently and correctly for an entire year (Trussell *et al.*, 1990). The **typical failure rate** is the pregnancy rate that can be expected for typical couples who will make some mistakes and have some slipups in the course of using the method over a year's time (Trussell *et al.*, 1990).

Note that the time frame of both failure rates is one year. But couples typically use contraception for many years, not one. What happens to failure rate estimates when multiple year usage is considered? Figure 3–6 (on page 102) indicates that, over a ten-year period, the risk of pregnancy increases for nearly every method. As the researcher who formulated Figure 3–6 points out, ". . . small risks taken repeatedly accumulate to very large risks over a long period" (Ross, 1989, p. 275). When looked at over the long term, only two methods—female sterilization and male vasectomy—have low failure rates (Ross, 1989).

Lowest expected failure rate
the lowest pregnancy rate expected among couples who use a method perfectly for one year.

Typical failure rate
the pregnancy rate typical of couples using a specific contraceptive method over a year's time.

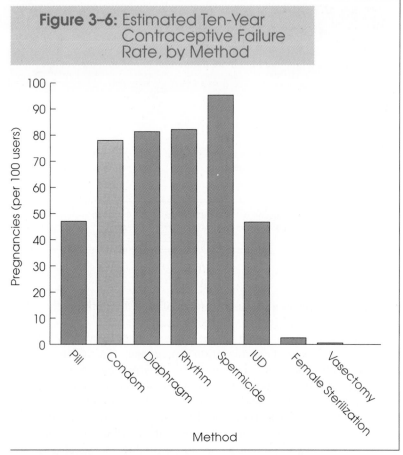

Figure 3–6: Estimated Ten-Year Contraceptive Failure Rate, by Method

Source: Ross, John, "Contraception: Short-term vs Long-term Failure Rates," *Family Planning Perspectives*, 1989, Vol. 21, No. 6, p. 276 © The Alan Guttmacher Institute.

This figure estimates the failure rate of various contraceptive methods over a ten-year period. For example, 95 of 100 couples using spermicide over a ten-year period can expect a pregnancy or "contraceptive failure." (The estimates assume the per year failure rate is constant for the ten years.)

Patterns of Contraceptive Use

Most couples able to have children, but not wanting to, practice contraception. About two-thirds of all women of childbearing age (15–44) are vulnerable to the risk of unintended pregnancy and using contraception; an additional 6 percent are vulnerable but are not using a contraceptive. The remaining 28 percent are not vulnerable to unwanted pregnancy because they are sexually inactive, sterile, or trying to become pregnant (Forrest & Fordyce, 1988, p. 116).

Table 3–2 indicates that marital status is clearly an important factor in determining whether people use contraception or not and which method they select. Married people are more likely to use contraception than unmarried people (97 percent use versus 87 percent use). Married couples, many of whom have undoubtedly had personal

Method	1987		
	Total	Married	Unmarried
All users	93	97	87
Sterilization	36	51	13
Female	22	28	12
Male	16	24	1
Pill	32	22	48
Condom	16	15	16
IUD	3	3	3
Diaphragm	4	4	4
Foam	1	3	1
Cream/jelly	*	*	*
Suppository	1	1	1
Sponge	3	1	4
Periodic abstinence	5	5	3
Withdrawal	5	5	6
Douche	1	1	1
Nonusers	7	3	13
Total	100	100	100

Table 3–2 Contraceptive Use by Marital Status, 1987

* Less than 0.5 percent.

Source: Jacqueline Forrest *et al.,* "U.S. women's contraceptive attitudes and practices: Have they changed in the 1980s?" *Family Planning Perspectives,* 1988, Vol. 20, No. 6, p. 117 © The Alan Guttmacher Institute.

experience with the "ten-year failure rates" shown in Figure 3–6, choose sterilization most often. Fifty-one percent of married couples rely on sterilization, 22 percent rely on the Pill, and 15 percent use a condom. Very few married couples depend on the other techniques.

The same three methods that are most popular for married couples are also most popular for nonmarried people. The rank order of use, however, is different. Almost half of the unmarried use the Pill, 16 percent use condoms, and 13 percent have been sterilized (Forrest & Fordyce, 1988, p. 117).

These patterns of contraceptive use are somewhat different from those existing at earlier periods in the twentieth-century United States. The Cohort Comparison on contraception in four cohorts details these earlier patterns, making the points that contemporary couples have better access to a greater variety of effective contraceptives than most other twentieth-century couples had, and that choices about contraception are shaped not only by technology but also by the law.

Cohort Comparison   Contraception in Four Cohorts

During the late 1800s and early 1900s, both federal and state laws prohibited the importation, mailing, or interstate shipment of contraceptive information and devices; doctors received no training about contraception and, in some states, were forbidden by law to give out the information they did have; and abortion was illegal in all states. Due to vigorous lobbying by birth control advocates, such as Margaret Sanger, some federal and state restrictions began to be lifted during the late 1920s and early 1930s, at about the time members of the New Century cohort (born 1910–1914) were becoming sexually active. This cohort, faced with a major economic depression during their early adulthood, had an economic incentive for limiting pregnancy and did so fairly successfully, having smaller families on average than the cohorts preceding and immediately following theirs. How did they do so? Those who had access to newly established birth control clinics or to sympathetic doctors were most likely to select the diaphragm as their method of choice (D'Emilio & Freedman, 1988). Those without such access had to resort to the secretive tactics of earlier generations to receive contraceptive information. One man described the process

like this:

> When I wanted a book on sex and contraception before (my wife and I) were married, it was illegal to sell them. To get Margaret Sanger's book (on contraception), I climbed a back stairway in New York (and) knocked on a door. A view panel was opened and someone asked, "What do you want?" I said, "The Book." The person looked at me, then said, "That will be four-fifty." I handed the money through the panel and the book was handed out and the panel closed. (Quoted in Brecher, 1984, p. 247)

Clinics, cooperative doctors, and even the more secretive ways of obtaining contraceptive information were available mostly to middle-class married couples living in urban areas in the North. Working-class couples, the unmarried, rural residents, and Southerners who wanted to prevent pregnancy tended to use less effective methods such as douching, withdrawal, or periodic abstinence.

Members of the Depression cohort (born 1930–1934), who became sexually active in the post-World War II years, tended to have their children (often as many as four or five)

early in their marriage. By the time they were in their early to mid-thirties in the early 1960s, they wanted dependable contraception. At about the same time, the last of the state laws that had prohibited doctors or others from providing contraceptive information and advice to married people was invalidated by the Supreme Court in its 1965 *Griswold v. Connecticut* decision. The early 1960s also brought the introduction of the birth control pill. Some of the Depression cohort couples used the Pill, but more of them, certain that they wanted no more children, chose voluntary sterilization. Within the cohort, blacks, Catholics, and those with less than a high school education were significantly less likely to use contraception and, consequently, typically had larger families (D'Emilio & Freedman, 1988).

By the time the Baby Boom cohort (born 1950–1954) became sexually active in the late 1960s and early 1970s, birth control pills and IUDs were in widespread use among married people but still sometimes difficult for the unmarried to acquire. The 1972 *Eisenstadt v. Baird* Supreme Court case invalidated the Massachusetts law forbidding the dissemination of contraceptive information to the unmarried and, thus, gave unmarried people the same *legal rights* (though not necessarily the same practical access) to contraceptive information that married people had (Hyde, 1990; Duncan, 1987). Abortion, illegal throughout the late nineteenth and most of the twentieth century, was legalized by the 1973 Supreme Court decision *Roe v. Wade* and provided a "backup" contraceptive method for the Baby Boomers. The differences in contraceptive use between blacks and whites, working class and middle class, and Catholics and non-Catholics virtually disappeared with this cohort. Almost all Baby Boom married couples used contraception to control family size;

after they had the number of children desired, sterilization became the contraceptive method of choice (D'Emilio & Freedman, 1988).

The Baby Bust cohort (born 1970–1974) reached adolescence and young adulthood during an era of concern about teenage pregnancy and sexually transmitted disease, especially AIDS. This concern lessened opposition to sex education (*The Gallup Report*, 1987, p. 19), meaning that the Baby Busters are more likely than previous cohorts to have learned about sexuality and contraception in junior high or high school. Even public schools that offer sex edu-

cation and have on-campus health clinics seldom dispense contraceptives, however (Kirby, Waszak, & Ziegler, 1991). Nonetheless, Baby Busters find it easier to acquire contraceptives from public clinics, private doctors, and drug store shelves than previous cohorts did; condom and Pill use are widespread. The changes that some states are making to restrict abortion may affect future Baby Buster access to this backup alternative (Kolbert & Mertus, 1991). All in all, however, this cohort has more contraceptive choices and easier access to contraception than any other twentieth-century cohort.

SEXUALLY TRANSMITTED DISEASES

Unwanted pregnancy is one risk associated with sexual intercourse; contracting a sexually transmitted disease is another. **Sexually transmitted disease (STD)** is the overall name applied to some twenty-five bacterial, viral, yeast, and protozoan infections spread primarily through sexual contact with an infected person (Hatcher *et al.*, 1990). STDs are most commonly contracted through genital-genital, oral-genital, and anal-genital contact. Some STDs can be passed from mother to newborn child as the baby passes through the birth canal and some, AIDS and syphilis in particular, can be passed from mother to fetus through the placenta. In addition, viral STDs, such as AIDS and hepatitis B, can be transmitted through blood transfusions or the use of infected needles. All but a few STDs are curable if discovered. But being "cured" does not prevent future infection; furthermore, people can contract and suffer from more than one STD at a time (Byer, Shainberg, & Jones, 1988; Crowe & Norsigian, 1984).

> Sexually transmitted disease (STD)
> infections spread primarily through sexual contact.

Table 3–3 The Most Common STDs and How They Can Affect You

STD	How it affects you	How treated
AIDS (Acquired Immuno-Deficiency Syndrome)	Long-lasting infections, diarrhea, night sweats, fever, weight loss, swollen glands, coughing or shortness of breath; leads to cancer, pneumonia, brain damage and death.	No satisfactory treatment at present time; usually fatal.
Chlamydia	Man—itching or burning during urination, whitish discharge from penis; woman—no symptoms, or burning during urination, whitish, cheesy vaginal discharge, and pain in the belly.	Can be cured with antibiotics; if untreated, can lead to pelvic inflammatory disease (PID), an infection of the uterus and tubes, which causes severe belly pain, fever, abnormal periods and tenderness of the female organs and can result in sterility in women.
Genital Herpes	Sores on penis or vagina, vaginal discharge, fever, fatigue, itching, and aches and pains; first attack may be very painful and later flare-ups less painful.	Symptoms disappear without treatment but once infected, there may be flare-ups averaging 4 to 7 times a year; no cure, can only treat symptoms.
Gonorrhea	Man—whitish discharge from penis, itching or burning during urination; woman—no symptoms or vaginal discharge, burning during urination, fever, pain in the belly.	Can be cured with antibiotics; without treatment, can cause arthritis, heart disease, blindness, pelvic inflammatory disease, sterility.
Syphilis	Sores on penis or vagina, mouth, anus, or elsewhere; low fever, sore throat, other sores or rashes.	Can be cured with antibiotics; if untreated, can spread and eventually cause blindness, heart disease, nervous disorders, insanity and death.
Venereal Warts	Fleshy growths, singly or in clusters, inside or outside of sex organs and anus; may cause rectal pain or pain during sex; become more prominent during pregnancy; increased risk of cervical cancer from some viruses that cause the warts.	Drug applied directly to warts, or surgical removal.

Source: March of Dimes Birth Defects Foundation, 1990.

We will focus on the six most common STDs (*Science Impact,* 1988b). Three of them—syphilis, gonorrhea, and chlamydia—are bacterially-based diseases treatable with antibiotics. The three viral STDs we will discuss—AIDS, genital herpes, and venereal warts (papilloma)—are not currently curable. Table 3–3 provides further information.

Bacterial STDs

Chlamydia, gonorrhea, and **syphilis** are the most common bacterially-based STDs. All are easily diagnosed and treatable with antibiotics. If left untreated, however, all three of these bacterial infections can spread to vital organs and produce permanent damage. Chlamydia and gonorrhea most often attack the reproductive organs and are leading causes of involuntary sterility; untreated syphilis can eventually destroy the circulatory and nervous systems (Allee, 1988; Byer, Shainberg, & Jones, 1988).

Although these STDs are easily diagnosable by medical tests, infected people often do not experience or recognize early symptoms. This is particularly true with chlamydia, currently the most common of all STDs in the United States (*Science Impact,* 1988b). On those unusual occasions when chlamydia symptoms do appear, they usually come in the form of painful urination and urethral (in males) or vaginal (in females) discharge. Females also might experience abdominal pain. In males, the initial symptoms of gonorrhea are similar to those of chlamydia and show up more frequently. Females infected with gonorrhea experience very slight initial symptoms, usually in the form of vaginal irritation and discharge (Byer, Shainberg, & Jones, 1988).

Syphilis shows up first in the form of painless but very infectious sores at the initial site of infection. The lesions are more likely to be visible in infected males, where they most often appear on the penis, than in infected females, where they are often hidden within the vagina. These lesions disappear within several weeks but, if untreated, the disease then progresses into its more serious stages (Byer, Shainberg, & Jones, 1988).

> **Chlamydia**
> the most common STD, bacterially based, most often attacks the reproductive system.
>
> **Gonorrhea**
> a common, bacterial STD, attacks primarily the reproductive system.
>
> **Syphilis**
> a common, bacterial STD, attacks primarily the circulatory and nervous systems.

Viral STDs

The three most common viral STDs—genital herpes, venereal warts, and AIDS—are diagnosable but not currently curable. **Genital herpes**, characterized by the appearance, disappearance, and reappearance of painful lesions in the genital area, is an embarrassing, but not usually life-threatening, disease. Medication can lessen the frequency and severity of the lesion attacks; limiting sexual contact and careful hygiene

> **Genital herpes**
> a common viral STD characterized by painful lesions in the genital area.

**Venereal warts
(Papilloma)**
a common viral STD,
the fastest growing
STD in the United
States.

**HIV (human
immunodeficiency
virus)**
virus that causes
AIDS.

**AIDS (Acquired
Immune Deficiency
Syndrome)**
virally based STD
characterized by loss
of the body's
immune response,
mental deterioration,
and eventual death.

during the periods when lesions are present can reduce the risk of spread (Byer, Shainberg, & Jones, 1988).

Venereal warts (papilloma) is the *fastest growing* STD in the United States (Byer, Shainberg, & Jones, 1988). The disease shows up first in the form of small, sometimes invisible, genital warts. Some forms of the papilloma virus are of major concern because they are heavily implicated in cervical cancer and may play a role in cancers of the vagina and penis as well (Byer, Shainberg, & Jones, 1988). There is no cure for papilloma although surgical removal and drugs can force the virus into hiding (*Science Impact*, 1988b).

HIV (human immunodeficiency virus), the virus which causes **AIDS (Acquired Immune Deficiency Syndrome)**, typically lies dormant for several years before AIDS symptoms emerge. HIV is unique among the STD viruses because it attacks the lymphocytes—white blood cells that produce immunity in the body—and also infects the brain (Byer, Shainberg, & Jones, 1988). The viral attack on the immune system leaves the body vulnerable to *all* disease and eventually leads to death; the attack on the brain means that AIDS victims gradually lose speech, memory, and other mental functions.

The federal Centers for Disease Control report that 206,400 persons in the United States had been diagnosed with AIDS as of January, 1992, and expect the total to reach 300,000 within two years (Associated Press, 1992). About 1 million people in the United States ("From the Centers . . . ," 1990, p. 1477) and 8 to 10 million men, women, and children worldwide are HIV-infected (Gillespie, 1991, p. 17); over the next decade or so, most are expected to develop AIDS ("Questions about AIDS," 1989).

HIV carriers can transmit the virus to others whether or not they have experienced any AIDS symptoms. HIV can be transmitted through semen or vaginal fluid during sexual contact—with oral sex being less risky than vaginal or anal intercourse—or through direct transfer of infected blood through transfusions or unclean needles. Early symptoms of AIDS are not particularly dramatic or distinctive. They include fever, weight and appetite loss, enlarged lymph nodes, or diarrhea. AIDS victims eventually die from cancer, pneumonia, or some other disease their decimated immune systems cannot handle and, as noted, may lose mental functioning prior to death. Although several experimental drugs are in use, there is no cure for AIDS ("Questions about AIDS," 1989; Byer, Shainberg, & Jones, 1988).

Preventing STDs

Although STDs vary in symptoms and seriousness, protection and prevention methods are similar. The best protection is sexual abstinence or a sexually monogamous relationship with an uninfected partner. Regardless of sexual orientation, individuals who have frequent sexual contact with many different partners are most at risk for all STDs. Sexual contact with current or former needle-using drug abusers is particularly risky. Once involved in a sexual contact, the use of a condom and of a spermicide containing Nonoxynol 9 can reduce the chances of acquiring an STD. Both provide a barrier between the infection and the vulnerable body parts, and spermicide is helpful in killing some viruses as well (Byer, Shainberg, & Jones, 1988). For those engaging in risky sexual behavior (frequent contact with many partners), such protection is necessary in *every encounter*. As one AIDS victim wrote:

> I practiced only safe activities since 1987. I was not infected, and made a strong [commitment] to stay uninfected. Unfortunately, several months ago, I slipped once.... I have never done it since, and I slipped just once, but I just found out that I am now infected with the AIDS virus (quoted in Chase, 1990, p. B1).

Finally, some sexual activities are safer than others. Consult the Personal Application entitled "Safer Sex Options" for suggestions.

**Personal
Application**

Safer Sex Options

Sexual feelings can be displayed in a wide variety of ways—not all of them involve intercourse, and not all of them are high risk. Consult the following list for suggestions about how to express sexual feelings while safeguarding your own health and that of your partner.

Safe
　massage
　hugging
　body rubbing
　kissing (dry)
　masturbation
　hand-to-genital touching (hand job) or mutual masturbation
　erotic books and movies

Possibly Safe
　kissing (wet)
　vaginal/rectal intercourse using latex condom (use spermicide for extra
　　safety)
　oral sex on a man using a latex condom
　oral sex on a woman who does not have her period or a vaginal infection
　　with discharge (use latex barrier such as dental dam for extra safety)

Unsafe
   any intercourse without a latex condom
   oral sex on a man without a latex condom
   oral sex on a woman during her period or a vaginal infection with dis-
       charge without a latex barrier such as a dental dam
   semen in the mouth
   oral-anal contact
   sharing sex toys or douching equipment
   blood contact of ANY kind, including menstrual blood, sharing needles,
       and any sex that causes tissue damage or bleeding

Source: Hatcher *et al*, 1990, p. 76.

Summary

People engage in sexual contact with one another for both reproductive and pleasurable reasons. Each sex has distinctive, specialized
sexual organs that produce sex cells, deliver the cells to a place where
they can unite to form a fertilized egg, and give people pleasure.
The female reproductive system, operating on a monthly, hormonally controlled cycle, is also capable of nourishing a fertilized egg
through nine months of development and delivering a new human
being.

Males and females experience similar physiological responses
when sexually aroused. Both go through a sexual response cycle that
includes four stages: excitement, plateau, orgasm, and resolution.

Sexual pleasure results from a rather complex confluence of
psychological and physiological factors, and problems in achieving
sexual pleasure are not unusual. Lack of interest in sex is a common
condition in both men and women from time to time. Other common female sexual problems are painful intercourse and inability to
reach orgasm; other common male sexual problems are impotence
and problems with the timing of ejaculation. The treatment of sexual
problems varies with their cause.

Contraception is important to most sexually active people today because, for most of their sexual lives, they do not want to repro-
duce. Contraceptive methods include self-control techniques, barrier
methods, hormonal intervention, surgical intervention, and post-
conception methods.

Sexually transmitted disease is another risk of sexual activity. The most common sexually transmitted diseases are the bacterial diseases chlamydia, gonorrhea, and syphilis, which are curable, and the noncurable viral diseases genital herpes, papilloma, and AIDS. AIDS is considered the most serious because it attacks the immune system and results in certain death. Limiting sexual activity, having a sexually monogamous relationship with an uninfected partner, and using condoms and spermicide offer the best protection against sexually transmitted disease.

CHAPTER 4

DATING AND PREMARITAL SEX

Here are some attitudes that different people have toward sex before marriage. Read each one carefully, and rank each philosophy in order of its importance to you. Put a 1 beside the attitude which exemplifies your position toward premarital sex most closely, a 2 next to the attitude which next best describes your philosophy, etc., ending with a 6 for the position which *least* reflects how you feel.

1. Virginity is a virtue. It is an assurance of sexual happiness. Premarital sex leads to feelings of guilt, regret, and recriminations. The social function of marriage has always been to legitimize parenthood, not sexuality. Hence, sex should be used only for the purpose of procreation. Unmarried adults should not indulge in sexual intercourse; those that do so are wrong and will be condemned.

2. Young adults should reserve themselves for their future marital partners. By doing so, they will be in harmony with their selves, their beliefs, and their families. Sex in marriage is a beautiful experience, fulfilling the satisfactions and needs of the partners. Remaining pure for your future husband or wife is the ultimate gift with which to consummate a marriage.

3. Sex outside of marriage is acceptable when the couple is engaged, or when there is a definite commitment to marriage. Sex should be saved to enjoy with one's marital partner. However, the couple need not wait until the marriage is legitimized by the ceremony. If both individuals feel that sexual intercourse, at this point, would enhance their relationship and fulfill interpersonal needs, then there is no reason why they should wait.

4. Premarital sex is all right if it increases the capacity to trust, brings greater integrity to personal relationships, dissolves barriers separating people, enhances self-respect, and fosters a zest for living. Concern for interpersonal relationships can provide a positive, meaningful setting for a consideration of sexual standards and moral behavior. The criterion for morality should not be the commission or omission of a particular act, but the consequences of that act upon the relationships of people, and upon their interaction with others and with society.

5. Every human being, just because he/she exists, should have the right to as much (or as little), as varied (or as limited), and as enduring (or as brief) sexual enjoyments as he/she prefers—as long as one does not needlessly, forcefully, or unfairly interfere with the sexual rights and satisfactions of others. The primary purpose of sex is enjoyment. The more sex fun a person has, the sounder he/she will be psychologically. Physical pleasure is reason enough for having sexual intercourse, and a person should be allowed to pursue such pleasure with any willing partner.

6. Chastity, in its obtuse ignorance, can only result in producing an incomplete and wretched type of life. Sexual enjoyment is an important part of life. To have remained chaste for a lifetime is to have been a self-deluded victim, living a wasted life. One must seize upon every opportunity to engage in sex with any partner available. Those who resist sexual experiences are not valuable or desirable members of society. They are nervous, restless, and unstable, begrudging others the pleasures they deny themselves.

Source: Murstein *et al.*, 1989, pp. 127–28.

In the following excerpt from their book *Marriage: East and West,* Vera and David Mace, U.S. marriage counselors married to one another, describe a discussion about love and marriage they had with a group of teenage girls in India. As you read, note how differently the Maces and the Indian girls feel about the practice of dating.

We gave as good an account as we could of how our young people are free to meet each other and have dates; how a boy and girl will fall in love; and how, after a period of going steady, they become engaged and then get married. We knew that young people in the East live a very restricted life, and have their marriages arranged for them by their parents, so we felt a little relieved that they had chosen to question us about our delightful romantic traditions. We didn't want to make them *too* envious, but we naturally were glad to demonstrate our superiority in this matter of finding a mate.

When we had finished, there was a meditative silence. Concluding that they had been impressed, we decided to start a discussion.

"Wouldn't you like to be free to choose your own marriage partners, like the young people do in the West?"

"Oh no!" several voices replied in chorus.

Taken aback, we searched their faces.

"Why not?"

"For one thing," said one of them, "doesn't it put the girl in a very humiliating position?"

"Humiliating? In what way?"

"Well, doesn't it mean that she has to try to look pretty, and call attention to herself, and attract a boy, to be sure she'll get married?"

"Well, perhaps so."

"And if she doesn't want to do that, or if she feels it's undignified, wouldn't that mean she mightn't get a husband?"

"Yes, that's possible."

"So a girl who is shy and doesn't push herself forward might not be able to get married. Does that happen?"

"Sometimes it does."

"Well, surely that's humiliating. It makes getting married a sort of competition in which the girls are fighting each other for the boys. And it encourages a girl to pretend she's better than she really is. She can't relax and be herself. She has to make a good impression to get a boy, and then she has to go on making a good impression to get him to marry her."

Before we could think of an answer to this unexpected line of argument, another girl broke in.

"In our system, you see," she explained, "we girls don't have to worry at all. We *know* we'll get married. When we are old enough, our parents will find a suitable boy, and everything will be arranged. We don't have to go into competition with each other."

"Besides," said a third girl, "how would we be able to judge the character of a boy we met and got friendly with? We are young and inexperienced. Our parents are older and wiser, and they aren't as easily deceived as we would be. I'd far rather have my parents choose for me. It's so important that the man I marry should be the right one. I could so easily make a mistake if I had to find him for myself."

Source: From *Marriage: East and West*, by David and Vera Mace. Copyright © 1960, 1959 by David and Vera Mace. Used by permission of Doubleday, a division of Bantam Doubleday Dell Publishing Group, Inc.

Although this discussion took place more than thirty years ago, the two very different ways of selecting a marriage partner it describes are both in use today. The dating and romance road to marriage promoted by the Maces prevails throughout the Western world—Europe, Australia, Canada, and the United States. The arranged marriage system favored by the Indian girls continues to be a prominent part of selecting a marriage partner in most Asian and African cultures. As the Indian teenagers explain, the arranged marriage method emphasizes the wisdom of parents and the importance of choosing a husband of good character, while downplaying the importance of youthful freedom, love, romance, and physical attractiveness. Accustomed to the arranged marriage system, the Indian youths see U.S. premarital rituals, such as dating and romance, as humiliating, competitive, and deceptive. The Maces, on the other hand, view the Indian parent-controlled system as restricting the freedom and fun of young people and find it hard to imagine how any young girl could turn down the liberating delights of dating and romance.

Chapter 4 focuses on dating and premarital sex, two intimate relationship activities frequently preceding marriage or long-term marriage-like arrangements in the contemporary United States and other Western cultures. We begin by discussing dating as a mate selection method, describing how it differs from the traditional Eastern ways of selecting a partner and explaining how it developed and changed. Then we will look at the choices people in the United States make about whom to date and whom to marry. The section on dating will close with discussions of conflict in dating relationships and of whether dating is good practice for marriage. The premarital sex portion of Chapter 4 will trace twentieth-century changes in sexual attitudes and behavior, discuss male and female differences regarding premarital sex, and explain why people choose to engage in first intercourse when they do. The chapter ends by discussing the "New Monogamy" as an alternative choice. Throughout the chapter, our focus will be on the intimate activities of the never married, especially never-married teenagers and young adults. The dating, sexual, and mate selection activities of the previously married will be described in Chapter 15.

DATING AS MATE SELECTION

Mate selection
the process of
finding and
choosing a
sexual or marriage
partner.

Dating
a mate selection
procedure in which
two individuals with
romantic interests in
one another share
prearranged
activities as a way of
getting to know one
another; the most
common mate
selection procedure
in the contemporary
United States.

Social scientists refer to the process of searching for and finding a sexual or marriage partner as **mate selection**. The mate selection process is very important to society as a whole. By grouping people into relatively stable reproductive units, mate selection is the first step in assuring society a continual supply of new people, something every society needs to survive. Mate selection is also important to individuals—after all, it determines whom one will live with and love with, share a home with and spend nights with, and work with and play with for years into the future.

Mate selection procedures vary from society to society. One of the major variations is in terms of *who* does the selecting: Should sexual or marriage partners select one another without any influence from others? Should parents control the entire selection process? Should parents select and give children veto power? Or should children do the initial selection and give parents the veto? A second source of variation concerns the criteria used in making the selection: Should potential partners evaluate each other on the basis of their feelings? On external criteria such as sexiness or stylishness? Or should more practical considerations such as economic status, ability to have children, and willingness to work hard prevail? Finally, mate selection procedures vary in terms of how intimately partners are expected to know one another prior to making a long-term commitment like marriage: Should the partners wait until after marriage to get to know one another intimately? Or should knowing one another in intimate ways precede marriage?

Dating is the prevailing mate selection procedure in the contemporary United States. Although most of you are probably very familiar with what dating is, you might never have considered its most essential elements—what makes dating different from other ways of finding a mate. The essential elements of dating can be summarized like this:

1. One person (typically, although not always, male) asks another (typically, although not always, female) to share some future, specified pleasurable activity. The person asked can choose whether to accept or reject the invitation. (This is where the competition and humiliation mentioned by the Indian girls comes in!)
2. During the date itself, the two partners focus on one another and on the shared activity, unsupervised by others.
3. Some intimate activity, broadly defined, is expected on a date, with partners who have dated one another many times expected to be the most intimate.

As a mate selection procedure, *dating maximizes individual choice while minimizing parental control, emphasizes emotional factors over practical ones, and assumes intimacy prior to long-term commitment.* Consider how this mate selection procedure differs from the arranged marriage system described by the Indian girls in the opening story. In **arranged marriage** systems, parents, or a combination of parents and other elders, control the initial and sometimes the final choices; practical criteria (Does he have a promising economic future? Is she healthy?) are more important than emotional ones; and the development of emotional and physical intimacy takes place *after* marriage, not before.

The characteristics of the arranged marriage method of mate selection conform well to the characteristics of the traditional family system described in Chapter 1. The arranged marriage method represents patriarchy in that older adults control the lives of younger ones. It is public in that the marriage negotiations are known to both extended families and often to the community as well and in that the betrothed couple has little, if any, privacy. And, with its attention to the practical characteristics of potential spouses, the arranged marriage method is clearly economically rather than intimately oriented. Conversely, the dating method of mate selection, at least in its purest form, typifies the

Arranged marriage a mate selection procedure in which parents or other older people select marriage partners for members of younger generations.

MATRIMONIAL.
Female

This advertisement shows one way Indian parents try to find a suitable husband for their daughter.

characteristics of modern family systems. Control by young people makes it egalitarian, at least insofar as age is concerned; the lack of supervision on dates makes it private; and the extreme emphasis on romance and emotional feelings clearly demonstrates the importance of intimacy.

When and how did dating develop in the United States? How has it changed? And to what extent is it really youth controlled, emotionally driven, and intimate?

The Development of Dating

Calling

a type of mate selection procedure that involves the man visiting the woman he wishes to marry in her parents' home; preceded dating as a mate selection procedure.

Dating is a twentieth-century development. When the twentieth century began, the most prominent U.S. mate selection procedure was **calling** (Bailey, 1988). Calling had some characteristics of arranged marriage and some of dating. In calling, a mate-seeking young man visited (or "called on") and got to know the young woman of his choice in her parents' home. The young man (not his parents) chose whom he wanted to call on, but the woman and her parents controlled whether or not he would be allowed to call. Men who had characteristics deemed valuable to the young woman and her parents—wealth, good family background, the potential to be a good father and husband—were in a better position to receive an invitation than were men with none of these characteristics. Once the man arrived at the home of the woman's parents, the young couple did not go out. They sat and talked, or they went for quiet walks, or she played the piano for him, or they had tea, or he had dinner with her family.

During the 1920s, dating began to replace calling as the major U.S. mate-selection procedure. Dating greatly lessened parental control over both partner choice and young peoples' intimate activities. Calling had an air of serious commitment about it, but dating was carefree fun.

Why did dating develop when it did? By the 1920s, more young adults than ever before went to coed colleges, and this is where dating first began. Soon the increasingly large numbers of teenage boys and girls attending public high schools together were dating as well. No longer confined to seeing one another only at church, community, or family gatherings, the young adults of the 1920s had more opportunities to scope one another out, talk to one another, and arrange future meetings away from direct adult supervision.

Two technological developments, the telephone and the automobile, also were important to the evolution of dating. As they spread, so did the practice of dating. Telephones became part of urban, middle-class homes beginning about 1910; by 1940, about 37 percent of all U.S. homes had a telephone; in the 1980s, 97 percent did (Beeghly &

Sellers, 1986, p. 323). In 1900, there were only 8,000 automobiles in the United States; by 1940, there were 27 million and by 1981, 106 million (Beeghly & Sellers, 1986, p. 323).

The telephone allowed young people to communicate in private and, more importantly, to make plans to meet somewhere away from the watchful eyes of parents and siblings. The car gave them the means to get there. Young men still had to "call" in order to pick up their dates, and young women received instructions about when to return home, but at least they did not have to spend the entire evening under adult supervision (D'Emilio & Freedman, 1988).

Throughout the 1920s and 1930s, young people sought, although they did not always achieve, "promiscuous popularity" in their dating: the more different people one dated, the more popular one was judged to be (Bailey, 1988). After World War II, security became more important than competitive popularity, and a new stage of dating—going steady—was added to the mate-selection process (Bailey, 1988). The men who had gone off to war came back wanting to settle down. The women, remembering the scarcity of men during the war, did not want to have to scramble to get dates again (Bailey, 1988). **Going steady**, a couple's agreement to date only one another, met both needs.

Going Steady
a couple's agreement to date only one another.

"Well, it's our first date. How does dinner, movie and a blood test sound?"

Changes in Dating

Dating became much more widespread between the 1920s and the early 1960s but, except for increased concern about security and the addition of going steady, basic dating patterns did not change very much during these 40 years. Throughout this period, men did the asking, usually selected the dating time and place, assumed responsibility for the transportation, and paid for the date. Women waited to be asked out, accepted or rejected the invitation, and, if they accepted, went along with the male's decisions regarding place and time. Both partners prepared extensively for the date, and the dates tended to be rather formal. As you will learn later in this chapter, sexual activity on dates throughout this period was mostly a matter of male-female compromise—men trying to go as far as they could, women trying to keep them from "going too far" (D'Emilio & Freedman, 1988).

Societal changes in sexual attitudes, sexual behavior, and women's roles that marked the 1960s and 1970s changed dating in two major ways: sexual intercourse became increasingly acceptable as part of the dating relationship, and cohabitation became established as a new phase in premarital intimate relationships. These two changes are so important that we will deal with both of them extensively later in the book: sexual activity changes will be dealt with in the second half of this chapter, and Chapter 5 will be devoted to cohabitation.

Have there been other, less major, changes in dating since the early 1960s? Perhaps so. The rigid gender roles that typified dating prior to the late 1960s seem to have become more flexible (Hutter, 1988; Korman, 1983). For example, one survey of college students done in the 1980s discovered that 90 percent of both males and females felt that it was equally appropriate for a female to approach a male on a first encounter as for a male to approach a female (Kleinke, Meeker, & Staneski, 1986, p. 596). Research done at the University of Florida at about the same time found that almost half the female students surveyed had initiated at least one date and that 56 percent had shared date expenses (Korman, 1983). Traditional dating patterns have not disappeared, however. At least in some parts of the country, men assume that women who initiate dates are more sexually active (Muehlenhard & Scardino, 1985); women, aware of this assumption, may respond by waiting for the man to ask first. Perhaps the most accurate statement we can make about changes in dating is that there is more *diversity* in terms of who does what in dating today than in the past—some dating couples maintain very traditional gender role patterns in dating while others have become more androgynous.

Dating also became more informal during the 1960s, 1970s, and 1980s. During these years, more young adults began to live independently and unsupervised in their own apartments or dorm rooms. This meant they no longer had to "go out" to spend private time with a dating partner; more dates involved informal activities such as eating, talking, or watching television (Knox & Wilson, 1981). Another fairly common recent pattern is for a man and woman to meet at a group gathering, such as a party or bar, and pair off as a "dating couple" later in the evening (Hutter, 1988). Both staying at home dates and pairing off after group activity dates are less prearranged, structured, and formal than earlier dating styles. The Cohort Comparison on dating in four cohorts provides further information about changes and continuities in dating.

Cohort Comparison   Dating in Four Cohorts

All four of the twentieth-century birth cohorts we are following through this book participated in dating. The New Century cohort (born 1910–1914), coming of age during the 1920s, were among the first young adults to date. The Depression cohort members (born 1930–1934) dated immediately following World War II, and the Baby Boom cohort (born 1950–1954) dated during the early days of the Sexual Revolution. Finally, the Baby Bust cohort (born 1970–1974) began their dating during an era marked by a partial return to conservatism. Now that we have placed our cohorts, let us compare them.

Our major source of information on the first three cohorts will be Martin K. Whyte's book, *Dating, Mating, and Marriage.* In his book, Whyte (1990) reports on three marriage cohorts of women in the Detroit area: women first married between 1925 and 1944, women first married between 1945 and 1964, and women first married between 1965 and 1984. These marriage cohorts do not, of course, correspond exactly to our birth cohorts, but they are close enough for comparative purposes. Most New Century women belong to Whyte's first marriage cohort, most Depression cohort women to his second, and most Baby Boom women to his third.

Whyte discovered that, in some ways, the women in the three cohorts had similar dating experiences. The median age at first date for all three cohorts was 16, and the median age for first dating the man they eventually married was 18. Women in these cohorts met their husbands in a number of different ways, but the most common husband-meeting method for women in all three cohorts was introduction by a mutual friend. There was little evidence that parents had become more lenient or stricter over the years; about half of the wo-men in each cohort said that their parents had tried to influence their choice of dates, typically by forbidding them to date certain boys.

Although they all began dating at about the same age, the New Century cohort women dated fewer men (4–7 was average) before marriage while the Depression cohort members dated an average of 10–14 different men and the Baby Boomers 12–15. As you might guess, the major way in which members of the three cohorts differed was in terms of sexual activities. As Figure 4–1 illustrates, the New Century cohort women generally moved through the stages of dating more slowly than later women—they first dated at age 16, first went steady at age 18, and first had sexual intercourse at age 20. Whyte estimated that only 24 percent had premarital intercourse, nearly all of these only with their future husband. Depression cohort women averaged one year between their

Cohort Comparison   Dating in Four Cohorts (cont'd)

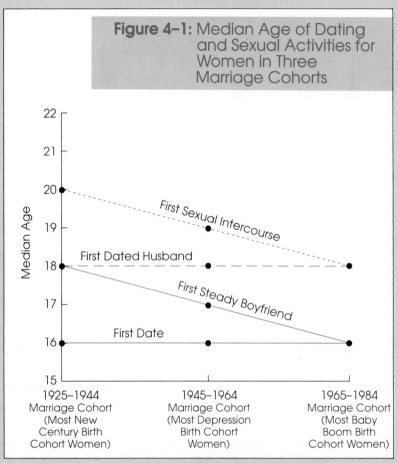

Figure 4–1: Median Age of Dating and Sexual Activities for Women in Three Marriage Cohorts

Source: Reprinted with permission from: Whyte, Martin King. *Dating, Mating, and Marriage,* p. 28. (New York: Aldine de Gruyter) Copyright © 1990 by Walter de Gruyter, Inc.

first date at age 16 and first going steady at age 17 and two more years before their first intercourse at age 19. According to Whyte's estimates, about half had intercourse before marriage, 17 percent with someone other than their husband. As might be expected, the Baby Boom women sped up the process—going steady during the same year (their sixteenth) that they began dating and engaging in first intercourse only two years later at age 18. Nearly three-quarters of them were nonvirgins at marriage and one-third had had sexual partners other than their husband prior to marriage. In addition, almost one-third of Whyte's final marriage cohort (essentially the Baby Boomers) had cohabited before marriage.

We cannot report with such precision on the Baby Bust cohort. Based on national figures and trends, they almost certainly experienced intercourse (and possibly dating) earlier than any of the other cohorts, although perhaps with fewer partners than the Baby Boomers (See Alternative Choice section on the New Monogamy). As noted, they are more likely than their predecessors to be informal, group-oriented, and androgynous in their dating behavior.

Choice in Dating and Mating

Dating involves much more individual choice and much less control by others than other methods for selecting a mate. How complete is individual control over dating and mate selection? How, if at all, are parents involved in the process? And what choices do individuals make about whom to date and whom to marry?

Parental Influence

Most parents in the United States today do not select a marriage partner for their son or daughter or accompany their children on dates. Nonetheless, many parents care a great deal about whom their children date and marry, so they attempt to exercise some type of control. Maintaining some control over mate selection is particularly important to parents who belong to an ethnic group with a long tradition of arranged marriages, like Vietnamese-Americans (Tran, 1988), and to those who are serious about preserving a particular religious or cultural heritage, like certain Native American groups (John, 1988). How can they maintain control in a culture that emphasizes individual choice and freedom for the young and in which their children quickly learn about the pleasures of dating?

People cannot make dates with those they do not have some way of meeting. Indirectly (and perhaps unconsciously), parents can exercise control over dating choices by channeling their children into situations in which they are likely to meet the types of people the parents consider suitable. Choosing to enroll a child in a private school, in ethnic-group based clubs and activities, or in a college where the child will be part of the racial, ethnic, or religious majority are all examples of this control. Parents also influence their children's dating choices by clearly indicating their approval or disapproval of particular dating partners. This influence is more often present for daughters than for sons. When a sample of college students was asked about parental influence in date selection, 40 percent of the men and 60 percent of the women acknowledged such parental influence (Knox & Wilson, 1981). Most of the students, especially the women, did not resent the involvement; they valued parental approval of their dating partners (Knox & Wilson, 1981).

Who Dates and Marries Whom?

Most people have considerable choice about whom to date and whom to marry even after parents have cut off or discouraged some of the possibilities. Whom do they choose to date? To marry? The answer to these questions seems obvious: people date those they like and they marry when they find a dating partner they love. At a very general level, these are accurate answers. There is a strong belief in the United States that the most important criterion for selecting a marriage partner is love (Goode, 1959). Marriage for money, social status, organizational advancement, or the creation of alliances is considered suspect in U.S. culture unless preceded by love.

But is love really blind and is the mate selection process essentially random? Or does love somehow operate in a nonrandom way? Are people more likely to date and marry those who are similar to or different from themselves? In the language of social scientists, is **homogamy** (marriage between similar people) or **heterogamy** (marriage between dissimilar people) more common? We will focus first on individual and then on social characteristics.

Homogamy
marriage between people who are similar.
Heterogamy
marriage between people who are different.

Individual Characteristics   People just beginning a dating relationship are not particularly concerned about either similarities or differences. Summarizing many studies on what people look for first in a dating partner, psychologist Bernard Murstein (1986) writes, " . . . the very first thing most people respond to in a dating situation is the physical attractiveness of the other. Men respond more to this quality than women" (p. 73).

Physical attractiveness may bring people together initially, but they are more likely to stay together if they are *physically similar*. In a study of physical attraction and the courtship process, White (1980) found that daters who had been most similar in physical attractiveness when they began dating experienced a deepening love over a nine-month period, while relationships involving the most physically dissimilar individuals had the highest chance of breaking up (White, 1980).

This connection between similarity in physical attributes and staying together apparently continues up until the time of marriage. People who marry tend to look alike in a variety of ways:

> . . . on the average, spouses resemble each other slightly but significantly on almost every physical feature. That goes not only for the traits you'd think of first, like skin and eye and hair color, but also for an astonishing variety of other traits, such as thickness of lips, breadth of nose, length of ear lobe and middle finger, circumference of wrist, distance between eyes, and lung volume. Experimenters have made this finding for peoples as diverse as Poles in Poland, Americans in Michigan, and Africans in Chad. (Diamond, 1986, p. 65)

Dating couples who end up as marriage partners are similar to one another in other ways as well (Buss, 1985). Research from the 1930s to the present finds that spouses' attitudes toward war, birth control, various political issues, technological growth, and sex roles are strongly similar (Buss, 1985). Perhaps daters "sort out" and reject those whose attitudes are very different from their own, or perhaps couples who become close in other ways also become close in their thinking.

What about personality traits? Do talkative men marry women who talk a lot? Are stubborn people especially attracted by other stubborn people? Only up to a point. None of the many studies on personality traits have shown a high correspondence between the personality traits of the husband and those of the wife, but many have shown weak to moderate matching on personality traits (Murstein, 1986). The research indicates that most people do not choose to marry their complete opposite in terms of personality but neither do they marry a person who has identical personality traits.

Social Characteristics   Daters who become spouses also tend to be closely matched in terms of social background characteristics such as race, socio-economic class, and religious denomination. Here again is evidence that mate selection is far from random.

Race is the clearest case of this nonrandom behavior. If mate selection were a purely random process, most blacks would marry whites since there are many more whites than blacks in the United States. In fact, interracial marriages, and especially black-white marriages, are rare (Whyte, 1990; Sandefur & McKinnell, 1986). About 1.8 percent of all U.S. married couples are interracial, but less than one-quarter of these interracial marriages are black-white combinations (U.S. Bureau of the Census, 1990a, p. 44). The interracial combinations of Native American and Caucasian and of Asian-American and Caucasian are more common (John, 1988; Kitano, 1988). In fact, some numerically small Asian-American groups, such as the Japanese-Americans, are as likely to marry outside their race as within it (Kitano, 1988). Nonetheless, most people continue to choose a marriage partner of the same race.

Homogamy is somewhat less common but still important when social class and religion are considered. Somewhere between 50 percent and 80 percent of all marriages are between people with similar social class backgrounds (Whyte, 1990; Eckland, 1985). If religious background is categorized as Protestant, Catholic, or Jewish, similar figures hold: more than 80 percent of Protestants marry Protestants, about 60 percent of Catholics marry Catholics (Murstein, 1986), and, since 1985, about 50 percent of Jews marry Jews (Freedenthal, 1992).

Marriage between people from different ethnic backgrounds, particularly if the two share race and religion and if each comes from a family that has been in the United States for several generations, is much more common in the United States today than in the past (Whyte, 1990; Murstein, 1986). As ethnic groups become more similar in terms of income, education, and occupation, the chances for inter-ethnic relationships increase and so do inter-ethnic marriages. In fact, one author concludes that "... ethnic homogamy could conceivably approach chance levels by the fourth generation" (Murstein, 1986, p. 30).

Propinquity
how close dating partners live to one another when they begin dating.

A final social background factor is propinquity—how far apart marriage partners lived at the time they began dating. Whyte (1990), in studying three marriage cohorts, found that even with rapid transportation available, people tend to date and marry those who live close to them. When asked how far they lived from their future husband when they first started dating, women marrying prior to World War II reported an average distance of three miles; those marrying between 1946 and 1964, an average distance of four miles; and those marrying between 1966 and 1984, an average of five miles (Whyte, 1990). Other studies reach similar conclusions: about half of all marriages are between people who lived within walking distance of one another at the time they started dating (Eckland, 1985).

Conflict in Dating Relationships

In most respects, then, people date, fall in love with, and marry those similar to themselves. But, with the exception of homosexual intimate relationships, all dating couples and all married couples are *heterogamous* for sex: they are composed of one male and one female. This difference is responsible for many of the challenges of modern dating.

Gender Differences

The different gender role training of females and males sometimes means that partners in a dating relationship are not always in sync with one another. For example, men and women tend to experience romantic love on somewhat different schedules. At the beginning of a relationship, men are more interested in romance, sex, and avoiding long-term commitment than are women. Once they have found a woman they find physically attractive, they "fall in love" quickly (Hendrick *et al.*, 1984). Women, on the other hand, are more interested in finding the kind of person they want based on a "shopping list" of characteristics, perhaps including physical attractiveness but also character and future educational and occupational prospects (Hendrick *et al.*, 1984). Once they identify such a person, they try to fall in love with him. Women are more cautious about falling in love initially than men are but, once in love, they are less cautious about experiencing and expressing romantic feelings. Women in love are more likely than men to report feelings such as "... floating on a cloud; wanting to jump, run, or scream; trouble concentrating; feeling giddy and carefree; general feeling of well being ... " (Murstein, 1986, p. 118).

You should be able to see the potential for conflict here. Early in the relationship a man, already in love, confronts a woman who seems to still be "shopping around" for a better deal; later on, the woman, now in love, is upset about the man's unwillingness to share his feelings of love and to make a long-term commitment. As you will learn in the next part of this chapter, men and women are also often on different schedules when it comes to sexual intimacy. In one college-based study, over 85 percent of the students acknowledged that they had experienced misunderstandings about the timing of sexual activities in their dating relationships (Knox & Wilson, 1981). Many couples break up over these or other misunderstandings, some handle their conflicts through reasoning and talking together, and still others become aggressive.

Dating Aggression

In the days when premarital romance was rather public, governed by strict rules of etiquette, and supervised by parents, couples had a number of checks on their aggressive tendencies. But as young people gained more control over their premarital relationships, these checks became less effective. Today physical aggression is estimated to be a part of one out of every three dating relationships, with verbal aggression present in nearly all of them (Lloyd, 1991; Stets & Henderson, 1991).

Figure 4–2 (on page 128) summarizes the results of a national study of verbal and physical aggression among young (18–30), never married daters. The vast majority of the daters surveyed had shown **verbal aggression** (defined as insulting or swearing at the other person; sulking or refusing to talk about an issue; or stomping out in the middle of a disagreement). A large minority had engaged in **minor physical aggression** (defined as pushing, grabbing, shoving, slapping or throwing something at their partner) and a smaller minority had used **severe physical aggression** against a partner (defined as kicking, biting, hitting, choking, or beating up on) (Stets & Henderson, 1991).

Figure 4–2 shows that, in a dating situation, women are more aggressive, especially more physically aggressive, than men: "They are 8 times more likely to kick or bite and 4 times more likely to hit than men" (Stets & Henderson, 1991, p. 32). These numbers measure only aggressive acts, not the injuries, if any, resulting from the actions. Research on family aggression suggests that, regardless of who commits the higher number of aggressive actions, females sustain the most injuries (Stets & Straus, 1990). This is almost certainly true in dating aggression as well.

Between 30 and 50 percent of couples involved in physical aggression while dating remain together, and many of them marry (Mayseless, 1991). Given that such premarital violence is predictive of marital problems later on, why do some violent couples stay together? Family

Verbal aggression
insulting, swearing at, sulking or refusing to talk to another person, or stomping out in the middle of a disagreement.

Minor physical aggression
pushing, grabbing, shoving, slapping, or throwing something at another person.

Severe physical aggression
kicking, biting, hitting, choking, or beating up on another person.

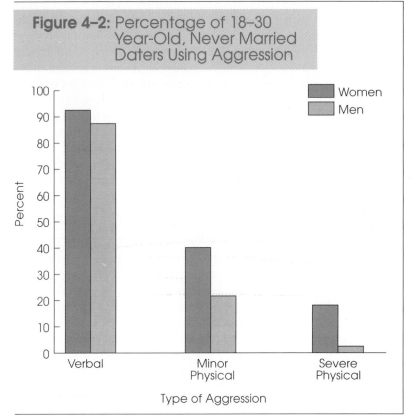

Figure 4–2: Percentage of 18–30 Year-Old, Never Married Daters Using Aggression

Verbal aggression includes insults, swearing, sulking, or stomping out; minor physical aggression includes pushing, slapping, or grabbing; severe physical aggression means kicking, biting, hitting, choking, or beating up. Women in dating situations use all types of aggression more often than men. Note that the figures measure actions taken, not injuries received. More women than men receive serious injuries from aggression.

Source: Stets and Henderson, 1991, p. 32. Copyrighted (1991) by the National Council on Family Relations, 3989 Central Ave. N.E., Suite #550, Minneapolis, MN 55421. Reprinted by permission.

science professor Sally Lloyd (1991) believes that the romanticism surrounding the dating period prevents couples from seeing the problems that underlie aggressive actions:

> Romanticism allows violence to be easily downplayed, as violence is attributed to external factors and not to a fundamental flaw in the relationship [and] . . . allows partners to believe that negative courtship behavior will disappear over time or be conquered by love. (p. 16)

Dating as Practice for Marriage?

Dating can be seen as a kind of practice period for intimacy in marriage. In dating, men and women have a chance to learn about a person of the opposite sex, to rehearse communication and conflict-resolution skills, and to practice sexual intimacy. Dating couples, in fact, spend a great deal of their time together talking, especially about their relationship (Knox & Wilson, 1981). As you will learn later in this chapter, they also spend a fair amount of time engaging in, although not talking about (Knox & Wilson, 1981), sexual intimacy.

Does this practice in intimacy make for better marriages later? Do people with more dating experience have better, longer lasting marriages? On the one hand, those with more dating experience have more opportunities to get to know and communicate with a variety of others. Such prior practice in intimacy, it might be argued, should make them better marriage partners. On the other hand, the romanticism surrounding dating might get in the way of realistic preparation for marriage; the intimate decisions and activities of dating couples might have little to do with married life. Perhaps those with lots of dating and romantic experience are *less* prepared than others for the realities of marriage.

Limited research on the topic suggests that, in general, dating experience has little impact on subsequent marriage. In his study of the three cohorts of Detroit women, Whyte (1990) found few differences between the marriages of women who dated extensively, had many marital prospects, and varied premarital sexual activity and those who dated only one man before marriage and had very limited premarital sexual experience. One dating-related factor made a slight difference: women who dated their future husband for a longer period of time were slightly more likely than those with a whirlwind courtship to have a marriage that stayed together, although not necessarily a more satisfying and problem-free marriage. In general, the practice in intimacy provided by dating does not seem to be especially helpful (or harmful) for later marriage and the romanticism of dating neither guarantees nor prevents a solid marriage later. Overall, what happens *after* marriage is more important for marital happiness and stability than what happens *before*. We will discuss this important idea in Chapter 7 on marital adjustment.

PREMARITAL SEX

The sexual activities associated with dating help explain the appeal of dating as a mate selection method—sex is what makes dating exciting and romantic for many young people. We use the term **premarital sex** to refer to the full range of sexual behavior (everything from holding hands to intercourse) of never-married young people and the term **premarital intercourse** to refer to sexual intercourse between never-married young people.

Premarital sex
the sexual behavior of young, never-married people.

Premarital intercourse
sexual intercourse between young, never-married people.

Our definitions of both premarital sex and premarital intercourse have their limitations because they assume that all sexually active, unmarried people eventually marry (the word *premarital* literally means *before marriage*) and that sex before marriage is restricted to young people. The more neutral terms **nonmarital sex** and **nonmarital intercourse** make neither assumption (Hyde, 1990) but are inappropriate for our discussion in this chapter because they also include extramarital sex and postmarital sex, topics we will discuss in Chapters 7 and 15.

Nonmarital sex
sexual activity between two people who are not married; the term does not distinguish between premarital sex, extramarital sex, and postmarital sex.

Nonmarital intercourse
sexual intercourse between two people who are not married.

Changes in Premarital Sex

Young people today have much more flexibility, freedom, and variety in their premarital sex lives than did their counterparts as recently as 30 years ago. They also may have more problems and uncertainties. Exactly how, when, and why have premarital sexual activities changed during the twentieth century?

1830–1920: Premarital Sex in the Era of Calling

Between 1830 and 1920, when calling was the prevailing method of selecting a marriage partner, U.S. standards for sexual behavior were at their strictest, most conservative level. Earlier in U.S. history, unmarried couples who intended to marry could get away with **bundling**, an activity which involved sharing a bed for warmth and companionship but not for sex. Parents devised a number of methods to keep the two young people physically separate: " . . . a wooden board might be placed in the middle of the bed; the young girl might be encased in a type of long laundry bag up to her armpits; or, her garments might be sewn together at strategic points" (Murstein, 1986, p. 65). By the early 1800s, bundling was considered highly immoral in most parts of the country (D'Emilio & Freedman, 1988) as were masturbation, pornography, sex for pleasure, and any kind of sex outside of marriage (Brecher, 1984; Gagnon, 1977). According to the prevailing standards of the time, the only legitimate purpose of sex was reproduction; only heterosexual, marital sexual intercourse was tolerated (Gagnon, 1977, pp. 23–26).

Bundling
a colonial era premarital activity in which an unmarried couple shared a bed but were not allowed sexual contact.

As in any society, some people broke the rules. However, the restrictions of the calling method, strong beliefs about the immorality of anything sexual, and regular adult supervision of young peoples' activities insured that a fairly high proportion of both men and women were sexually inexperienced at marriage. As you will see, things changed quickly once dating began.

1920–1965: Premarital Sex in the Double Standard Years

Dating, which became a prominent part of young adult life during the 1920s and 1930s, brought decreased parental supervision of young couples and less rigid ideas about sexual activity prior to marriage. Daters took advantage of their increased freedom and quickly adopted two sexual innovations: **necking** and **petting** (D'Emilio & Freedman, 1988). While definitions varied across the United States, necking was generally defined as sexual caresses above the neck, primarily of the lips, ears, and neck, while petting referred to sexual caresses below the neck (Bailey, 1988, p. 80). Necking and petting represented a compromise between the desires of young couples for sexual intimacy and their reluctance to "go too far" in violating strict rules forbidding premarital intercourse for women (Bailey, 1988; Caplow *et al.*, 1985).

> **Necking**
> sexual caresses above the neck, primarily of the lips, ears, and neck.
> **Petting**
> sexual caresses below the neck.

Although the introduction of dating brought about a small revolution in sexual values and behavior, the old rules condemning sexual intercourse outside of marriage still applied—but much more to women than to men. By the 1930s, the double standard of sex was fully established (D'Emilio & Freedman, 1988; Darling, Kallen, & VanDusen, 1984). The **double standard of sex** declared that men were innately much more interested in sex than women were and that premarital intercourse was acceptable for men but not for women. One girl, sixteen years old and pregnant, bitterly recounted her experience with the double standard:

> **Double standard of sex**
> the belief that males are innately more interested in sex than females are and that premarital intercourse is more acceptable for males than for females.

> How are you supposed to know what they want? You hold out for a long time and then when you do give in to them and give your body they laugh at you afterwards and say they'd never marry a slut, and that they didn't love you but were just testing because they only plan to marry a virgin and wanted to see if you'd go all the way. (quoted in D'Emilio & Freedman, 1988, p. 262)

Studies done by Kinsey and his team in the 1940s confirmed that both men and women were affected by the message conveyed by the double standard. Figure 4–3 (on page 132) presents some of the Kinsey study results. Note that, in every age group, a much higher proportion of nonmarried men than of nonmarried women had engaged in premarital intercourse. This pattern would continue into the 1960s.

1965–1980: The Sexual Revolution

Sexual attitudes and behavior remained stable during the middle decades of the twentieth century, from the 1930s until the mid-1960s.

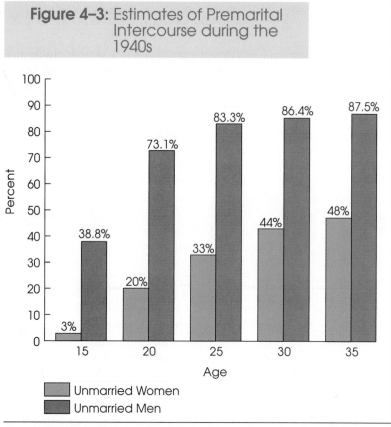

Figure 4–3: Estimates of Premarital Intercourse during the 1940s

Unmarried Women
Unmarried Men

Even before the Sexual Revolution, premarital sexual experience was quite common for men. The difference in rates between men and women illustrates one consequence of the "double standard."

Source: Kinsey *et al.,* 1953, p. 333; Kinsey, Pomeroy, and Martin, 1948, p. 550. Reprinted by permission of the Kinsey Institute for Research in Sex, Gender, and Reproduction, Inc.

People responding to sexual attitude surveys in the early 1960s gave essentially the same answers Kinsey's respondents had in the 1930s and 1940s (Reiss & Miller, 1979). Profound changes took place between 1965 and 1980, however. Premarital sex, including premarital intercourse, became acceptable for women as well as for men and female premarital virginity declined drastically. So profound and overreaching were the changes that they are commonly referred to as the **Sexual Revolution**.

Changes in Attitude   In 1965, national survey data showed that a majority of men and women, both young adults and older ones, felt that premarital intercourse was wrong (Thornton, 1989). By 1975, the majority of young people of both sexes and increasing proportions of older people as well believed that premarital intercourse was acceptable. Review the results shown in Table 1–2, Question 4, to remind yourself of how quickly this attitude change took place.

Sexual Revolution
the period between 1965 and 1980 when attitudes and behavior having to do with premarital sex changed in a more liberal direction.

The rapid change in opinion about the morality of sexual intercourse before marriage showed up especially strongly on college campuses and especially among college females. For example, in 1965, researchers at the University of Georgia found that 70 percent of the women and 33 percent of the men surveyed felt that premarital intercourse was immoral; in just five years, these percentages dropped to 34 percent for the women and 14 percent for the men (King, Balswick, & Robinson, 1977; Robinson, King, & Balswick, 1972).

Changes in Behavior   Change was even more striking, profound, and lasting in the realm of premarital sexual behavior. In the early 1970s and before, only a minority of teenage women had experienced sexual intercourse, with black women more experienced than white. By the late 1980s, white, black, and Hispanic teenage women were more likely to be nonvirgins than virgins, and differences in sexual behavior among the races had nearly disappeared (Forrest & Singh, 1990; Heaton, Lichter, & Amoateng, 1989; Simon, 1989).

The behavioral changes for men were less profound but similar to those of women. Both before and after the Sexual Revolution, the majority of young adult males had premarital intercourse experience; the Sexual Revolution simply made this majority a larger one. For example, Figure 4–4 (on page 134) shows that in 1965, about 65 percent of male college students had engaged in premarital intercourse; by 1985, almost 80 percent had.

What Caused the Sexual Revolution?   Why did the Sexual Revolution occur when it did and, once started, what kept it going? The introduction of the birth control pill and the increasing availability of other types of contraceptives, the legalization of abortion in 1973, the increased participation of women in the labor force, and new knowledge that women as well as men are "designed" for pleasurable sex have all been offered as explanations (Darling, Kallen, & VanDusen, 1984; Bell & Coughey, 1980). Some feel, however, that a demographic explanation works best: the Sexual Revolution occurred when it did because the huge Baby Boom birth cohort appeared on the scene as teenagers and young adults.

The Sexual Revolution lasted roughly from 1965 to 1980. These were the precise years that the Baby Boomers, the whole set of children born between 1946 and 1964, entered young adulthood. Whenever a birth cohort is as large as the Baby Boom cohort was, its ideas and actions take on increased importance and often become the accepted standard for the whole society. The fact that so many Baby Boomers attended college meant that large numbers of young adults were in intimate day-to-day contact with one another and somewhat removed from adult authority throughout the period from 1965 to 1980. Together these young adults developed a strong youth culture

Figure 4–4: Percentage of College Students with Premarital Intercourse Experience 1965–1985

Percent

Year of Survey

■ Men
□ Women

As the Sexual Revolution proceeded during the late 1960s and the 1970s, more college students had premarital sexual intercourse and previous differences between male and female rates diminished.

Source: Robinson *et al.*, 1991, p. 217. Copyrighted (1991) by the National Council on Famiy Relations, 3989 Central Ave. N.E., Suite #550, Minneapolis, MN 55421. Reprinted by permission.

that questioned traditional assumptions about almost everything, including sexual behavior and the double standard. The effect of so many teenagers becoming adults all at once, when combined with the factors mentioned previously, was critical in developing and sustaining the Sexual Revolution (Darling, Kallen, & VanDusen, 1984). By the time the youngest of the Baby Boomers settled into adult life, the Sexual Revolution, although not all of its consequences, had come to an end.

1980 to Present: A Return to Conservatism?

Young adults of the late 1970s and early 1980s expressed more conservative views on political, religious, and social issues than had their counterparts in the 1960s and early 1970s (Astin, Green, & Korn, 1987;

Clatworthy, 1985; Hastings & Hoge, 1986, 1981). Some analysts saw strong similarities to pre-Sexual Revolution days and suggested that the post-Sexual Revolution young adults had embarked on a "return to the fifties," more interested in narrow personal issues and less concerned with broader social issues (Hastings & Hoge, 1986, p. 376). The late 1980s and early 1990s saw a return to somewhat more interest in broad social issues and somewhat more liberal political views, but young adults remained more conservative than they had been during the Sexual Revolution days ("This Year's College . . . ," 1991; Hirschorn, 1988).

Have young adults also become more conservative in terms of sexual attitudes and behavior? Several studies note that college students' attitudes about sex did move in a more conservative direction in the 1980s (Murstein *et al.*, 1989; Hastings & Hoge, 1986; Clatworthy, 1985; Robinson & Jedlicka, 1982). The University of Georgia surveys that documented the beginning of the Sexual Revolution documented its end as well, at least when attitudes are considered. The 1980 and 1985 waves of the survey found that students had not only halted the trend towards more sexually liberal attitudes, but were moving in the opposite direction and becoming more sexually conservative (Robinson *et al.*, 1991; Robinson & Jedlicka, 1982). For example, in 1975, only 19.5 percent of the male students and 30.1 percent of the female students felt that it was immoral for a man to have sexual intercourse with a great many women; by 1985, 31.7 percent of the male students and 51.8 percent of the female students saw this behavior as immoral (Robinson *et al.*, 1991).

Figure 4–4 indicates that the movement towards more conservative *attitudes* about sex did not result in more conservative *behavior*, at least if the probability of engaging in premarital intercourse is the measure used. Despite increased attention to the disease and pregnancy risks associated with sexual intercourse, both teenagers and college students of the 1980s were more likely to have experienced premarital intercourse than their Sexual Revolution counterparts (Robinson *et al.*, 1991; Forrest & Singh, 1990).

The Alternative Choice section on the "New Monogamy" indicates that some young adults are becoming more conservative in terms of the conditions under which they become sexually active. And somewhere between 30 percent and 50 percent of young people report that they have changed their sexual behavior in some way in response to the AIDS crisis (Roscoe & Kruger, 1990; Carrol, 1988). However, more detailed investigation reveals few real changes in behavior (Thurman & Franklin, 1990; Moffatt, 1989; Carrol, 1988). For example, young adults report that they are "more selective" about their sexual partners than they used to be, but very few actually quiz potential partners on their sexual past (Roscoe & Kruger, 1990). Those that do go to the trouble of quizzing partners may not receive a truthful answer. Forty-seven percent of the men and 42 percent of the women in a survey of California college students admitted that they would lie to a new partner about how many sexual partners they had previously had (Wheeler, 1990).

One area in which there has been significant behavioral change is condom use. In a national study of never-married young men ages 17–19, self-reported condom use during the last sexual intercourse more than doubled from 1979 to 1988 for both black and white males (Sonenstein, Pleck, & Ku, 1989). Similar increases in condom use are reported when teenage girls are the respondents (Forrest & Singh, 1990).

Conflict in Premarital Sexual Relationships

Throughout the twentieth century, before, during, and after the Sexual Revolution, males and females have struggled with premarital sexual behavior. In the era of the double standard, the conflict emerged because couples were trying to fulfill two inherently contradictory goals: satisfying the male's perceived sexual needs for intercourse and preserving the female's virginity. As you will learn, the Sexual Revolution decreased the importance of the double standard but not the conflict about premarital sex.

Is the Double Standard Dead?

As the Sexual Revolution progressed, some researchers declared that the double standard was dead or dying (King, Balswick, & Robinson, 1977). In some respects, these researchers were right. Look at Figure 4–4 again. The *difference* between the proportion of men having premarital intercourse and the proportion of women having premarital intercourse has shrunk year by year: men and women are becoming more alike in their sexual behavior (Robinson *et al.*, 1991; Darling, Kallen, & VanDusen, 1984; King, Balswick, & Robinson, 1977). Male and female opinions about the morality of premarital intercourse in general have become more and more alike; where there was once a giant gap, there is now only a slight difference (Robinson *et al.*, 1991; Beeghly & Sellers, 1986).

The double standard is not completely dead, however. While most people today believe that premarital intercourse is equally acceptable behavior for women and for men, they adopt harsher standards for women when the question of **promiscuity**—having sexual intercourse with more than one partner—is raised. For example, both male and female college students are much more likely to think that a promiscuous woman is sinful or immoral than that a promiscuous man is (Robinson *et al.*, 1991). Women can go farther than they once could in terms of premarital sex without being harshly judged, but having intercourse with many partners is still, apparently, "going too far."

These double standard attitudes are reflected, to some extent, in behavior. A 1986 college student study found that, for those students who were not virgins, about half of both males and females had had between two and five partners. The differences appeared at the extremes; about twice as many males as females reported six or more partners, and far more females than males reported only one partner (Earle & Perricone, 1986).

Promiscuity
sexual intercourse with more than one partner.

Dual Meanings of Sex

Recall the "What Do You Think?" question at the beginning of the chapter. Table 4–1 shows how men and women students at one northeastern liberal arts college responded to it. Note that, although the majority of both men and women selected the "sex as part of a good relationship" (response 4) as their primary philosophy, men were more likely than women to select the "fun" and "as much as possible" responses (responses 5 and 6).

These survey results reflect what other researchers have found as well. Men and women tend to attach different meanings to premarital sex and particularly to premarital intercourse. With the development of this **dual meaning of sex**, men define sexual intercourse as a casual,

Dual meanings of sex
the tendency for males to see sexual intercourse as a casual, pleasant activity and for females to regard it as a sign of commitment.

Table 4–1 Primary Choice of Sexual Philosophy, Women and Men, 1986		
Philosophy of Sex	**% of Women Selecting**	**% of Men Selecting**
1. Procreation	0.0	0.0
2. Valid in marriage only	6.5	6.8
3. OK with fiance	7.9	8.3
4. As part of good relationship	72.4	63.1
5. As fun w/consenting other	12.4	17.7
6. As much as possible w/anyone	1.3	3.9

Source: Murstein *et al.*, 1989, p. 130.

pleasant activity and women define it as a sign of commitment. And unlike in the days of the double standard, neither men nor women currently apply a different standard to the other sex than to their own. Rather, they expect the other to adopt their meaning of sex—men expect women to adopt the male definition and women expect men to adopt the female definition.

The dual meanings seem to arise as a result of differential sexual training. The average male is trained to see premarital intercourse as a casual, pleasurable activity that should be done as often and as early as possible *and so he pushes for sex.* Meanwhile, the average female is trained to see sexual intercourse as a sign of commitment, reserved for those relationships that are serious and future-oriented, *and so she resists casual sex* (Christopher & Cate, 1988). Asked when in a relationship intercourse became acceptable, the males in one study were *ten times* more likely than females to accept it on a date with a "casual acquaintance," *four times* as likely when "dating occasionally," and *twice* as likely when "dating regularly" (Earle & Perricone, 1986).

Thus, particularly in the early stages of a relationship, males and females have frequent disagreements about the timing of premarital intercourse because they hold different, although not always expressed, ideas about what sexual intercourse means.

Date Rape

The idea of dual meanings might help you better understand an issue of major interest on many college campuses today—the issue of "date rape." The term **date rape** is often used to refer to any forced sexual intercourse committed by an acquaintance as opposed to a stranger (Ward *et al.*, 1991).

Date rape
any forced sexual intercourse committed by a non-stranger.

Curious about the actual relationship between rapists and their victims, Ward and her colleagues (1991) surveyed the students on the campus of a New England state university. These researchers asked women respondents to describe the most serious incident of unwanted sexual aggression, if any, they had experienced in the previous academic year. Based on the self-reports they received, the researchers estimated that one out of three women had experienced unwanted sexual contact (actual or attempted kissing, touching, or fondling in a sexual or intimate way) and that one in five had experienced unwanted attempted intercourse. About one woman in ten had been the victim of unwanted, completed sexual intercourse (vaginal, oral, or anal penetration) (Ward *et al.*, 1991).

The typical woman who reported unwanted sexual aggression said that the perpetrator had been a friend or acquaintance and that the incident had occurred in a dorm room during a party at which both partners had been drinking (Ward *et al.*, 1991). In other words, the most typical scenario for sexual aggression was neither the stranger in a dark alley nor a traditional date but rather a group gathering. Even so, nearly one-third of the unwanted intercourse incidents had involved a boyfriend. In most cases, the woman had reported the incident to a close friend or roommate but not to anyone else (Ward *et al.*, 1991).

When these same researchers asked the male students on campus if they had ever been sexually aggressive toward a female student who had rejected their advances, very few said "yes." Perhaps the males were simply denying their aggression, but the researchers felt something else was at work as well. They suggested that the different pictures of sexual aggression painted by males and females—males reporting very little and females reporting a lot—could be accounted for by male-female differences in communication: " . . . men and women read sexual cues and form sexual expectations on very different bases. The result is that males are much less likely than females to perceive that the woman does not want the sexual interaction" (Ward *et al.*, 1991, p. 70). In other words, the females were trying to reject the advances of the males in line with their belief that sex should indicate commitment, but the males, convinced that casual sex is fun for everyone, did not perceive the rejection as such.

The decision to become sexually active is often filled with uneasiness. The concept of New Monogamy—sex as part of a committed, rather than casual, relationship—can help.

Choosing Premarital Intercourse

Thus far, we have written about premarital sex and particularly premarital intercourse in terms of long term social changes, trends, rates, and meanings. But, within every relationship, premarital sex and premarital intercourse are also highly significant personal experiences involving individual choice. The Personal Application in this chapter gives one psychologist's suggestions for making this important choice.

For many people, their first intercourse is a particularly important event, looked back on and remembered for years. Anthropologists call such events, those marking a change from one life stage to another, **rites of passage**.

Rite of passage
an event that marks a change in one's personal life from one stage to another.

In the United States today, the rite of passage from virginity to nonvirginity typically occurs in middle adolescence. Studies on a variety of diverse groups suggest that the average female first experiences intercourse somewhere between her sixteenth and eighteenth birthday (Murstein *et al.*, 1989; Rowe, Rodgers, & Meseck-Bushey, 1989; Simon, 1989; Wyatt, 1989; Earle & Perricone, 1986). Males typically lose their virginity anywhere from several months to one year before females do, at an average age of fifteen and a half to seventeen and a half years (Murstein *et al.*, 1989; Simon, 1989; Earle & Perricone, 1986). Although white patterns for premarital intercourse have become more similar to black patterns in recent years, the average black teenager still becomes involved in intercourse earlier in adolescence than the average white teenager. By age sixteen, more than one half of all the black males, black females, and white males but only one-third of the white females have experienced first intercourse (Rowe, Rodgers, & Meseck-Bushey, 1989).

These, though, are the average patterns. Although most people today make the transition to nonvirginity prior to marriage, they do so at different ages and at different stages in their lives. And some, called "adamant virgins" and estimated to make up from 10 percent to 34 percent of the young adult population, choose virginity until marriage (Robinson *et al.*, 1991; Herold & Goodwin, 1981). What factors influence whether a young person has premarital intercourse earlier than average, later than average, or not at all?

Biological Factors

Both young adults and older ones often credit (or blame) biological factors when discussing the sexual activities of the young—"It's his hormones talking," "raging hormones," or "I need sex just like I need food." Biology does have something to do with the initiation of sexual interest and activity. At puberty, the sexual organs necessary for intercourse mature and the production of androgens, hormones known to influence the sex drive in both males and females, increases markedly. As a result of these changes, young people are biologically primed for sex.

In adolescent boys, production of the androgen testosterone is highly correlated with sexual activity (Udry *et al.*, 1985). The higher the amount of testosterone in a young male's body, the more sexually active (in terms of sexy dreams, non-intercourse sex, and sexual intercourse) he is. Even for virgins, the level of sexual activity (holding hands, hugging, kissing, breast and genital contacts with the opposite sex) is strongly associated with testosterone level. Thus, some of the variation between individual males in terms of sexual interests and activity is tied to biology.

Social Factors

Biology cannot completely explain the timing of first intercourse, however. Some young people, particularly males, are sexually active before they pass through puberty (Rowe, Rodgers, & Meseck-Bushey, 1989). Along the same lines, females typically reach physical maturity before males but begin their sexual lives somewhat later. Clearly, factors other than biology are at work here.

Parental Influence   Like most other choices in life, the choice to have first sexual intercourse is heavily influenced by other people and particularly by those whose approval is most important. Thus, teenagers, especially middle-class, female teenagers, who are close to their parents and who perceive that their parents disapprove of premarital intercourse, are likely to delay first intercourse until their late teens, their twenties, or marriage (Wyatt, 1989; Udry & Billy, 1987). The key here is the importance of the parent-child tie to the child, not the time and energy the parent puts into explicitly lecturing on sex and contraception. In fact, several studies have found that parental communication about sex and contraception, by itself, has no impact on the timing of first intercourse (Moore, Peterson, & Furstenberg, 1986; Newcomer & Udry, 1985).

Certain maternal attitudes and behavior (the impact of father's attitudes and behavior have not been studied) are associated with earlier sexual intercourse. Mothers who have liberal sexual attitudes themselves, who married young, who have been divorced, or who have remarried tend to have children who start sexual intercourse earlier than their peers (Thornton & Camburn, 1987).

Personal Application

Are You Ready for Sex?

You Are Ready If:

1. You feel guiltless and comfortable about your present level of involvement.
2. You are confident that you will not be humiliated and that your reputation will not be hurt.
3. Neither partner is pressuring the other for sex.
4. You are not trying to:
   a. prove your love for the other person;
   b. increase your self-worth;
   c. prove that you are mature;
   d. show that you can attract a sexual partner;
   e. get attention, affection, or love;
   f. rebel against parents, society, etc.
5. It will be an expression of your current feelings rather than an attempt to improve a poor relationship or one that is "growing cold."
6. You can discuss and agree on an effective method of contraception and share the details, responsibilities, and costs of the use of the method.
7. You can discuss the potential of contracting or transmitting sexually transmitted diseases.
8. You have discussed and agreed on what both of you will do if conception occurs, because no contraceptive method is 100% effective.

Source: Allgeier, 1985, pp. 8–9. Reprinted with permission from the *SIECUS Report* July 1985 Vol. 13, No. 6. Copyright © Sex Information and Education Council of the U.S., Inc. 130 West 42nd Street, Suite 2500, New York, NY 10036.

Peer Influence   Those teenagers who desire independence from parents and who identify more with friends than with parents typically become nonvirgins earlier than teenagers who continue to maintain close ties with parents (Jessor & Jessor, 1975). The characteristics of the particular peer group are also important. Generally, the higher the proportion of nonvirgins in a young person's peer group and the more social interaction the young person has with those nonvirgins, the more likely he or she is to engage in sexual intercourse (Rowe, Rodgers, & Meseck-Bushey, 1989; Furstenberg *et al.*, 1987). Peer group experience with sexual intercourse is an extremely important influence on individual decision making about sexual behavior: "Those [teenagers] who say most of their friends have had intercourse are estimated to be *100 times more likely* to have had intercourse than those who say none have" (Furstenberg *et al.*, 1987, pp. 515–16, emphasis added).

The importance of the peer group subculture helps explain why males and blacks tend to have first sexual intercourse earlier than females and whites. Male peer groups generally emphasize that sexual intercourse is a pleasurable, recreational activity and a sign of maturity, whereas female peer groups are more likely to emphasize sex as part of a total, committed relationship. Black subculture tends to be more tolerant of earlier sexual involvement than white subculture; thus, the relative proportions of blacks and whites in a peer group can also make a difference in teenage involvement in sexual intercourse. Focusing on the black-white ratio of high schools, Furstenberg *et al.* (1987) found that both female and male blacks in predominately black schools were *ten times* as likely to have had intercourse as were whites in predominately white schools, but only *1.6 times* as likely if they were in predominately white schools. Clearly, one crucial factor is differences in subgroup attitudes and values.

Choice and Risk   Another way of explaining differences among social groups and among individuals in the timing of first intercourse is to consider intercourse as a risky activity. Sexual intercourse *is* risky, carrying with it the risks of sexually transmitted diseases, unwanted pregnancy, and, for those who believe premarital intercourse is wrong, guilty consciences and loss of self-respect. One widely applicable principle about risky behavior states that those who have less to lose will be more willing to engage in risky activities. Let us see how this general principle can be applied to the timing of first sexual intercourse.

Throughout the twentieth century, young people from middle-class homes have delayed first intercourse longer than young people from working-class homes (Weinberg & Williams, 1980). Traditionally, most working-class teenagers have expected to begin working and adult life immediately after high school graduation, while more middle-class teenagers have planned to go to college. The risk of early parenthood may well be perceived as a more acceptable risk to those who plan to begin full adult life early anyway than to those who face many more years of formal education before obtaining a job adequate to support a family. Thus, despite the fact that college students are often thought of as "party animals," they are actually more conservative in terms of sexual intercourse than same-age peers not attending college. Data from the 1940s indicated that those with no more than a high school education had first intercourse almost two years earlier than those with a college education; by the 1970s, the non-college-educated began sexual intercourse more than three years earlier than those attending college (Weinberg & Williams, 1980).

Along similar lines, minority group members living in the poorest urban neighborhoods with few job opportunities and much higher than average death rates are among those most likely to be sexually active at an early age, most likely to engage in high risk sexual activities, and most likely to suffer from sexually transmitted diseases (Aral & Holmes, 1991). These same young people, who feel that they have little future and little to lose, also are likely to engage in other types of risky activities—crime, drug use, and other forms of deviance (Udry & Billy, 1987; Jessor & Jessor, 1975).

Opportunity   Finally, as with other forms of human behavior, some people have more opportunities for premarital intercourse than others. Simply put, those with more opportunities begin sexual intercourse earlier. Teenagers and young adults escalate their sexual involvement through a series of increasingly erotic behaviors—kissing, light petting, heavy petting, intercourse (Spanier, 1975). The earlier a person starts dating and the more he or she dates, the quicker the progression through the categories of erotic behaviors (Spanier, 1975). And the quicker the progression through the categories, the earlier the age at first intercourse. Thus, age at first date and frequency of dating are both good predictors of age at first intercourse.

Alternative Choice

The New Monogamy

During the 1970s and early 1980s, many dating couples were guided by a standard of premarital sexual intercourse that emphasized the pleasurable aspects of intercourse and assumed that both men and women would have numerous casual sexual partners prior to marriage. Even at the time, not everyone followed this standard: some remained virginal until marriage and others reserved premarital intercourse for emotionally committed relationships. This latter alternative, sometimes called the "New Monogamy," was and is an important alternative choice.

New Monogamy
the practice of delaying intercourse until the dating relationship has reached a high degree of emotional commitment, committing to one partner at a time, and having few sexual partners.

We use the term **New Monogamy** to indicate the practice of delaying intercourse until the dating relationship has reached a high degree of emotional commitment, committing to one partner at a time, and, as a result, having few sexual partners. The "New Monogamy" as an alternative fits well with several recent trends and current concerns. With its emphasis on sex as part of a committed relationship rather than on sex as a casual pleasure, the New Monogamy is highly compatible with the shift to more conservative sexual attitudes that has been noted in recent years. In addition, limiting sexual intercourse to one well-known partner at a time decreases the chances of contracting AIDS or other STDs. And, finally, commitment to a New Monogamy standard decreases the chances that unexpected, unprotected intercourse will occur, thus cutting down on unplanned pregnancies. In short, the New Monogamy can lessen the risks of sexual intercourse.

College students, always more sexually conservative than others their age, may be most affected by the New Monogamy. One study

comparing college students in 1979 to those at the same college in 1986 found that the proportion of sexually active students had declined, that the age of first intercourse for both females and males had risen, and that the sexual philosophies of both had become more conservative (Murstein *et al.*, 1989). The 1986 students in this study were less likely than the 1979 students to have had their most recent sexual experience in a "casual" or "close but not exclusive" relationship (Murstein *et al.*, 1989). Instead, the majority of both men (61.9 percent) and women (73.8 percent) indicated that their most recent sexual experience had taken place within a "steady" relationship. Other researchers report that college students of the late 1980s and early 1990s were "more selective" in choosing their sexual partners (Roscoe & Kruger, 1990), had reduced the amount of casual sex (Moffatt, 1989), and were dating less (Carrol, 1988). All of these could be taken as indications that the New Monogamy is increasingly accepted as an alternative standard among at least some college students.

Summary

Dating, the most common method for meeting and selecting a marriage partner in the United States today, is different from other methods of mate selection in its emphases on individual choice, on intimacy prior to marriage, and on couple privacy. Dating began to replace calling, a mate selection method during the 1920s that involved more parental supervision. By the 1950s, both dating and going steady were well established practices. Since the 1960s, dating has become less formal and less rigid in terms of gender roles.

Despite their limited formal control, parents continue to influence their children's choices of dating and marriage partners by channeling their children into some activities and away from others and by bestowing or withholding approval. Daters, especially males, make their initial dating choices based on physical attractiveness. When it comes to selecting serious dating partners and marriage partners, however, most people select someone with a similar physical appearance and similar attitudes, although not necessarily a similar personality. Most also tend to marry someone who lives close to them and belongs to the same race, religion, and social class.

Dating offers the opportunity for couples to practice intimacy before marriage, but gender differences in socialization and perception mean frequent conflicts as well, especially early in the dating relationship. Most dating relationships include verbal aggression, and a substantial minority involve physical aggression as well. Despite the opportunity dating offers for practicing communication, conflict resolution, and sex, those with extensive dating experience are neither more nor less successful in marriage than those with limited dating experience.

The greatest changes in mate selection over the course of the twentieth century have been those associated with premarital sex. During the early part of the century, before dating began, premarital sexual activity of any kind was strictly limited and sexual standards prohibited premarital intercourse for both females and males. The greater freedom allowed by dating meant that necking and petting became common premarital activities and that the strict standards prohibiting premarital intercourse were relaxed for men, though not for women. Throughout the middle years of the century, few men were virgins at marriage, but they expected their wives to be. The Sexual Revolution of the late 1960s and the 1970s brought changes in both attitudes and behavior. Premarital intercourse came to be seen as acceptable for both men and women; the sexual behavior of women came to approach that of men. The 1980s brought a return to somewhat more conservative sexual attitudes, although sexual behavior did not change.

Male and female sexual attitudes and behavior are more similar than they once were, but women continue to be judged more harshly than men for having multiple partners. Men tend to want sexual intercourse earlier in the relationship than women do and, compared to women, see it more as a source of pleasure than as a sign of commitment. These dual meanings often lead to conflict and sometimes to date rape.

The median age for first sexual intercourse is the mid-teenage years, but individuals show a great deal of variation in this respect, with some remaining virgins until marriage. Males typically experience first intercourse earlier than females, and males with the highest testosterone levels are generally the most sexually active. Social factors are more important than biological ones, however. Teenagers who feel close to their parents and whose parents disapprove of premarital intercourse delay first intercourse longer than teenagers who identify with peers and want to feel independent of parents. The norms and values of the peer group are also tremendously influential. Generally speaking, male peer groups, black peer groups, and working-class peer groups favor earlier involvement in sexual intercourse than do female, white, or middle-class peer groups, who tend to delay first intercourse. Those who feel they have less to lose, in terms of clear conscience or future opportunities, are more willing to risk disease and unplanned pregnancy to obtain the pleasures of sex. Those who start dating earlier and who date often also tend to experience first intercourse earlier.

The New Monogamy, a sexual standard emphasizing emotional commitment, one partner at a time, and fewer partners overall, is one way for young people to balance the pleasures and risks of premarital intercourse. This alternative choice fits well with the conservative attitudes and the greater risks of sexual disease characterizing the United States in the 1990s.

CHAPTER 5

COHABITATION

Should you and your intimate partner live together without getting married? These questions will help you think about cohabitation (living together) with respect to your own circumstances. Answer the first set of questions if you want to consider cohabitation as a trial marriage or as an alternative to dating. Answer the second set if you want to consider cohabitation instead of marriage.

Cohabitation as Trial Marriage or as an Alternative to Dating

1. How important is it to you to get to know your partner in a wide variety of situations?
2. How important is it for you to have easily available, relatively safe sexual intercourse?
3. How important is it for you to test your partner under marriage-like conditions, but without the legal commitment?
   (If these are very important to you, cohabitation might be a good choice. But consider your answers to questions 4–8 first.)
4. How important is it to you to obey the laws regarding sexual behavior? Are you willing to risk legal prosecution?
5. Is living together without marriage generally approved or disapproved in the area in which you live? How important is it to you that you conform to approved behavior?
6. Will you risk disapproval from parents, other relatives, or friends if you cohabit? How important is their approval to you?
7. Do you have children who will be involved in the cohabitation arrangement? How will it affect them?
8. Will you feel immoral or guilty if you cohabit?

Cohabitation as a Permanent Alternative to Marriage

1. How important is it to you to be free of financial obligations to your intimate partner?
2. How important is it to you to be able to leave a relationship without legal or financial obligations?
3. How important is it to you to maintain a social life independent from your partner?
   (If these are very important to you, cohabitation might be a good choice. But consider your answers to questions 4–10 first.)
4. How important is it to you to obey the laws regarding sexual behavior? Are you willing to risk legal prosecution?
5. Is living together without marriage generally approved or disapproved in the area in which you live? How important is it to you that you conform to approved behavior?
6. Will you risk disapproval from parents, other relatives, or friends if you cohabit? How important is their approval to you?
7. Do you have children who will be involved in the cohabitation arrangement? How will it affect them?
8. Will you feel immoral or guilty if you cohabit?
9. How important is it for you to be able to receive the financial benefits (for example, health insurance) attached to your partner's job?
10. How important is it for you to have legal and financial protection if your partner dies or the relationship ends?

Judy and Michael, two young people who had each been married and then divorced, enjoyed being with one another. Their relationship evolved through dating, to cohabitation, and eventually to marriage. Cohabitation was an important step in their developing relationship.

Judy on cohabitation:

I'd been the one to invite him to move in—though at the time I didn't know his idea of domestic happiness was sitting at the oak table in the kitchen with his feet up on another chair (mine), munching oyster crackers, the crumbs floating about like dandelion seeds, while we read the newspaper together. But who can know such things until they share bed, board, and kitchen?

I wasn't sure I was in love with him. We did have wonderful times together, though, and going out on dates suddenly seemed silly—playing games when we were grown up. We all reach a time when we are ready for our next step, and I was ready for more than dating.

Was I thinking about marriage? Probably. Don't we all when we find someone who makes each day golden? But I didn't want to. I had been married, and my image of myself as a successful wife had been shaken. I wasn't in a hurry to try out a new husband. Besides, I enjoyed living alone. I had friends, places to go, and private space for sorting out thoughts. In short, I didn't invite Michael out of desperation to nestle his toothbrush next to mine.

Michael on cohabitation:

I wasn't in love. I never thought of marriage. We were two mature people who enjoyed each other and so decided to live together. No one asked for how long.

Caution, it seemed, hadn't been necessary. Each step felt natural and right—carrying in suitcases and books; putting my feet up to read the paper in Judy's kitchen (later it would feel like our kitchen); more important, being myself. . . .

Then my son, Eric, came for a visit, his first since I had moved in, and it was a tense one. Judy got upset at little things; Eric kept finding ways to annoy her. One night she asked me if I had told Eric I loved her. I hadn't—how could anyone, even a child, miss how I felt about her?—but the next day I did.

Eric listened in silence. It occurred to me that he might be wondering when Judy would go home (like a baby sitter) and leave us together, as we'd been before I met her. "Listen, Eric," I said, "we're a family." And I told him carefully (because I figured he'd understand at least some of it) what it meant to me in love and strength and security to live with this woman.

"Well," Eric said when I finished, "but she isn't my step-mother because you aren't married."

I paused. That was true but unimportant. "We don't need to be married to love each other and be a family." (Barnard, Judith & Fain, Michael. *Redbook Magazine*, June 1980, p. 31+).

Judy and Michael are part of a quiet revolution that has taken place in the United States during the last two decades. Individuals of all ages have participated in this continuing revolution, one which has substantially changed the way unmarried intimate partners relate to one another. This quiet, ongoing revolution is the addition of nonmarital cohabitation (or living together) as an important stage in the development of many intimate relationships. Chapter 4 described dating as the early twentieth century's contribution to U.S. courtship rituals. Cohabitation holds a comparable place in the late twentieth century (Spanier, 1983).

Today, as many as four out of ten of all the people in the United States who marry live together first (Bumpass & Sweet, 1989, p. 619). Like Judy, many trying this new stage of courtship do so because they are uncertain about love and marriage but feel the need for something more than dating. Like Michael, many "drift" into the arrangement. Once established, a cohabitation relationship can go in any one of several directions. Judy and Michael grew closer together as the result of living together and eventually married, but not all cohabitation arrangements have such an outcome. Cohabitation is not completely like dating; neither is it completely like marriage. As Michael explains to his son Eric, cohabitation has some characteristics of marriage and family. But as Eric points out to his dad, cohabitation is *not* marriage. Its unique characteristics mean that cohabitation has both interesting advantages and challenging disadvantages.

Chapter 5 deals with cohabitation. The chapter begins by defining cohabitation and by discussing several types of cohabitation relationships. Then we focus on social change and cohabitation, explaining the tremendous increase in cohabitation and the reasons behind it. The next section, "The Cohabitation Experience," traces cohabitation from its beginning stages to its end, with subsections on sexual interaction, gender roles, and duration. Then we assess the consequences of cohabitation: Does prior cohabitation lead to higher quality, more stable subsequent marriages? Are children living with cohabiting adults different from other children? How does cohabitation affect society? The chapter ends by discussing Homosexual Unions as an Alternative Choice.

WHAT IS COHABITATION?

Defining the term cohabitation is a difficult task. How many people are involved in a cohabitation arrangement? Are they always of opposite sexes? Are they sexually intimate? How many days and nights a week (one? three? seven?) must they spend together and for how long a time (one month? six months? two years?) to be considered cohabitors? Such questions have no easy answers.

In an important early discussion of cohabitation, sociologist Jan Trost (1975) argued that the crucial difference between a married couple and a cohabiting couple is their *legal status*. Marriage relationships have been declared "legal" by an official governmental agency; cohabitation relationships have not. Following Trost, we define **cohabitation** as an intimate union in which two opposite sex individuals live together under "marriage-like" conditions. The only distinction between a cohabiting couple and a married couple is the legal relationship of marriage.

Intimate homosexual partners who share a residence have many legal similarities with cohabiting couples. We do not include such couples in our definition of cohabitation because their relationship differs from marriage not only in its legal status but also in its composition (two partners of one sex rather than one of each sex). Rather, homosexual partners who share living quarters will be discussed in the Alternative Choice section at the end of the chapter.

Types of Cohabitation

Cohabiting couples differ from one another in their reasons for living together, in their commitment to the relationship, and in the perma-

Cohabitation

An intimate union in which two opposite sex individuals live together under marriage-like conditions

Cohabitation **5**

nence of the cohabitation arrangement. Researchers have identified at least five different types of cohabitation (Macklin, 1978). These are:

1. Temporary, casual, and convenient. Some couples live together for *practical* reasons. Perhaps the arrangement starts when each partner wants to share an apartment with someone but neither can find a same sex roommate. Or maybe the two want to take advantage of a gender-based division of labor—he maintains her car and she cooks for him. Or they may be living together to obtain quick, easy, and relatively safe sex. As one male respondent in an early study on cohabitation stated, "It's less of a hassle to get laid" (quoted from Arafat & Yorburg, 1963, p. 101). Whatever their practical reasons for cohabiting, the partners in this type of cohabitation arrangement are not committed to one another and assume that living together is a temporary convenience.

2. Affectionate-dating, going together. Couples who date and enjoy each other's company often want to spend more time together than dating allows. In choosing to live together, they add a new stage to their dating relationship. The commitment and duration of this type of cohabitation is like that of a dating relationship: the partners will stay together as long as they both desire.

3. Trial marriage. Some couples choose to cohabit because they are "engaged to be engaged" and want to "test" whether their relationship will survive the intensity of being full-time. This motivation for cohabitation may be particularly common among previously married cohabitors. Over six out of ten couples who *remarried* during the 1980s cohabited first (Bumpass & Sweet, 1989, p. 619). We suspect that at least some of these formerly married people wanted to test their new partner under marriage-like conditions before they committed to a marital relationship again.

4. Temporary alternative to marriage. Couples who use cohabitation as a temporary alternative to marriage are highly committed to staying with one another. They plan to marry, often at some already designated future time (for example, after they both graduate from college), but they find marriage an inconvenient alternative at the moment. In the meantime, they see few disadvantages and many advantages to a temporary cohabitation arrangement.

5. Permanent alternative to marriage. Partners in permanent cohabitation arrangements are highly committed to each other but have decided, for whatever reason, that they do not want to marry. They assume that their relationship will be

permanent, but also that it is the final stage of their courtship. According to the tabloids, many actors and actresses are involved in such long-term, highly stable nonmarital relationships. Such celebrities frequently choose to have children together but not to marry.

Researching Cohabitation

Although researchers recognize many types of cohabitation, they often fail to distinguish between the types when doing cohabitation research. This failure may have important effects on research results. For example, social scientists frequently ask the question, "Will cohabitation lead to more successful marriages?" Studying the temporary, casual, convenient type of cohabitation may produce different answers to this question than studying couples living together as a temporary alternative to marriage. Thus far, researchers have dealt only with cohabitation in general, not with cohabitation by type.

In dealing with cohabitation in general, social scientists have examined some categories of cohabiting people extensively and some hardly at all. Almost all of the early cohabitation research, and a large proportion of current research, focuses on college students, probably because they are easily accessible subjects for college professor-researchers. Although one in four college students cohabit at some time during their college career (Newcomb, 1979), they have never been the major category of cohabitors. Most cohabiting couples do not include a college student.

In paying attention mostly to *premarital* college student cohabitation, researchers have failed to note the importance of cohabitation as an *after* or *between* marriage stage. As you will see, the previously married were trying cohabitation in large numbers several years before it caught on among the never-married (Bumpass & Sweet, 1989, p. 619). Yet, until rather recently, the previously married were an understudied category of cohabitors.

Besides the difficulties involved in defining cohabitation and in studying all the diverse categories of cohabitors, researchers have had a difficult time even finding out how many cohabitors there are. The 1980 Census form provided a "partner/roommate" category but did not attempt a further breakdown. On the 1990 Census form, unrelated respondents who shared living quarters could specify whether they were "roommates" or "unmarried partners." The information made available by this distinction will allow researchers to count, rather than simply estimate, the number of cohabiting couples (*American Demographics*, 1989a).

Because of the definition, sample selection, and counting difficulties involved in doing past cohabitation research, you should take care in interpreting the research results described in this chapter. Remember that the numbers given for how many people cohabit are estimates. Keep in mind also that many of the research results apply best to college student cohabitors and may or may not be equally applicable to cohabitors in general.

SOCIAL CHANGE AND COHABITATION

In 1970, there were about 500,000 cohabiting couples in the United States; 20 years later, there were more than 2.7 million. Two sociologists who have made a career of tracking changes in the United States note: "Rarely does social change occur with such rapidity. Indeed, there have been few developments relating to marriage and family life which have been as dramatic as the rapid rise in unmarried cohabitation" (Glick & Spanier, 1980, p. 20). The dramatic rapidity of cohabitation's spread justifies the use of the term "cohabitation revolution." So does the fact that cohabitation affected so many people from so many social categories. The cohabitation revolution represents an important social change in and of itself. But cohabitation also reflects, and perhaps can be explained by, other significant social changes occurring at the same time.

Changes in How Many Cohabit

You can see the rapid increase in cohabitation by glancing at Figure 5–1. It provides estimates of the number of unmarried-couple households in the United States from 1970 to 1989. Unmarried-couple households *doubled* from 1970 to 1978, and *doubled again* by 1986. At present, there is no evidence that the increase in cohabitation is leveling off.

Even with this rapid increase, the actual number of unmarried-couple households at any given time is relatively small when compared to the number of married-couple households. The 2.7 million unmarried-couple households make up about five percent of the "couple" households in the United States; the 52 million married-couple households constitute the other 95 percent (U.S. Bureau of the Census, 1990a).

The numbers in Figure 5–1 indicate how many people are cohabiting at any given time; those in Figure 5–2 (on page 157) show the proportion of individuals who cohabited before marriage. The proportion of people marrying for the first time who had cohabited *quadrupled* from the mid-1960s and early 1970s to the 1980s, when it reached 44 percent. The percentage increase for those who had been previously

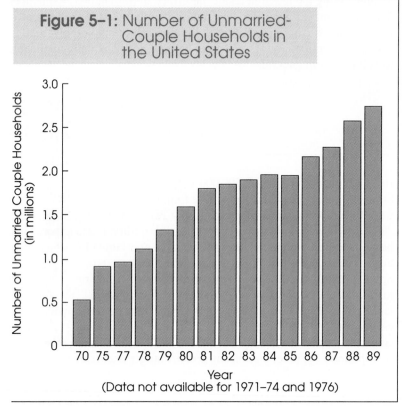

Figure 5-1: Number of Unmarried-Couple Households in the United States

The number of couples cohabiting has increased dramatically in the last two decades. Almost six times as many couples were cohabitors in 1989 as in 1970. (Data not available for 1971–1974 and for 1976.)

Source: *World Almanac,* 1990, p. 841; Saluter, 1989, p. 9; U.S. Bureau of the Census, 1989b, p. 44 and 1980 p. 44; Thornton, 1988, p. 501; and Glick & Spanier, 1980, p. 21.

married, while not as large, is still dramatic. As of the mid-1980s, about 60 percent of those remarrying had cohabited first. Given these trends, *it is highly likely that in the very near future more than one out of every two people who marry will have cohabited first* (Bumpass & Sweet, 1989).

Changes in Who Cohabits

The cohabitation revolution of the 1970s and 1980s was a significant social change not only because it happened so rapidly, but also because it affected so many different social groups. Prior to the early 1970s, most cohabitors were poor (Newcomb, 1979; Trost, 1975) and cohabited as a response to economic stress and uncertainty. Cohabitation was especially common among low income, older blacks with little education (Glick & Spanier, 1980).

Beginning in the early 1970s or slightly earlier, formerly married people from all racial, age, and socio-economic backgrounds started to cohabit, many of them for noneconomic reasons. Data in Figure 5–2

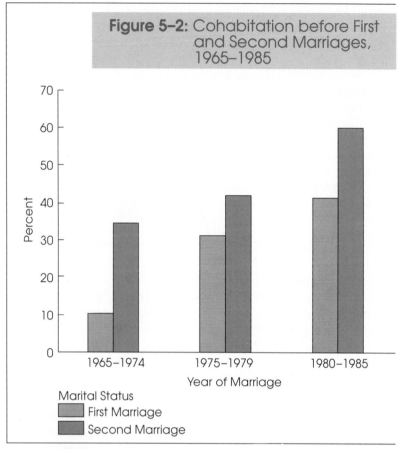

Figure 5–2: Cohabitation before First and Second Marriages, 1965–1985

Year of Marriage

Percent

Marital Status
First Marriage
Second Marriage

Almost one out of every two individuals marrying for the first time and six out of ten marrying for a second time during the early 1980s had cohabited (generally, but not always, with their future spouse) before the marriage.

Source: Bumpass & Sweet, 1989, p. 619.

confirms that the previously-married led the cohabitation revolution with the never-married following somewhat later (Bumpass & Sweet, 1989). These new, never-married cohabitors were mostly white and often were from middle-or upper-class backgrounds.

By the 1980s, cohabitation was no longer associated with any one racial, economic, or social group (Spanier, 1983). A 1983 nationwide survey of never-married women in their twenties, for example, found only slight differences between the cohabitation rates of blacks and whites (Tanfer, 1987). The results of this study indicated that about three out of ten of the young women surveyed had past or current experience with cohabitation. Those in their late twenties, having had more possible years to cohabit, had higher rates than those in their early twenties.

Detailed studies of more localized populations also indicate the absence of social and economic differences between cohabitors and noncohabitors. A Lane County, Oregon study of marriage license applicants noted that cohabitation was not concentrated in any particular racial, age, or occupational group (Gwartney-Gibbs, 1986). Similarly, Whyte (1990) found no social class or ethnic differences between those who had and those who had not cohabited before marriage in his Detroit study.

When a behavior once limited to a small, specialized segment of the population spreads throughout a society and becomes acceptable to large numbers of people, sociologists say the behavior has become "institutionalized." Some cohabitation researchers (Gwartney-Gibbs, 1986; Spanier, 1983) feel that cohabitation is undergoing such an **institutionalization** process. They contend that cohabitation, once considered a deviant behavior practiced only by those with few alternatives, is fast becoming a legitimate, accepted part of the courtship ritual in the United States and several other countries.

Why Cohabitation and Why the Increase?

What caused so many diverse people to embrace a new stage in intimate relationships so rapidly? Because so many types of people cohabit for so many reasons, there is no one answer to the question. All of the proposed answers, however, suggest that the cohabitation revolution resulted from other social changes occurring at the same time.

Changes in College Rules

One explanation for the 1970's and 1980's increase in cohabitation is that college rules changed. Prior to 1970, most colleges and universities operated formally under the legal principle of *in loco parentis*, a phrase roughly translated as "parents in residence." Colleges, acting in the place of parents, provided only single sex dorms and imposed rather strict curfews, especially for female students. During the 1970s, many colleges effectively abandoned the principle of *in loco parentis*, allowing coed dorms and discontinuing or greatly liberalizing curfews (Moffatt, 1989; Horowitz, 1987). These changes in the operating procedures of colleges and universities made it easier for students to cohabit and undoubtedly account for some of the increase in cohabitation among college students. They do not explain why so many noncollegians also cohabit.

The Sexual Revolution

The increase in cohabitation began only slightly after the Sexual Revolution of the late 1960s and early 1970s discussed in Chapter 4. Some researchers (Bumpass & Sweet, 1989) suggest that the roots of the co-

---

Institutionalization

The process through which a behavior once limited to a small, specialized segment of the population spreads thoughout a society and becomes acceptable to large numbers of people

---

In Loco Parentis

A phrase meaning "parents in residence," applied to the attempt by colleges and universities to stand in for parents by restricting student behavior through activities such as housing arrangements and curfews

habitation revolution lie in the changes that occurred in premarital sex attitudes and behavior during the Sexual Revolution. According to this point of view, once people lowered their moral opposition to premarital sex, they also became more tolerant of alternative courtship styles such as cohabitation.

Attitudinal changes associated with the Sexual Revolution may explain the earliest phases of the cohabitation revolution, but they do not explain its continuation. Peoples' attitudes toward premarital sex have stayed at about the same level of acceptance for the last decade or more (Thornton, 1989). Some researchers, in fact, report an increasing *conservatism* in attitudes about premarital sex since the late 1970s (Clatworthy, 1985; Robinson & Jedlicka, 1982). Yet, cohabitation rates continued to increase throughout the 1980s and show no signs of slowing down. Once started, cohabitation seemed to provide some of its own momentum to continue, with or without continuing liberalization of attitudes.

Concerns about Marriage

The 1970s were a time of increasing concern about the quality of marriage. The rates of divorce and separation rose to their highest levels ever; people became aware of spouse abuse and of marital dissatisfaction. The third explanation of the increase in cohabitation sees cohabitation as a response to increased concern about marital problems. According to this explanation, many unmarried and formerly married people noted that dating, the old mate selection pattern, no longer seemed to assure good marriages. They worried about their own future marriages and began to use cohabitation as a new way of screening potential marriage partners. The Lane County, Oregon study referred to earlier (Gwartney-Gibbs, 1986) and case studies of "trial marriage" couples provide tentative evidence that some individuals do indeed use cohabitation as a mate-screening method. However, not all cohabitation arrangements are of the trial marriage type and require other explanations.

Changes in Values

The final explanation for the cohabitation revolution attributes increased cohabitation to a general change in values concerning personal and family life. Formulated by Dirk van de Kaa (1987), a European scholar, to explain high European cohabitation rates, the explanation might also apply to some U.S. cohabitors. van de Kaa (1987) argues that substantial numbers of adults have moved away from **altruism**, a value system emphasizing the needs of society and of family members

> **Altruism**
> A value system emphasizing the needs of society and of family members over personal desires

Individualism
A value system emphasizing individual rights and self-fulfillment over the needs of others

over personal desires, and toward **individualism**, a value system emphasizing individual rights and self-fulfillment over the needs of others. As individualism takes hold, both women and men seek fulfillment through paid work, are sexually active before marriage, and want to delay or forego having children. These individualistic behaviors and attitudes effectively do away with three of the major traditional reasons for marriage: economic interdependence, sex, and procreation. According to van de Kaa (1987), increasing numbers of people see cohabitation as providing some of the same benefits as marriage—an easily available sex partner, the economic efficiency of pooled financial resources, and the labor efficiency of a household division of labor—without the obligations and sacrifices. The shift to a more individualistic value system means an increased acceptance of, or even preference for, cohabitation (van de Kaa, 1987; Macklin, 1980).

Most of the basic elements of van de Kaa's explanation apply to the United States as well as to Europe: both men and women pursue personal fulfillment through paid work, premarital sex has increased, more couples are choosing to have very small families, and the cohabitation rates have increased dramatically. In addition, several prominent national studies of the United States claim that its citizens are less altruistic and more individualistic than ever before (Bellah *et al.*, 1985; Veroff, Douvan, & Kulka, 1981). Yet, part of the explanation does not ring true. As Chapters 6 and 15 will make clear, *people in the United States are not giving up on marriage.* Recall the types of cohabitation in the United States. With the exception of cohabitors who live together as a permanent alternative to marriage, U.S. cohabitors see living together as a short, temporary stage on the way to marriage or as a kind of substitute for dating. Living together may delay marriage but, in most types of U.S. cohabitation, it does not provide a permanent substitute.

All four of these explanations of the cohabitation revolution—the change in college rules, the Sexual Revolution, increased concern with marital problems, and changes in societal values—provide partial answers to the question, "Why cohabitation and why the increase?" No one of them alone is adequate in explaining all types of cohabitation.

THE COHABITATION EXPERIENCE

Cohabitation is a rather new form of behavior and one that is often fairly well hidden; cohabiting couples can easily "pass" as either married or dating couples. As a result of its newness and secrecy, few people who have not cohabited have a clear idea about what cohabitation is like. If you have never cohabited, this section will let you in on some of the details—how cohabitation begins and ends, whether cohabitors are satisfied with their choice, and how cohabitors compare to married couples in terms of gender roles and sexual behavior. Perhaps the information will help you make your own choices about cohabitation. If you are now cohabiting or have previously done so, you will be able to compare your own experiences to those of other cohabitors.

How Does Cohabitation Begin?

Perhaps the most interesting question about cohabitation is how such arrangements get started in the first place. Do couples considering cohabitation agonize and negotiate over the legal, economic, and familial consequences of cohabiting? Or does one member of the dating couple simply ask, "Do you want to move in with me?"

Couples who end up living together seldom make a well-considered, formal decision to do so (Jackson, 1985; Moeller & Sherlock, 1981; Macklin, 1974). An early study on cohabitation among college students found that only one in four cohabiting couples had even discussed whether to live together before actually doing so (Macklin, 1974). Even this small percentage discussed it only when nudged by some external event—pregnancy, graduation, the need to make plans for summer or fall, or the need to change housing arrangements. In most cases, then, cohabitation is the end result of several little decisions to spend more and more time together. Researcher Patrick Jackson (1985) notes:

> The most adequate metaphor to describe this movement is *drift* . . . in which couples spend an increasing amount of time in the mundane activities of everyday life: eating, entertainment, sleeping, studying, and occasionally visiting friends . . . (p. 254; emphasis added).

A respondent in another study of cohabitation described the "decision" in a way that sounds very similar to "drift":

> It was real quick. . . . In a lot of ways it seemed to be almost convenient timing. We both needed a place to live; we seemed to like each other quite a bit, more than usual; we were together a lot daily, getting along on a day-to-day basis. . . . It seemed like a good thing to try. So we did. . . . (Blumstein & Schwartz, 1983, p. 418)

If cohabitors drift into cohabitation, do noncohabitors make a definite decision *not* to cohabit? Researchers seldom pose the question in this way. They have, however, tried to distinguish cohabitors from noncohabitors. In most ways, those who choose to drift into cohabitation and those who choose not to are very comparable (Newcomb &

Bentler, 1980a; Macklin, 1978). However, some categories of people are less likely to cohabit than others. Although both young and middle-aged adults cohabit, very few people over 65 do so (Bumpass & Sweet, 1989). Women in their twenties are significantly less likely to cohabit if they come from a nonwestern state or if they have finished high school and attended college (Tanfer, 1987). Religion is also an important factor, at least among young women. Those who identify with a particular religious denomination have substantially lower cohabitation rates (29 percent vs 48 percent) than those who do not, and the cohabitation rates of regular churchgoers are much lower than those of nonchurchgoers (Tanfer, 1987). Perhaps religious beliefs prevent some people from even considering cohabitation, perhaps the more religiously oriented simply avoid situations that allow the "drift" into cohabitation, or perhaps churchgoers fear losing the approval of other church members.

What about Sex?

Cohabitation is not always *only* about sex. Macklin (1974) found that almost 10 percent of her sample of college cohabitors lived together for three or more months before they began having intercourse. Nonetheless, sex is an important part of most cohabitation arrangements. College students who cohabited during the 1970s listed sex, companionship, and the economic advantages of living together as the most positive aspects of cohabitation (Newcomb, 1979). The importance of sex in cohabitation holds for noncollege students as well; generally, the more frequent the sex, the more satisfied the cohabitors are with their relationship (Blumstein & Schwartz, 1983).

Regardless of how long they have been together, cohabitors engage in sex more often than either dating couples or married people (Tanfer, 1987; Blumstein & Schwartz, 1983, p. 195; Risman *et al.*, 1981; Newcomb and Bentler, 1980a). Figure 5–3 shows the sexual habits of women surveyed in a nationwide study. Virtually no cohabiting women were sexually inactive, in contrast with about three in ten of the unmarried, noncohabiting women. Married women were just as likely as cohabiting women to be sexually active but more of the cohabitors had sexual intercourse several times a week or every day (Bachrach, 1987).

Cohabitors have sexual intercourse more often and for longer at a time than do married couples (Huey, Kline-Graber, & Graber, 1981). They also have less conventional sex lives, engaging more often in both female-initiated sex and in oral sex (Newcomb & Bentler, 1980a).

Like married couples, the longer cohabiting couples have been together, the lower their frequency of sexual intercourse (Blumstein &

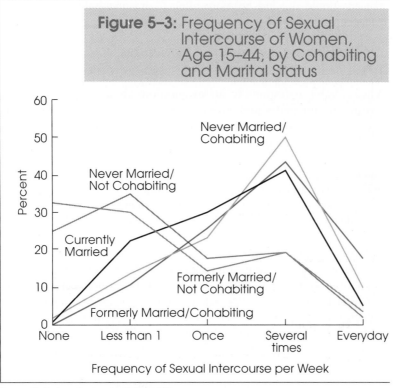

Figure 5–3: Frequency of Sexual Intercourse of Women, Age 15–44, by Cohabiting and Marital Status

Never Married/ Cohabiting

Never Married/ Not Cohabiting

Currently Married

Formerly Married/ Not Cohabiting

Formerly Married/Cohabiting

Percent

60
50
40
30
20
10
0

None   Less than 1   Once   Several times   Everyday

Frequency of Sexual Intercourse per Week

Source: Data from Bachrach, 1987, p. 630.

Researchers asked women in a variety of living situations to state how often they had sexual intercourse in the average week over the past three months. Women who are married or cohabiting are far more likely to be sexually active than are nonmarried noncohabitors. Note that more cohabitors than married women have sexual intercourse many times a week.

Schwartz, 1983). While this diminished frequency is sometimes a sore spot for both married and cohabiting couples, most are comfortable with their current rate. As one female cohabitor stated:

> We used to have sex a lot more often; in the first six months we were having sex five times a week at least, if not six. Maybe seven. . . . We've come down to twice a week. We're both busy and we're tired a lot and have different schedules and that's fine for both of us. I don't think either of us goes around sexually starved. (Blumstein & Schwartz, 1983, p. 199)

What about Gender Roles?

As you have seen, cohabiting couples are innovative in both their courting behavior and their sex lives. Do their innovative, somewhat unconventional ways extend to gender role behavior and attitudes as well? Do cohabitors challenge traditional ideas about what men and women should do and be more often than noncohabitors? There is evidence on both sides.

Cohabitors as Gender Role Innovators

When cohabitors respond to survey questions about what activities are appropriate for males and females in general, they are less bound by traditional definitions than are noncohabiting couples (Tanfer, 1987; Newcomb, 1983; Moeller & Sherlock, 1981; Newcomb & Bentler, 1980a). One researcher, summarizing the results of many surveys, concluded that "... cohabitors perceive themselves as more androgynous and counter-traditional than noncohabitors" (Newcomb, 1983, p. 89).

At least some cohabitors make efforts to carry out their androgynous ideas in day-to-day life (Blumstein & Schwartz, 1983; Moeller & Sherlock, 1981). The cohabiting couples interviewed for the study *American Couples* went to great lengths to avoid the traditionally defined female-male relationships (Blumstein & Schwartz, 1983). The men wanted the women with whom they lived to be economically independent and to "pull their own weight," and the women agreed. As the women attempted to contribute their fair share economically—a difficult task because of the different pay scales of men's and women's jobs in the United States—they expected the men to assume responsibility

Cohabiting couples generally try to maintain a fair division of household labor.

for half the housework tasks. Furthermore, the women wanted equal say in decisions affecting their own lives. In short, these cohabiting women wanted equality in economics, task assignment, and power, and they were pushing to attain that equality.

The Persistence of Traditional Gender Roles

While cohabiting couples express nontraditional *attitudes*, traditional gender roles persist in some areas of their lives. Evidence of traditional gender roles among cohabitors is strongest in two areas: the division of household work and the meanings attached to cohabitation.

Division of Household Work   When it comes to dividing up household chores, cohabiting couples are not substantially different from married couples. Cohabiting men tend to do traditional male chores such as maintaining the yard and the car, and cohabiting women do most of the traditionally female, inside, household work (Jackson, 1985; Newcomb, 1983; Newcomb, 1979; Stafford, Backman, & Dibona, 1977). Despite some attempts to resist the traditional patterns, cohabiting couples tend to fall into the same gender role-based routine that married couples do early in their relationship. This female cohabitor tells how the traditional division of labor developed in her cohabiting relationship and how difficult it was to change:

> I wanted to show him that I was a good cook and that I knew how to keep care of the house. . . . He never asked me to. It's just that I really liked him and felt that it was important he knew I was competent in doing those things. . . . I finally figured out that I blew it when we first started living together because it's really hard to break out of old habits. If I quit doing most of the things I do, who knows what will happen? I don't want him to leave, although I don't think he'd go that far. He might even do some of the housework, but he does such a shitty job I'd have to do it again, and he knows that. He really has a good thing going. (Jackson, 1985, p. 255)

The Meanings of Cohabitation   The persistence of traditional gender roles also shows up in the *meanings* cohabiting men and women attach to the cohabitation experience. Male and female views of initial cohabitation parallel male and female views of premarital sex. Initially, men tend to see cohabitation as an enjoyable, temporary, convenient arrangement and sex as a very important part of the whole relationship, while women tend to view cohabitation as an important emotional commitment that could lead to marriage and see sex as less important (Jackson, 1985; Blumstein & Schwartz, 1983). The two co-habitors quoted below, the first a man and the second a woman, illustrate these contrasting meanings:

> When I first asked her she looked at me like I was asking her a momentous thing. And I scratched my head, because it wasn't momentous to me . . . I think we discussed that once, and she said, "You don't attach much importance to this," "No" (he said), "it's just that you can come and stay with me, that's all" (Jackson, 1985, p. 254).

> When we first moved in together I told him that I would never bring marriage up, that it would be up to him when he was ready to get married, and it was . . . I went into the relationship as if it were a marriage, a commitment. I never had any desire to date anybody else . . . (Jackson, 1985, p. 254).

"Commitment? I think I'm going to let that idea marinate awhile."
Source: *New Yorker*, June 11, 1990, p. 35.

Because of these differences in how cohabitation is defined, men and women show different cohabitation patterns. One early study, based on a mail questionnaire sent to a random sample of 1100 students at one university, found that more men than women had engaged in multiple cohabitation relationships and reported "short" cohabitation experiences (Peterman, Ridley, & Anderson, 1974). According to their own self-reports, 62 percent of the men but just 41 percent of the women in this study had cohabited more than once. Half the males had never cohabited longer than one month, compared with only three out of ten females (Peterman, Ridley, & Anderson, 1974).

The male-female differences in the meaning attached to cohabitation are much more apparent among cohabiting couples who have been together a short time than they are among long-term cohabitors (Peterman, Ridley, and Anderson, 1974). This phenomenon might well occur because those who define cohabitation in similar ways from the beginning are more likely to stay together long term, while those who start with very discrepant meanings break up quickly (Peterman, Ridley, & Anderson, 1974). Another possibility is that, through the day-to-day experiences of talking, playing, and working together, cohabiting partners change one another, and two partners who initially defined cohabitation quite differently come to view the experience in similar ways (Jackson, 1985).

How Long Does Cohabitation Last?

Cohabiting couples typically split up or marry rather quickly. In her national study of 20–29 year-old never-married women, Tanfer (1987) found that cohabitation relationships that did not end in marriage lasted an average of 18 months. Another national cohabitation study found that about 40 percent of cohabitation arrangements lasted less than a year, about one third lasted two years, and only 10 percent survived into a tenth year (Bumpass & Sweet, 1989).

Table 5–1 presents more detailed information about cohabitation. These results, from a study of cohabitation among young adults under

Table 5–1 How Cohabitation Ends: Splitting up versus Marriage					
	State of the Cohabitation Relationship	Length of the Cohabitation Relationship in Months			
		6	12	18	24
Females	Relationship Continuing	77	52	43	40
	Couple Split Up	13	20	22	23
	Couple Married	10	28	35	37
Males	Relationship Continuing	74	56	45	37
	Couple Split Up	18	29	37	40
	Couple Married	8	15	18	23

Source: Data from Thornton, 1988, p. 505.

age 25 in Detroit, confirm the short-term nature of most cohabitation in the United States. Note that, for both men and women, over 60 percent of the cohabitation unions ended, through marriage or through splitting up, within two years.

What Happens When the Cohabitation Relationship Ends?

Even though most cohabiting couples stay in the cohabitation arrangement for only a short time, they are content with it at the time. They report higher levels of relationship satisfaction and fewer problems than dating, noncohabiting couples (Risman *et al.*, 1981). In fact, cohabiting couples are similar to married couples in terms of contentment, satisfaction, and adjustment in their relationships (Newcomb, 1983; Macklin, 1978). The pain of splitting up is also similar. As Macklin (1978) notes, "Cohabitants can expect to experience the same process of denial, depression, anger, ambivalence, and reorientation to single-hood associated with the dissolution of any serious relationship" (p. 220).

Other researchers agree. Mika and Bloom (1980) found that, in many ways, the breakup of a cohabitation relationship was just as emotionally disruptive and psychologically painful as a divorce. Cohabitors splitting up listed the same problems as married people undergoing divorce—loneliness, questioning of self-identity, sexual satisfaction, the relationship with ex-partner, financial stress, social reintegration, and new relationships. But many respondents also indicated they had gained from the experience. Both men and women felt they benefitted substantially in terms of personal growth and increased self-knowledge and women reported postseparation benefits in terms of increased independence and happiness (Mika & Bloom, 1980). While painful, the termination of the cohabitation arrangement was not without benefit.

CONSEQUENCES OF COHABITATION

Cohabitation, as a new form of courtship, has consequences for many people. Cohabiting couples themselves are most affected by the experience. During the cohabitation period, the couple exists in a rather peculiar legal situation. If they marry, the prior cohabitation experience may well affect their marital relationship. Some children live with parents in cohabitation situations, and these children, too, can expect to be affected in some ways. Finally, cohabitation has implications for the institutions and laws of the larger society.

Many cohabiting arrangements include children brought into the relationship by one or both partners. This combination can affect the couple and the children in various ways.

The Legal Consequences of Cohabitation

Cohabitation, unlike marriage, has no legal tradition within the United States (Newcomb, 1979). Depending on the state and on the circumstances of their cohabitation, cohabiting couples can be prosecuted for adultery (if one of the two is married and if they have sexual intercourse), for fornication (if neither is married and if they have intercourse), or for the statutory offense of "living in adultery or fornication" (two opposite sex people not married to each other who cohabit openly and who have intercourse at least once) (*American Jurisprudence*, 1962). In Florida, for example, nonmarital cohabitation is a misdemeanor, and adultery is an offense subject to criminal penalties (Abrams, 1986).

In addition to the possibility of legal prosecution, cohabiting partners risk losing certain benefits by living together. For example, a cohabitor receiving alimony may risk the reduction or elimination of alimony payments, in part because of the cohabitation and in part because of changed financial circumstances (Langbein, 1988; NOW Legal Defense and Education Fund & Cherow-O'Leary, 1987; Vanagle, 1987). Cohabitation might also affect a parent's rights to child custody.

According to *Parrillo v. Parrillo*, a Rhode Island case, courts can legitimately prohibit a custodial mother from allowing an unrelated male to spend the night when her children are present (Knauerhose, 1989).

Cohabiting couples seldom qualify for benefits and privileges routinely extended to married couples. Spouses can receive child care assistance, employment-based health insurance, pensions, military survivor's benefits, worker's compensation, or unemployment compensation based on their marital relationship to a covered worker. Cohabiting partners have no claim on such benefits. In addition, cohabiting partners may not be allowed to authorize emergency medical procedures for one another, to have family visiting privileges in a hospital, or to take bereavement leave if their partner dies (Peck, 1988). Except by special provision, cohabiting partners lack inheritance rights to a partner's property and can expect no compensation if they dissolve the relationship. Finally, cohabiting couples also may lose the opportunities to live in neighborhoods zoned for single families and to qualify for family rates on recreation and museum memberships (Postel, 1990; Peck, 1988).

During the 1970s and 1980s, state laws regarding cohabitation were challenged and sometimes changed. One U.S. district court in 1986, for example, declared that an old Virginia law prohibiting fornication and cohabitation violated constitutional rights to privacy (Duncan, 1987). Other state actions have moved towards abolishing the legal distinction between cohabiting and married couples (Anderson, 1987–1988; Blanc, 1984). For example, in a 1970s precedent-setting decision, the California Supreme Court ruled that cohabitation arrangements can include financial obligations and that the value of the services of a cohabitor (including emotional support but excluding sex) can be used in the determination of the property settlements (NOW Legal Defense and Education Fund & Cherow-O'Leary, 1987; Newcomb, 1979). In 12 states, cohabitors are also treated as marriage partners when it comes to prosecution for rape: if they rape their cohabitation partner, they are immune from prosecution under marital rape exemption provisions (NOW Legal Defense and Education Fund & Cherow-O'Leary, 1987).

A number of cities—among them, West Hollywood and San Francisco, California, Ithaca, New York, and Madison, Wisconsin—allow nonfamily households of all types (cohabitors, gay and lesbian couples, communal arrangements) to register as "domestic partners" (Lewin, 1990). Appropriately enough, San Francisco's domestic partner statute took effect on Valentine's Day, 1991 (Bishop, 1991). Registration confers no formal privileges or obligations but might help some nonfamily units qualify for "family memberships" and for hospital visiting privileges (Lewin, 1990). Some feel that such registration could represent a first step in extending married couple rights for health, life insurance, and retirement benefits to unmarried, intimate couples

(Anderson, 1987–1988). Indeed, a few cities, most of them in California, have extended family leave and health insurance benefits to city employees with domestic partners (Larson & Edmundson, 1991).

Cohabitation Consequences for Subsequent Marriage

Many cohabitors decide to marry after cohabiting. Are their marriages different from those of their counterparts who married without prior cohabitation? Are they more likely to be happy with marriage? To stay together? To have children? Here we focus on how cohabitation affects first marriages. The effects of cohabitation on remarriages will be discussed in Chapter 15.

Cohabitation and Marital Quality

At least some people who cohabit do so hoping that cohabitation will lead them to make a wise marital choice and that living together prior to marriage will result in a high quality, lasting marital relationship. Are their hopes realistic? Not according to most of the research done thus far. Researchers studying the effects of prior cohabitation on the *quality* of subsequent marriage agree that, overall, *couples who lived together before marriage do not have higher quality marriages than those who lived apart.*

Numerous researchers conclude that cohabitation simply makes no difference, positive or negative, on subsequent marital quality (Crohan & Veroff [for white respondents only], 1989; Watson & DeMeo, 1987; Watson, 1983; Newcomb & Bentler [for those married longer than four years], 1980b). Others find that couples who cohabited prior to marriage have *lower* quality marriages, at least in some respects. Black respondents with cohabitation experience had less happy marriages than those without, according to Crohan and Veroff's study (1989). Booth and Johnson (1988) discovered that prior cohabitors had less marital interaction and more marital problems than other married couples, and Demaris and Leslie (1984) found that cohabitors were more often dissatisfied with their marriages. In sum, there is little evidence that prior cohabitation improves marital quality.

Cohabitation and Marital Stability

Prior cohabitation does not help first marriages stay together. Indeed, those who cohabit prior to first marriage have substantially higher rates of subsequent separation and divorce than those who entered first marriage without prior cohabitation (Bumpass & Sweet, 1989; Booth & Johnson, 1988; Thornton, 1988). This finding holds true not only in the United States but also in other countries with high cohabitation rates. Canadian women who cohabit have a 50 percent higher risk of divorce than women who do not (Balakrishnan *et al.*, 1987); in Sweden, the marital collapse rate (both divorce and separation) is 80 percent higher for cohabiting women (Bennett, Blanc, & Bloom, 1988). Among Swedish women, the longer the cohabitation prior to marriage, the higher the chances of subsequent marital dissolution—women cohabiting longer than three years had marital dissolution rates 50 percent higher than those cohabiting less than three years (Bennett, Blanc, & Bloom, 1988).

Cohabitation and marital dissolution may be connected in another way. In this section, we have considered only people who *marry* after cohabitation. What about individuals who cohabit but break up without marrying? Some experts suggest that these people, who used cohabitation as a way of screening out "bad" marriage partners, may be responsible for the slight decline in the divorce rate during the 1980s: "... if it were not for the high prevalence of cohabitation, the marital dissolution rate might well be higher than it is" (Bumpass & Sweet, 1989, p. 621).

Why the Negative Consequences?

Cohabitation may prevent some bad marriages from taking place and may help some second marriages stay together. For the most part, though, cohabitation has negative effects on the quality and stability of subsequent marriage. Why?

Most of the limited research done so far concludes that cohabitors are simply less committed to family and marriage as a way of life than are those who do not cohabit (Bennett, Blanc, & Bloom, 1988; Lewis *et al.*, 1977). There are several indications of this lower commitment. Compared to their noncohabiting unmarried counterparts, cohabitors express desires for fewer children after marriage (Bower & Christopherson, 1977). And once married, former cohabitors are much less likely than married couples who did not cohabit to have children, at least during the early years of marriage (Newcomb & Bentler, 1980b).

A second indication of lower commitment to marriage and family among cohabitors is their reaction to marital problems and unhappiness. In comparing divorcing couples who had cohabited first to divorcing couples who had not, Newcomb and Bentler (1980b) found that the former cohabitors reported less marital unhappiness and fewer problems at the time of their divorce than did the noncohabitors. The former cohabitors, in short, had a lower threshold for marital problems and marital unhappiness; when they faced problems, they divorced. Noncohabitors, characterized by a stronger commitment to marriage and parenthood, were willing to endure more problems and more unhappiness before making the decision to divorce.

This "less commitment" explanation of higher divorce rates among former cohabitors suggests that lower commitment to marriage and family leads some people to cohabit in the first place and, later, makes these same people less hesitant to dissolve the subsequent marriage. In other words, the "less commitment" explanation implies that it is something about the people who cohabit that explains their higher rates of marital breakup. It is also possible, of course, that something about the cohabitation experience itself contributes to less stable marriages after cohabitation. The question of whether the nature of the individuals who cohabit or the experience of cohabiting itself explains higher subsequent breakup rates is still an open one, awaiting further well-designed research (Booth & Johnson, 1988).

Cohabitation and Children

Overall, cohabitors are much less likely than married couples to become parents (Newcomb, 1986; Blanc, 1984; Moeller & Sherlock, 1981). Nonetheless, there are children in some cohabitation households. Figure 5–4 (on page 174) indicates that even though most 1987 cohabitation households were childless, between 1970 and 1987 the *number* of cohabiting households with children increased almost fourfold.

To see how children are affected by cohabitation, you need to understand something about the formal relationship between adults and children in cohabitation households. These formal relationships vary. Some children living in cohabitation households are the children of cohabiting women who have never been married. A national 1983 study of never-married women found that, when compared to never-married noncohabiting women, never-married cohabiting women were far more likely to have been pregnant (54 percent versus 23 percent) and to have had children (34 percent versus 13 percent) (Tanfer, 1987). Some of these cohabiting mothers are living with the father of their child(ren); others are cohabiting with a man who is not biologically related to their child(ren). Thus, some children in cohabitation households are illegitimate children living with both biological parents, while others are illegitimate children living with one parent and one nonparent.

Many children living in cohabitation households, however, were born within wedlock but no longer live with both biological parents. The most usual case is one in which a divorced woman and the child(ren) of her previous marriage share a home with the mother's intimate partner. In this case, the child is legitimate but lives, on a

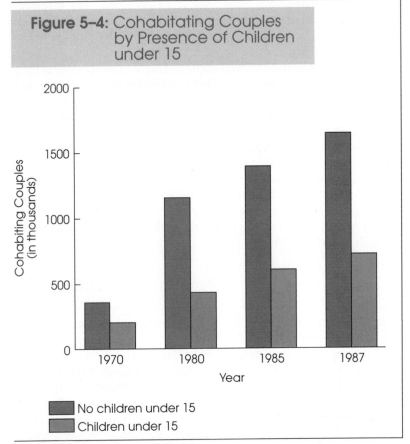

Figure 5-4: Cohabiting Couples by Presence of Children under 15

No children under 15
Children under 15

Source: U.S. Bureau of the Census, 1989b, p. 44.

The figure indicates that, while most 1988 cohabitation households were childless, the *number* of cohabiting households with children increased from slightly less than 200,000 to slightly more than 800,000 between 1970 and 1988. For 1970, the "children" bar refers to children under age 14.

day-to-day basis, with an unrelated male. The relationship is *like* a stepfather-stepchild relationship but, because the adults are not married, cannot truly be referred to in that way.

The Legal Status of Children in Cohabitation Households

The legal status of children in cohabitation households depends on their biological relationship to the adults with whom they are living. Legitimacy (whether the child was born within or outside of marriage) makes much less difference today than it did prior to the 1960s. Since the 1960s, courts have ruled in separate decisions that illegitimate children have the same rights as legitimate children to recover financial benefits from the wrongful deaths of their mother or father, to receive Social Security benefits at the death of a parent, and to receive child support from their father (Douthwaite, 1979; Newcomb, 1979). Such benefits are typically available, however, only if there has been some type of formal declaration of the parent-child relationship. For example, illegitimate children with one or two parents in the military are eligible to receive the same military benefits as legitimate children of military personnel, *but only* if the requisite military procedures are followed and the child is officially designated as the child of a military employee.

Children in cohabitation households who are living with their mother and her intimate partner and whose father lives elsewhere remain the legal children of their two biological parents. Their legal situation is somewhat similar to that of stepchildren who have not been legally adopted by their stepparent, a topic which we will discuss in Chapter 15.

Childrearing and Cohabitation

Research on the consequences of being reared in a cohabitation-based household is very limited. Here we focus on one long-term study that began in 1973 and followed children for a seven-year period. One part of this UCLA study compared the socialization experiences of children raised in traditional two-parent families to children raised in cohabitation families (Alexander & Eiduson, 1980; Eiduson & Alexander, 1978). The study focused on white, middle-class individuals and began six months before the children to be studied were born.

An early project report, done when the children were less than two years old, discovered that, although the cohabiting parents had very different values from the married parents, they were rearing their children in similar ways. In both types of households, the mothers provided the primary care, the parents were very good at being parents, and the children were doing well. Cohabiting fathers were far more active parents than were traditional fathers but, overall, the researchers found few differences in the children or in how they were being reared (Eiduson & Alexander, 1978).

A followup report, done when the children were seven, reinforced the original findings (Alexander & Eiduson, 1980). The children in both types of households were being reared in comparable ways. The researchers stated:

> With the explicit diversity of parental perspectives, it is surprising that actual childrearing has been neither so diverse nor so casual. Instead, the predominant parental behavior during infancy was the "middle-class" orientation of parenting practices—parents parenting as they had been parented. Interest in child development was intense, and in all the families, *the baby's needs seemed to shape the families more than the diversity in families shaped the children.* (emphasis added, Alexander & Eiduson, 1980, p. 43–44)

Researchers did discover a few differences at the time of the seven-year followup, however. Children in marriage-based families were exposed to more stable and consistent relationships with their parents because cohabitation-based families moved and changed family make-up more often. Interestingly, the traditional families more often displayed nontraditional gender roles. Mothers in traditional families went back to work relatively quickly while mothers in cohabiting families stayed home much longer to raise the children. In other words, married mothers did not play the traditional stay-at-home mothering role, while cohabiting mothers did. As noted above, neither the greater instability nor the more traditional mothering found in cohabitation households affected how the children were reared.

Cohabitation and Society

As noted earlier in this chapter and also in Chapter 1, the increase in family-like nonfamilies, such as cohabiting couples, has led both ordinary citizens and lawmakers to look again at just what "marriage" and "family" really mean. A change in the entire system of U.S. family law *may* be one long-term societal consequence of increasing cohabitation. We have also pointed out that, for a little less than half the population, cohabitation has become a regular step in the courtship process. This represents another societal consequence of cohabitation. Do the societal consequences of cohabitation go even further? Is cohabitation becoming a replacement for marriage?

In some European countries, cohabitation *has* become a permanent substitute for marriage for a substantial minority of couples (Blanc, 1987; van de Kaa, 1987). Writing about Sweden, van de Kaa (1987) states, " . . . for at least 10 percent of young people who started cohabiting after the mid-1970s, unmarried cohabitation will be a permanent status" (p. 17).

Is cohabitation becoming a permanent status in the United States as well? The answer seems to be "no." Although many people, both young and not so young, are choosing to cohabit, there is little evidence *as of right now* that they are following the Swedish example and choosing cohabitation instead of marriage. In a study of attitudes on family issues in the United States covering several decades, Thornton (1989) found strong shifts toward a greater acceptance of family alternatives such as cohabitation but did not find any strong shift away from the personal desire to get married or to have a family. Although respondents rejected moral imperatives telling them they "had" to get married and that they "had" to have children, they still wanted to do both. They did not, in other words, consider cohabitation as a permanent substitute for marriage in their own lives.

Most researchers agree that cohabitation in the United States still represents a transitional stage in the development of intimate relationships, not an ending stage (Tanfer, 1987; Newcomb, 1986). People in the United States may want to cohabit, but they also want to marry. As Thornton (1988) states, " . . . even though cohabitation is an important transitional state for many, marriage represents the bulk of the union experience for the great majority of Americans" (p. 506). At this point, at least, cohabitation has added a new dimension to the courtship process, but the process ultimately ends in marriage.

Alternative Choice

Homosexual union
Two gay males or two lesbians who are emotionally and physically committed to one another and share a living space

Homosexual Unions

Cohabitation is one type of intimate, nonmarital, residential relationship in the United States today. **Homosexual unions**—two gay men or two lesbians who are emotionally and physically committed to one another and who share a living space—are another. The number of people living together as homosexual couples is, of course, very difficult to determine. One study of homosexuals in the six counties in the San Francisco area determined that almost 40 percent of the classifiable gay men and over 60 percent of the classifiable lesbians were "coupled." While women often formed couple relationships soon after accepting their lesbian sexual orientation, men generally became interested in this type of relationship only after a number of years of nonexclusive homosexual activity (Bell & Weinberg, 1978).

Homosexuals enter into and try to sustain couple relationships for many of the same reasons that heterosexuals do: companionship, emotional commitment, intimate communication, and dependable sex. As the authors of the San Francisco study concluded:

> . . . our data tend to belie the notion that homosexual affairs are apt to be inferior imitations of heterosexuals' premarital or marital involvements. . . . From our respondents' descriptions, these affairs are apt to involve an emotional exchange and commitment similar to the kinds that heterosexuals experience, and most of the homosexual respondents thought that they and their partners had benefited personally from their involvement and were at least somewhat unhappy when it was over. (Bell & Weinberg, 1978, p. 102)

Although homosexual unions are "marriage-like" in their emotional closeness, most are *not* marriage-like in the sense of assigning each partner a separate role based on traditional gender role distinctions. That is, most homosexual couples do *not* include a passive, dependent, stay-at-home, nurturant partner (the "female" role) and a dominant, independent, provider partner (the "male" role). Both gay male and lesbian couples tend to believe that both partners should work outside the home and try to avoid situations in which one partner is "provider" and the other "dependent" (Blumstein & Schwartz, 1983, pp. 125–31). In addition, although one partner (particularly in gay male couples) may do more of the household work than the other, the work is not generally divided along traditional gender role lines. Partners are equally likely to cook, clean, do household repairs, and take care of the yard (Bell & Weinberg, 1978, pp. 91, 99).

Homosexual couples avoid modeling their relationship on the traditional heterosexual marriage with its rigid gender roles. Gender roles are important, though. Gay male relationships are frequently shaped by the traditional male emphasis on economic success, competition, and genital sex and lesbian relationships by a traditional female emphasis on sharing, avoiding competition, and nongenital sexual closeness (Blumstein & Schwartz, 1983).

Homosexuals who have children from a former relationship face many legal and social obstacles. Obtaining custody of their children is often difficult.

This adherence to traditional gender roles sometimes causes friction within homosexual relationships. For example, like other men, gay men tend to associate economic success with power. The partner earning more money tends to dominate decisionmaking in gay male couples, making the partner who earns less feel resentful (Blumstein & Schwartz, 1983, p. 65). A second example involves the sexual lives of lesbians. Raised with the idea that females should not initiate sexual activity and that oral sex is wrong, older lesbians often have less sexual activity than they desire because neither partner is comfortable with the initiator-innovator role (Blumstein & Schwartz, 1983).

At the same time, having a partner of the same sex can contribute to couple closeness. In their study of married, cohabiting, gay male, and lesbian couples, Blumstein and Schwartz (1983) found that same-sex couples were more likely to spend large amounts of leisure time together than were opposite-sex couples. Spending time together in mutually satisfying activities is one important way for all intimate couples to remain close. Homosexual couples are apparently more successful at this aspect of intimacy than are many husbands and wives who spend leisure time with same-sex friends pursuing very different activities.

Homosexual couples face many of the same legal dilemmas that cohabitors do. They lack the legal standing of married couples and, thus, are unable to qualify for most spouse or family-based benefits. In twenty-four states, homosexual activity is technically a crime and homosexual couples risk prosecution (Greenberg, 1988, p. 455). There is one critical difference between cohabitors and homosexual couples: cohabitors have the legal option of getting married; homosexual couples do not. For many cohabitors, cohabitation is an intermediate step between dating and marriage; for gay men and lesbians in couple relationships, living together in a quasi-marriage, legally ambiguous relationship is the final stage in the relationship.

Summary

Cohabitation is a courtship stage in which two opposite-sex persons live together in marriage-like conditions. The five types of cohabitation are: 1. temporary, casual, convenient; 2. affectionate-dating, going together; 3. trial marriage; 4. temporary alternative to marriage; and 5. permanent alternative to marriage. The many types of cohabitation, the diversity of people who cohabit, and the difficulties in counting cohabitors all make research results on cohabitation tentative in nature.

The rate of cohabitation increased very rapidly between the early 1970s and the late 1980s and shows no signs of slowing down.

Once limited to older, racial minority, or economically deprived groups, cohabitation today involves people of all socioeconomic statuses, races, and ages. Changes in college rules, the Sexual Revolution, increased recognition of marital problems, and general value shifts from altruism to individualism have all been proposed as social changes that help explain cohabitation increases.

Those who choose the cohabitation experience frequently drift into it and typically cohabit for only a short period of time before marrying or breaking up. Men tend to define cohabitation much less seriously than women in its early phases, though male-female definitions converge in longer term cohabitation. Although cohabitors are egalitarian in gender role attitudes and resist some pressures to be traditional, the conventional division of household labor persists in most cohabitation arrangements. Cohabitors enjoy their living arrangement, are very sexually active and innovative, and feel that cohabitation is a worthwhile experience. Like the collapse of any type of intimate relationship, the end of a cohabitation arrangement is painful, often as emotionally and psychologically unsettling as a divorce.

Cohabitation has numerous consequences for those who choose it. Technically, cohabitors are often violating one or more state laws; more practically, they forego many of the employment, government, and local zoning benefits that go automatically to married couples. Laws on some of these matters are changing. Cohabitation may have resulted in a lower overall proportion of bad marriages, but prior cohabitation does not improve the quality of first marriages and, in fact, is associated with higher dissolution rates in such marriages. Lower commitment to marriage and family seems to explain both why some people cohabit in the first place and why these same people are less hesitant to divorce. Today, the legal status of children in cohabitation arrangements depends more on their biological relationship to the cohabiting partners than on their legitimacy. Overall, children in cohabitation arrangements are not much different from children reared by married parents. On a societal level, the prevalence of cohabitation may eventually change legal definitions of marriage and family. Cohabitation is fast becoming institutionalized as a part of the U.S. courtship process but, at present, shows few signs of replacing marriage.

Homosexual unions are another intimate alternative to dating and marriage. These relationships are fairly widespread among both gay men and lesbians, although they are more frequent and more often sexually exclusive for lesbians. Homosexuals receive the same emotional rewards from their couple relationships that heterosexuals do. They tend not to assign "male" and "female" roles within the relationship; rather, traditional gender role socialization prevails, sometimes causing friction and sometimes enhancing closeness. The legal situation of homosexual couples is similar to that of cohabitors. However, since homosexual couples cannot marry, their relationship is often considered to be permanent rather than temporary.

CHAPTER 6

THE DECISION TO MARRY

The following questions ask for your opinions concerning the legal requirements for marriage. After answering the questions, you might want to check the laws that apply in your state of residence. Information on some of these matters can be found in Table 6-1 (on pages 199-200).

1. Should there be a minimum age requirement for marriage without parental consent? If so, what should it be? Should this age be different for males and females? Should people be able to marry at a younger age with parental consent? What age?
2. Should first cousins be able to marry one another?
3. Should the law require that people be tested for sexually transmitted diseases before receiving a marriage license?
4. Should premarital counseling be required before certain people are allowed to marry? If so, which people?
5. Should there be a waiting period between applying for a marriage license and receiving one? If so, how long? Once received, for how long should the marriage license be valid?

The following passages, from family therapist Michael P. Nichol's book, *The Power of the Family*, describe some of the feelings of Sharon and Stewart, a couple in their twenties, as they prepare for and participate in their wedding ceremony.

> Sharon never imagined how much there was to be done to arrange a wedding. There were caterers, flowers, a band to pick, what music to play, who to invite, choosing the invitations, who should sit where ("You can't put Aunt Adele at *that* table!" her mother said), and on and on. Weddings were supposed to be romantic. This was turning into a chore.
>
> The night before the real thing, after the rehearsal, Sharon's father staged a big family dinner at the Empire Room. While everyone was eating and drinking and laughing and making toast after toast, Sharon watched Stewart. He was smiling and talking but he seemed out of place, uncomfortable with all these people—her family. *It's a mistake*, she thought. *I don't love him. He's just a boy.*

Later, at the wedding itself . . .

> Stewart was aggravated by all the picture-taking. Every time he tried to talk with somebody or have some champagne, the photographer was dragging him away. "Okay, let's have the bride and groom and the bride's parents." *Whose wedding is this?* Stewart thought. But then he knew the answer. It was Sharon's family's wedding. So he allowed himself to be pushed along like a leaf in the wind. He just kind of stood outside and watched. The photographer was not content to record what was really happening, she had to stage it. Everything was posed—this group, that group—and some of it much too precious for Stewart's taste. Pictures of him kissing Sharon, pictures of her feeding him cake. These things should be private.
>
> Once Stewart stood next to Sharon under the canopy of flowers, everything stopped. All the noise, the pushing and pulling, and the loudness, all the foolishness. It was quiet. His heart was full. The rabbi's words sounded right. Sharon was beautiful. She looked like a woman and a little girl all at the same time. "Do you . . . ?" "Yes, I do!" he said with all his mind. (Michael P. Nichols, author of *The Power of the Family*, 1988, pp. 82–83).

Marriage
a legally and socially recognized union between two opposite-sexed adults involving certain obligations and privileges.

Like many couples marrying for the first time, Sharon and Stewart are shocked by the realization that their decision to marry is more than just a private agreement. Rather, they find, both before and during the wedding, their marriage is *everybody's business*. On a small scale level, Sharon and Stewart illustrate one of the text's major themes: **marriage**, a legally and socially recognized union between two opposite-sexed adults involving certain obligations and privileges, is both a highly personal experience and an important societal institution.

Chapter 6 deals with marriage on both the personal and the societal level but focuses on the latter. Our emphasis will be on first marriages, although many of the topics we discuss are equally applicable to remarriages. The special features of remarriages will be dealt with in Chapter 15. We begin Chapter 6 by examining variations in the prevalence of marriage both over time and between racial groups. Then we discuss how the meaning of marriage has changed. Next we look at marriage as a legal, religious, and community institution, paying special attention to the laws about marriage. The next section returns to the individual level, discussing how marriage affects the mental, emotional, and physical health of husbands and wives. The Alternative Choice section of the chapter deals with the choice to remain single.

SOCIAL CHANGE AND MARRIAGE

Marriage in the United States in the 1990s is different than it was 100 years ago, 50 years ago, or even 20 years ago. Some social changes in marriage—for example, changes in the age at which people first marry—seem to be somewhat cyclical in nature, tied to the particular circumstances of a given era and society. Other changes—for example, ideas about what constitutes an ideal marriage—evolve slowly over hundreds of years and are not limited to a single society. We will focus on two broad types of social change: 1. changes in the prevalence of marriage and 2. changes in the meaning of marriage.

Changes in the Prevalence of Marriage

Every year, close to two and one-half million U.S. couples marry, two thirds of them for the first time (Saluter, 1989). Does this figure indicate that marriage is more popular than ever? Or does it actually represent a decline in the prevalence of marriage?

Changes in Marriage Rates

Marriage rate
a ratio of the number of people who marry in a given year to the total number eligible for marriage.

One way to answer these questions is to look at the **marriage rate**, a ratio comparing the number of people who actually married in a given year to the total number eligible (that is, unmarried and of appropriate age) for marriage. Figure 6–1 gives an overall picture of first marriage rates for unmarried women aged 14 to 44 in the United States since 1921. You should be able to tell from the figure that first marriage rates are subject to a lot of fluctuation. People were *least* likely to

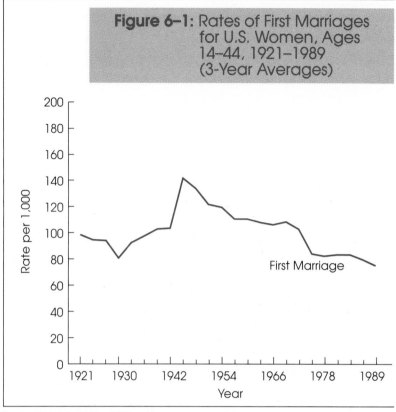

Figure 6–1: Rates of First Marriages for U.S. Women, Ages 14–44, 1921–1989 (3-Year Averages)

First Marriage

"Rates of first marriage" are calculated by dividing the number of first marriages performed in a given year by the number of single women, aged 14–44 (the age group most likely to be marrying for the first time) in the population and multiplying by 1000. The marriage rate peaks and valleys shown in the figure are closely tied to social and economic conditions.

Source: Norton and Miller, 1989, p. 23.

undertake marriage during the early 1930s, the beginning years of the Great Depression, and were most likely to marry in the years immediately following World War II. During the 1980s, first marriage rates were on the low side, but not at the lowest point ever.

Changes in Median Age at First Marriage

A second way of measuring the relative prevalence and popularity of marriage is to see how early in life people marry. If marriage is extremely popular, people will marry young; if it is less popular, people will delay marriage and pursue other opportunities (Espenshade, 1985, p. 205). Figure 6–2 (on page 188) traces trends in the median age at first marriage since 1890. As you can see, between 1890 and the early 1950s, the median age at first marriage declined substantially. To get a better understanding of just how *young* people were when they married in the 1950s, pretend you are a female, twenty years and six months old,

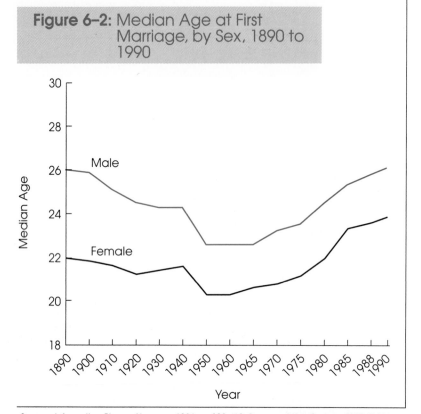

Figure 6–2: Median Age at First Marriage, by Sex, 1890 to 1990

Source: *Information Please Almanac*, 1991, p. 808; U.S. Bureau of the Census, 1989, Table A–2.

The median age at first marriage declined throughout the first half of the twentieth century but rose during the second half. Note that the difference in age between husband and wife has decreased as compared to one hundred years ago.

living in the United States in 1950. Chances are about 50–50 that you would already be married! The median age at first marriage remained low throughout the 1950s and 1960s. However, it began rising precipitously after about 1970. Today, women on average wait until almost age 24, longer than women in any previous era, to marry, and men first marry at about age 26, the same age their counterparts of 100 years ago did (*Information Please Alamanac*, 1991, p. 808). These figures, along with the marriage rate figures, suggest that marriage was extremely popular in the 1950s and 1960s but it is much less popular today.

Marital Status and Race

The relatively low current rate of marriage and the tendency to delay marriage until the mid-to-late twenties, when combined with the high divorce rates of the 1970s and 1980s, mean that there is considerable diversity among adults in terms of marital status. Figure 6–3 illustrates

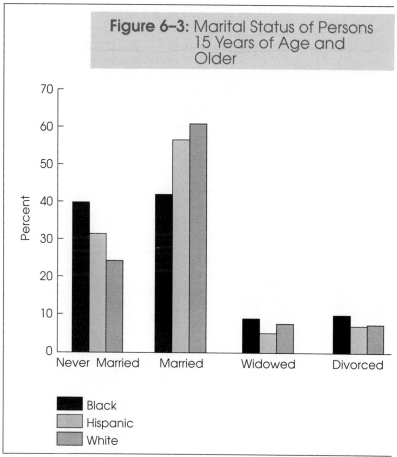

Figure 6–3: Marital Status of Persons 15 Years of Age and Older

The figure shows the current marital status of blacks, Hispanics, and whites. Note that "married" is the most common marital status for all three groups but also that blacks are more likely than whites or Hispanics to be widowed, divorced, or never married. The proportion of married and never married Hispanics falls between white and black proportions.

Source: Data from U.S. Bureau of the Census, 1989c, Table 1.

this diversity; "married" is still the most common situation for those over age fifteen, but there are also substantial numbers of never married, widowed, and divorced people.

Figure 6–3 also shows substantial differences in marital status between Hispanics, blacks, and whites. Persons of Hispanic origin are almost as likely as whites to be married and less likely than either blacks or whites to be divorced. About one out of three Hispanics has never married, due, at least in part, to the fact that the Hispanic population is a young one (Becerra, 1988, p. 151). The "youth" of the Hispanic population also accounts for the low proportion in the widowed category. These patterns are more characteristic of Mexican-Americans than of Puerto Rican-Americans, whose marital patterns are more like those of blacks (Becerra, 1988; Sánchez-Ayéndez, 1988).

The black-white differences in Figure 6–3 are particularly striking. While six out of ten whites are currently married, only slightly more than four out of ten blacks are. A randomly selected black adult is almost as likely to be "never married" as to be married; blacks also have the highest proportions in the widowed and divorced categories. In short, blacks show a great deal of diversity in marital status.

Many more blacks than whites choose never to marry. Among whites born in 1954, for example, 90 percent of the females and 91 percent of the males are expected to have been married at least once by the age of 44. However, among blacks born in the same year, only 86 percent of the males and 70 percent of the females are expected to have had such experience (Rodgers & Thornton, 1985). The Cohort Comparison in this chapter illustrates that this difference in black-white marriage patterns is a rather recent development.

Cohort Comparison   Propensity to Marry by Birth Cohort and Race

Although the majority of people in every birth cohort marry, the size of the majority varies considerably from cohort to cohort. In this Cohort Comparison, we will look at the proportion of the men and women of the New Century, Depression, and Baby Boom cohorts who married by age 44. We will consider blacks and whites separately.

Our information comes from a statistical study done by Willard L. Rodgers and Arland Thornton (1985). Rodgers and Thornton used statistical methods to estimate how many black males and females and white males and females from selected one-year birth cohorts married (or will marry) by their middle forties. Although they investigated 16 different one-year birth cohorts (beginning with the 1880 cohort), we will focus on the three that best represent the birth cohorts we have been tracing: the 1910 birth cohort (representing the New

Century cohort), the 1934 cohort (representing the Depression cohort), and the 1954 cohort (representing the Baby Boom cohort).

Figure 6-4 summarizes Rodgers and Thornton's results. Note that the birth cohort members most likely to marry were those born in 1934, who would have been marrying in the 1950s and 1960s. Over 90 percent of each category represented in the 1934 cohort married; in the case of white females, the marriage probability was nearly 97 percent. This group is considered somewhat unusual in its propensity to marry since its overall marriage rate was higher than any group that preceded or followed it (Rodgers & Thornton, 1985; Cherlin, 1981).

No matter what their race or sex, members of the 1954 birth cohort, marrying mostly in the 1970s and 1980s, have the lowest probability of marriage. For whites and for black

males, the proportion of 1954 cohort members expected to marry is somewhat lower than the proportion of 1934 cohort members who married, but it is about the same as the proportion of the 1910 cohort that eventually married. Black females born in 1954 are *much* less likely to marry than any previous cohort, with only 70 percent expected to marry before their mid-forties. The changes seen in the black female propensity to marry are even more striking when one considers that in birth cohorts prior to 1905, black females were more likely to marry than the other categories. For example, 93 percent of the black females born in 1890 married while 90 percent of the white females born in that year did so (Rodgers & Thornton, 1985, p. 274). In short, different cohorts of black females have shown considerable variation in their propensities to marry. The text suggests some reasons why.

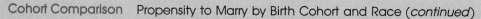

Cohort Comparison   Propensity to Marry by Birth Cohort and Race (*continued*)

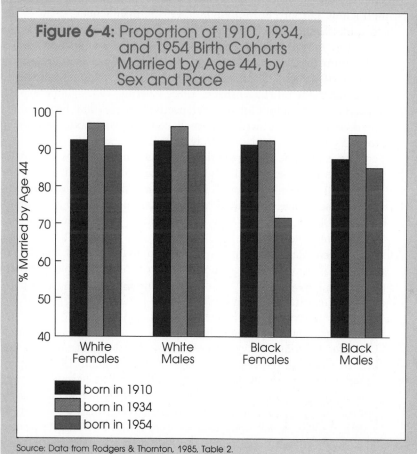

Figure 6–4: Proportion of 1910, 1934, and 1954 Birth Cohorts Married by Age 44, by Sex and Race

Source: Data from Rodgers & Thornton, 1985, Table 2.

Explaining Changes in the Prevalence of Marriage

We have given you a great deal of information about the prevalence of marriage in different time periods and among different subgroups in the population. Now it is time to make sense of it all. Specifically, why is marriage more prevalent in some historical periods than others? Why is it less prevalent today among blacks than whites? Among black females than among black males? We will consider two explanations here: an economic opportunities explanation and a sex ratio explanation.

Economic Opportunities Explanation   The **Economic Opportunities Explanation** for variations in the prevalance of marriage simply states

Economic Opportunities Explanation
an explanation for variations in the prevalence of marriage stating that the economic opportunities available to young men and women influence their decisions about when to marry and whether to marry at all.

E.O.E.

Ⓐ More Money
more Marriage

Ⓑ Less gain for
women less marriage

that the economic opportunities available to young men and women influence their decisions about when to marry and whether to marry at all (Lichter, LeClere, & McLaughlin, 1991; Oppenheimer, 1988). When job opportunities and pay scales for young men are good (as in the 1950s and 1960s), couples are more likely to marry and to do so at a fairly young age; when economic prospects for young men are poorer (as in the 1930s and 1970s), people delay marriage and are more likely not to marry at all (Espenshade, 1985; Cherlin, 1981). Some experts (Easterlin, 1987) adopting this perspective believe that birth cohort size is an important variable—small cohorts have better economic prospects and, thus, higher marriage rates.

The Economic Opportunities Explanation also helps to explain why blacks have been less likely than whites to marry in recent years. As you will learn in Chapter 10, the economic downturns of the 1970s affected black males much more strongly than they affected white males (Bennett, Bloom, & Craig, 1989; Oppenheimer, 1988). Blacks consider the provider role of a husband/father as very important. Therefore, when black males cannot find well-paid employment, they tend not to marry and are not considered good marriage prospects by black females (Tucker & Taylor, 1989). This is exactly what happened in many parts of the United States during the 1970s and 1980s.

A second part of the Economic Opportunities Explanation concerns women and states that when women have less to gain economically from marriage, they are more likely to delay marriage and less likely to marry at all (Lichter, LeClere, & McLaughlin, 1991; Oppenheimer, 1988; Becker, 1981). This explanation works particularly well in explaining why women in the 1970s and 1980s, who had many more opportunities to work in paying jobs, married later than women in the 1950s and 1960s, when opportunities were fewer. Most white women still earn considerably less than most white men; marriage is still "profitable" for them and they continue to marry in fairly high numbers. The gap between the wages of black women and those of black men is much less, however, and black women tend to be in higher prestige occupations than black men (Espenshade, 1985). Because black women, overall, have less to gain from marriage than white women, they marry in much smaller numbers.

Sex Ratio Imbalances   A second explanation of variations in marriage prevalence, the **Sex Ratio Imbalance Explanation**, states that when there is a relative shortage of appropriately aged males to females, men are less likely to commit to marriage, particularly at an early age, and the overall marriage rate goes down (Guttentag & Secord, 1983). To put it a slightly different way:

> When men are in short supply they have more bargaining power in a potential relationship because there are more women among

Sex Ratio Imbalance Explanation
an explanation for variations in the prevalence of marriage stating that, when there is a relative shortage of appropriately aged males to females, men are less likely to commit to marriage, particularly at an early age, and the overall marriage rate goes down.

whom they can choose. Conversely, women have relatively less leverage because they have fewer alternatives. Transient relationships between men and women become important, and women do not expect men to remain with them for many years. (Espenshade, 1985, p. 232)

The Sex Ratio Imbalance Explanation helps explain why women born at the very beginning of the Baby Boom are more likely to remain single. If they follow the time-honored tradition of considering only men slightly older than themselves as potential husbands, they face a distinct shortage of eligible marriage partners. This phenomenon is known as the **marriage squeeze** (Parke & Glick, 1967). The Sex Ratio Imbalance Explanation is also extremely helpful in explaining lower rates of marriage among blacks, especially black females (Bennett, Bloom, & Craig, 1989). In 1970, there were 57 unmarried black males, aged 23–27, for every 100 unmarried black females, aged 20–24 (Espenshade, 1985, p. 233). Why this extreme imbalance? Blacks have lower sex ratios at birth than whites (102 male births per 100 female for blacks versus 106 males per 100 females for whites). Also, young black males have much higher death rates than young white males, and black males experience higher rates of institutionalization. Finally, the tendency for black males to marry outside their race much more often than black females further decreases the supply of potential husbands for black females (Bennett, Bloom, & Craig, 1989; Espenshade, 1985). Meanwhile, Mexican-Americans, although subject to many of the same economic pressures as blacks, have fairly high marriage rates because, in that population, females are in short supply since they are less likely to immigrate to the United States than males (Becerra, 1988, p. 151).

Marriage squeeze the situation in which women have a shortage of potential marriage partners because they are part of a large cohort following a smaller one.

Changes in the Meaning of Marriage

When individuals marry, their personal expectations about what marriage should be like are influenced, at least in part, by the meanings marriage has in their particular society. As family life changes, so do these societal meanings of marriage. In Chapter 1, we noted that over the centuries in Western societies family life has become less economically based and more intimately based, less patriarchal and more egalitarian, and less public and more private. Thus, the meaning of modern (as opposed to traditional) marriage is that it is—or ideally should be—intimate, egalitarian, and private. Here we will give a few concrete examples of how these ideas are reflected in modern marriages by contrasting them with traditional marriages of the past. After reading the examples, perhaps you will be able to think of other ways in which modern marriages are intimate, egalitarian, and private.

Marriage as Intimate

By looking at the changing meaning attached to marital sex, we can recognize the decreased importance of economic necessity as well as the increased importance of intimacy in marriages. Husbands and wives in traditional marriages felt that reproduction was the major reason for sexual intercourse. Sexual intercourse was an important part of marriage because it benefited both the couple and the society economically—new babies very soon became new workers (Gagnon, 1977).

Modern marriage no longer, by definition, implies procreation (Davidson & Darling, 1988; D'Emilio & Freedman, 1988; Hunt, 1983). Some couples choose to have no children at all; even those who choose to have children seldom define reproduction as the sole reason for sexual activity. Rather, modern marital sex is seen primarily as a pleasurable activity that brings husband and wife closer together and enhances feelings of intimacy. Modern couples are concerned about providing mutual sexual satisfaction for one another; sexual satisfaction is an important component of overall satisfaction with marriage (Blumstein & Schwartz, 1983; Levin & Levin, 1975); and married couples continue their sexual relationship even when they are no longer capable of reproduction (Brecher, 1984).

Unplanned pregnancies sometimes force young people to make decisions about marriage long before they are ready.

Marriage as Egalitarian

In traditional marriages, the husband was assumed to be in control (Jacob, 1988). This husband-control assumption is most clearly illustrated by examining the law. Marriage laws once gave husbands the prerogative of deciding how to spend family resources, of determining where the family would live, and of having final say in family conflicts. If a husband decided to move and his wife refused to go with him, she (but not he) could be charged with desertion. Further, the law required that women give up their maiden name and take their husbands' surname as their own. The basic principle underlying these and other laws was " . . . that a married woman had no legal or civil identity separate from her husband" (Schroeder, 1986, p. 291). At the same time, the law defined family support as a husband-only obligation, and only husbands could be required to pay alimony if the marriage broke up.

Modern marriages are more often based on the value of egalitarianism. Since the marriage is between two independent adults, neither spouse is expected to make major decisions unilaterally. In the past thirty years, many marriage laws have changed in a more egalitarian, gender-neutral direction (Jacob, 1988). But many individual couples had adopted this egalitarian approach long before marriage laws changed (Weitzman, 1977). Today, husbands can no longer unilaterally determine where the couple lives (NOW Legal Defense and Education Fund & Cherow-O'Leary, 1987), both husbands and wives can be required to pay alimony (Price & McKenry, 1988), and both husbands and wives can use whatever name they wish as long as the use of the name is not for illegal purposes (Schroeder, 1986; Douthwaite, 1979).

Interestingly enough, as men and women have grown more equal under the law, they also have tended, on average, to select first marriage partners closer to their own age. Look again at Figure 6–2. At the beginning of the twentieth century, a woman following the median pattern married a man four years older than herself. This practice might well have reinforced the husband's authority. Today, at the end of the century, women marrying in their early twenties typically marry men only two years older than themselves. And women marrying for the first time when they are 30–44 years old are actually more likely to marry a slightly younger man than an older one (Oppenheimer, 1988). In this and in many other ways, husband superiority is no longer one of the major meanings of marriage.

Marriage as Private

Marriage was once considered a moral obligation; everyone was expected to marry and to stay married for the good of society (van de

Kaa, 1987). In Puritan New England, for example, single people were heavily discouraged from living alone—a situation considered inevitably "sinful." Rather, they were placed with a family and, if they refused, taxed or imprisoned (Morgan, 1966, pp. 144–46). As recently as one generation ago, remaining single was considered an "odd" or deviant behavior. A 1957 survey asked adults, "Suppose all you knew about a man/woman was that he/she did not want to get married. What would you guess he/she was like?" More than half the respondents described the person as sick, immoral, or too selfish or neurotic to marry. Only about one in ten of the respondents gave an answer that could be considered positive (Veroff, Douvan, & Kulka, 1981, p. 147).

Single people are no longer judged so harshly (Veroff, Douvan, & Kulka, 1981), and decisions to stay single or to marry are considered private choices. People marrying today no longer do so with the sense that they are aiding the best interests of society. Rather, they wed to promote their own individual self-interests (Gove, Style, & Hughes, 1990; van de Kaa 1987; Blumstein & Schwartz, 1983). Neither do those involved in modern marriages *stay* married out of a sense of societal obligation. Personal happiness and self-fulfillment are the criteria for marrying in the first place and for remaining in a marriage (Gove, Style, & Hughes, 1990; Jacob, 1988; Blumstein & Schwartz, 1983). Marriage has changed from being a relationship controlled by society (through numerous laws and strong norms prescribing what could and could not be done) to being one increasingly controlled by the couple themselves (Schröter, 1987).

In sum, modern marriages are based on a very different set of principles than traditional marriages were. To the extent that modern couples embody the modern principles of intimacy, egalitarianism, and privacy in their marriages, they will have marriages different in nature and in day-to-day functioning than couples living in traditional marriages of the past.

MARRIAGE AND SOCIETY

Despite the fact that what goes on between husband and wife has become more private over time, modern marriage is still "everybody's business" in a number of ways. State laws define who can marry, set limits on what can be done within marriage, and specify the conditions under which marriage can be dissolved. Most couples make public announcements of their decision to marry and prepare public reports for the local newspaper of the marriage ceremony itself. Numerous businesses—flower shops, tuxedo rental businesses, and catering concerns before the marriage and real estate, appliance, and credit card companies afterwards—have a major economic interest in peoples' decision to marry. Religious organizations devote large amounts of energy to educating couples about the religious aspects of marriage, presiding over marriage ceremonies, and providing marital counseling. In all these ways and more, marriage is tied to the major social institutions of society.

Marriage and the Law

Engaged couples are generally more concerned about planning the details of their marriage ceremony than about contemplating the legal meaning of marriage. Nonetheless, marrying in the United States means entering into and accepting the conditions of *an indefinite, legally-binding contract* (Douthwaite, 1979). Lenore J. Weitzman (1977) explains that the marriage contract is different from others, "The legal marriage contract is unlike most contracts: its provisions are unwritten, the terms are unspecified, and the terms of the contract are typically unknown to the contracting parties" (p. 287).

The fact that marriage begins with an indefinite, legally-binding contract has two important consequences: first, those who violate the contract can be punished with fines or incarceration, and second, only the state—not the couple—can break the contract. If no state agrees to set the contract aside, the couple cannot become "unmarried" (that is, divorced).

In this section of the book, we will deal with two types of laws governing marriage. First, we will consider laws regarding the requirements for getting married and then discuss a few of the laws that apply to being married. Laws about the breakup of marriage will be dealt with in Chapter 14.

Laws about Getting Married

Every state sets numerous conditions and requirements that men and women must meet before being granted permission to marry. The legal right of the state to specify the conditions under which couples can marry was affirmed in the case of *Reynolds v. United States*. In this 1878 case, the U.S. Supreme Court declared that George Reynold's claim that his religion allowed him to be a bigamist could not supercede the law stating that no person could be married to more than one person (Cohen, Schwartz, & Sobul, 1968). In essence, the Supreme Court reaffirmed the right of the *state*—not religion, ethnic group, or individual—to establish standards for the marriage contract.

DUNAGIN'S PEOPLE

"AND DO YOU BOTH PROMISE TO ABIDE BY THE TERMS SET FORTH IN PARAGRAPH B OF SECTION TWO OF THIS AGREEMENT?"

Table 6–1 summarizes the minimum requirements for obtaining a marriage license in each state. Some requirements are universal while others vary. For example, every state specifies a minimum age at which persons can marry without parental permission, but three states—California, Georgia, and Mississippi—have no minimum age if parental permission has been granted. Some states require tests for sexually transmitted diseases or sickle cell anemia or infectious tuberculosis, and one (New York) will deny a license to reproductively capable couples if the test for sickle cell anemia is positive. While some states require a waiting period between the time the license is applied for and the time it is issued, others require a waiting period after the license is issued. Utah authorizes counties to provide premarital counseling to those marrying before age 19 and to the previously divorced. In addition, each state specifies who can marry whom. Marriage to a person of the same sex, an immediate family member, a grandparent, or an aunt or uncle is invalid in every state. About half the states allow first cousin marriage; the others prohibit it.

Despite the state-to-state variations in requirements, any marriage considered legal in one state or U.S. territory is generally considered

					Physical Exam &			
					Blood Test for Male and Female			
					Maximum			
					Period		Waiting Period	
	Age with		Age without		Between	Scope of	Before	After
	Parental Consent		Consent		Exam and	Medical		
State	Male	Female	Male	Female	License	Exam	License	License
Alabama*	14a	14a	18	18	—	b	—	s
Alaska	16z	16z	18	18	—	b	3 da., w	—
Arizona	16z	16z	18	18	—	—	—	—
Arkansas	17c	16c	18	18	—	—	v	—
California	aa	aa	18	18	30 da., w	bb	—	h
Colorado*	16z	16z	18	18	—	—	—	s
Connecticut . . .	16z	16z	18	18	—	bb	4 da., w	ttt
Delaware	18c	16c	18	18	—	—	—	e. s
Florida	16a, c	16a, c	18	18	—	b	3 da.	s
Georgia*	aa	aa	16	16	—	b	3 da., g	s*
Hawaii	16d	16d	18	18	—	b	—	—
Idaho*	16z	16z	18	18	—	bb	—	—
Illinois	16	16	18	18	30 da.	b. n	—	ee
Indiana	17c	17c	18	18	—	bb	72 hrs.	t
Iowa*	18z	18z	18	18	—	—	3 da., v	tt
Kansas*y	18z	18z	18	18	—	—	3 da., w	—
Kentucky	18c, z	18c, z	18	18	—	—	—	—
Louisiana	18z	18z	18	18	10 da.	b	72 hrs., w	—
Maine	16z	16z	18	18	—	—	3 da., v. w	h
Maryland	16c, f	16c, f	18	18	—	—	48 hrs., w	ff
Massachusetts . .	16d	16	18	18	60 da.	bb	3 da., v	—
Michigan	16c, d	16c	18	18	30 da.	b	3 da., w	—
Minnesota	16z	16z	18	18	—	—	5 da., w	—
Mississippi	aa	aa	17gg	15gg	30 da.	b	3 da., w	—
Missouri	15d, 18z	15d, 18z	18	18	—	—	—	—
Montana*yy	16	16	18	18	—	b	—	ff
Nebraska*yy	17	17	18	18	—	bb	—	—
Nevada	16z	16z	18	18	—	—	—	—
New Hampshire .	14j	13j	18	18	30 da.	b, l	3 da., v	h
New Jersey . . .	16z. c	16z. c	18	18	30 da.	b	72 hrs., w	s
New Mexicoy . . .	16d	16d	18	18	30 da.	b	—	—
New York	14j	14j	18	18	—	nn	—	24 hrs., w. t
North Carolina . .	16c, g	16c, g	18	18	—	m	v	—
North Dakota . .	16	16	18	18	—	—	—	t
Ohio*	18c, z	16c, z	18	18	30 da.	b	5 da.	t. w
Oklahoma*	16c	16c	18	18	30 da., w	b	—	s
Oregon	17	17	18	18	—	—	3 da., w	—
Pennsylvania* . .	16d	16d	18	18	30 da.	b	3 da., w	t
Puerto Ricoy	18c, d, z	16c, d, z	21	21	—	b	—	—
Rhode Island* . .	18d	16d	18	18	—	bb	—	—
South Carolina* .	16c	14c	18	18	—	—	1 da.	—
South Dakota . .	16c	16c	18	18	—	—	—	tt
Tennessee	16d	16d	18	18	—	—	3 da., cc	s

(continued)

Table 6-1 (continued)

State	Age with Parental Consent		Age without Consent		Physical Exam & Blood Test for Male and Female			
					Maximum Period Between Exam and License	Scope of Medical Exam	Waiting Period	
	Male	Female	Male	Female			Before License	After License
Texas[*][y]	14j, k	14j, k	18	18	—	—	—	s
Utah	14	14	18x	18x	30 da.	b	—	s
Vermont	16z	16z	18	18	30 da.	b	3 da., w	—
Virginia	16a, c	16a, c	18	18	—	b	—	t
Washington . . .	17d	17d	18	18	—	bbb	3 da.	t
West Virginia . . .	18c	18c	18	18	—	b	3 da., w	—
Wisconsin	16	16	18	18	—	b	5 da., w	s
Wyoming	16d	16d	18	18	—	bb	—	—
Dist. of Columbia[*]	16a	16a	18	18	30 da., w	b	3 da., w	—

* Indicates 1987 common-law marriage recognized; in many states, such marriages are only recognized if entered into many years before. (a) Parental consent not required if minor was previously married. (aa) No age limits. (b) Venereal diseases. (bb) Venereal diseases and Rubella (for female). In Colorado, Rubella for female under 45 and Rh type. (bbb) No medical exam required: however applicants must file affidavit showing non-affliction of contagious venereal disease. (c) Younger parties may obtain license in case of pregnancy or birth of child. (cc) Unless parties are 18 years of age. (d) Younger parties may obtain license in special circumstances. (e) Residents before expiration of 24-hour waiting period; non-residents formerly residents, before expiration of 96-hour waiting period; others 96 hours. (ee) License effective 1 day after issuance, unless court orders otherwise, valid for 60 days only. (f) If parties are under 16 years of age, proof of age and the consent of parents in person is required. If a parent is ill, an affidavit by the incapacitated parent and a physician's affidavit to that effect is required. (ff) License valid for 180 days only. (g) Unless parties are 18 years of age or more, or female is pregnant, or applicants are parents of a living child born out of wedlock. (gg) Notice to parents necessary if parties are under 21. (h) License valid for 90 days only. (j) Parental consent and/or permission of judge required. (k) Below age of consent parties need parental consent and permission of judge. (l) With each certificate issued to couples, a list of family planning agencies and services available to them is provided. (m) Mental incompetence, infectious tuberculosis, venereal diseases, and Rubella (certain counties only). (n) Venereal diseases; test for sickle cell anemia given at request of examining physician. (nn) Tests for sickle cell anemia may be required for certain applicants. Marriage prohibited unless it is established that procreation is not possible. (p) If one or both parties are below the age for marriage without parental consent (3 day waiting period). (s) License valid for 30 days only. (t) License valid for 60 days only. (tt) License valid for 20 days only. (ttt) License valid for 65 days. (v) Parties must file notice of intention to marry with local clerk. (w) Waiting period may be avoided. (x) Authorizes counties to provide premarital counseling as a requisite to issuance of license to persons under 19 and persons previously divorced. (y) Marriages by proxy are valid. (yy) Proxy marriages are valid under certain conditions. (z) Younger parties may marry with parental consent and/or permission of judge. In Connecticut, judicial approval. (zz) With consent of court.

Source: Gary N. Skoloff. Skoloff & Wolfe, Livingston, N.J.: as of June 1, 1990. Reprinted by permission of *The World Almanac & Book of Facts, 1991,* copyright Pharos Books 1990, New York, NY 10166.

legal in all others (Douthwaite, 1979). Thus, for example, when first cousins John Settinerri, age 83, and Josephine Isgro, age 73, married in New York (a state permitting first cousin marriage) and then moved to Michigan (a state forbidding first cousin marriage at the time), their marriage was still valid (Hofsess, 1988). However, some states reserve the right to annul the marriages of state residents who marry in another state specifically to avoid certain requirements and then return to their state of residence (Very, 1982, p. 197).

Common Law Marriage

In Alabama, Colorado, Georgia, Idaho, Iowa, Kansas, Montana, Ohio, Oklahoma, Pennsylvania, Rhode Island, South Carolina, Texas, and the District of Columbia, couples need not necessarily obtain a marriage license to be considered legally married. These fourteen localities recognize **common law marriages**, marriages created by certain activities on the part of the couple rather than by a state approved legal contract.

Common law marriage requires two distinct actions. First, two people meeting the minimum requirements for marriage in the state in which they reside must represent themselves to the outside world as a married couple (Douthwaite, 1979). They can do so by living together for a significant time period (varying from state to state), by having signed documents as a married couple, or by passing themselves off as a married couple in some other way. Secondly, a representative of the state—for example, a state judge—must declare the couple to be married. Without both actions, the couple is not considered to have a common law marriage.

Because common law marriages must be officially recognized as such to count as marriages, they do not violate the basic principle that only the state can designate a couple as married. The only difference between marriage-license marriages and common law marriages is in their origin: in one case, the couple petitions the state to be married; in the second, the state responds to a situation (for example, the pending birth of a child to an unwed couple) and declares the couple married.

Once recognized, a common law marriage is equivalent to any other marriage. This means that it counts as a marriage even in states that do not recognize common law marriages and that it can be terminated only by death or divorce (Douthwaite, 1979).

> **Common law marriage**
> marriage created by certain activities on the part of the couple and declared valid by the state through judicial decree rather than through a marriage license.

Laws about Being Married

There are any number of laws applying to the conduct of husbands and wives once they are married. We mentioned some of these when discussing egalitarianism in marriage; others will come up in a later chapter when marital sexuality is discussed. Here we will restrict our discussion to laws about property-holding within marriage.

In 41 states, typically referred to as "common law" or **separate property** states, each partner maintains separate ownership of all property he or she brought into the marriage as well as any property acquired after marriage (Mennell & Boykoff, 1988; Nicholas, Price, & Rubin, 1979). Separate property provisions were passed in the nineteenth century as a way of giving women some protection from unfair

> **Separate property**
> a provision whereby each marriage partner separately owns all property he or she brought into the marriage and any property he or she acquired after marriage.

Community property
a provision stating that all property accumulated during the course of the marriage belongs equally to both spouses regardless of which one actually earned it.

Antenuptial or prenuptial agreement
an agreement made prior to marriage in which both partners disclose all assets and agree on how they will be divided in case the marriage dissolves.

treatment by their husbands. Prior to that time, the husband gained ownership of anything his wife brought into the marriage and also owned whatever she acquired after the marriage (Nicholas, Price, & Rubin, 1979).

The other nine states—Arizona, California, Idaho, Louisiana, Nevada, New Mexico, Texas, Washington, and Wisconsin—are **community property** states (Mennell & Boykoff, 1988). In these states, all property accumulated during the course of the marriage belongs equally to both spouses regardless of which one actually earned it (Jacob, 1988). "Community property systems recognize . . . the contribution of both spouses to the acquisitions during marriage. The theory presumes equal contribution by husband and wife to the family wealth" (Mennell & Boykoff, 1988, p. 7).

For the purpose of dividing property after a divorce, separate property states and community property states are moving toward using similar criteria, however. In recent years, the needs, financial abilities, and contributions of each spouse have become the major criteria judges use in deciding who gets what (NOW Legal Defense and Education Fund & Cherow-O'Leary, 1987; Nicholas, Price, & Rubin, 1979).

Some couples bypass the property ownership, division, and inheritance statutes of their state by entering into an **antenuptial** (or prenuptial) **agreement** prior to marriage. In such an agreement, each partner makes full disclosure of all assets and the couple agrees on who will get what if the marriage dissolves. The Personal Application on antenuptial agreements provides further information.

Personal Application

Antenuptial Agreement

Do you have now or expect to acquire something of sentimental value—family land, a family heirloom, your first car—that you want to always own personally? Do you expect to acquire substantial assets during your marriage that you do not necessarily want to split evenly with your future spouse? Would you like to guarantee that your parents will be able to receive a portion of your assets if you die first? If you have children from a previous relationship and are marrying a person who also has children, how can you assure that both children and stepchildren will get those assets of yours you want them to have? As a prospective spouse, would you feel more comfortable knowing that the details of a possible future divorce settlement—child custody, child support arrangements, conditions for spousal support, and division of family and personal property—had been worked out ahead of time?

All of these questions point to situations in which an antenuptial agreement, drawn up with the help of lawyers prior to the marriage, might be valuable. Here is an example:

Antenuptial Agreement

1. **Introduction.** Agreement dated [*date*] between [*name*], residing at [*address*] (Prospective Wife), and [*name*], residing at [*address*] (Prospective Husband).
2. **Reason for Agreement.** The parties intend to marry and in anticipation of their marriage wish to arrange and determine the status of all property presently owned by them and that may be acquired by each of them during the marriage.
3. **Prospective Husband's Net Worth and Income.** Prospective Husband estimates his present net worth to be . . . dollars ($ . . .), the details of which are set out in Exhibit A [*omitted*] attached to and made a part of this Agreement. Prospective Husband's gross income from all sources in [*year*] was . . . dollars ($ . . .). Prospective Husband expects that his net worth and gross income will increase in future years [*or*, expects no substantial increase in his net worth or gross income in future years].
4. **Prospective Wife's Net Worth and Income.** Prospective Wife estimates her present net worth to be . . . dollars ($ . . .), the details of which are set out in Exhibit B [*omitted*] attached to and made a part of this Agreement. Prospective Wife's gross income from all sources in [*year*] was . . . dollars ($ . . .). Prospective Wife anticipates no substantial increase in her net worth or gross income in future years [*or*, expects that her net worth and gross income will increase in future years].
5. **Neither Party to Have an Interest in the Other's Property.** Each party releases any claims that he or she may acquire by reason of their forthcoming marriage in the property of the other, whether presently owned or hereafter acquired, and whether characterized as community or quasi-community property in the State or States in which the parties reside after their marriage. Each party shall be free to dispose of his or her property free of any claims of the other.
6. **Waiver of Rights in Each Other's Estate.** Each party waives any right that he or she may have to elect to take an intestate share of the other's estate in contravention of the terms of the deceased party's will. Each party will refrain from any action that might change or abrogate any provision of the other party's will.
7. **Transfer of Property by Prospective Husband to Prospective Wife.** In consideration of their marriage, Prospective Husband will transfer to Prospective Wife the real and personal property set out in Schedule C [*omitted*] attached to and made a part of this Agreement. The property shall be transferred no later than [*date*], and the transfer shall be absolute and free of any claim by Prospective Husband or any third party.
8. **Prospective Husband to Make Bequest in Favor of Prospective Wife.** If the parties marry, Prospective Husband will include a bequest to Prospective Wife in Prospective Husband's will of . . . dollars ($ . . .), free of

all taxes and charges, provided: (a) Prospective Wife survives Prospective Husband and (b) the parties are not divorced nor has the marriage been annulled at the time of Prospective Husband's death.

9. **No Warranties or Representations Other Than Those Contained in This Agreement.** Neither party has made any representation or warranty to other with regard to his or her present net worth and income and his or her future expectations other than those contained in this Agreement.

10. **Parties Represented by Counsel.** Each party is represented by counsel of his or her choice, and each has been independently informed of the legal import of this Agreement. Prospective Wife is represented by [*name*], Esq., whose offices are at [*address*], and Prospective Husband is represented by [*name*], Esq., whose offices are at [*address*].

11. **Parties to Execute Further Instruments and Take Acts to Effectuate Purpose of Agreement.** Each party, when requested by the other, shall execute such further instruments and take such further steps as may be reasonably necessary to effectuate the purpose of this Agreement.

12. **Governing Law.** This Agreement shall be governed by and interpreted in accordance with the laws of [*state*].

[*signature*]
Prospective Wife

[*signature*]
Prospective Husband

Source: Reprinted by permission of the publisher from *Basic Legal Forms with Commentary*, 2nd Edition, Warren, Gorham & Lamont, © 1991.

The Social Significance of the Wedding

The laws pertaining to marriage make clear that society has an abiding interest in marriages for their entire duration and beyond. The ties between the individual couple and the rest of society show up most clearly, however, in the marriage ceremony itself and in the events preceding it. We use the term **wedding** to refer to the legally approved, and in most cases religiously sanctioned, ceremony two individuals participate in to create a marriage. The events leading up to and including the wedding are the most public part of marriage for most couples.

Logic suggests that the prewedding rituals and the public wedding ceremonies should have become less important over the years. After all, many couples are sexually intimate before the marriage, an increasing number actually live together before they marry, overall marriage rates are down, and marriage itself has become more private. In light of all this, why bother with prewedding activities such as bachelor parties and bridal showers? And given their expense—in time, energy, and money—why have elaborate wedding ceremonies at all? Why not just

Wedding
the legally approved, and in most cases religiously sanctioned, ceremony two individuals participate in to create a marriage.

have a civil ceremony that satisfies the requirements of the state and get on with married life?

But that is not what is happening; both prewedding public rituals and public wedding ceremonies have become more widespread and more elaborate. Martin K. Whyte (1990) studied three marriage cohorts—those marrying between 1925 and 1944, those marrying between 1945 and 1964, and those marrying between 1965 and 1984. He found that the majority of each marriage cohort had been engaged, but that the later-marrying cohorts were more likely to have received an engagement ring, a highly visible symbol of impending marriage. The number and diversity of prewedding parties have also grown over time. All-male bachelor parties and all-female bridal showers have become even more common than in the past (Whyte, 1990). In addition, "bachelorette" parties for the bride, "groomal" showers for the groom, and "couple" showers for both have also been added to the prewedding party agenda (Berardo & Vera, 1981).

As for the marriage ceremonies themselves, Whyte (1990) found that each marriage cohort he studied was more likely than the preceding one to have participated in a traditional, elaborate wedding followed by a reception for a large number of people. A minister, priest, rabbi or other religious official had presided over 80 percent of the weddings in each marriage cohort, but the later cohorts were more likely to have had a church or synagogue wedding. In other words, contrary to what logic might suggest, weddings have become more prominent and more public.

But why? Whyte (1990) cites five reasons, all of which highlight the social significance of the wedding ceremony. First, the ceremony is an announcement. The wedding, along with its pictures and writeup in the local newspaper, announces to the couple's social world they are no longer two single individuals—they are now one social unit. The announcement also indicates that neither is a legitimate dating partner. For the parents of the couple, the wedding ceremony announces to the world that their children are now married.

Second, in an age of premarital sexuality and cohabitation, the "announcement" aspect of the wedding is probably *more* important now than ever before because it distinguishes the new relationship of the couple from their old one. A simple ceremony presided over by a justice of the peace provides no definitive break between the premarriage "marriage-like" state and the beginning of the actual marriage. An elaborate, public wedding is a more dramatic way of announcing that the relationship of the couple has changed.

Third, the elaborate wedding rituals also represent a way for older generations to help "fund" younger ones. An invitation to the wedding reception is, at least in part, a request for a gift. The gift is often a resource useful in furnishing a new home. Since newly married couples

The wedding ceremony of this Algonquin couple provides an opportunity for friends and relatives to celebrate a new marriage and to welcome the couple into married life.

seldom live with parents following the wedding, the gift-giving rituals provide a way for the older generation to help the couple establish and furnish an independent household.

Fourth, wedding rituals also provide family, friends, and community a chance to give their approval to the new marital union. By participating in the ceremonies, by congratulating the couple, and by giving gifts, the community members provide public recognition and approval of the couple's new status.

Finally, elaborate marriage rituals provide families with a legitimate opportunity to engage in status competition. By having many bridesmaids and groomsmen, buying very expensive flower arrangements, inviting many people to the wedding reception, and "giving their daughter (or son) a wedding the community will not soon forget," families demonstrate their own economic success. Anthropologists describe similar competitions among tribal leaders who try to gain status by giving the biggest feast and by giving away the most presents. In a sense, marriage rituals in the United States are an equivalent social phenomena—an attempt to gain status by spending lots of money on ceremonial activities. Figure 6–5 gives an estimate of just how much money is involved.

For some couples, the wedding ceremony is not only (or perhaps even primarily) a social event and a way to spend money and receive gifts. It is, rather, a way of solemnizing their union before God. The

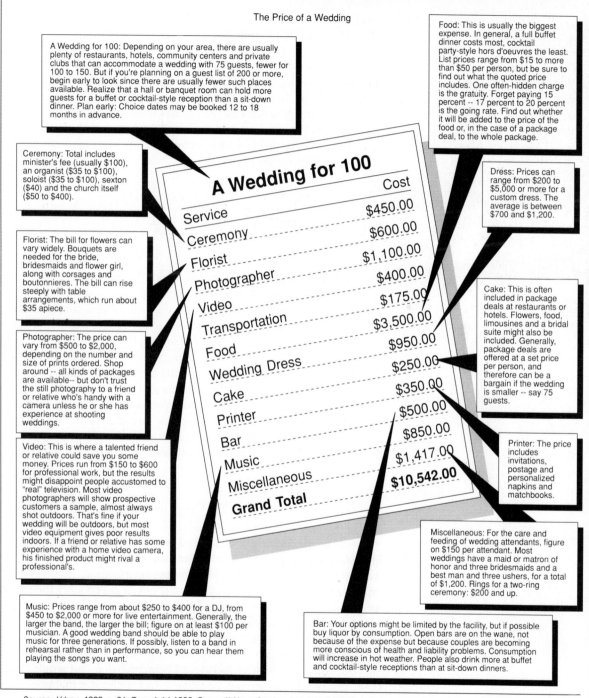

Figure 6–5: The Price of a Wedding

The Price of a Wedding

A Wedding for 100: Depending on your area, there are usually plenty of restaurants, hotels, community centers and private clubs that can accommodate a wedding with 75 guests, fewer for 100 to 150. But if you're planning on a guest list of 200 or more, begin early to look since there are usually fewer such places available. Realize that a hall or banquet room can hold more guests for a buffet or cocktail-style reception than a sit-down dinner. Plan early: Choice dates may be booked 12 to 18 months in advance.

Food: This is usually the biggest expense. In general, a full buffet dinner costs most, cocktail party-style hors d'oeuvres the least. List prices range from $15 to more than $50 per person, but be sure to find out what the quoted price includes. One often-hidden charge is the gratuity. Forget paying 15 percent -- 17 percent to 20 percent is the going rate. Find out whether it will be added to the price of the food or, in the case of a package deal, to the whole package.

Ceremony: Total includes minister's fee (usually $100), an organist ($35 to $100), soloist ($35 to $100), sexton ($40) and the church itself ($50 to $400).

Dress: Prices can range from $200 to $5,000 or more for a custom dress. The average is between $700 and $1,200.

Florist: The bill for flowers can vary widely. Bouquets are needed for the bride, bridesmaids and flower girl, along with corsages and boutonnieres. The bill can rise steeply with table arrangements, which run about $35 apiece.

Photographer: The price can vary from $500 to $2,000, depending on the number and size of prints ordered. Shop around -- all kinds of packages are available-- but don't trust the still photography to a friend or relative who's handy with a camera unless he or she has experience at shooting weddings.

Cake: This is often included in package deals at restaurants or hotels. Flowers, food, limousines and a bridal suite might also be included. Generally, package deals are offered at a set price per person, and therefore can be a bargain if the wedding is smaller -- say 75 guests.

Video: This is where a talented friend or relative could save you some money. Prices run from $150 to $600 for professional work, but the results might disappoint people accustomed to "real" television. Most video photographers will show prospective customers a sample, almost always shot outdoors. That's fine if your wedding will be outdoors, but most video equipment gives poor results indoors. If a friend or relative has some experience with a home video camera, his finished product might rival a professional's.

Printer: The price includes invitations, postage and personalized napkins and matchbooks.

A Wedding for 100	Cost
Service	$450.00
Ceremony	$600.00
Florist	$1,100.00
Photographer	$400.00
Video	$175.00
Transportation	$3,500.00
Food	$950.00
Wedding Dress	$250.00
Cake	$350.00
Printer	$500.00
Bar	$850.00
Music	$1,417.00
Miscellaneous	$10,542.00
Grand Total	

Miscellaneous: For the care and feeding of wedding attendants, figure on $150 per attendant. Most weddings have a maid or matron of honor and three bridesmaids and a best man and three ushers, for a total of $1,200. Rings for a two-ring ceremony: $200 and up.

Music: Prices range from about $250 to $400 for a DJ, from $450 to $2,000 or more for live entertainment. Generally, the larger the band, the larger the bill; figure on at least $100 per musician. A good wedding band should be able to play music for three generations. If possibly, listen to a band in rehearsal rather than in performance, so you can hear them playing the songs you want.

Bar: Your options might be limited by the facility, but if possible buy liquor by consumption. Open bars are on the wane, not because of the expense but because couples are becoming more conscious of health and liability problems. Consumption will increase in hot weather. People also drink more at buffet and cocktail-style receptions than at sit-down dinners.

minister (or other religious official) presiding at a wedding has a double function. He or she acts first as a representative of the state, as indicated by the phrase, "And now by the power vested in me by the state of _____, I pronounce you husband and wife." If the minister is not specifically empowered by the state to perform the wedding, the marriage is not legal. At the same time, the religious official presiding over a wedding is the representative of a particular religion. In this position, the religious official can remind the marrying couple that they are married "in the eyes of God" and, either during or before the ceremony, inform them of their obligations as married members of a particular religious tradition.

CHOOSING MARRIAGE

Being married is one adult style of life. Today, especially, it is one choice among many others: adults can choose to remain single and live alone or with family members, become half of a homosexual couple, cohabit, or join a religious or other communally living group. Most adults continue to choose marriage, at least for some part of their adulthood. We have already dealt somewhat with *how* people choose a marriage partner in Chapter 4 and with some of the advantages of marriage over cohabitation in Chapter 5. Much of the rest of the text deals with the consequences—both beneficial and problematic—of choosing marriage. This section is, then, in part review and in part preview. We will look first at the marriage choice from the push-pull perspective and then consider the mental and physical health consequences of marriage.

Pushes and Pulls toward Marriage

Why do people marry? When asked why *they* married, most already married couples in the United States are apt to answer "because we were in love" (Trost, 1986). While this answer encapsulates the individualistic, intimate nature of modern marriage, it is probably too simple an answer.

Sociologist Peter Stein (1976) approached the question of why people marry by asking never-married people what future circumstances might lead them to marry. He sorted their varied responses into two categories—attractive features of being married that would "pull" them towards marriage and negative features about remaining single that would "push" them out of singlehood and into marriage. If you are currently single, you might try to develop such a list before looking at Table 6–2. What circumstances in your life might make marriage a much more attractive option to you than it is now? What negative changes could occur in your single status that might push you into marriage?

Table 6–2 summarizes Stein's (1976) findings. Among the attractions that single people said might pull them into marriage were love, the desire for a family, parental and societal approval, physical attraction, the legitimization of sex, and social policies favoring married people. Stein's respondents felt that pressure from parents to marry, the desire to leave home, loneliness and isolation, and fear of independence were negative characteristics of remaining single that might push them into marriage.

Stein (1976) suggested that the importance of these factors varies with age, relationship to parents, relationship with friends, and the perception that there is a legitimate choice between marriage and singlehood. For example, the desire for children might be an insignificant factor at age 20 but a very important one at age 30 for some individuals.

Table 6–2 Pushes and Pulls toward Marriage

Pushes	Pulls
(Negatives in Present Situations)	(Attractions in Potential Situations)
Pressure from parents	Approval of parents
Desire to leave home	Desire for children and own family
Fear of independence	Example of peers
Loneliness and isolation	Romanticization of marriage
No knowledge or perception of alternatives	Physical attraction
Cultural and social discrimination against singles	Love, emotional attachment
	Security, social status, social prestige
	Legitimation of sexual experiences
	Socialization
	Job availability, wage structure, and promotions
	Social policies favoring the married and the responses of social institutions

Source: Stein, 1976, p. 65 © Peter J. Stein.

Marriage and Health

In terms of physical and mental health, most people benefit from marriage. Research on the relationship between marital status and health has consistently found that married people are healthier in virtually every way than those who are not married (Gove, Style, & Hughes, 1990). We will deal first with physical health, then with mental health, and finally with explaining the good health-marriage connection.

Physical Health

The connection between good health and marriage is clearest for physical health. A massive study of health and mortality done in the United States during the 1970s found that married people are the healthiest, followed in descending order by single people, the widowed, and, finally,

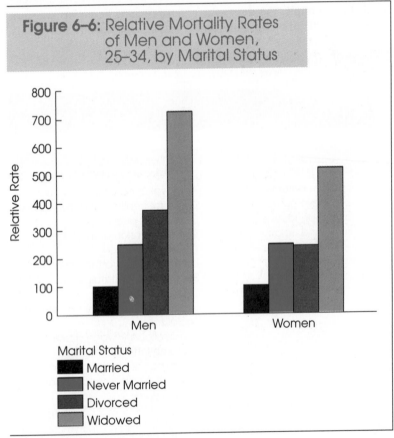

Figure 6–6: Relative Mortality Rates of Men and Women, 25–34, by Marital Status

Marital Status
- Married
- Never Married
- Divorced
- Widowed

Being married is associated with good health and continued survival. This figure standardizes the mortality rate of married men and women, aged 25–34, at 100 and compares the mortality rates of never married, divorced, and widowed. Thus, for example, widowed men, aged 25–34, have a relative mortality rate of over 700, meaning that they are more than 7 times as likely to die as married men of the same age.

Source: Gove, Style, & Hughes, 1990, p. 8.

the divorced and separated (Verbrugge, 1979). Mortality rates show a similar pattern.

Figure 6–6, comparing the mortality rates of young married adults to those of young, unmarried people, clearly shows the difference marriage can make in survival. In the 25–34 year old age group, single men have mortality rates *twice* as high, divorced men have rates over *three* times as high, and widowed men have rates over *seven* times as high as married men. A similar pattern can be seen for women: single and divorced women have mortality rates over *twice* as high and widowed women have rates over *five* times as high as married women. Figure 6–6 does not include data on older people but the pattern is much the same, though somewhat less strong, for them: *marriage helps people of all ages stay alive* (Gove, Style, & Hughes, 1990).

Marriage can even help people survive deadly diseases. A study of the long-term survival from breast cancer found that women who were married at the time of their diagnosis had a 10 year survival rate over 33 percent higher than women who were widowed at the time of the diagnosis (Neale, Tilley, & Vernon, 1986). And a report published in the *Journal of the American Medical Association* concluded that the beneficial effects of marriage on cancer survival rates applied to many other types of cancer as well: "The percent of persons surviving at least five years is greater for married than unmarried in almost every category of age, gender, and stage (of the cancer's development)" (Goodwin *et al.*, 1987, p. 3128).

Mental Health

Whether or not marriage is also associated with good mental health is a subject of some controversy. The controversy stems, in part, from sociologist Jessie Bernard's 1972 book, *The Future of Marriage*. In the book, Bernard collected the results of studies done on marital status and mental health between the late 1930s and 1970. Bernard concluded on the basis of these studies that marriage enhanced the mental health of men but had a slight but consistently negative effect on women's mental health. In comparing married men to never-married and widowed men, Bernard (1972) wrote:

> . . . the husbands' marriage, whether they like it or not (and they do) is awfully good for them. . . . their mental health is far better, fewer show serious symptoms of psychological distress, and fewer of them suffer mental health impairments. (pp. 17–18)

Bernard argued that married women, particularly those who were full-time housewives after marriage, had to make many more adjustments in their daily lives after marriage than married men did; in adapting to marriage, wives experienced a kind of "shock" which resulted in impaired mental health. She concluded:

> It is not necessarily the magnitude of the statistical differences between the mental health of married and single women or between married men and married women that is so convincing; it is, rather the consistency of the differences. No one difference or even set of differences by itself would be definitive; but the cumulative effect of so many is. The poor mental health of wives is like a low-grade infection that shows itself in a number of scattered symptoms, no one of which is critical enough to cause an acute episode. (1972 p. 37)

In sum, Bernard argued that marriage was very good for men and, if not actually bad for women, was not as good for women as it was for men.

Was she right? Do such findings hold for marriages of the 1970s, 1980s, and 1990s? Subsequent tests of Bernard's hypothesis have met with mixed results. Using national data for white respondents and writing at about the same time as Bernard, Glenn (1975) found that married men and women were comparable in marital satisfaction and that marriage contributed to higher personal happiness for women than for men. These results led him to reject Bernard's hypothesis.

A second and more recent test had more equivocal results. Lowe and Smith (1987) found that married women have better mental well-being than married men—a finding at odds with Bernard's. At the same time, these researchers noted that the *difference* between the mental well-being of married men and the mental well-being of nonmarried men was far greater than the difference between the corresponding categories for women. In other words, marriage contributed far more to the mental well-being of men than to that of women—a conclusion similar to Bernard's.

In fact, the controversy over Bernard's findings may not be so much of a controversy after all. Bernard (1972) specified that her findings were tied to a particular type of marriage—one in which wives became housewives upon marrying while husbands continued to work. Women have more options today, both before and during marriage (Schröter, 1987), and these increased options might well explain contrasting findings about the mental health of married women.

Explaining the Healthy Effects of Marriage

What is it about marriage that "protects" married men and women from physical and mental problems? Researchers offer two explanations: 1. social selection and 2. the nature of the marital relationship itself (Gove, Style, & Hughes, 1990). The **social selection** explanation suggests that married people were mentally and physically healthy before marriage and that this good health, in fact, added to their attractiveness as marriage partners. Proponents of this explanation argue that those with poor emotional or physical health have much more difficulty getting or staying married. Thus, the reason married people are healthier has nothing to do with marriage but rather with the types of people who do or do not get married.

Researchers who have carefully evaluated the social selection explanation conclude that it is probably invalid (Gove, Style, & Hughes, 1990). When married and single people with *similar* characteristics are compared, married people are healthier and live longer than nonmarried people. Unmarried people involved in strong intimate (including cohabitation) relationships who do not marry continue to have poorer health than the married (Gove, Style, & Hughes, 1990). Based on these findings, Gove, Style, and Hughes (1990) argue that the marital relationship explanation provides a more adequate explanation of good health among the married.

The **marital relationship** explanation states that something about the marital relationship itself enhances the physical and mental health of married people. But what? The answer has to do with both the nature of modern marriage and the nature of modern life. According to Gove, Style, and Hughes (1990), modern society is complex and is characterized by large "ends-oriented" organizations. In such organizations, individuals have a difficult time developing a sense of who they are—a "self-image." They increasingly turn to their marriage and family for the one-on-one personal interaction necessary to develop and maintain a consistent, stable self-identity. Marriage also provides privacy and security—probably more security than can be found in nonmarital, intimate relationships.

Married people recognize these characteristics of marriage. When asked to enumerate the advantages of being married, married men and women come up with this list: " . . . (a) sharing problems, (b) sharing pleasures, (c) having someone who cares about you and (d) having someone to care about" (Gove, Style, & Hughes, 1990, p. 14). The intimacy, privacy, and security of modern marriage, according to the research, play an important part in maintaining the physical and mental health of married men and women.

Not all marriages are intimate, private, and secure, however. Do people in nonintimate, insecure, or otherwise unhappy marriages have better health than the nonmarried? Quite the contrary: the well-being of unhappily married people is particularly low (Gove, Style, & Hughes, 1990). Individuals in such unhappy marriages are especially vulnerable to high levels of both mental and physical distress. In short, while being

Social selection
an explanation of the health benefits of marriage suggesting that people who eventually marry are mentally and physically healthier than those who do not marry.

only Crazies don't get married [handwritten]

Marital relationship
an explanation of the health benefits of marriage that states that the intimate, secure nature of marriage makes married people healthier.

Marriage makes all better people [handwritten]

in a secure, intimate marriage can enhance one's mental and physical health, being in an insecure, nonintimate marriage can contribute to poor mental and physical health.

Alternative Choice

Ambivalents
young people who are voluntarily and temporarily single.

Wishfuls
young people who are involuntarily, temporarily single and actively seeking a mate.

Resolved
people, mostly older, who are voluntarily single and expect to stay that way.

Regretfuls
people, mostly older, who are involuntarily single and expect to stay that way.

Staying Single

Most people in the United States choose to be married for at least part of their adulthood. At the same time, the relatively late age at first marriage, the high divorce rate, and the higher life expectancy for women than for men all mean that few people in the United States today spend their entire adulthood as married people. The term "single," used in its broadest sense, includes many types of people. The 24-year-old who expects to marry within a few years, the 54-year-old who has never married and never intends to, the 30-year-old divorced person who is trying to decide whether to remarry or remain single, and the 75-year-old who spent fifty years in marriage and is now widowed are all "single." In this alternative choice section, we focus on never-married singles, especially on those who are older, although some of our comments apply to formerly married singles as well.

Table 6–3, developed by Stein (1981), provides one way of categorizing single people. His four categories are based on whether single status is voluntary or involuntary, and on whether singleness is permanent (stable) or temporary. Psychologist Arthur Shostak (1987) refined the typology somewhat by attaching labels to each of Stein's categories. Shostak (1987) refers to those in the "voluntary, temporary" category as **ambivalents**. The ambivalents are mostly young people postponing marriage; many of them are in cohabitation or dating relationships. Those in the "involuntary, temporary" or **wishful** category also tend to be young. Desirous of marriage, they are actively seeking mates. Shostak (1987) refers to the "voluntary, stable" singles as **resolved**, and includes those in religious orders, single parents who desire to remain single, confirmed homosexuals, and older heterosexual singles who have come to prefer the single way of life. Finally, people in the "involuntary, stable" category or **regretfuls** tend to be older but regard their singleness as a "life sentence" rather than as a choice they consciously made (Shostak, 1987, p. 357).

It is impossible to say how many singles fit into each category—for one thing, people move between the categories as their circumstances change. However, the majority of never-married singles are young and are probably best categorized in the ambivalent or wishful

Table 6–3 Typology of Singlehood		
	Voluntary	Involuntary
Temporary	Never-married and formerly married who are postponing marriage by not currently seeking mates, but who are not opposed to the idea of marriage	Those who have been actively seeking mates for shorter or longer periods of time, but have not yet found mates Those who were not interested in marriage or remarriage for some period of time but are now actively seeking mates
Stable	Those choosing to be single (never-marrieds and formerly marrieds) Those who for various reasons oppose the idea of marriage Religionaries	Never-marrieds and formerly marrieds who wanted to marry or remarry, have not found a mate and have more or less accepted being single as a probable life state

Source: Stein, 1981, p. 11. Copyright (c) 1981. From *Single Life: Unmarried Adults in Social Context*. By Peter J. Stein. Reprinted with permission of St. Martin's Press, Inc.

categories. Less than 10 percent of high school and college students say that they expect to remain single for life (Long, 1983; Thornton & Freedman, 1982). In fact, throughout the twentieth century, the proportion of people remaining single into their mid-forties has hovered somewhere between 5 and 10 percent overall. As you can ascertain from looking back at Figure 6–4, the proportion has been somewhat lower for white women than for white men, lower for some cohorts than for others, and generally higher (and subject to more fluctuation) for blacks than for whites.

Which people are most likely to reach middle age without marrying? Women with high levels of education, income, occupational prestige, and intelligence are less likely to marry than are other women (Leppel, 1987; Spreitzer & Riley, 1974). A study of women who had received graduate degrees from a large midwestern university between 1964 and 1974 found that more than one in four had never been married—a rate *five times* that for other women (Houseknecht, Vaughan, & Statham, 1987). There is no such relationship between education and singleness for men. Highly educated men and men with less education have about the same level of singleness—about eight percent (Houseknecht, Vaughan, & Statham, 1987). Males with high incomes are more likely to marry than other males; in fact, the higher the income, the higher the probability a male will marry.

Thus, women who reach middle age without marrying tend to be better educated, have higher incomes, and hold higher prestige jobs than married women of the same age, but the same cannot be said of middle-aged, never-married men. There are a number of factors at work here. On the one hand, highly educated women with good incomes have more options than other women—they are less likely to be "pushed" into marriage by economic need (Bennett, Bloom, & Craig, 1989) or because marriage is the only way they can afford to have a child. Some of these women make a conscious choice not to marry so that they can dedicate more time and energy to their careers (Loewenstein *et al.*, 1981). Highly educated, well-paid women can also afford to be "pickier" in their choice of a mate; one woman explained her singleness this way: "I just couldn't find the right person, with similar high standards and values, and was not willing to settle for second-best" (Loewenstein *et al.*, 1981, p. 1134).

On the other hand, the cultural tradition of male dominance in marriage may encourage males to accept (and perhaps even to seek out) women with lower levels of income, education, and occupational status than they themselves have as marriage partners. The same tradition means that women—both black and white—want to marry men they consider at least their equals (if not their superiors) in these attributes (Lichter, LeClere, & McLaughlin, 1991; Bennett, Bloom, & Craig, 1989; Tucker & Taylor, 1989; Higginbotham, 1981). As long as these cultural patterns prevail, economically successful men will have a large pool of women from which to choose, *increasing* their chances of marriage, and economically successful women will face a relative shortage of acceptable partners, *decreasing* the probability they will marry.

These economic factors alone do not determine who will stay single and who will marry. Family influence and individual circumstances can also be important. Men who marry late in life or not at all report that they were under less family pressure to date and marry than their friends were (Darling, 1981). In one study, never-married women noted that some significant family member had, at some point, indicated to them that staying single was "permissible" (Peterson, 1982). During the years when their contemporaries were marrying, never-marrying men and women were often heavily involved in family obligations to their parents or to younger siblings, enmeshed in their careers, or active in meaningful same-sex friendship groups (Peterson, 1982; Darling, 1981). Some never-marrying people experienced "bad luck" in relationships that might otherwise have ended in marriage—their "true love" died, deserted them, or was deemed unacceptable by their family (Peterson, 1982; Loewenstein *et al.*, 1981).

Once "out-of-sync" with their marrying contemporaries, many nonmarrying men and women (the "resolved" in the typology) come to be affected by the "pulls" of the single way of life listed in Table 6–4—freedom and independence, privacy, opportunities to pursue personal growth and career goals—and choose it permanently (Peterson, 1982; Loewenstein *et al.*, 1981). They recognize that remaining single can mean " . . . no mate or children, financial problems, lack of companionship or sexual partner, sole care of family members, making decisions alone, maintenance problems, attitudes of society, and loneliness" (Loewenstein *et al.*, 1981, p. 1133). However, most are able to build up a network of friends, fellow workers, or family members, or establish a nonmarital intimate partner relationship to deal with these disadvantages (Cockrum & White, 1985; Loewenstein *et al.*, 1981). All in all, only 13 percent of the never-married report that they are unhappy about their lives (Shostak, 1987). While this rate of dissatisfaction is slightly higher than among the married, it is lower than among widowed, separated, and divorced people (Shostak, 1987).

Table 6–4 Pushes and Pulls toward Singlehood

Pushes	Pulls
(To Leave Permanent Relationships)	(To Remain Single or Return to Singlehood)
Lack of friends, isolation, loneliness	Career opportunities and development
Restricted availability of new experiences	Availability of sexual experiences
Suffocating one-to-one relationship, feeling trapped	Exciting life style, variety of experiences, freedom to change
Obstacles to self-development	Psychological and social autonomy, self-sufficiency
Boredom, unhappiness, and anger	Support structures: sustaining friendships, women's and men's groups, political groups, therapeutic groups, collegial groups
Poor communication with mate	
Sexual frustration	

Source: Stein, 1976, p. 65 © Peter J. Stein.

Summary

Although there have been some fluctuations in the marriage rate and in the median age at first marriage during the twentieth century, marriage remains a prevalent and popular choice. Over 90 percent of the people in the United States are married for some part of their adulthood. Whites and Hispanics are more likely to marry than blacks, especially in recent cohorts. Black women currently have the lowest marriage rates. Economic opportunities for young adults and the ratio between men and women both help to explain historical and racial differences in the prevalence of marriage.

Over time, idealized conceptions of marriage have come to emphasize intimacy, egalitarianism, and privacy over economic survival, patriarchy, and public influence. These changed conceptions are reflected in the law, in the way in which modern couples think about sexuality, and in peoples' reasons for marrying.

Marriage continues to be influenced by society, however. Marrying requires state approval and each state has its own rules about requirements for marriage. A few states allow for common law marriages, but even these must be officially recognized to be valid. State law also determines the ownership of property within marriage—some states are separate property states and others are community property states.

The wedding ceremony is a public announcement of a couple's transition to "married couple." Weddings, and the rituals preceding them, provide engaged couples with public recognition and approval, help them start a household, and allow their families to gain social status. Weddings also remind couples of their religious ties and traditions. Far from becoming less important, such elaborate and costly rituals accompany more weddings than ever before.

Individuals marry both to escape the negative consequences of remaining single—loneliness, undesired independence, and parental pressure—and because they are attracted to the benefits of marriage—emotional attachment, chance to have legitimate sex and children, and social, economic, and political advantages. An often unforeseen side benefit of marriage is the advantage marriage carries in terms of health. Married people are healthier, have better survival rates from deadly diseases like cancer, and live longer than the unmarried. Married people, particularly husbands, also tend to have better mental health and fewer symptoms of psychological distress. The marriage advantage, however, is lost if the marriage is nonintimate, insecure, and unhappy.

Staying single is an increasingly acceptable lifestyle. The majority of the never-married singles are ambivalents—young people postponing marriage—or wishfuls—young people actively seeking a mate. About 10 percent of the population remains single into middle age or beyond. A few of the older never-married regret their status, but most appear to be resolved to their single status and have built satisfying lives around work, friends, family, or intimate partners.

CHAPTER 7

THE TASKS OF MARRIAGE: ADJUSTMENT FOR MARITAL SUCCESS

When two people marry or establish a long-term living together arrangement, many potentially controversial day-to-day issues emerge. Here are some that will be discussed in the next several chapters. Answer each question first from your point of view, and then have the person to whom you are emotionally closest answer the same question. Are there substantial differences between the two sets of answers? If so, how might you reach a compromise position?

1. Are you a "morning person" (that is, are you "raring to go" in the morning) or a "night person" (do you think mornings are for sleeping and that evenings are for getting things done)?

2. Do you feel comfortable "opening up" about feelings or about things that worry you, or do you prefer keeping things to yourself?

3. How do you feel about expressing affection in public places? Should partners kiss, hold hands, and hug each other in front of others or should such signs of affection be shown only when the two are alone? Should partners act differently in public after marriage than before marriage?

4. How and with whom should leisure time be spent? Should partners spend their leisure time together or with friends of both partners? Should each spend time separately, each with his or her own circle of friends, or alone?

5. Should partners keep their money separate and each accept responsibility for paying half the bills? Or should they combine their earnings into a joint account and pay the bills (and perhaps an allowance for each) from the joint account? Who should make decisions about spending money on the "big ticket items"—cars, stereos, furniture, vacations, and so forth?

6. Should partners have sexual intercourse only with one another? What if the two have very different sex drives? Or what if one suffers an injury that prevents sexual intercourse? Is there any situation in which it is acceptable for married people to have sexual relationships outside of marriage?

7. Should both partners have the right to initiate sex? Do they both have the right to refuse? If one refuses, does he or she have to explain why?

8. Do you want children? If you do, how many?

9. Read the introductory section about newlyweds Charles and Raney. Who do you think is right? Is Charles right to insist that Raney's family visit only when they (Charles and Raney) are home? Is Raney right to grant her family unrestricted access to the house? Is it right for Raney to expect that they eat dinner every Sunday with her family even though Charles does not enjoy it? Should Charles show his boredom so openly?

Charles and Raney, characters in Clyde Edgerton's novel *Raney*, have been married six weeks when the incident described in the following passage occurs. The two have just finished eating Sunday dinner with Raney's family. During the meal, Raney's mother had mentioned stopping by their house on the previous day. Charles and Raney had not been home, but Raney's mother and aunts had entered the unlocked house to use the phone and get something to drink. Charles was irritated to learn about this "visit"; Raney, who narrates the story, thought nothing of it. Here is what happened after the meal:

> We finished eating and set in the den and talked for a while and the subject didn't come up again. Charles always gets fidgety within thirty minutes of when we finish eating. He has no appreciation for just setting and talking. And I don't mean going on and on about politics or something like that; I mean just talking—talking about normal things. So since he gets fidgity, we usually cut our Sunday visits short. "Well, I guess we better get on back," I say, while Charles sits over there looking like he's bored to death. I know Mama notices.
>
> Before we're out of the driveway, Charles says, "Raney, I think you ought to tell your mama and Aunt Naomi and Aunt Flossie to stay out of our house unless somebody's home."
>
> To stay out of *my* own house.
>
> He couldn't even wait until we were out of the driveway. And all the car windows rolled down.
>
> When we got on down the road, out of hearing distance, I said, "Charles, you don't love Mama and never did."
>
> He pulls the car over beside the PEACHES FOR SALE sign across from Parker's pond. And stares at me.
>
> The whole thing has tore me up. "Charles," I said, and I had to start crying, "you don't have to hide your life from Mama and them. Or me. You didn't have to get all upset today. You could understand if you wanted to. You didn't have to get upset when I opened that oil bill addressed to you, either. There ain't going to be nothing in there but a oil bill, for heaven's sake. Why anyone would want to hide a oil bill I cannot understand."
>
> He starts hollering at me. The first time in my life anybody has set in a car and hollered at me. His blood vessels stood all out. I couldn't control myself. It was awful. If you've ever been hollered at, while you are crying, by the one person you love best in the world, you know what I mean. This was a part of Charles I had never seen. (Edgerton, 1985, pp. 24–25).

Charles and Raney are in the process of learning new, not always pleasant, things about one another. As they live together day-to-day, they discover areas of disagreement that never arose during their dating days: what are proper subjects of conversation, how open should their home be to relatives, what is private and want is not, and how long should one stay at the in-laws' home after Sunday dinner. Like other newlyweds, Charles and Raney find that marriage involves a whole series of adjustments, both to one another and to marriage itself.

All newly married husbands and wives confront many challenges as they try to build a successful marriage. And the challenges do not end once the conflicts of early marriage are resolved. A strong, successful marriage requires that husband and wife make a never ending series of adjustments as they encounter new situations or old ones in new forms. This constant necessity to adjust means that every successful marriage is a process rather than a product—it is always being built, but never finished.

Chapter 7 introduces the topic of adjustment in marriage. First, we discuss the types of adjustment newly married couples face, describe why adjustment is sometimes difficult, and introduce the concept of family culture. Then we focus on strong marriages and strong families, distinguishing between marital quality and marital success and reviewing the research on how high-quality marriages and strong families are different from others. In the second half of the chapter, we begin a multi-chapter discussion about adjustment to particular "tasks" of marriage by discussing marital sexual adjustment. This sexual adjustment section will assess the importance of sex in achieving marital satisfaction, discuss why sexual adjustment is sometimes difficult, describe typical patterns of marital sex, and deal with the issue of extramarital sex. The next three chapters of the text will continue our discussion of adjustment to the tasks of marriage by describing the adjustment challenges involved in marital communication, dividing marital work, and managing money.

MARITAL ADJUSTMENT

Marital adjustment
the complex set of
compromises and
changes each
partner makes to
accommodate the
other and to fulfill
the obligations of
marriage.

Marital adjustment is an overall term referring to the complex set of compromises and changes each partner makes to accommodate the other and to fulfill the obligations of marriage. Early within marriage, each spouse confronts three types of adjustment: psychological adjustment to a new interdependent way of living, pragmatic adjustment to a unique partner with his or her own way of doing things, and social adjustment to the social status of "married person."

Both new spouses must *personally* and *psychologically* adjust to the interdependent style of life that marriage implies. Marriage affects virtually every aspect of their lives—the way they do their jobs, the hours they keep, where they spend vacations, their recreational activities, and even how and when they sleep. No longer can each partner think of herself or himself as an independent actor: an "I" who can do whatever "I" want whenever "I" want. Now each is part of a team, one-half of a "we," whose behavior will affect the life of the spouse. Instead of thinking "How will this behavior affect *me*?" or "Do *I* really want to tell my boss to take this job and shove it?" or "Do *I* want to go bar-hopping all night long?", the newly married person asks, "How will this behavior affect *us*?" or "Do *we* want me to tell my boss to take this job and shove it?" or "Do *we* want to go bar-hopping all night long?"

Each person in a marriage is not only married; he or she is also married to a particular other person with idiosyncratic thoughts, feelings, and ways of doing things. Both spouses face the challenge of adjusting to the specific quirks, habits, and idiosyncrasies of the other. Although the habits at issue are often trivial, they may be tremendously important to those involved. A simple term, "tremendous trifles," beautifully captures the essence of the situation. Tremendous trifles are rel-

The Tasks
of Marriage:
Adjustment for
Marital Success

7

atively minor characteristics or habits of one spouse that drive the other spouse crazy (Rice, 1983). Consider, for example, the issue of how quickly a meal should be eaten. Ultimately, the speed with which either spouse eats is just not that important. But the spouse who eats faster is often forced to sit for what seems like an eternity quietly watching his or her spouse finish a meal. Or consider differences in the length of time it takes to shower, or whether drinking glasses go open end up or open end down in the cupboard, or whether one sleeps with the windows open or closed, or whether the toilet seat is left up or down. Early marriage is filled with discovering, arguing about, and sometimes compromising on such idiosyncratic partner differences.

The first two types of adjustment—to an interdependent style of life and to a particular other person—are involved, at least to some extent, in other types of relationships as well. Cohabiting partners or roommates, for example, must adjust in both ways. But the final type of adjustment—adjusting to the new social status of husband or wife— is limited to marriage. The societal expectations associated with marriage are different and much more complex than those associated with being single. The process of marrying and becoming a husband or wife carries with it legal obligations of emotional and financial support and promises of commitment to the spouse ("to love, honor, and cherish" him or her, while "forsaking all others"). Marriage means not only taking on the role of husband or wife but also the role of daughter-in-law or son-in-law and sister-in-law or brother-in-law, with all the informal and ambiguous obligations these roles imply.

Building a Family Culture

How is marital adjustment achieved? How do newly married couples learn to live interdependently, tolerate each other's habits, and fulfill the societal expectations associated with marriage? In effect, they adjust by creating their own family culture. **Family culture** is the set of rules, values, behavior patterns, and language negotiated by a married couple

Family culture
a set of rules, values, behavior patterns, and language negotiated by a married couple that sets their family apart from others.

that sets their family apart from others. Family culture includes agreements about serious matters (for example, "Extra-marital sex is forbidden") but also understandings about relatively trivial things (for example, "Family members can have the dinner of their choice on their birthday"). The clarification of important values is part of building a family culture (for example, "Joint decision-making within the family is good" or, alternatively, "The husband should make all the important decisions") but so is the development of a family language (for example, nicknames for one another, shorthand terms for things that are said again and again, what to call body parts and bodily functions, and so forth).

Couples draw upon what they have learned from their parents and relatives, the mass media, and friends in making choices about their family culture. Agreement on some issues comes easily because the spouses hold similar personal views. Indeed, these similar views might well have brought them together in the first place. In the case of some other issues—for example, that families should eventually have children and that husbands should work outside the home—societal expectations are so strong that the standard view almost automatically becomes part of most couples' family culture. Note, however, that there is less societal agreement on these issues now than in the past, making it somewhat more likely that partners within an individual marriage will hold different views.

Even if husband and wife are very much alike when they marry, they still have many issues to negotiate. For some choices they face, neither spouse has firm ideas coming into the marriage and people outside the marriage are of little help. For example, couples frequently enter marriage with no "standards" about marital sex (Greenblat, 1983). Parents, sex education classes, and the mass media provide few if any guidelines about how often to engage in sexual intercourse or how to initiate, accept, or reject sexual activity within marriage. As you will learn later in the chapter, each individual couple negotiates its own agreements on such issues.

On other issues, both partners hold strong views but the views of one partner are in direct opposition to the views of the other. Family therapist Michael Nichols (1988) argues some amount of marital conflict is inevitable because each spouse comes into marriage with their own individual perspectives.

> The idea of a "family unit" suggests happy harmony. Actually, the family unit is an organism in conflict, an organism in unstable balance. Two people come to marriage with different perspectives and different dispositions. Thus conflict is inherent in the nature of the organism. Conflict is neither good nor bad; *it is inevitable.* (Nichols, 1988, p. 91, emphasis added)

One reason that building a family culture presents such a challenge and is the source of so much conflict is that each spouse comes into marriage from another family. The family in which each partner grew up, called the **family of orientation**, had its own set of rules, values, behaviors, and language. Each spouse, in some way or another, brings the family culture of his or her family of orientation into the family being created, the **family of procreation**. Even those who marry to escape their family of orientation or who resolve to have a different kind of marriage than their parents carry elements of their old family culture into their new marriage.

Since it is virtually inconceivable that the family cultures of two different families of orientation will be exactly alike, disagreements are bound to arise. Such disagreements may not surface before marriage because neither spouse fully recognizes the impact of family culture until confronted with a family culture that is very different. This confrontation frequently does not arise until after marriage. Consider a breakfast time example. The husband comes from a family in which all family members come to the breakfast table wearing nightclothes and eat a large breakfast together while discussing plans for the day. The wife comes from a family in which family members wander to the breakfast table one-by-one, but always dressed in daytime clothing, pick up a section of the newspaper to read, and eat a small breakfast without speaking to one another. Each spouse, prior to marriage, might well have thought that "all families" ate breakfast the way theirs did; each may experience minor shock at the other spouse's "strange" breakfast customs. Together, they must establish their own family culture about breakfast.

The list of potential areas of disagreement between married partners from different families of orientation is virtually limitless. Some of the common areas of disagreement include how to disagree (Should disagreements be open, loud, and confrontational, or should they be quiet and restrained?), how to use leisure time (Should husband and wife spend all their leisure time together, or should they have leisure activities that do not include the other?), and how to show affection (Should family members express their affection openly with little restraint even in public, or should they reserve demonstrations of affection to private family times?).

Husbands and wives involved in interfaith, inter-ethnic, or interracial marriages may be confronted with additional areas of disagreement because their marriage is not only a blending of two families of orientation but also a blending of different cultural traditions. Paul and Rachel Cowan (1987), writing about Jewish-Christian marriages, note that certain incidents—the first December holiday season after the marriage, the birth of a child, the death of a close family member—are "timebombs" that bring cultural differences between spouses into direct

Family of orientation
the family in which one grows up.

Family of procreation
the family one forms by marrying.

confrontation. Differences in social background do not necessarily hamper adjustment, however. Respondents in one study of black-white marriages reported that their differences in racial background helped them develop "a keen sense of awareness of each other's feelings" that aided in marital adjustment (Porterfield, 1978, p. 105). Since partners in intergroup marriages of all types sometimes face rejection from their families of orientation (Cowan & Cowan, 1987; Porterfield, 1978), building a strong family culture of their own is even more important.

Couples of all types who stay together and have satisfying marriages have learned to compromise and adapt in the face of initial disagreements and differences (Nichols, 1988). The family culture they build together is different from that of either partner's family of orientation; it sets their family of procreation apart as something special, gives them something to pass on to their children, and influences how well they cope with the challenges of family life.

Building Strong Marriages

Do the decisions couples make in building their own family culture make a difference in terms of marital success? What is marital success, anyway? What makes some people "happily married" and others "unhappily married"? Questions like these are of interest to both the general public and to social science researchers. In fact, scholarly journals focusing on family issues—such as *Journal of Marriage and the Family, Family Relations*, and *Journal of Family Issues*—are filled with studies about the factors that make some marriages successful and others less so.

Marital Success

What exactly is a successful marriage? A restaurant in the town where one of the authors lives gives a percentage discount for every year a couple celebrating a wedding anniversary has been married. The restaurant manager then takes a picture of the anniversary couple and posts it under the heading "Successful Marriages." Are all these marriages truly successful? Is success measured only in terms of length? Should we consider a marriage successful just because it has lasted 25, or 30, or maybe 35 years?

Marital quality
how good a
marriage is
according to the
spouses at a given
point in time.

Those who do research on marriage make a critical distinction between marital quality and marital success (Glenn, 1990) that we will also adopt. **Marital quality** (also referred to as marital satisfaction or marital happiness) is defined as how good the marriage is *according to the spouses at a given point in time*. Marriages in which partners say they are happy and satisfied are judged to be of higher quality than those marriages in which partners express unhappiness or dissatisfaction. **Marital success** (sometimes also called marital stability), on the other hand, refers to *what happens to the marriage over a period of time.* Marriages that last until the death of one spouse are judged more successful than those that end through divorce or separation. In this chapter and to a lesser extent in those that follow, we are interested in marital quality. We will address the issue of marital success in Chapter 14.

> **Marital success**
> what happens to a marriage over a period of time, whether it lasts until death or ends in divorce.

Marital Quality

Researchers agree that marital quality has numerous components (Whyte, 1990; Johnson *et al.*, 1986; Norton, 1983). Commonly identified

Long-lasting marriages are often thought to be successful. Is marriage duration a good criterion for evaluating the success of a marriage?

dimensions of marital quality include: marital happiness, marital interaction, marital disagreements, marital problems, and marital instability (Johnson *et al.*, 1986). These can be further consolidated into two overall dimensions—a positive one, consisting of marital happiness and marital interaction, and a negative one, consisting of marital disagreements, problems, and instability (Johnson *et al.*, 1986). The Personal Application entitled "Dyadic Adjustment Scale" presents one scale that many social scientists have used for measuring marital quality.

Personal Application

Dyadic Adjustment Scale

The Dyadic Adjustment Scale reprinted below is one of the most widely used measures of marital quality. The higher the score, the better adjusted the couple is.

Most persons have disagreements in their relationships. Please indicate below the approximate extent of agreement or disagreement between you and your partner for each item on the following list.

	Always agree	Almost always agree	Occasionally disagree	Frequently disagree	Almost always disagree	Always disagree
1. Handling family finances	5	4	3	2	1	0
2. Matters of recreation	5	4	3	2	1	0
3. Religious matters	5	4	3	2	1	0
4. Demonstrations of affection	5	4	3	2	1	0
5. Friends	5	4	3	2	1	0
6. Sex relations	5	4	3	2	1	0
7. Conventionality (correct or proper behavior)	5	4	3	2	1	0
8. Philosophy of life	5	4	3	2	1	0
9. Ways of dealing with parents or in-laws	5	4	3	2	1	0
10. Aims, goals, and things believed important	5	4	3	2	1	0
11. Amount of time spent together	5	4	3	2	1	0
12. Making major decisions	5	4	3	2	1	0
13. Household tasks	5	4	3	2	1	0
14. Leisure time interests and activities	5	4	3	2	1	0
15. Career decisions	5	4	3	2	1	0

	All the time	Most of the time	More often than not	Occa- sionally	Rarely	Never
16. How often do you discuss or have you considered divorce, separation, or termina- ting your relationship?	0	1	2	3	4	5
17. How often do you or your mate leave the house after a fight?	0	1	2	3	4	5
18. In general, how often do you think that things between you and your partner are going well?	5	4	3	2	1	0
19. Do you confide in your mate?	5	4	3	2	1	0
20. Do you ever regret that you married? (*or lived together*)	0	1	2	3	4	5
21. How often do you and your partner quarrel?	0	1	2	3	4	5
22. How often do you and your mate "get on each other's nerves?"	0	1	2	3	4	5

	Every day	Almost every day	Occa- sionally	Rarely	Never
23. Do you kiss your mate?	4	3	2	1	0

	All of them	Most of them	Some of them	Very few of them	None of them
24. Do you and your mate engage in outside interests together?	4	3	2	1	0

How often would you say the following events occur between you and your mate?

	Never	Less than once a month	Once or twice a month	Once or twice a week	Once a day	More often
25. Have a stimulating exchange of ideas	0	1	2	3	4	5
26. Laugh together	0	1	2	3	4	5
27. Calmly discuss something	0	1	2	3	4	5
28. Work together on a project	0	1	2	3	4	5

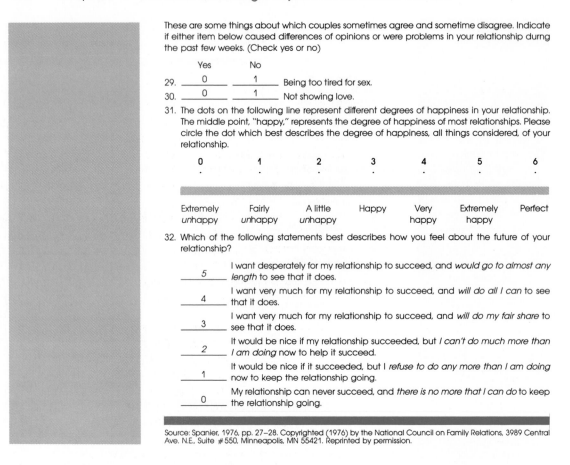

These are some things about which couples sometimes agree and sometime disagree. Indicate if either item below caused differences of opinions or were problems in your relationship durng the past few weeks. (Check yes or no)

	Yes	No	
29.	0	1	Being too tired for sex.
30.	0	1	Not showing love.

31. The dots on the following line represent different degrees of happiness in your relationship. The middle point, "happy," represents the degree of happiness of most relationships. Please circle the dot which best describes the degree of happiness, all things considered, of your relationship.

0	1	2	3	4	5	6
Extremely *unhappy*	Fairly *unhappy*	A little *unhappy*	Happy	Very happy	Extremely happy	Perfect

32. Which of the following statements best describes how you feel about the future of your relationship?

____5____ I want desperately for my relationship to succeed, and *would go to almost any length* to see that it does.

____4____ I want very much for my relationship to succeed, and *will do all I can* to see that it does.

____3____ I want very much for my relationship to succeed, and *will do my fair share* to see that it does.

____2____ It would be nice if my relationship succeeded, but *I can't do much more than I am doing* now to help it succeed.

____1____ It would be nice if it succeeded, but I *refuse to do any more than I am doing* now to keep the relationship going.

____0____ My relationship can never succeed, and *there is no more that I can do* to keep the relationship going.

Source: Spanier, 1976, pp. 27–28. Copyrighted (1976) by the National Council on Family Relations, 3989 Central Ave. N.E., Suite #550, Minneapolis, MN 55421. Reprinted by permission.

The highest quality marriages, according to research of this type, are those scoring high on the positive dimensions and low on the negative dimensions; the lowest quality marriages are those low on the positive dimensions and high on the negative ones. Interestingly enough, the positive and negative dimensions of marital quality are relatively independent of one another (Johnson *et al.*, 1986). That is, any given marriage can be a mixture of positives and negatives. Recent marriages, for example, tend to score high on both the positive and negative dimensions: the spouses communicate a great deal and express great happiness with one another but also have a lot of disagreements and problems (Whyte, 1990; Johnson *et al.*, 1986; Schafer & Keith, 1981). Meanwhile, longer-lasting marriages tend to score lower on both dimensions, showing less positive intensity but also fewer disagreements and problems (Whyte, 1990; Johnson *et al.*, 1986; Schafer & Keith, 1981).

What factors contribute to high marital quality? Generally speaking, researchers have found that how spouses deal with one another after marriage is more important to marital quality than the background characteristics they had going into marriage. Specifically, marriages between people of similar socioeconomic, ethnic, religious, and racial backgrounds are no more or less likely to be of high quality than marriages between people from dissimilar social backgrounds (Whyte, 1990; Porterfield, 1978). As noted in Chapter 4, extensive dating experience has no effect on later marital quality. And beyond a certain minimum level, neither does income (Brinkerhoff & White, 1978). A few background characteristics do make a difference—women who had severe conflicts with their parents have a more difficult time achieving a high quality marriage, and those who married in opposition to parents experience more marital problems (Whyte, 1990).

After marriage, couples who emphasize or develop shared personal traits, a common value system, shared leisure activities, and joint friends generally have higher quality marriages (Whyte, 1990). However, some kinds of attitudinal incompatibility apparently affect marital quality less than others. Take the issue of gender role ideology— attitudes about the proper roles of men and women. Marriages in which the husband holds traditional attitudes about gender roles and the wife holds nontraditional attitudes tend to be of lower quality than those in which the spouses share gender role attitudes (Li & Caldwell, 1987; Bowen & Orthner, 1983), with the women in such marriages being particularly unhappy (Lueptow, Guss, & Hyden, 1989). However, the nontraditional husband-traditional wife couple is just as likely to have high marital quality as couples who share gender role attitudes (Li & Caldwell, 1987; Bowen & Orthner, 1983). Insofar as behavior follows from attitudes, perhaps both spouses perceive such marriages as satisfying because each is getting more from the other than their attitudes led them to expect.

In addition to shared values, friends, and activities, shared participation in decision making and shared control over earnings also contribute to higher marital quality (Whyte, 1990). Couples with supportive ties to parents and other kin tend to have more satisfying marriages as well (Whyte, 1990). Since marital quality is a measure of marital satisfaction at one point in time, it may fluctuate over the course of the marriage. The effect of employment patterns, pregnancy, parenthood, and aging on marital quality will be dealt with in future chapters.

In addition to the factors already mentioned—shared personality traits, common value systems, shared leisure activities, and joint friends—the *emotional attachment* ("commitment" or "love") of each partner to the marriage as a unit and to the other partner is crucial to marital quality. Several researchers suggest that commitment may be the most important factor in a good marriage (Whyte, 1990; Stinnett & DeFrain, 1985).

Do some racial and ethnic groups have higher quality marriages than others? The question has received little research attention. Neither the review of research on Hispanic families (Vega, 1990) nor the review of research on black families (Taylor *et al.*, 1990) appearing in the *Journal of Marriage and the Family* end-of-the-decade review issue mentioned marital quality as a topic. Some researchers believe that the measures of marital quality typically used reflect white, middle-class attitudes about what marriage should be (Skolnick, 1983); perhaps those researching minority marriages feel that such measures are inappropriate. Whyte (1990) compared marital quality in black and in white marriages and found that black women were more often dissatisfied with their marriages than white women. His explanation of the differences suggests that blacks have somewhat different criteria for what makes a "good" marriage than do whites.

> . . . the black wives in the sample differed from the white wives—in holding somewhat different marital values (e.g., stressing a good income more and sexual fidelity less), exhibiting less mutuality and togetherness (in spending free time together, confiding, speaking to the husband first about a problem, and so forth), less often pooling income into a joint account, and in general expressing less satisfaction with the marriage and being more likely to have experienced a marital separation. In general these differences point to a more incomplete "merger" of the two spouses into the conjugal relationship in black than in white marriages, producing a greater maintenance of separate activities and resources. (Whyte, 1990, pp. 161–62)

Secrets of Strong Families

Most family culture features associated with high quality marriages are also present in strong families—parents and children who are able to adapt to, deal with, and survive the difficulties of family life. After years of trying to understand and help troubled families, family counselors and researchers Nick Stinnett and John DeFrain (1985) decided to focus on discovering what made some families strong, able to stick together, and deal with problems. To accomplish their aim, they established a National Center for Family Strengths at the University of Nebraska and, with their research staff, collected data on over 3000 families over a period of years.

Their findings led to the identification of six characteristics crucial for building family strength. As you read through the list, note that none is an "objective" characteristic like income, educational attainment, or power. Rather, all refer to patterns of interaction among family members; all are components of family culture established sometime after the marriage began. Here is their list:

1. *Commitment* "Members of strong families are dedicated to promoting each other's welfare and happiness. They value the unity of the family" (Stinnett & DeFrain, 1985, p. 14). When pushed, Stinnett and DeFrain say that commitment is the most important of the six characteristics. They point out that commitment implies that individual family members put the welfare of the family first and work hard to ensure it remains strong. Such commitment sometimes entails sacrifices by family members. Commitment might mean cutting back on career involvement or curtailing involvement in sports, for example. Such commitment and sacrifices help build stronger families.

2. *Appreciation* "Members of strong families show appreciation for each other a great deal" (Stinnett & DeFrain, 1985, p. 14). Family members are like everyone else; they like to be appreciated. Members of strong families go out of their way to show appreciation of one another. They do not assume that others know they are appreciated but demonstrate their appreciation through compliments, praise, "thank yous," and gifts. Recipients of the appreciation are careful to graciously accept and acknowledge it, neither deflecting praise ("I was lucky") nor undermining compliments ("Oh, it was nothing").

3. *Communication* "Members of strong families have good communication skills and spend a lot of time talking with each other" (Stinnett & DeFrain, 1985, p. 14). Because communication is the focus of the next chapter, we will delay full discussion until then.

4. *Time* "Strong families spend time—quality time in large quantities—with each other" (Stinnett & DeFrain, 1985, p. 14). The strong families Stinnett and DeFrain (1985) studied were not convinced that a family could make up for a low *quantity* of time by achieving a high *quality* of time. Members of strong families did the same kinds of things that most adults and children do—eat meals, do chores, play, participate in religious activities, and celebrate birthdays and holidays—but did them as a family unit, not as individuals.

   Stinnett and DeFrain (1985) concluded that the time spent with the family had very important individual consequences for family members. People who spent time with other family members were spending time with people who cared about them, and, as a consequence, were seldom lonely. Spending time together helped family members develop a sense of identity—a feeling they were a part of something special. Finally, spending time together nurtured the close relationship among family members.

5. *Spiritual Wellness* "Whether they go to formal religious services or not, strong family members have a sense of a greater good or power in life, and that belief gives them strength and purpose" (Stinnett & DeFrain, 1985, p. 14). Not all the strong families Stinnett and DeFrain (1985) studied were religious, but a spiritual dimension of some sort was crucial to family strength. This spiritual dimension was important for both family well-being and for individual psychological well-being. Spiritual wellness is important for the well-being of the family because it promotes caring, love, and compassion of each family member for the others. It is important for individuals because it helps them find a sense of purpose and meaning in life, a positive confident outlook, guidelines for living, and a sense of peace and freedom.

6. *Coping Ability* "Members of strong families are able to view stress or crises as an opportunity to grow" (Stinnett & DeFrain, 1985, p. 14). Strong families have the skills, knowledge, and resilience necessary to cope with the problems, disappointments, and disasters of life. The very fact that they are a strong family is a tremendously important resource. And the attributes they possess as a strong family—commitment, appreciation for each other, good communication, willingness to devote ample amounts of quality time to each other, and spiritual well-being—are all resources they can draw on in times of need.

Strong families approach problematic situations with a positive point of view. Families who take a confident, optimistic approach to any problem the family faces are able to do so because they believe that, as a family, they can develop strategies that will allow them to deal with whatever happens (Antonovsky & Sourani, 1988; McCubbin *et al.*, 1980). Rather than being overwhelmed by crises, they have confidence that their family will ultimately prevail. The Personal Application entitled "Family Sense of Cohesion" offers you an opportunity to think about your own family in this respect.

Family Sense of Cohesion Scale

Personal Application

These six questions about the problems of daily family life are from a longer questionnaire. Answer each of the following for your own immediate family, trying to think of the behavior of the entire family (excluding little children) rather than the behavior of only specific individuals. For each item, circle the number that best represents where you think your family would fall between the two indicated extremes. There are no right and wrong answers; each family has its own way of handling problems.

1. Let's assume that unexpected guests are about to arrive and the house isn't set up to receive them. Does it seem to you that . . .

1	2	3	4	5	6	7
The job will fall on one person.						All members of the family will pitch in to get the house ready.

2. When a problem comes up in the family (like unusual behavior of a family member, an unexpected overdraft in the bank account, being fired from work, unusual tension), do you think you can clarify how it happened?

1	2	3	4	5	6	7
Very little chance						To a great extent

3. Let's assume that your family has been annoyed by something in your neighborhood. Does it seem to you that . . .

1	2	3	4	5	6	7
Nothing can be done to prevent the annoyance.						It's possible to do a great deal to prevent the annoyance.

4. Let's say you're tired, disappointed, angry, or the like. Does it seem to you that *all* members of the family will sense your feelings?

1	2	3	4	5	6	7
No one will sense my feelings.						All the family members will sense my feelings.

5. Think about your feeling about the extent of planning money matters in your family . . .

1	2	3	4	5	6	7
There's no planning about money matters at all in the family.						There's full planning of money matters.

6. To what extent do family members share sad experiences with each other?

1	2	3	4	5	6	7
We don't share our sad experiences with family members.						There's complete sharing with all family members.

Add up your answers. The higher the number, the higher the sense of coherence in your family.

Source: Antonovsky & Sourani, 1988, pp. 91–92. Copyrighted (1988) by the National Council on Family Relations, 3989 Central Ave. N.E., Suite #550, Minneapolis, MN 55421. Reprinted by permission.

In later chapters, we will explain how these components of family culture enable families to deal with specific family changes, such as parenthood, unemployment, and aging. For now, we turn to another important component of marital quality in the early years of marriage—sexual adjustment.

SEXUAL ADJUSTMENT IN MARRIAGE

One of the first adjustments recently married couples face is sexual adjustment. Even couples sexually experienced with one another before the honeymoon night have to work out a sexual life within the overall context of married life and must continue adjusting to one another's individual preferences. As with so many other marital adjustments, sexual adjustments are not made once and forgotten. Rather, marital sexuality is negotiated again and again as couples make changes in their work situations, become parents, deal with the stress of family problems, and grow old.

This section focuses on sexual adjustment in recent marriages. In later chapters, we examine how couples adjust their sexual patterns during later stages of marriage.

How Important Is Sex for Marriage?

Marital sexual adjustment is important because a satisfactory marital sexual relationship is an important component of overall satisfaction and happiness in modern marriages. Several studies confirm that sexual satisfaction and marital satisfaction tend to go together. In 1975,

100,000 women responded to a published survey on the importance of sex for their marriages (Levin & Levin, 1975). Respondents were younger, better educated, and more affluent than U.S. women in general and, therefore, not a representative sample. Still, the study results were compelling: women who rated their sex lives positively also rated their marriages positively, and those who rated their sex lives negatively rated their marriages negatively as well. Later studies support these findings. Ammons and Stinnett (1980) studied 72 especially strong, vital marriages to see how they differed from others. They found three factors critical in explaining the high quality of unusually vital marriages: the *quality of the sex in the marriage*, concern about the spouse, and commitment to a quality marriage. Finally, in their study of U.S. couples, Blumstein and Schwartz (1983, p. 201) found that "both the quantity and quality of sex" were central to a good overall relationship for all types of couples—married and cohabiting, heterosexual and homosexual.

Sex remains important throughout the marriage. Both men and women over age 50 consider sex to be very important for marriage and older couples who enjoy having sex are far more happily married than those who do not (Brecher, 1984). Among older wives, in fact, a report that sex is unimportant is the single best predictor of an unhappy marriage (Brecher, 1984).

Researchers believe that older couples who enjoy having sex are far more happily married than those who do not.

But what about Stinnett and DeFrain's (1985) work on "strong families"? Their list of the six factors characteristic of strong families includes neither high quality nor frequent marital sex. Stinnett and DeFrain (1985) do bring up the topic, however. When writing about the importance of *appreciation*, they state, "We discovered another benefit of appreciation from our strong families; *the folks in our research report healthy sex lives*" (1985, p. 48, emphasis added). In the passage quoted, Stinnett and DeFrain imply that high quality marital sex is an outcome or "benefit" of a broader family behavior pattern. But marital sexuality might also be seen as one way of building the qualities characteristic of strong families. After all, marital sexuality provides the couple with a shared physical activity, time together, an opportunity to talk intimately, a way of showing appreciation for one another, and a symbol of commitment (Reiss, 1986). As one couple in the Family Strengths study reported, "What do we enjoy doing together as a couple? Talking and sex—not necessarily in that order!" (Stinnett & DeFrain, 1985, p. 48)

No study states that a high quality sex life is an absolute requirement for a high quality marriage, nor that a good sex life guarantees a good marriage. As noted, Stinnett and DeFrain (1985) do not include a high quality marital sexual relationship among the six most important characteristics of strong families. Nonetheless, studies consistently suggest that quality of sex and quality of marriage do go together in most cases—most highly satisfying marriages include a very good marital sex life, and most couples with a very good marital sex life have a satisfying marriage as well.

Difficulties in Sexual Adjustment

Like other types of adjustment in marriage, satisfactory sexual adjustment seldom comes automatically. Rather, it requires understanding and negotiation between two spouses. Marriage partners may have difficulties with sexual adjustment for a variety of reasons. Here, we focus on two major categories—gender roles and individual differences.

Gender Roles and Sexual Adjustment

One reason that husbands and wives sometimes have a difficult time adjusting sexually is that they are of opposite sexes, and, therefore, are socialized in different ways about sexuality and marriage. As noted in Chapter 4, men and women often think about sex differently prior to marriage—men see it as a pleasurable, physical activity, while women see it as a sign of emotional commitment. To an extent, these separate meanings are carried over into marriage and become the source of much miscommunication and misunderstanding. Consider the following comments made by a wife and husband, both in their twenties, and married for nine years:

The wife . . .
I don't understand him. He's ready to go any time. It's always been a big problem with us right from the beginning. If we've hardly seen each other for two or three days and hardly talked to each other, I can't just jump into bed. If we have a fight, I just can't turn it off. He has a hard time understanding that. I feel like that's all he wants sometimes. I have to know I am needed and wanted for more than just jumping into bed.

The husband . . .
She complains that all I want from her is sex, and I try to make her understand that it's an expression of love. I'll want to make up with her by making love, but she's cold as the inside of the refrig. Sure I get mad when that happens. Why shouldn't I? Here I'm trying to make up and make love, and she's holding out for something—I don't know what.

The wife . . .
He keeps saying he wants to make love, but it doesn't feel like love to me. Sometimes I feel bad that I feel that way, but I just can't help it.

The husband . . .
I don't understand. She says it doesn't feel like love. What does that mean, anyway? What does she think love is? (quoted in Rubin, 1976, p. 146)

In this marriage, the husband sees sexual activity as a *sign* of love, a way of showing emotional commitment, and a satisfactory way of "making up" after an argument or reestablishing contact after being apart. The wife, on the other hand, sees sexual activity as something that should *follow* verbal expressions of appreciation and love, as something that a couple should work up to rather than "jumping into," and as a small part of a total relationship. In this marriage, as in many others, the husband prefers to show his love instrumentally by engaging in a physical activity while the wife wants expressive signs of love as well (Cancian, 1986).

Husbands generally desire more sexual activity than their wives do and are better able to enjoy sex as a physical experience (Blumstein & Schwartz, 1983; Udry & Morris, 1978). They are also more willing

Fellatio
stimulation of
the penis
by a partner's lips,
mouth, and tongue.

Cunnilingus
stimulation of the
female genitalia
using lips, mouth,
and tongue.

and ready than wives to experiment with new sexual positions and with nonintercourse forms of sex (Blumstein & Schwartz, 1983; Rubin, 1976). For example, oral sex was important to heterosexual men in the Blumstein-Schwartz study (1983) who said their sex lives were happy. The men enjoyed both receiving **fellatio**, stimulation of the penis by a partner's lips, mouth, and tongue, and performing **cunnilingus**, stimulation of the female genitalia using lips, mouth, and tongue. The presence or absence of oral sex did not affect women's sexual satisfaction, however. They preferred sexual activities, such as kissing and intercourse, that involved mutual participation in equivalent roles (Blumstein & Schwartz, 1983).

According to research done in the 1960s and 1970s, the differences between male and female sexual attitudes and sexual preferences may be greater in lower- and working-class marriages than in middle-class marriages, making sexual adjustment more difficult for the lower and working class. Writing just as the Sexual Revolution was beginning, Rainwater (1965) revealed that the overwhelming majority of husbands had positive feelings toward marital sex, with middle-class men being somewhat more positive than lower-class men. Almost 90 percent of the middle-class wives, but less than 60 percent of the lower-class wives, had positive feelings about marital sex. Thus, there was a much larger sexual "gender gap" in lower-class than in middle-class marriages.

Ten years later, in the midst of the Sexual Revolution, the story was much the same. Lillian Rubin (1976), in an interview study of blue-collar marriages, detailed how working-class males and females still had very different attitudes toward sex. Men dominated sexual issues and distinguished between "good girls" (who are not sexually experienced, do not especially like sex, and are the kinds of women men want to marry) and "bad girls" (who are sexually experienced, like sex, are fun to play with, but whom men would never marry). Working-class husbands often claimed they wanted their wives to be innovative sex partners (like "bad girls"), yet did not want them to be unfeminine or aggressive in sex (like "bad girls"). Their wives, fearful of being thought of as bad girls by their own husbands, were understandably reluctant to be innovative or to express much enjoyment in sex. Thus, both men and women expressed dissatisfaction with their marital sex lives; husbands because their interest and spirit of innovation were so much greater than those of their wives, wives because they feared being thought of as "cheap" if they acted out sexual desires and because they yearned for other signs of affection (Rubin, 1976).

Generally speaking, middle-class husbands and wives start out closer in their sexual attitudes and more experienced at understanding the other sex's point of view than working- and lower-class husbands and wives. Thus, middle-class women are more likely than working-class women to be willing to experiment sexually, and middle-class men are more practiced than their working-class counterparts in expressing their love verbally as well as physically (Rubin, 1976).

Many of the differences between men and women that created sexual adjustment difficulties in the past may be lessening. Men and women marrying today are closer in experience and in attitudes about sex than their predecessors. Movies, magazine articles, television talk shows and advice programs, and books promoting a varied and active sex life permeated the "sexualized society" of the 1980s and reached people of both sexes in all social classes (D'Emilio & Freedman, 1988). However, husbands and wives still have conflicts about sex because of differential socialization. Furthermore, social class differences in sexual adjustment have probably not disappeared (Weinberg & Williams, 1980; Mahoney, 1978).

Individual Differences

Some husbands and wives find sexual adjustment difficult because of individual differences in sexual desire or sexual preferences not necessarily related to gender. Individuals with varying hormonal levels, sexual experiences, and upbringing vary in level of sexual desire. As noted in Chapter 3, sexual desire is affected by a variety of factors external to the couple relationship—everything from pregnancy and childbirth, to working long hours, to alcohol use, to grieving for a deceased relative can affect sexual desire. To make a satisfactory sexual adjustment, marital partners have to realize that their sexual desires will not always be "in sync" with one another and that they will have to work to reach some sort of compromise.

Satisfactory sexual adjustment is hampered in some marriages because one or both partners have a sexual problem like those described in Chapter 3. For example, in a marriage in which simultaneous orgasm is important to both partners, an anorgasmic wife or a prematurely ejaculating husband can hamper sexual satisfaction. Such couples might benefit from sexual therapy.

Patterns of Marital Sex

Most married couples eventually develop some kind of working agreement about what types of sexual activity to share, about how often to do so, and about who initiates and who has the right to refuse. Individual couples have a great deal of leeway in the choices they make; there are many possible ways to be a sexually adjusted couple. In the paragraphs which follow, we describe some of the "average" patterns, as revealed by the research of social scientists and sexologists. Keep in mind that these "averages" conceal a great deal of couple-to-couple variation.

Types of Sexual Activity

Today, the average married couple engages in a variety of sexual activities together. Extended foreplay, kissing, and the use of sexual aids such as sexy lingerie or erotic videos—all of which reflect an increased concern for mutual sexual pleasure—are important parts of marital sex for many couples (D'Emilio & Freedman, 1988; Rubenstein & Tavris, 1987; Levin & Levin, 1975; Hunt, 1974). Having used such arousal techniques, husbands and wives are willing to experiment with a variety of intercourse positions in addition to the traditional "man on top, woman on bottom" position. And marital intercourse lasts longer, on average, than it did thirty or forty years ago—ten minutes versus two, according to one study (Hunt, 1974).

Most married couples engage in cunnilingus, fellatio, or both at least occasionally (Wyatt, Peters, & Guthrie, 1988a, 1988b; Rubenstein & Tavris, 1987; Blumstein & Schwartz, 1983; Levin & Levin, 1975). The summary of one large-scale survey of marital sex reported that "Oral-genital sex is an almost universal experience. It is practiced in varying frequency by 9 out of 10 women under the age of 40 and by 8 out of 10 women who are 40 or older" (Levin & Levin, 1975, p. 52). Oral-genital sex is more common among white couples than among black couples, however. The 90 percent figure reported above applies to whites; about 70 percent of black couples engage in cunnilingus and fellatio (Wyatt, Peters, & Guthrie, 1988a, 1988b).

Overall, modern married couples pay more attention to sex, are more playful and experimental in pursuing it, and are more concerned about mutual satisfaction than were their parents and grandparents. The Cohort Comparison provides further insight into twentieth-century changes in marital sex.

Cohort Comparison   Advice on Marital Sex from _The Reader's Digest_

Throughout the twentieth century, and especially in the latter half, married couples have had available numerous magazine articles, books, and educational films to give them information and advice about how to achieve sexual satisfaction in marriage. This cohort comparison will help you get a feel for what different twentieth-century birth cohorts might have learned about marital sexual adjustment from popular magazines. We selected one popular magazine article on marital sexual adjustment from 1937, one from 1957, and one from 1978 for analysis and comment. These years correspond to the times when most members of the New Century, Depression, and Baby Boom cohorts would have been fairly recently married. The articles selected were all published in *The Reader's Digest*, a widely read magazine that selects and reprints articles from popular magazines and books. All addressed marital sexual adjustment in general terms.

New Century cohort members might have read a 1937 article, entitled "The Sexual Relationship in Marriage." The article notes that, for many married couples, the sexual relationship ". . . remains a generally disappointing and recurrently a disruptive element in the partnership" (Harris, 1937, p. 23). The author advises both sexes, but particularly men, to learn about their partner's body and needs, to be "utterly frank" about sex, and to strive for mutual rather than individual sexual satisfaction. Here is a passage that captures the essence of the author's message:

Sexuality as it appears in acts whose purpose is merely to satisfy one's own demands tends to be cruel and relentless; but when it appears as a purpose of two partners to share an experience with each other, it is the handmaid of tenderness. This is the ideal experience. (Harris, 1937, pp. 24–25)

The 1957 article, one that might have been read by young Depression cohort members, also stresses the need for couples to learn about one another and to strive for mutuality in sexual relations. However, the article, entitled "The Act of Love: Woman's Greatest Challenge," places major responsibility for achieving such mutuality on wives. Other articles published at about the same time also reflect this theme, at least in their titles ("How to Love Your Husband," "What Keeps a Husband Faithful?"). In the following passage, the author, a female doctor, suggests that, in striving to satisfy their husbands (even if it means faking orgasm), wives also reach satisfaction themselves:

A man can feel kinship with the gods if his wife can make him believe he can cause a flowering within her. If she doesn't feel it she must bend every effort to pretend. This is the worthiest duplicity on earth; I heartily recommend it to discontented wives. It gives a man his manhood, a quality of glorious robustness that cannot fail to reward the giver. Thousands of women who have begun this sort of benign sham have discovered that their pretended delight rapidly became real. (Hilliard, 1957, p. 45)

Baby Boom birth cohort members might have read a 1978 article entitled "To Increase the Enjoyment of Sex in Marriage" in *The Reader's Digest*. The old themes of the importance of learning about one another's needs and striving for mutuality appear again. The author, a sociologist-novelist-priest, further asserts that each partner has a responsibility to teach the other and that sexual intimacy in marriage should be a growth experience. Here is part of what he says:

The sensitivities and capacities of being effective bed partners come only through practice, trial and error, through the ability to laugh at blunders, and of course from getting feedback. The lover needs to be told what he is doing right and what wrong. Fidelity means, then, that a lover asks for, indeed demands, such feedback— but in such a way that the instructions, be they in word or action, are a pleasure to give. (Greeley, 1978, p. 112)

Frequency Patterns

For most couples, achieving a satisfying marriage is dependent to a great extent on the development of a pattern of mutually satisfying, frequent sex. Based on the results of their large scale study, Blumstein and Schwartz (1983) stated, "Married couples feel so strongly about having sex often that those who say they have it with their partner infrequently tend to be dissatisfied with their entire relationship" (1983, p. 201). Other major survey studies find the same thing—the more sex a married couple has, the greater the satisfaction with their marital relationship (Rubenstein & Tavris, 1987; Levin & Levin, 1975).

Frequency in Early Marriage   Despite the general knowledge that "sex is important to marriage," recently married couples have few guidelines about "how often is often enough." As a result, each couple negotiates its own guidelines as part of building their family culture during the first years of their marriage (Greenblat, 1983). As Table 7–1 illustrates, different couples came to widely varying conclusions, especially during the first year of marriage. While some couples had intercourse an average of once a week, others reportedly did so an average of more than once a day. Clearly, four times a month to forty-five times a month is a very broad range. But a number of studies confirm that newly married couples have widely divergent frequency rates (Rubenstein & Tavris, 1987; Frank & Anderson, 1985; Levin & Levin, 1975). Kinsey et al. (1953), for example, found that as many as 6 percent of married women in their early twenties reported sexual intercourse as infrequently

Table 7–1 Frequency of Intercourse per Month, by Years Married

Years Married	N	Mean Frequency	Range
1	12	14.8	4–45
2	10	12.2	3–20
3	19	11.9	2–18
4	7	9.0	4–23
5	18	9.7	5–18

Source: Data from Greenblat, 1983, p. 292. Copyrighted (1983) by the National Council on Family Relations, 3989 Central Ave., N.E., Suite #550, Minneapolis, MN 55421. Reprinted by permission.

as once every two weeks while a similar number claimed to have intercourse six or more times a week.

What about the "average" newly married couple? Greenblat (1983) found that the couples in her study married one year or less averaged about 15 times a month; James (1981) reported a mean rate of slightly more than 17 times per month for newly married couples; and Blumstein and Schwartz (1983) found that, among couples married two years or less, about half had sex three or more times a week while the other half had sex less than three times a week. Based on these results, the average couple has sexual intercourse about 15 times a month during the early years of marriage.

Declines in Frequency   After the first year or so, most married couples have sexual intercourse less often (Blumstein & Schwartz, 1983; James, 1981; Udry, 1980; Udry & Morris, 1978). In Greenblat's (1983) sample, for example, 30 percent of the couples maintained or increased their first year's sexual intercourse rate into the second year, but fully 70 percent experienced declines, ranging from small to drastic, in frequency of intercourse. Many of those reporting no decline had lived together before marriage and had reduced their sexual frequency before they ever married.

Why the decline? Increasing age, with an accompanying decline in sexual interest, is, of course, one possible explanation. Figure 7–1 (on page 248) clearly illustrates the connection between increasing age and decreasing participation in marital intercourse. However, the decline cannot be attributed solely to the aging process since it occurs regardless of how young or how old the partners are when they marry (Blumstein & Schwartz, 1983; Udry, 1980). What other factors are at work?

When married couples are asked to explain the decline of sexual frequency in their own marriages, they typically point to four types of factors: pregnancy and fear of becoming pregnant, work, children, and familiarity and availability (Greenblat, 1983). The first three factors are dealt with at greater length in later chapters; here we focus on the factor of familiarity and availability.

After a couple establishes a pattern in their sex life, sexual activity tends to become routine and to be taken for granted; sex is always with the same person and it is easily available. This familiarity and availability leads some couples to engage in intercourse less often because they find it less exciting than they once did — "We've gotten into a routine with each other and it's not as exciting any more," and "the spark isn't as big" (quoted in Greenblat, 1983, p. 297). Other couples, however, see familiarity and their reduced frequency of intercourse as a positive development. Once accustomed to one another and assured of the availability of a partner, they do not perceive frequent sexual intercourse

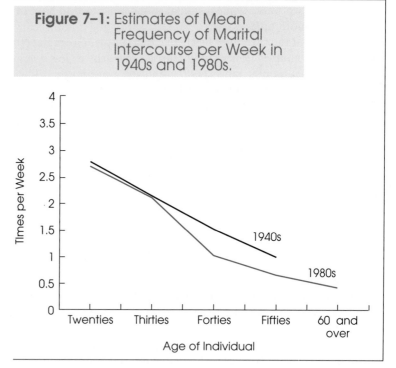

Figure 7-1: Estimates of Mean Frequency of Marital Intercourse per Week in 1940s and 1980s.

"Mean frequency" refers to the average number of times per week married couples have sexual intercourse. Age is clearly related to frequency of marital intercourse. During the 1980s, young married couples averaged 3 times a week while couples in their sixties averaged once every two weeks.

Source: 1980s data: Smith, 1991. 1940s data: Kinsey *et al.*, 1953, p. 394 and Kinsey, Pomeroy, and Martin, 1948, p. 252; reproduced by permission of The Kinsey Institute for Research in Sex, Gender, and Reproduction, Inc.

to be as important as they did initially. Some couples develop nonintercourse ways of showing sexual affection, having intercourse less frequently but making it more meaningful. According to these couples, "[Intercourse] is better because it's more relaxed" and "not having it regularly or daily makes it more interesting" (Greenblat, 1983, p. 297).

The familiarity brought about by marriage can also lead husbands and wives to reduce efforts to keep themselves physically attractive and this, in turn, can affect their sex lives. Human sexuality expert John Gagnon (1977) notes that:

> For many of us the important game is over when we get married. What made most of us attractive before we got married is not what we work at after we get married. Thus a young woman and a young man may keep themselves attractive while they are in the marriage market. Finally they get somebody. After the honeymoon she starts gaining weight or wearing curlers; he starts to get a paunch. They were on the hunt, but once the hunt is complete, they do not have to put up a front any more. (pp. 209–210)

But physical attraction is an important source of sexual arousal for both males and females and its importance continues into marriage (Gagnon, 1977). If one or both spouses lose the physical characteristics their partner once found attractive, some decline in sexual activity is an expected outcome.

Continuing physical attractiveness is important in assuring frequent sexual activity in marriage. It also influences the couples' satisfaction with marital sex, their satisfaction with the overall relationship, the possibility of extramarital affairs, and the actual survival of the relationship (Margolin & White, 1987; Blumstein & Schwartz, 1983). While important for both spouses, the continued physical attractiveness of the partner is more important to husbands than to wives (Margolin & White, 1987).

Patterns of Initiation and Refusal

Besides establishing the types of sexual activity they will share and how often they will do so, husbands and wives also develop patterns of initiation and refusal. That is, they come to some type of agreement (often unstated) about who initiates sexual interaction and how he or she does it, and about who has the right to refuse and for what reasons. Traditionally, husbands controlled the sexual part of the marriage just as they controlled all other aspects of it. "Sexual adjustment" essentially meant that the wife adjusted to the husband's sexual needs, whatever they were. With an increasing emphasis on mutual sexual pleasure during the twentieth century, most husbands came to respect their wives' right to refuse sexual intercourse and a new pattern of "husband initiates but wife has the right of refusal" came to dominate (D'Emilio & Freedman, 1988).

In recent years, initiation of sexual activity has become more of a shared activity in many marriages—sometimes the husband makes the suggestion, sometimes the wife does. Survey research reveals that a majority of younger wives at least occasionally take the lead in suggesting intercourse or in trying out sexual innovations on their husbands (Blumstein & Schwartz, 1983; Levin & Levin, 1975).

Drastic changes in the male initiation-female right of refusal pattern are not common, however, because of the persistence of traditional ideas about gender roles and differing male-female perceptions about the meaning of sexual activity. In particular, reversing the traditional gender roles regarding sexual initiation and refusal can create conflict. When a husband initiates sex and is turned down (the traditional pattern), he can shrug off the refusal as an indication of his wife's lower sex drive; she is not rejecting him personally, she is only rejecting sex.

But when a wife initiates sex and is turned down (a nontraditional pattern), she may feel that her husband is *uninterested in her* rather than being uninterested in sex. Wives more often perceive refusal as a personal rejection. The husband who turns down his wife, meanwhile, often feels guilty because he is not fulfilling the expectation that males are more interested in sex than are females. Wishing to avoid these potential conflicts, wives in most marriages tend to initiate sexual activity only when they feel it will not undermine their husband's feeling of being in control; most husbands continue to initiate and determine the form of most marital sexuality; and most wives still control sexual frequency through their right of refusal (Szinovacz, 1984; Blumstein & Schwartz, 1983).

Extramarital Sex

Marriages in the United States are built on the assumption of **sexual monogamy**: spouses are expected to have a sexual relationship with one another and *only* with one another. Most of the U.S. population, married and unmarried, endorse this assumption. Surveys about sexual attitudes consistently indicate that about nine out of ten women and about eight out of ten men feel that **extramarital sex**, sexual involvement of a married person with someone other than the spouse, is "Always" or "Almost Always" wrong (Thornton, 1989, p. 886). Twenty-seven states have laws prohibiting **adultery**, the legal term applied when a married person has intercourse with someone other than his or her spouse. Such laws are only occasionally enforced (Associated Press, 1990, p. 12). However, their persistence indicates that sexual monogamy within marriage is an important societal as well as personal concern.

Incidence

Despite the near-unanimous sentiment against it, involvement in extramarital sex is not particularly unusual. Because the topic is a sensitive one, researchers have a difficult time knowing how many married people are or have been involved in extramarital sex. Table 7–2 reflects some of these difficulties. The table presents a compilation of research results on estimated rates of extramarital sex. As you can see, the method of obtaining respondents and the age and length of marriage of the respondents for these studies vary widely. So do the estimates of extramarital involvement—from 8 percent (married women who have had extramarital sexual intercourse since age 50) to 69 percent (married female *Cosmopolitan* readers over age 35). In attempts to come up

---

Sexual monogamy
restricting one's sexual activity to one partner only; in the case of marriage, the one partner is the spouse.

Extramarital sex
sexual involvement of a married person with someone other than the spouse.

Adultery
the legal term applied when a married person has intercourse with someone other than his or her spouse.

Table 7–2 Incidence of Extramarital Behaviors in Selected Studies			
	Study, Behavioral Referent, Sample	Married Men	Married Women
Kinsey (1948, 1953), extramarital intercourse.	Approximately 3088 married men of all ages. Approximately 2000 married women up to the age of 40.	50%	26%
Anthanasiou, Shaver, and Tavris (1970), extramarital intercourse.	Approximately 8000 married men and women of all ages, but three-quarters of the sample younger than 35 years.	40%	36%
Johnson (1970a, 1970b), extramarital intercourse.	100 middle-aged couples, well educated, fairly affluent, and, as a group, experienced consider-able stability in their marriages.	20%	10%
Hunt (1974), extra-marital intercourse.	982 males and 1044 females, 18 years of age and over, representative of the adult American population.	41%	18%
Bell, Turner, and Rosen (1975), extra-marital intercourse.	2262 married women, average age of 34.5 years, average length of marriage 13.2 years, reasonably distributed by education and religious affiliation.	—	26%
Levin (1975); Tavris and Sadd (1975), extramarital sex.	Married female *Redbook* readers in the United States, 40 years of age and older.	—	39%
Maykovich (1976), extramarital sexual relations.	100 white, middle-class, married American women, aged 35 to 40.	—	32%
Pietropinto and Simenauer (1976), cheating on wife or steady girlfriend.	4066 men in a nationwide United States sample.	47%	—
Yablonsky (1979), extramarital sex/ affairs.	771 married men from various United States geo-graphic regions; average age 36 years, average marriage approximately 11 years.	47%	—
Wolfe (1980), extra-marital sex.	Married females *Cosmopolitan* readers; age 35 and older.	—	69%
Hite (1981), extra-marital sex.	Married men in an overall sample of 7239 men representative of the male population of the United States.	66%	—
Blumstein and Schwartz (1983)	3574 married couples from all parts of the United States; married at least 10 years as —	30%	22%

(*continued*)

Table 7-2 (continued)

Study, Behavioral Referent, Sample	Married Men	Married Women
Brecher (1984), extramarital sex	4246 men and women aged 50 or older from all parts of United States; percent who have had extramarital sex since age 50	23%	8%
Wyatt, Peters, and Guthrie (1988a and 1988b), extramarital sex	122 white women age 18–36 chosen as representative sample of all 18–36 year old white women in L.A. County, CA; percent of 89 ever-married women who have had an affair.	—	37%
	126 black women age 18–36 chosen as representative sample of all 18–36 year old black women in L.A. County, CA; percent of 40 ever-married women who have had an affair.	—	40%

Note: The designation "married" frequently includes presently married as well as previously married.

Source for summaries prior to 1983: Thompson, 1983, pp. 5–6. Published by permission of *The Journal of Sex Research*, a publication of the Society for the Scientific Study of Sex.

with an accurate figure, several researchers, *projecting from their studies,* suggest that as many as 50 percent of all husbands and almost as many wives will engage in extramarital sex *at some point during their marriage* (Thompson, 1983).

As shown by Figure 7–2, almost equal proportions of males and females in fairly recent marriages choose to have extramarital sexual affairs. In couples who have been married longer, however, men are more likely than women to have had extramarital experience (Blumstein & Schwartz, 1983). This male-female disparity in behavior apparently increases with age. In his study of sex among the elderly, Brecher (1984) found that only eight percent of wives but fully 23 percent of husbands had engaged in extramarital sex since age 50.

These findings might mean that older, longer married men have more opportunities or desire for extramarital sex than older women do, whereas the opportunities and desires of younger men and women are more nearly equal. They might also, however, reflect a cohort difference. Young married women today, products of the Sexual Revolution, are far more willing to engage in extramarital intercourse than are their pre-Sexual Revolution counterparts (Blumstein & Schwartz, 1983). As these women grow older, the existing disparity between older females and males will probably diminish or perhaps disappear entirely.

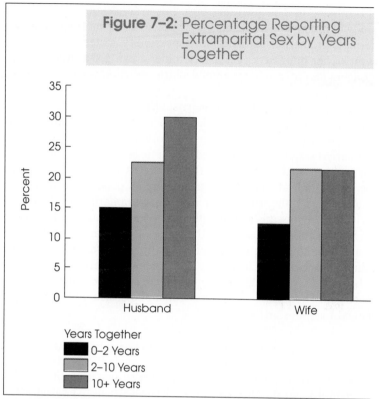

Figure 7–2: Percentage Reporting Extramarital Sex by Years Together

Years Together
- ■ 0–2 Years
- ▨ 2–10 Years
- ▨ 10+ Years

Extramarital affairs can happen any time. For couples married recently, men and women have similar rates of extramarital involvement. For those married more than ten years, men have substantially higher rates. After the tenth year of marriage, three in ten husbands and more than one in five wives report engaging in extramarital sex at some time during their marriage.

Source: Philip Blumstein & Pepper Schwartz, *American Couples: Money, Work, and Sex,* p. 274. © William Morrow and Company, Inc, 1983. Used by permission of William Morrow and Company, Inc./Publishers, New York.

Why Extramarital Sex?

Believing as they do in marriage and in sexual exclusivity within it, why do up to half of all husbands and wives eventually get involved in adultery? In an extensive review of the research, Thompson (1983) reports that two general factors are consistently linked to such behavior: characteristics of the marriage and personal readiness.

Marriages characterized by dissatisfaction on the part of one or both partners are more likely to be affected by extramarital sex. Individuals who are dissatisfied with their marriage in general or who are disappointed with the quality and frequency of their marital sexual intercourse are more likely than others to fantasize about extramarital involvement; some of them pursue involvement beyond the fantasy level (Thompson, 1983). They seek in extramarital relationships what they feel is missing in their own marriage. For example, one respondent in a study of intimate relationships, unhappy with her marriage, and considering extramarital sex as a future possibility, stated "Maybe when the girls [her daughters] get a little older I can get a little more independent and try my wings and fly a little bit" (Blumstein & Schwartz, 1983, p. 284).

Personal readiness for extramarital affairs is a second factor which distinguishes those married people who depart from sexual monogamy from those who do not. Contact with others who have experienced extramarital sex, the ability to easily separate sex from love, a perceived need for more sexual variety, or the belief that an extramarital sexual experience can lead to personal growth are all personal readiness factors associated with greater involvement in extramarital sex. Husbands or wives whose dissatisfaction with their own marriage leads to isolation or alienation represent another type of "personally ready" individuals likely to engage in adultery. Finally, some reach the personal readiness stage, not because they are specifically missing something, but because they come to believe that there could be something more to their life (Thompson, 1983). One woman described how she reached personal readiness as follows:

> I began to realize that I had made a mistake by not having sex before marriage. It suddenly hit me that I—who was only 28—would die having sex with only one man. I decided that was not what I wanted to do with my body, and after that the idea of having sex with another man became something possible, even desirable. But I had nobody in mind at the time. (Atwater, 1982, p. 39)

Thus far, researchers know little about *how* people become extramaritally involved or about how the two general factors—the characteristics of the marriage and personal readiness—are related to one another. Perhaps people do not become personally ready for extramarital sex unless and until their own marriage is dissatisfying to them. Or, perhaps they do not become dissatisfied until they come to believe that an extramarital affair is an option for which they are ready (Thompson, 1983).

Some researchers believe that extramarital sex, like sex in general, has different meanings for men than for women and imply that the process of getting involved might also be different (Blumstein & Schwartz, 1983). Women, trained to see sex as part of an intense emotional relationship, might seek extramarital sex when they feel their own marriage is emotionally deficient and attach great importance to the extramarital affair. Men, taught that sex and love are separable, might start out more personally ready for extramarital intercourse than women and perceive it as a pleasurable but insignificant recreational activity, not necessarily indicating dissatisfaction with their own marriages. Such speculation awaits more systematic examination.

Effect on the Marriage

How does adultery affect the marriage? Research on this question is very limited, but suggests that the extramarital affairs of one or both partners has no single effect on the existing marriage. For example, one study of extramaritally active women asked respondents to assess the effect of their extramarital experience on their marriages (Atwater, 1982). The women, a volunteer and probably nonrepresentative sample, reported effects on their marriages that ranged "... from mostly positive to decidedly negative to none" (Atwater, 1982, p. 77). Even the effect of the extramarital affair on the frequency of intercourse with their husbands varied; some reported no change in frequency, some reported a decline in marital intercourse, and some said that frequency of marital intercourse increased as a result of extramarital involvement.

Much extramarital sexual intercourse goes undiscovered by the nonactive partner; in such cases, the extramarital relationship is a personal issue to the involved partner but not truly a marital issue. If and when the nonactive partner finds out, the adultery becomes a marital issue and often a marital crisis. How do couples deal with the crisis? Divorce is a common response to the discovery that a partner has been or is involved with somebody else. In an eighteen-month follow-up to their original survey, Blumstein and Schwartz (1983) found that extramarital sex was associated with marital collapse. Husbands and wives who had been involved in extramarital affairs were more likely to break up during the eighteen-month period than were married couples who had been monogamous. Recent and long-term marriages were affected in similar ways; extramarital sex increased the likelihood of separation and divorce in both (Blumstein & Schwartz, 1983). Although infidelity is not the major reason most people divorce, it does contribute to a substantial minority of divorces. When divorced people are asked about the causes of their divorce, 10–35 percent of the husbands and 21–37 percent of the wives mention spousal infidelity as a contributing cause (Cleek & Pearson, 1985; Burns, 1984; Kitson & Sussman, 1982).

But divorce is not the inevitable outcome of extramarital affairs. Brecher (1984) found that 524 of his elderly respondents acknowledged having had extramarital sex during their current marriage. Of these 524, at least 149 and possibly as many as 246 had had sex outside of marriage *with their spouse's knowledge* and had remained married (Brecher, 1984, p. 128). Researchers know little about how couples who stay together adjust to the knowledge of marital infidelity or about the quality of their marriages after the adjustment is made. Some couples may adjust by changing their family culture from one that prohibited extramarital sex to one that openly and mutually allows it. One small-scale study of 41 sexually open marriages (marriages in which extramarital sex by either partner is considered a possibility) found that only one such marriage began as sexually open; the other 40 shifted from endorsing sexual monogamy to accepting sexual openness at some point after the marriage began (Rubin & Adams, 1986). When marital quality and marital stability were assessed, the sexually open couples were not significantly different from couples who believed in sexual monogamy (Rubin & Adams, 1986). All of the findings taken together indicate that extramarital sex, like any other marital challenge, affects different couples in very different ways.

Summary

Every newly married couple must adjust both to one another and to the new status of married person through a process of compromise, change, and building a unique family culture. The process may be difficult because each partner tends to be influenced by the family culture of the family of orientation. However, research on marital quality indicates that what couples do after marriage in attempting to build a strong, committed marriage matters more than events or characteristics preceding the marriage. High quality marriages and strong families tend to embody certain common characteristics— being committed to the marriage and the family, communicating well and often, showing appreciation, spending time together, sharing of a strong sense of spiritual well-being, and believing that the family as a unit can overcome the problems it faces.

Satisfactory sexual adjustment is one important component of a satisfying marriage. Couples sometimes have difficulty adjusting to one another sexually because they lack sexual knowledge and guidelines, because males and females are socialized differently, and because of individual sexual differences. Most married couples today engage in a variety of sexual activities, have intercourse 15 or so times a month in the early years of marriage and less often thereafter, and rely mostly on the husband to initiate sex and on the wife to set the level of frequency. A substantial minority of married people, perhaps close to one half, engage in extramarital sex at some time during their marriage. Some do so because they are in search of something missing in their own marriage; others because they reach a state of personal readiness for it. Extramarital sex, when discovered, often, but not inevitably, leads to divorce. In fact, some marriages stay together and apparently adjust to the extramarital indiscretions of one or both partners.

CHAPTER 8

THE TASKS OF MARRIAGE: COMMUNICATION AND CONFLICT

Answer each of the following questions in as detailed a manner as possible before reading the chapter and then reconsider your answers after you read the chapter. You might also want to see how your partner responds.

1. What would you do or say if your partner made a major purchase (for example, a car, or an expensive piece of furniture, or a vacation cruise for both of you) without discussing the purchase with you first? Would it matter if your spouse used money you both had earned? What would you do in that case?
2. What do you say if your partner, modeling a new outfit he or she just bought, asks you "How does it look?" and you think it looks terrible?
3. How do you respond when your partner buys you a surprise gift that you really don't like and really don't want?
4. What would you do or say if you believe your partner is flirting with someone else at a party?
5. What do you do or say if you are unhappy with the sexual relationship you have established with your partner?
6. What should you do or say if your partner strikes you in anger or frustration? Does it make a difference if you require medical attention because of the blow?

Linguist Dr. Deborah Tannen (1990), in her book *You Just Don't Understand!*, tells the following story about differences in female and male communication and how important understanding the differences is:

> A woman who had heard my interpretations of these differences between men and women told me how these insights helped her. Early in a promising relationship, a man had spent the night in her apartment. It was a weeknight, and they both had to go to work the next day, so she was delighted when he made the rash and romantic suggestion that they have breakfast and report late for work. She happily prepared breakfast, looking forward to the scene shaped in her mind: They would sit facing each other across her small table, look into each other's eyes, and say how much they liked each other and how happy they were with their growing relationship. It was against the backdrop of this heady expectation that she confronted an entirely different scene: As she placed on the table an array of lovingly prepared eggs, toast, and coffee, the man sat across her small table—and opened the newspaper in front of his face. If suggesting they have breakfast together had seemed like an invitation to get closer, in her view (or obstructing her view) the newspaper was now erected as a paper-thin but nonetheless impenetrable barrier between them.
>
> Had she known nothing of the gender differences I discuss, she would simply have felt hurt and dismissed this man as yet another clunker. She would have concluded that, having enjoyed the night with her, he was now availing himself of her further services as a short-order cook. Instead, she realized that, unlike her, he did not feel the need for talk to reinforce their intimacy. The companionship of her presence was all he needed, and that did not mean he didn't cherish her presence. By the same token, had he understood the essential role played by talk in women's definition of intimacy, he could have put off reading the paper—and avoided putting her off. (pp. 85–86)

Tannen's example illustrates that human interaction, especially male-female interaction, is often subtle, complex, and fraught with possibilities for misunderstanding. To the man in the example, reading the newspaper was a sign that he felt comfortable and relaxed spending time with the woman; to the woman, his newspaper reading symbolized withdrawal and lack of interest in her. The quality and complexity of human interaction is one attribute that sets human beings apart from other animals. By interacting in subtle and sophisticated ways, people can communicate far more complex ideas and emotions than other animals. The subtlety and sophistication of human interaction cuts both ways: when done well, interaction can be the building block of human relationships; when done poorly, it can undermine and destroy relationships.

These issues are relevant to marriage in a number of ways. As noted in previous chapters, modern marriages are increasingly based on intimacy. And many experts consider frequent, high quality, self-disclosing interaction an important component of intimacy. At the same time, every marriage contains a man and a woman, a combination of people particularly prone to misinterpreting one another in interaction. No wonder married couples who split up often attribute their breakup to "poor communication."

Marital communication and its inevitable companion, marital conflict, are the main topics of this chapter. To understand the complexities of marital communication, you first need to understand human communication processes in general. The first section of this chapter provides such a discussion. In it, we consider the symbolic nature of human communication, the human communication process, and sources of "noise" or disruption in human communication.

In the second section of the chapter, we apply some of these general principles to marital communication, describing the characteristics of good marital communication, exploring some of the factors that affect the quality of marital communication, and assessing just how important marital communication is to overall marital quality.

The third section of this chapter deals with marital conflict. Here we discuss three nonaggressive ways of handling marital disagreements—avoidance, confrontation, and resolution. The fourth section focuses on aggression as a way of dealing with marital conflict. We discuss the forms aggression takes, the reasons for it, and the damage it does. Gender and racial differences in the use of aggression are described as well.

HUMAN COMMUNICATION

Communication is an interactive process in which at least two people continually send and receive information. Communication always takes place within group situations, and group situations always involve some type of communication. Here we focus on the smallest communication group—a two person group, with special attention to husband-wife communication.

Two-person communication always involves a sender of messages and a receiver of messages. Neither the sender role nor the receiver role is exclusive to one individual, however. Rather, the two interacting people switch back and forth between the two roles, taking turns being sender and receiver. What kinds of "messages" do people send and receive? How do they prepare their messages, and what do they do with the messages they receive? Why are messages so often misunderstood?

Communication
an interactive process in which at least two people continually send and receive information.

The Symbolic Nature of Human Communication

Human communication is different from the communication of most other animals in that human communication is largely symbolic. A **symbol** is something (a series of pencil strokes, a word, a sound, a gesture, or an object) that has a certain meaning because people agree that it should have that particular meaning. A symbol represents something other than itself. For example, within a school context, the three pencil strokes that make up the letter "A" symbolize that a student has performed well. Because symbols are arbitrary creations, the same symbol can mean different things to different people and the meaning of symbols can change.

Symbol
a word, sound, gesture, or object that has a certain meaning because people agree that it should.

Human beings use three major symbolic "channels" when communicating with one another: a **verbal channel**, consisting of words; a **vocal channel**, consisting of speaking tone and inflection; and a **visual or nonverbal channel**, consisting of body movements and facial expressions (Noller, 1982). Each channel can be used alone or in combination with other channels to communicate information, ideas, and emotions (Gaelick, Bodenhausen, & Weyer, 1985). For example, the phrase "I'm going to the grocery store now" (the verbal channel) said in a neutral tone (the vocal channel) and accompanied by movement towards the door with keys and money (the visual channel) conveys information. The phrase "I'm very upset about this" (the verbal channel) said in an angry tone (the vocal channel) and accompanied by tightly gripping the other person's arm (the visual channel) conveys both emotion and information. In these examples, the symbolic messages conveyed by each of the three channels is consistent. Later in the chapter, we will discuss situations in which the channels are inconsistent with one another.

> **Verbal channel**
> the words used in sending a message.
>
> **Vocal channel**
> the speaking tone and inflection used in sending a message.
>
> **Visual or nonverbal channel**
> the body movements and facial expressions used when sending a message.

The Communication Process

The process of sending and receiving symbolic messages over the verbal, vocal, and visual channels involves several steps. These steps are

Good family communication involves various forms of expression, including such nonverbal cues as eye contact.

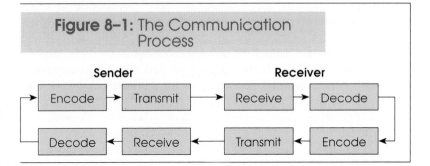

Figure 8–1: The Communication Process

Sender · Receiver

Encode → Transmit → Receive → Decode

Decode ← Receive ← Transmit ← Encode

Communication is a complex process, consisting of many steps. Errors in any of the steps can cause misunderstandings and conflict.

diagrammed in Figure 8–1. Start at the point marked "sender" on the diagram to follow the process. The sender first *encodes* his message into a sendable form—a sentence, gesture, facial expression, or all three. Then he *transmits* his encoded message (for example, by speaking a sentence aloud). The receiver *receives* (hears the spoken sentence) and *decodes* (determines what the message means) the transmission prior to encoding and transmitting her response. The original sender, in turn, receives and decodes the original receiver's transmitted message.

Clearly, the encoding, transmitting, receiving, and decoding of messages is a complicated process. This complexity increases the possibility of mistakes since errors can be made during any step of the process. We will deal with some of the complexities in the section on "Noise." First, however, let us apply the process described in Figure 8–1 to a husband-wife interaction that worked very well. The basic outline of this example comes from a student; we have elaborated on it somewhat to illustrate the separate components of the communication process.

The student, a married woman, wanted to have sexual intercourse with her husband (*the message*) as soon as he got home. She decided that she needed to get his attention immediately and strikingly and decided to communicate using the visual channel. When the husband arrived at their apartment, he was greeted by a wife dressed only in clear plastic wrap (her way of *encoding* and *transmitting* her message). The husband, in this case, correctly *received* and *decoded* his wife's message. Perhaps his thought process went something like this: "She has never done *this* before but then she always has been full of surprises! I haven't seen any other signs that she's losing her mind and, come to think of it, she has been reading that book on pleasing your husband. I think she is eager for sex right now and I feel the same way!" He transmitted his response by saying "Yes!" and eagerly followed her into the bedroom.

Noise in Communication

Human messages are sometimes disrupted by "noise" in the same way that telecommunication messages are; in each case, eliminating the noise improves the chances of the message being sent and received accurately (Broderick, 1988). Human communication can break down because of noise due to sender error, receiver error, the use of meta-messages, and interchannel inconsistency.

Sender Error

The sender can be the source of noise and consequent misunderstanding by selecting a word or phrase that means something different to the receiver than it does to the sender. For example, students who want to ask their professors for permission to miss class often encode their message like this: "Are we doing anything important in class today?" The student wants to send the message that he is not an habitual, unselective absentee. The professor is likely to decode the message as "This student does not take my class very seriously if he thinks that some class days are less important than others!"

Senders might also send ambiguous "noisy" messages because they have mixed feelings about what they want to communicate. Imagine that you are physically attracted to a person who is totally different from you in terms of values and interests. What message do you encode and transmit? One that says "I'd like to know you better" or one that says "Stay away from me"? In such situations, people often send mixed messages—for example, avoiding the person but sneaking a glance (with eyes that glow) at her whenever she comes near. The receiver, in this case, is likely to be very confused.

In other cases, the sender is clear about feelings and knows how to encode the message accurately but realizes that an honest, accurate message is negative and might hurt the receiver. Such situations occur often in male-female relationships. Let us say that you are a man and your girlfriend is wearing a new perfume that smells (to you) like the monkey house at a zoo. Since there are few guidelines on how to encode and transmit a negative but true message, you will probably try to: 1. ignore the perfume, 2. make a noncommital response such as "That perfume has an interesting aroma", or 3. lie and say that you like the perfume.

Receiver Error

Accurate reception of sent messages is an undervalued skill in human communication. When the receiver accurately and perceptively understands the message the sender has sent and responds appropriately, the interaction is off to a very promising start. But inattention, inaccurate reception, or incorrect interpretation can lead to bad feelings and breakdowns in communication. Look back to Figure 8–1. Note that the receiver's response is based *not* on the sender's message, but rather on the receiver's *perception and interpretation* of the sender's message during the decoding stage (Kinch, 1963). In decoding a message, the perceptive receiver is aware of not only *what* the sender is saying (the verbal channel), but also *how* it is said (the vocal channel), and what body and facial movements accompany it (the visual channel). In addition, the perceptive receiver may try to remember similar messages and their meanings in the past. Only then does the sender encode and transmit a response.

Let us take a case in which the encoded message was inaccurately decoded. Again, the story involves a student wife and her husband. After a rough day, the wife wanted to feel better and thought that being held by her husband would help (wanting to be held was *the message* she wanted to send). She *encoded* and *transmitted* the message by telling her husband that she wanted to "snuggle," a term she had used in the past to refer to hugging. He *received* the message "snuggle," but *decoded* it to mean that his wife wanted to have sex (perhaps he was not paying attention to the visual and vocal channels, perhaps he had forgotten what she meant by "snuggle," perhaps she was giving a mixed message, perhaps he wanted sex himself). His subsequent actions, based on his misinterpretation of the situation, only angered the wife and made her feel more misunderstood than ever.

Meta-Messages

Meta-message
a message that has a meaning other than what it symbolizes on the surface.

A **meta-message** is a message that has a meaning other than what it symbolizes on the surface; it is a "hidden message" or a "message behind the message." Senders sometimes purposely hide their true message, perhaps one touching their deepest feelings and insecurities, in a series of messages that seem, on the surface, to be simply informational. Consider the following wife-to-husband messages, scattered over a period of several days or weeks:

1. "Times have sure changed. My father was able to buy his wife a new car every year."
2. "My brother and his wife just got back from a two-week Hawaiian vacation. Wouldn't it be great to be able to afford that?"
3. "You should see that new house going up in the next block—it's going to be a mansion. The main floor of our house would fit into their master bedroom suite."

Perhaps this wife simply liked to pay attention to and report on the economic well-being of others. However, she might also be sending her husband the meta-message, "Honey, I love you but I wish you were more financially successful."

Receivers of all messages are faced with the task of sorting out which messages to receive and respond to at face value and which messages to interpret as meta-messages with deeper meanings. Consider a few of the possibilities in the case above:

1. The wife was merely making comments about luxuries different acquaintances had. The husband interprets the message correctly and responds by giving other examples of well-off people.
2. The wife intended a meta-message and the husband interpreted it correctly. He responds by telling her that he wishes he could be a better provider, too, and invites her to come up with suggestions.
3. The wife intended a meta-message but the husband missed it. She cannot figure out why he responds to her deeply-felt concerns with trivial conversation.
4. The wife did not intend a meta-message, but the husband thinks she did. She can understand neither his defensiveness nor his apologies.

Interchannel Inconsistency

A final type of communication "noise" is **interchannel inconsistency**, the lack of correspondence between verbal, vocal, and visual communication. Some people are very cognizant of all three communication channels and work hard to assure that their spoken message, their way of speaking, and their overall appearance and gestures convey a clear and consistent message. The receivers of such messages can feel confident that they have received and decoded the message correctly because all three channels "match" and reinforce one another. For example, a wife whose husband embraces her while tenderly saying "I love you" is likely to feel loved.

Sometimes, however, the messages sent on the visual, vocal, and verbal channels do not match. This can occur when the sender is unsure of which message to send, when the sender pays much more attention to one channel than to the others, or when an honest message would be a hurtful one. The receiver in such situations is confused about which message to accept and decode. Take our earlier perfume example. The boyfriend *says* "I really like that perfume" but says it in a sarcastic way and spends the rest of the afternoon trying to sit apart from his girlfriend. If the girlfriend pays attention to the vocal and visual channels and wants the approval of her boyfriend, she is unlikely to wear the perfume in his presence again. If she focuses only on his verbal message, however, she will keep wearing the perfume.

> **Interchannel inconsistency**
> lack of correspondence between verbal, vocal, and visual communication.

COMMUNICATION IN MARRIAGE

Marital communication is a type of two-person communication. Although we might expect husbands and wives to be somewhat more successful at accurately encoding, transmitting, and decoding messages than people in a less intimate relationship, getting married does not make the confusion inherent in two-person interaction disappear. Some married couples are very successful communicators and some are quite unsuccessful. Marital specialists, recognizing the importance of communication for the success of marriage, have asked the question, "What types of marital communication enhance marital happiness and facilitate marital success?" Their answers, detailing the characteristics of good marital communication, are summarized in this section. As you read through the characteristics, note that many of them represent *choices* that couples make about how they will communicate with one another. Some choices lead to enhanced communication and relationships; others discourage continued communication and, indirectly, the continuation of the relationship.

Choosing Good Marital Communication

In Chapter 7, we introduced you to the writings of Stinnett and DeFrain (1985) regarding the characteristics of strong marriages and families. These two authors pay considerable attention to the importance of good marital communication in strengthening family life. According to them, good marital communication requires time, good listening skills, and understanding the other person's point of view. It takes place in a caring environment and is honest but kind (Stinnett & DeFrain, 1985).

Time

Good marital communication requires time together and cannot be hurried. The topics of communication do not matter much, as long as couples take some time to converse with one another. Some couples with strong marriages set aside some time each day or week strictly for conversation; others converse while they are doing chores, having dinner, or driving to work. Many married couples, however, spend very little time talking to one another. One study cited by Stinnett and DeFrain (1985) found that the average married couple spends only 17 minutes a week in conversation. This means, of course, that some spend even less.

Good Listening Skills

Although some husbands and wives have difficulty letting their partner talk, good marital communication requires that both partners talk and that both listen. One wife in a strong marriage recounts how she trained her husband not to monopolize their conversations: "We used a timer at home to take turns—kind of like you do with children. I'd set it for three minutes and he'd talk; then I'd get the next three—with no unnecessary interruption. As he learned to listen, we put the timer away" (Stinnett & DeFrain, 1985, p. 65).

Accuracy

As noted earlier, misunderstandings can creep into any two-person communication. In good marital communication, each spouse accurately encodes, transmits, receives, and decodes the messages. Each is careful to avoid meta-messages, and each asks for clarification about confusing messages. For example, a mutual friend continually gets into trouble when he and his wife are traveling and she says, "Look, there is a garage sale (or a discount mall or a craft show)." He always says "I see it" and drives on by. And as he travels down the road, his wife becomes incensed because he does not stop and let her shop. The husband, however, is responding to what she says, not what she means. And she is not saying what she means. If she would say "I'd like to stop and shop there" or if he would ask "Would you like to stop here and shop?," this particular misunderstanding would not occur.

You might argue "He should have known that's what she meant." Stinnett and DeFrain (1985) are especially critical of this approach to communication. They suggest that couples avoid **mind raping**, assuming knowledge about what the other person is thinking without taking the time to find out, and insist that people be sure they really know what the other means rather than just assuming they do. Queries such as "I don't understand. Would you explain that to me again?" or "Do you mean . . .?" help to insure each knows what the other means.

Mind raping
assuming knowledge of what another person is thinking without taking the time to find out what that person really means.

Understanding the Other's Point of View

Each person sees the world from a point of view derived from his or her own upbringing and prior experiences. In a marriage, the husband has his own unique point of view and the wife has hers. Differences in points of view can interfere with good marital communication. Building good communication patterns, then, means trying to understand the other's point of view and taking that view into consideration when encoding and decoding messages. One wife reported:

> He and I had fought over housekeeping—I'd fuss that our place was messy; he'd say it was comfortable. When I got it cleaned to suit me, he'd say it was too tidy, too sterile. One day it dawned on me that Hank's folks are more relaxed about housekeeping. They are clean—don't get me wrong—but they like to have books and magazines handy. She always has needlework materials out—on the table or scattered about the living room. (Stinnett & DeFrain, 1985, p. 69)

Once this wife viewed the living room through her husband's eyes, the couple came to understand how each felt about neatness and livability and were able to work out compromises that eliminated the conflict.

A Caring Communication Environment

Spouses in strong marriages value each other and care about what the other is going through. By showing their willingness to share both good and bad times in caring ways, they help each other feel good about themselves and their marriage. Creating a caring communication environment also encourages continued positive communication. One salesman, worried about his family's financial security during his early career, initially told his wife there was "nothing wrong" when she asked why he looked so worried. His wife persisted, however, by saying "Yes, you are worried . . . and I think it's only natural. But I hate to see you feel that way. Let's talk about it and see if the situation is as bad as it seems and what actions we can take to make things better" (quoted in Stinnett & DeFrain, 1985, p. 70). The care and concern in this wife's comments are obvious. With the caring atmosphere she established, she and her husband were successful in addressing the problems that had him so worried.

Creating a caring atmosphere also helps each member of the couple to "open up" to the other and to disclose innermost thoughts and feelings. As noted, such self-disclosure is a major component of intimacy. In addition, self-disclosure is a major contributor to marital satisfaction; the greater the self-disclosure of both husband and wife to the other, the greater the marital satisfaction (Schumm et al., 1986; Davidson, Balswick, & Halverson, 1983; Hendrick, 1981).

Honest, yet Kind

People often face situations of wanting to be honest with another person but fear that honesty will cause pain or discomfort. The desire to avoid hurting the other is perhaps especially strong between intimate partners. Nonetheless, married couples with strong relationships are honest, yet not brutal, in the messages the partners send to one another. They maintain a delicate balance between honesty and kindness. Fear of offending his wife does not prevent an honest, yet kind husband from gently pointing out when he thinks she is about to make an unwise career decision. Nor does such fear inhibit a woman who knows that her husband is about to make a foolish purchase. Such honesty is best expressed in the caring and sympathetic way of two people who are really concerned about the other's welfare. Look at the Personal Application in this chapter for additional ideas about good communication practices.

Personal Application

Good Communication Practices

Good marital communication is built on good communication practices. Think about your own communication style. How often do you use the good communication practices listed here with those to whom you feel closest—parents, children, siblings, or intimate partner? Do you sometimes get careless and forget to use them? What happens when you fail to use them?

1. *Send clear and accurate messages.* Precise and unambiguous statements facilitate good communication, while imprecise and ambiguous statements hinder it. Consider the difference between these two statements: "You hurt me tonight at the party." versus "I was hurt when you told your friends that the most exciting part of your life ended when you married me."
2. *Avoid double bind messages.* Do not send simultaneous messages with mutually exclusive meanings. How many messages are contained in the following sequence of statements? "No! There is nothing wrong! And I don't want to talk about it!"
3. *Be empathetic.* Empathy can be defined as the sympathetic understanding of what another person is thinking, feeling, and experiencing. The meaning of empathy is captured in the sentence: "In order to really know what I am going through, you have to put yourself in my place." By trying to put yourself in his or her place, you can better understand what he or she is trying to say.
4. *Provide feedback.* Communication involves an exchange of information. The response (or feedback) to the message the other person has sent indicates the message was (or was not) received and was (or was not) understood. "Yes, go on, I'm listening." "No, I don't understand that. Would you please repeat it?"
5. *Be generous with supportive and positive statements.* Accuracy, empathy, and feedback are all important. But we all like to feel good about ourselves. When we give recognition to the worth of another person, when we compliment their accomplishments, and when we reassure them of how important they are to us, we not only make them feel better, we build a stronger foundation for communication.

Factors Affecting Marital Communication

Couples can choose whether or not to incorporate the characteristics associated with good communication into their own communication patterns. Choices are not without limitations, however, nor are the communication-enhancing choices always easy to implement. Three major factors—gender role socialization, marital power, and situational constraints—impinge on communication choices.

Gender Role Socialization

The differential socialization of men and women shows up clearly in the problems they encounter when they communicate with one another. As noted in Chapters 4 and 5, men and women often have communication problems long before they marry. One study of such problems investigated how often the normal, "nonflirtatious" friendly behavior of young men and women was misperceived by the opposite sex as being sexually oriented (Abbey, 1987). Two out of three college students (72 percent of women and 60 percent of men) reported instances in which their friendly behavior had been misunderstood as being sexually motivated. Men and women responded to the misperception in different ways. Men were much more likely than women to be indifferent to, or actually happy about, the misunderstanding. Women were likely to be upset, angry, embarrassed, insulted, or to feel used when their behavior was misperceived as sexual. Figure 8–2 illustrates the study's findings.

Misperception problems related to differential gender role socialization continue into marriage and can produce substantial communication problems for husbands and wives. Francesca Cancian (1987) identifies two conceptions of love related to traditional gender role socialization: the **feminine conception of love** emphasizes the importance of talking, emotional expression, and self-disclosure, and the **masculine conception of love** emphasizes spending time together, doing specific chores for one another, and sex. As noted in Chapter 2, not everyone incorporates traditional gender roles into their own gender identity—some men hold "feminized" conceptions of love and some women hold "masculinized" conceptions. However, men and women who identify with and incorporate traditional gender roles end up with different ways of expressing love. What happens when such men and women marry one another?

Prepared by socialization to be more emotionally expressive, wives holding a feminized conception of love tend to communicate their emotions to their husbands through direct verbal messages (for example, saying "I love you") or through affectionate actions (spontaneously

Feminine conception of love
definition of love emphasizing the importance of talking, emotional expression, and self-disclosure.

Masculine conception of love
definition of love emphasizing spending time together, doing specific chores for one another, and sex.

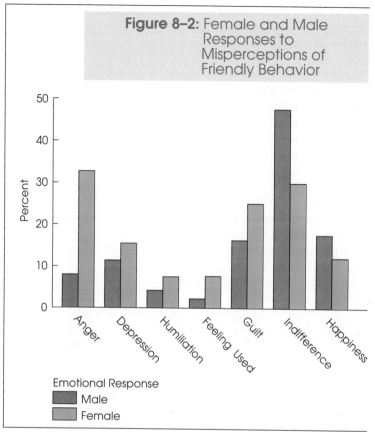

Figure 8–2: Female and Male Responses to Misperceptions of Friendly Behavior

Percent

Anger   Depression   Humiliation   Feeling Used   Guilt   Indifference   Happiness

Emotional Response
■ Male
■ Female

How do you feel when behavior you define as being "friendly" is misperceived as being sexually oriented by a member of the opposite sex? Most male college students in one survey said they felt indifferent about being misperceived; many female students felt angry.

Source: Abbey, 1987, p. 186. Antonio Abbey, "Misperceptions of Friendly Behavior as Sexual Interest: A Survey of Naturally Occurring Incidents," *Psychology of Women Quarterly*, Cambridge University Press.

hugging or kissing their husband) (Thompson & Walker, 1989; Cancian, 1987). Husbands, to the extent that they accept the masculinized conception of love, more often communicate their feelings of emotional attachment through sex, shared activities, practical help, or just being in the spouse's presence. Each spouse might well be unaware of the socialization of the other and assume that, since the partner is not showing emotional attachment in the "appropriate" way, the attachment simply is not there. Consider the husband who washed his wife's car as a way of showing his affection and was surprised when she did not accept the act as an affectionate one (Cancian, 1987).

Deborah Tannen (1990) in her book *You Just Don't Understand!* (from which we quoted at the beginning of this chapter) focuses on related female-male differences in communication. She asserts that males and females are trained differently, and that each sex has its own

Genderlect
gender-associated
style of
using language,
equivalent to
regional dialects.

dialect, or **genderlect**, equivalent to regional variations in English. That is, women learn a certain style of English that they typically (but not necessarily) use, and men learn another style that they typically (but again, not necessarily) use.

Typical female genderlect is based on several assumptions, the most important of which are *equality* and *community*. Women who accept these assumptions (and not all do) use language to create a sense of equality among the people with whom they are talking ("No matter what our particular strengths and weaknesses are, we are all ultimately the same") and to try to build a sense of closeness, intimacy, and caring in the group ("We are all in this together").

Men's genderlect is based on very different assumptions: *independence* and *hierarchy*. Men who accept these assumptions (and again, not all do) use language to assert that they are independent actors in the real world, not tied down or dependent on anyone. Secondly, they use language as a weapon in their constant struggle to establish their place in life's hierarchy. In speaking, they try to be in a "superior" position to as many people as possible and in an "inferior" position to as few people as possible.

The net result of these differences in genderlect, according to Tannen (1990), is that many husbands and wives have very different goals when they talk. Wives who accept female genderlect assumptions talk for the sake of talking with the subject matter being irrelevant. The very act of talking is, for them, a way of creating and maintaining an equal, "we're in this together", intimate relationship with their spouse. Husbands, on the other hand, do not see "just talking" as a way of building and maintaining relationships. Those husbands who accept male genderlect assumptions will listen only when their wives have something useful (perhaps for an upcoming status battle) to say.

Researchers who record and analyze conversations between married people find that Tannen's assumptions ring true. When Fishman (1978) analyzed hours of "everyday", at-home, husband-wife conversation, she found that wives worked much harder trying to establish and maintain conversation with their spouses than husbands did. Wives asked their husbands questions about some topic to get a response and used phrases such as "D'ya know?" and "This is interesting" to involve husbands in a dialogue. For their part, husbands frequently ignored or actively discouraged their wives' attempts to engage them in conversation. In doing so, they asserted their independence.

When husbands initiated conversations, regardless of topic, wives worked hard to sustain a dialogue. They actively participated in the conversation by commenting on the husband-chosen topic, encouraged further talking by showing interest in the topic, and otherwise indicated their desire that the dialogue continue (Fishman, 1978).

In short, *spoken words* are really critical for women in intimate relationships but are just not that important for men (Tannen, 1990; Thompson & Walker, 1989; Rubin, 1983; Fishman, 1978). Wives typically want extensive, self-disclosing conversation because that is such an important component of how they define love. Men do not put that much emphasis on talking because conversation is not that important in the masculinized definition of love. The different value that men and women place on conversation causes problems in many relationships.

Men and women attach differential importance not only to verbal communication, but also to nonverbal communication. In particular, wives seem more concerned than husbands that their nonverbal messages be received and decoded accurately. One study found that marriages in which the husband had become skilled at understanding the nonverbal messages sent by the wife were more satisfying for both spouses. Husbands who were not skilled at interpreting their wives' nonverbal cues were less often satisfied with their marriages. Their wives were also less satisfied (Gottman & Porterfield, 1981). Wives' ability or inability to read their husbands' nonverbal cues, however, was unrelated to the marital satisfaction of either spouse (Gottman & Porterfield, 1981).

Marital Power

The distribution of marital power affects both how spouses communicate and who wins conflicts. Here we deal with the effects of power on communication; effects on conflicts will be discussed in the second half of the chapter. What is marital power? **Marital power** is the ability to get one's own way within the marriage. Specifically, the spouse with more marital power has greater influence in important family decisions.

What determines who has marital power and who does not? One critical factor is the control of resources, especially economic resources. Spouses who have much more education or who have higher status, better-paying jobs than their partners tend to have more marital power, as do employed spouses married to nonemployed or unemployed partners. A good example of the importance of economic resources for marital power is the control of one's own money. Both men and women typically believe that the right to dominate the decision-making process is based on one's financial contribution to the relationship; the more money one person contributes relative to the amount the other contributes, the more power that person is expected to have (Blumstein & Schwartz, 1983). Since married men generally earn more than their wives, they often have the power advantage.

> Marital power
> the ability to get
> one's own way
> within the
> marriage.

Wives who earn an outside income gain marital power; the more they earn relative to their husband, the more power they have (Blumstein & Schwartz, 1983; Bell, Chafetz, & Horn, 1982). They feel freer to spend money however they choose and feel less accountable to their husbands for the financial decisions they make. The importance of having one's own money and one's own job can be seen in the following statement made by a wife about her frequently unemployed husband:

> He had trouble getting a job and almost never could keep one. If I didn't have my job as a waitress, we would have starved. Even though he didn't make no money, he still wanted to control the house and the kids. But it was my money, and I wasn't about to let him spend it on booze and gambling. That really used to tee him off. (quoted in Gelles & Straus, 1988, p. 82)

A second factor affecting marital power is the acceptance of traditional gender role ideology. Couples who accept the philosophy that the husband is the principal provider generally accord him more power within the marriage. Indeed, if *either* spouse endorses the male-provider role philosophy, the husband has more power (Blumstein & Schwartz, 1983). This is true even in cases where the wife works and makes more money than her husband. As long as she accepts the male-provider role philosophy, her husband continues to be the most influential in couple decisions, especially financial ones.

Some couples, particularly those who split up household duties in traditional ways (basically, she does the inside work and he does the outside work), also divide marital power along such lines. Each spouse has areas of expertise and, at least up to a point, holds more marital power in those areas (Bell, Chafetz, & Horn, 1982). Thus, the wife in a traditional marriage might have more marital power when deciding what type of kitchen curtains to buy, and her husband might have more power when deciding what color to paint the exterior of the house.

Finally, physical stature and strength can influence marital power. Spouses who are physically larger and stronger than their partners can use their physical advantage to have their own way. Physical strength is especially important in situations of conflict and violence, topics discussed in the last part of this chapter.

Resources, acceptance of traditional gender ideology, and physical strength can all influence who has marital power. But how does marital power influence day-to-day couple communication? Research focusing on marital power and its effects on marital communication finds that the relative power of husband and wife within a marriage is an important determinant of marital communication patterns (Kollock, Blumstein, & Schwartz, 1985). If the husband is the more powerful partner, he dominates marital conversations. He talks the most, talks about what he wants to talk about, and frequently interrupts his wife. Similarly, if the wife is the more powerful, she dominates marital interaction. Husbands and wives who are equal in power also tend to be equal participants in marital communication, with neither being dominant (Kollock, Blumstein, & Schwartz, 1985).

Situational Constraints

Most husbands and wives have interests and obligations outside their immediate marital relationship. At times, these extra-marital activities can interfere with marital communication. For example, a wife's bowling league or her husband's volunteer work at a shelter for the homeless might keep them from spending the time together that is required for good communication. Sometimes the expectations of others affect how much quiet, intimate time a couple shares. For example, for many years there was a White House tradition that the President and First Lady should sleep in separate bedrooms. The extent to which this tradition affected the marital relationship of First Families is unknown. However, there must have been at least some disenchantment with the tradition since it no longer exists; President Gerald Ford and First Lady Betty Ford broke the tradition, announcing that they would share both bedroom and bed.

As you will learn in more detail in Chapter 12, children constitute a special barrier to marital communication. Children, especially young ones, require time, energy, and often immediate attention on an unpredictable schedule. All this can limit the opportunities husband and wife have to spend time with each other. One in-depth study of interaction in a family consisting of husband, wife, and three preschool children found that only 4 percent of the total verbal interactions in the family were between the two adults (Piotrkowski, 1979). Larger scale studies find much the same thing; the greater the number of children in a family, the less the interaction between husband and wife (White, 1983).

In addition, work obligations can interfere with marital communication. Some jobs—like management and teaching—require a large investment of hours, including hours spent at home at night preparing for the next day. Others—like some sales and transportation jobs—require extensive travel. Military service requires both extensive time and frequent travel. If you followed the human interest stories of the United Nations-Iraq War of 1991, you are probably aware of numerous couples who had to virtually suspend their relationship because of military assignment.

What happens when marital communication is interrupted or when opportunities to spend time together are limited? Numerous studies

Work that takes a spouse a long way from home—like an overseas military assignment—can seriously inhibit marital communication.

suggest that these relationships suffer. One study of couples in which one partner was involved in evening or nighttime shift work found that such arrangements did modest but measurable damage to marital quality and increased the probability of divorce (White & Keith, 1990). Dual-earner couples, even without shift work complications, spend less time together in play, conversation, watching TV, eating, taking care of the household, and raising the children than couples with only one earner. Such time constraints might, when combined with other factors, lead to reduced marital satisfaction (Kingston & Nock, 1987). These effects will be considered in more detail in Chapter 9.

Marital Communication and Marital Quality

How important is good marital communication to overall marital quality? Much research published during the 1980s concluded that good communication is one of the most important contributors to high marital quality (Noller & Fitzpatrick, 1990; Stinnett & DeFrain, 1985; Ting-Toomey, 1983). In fact, some research suggests that communication is *the key factor* in marital quality, surpassing such competing factors as marital sex, family finances, and leisure time spent together (Ting-Toomey, 1983).

Good communication is associated with marital satisfaction for both younger people and older ones. Brecher (1984), in his study of people over fifty years of age, found that of fifteen nonsexual marital qualities he studied, communication was the most important for marital satisfaction. He stated:

> Wives and husbands who rate the quality of communication in their marriages as excellent to very good enjoy an astonishingly high proportion of happy marriages—the highest for any group in this study.... Open communications between husband and wife thus provide *an almost iron-clad guarantee* of a happy marriage for our respondents. It is almost impossible for a couple to be unhappily married if communications between them are excellent or very good. (p. 82; emphasis added)

While marital communication and marital quality are clearly related to one another, it is difficult to determine which comes first. Is a couple happily married because they communicate well, or do they communicate well because they are happily married? Or is the relationship between communication and marital quality best visualized as a circle—they communicate well because they are happily married and they are happily married because they communicate well? While the issue is still being studied (Noller & Fitzpatrick, 1990), existing evidence suggests that the relationship is circular (the two influence each other) and that marital quality is more important for marital communication than the reverse (Krokoff, Gottman, & Roy, 1988; White, 1983).

In general, then, good communication and high marital quality go together. There are exceptions, however. Some couples are happily married even though their communication patterns are not particularly good (Brecher, 1984). This may be because good communication is simply a more important criteria for judging the quality of the marriage for some couples than for others. For example, couples who want to handle marital problems by communicating with one another about them have happier marriages when their communication is good. For these couples, poor communication disrupts marital happiness because they place a high value on good communication (Krokoff, Gottman, & Roy, 1988). But some couples, including some who are happily married, feel uncomfortable openly communicating with one another about marital problems and prefer to handle conflict by *not* communicating about it (Krokoff, Gottman, & Roy, 1988). For these couples, good communication and marital happiness are unrelated.

There is also evidence that good marital communication cannot compensate for an unhappy marriage. Poor marital communication can lead to lowered marital quality, but enhanced marital communication is not enough by itself to produce marriages of high quality (Noller

& Fitzpatrick, 1990; Schumm *et al.*, 1986). How the self-disclosure aspect of communication affects marital satisfaction, for example, depends on how two spouses feel about one another. For partners who have very positive feelings (care, respect, empathy, and appreciation) toward one another, self-disclosure enhances marital satisfaction; the more they open up and express the positive feelings, the happier their marriage. But for those who do not have such positive feelings about their spouse, self-disclosure does not always lead to a happier marriage. In fact, husbands and wives who have negative feelings toward one another might actually be worse off if they are encouraged to engage in more extensive, self-disclosing marital communication (Schumm *et al.*, 1986).

Thus, good marital communication is not a panacea. It is one of many aspects of a marriage that can improve or hurt a marriage—but only one.

MARITAL CONFLICT

The marital relationship sometimes involves disagreement and conflict. Every marriage, after all, consists of two independent people with their own beliefs, values, attitudes, and desires. The fact that the two received different gender role socialization and grew up in different family cultures adds further potential for conflict. Frequent sources of marital conflict include how to spend money, where to go on vacations, relationships with in-laws, and how to raise the children.

Marital conflict is not necessarily bad. In fact, recognizing and dealing with minor conflicts can have positive effects for a marriage by bringing issues out into the open, clarifying each person's point of view, and preventing the buildup of smaller conflicts into larger ones (Lauer & Lauer, 1991). The critical issue is not that conflicts exist, but rather how couples choose to deal with them. What options are open to a husband and wife who have very different ideas on an important issue? In this section, we will discuss three nonaggressive strategies for dealing with marital disagreements: avoidance, confrontation, and resolution.

Avoiding Conflicts

Some couples deal with potential marital conflict by avoiding issues about which they might disagree. Essentially, this means they often fail to confront actual marital or family problems. There are several avoidance methods. A couple might *postpone* discussion about a problem to a later time ("It's late, we can talk about this tomorrow") or might *ig-*

nore-the problem ("Let's don't think about the credit card bills—this vacation is too much fun.") They might _deny a problem exists_ ("My husband does not beat me—he just slaps me too hard sometimes.") Or they might _withdraw from the conflict_ by threatening to leave or by actually leaving ("If you insist on talking about my mother's interference in our marriage, I'm leaving!")

How does avoidance of conflict ultimately affect the marriage? The effect depends on the answers to two crucial questions: Who chooses the tactic? and How long are problems avoided?

Husband and wife can choose the avoidance tactic jointly as a way of dealing with conflict, or avoidance can be chosen by one partner and then imposed on the other (Fitzpatrick, Fallis, & Vance, 1982). Some married couples jointly agree to handle conflict by avoiding it because each feels very uncomfortable fighting with the other (Krokoff, Gottman, & Roy, 1988). Jointly agreed-upon avoidance tactics can be beneficial for some marriages. But when only one partner chooses avoidance and imposes it on the other, the marriage is more threatened. Such one-sided avoidance might actually become another source of conflict. A male respondent in Rubin's (1983) study of intimate communication illustrates how avoidance can become an additional source of conflict when he describes his reaction to his wife's attempt to discuss problems they are having:

> So lots of time when she starts, I'll back off figuring her talking is only going to make it worse. (With a crooked smile) But that doesn't work so well either because she gets mad because I don't want to hear and then _that's_ the problem. (p. 76)

The question of how long avoidance goes on is also critical to the long-term prospects for the marriage. Temporarily avoiding problems, providing they are addressed later, does not necessarily have a negative impact on the marriage. However, indefinitely avoided and thus unsolved marital conflicts can ultimately lead to further problems (Bowman, 1990). A three year study of the effects of communication on the quality of marriages found that when couples tried to maintain marital peace by avoiding disagreements, the quality of the marital relationship itself was threatened (Gottman & Krokoff, 1989). Avoiding disagreements was sometimes good for the relationship _in the short run_, but, _in the long run_, it often led to the relationship's deterioration.

The avoidance of conflict-inducing problems not only reduces marital satisfaction but may endanger the survival of the marriage itself. In her book on the collapse of relationships, Vaughan (1986) described what happens when couples fail to communicate about their dissatisfaction. In her study, couples began to "uncouple" when one partner became dissatisfied with the relationship but refused to discuss the dissatisfaction openly with the partner. Instead, the unhappy spouse tried to "fix" the relationship (for example, by trying to get the partner to change in some way) without talking to the partner about the problem. When attempts to fix the relationship in this way failed, the dissatisfied partner became convinced the relationship was unsaveable and began to look for a way to end the relationship.

Vaughan's (1986) work suggests that the lack of open discussion about problems dooms many relationships. In the uncouplings she studied, *the dissatisfied partner had given up on the relationship before the other partner was aware there was a serious problem.* By the time the other partner discovered there was a problem, the dissatisfied partner already wanted out.

Confronting Conflicts

Couples who confront their conflicts directly tend to have higher marital satisfaction and fewer problems in the long run than couples who do not (Gottman & Krokoff, 1989; Menaghan, 1982). However, confronting important marital disagreements is not a pleasant task. Couples who choose to confront conflicts and bring them out into the open must sometimes endure short-term marital disharmony. Nonetheless, such couples are happier in the long run (Gottman & Krokoff, 1989).

Which particular techniques work best in confronting conflicts? Stinnett and DeFrain (1985) identify six conflict confrontation techniques used by couples with strong marriages:

1. *Strong couples deal with disagreements when they come up; they do not delay facing them.* As noted, research suggests that indefinite avoidance leads to marital problems and possibly to marital collapse. Couples with strong marriages prefer *no* delay—short-term or indefinite—in addressing their problems. After all, the more they delay, the greater the number of contentious issues that might build up. One husband reports: "We cannot stand to have any contention between us. It bothers both of us to be at odds with each other. As a result we deal with sore spots as quickly as they come up" (quoted in Stinnett & DeFrain, 1985, p. 75).

2. *Strong couples deal with only one conflictual issue at a time.* In most cases, husbands and wives who face each problem as it comes up have the advantage of having to deal with only one issue at a time. Trying to manage one problem is far easier than trying to manage many. Even when confronted with many problems simultaneously, strong couples choose to deal with just one at a time. They select the one they are going to work on and put the rest on hold temporarily. Con-

trast this situation to its opposite: a couple who lets problems pile up, decides to deal with them all in a marathon argument, and ends up overwhelmed and exhausted.

3. *Strong couples try to get to the core of the conflict by focusing on specific issues.* Conflicts over general issues are very difficult to address, but conflicts over specific issues are often much more amenable to solution. One couple continually fought over how much money the wife spent. When they sat down and worked on the specifics of the conflict, they found agreement about all expenditures but one. Once they uncovered the specific area of conflict—the husband felt the wife spent too much on children's clothing—they easily negotiated a solution acceptable to both (Stinnett & DeFrain, 1985).

4. *Strong couples work hard to insure that they know what their conflicts are really about.* Before investing time and energy in lengthy negotiations, couples who use communication to resolve conflicts are careful that they are not simply misunderstanding one another. For example, one husband was furious at his wife when she objected to sending a check to his parents who were in desperate need of money. It turned out she had no objection to her husband sending money to his parents, she just wanted him to wait a couple of days until payday so there would be money in the checking account to cover the check. They avoided an argument and saved negotiation time by clearing up the misunderstanding first (reported in Stinnett & DeFrain, 1985).

5. *Strong couples work as allies to solve their problems.* They avoid "zero-sum" conflicts where one spouse must lose in order for the other to win. Their goal is to develop solutions that benefit the marriage, not either spouse alone. "We try to see ourselves as being on the same side—as a team. The enemy is the problem. We're fighting it—not each other" (quoted in Stinnett & DeFrain, 1985, p. 77).

6. *Spouses in strong marriage do not use their intimate knowledge about each other to hurt one another.* Couples who are emotionally close know enough about one another to inflict great emotional pain; each knows what the other is most sensitive about and fears most. Some couples use such knowledge as "ammunition" in fights. Couples in truly strong marriages do not use such knowledge because they care about each other and because they care about the marriage. As one wife succinctly stated, "To use sensitive areas as attack points is a good way to destroy a marriage . . ." (quoted in Stinnett & DeFrain, 1985, p. 77).

Resolving Conflicts

Confronting conflicts brings them out into the open but does not, in itself, bring about a resolution. How can conflicts be resolved? Experts identify three types of conflict resolution: acceptance of legitimate differences, giving in, and negotiation.

Acceptance of Legitimate Differences

After bringing their disagreements out into the open and discussing them at great length, some couples discover that, in some of areas of life, their differences are simply unresolvable. Each understands the nature of the conflict and each is able to see that the other person's point of view is legitimate. However, both continue to hold their original beliefs and both recognize that mutually acceptable compromise is impossible. In such situations, couples "agree to disagree." They accept both points of view as legitimate and learn to live with their differences.

Note the differences between the "acceptance of legitimate differences" tactic and the avoidance strategy mentioned earlier. For example, a Southern Baptist husband and a Catholic wife who *avoid* religious conflicts never discuss their religious differences and never try to understand their partner's religious beliefs. They never acknowledge to one another that they disagree about religion; their religious differences remain below the surface, perhaps feeding into other conflicts. On the other hand, a Southern Baptist husband and Catholic wife who "agree to disagree" about religion *have* discussed and confronted their differences before concluding that compromise is impossible. They openly acknowledge that they disagree about religion.

Giving In

A second way of resolving conflicts is for one partner to give in and accept the other partner's position. For example, the husband may conclude that continuing conflict about whether the wife should shift from part-time work to full-time work is dangerous for the long-term health of the marriage and give in to her desire to work full-time. Or the wife might realize that her religious beliefs are much less important to her than her husband's religious beliefs are to him and give in to his request that their children participate in his religion. The "giving in" tactic works best when it is noncoercive, when one partner voluntarily gives in without being pressured or threatened by the other.

Negotiation

Some marital disagreements cannot be resolved by agreeing to accept the difference or by one partner giving in. Another conflict-resolution option is negotiation, or working out a mutually agreeable solution to the conflict. Cox (1990, p. 202) suggests that couples approach negotiation in the same way that a team of scientists approaches a scientific investigation. In particular, couples should:

1. Recognize and define the problem.
2. Set up conditions supportive of problem solving.
3. Brainstorm for possible solutions.
4. Select the best solution.
5. Implement the solution.
6. Evaluate the solution.
7. Modify the solution if necessary.

Note that the negotiation process involves teamwork and a certain amount of trial-and-error experimentation. The whole process of brainstorming, implementation, evaluation, and modification works best if husband and wife are approximately equal in resources and marital power. In such a situation, both partners can feel like winners. In cases in which one spouse clearly has more marital power than the other, however, resolutions that look like "negotiated settlements" do, in fact, have a winner and a loser (Bell, Chafetz, & Horn, 1982). The immediate conflict is resolved, but only one partner feels truly satisfied with the resolution.

Couples who find it difficult to negotiate mutually agreeable resolutions on their own sometimes benefit by going to a counselor or therapist. These alternatives are discussed in the Alternative Choice section of Chapter 14.

MARITAL AGGRESSION

Some married couples deal with marital conflict by threatening one another, hurling verbal insults at one another, assaulting one another, and even killing one another. These tactics are known collectively as **marital aggression**, the intent or perceived intent to cause physical or psychological harm or injury to a spouse (Gelles & Straus, 1979). Note that marital aggression includes both violent and nonviolent attacks, threatened attacks, and attacks carried out. Both attacks on one's ego

> **Marital aggression**
> the intent or perceived intent to cause physical or psychological harm or injury to a spouse.

and threatened attacks are nonviolent and leave no physical traces, but they are nonetheless very aggressive and damaging. Like the dating aggression discussed in Chapter 4, marital aggression can be divided into four major categories: verbal aggression, minor physical aggression, severe physical aggression, and marital rape.

Verbal Aggression

When husbands and wives use their intimate knowledge to belittle, scare, or hurt their spouse, they are engaging in verbal aggression (Straus, 1979). Threatening physical harm is another form of verbal aggression. Finally, staring, "giving the finger," sulking, or stomping out of the room are nonverbal but communicative behaviors also classified here as "verbal aggression."

To what extent do married couples in the United States use verbal aggression as a conflict tactic? Stets (1990) employed data from a nationally representative sample to answer the question. After she totaled the reported frequencies of six specific verbal aggression behaviors, she

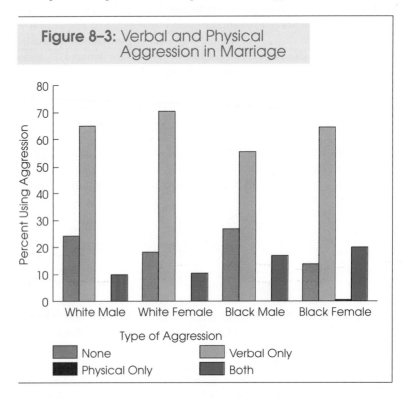

Figure 8–3: Verbal and Physical Aggression in Marriage

During marriage verbal aggression frequently occurs in the absence of physical aggression, but physical aggression virtually never occurs in the absence of verbal aggression.

Source: Stets, 1990, p. 508. Copyrighted (1990) by the National Council on Family Relations, 3989 Central Ave. N.E., Suite #550, Minneapolis, MN 55421. Reprinted by permission.

estimated that as many as *three out of every four* married people engaged in some form of verbally aggressive behavior toward their spouse each year. As illustrated in Figure 8–3, wives are somewhat more likely to use verbal aggression than husbands (Stets, 1990).

At one time, some counselors and many lay people thought that using verbal aggression was a good way to prevent physical aggression. According to this belief, "letting it all hang out" by being verbally aggressive reduced animosity and released pent-up tension. Most research no longer supports this position (Stets, 1990). Instead, the opposite may be true: verbal aggression may lead to physical aggression. What family violence researchers find is an escalating hierarchy of aggression from nonaggression to verbal aggression to physical aggression (Stets, 1990). Verbal aggression almost invariably comes before physical aggression. If verbal aggression is not present, typically neither is physical aggression.

Figure 8–3 illustrates these research results. Note by examining Figure 8–3 carefully that the columns representing "physical aggression only" are almost totally blank. Black males report no "physical aggression only" at all, while the other three categories of respondents report very little. Verbal aggression occurs without physical aggression, but *physical aggression does not occur in the absence of verbal aggression*. While verbal aggression cannot be considered the *cause* of physical aggression, it does seem to be a prerequisite (Stets, 1990).

Minor Physical Aggression

All physical aggression carries some risk of injury, but some types of physical aggression (for example, beating up, kicking, or using a gun or knife) carry considerably more risk than others (for example, throwing something or slapping). For our purposes, aggressive behaviors with a low risk of producing serious injury are considered "minor" while those with a high risk are considered "severe."

Many people believe that minor physical aggression not intended to do serious bodily injury is a "normal" part of married life (Straus, Gelles, & Steinmetz, 1989). For example, a substantial minority of husbands and wives consider slapping and hitting to be "normal" between married partners. In addition, as many as one in four wives and one in three husbands accept the proposition that while marital violence may not be good, it is one of those things that happens in marriage (Straus, Gelles, & Steinmetz, 1989).

Given such attitudes, the data presented in Figure 8–4 (on page 288) are not particularly surprising. Note that nearly one out of ten husbands and wives had pushed or grabbed one another and that somewhat fewer had thrown something at, or had slapped, a spouse.

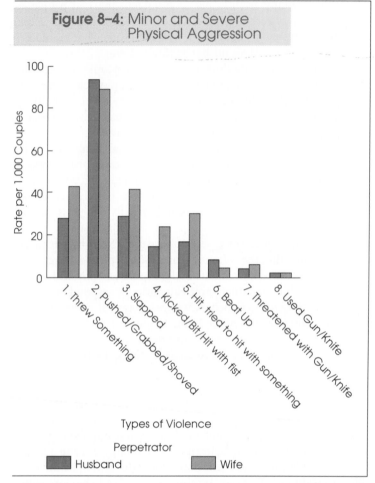

Figure 8-4: Minor and Severe Physical Aggression

Y-axis: Rate per 1,000 Couples

X-axis (Types of Violence):
1. Threw Something
2. Pushed/Grabbed/Shoved
3. Slapped
4. Kicked/Bit/Hit with fist
5. Hit, tried to hit with something
6. Beat Up
7. Threatened with Gun/Knife
8. Used Gun/Knife

Perpetrator: Husband   Wife

Categories 1-3 are defined as "minor" physical aggression; categories 4-8 as "severe" physical aggression. As with dating, more females than males use physical aggression toward their marriage partner. But just as with dating, the consequences of male aggression are more severe than are the consequences of female aggression.

Source: Straus & Gelles, 1986, p. 471. Copyrighted (1986) by the National Council on Family Relations, 3989 Central Ave. N.E., Suite #550, Minneapolis, MN 55421. Reprinted by permission.

Figures 8–3 and 8–4 show that wives are somewhat more likely to direct physical aggression at husbands than vice-versa; Figure 8–3 shows that black couples engage in physically aggressive conflict more often than white couples.

Severe Physical Aggression

As noted, severe physical aggression includes actions that carry a high risk of substantial physical injury or even death. Kicking, biting, or hitting the spouse; hitting or trying to hit the spouse with something;

beating up the spouse; threatening the spouse with a gun or knife; or using a gun or a knife on the spouse are examples of severe physical aggression, also called **spouse abuse**. Few people consider actions such as these a "normal" part of married life. Nonetheless, national surveys show that about three percent of U.S. husbands and four percent of U.S. wives engage in one or more of these violent acts toward their spouse every year. The combined risk for these five behaviors occurring in any one family is about six percent. That is, about six out of every 100 marriages in the United States is marked by at least one episode of severe physical aggression every year (Straus & Gelles, 1986). This means, assuming rates have not changed since 1985, that about 3,200,000 of the 53,000,000 married couples in the United States experience spouse abuse each year.

> Spouse abuse
> acts of severe
> physical aggression
> directed against a
> marriage partner.

Figure 8–4 indicates that, even in the general category of severe physical aggression, wives have higher rates than husbands. The data on sex differences in marital aggression can be easily misunderstood, however, since more acts of aggression do not necessarily mean more damage inflicted (Hampton, Gelles, & Harrop, 1989). Given average sex differences in size, strength, marital power, and aggressiveness, husbands' marital aggression undoubtedly causes more damage to wives than wives' does to husbands. Note also that husbands have higher rates of the most dangerous and injurious forms of violence such as beating up their spouse (Straus, Gelles, & Steinmetz, 1989). Experts believe that much of the aggressive behavior of wives, in fact, stems from self-defense, self-preservation, or retaliation (Hampton, Gelles, & Harrop, 1989; Straus, Gelles, & Steinmetz, 1989).

But husbands are not always bigger, stronger, and more powerful than their wives, and some husbands are clearly victims of spouse abuse. Consider this case of husband abuse:

> A wealthy, elderly New York banker was finally granted a separation from his second wife, 31 years his junior, after 14 years of marriage and physical abuse. According to the presiding judge, the wife had bullied him with hysteria, screaming tantrums and vicious physical violence.
>
> The husband wore constant scars and bruises. His ear had once been shredded by his wife with her teeth. She had blackened his eyes, and on one occasion injured one of his eyes so badly that doctors feared it would be lost. (Straus, Gelles, and Steinmetz, 1989, pp. 308–309)

Marital Rape

> Marital rape
> one spouse forces
> the other to have
> sex by the use
> of intimidation
> or violence.

One of the most extreme forms of severe spouse abuse is **marital rape**. Here, one spouse (typically, but not always, the husband) forces the other spouse to have sex through intimidation or violence. While reliable estimates of marital rape are difficult to obtain, two separate studies produced remarkably similar results: about 10 percent of wives have been raped by their husbands (Gelles & Cornell, 1985, p. 70). The 10 percent estimate may be a very conservative one, however, since many women do not define forced sex with their husband as rape (Gelles & Cornell, 1985). Just as spouses are more likely to be assaulted by one another than by a stranger (Straus, Gelles, & Steinmetz, 1989), wives are more likely to be subjected to forced sex by their husbands than to be victims of rape by a stranger (Gelles & Cornell, 1985).

Spousal exemption laws

laws that prevent one spouse from charging the other with rape.

Traditionally, the states have not considered forced sex within marriage to be "rape" and, in fact, had **spousal exemption laws** on the books preventing one spouse from charging the other with rape. Recent attention to marital rape has resulted in changes in relevant state laws. At least 18 states throughout the United States—for example, Georgia, Nebraska, New York, Oregon, and Wisconsin—have abolished the marital rape exemption (Nyberg, 1989, p. 286; "Rape and Marriage," 1990). In these states (and maybe more by now), one spouse can charge the other with rape.

Explaining Spouse Abuse

Popular images of marriage and family life may include arguments and perhaps even mock physical fights but seldom feature the more severe aggressive acts known as spouse abuse. After all, intimate relationships are supposed to be based on love, caring, and mutual support. Spouse abuse does not seem to fit into this picture of intimacy. Why, then, does it occur? We will first discuss several factors associated with spouse abuse and then present one theory of intimate violence.

Factors Associated with Spouse Abuse

Some couples are more likely to be involved in spouse abuse than others. Although spouse abuse can occur in marriages involving spouses of all ages, it occurs most often among young married couples (Stets, 1990). In fact, those younger than 30 have spousal abuse rates more than twice as high as those over 30 (Stets, 1990; Gelles & Cornell, 1985). Perhaps young marriages exhibit more spouse abuse because they are more often under financial pressure, perhaps couples eventually learn other tactics for handling conflict, or perhaps most young, violent marriages simply do not survive long enough to become long-lasting, violent marriages.

Spouse abuse occurs more often in low-socioeconomic-status, low-income households. Some of this observed difference is undoubtedly a difference in reporting. Middle- and upper-class families live in more private, isolated homes where neighbors cannot hear what is occurring. Such families are better able to hide spouse abuse from police, medical authorities (by going to private physicians rather than to hospital emergency rooms when injured), and researchers. Nonetheless, lower-income families appear to have higher rates of spouse abuse than families from other income levels, even when reporting differences are taken into account (Gelles & Cornell, 1985; Gelles, 1980). Greater financial pressures and the lack of affordable escapes (the poor have fewer places than others to go to "cool off" in the midst of marital strife) probably contribute to the higher spouse abuse rates among lower-income families.

For some families, violence seems to be part of a family culture passed from one generation to the next. Children exposed to the abuse of one parent by the other (**parental spouse abuse**) are more likely than other children to be abused or to abuse within their own marriages (Stets, 1990; Wallerstein & Blakeslee, 1990; Seltzer & Kalmuss, 1988; Gelles & Cornell, 1985; Kalmuss, 1984; Gelles, 1980). Apparently, some children who observe their parents using physical aggression against one another grow up believing that physical aggression between spouses is a "normal" part of married life (Wallerstein & Blakeslee, 1990).

Both perpetrators and victims of spousal abuse often "blame" alcohol or drugs—"We were both drunk and didn't know what we

> **Parental spouse abuse**
> exposure of a child to the abuse of one parent by the other parent.

Love is not always enough to prevent one spouse from verbally or physically abusing the other spouse.

were doing" or "It's the drugs that make him act that way." There is an association between alcohol/drug consumption and family violence; about half of all family violence incidents involve alcohol use. However, drugs and alcohol cannot be directly blamed; they do not typically produce chemical changes within the body that lead to violent behavior (Gelles & Straus, 1988). Rather, drug and alcohol use seem to give people an ex-post-facto excuse for their violence since, in the United States, people learn that they will not be held accountable for actions done while under the influence of alcohol or drugs. Family violence experts conclude that the belief that "alcohol and drugs are the real causes of violence in the home" is a *myth* (Gelles & Straus, 1988).

A Theory of Intimate Violence

Knowing the factors associated with spouse abuse does not truly explain *why* some couples develop and sustain patterns of spousal abuse. One possible explanation for spousal abuse involves rewards and costs. Specifically, for some individuals in certain situations, the rewards of family violence far exceed its costs (Gelles & Straus, 1988).

How can spousal abuse be rewarding? The possible *rewards* of family violence to the abuser come out in interviews with victims. Those who beat their spouse, or threaten to do so, can force the abused to accede to his or her demands, are able to show who is in control, and, in general, can get his or her own way. As one wife (a victim of two years of abuse) stated:

> I would do anything. I would try to anticipate his moods. Cook his favorite dish. Dress the way he liked. I would have the kids washed and in bed when he got home from work so there wouldn't be any stress at home. I gave up my first job so I could be home, but then he got too worried about money, so I got another job as a teacher. I think I spent twenty-four hours a day either doing things to please him or thinking ahead to prevent his getting mad. (quoted from Gelles & Straus, 1988, p. 34)

Clearly, this woman's husband was rewarded for his abusive behavior. The *costs* of spousal abuse are often very low or nonexistent. Since abusers strike those who generally cannot or will not strike back, they run only a small risk of being injured themselves, especially in the short run. In many communities, abusers also have nothing to fear from official intervention. Police are frequently reluctant to intervene in domestic violence cases. When they do intervene, they arrest the abuser in less than 10 percent of the cases. Consider the case of the wife who called the police and heard them advise her husband to go for a walk around the block so that he could calm down. Here is what happened next, according to the wife:

> Well, Dan was back in about forty-five minutes. He had calmed down, but he had a kind of mean look on his face. When he came in he said, "Well, you played your ace—see what happened—nothing! Now you know who's out there to help you." Christ, calling the cops made it worse. Now he figured he could really beat the shit out of me and no one would do a thing. (quoted in Gelles & Straus, 1988, p. 25)

In this case, there were no costs and, in fact, official intervention left the victim in a more vulnerable position than ever.

Two separate studies suggest that increasing the cost of spousal abuse might indeed reduce its attraction. In a field experiment of domestic violence (of either married or unmarried partners) in Minneapolis, Minnesota, police were randomly assigned one of three ways to respond to accusations of the abuse of the female: give the male a warning, order him to leave the house, or arrest him (Sherman & Berk, 1984). A six-month followup of the cases found that males who had been arrested were far less likely than other abusive males to be arrested again for abuse or to be reported by their partner as abusive.

A second study, done in southern California using police records on wife battery, reported comparable results: arresting a husband for spouse abuse resulted in lower rates of arrest for subsequent spouse abuse (Berk & Newton, 1985). In both studies, increasing the costs of the abuse reduced its chance of recurrence.

Social Change and Marital Violence

The long-term historical record of spouse abuse in the United States shows little change in how often it occurs; what has changed is how much attention the public pays to it, who or what is blamed for it, and what solutions or treatments are proposed (Gordon, 1988). As one historian noted about family violence in general, "Its incidence has not changed as much as its visibility" (Gordon, 1988, p. 2). The Cohort Comparison in this chapter deals with how social work agencies responded to spouse abuse earlier in the twentieth century. In the following paragraphs, we focus on changes in the past fifteen years.

Prior to the mid-1970s, spouse abuse received little public attention; social workers, abused spouses, and victims' families knew about its existence, but for others it remained a hidden problem. The Women's Movement, public concern about families, and increasing interest in all types of family violence have contributed to the explicit recognition of marital violence as a legitimate social problem in recent years. Since the "discovery" of marital violence, research on the topic has greatly increased, some laws governing spouse abuse have been changed, some police departments have changed the ways in which they handle domestic violence calls, and private agencies have established spouse abuse shelters for victims (Straus & Gelles, 1986).

Some sociologists (Hampton, Gelles, & Harrop, 1989; Straus & Gelles, 1986) argue that the explicit concern about marital aggression toward wives during the past decade and a half has had the effect of substantially reducing rates of wife abuse. Table 8–1, based on the findings of national surveys, documents that white wives, white husbands, and especially black wives were less often victims of severe spousal aggression in 1985 than in 1975 (Hampton, Gelles, & Harrop, 1989; Straus & Gelles, 1986). Curiously enough, black husbands were more often reported as victims of severe spousal aggression in 1985 than in 1975, a phenomenon for which there is currently no satisfactory explanation (Hampton, Gelles, & Harrop, 1989).

Despite all the concern about marital violence and all the programs that have been developed to address marital violence, there is still an enormous amount of spouse abuse in marriages. The results of

Table 8–1 Instances of Marital Violence per 1000 Couples, 1975 and 1985, by Race

	1975	1985
Black Husband to Wife		
Overall	169	169
Severe	113	64
Black Wife to Husband		
Overall	153	204
Severe	76	108
White Husband to Wife		
Overall	112	107
Severe	30	28
White Wife to Husband		
Overall	106	116
Severe	41	39

Source: Hampton, Gelles, & Harrop, 1989, p. 974. Copyrighted (1989) by the National Council on Family Relations, 3989 Central Ave. N.E., Suite #550, Minneapolis, MN 55421. Reprinted by permission.

the 1985 Second National Family Violence Surveys—extrapolated to the U.S. population as a whole—suggest that about 1.6 million wives and 2.4 million husbands are subject to physical abuse from their spouses every year (Straus, Gelles, & Steinmetz, 1989, p. 309; Straus & Gelles, 1986, p. 470). The majority of couples engage only in verbal or minor physical aggression or entirely forego aggression as a conflict-handling tactic. But, for a persistent minority, handling marital conflict is a potentially deadly ordeal.

Cohort Comparison   Social Work Handling of Wife Abuse

Spouse abuse was a hidden problem for many years. As historian Linda Gordon (1988) points out, however, women victims of spouse abuse have long tried to get help from family members, neighbors, and social workers. Gordon (1988) examined the records of several Boston social work agencies to learn how family violence was handled in different historical periods. This cohort comparison is based on Gordon's research. We focus specifically on one question: What reception were abused women of each birth cohort likely to get from social workers when they asked for help?

New Century cohort members (born 1910–1914) were young husbands and wives during the Depression years of the 1930s. Wives more often complained to social workers about their husbands' inability to provide financial support than about physical abuse, even when they were visibly the victims of such abuse. Social workers urged the abused wives to try to understand the strain their husbands were under and to become better wives themselves. This tendency to "blame" the wives for their abuse marked a change from the early twentieth century when social workers and other activists worked on reforming abusive husbands by threatening, cajoling, urging short jail sentences, and visiting abusive homes unexpectedly.

Female Depression cohort members (born 1930–1934) were even more likely to be blamed when their husbands abused them. When they sought help in the 1950s and 1960s, an era in which all types of family violence were covered up, their abuse was most likely referred to as "marital discord" or "marital disharmony." Social workers were trained to assume that wives who "allowed themselves" to be abused by their husbands were psychologically abnormal, were excessively dependent or masochistic, or rejected their femininity. At the same time, marital separation came to be seen as a more acceptable alternative than previously.

By the time the Baby Boom cohort women (born 1950–1954) were marrying in the 1970s and 1980s, a larger number of options were open to abused wives, at least in some communities. Spouse abuse was more often seen as resulting from differences in marital power and reflecting conditions in the larger society rather than as a private or psychological problem. Abused Baby Boom cohort wives might be advised to get away from their abusive husband, seek refuge in a battered women's shelter, and learn the skills necessary to support themselves.

There is little question that some members of the Baby Bust cohort (born 1970–1974) will also experience spousal abuse within marriage. The treatment they receive will depend upon how the laws change and whether the reforms started in the 1970s and 1980s continue.

Summary

Marital communication shares many characteristics with human communication in general. Human beings use symbols to communicate with one another and transmit the symbols over three channels: a verbal channel, a vocal channel, and a visual channel. Each two-person communication group includes a sender role and a receiver role with the two people trading roles throughout the interaction. The sender encodes and transmits a message and the receiver receives and decodes it. Noise, in the form of sender error, receiver error, the use of meta-messages, or interchannel inconsistency, often interferes with clear and accurate communication.

The ability of a husband and wife to express their feelings, desires, hopes, and frustrations can facilitate marital success or can contribute to marital failure. Couples who spend lots of time with each other, listen well, work on accuracy in their communication, try to understand the other person's point of view, create a caring communication environment, and are honest in a caring way have the opportunity to enjoy an intimate relationship that will continue to remain strong. Good marital communication does not occur in a vacuum. There are factors that affect its impact and limit what it can do. The differential socialization of men and women, differences in marital power, and situational factors all have an impact on communication.

Despite the benefits of good marital communication, even good communication cannot prevent all marital conflicts. Couples have choices in how they handle conflicts. They can avoid them, confront them, or engage in marital aggression. Couples who choose to confront and resolve their conflicts may have to endure some marital disharmony in the short run. But, by choosing to work through their problems, they have the potential of enhancing their marriage in the long run.

Some couples deal with their conflicts through aggression. Generally, couples who are physically aggressive toward one another are verbally aggressive first. About 10 percent of husbands and wives exhibit minor physical aggression toward their spouses, and three to four percent engage in some form of severe physical aggression toward their spouses each year. Wives are verbally and physically aggressive more often than husbands but also suffer more injury from spousal abuse; blacks have higher levels of marital violence than whites. Marital aggression tends to be concentrated among young couples, those who observed physical aggression between their parents, and those who are currently experiencing severe economic stress. One prominent theory suggests that some people abuse their spouses because the rewards they receive from the abuse far exceed the costs. One special type of marital physical aggression—marital rape—is currently receiving increased legal attention. Once excluded from the rape laws, forced sex between married partners increasingly is considered to be a legally unacceptable form of violence; some states have now declared marital rape to be no different than nonmarital rape.

CHAPTER 9

THE TASKS OF MARRIAGE: DIVIDING MARITAL WORK

WHAT DO YOU THINK?

Here are some statements about men, women, and work. Record your opinion by circling the "agree" or the "disagree" response for each statement.

Statement	Response	
1. It is much better for everyone involved if the man is the achiever outside the home and the woman takes care of the home and family.	Agree	Disagree
2. Women are more capable of managing a household than men.	Agree	Disagree
3. Men are more capable of being successful in the business world than women.	Agree	Disagree
4. Women who have successful careers end up sacrificing too much of their family and personal life.	Agree	Disagree
5. Men who have successful careers end up sacrificing too much of their family and personal life.	Agree	Disagree

Source: *The Gallup Poll Monthly*, February 1990, p. 32.

DEAR ANN LANDERS: I am tired — not just "tired," but bone-weary exhausted. I'm the female of the '80s, a professional woman with a good husband and three wonderful children. I put in 40 hours a week downtown and just as many at home. When people like me are written up in a women's magazine or a newspaper article, you'd think we had the world by the tail. Baloney.

My job as a supervisor is stressful. The demands on me are awesome. Everyone wants something. When I come home I must prepare supper, clean the house, wash clothes, pick up the kids from the activity of the day, help them with homework, see that they are bathed and put to bed. By then, I am totally shot. My body says rest, but my mind says I must get ready for tomorrow.

I am 45 pounds overweight, and every week I add another pound or two. This is another area of my life that I can't seem to control. I know I should go on a diet, but I don't feel like tackling another big job right now.

My husband helps more than most husbands, and the children are our top priority. I truly wish I didn't have to work, but there's no way we could make it if I stayed home. I'm not working so we can have a Mercedes, a pool or fancy vacations. I work so we can meet our house and car payments, buy decent clothes and put food on the table. We are not extravagant people. Even though my husband and I are both professionals, we don't make a great deal of money. If I quit work, it would cut our income in half.

I miss not picking up my kids after school. I was depressed all summer because I couldn't stay at home with them. Before I know it, these children won't need me and I'll have missed it all.

My parents live across town. They are retired and depend on me a lot. This is another heavy burden. They were terrific parents. I feel guilty that I can't do more for them.

My point is this: I'm being pulled every which way by people I feel responsible for. I know you will suggest counseling, Ann, but I live in a rural area and the closest counselor is 55 miles away. With my work and family and limited income, counseling isn't possible.

My pastor tells me I should "pray about it." My doctor says other than occasional hypertension due to my weight and stress, I'm as healthy as a horse.

So, there you have it. Each day is busier than the day before. I feel as if I am sinking in quicksand. I know I have a lot of company. More and more women are juggling jobs and families. Are there any answers for us? I'd like to know what Ann Landers has to say. How in the world did YOU do it?—TIRED IN TEXAS

Source: "Landers." 1989, p. 2-E. Permission granted by Ann Landers and Creators Syndicate.

In her letter to advice columnist Ann Landers, "Tired in Texas" expresses the frustration, stress, and fatigue she feels as she tries to balance the many types of work associated with modern family life. As she worries about how her harried life is affecting her children and her own health, she feels guilty about not doing even more. "Tired in Texas" is a typical modern wife and mother in several respects: she works full-time outside the home, contributes a substantial share of the family income, and assumes major responsibility for housework and care of family members. Is her frustration also typical? Does her husband have similar frustrations? How does their busy, work-filled life affect their marriage?

Chapter 9 will help you understand the personal problems of "Tired in Texas" in light of larger social, economic, and technological changes. The first part of the chapter describes the three types of work associated with marriage: money production, people production, and household production. Married couples in different historical eras have divided up these types of work according to different patterns. We will examine two such historical patterns—economic partnership and separate spheres. Then we will discuss a third pattern of dividing marital work, dual helpers. The dual-helpers pattern dominates contemporary life and is aptly described by "Tired in Texas" in the chapter opening. We will discuss how the dual-helpers pattern evolved, how it represents both change and continuity with earlier patterns, and how it affects both individual family members and marriage. Finally, the Alternative Choice section will focus on symmetrical work sharing, an alternate contemporary way of dividing marital work that may be the predominant pattern in the future.

The Tasks of
Marriage:
Dividing
Marital Work **9**

TYPES OF MARITAL WORK

Work can be defined very broadly as "an activity that produces something of value for other people" (U.S. Department of Health, Education, and Welfare, 1973, p. 3). Clearly, married couples spend much of their time "producing something of value for other people" or working. Selling shoes in a mall shoe store to make money, wiping a three-year-old's nose, and clipping an overgrown hedge all produce something of value to the family and yet are very different kinds of work. Married couples in the United States today are involved in three types of work: 1. money production, 2. people production, and 3. household production.

Work
an activity that produces something of value for other people.

Money Production

Money production is the production of goods and services in exchange for pay. Most people refer to money production as "my job" or "working." Besides money, work for pay can also provide status, self-esteem, and a sense of identity and usefulness to individuals. However, even those who say "I'm not working for the money" probably really do need the money the job provides. Most adults *simply have no choice* about whether or not to participate in money production during some part of their lives. Except for a very few people who are able to produce by themselves what they need to live, surviving in the United States today requires a good deal of money. A few people inherit enough money to live well, but most must participate in the paid labor force to earn this money.

Money production
the production of goods and services in exchange for pay.

In industrialized societies, money production is typically done away from home and requires workers to give up some measure of individual freedom, control, and creativity. Most people who work for money are employees of large organizations under the supervision of other people. The details and future of their jobs may well be decided by people they will never meet. Many paid jobs require that employees adhere to a schedule, work without interruption except for scheduled breaks, and work on part of a project without ever seeing the end result. In addition, most paid workplaces discourage open expression of emotions.

Jobs and workplaces vary tremendously, of course. Some occupational positions do offer opportunities for individual decision making, ever-increasing responsibilities, supervision of others, and creativity. Most that do, however, also require advanced education, long hours of work, especially during the early years, long-term commitment, and competing with others for promotion. These high-demand, high-reward occupational positions are often referred to as **careers**. A relatively small proportion of paying jobs are careers in this sense (Krause, 1971, p. 41).

Because of the kinds of scheduled demands they impose and because of their nonemotional qualities, both noncareer jobs and careers differ from the two types of marital work done at home. Marital work at home includes the other two types of work we will discuss: people production and household production.

> **Career**
> a type of money production requiring long years of preparation and concentrated dedication, which has an established system of promotion opportunities.

People Production

People production, as used in this chapter, refers to activities directed toward giving physical, psychological, and emotional care to family members. Economist Linda Murgatroyd (1985) provides this definition:

> ... Those who nurture, procreate, feed, educate, give physical care (medical or otherwise) or manipulate others psychologically in such a way as to increase the amount, or ameliorate the quality of human energy and potential labor power embodied by directly manipulating people, are doing people-producing work. (pp. 58–59)

People production typically takes place at home and is, in a real sense, what modern couple relationships and parent-child ties are all about. Rather than thinking about people production as "work," married couples are likely to think of it as an essential part of their identity as spouses and parents. As Murgatroyd's definition suggests, people production includes both nurturant and physical activities. Intimate, nurturing activities such as hugging, offering emotional support, and

> **People production**
> unpaid activities directed toward giving physical, psychological, and emotional care to family members.

sharing a secret joke are part of people production. In a sense, we have already dealt with people production in Chapters 3 (sex), 7 (adjustment), and 8 (communication) and will deal with it further in Chapter 12 (parents and children). People production also involves physical activities directed toward practical ends. For example, taking an elderly relative to a doctor's appointment, changing a baby's diaper, and having intercourse at the "right time of the month" in order to conceive are all people production activities.

In contrast to money production, people production often involves the full range of emotions—love, trust, anger, and envy. People production cannot always be done on a schedule. It frequently interrupts and is interrupted by other demands and is often combined with other home-based work. In addition, individuals have considerable choice about the amount and nature of people production they do (Beutler et al., 1989).

Household Production

Household
production

the production,
acquisition, and
maintenance of the
possessions needed
to live.

Household production refers to the production, acquisition, and maintenance of the possessions married couples need to live their day-to-day lives at home. It includes much of what most people call "housework," "home repairs," "yard work," and "shopping." Household production encompasses everything from planning and preparing an entirely different, unique, delicious family meal to reinsulating the attic to scrubbing the bathroom floor. Economist Gary Becker (1976) defines household production as "unpaid activities carried on by and for household members but which could be replaced by market goods and services" (p. 138).

All couples "hire out" some parts of their household production work. For example, every time you order a pizza instead of making one or pay the city for your water rather than lugging water from a hand-dug well, you are turning some potential household production work over to somebody else. Married couples who are rich enough can, of course, pay someone else to do almost all of their household production tasks. But making such arrangements is itself a kind of work. Meanwhile, less wealthy married couples continue to produce home-cooked meals, insulate attics, and clean bathrooms. Household production clearly has practical survival value. But many families see their home as more than just a shelter, viewing it as an extension of themselves and as a symbol of their success. For these families, the household production necessary to create and maintain their home has psychological and symbolic value as well as survival value.

Household production has some of the individual choice, control, and scheduling features of people production and often occurs simultaneously with it. For example, a mother who teaches her child about

	Table 9-1 Types of Marital Work		
	Money Production	People Production	Household Production
What Is It?	Production of goods and services in exchange for pay.	Giving physical, emotional, and psychological care to family members.	Production, acquisition, and maintenance of possessions needed for daily life.
What Are Its Characteristic Features?	away from home; scheduled; often supervised; paid; nonemotional	at home; unscheduled; unsupervised; unpaid; emotional	at home; unscheduled; unsupervised; unpaid; nonemotional
Examples	factory work; office work; selling home-made crafts	comforting child; kissing spouse; bathing child	washing dishes; fixing lunch; shopping

colors while sorting the laundry is combining people production and household production. Household production also has some characteristics of the least satisfying types of money production work. One review summarized the situation of household production workers, especially women, as follows:

> . . . they [home workers] are unsupervised and rarely criticized, plan and control their own work, and have only their own standards to meet. [The work] is also worrisome, tiresome, menial, repetitive, isolating, unfinished, inescapable, and often unappreciated. (Thompson & Walker, 1989, p. 855)

Table 9-1 offers a convenient summary of the three types of marital work. Refer back to it as you read through the chapter.

PAST PATTERNS OF MARITAL WORK

All married couples make choices about which types of marital work to emphasize or de-emphasize and about who—husband, wife, child, other family member, or hired help—should do each type of work.

Negotiating and implementing these choices are important parts of building a family culture. As you will learn, making satisfactory choices about work is important to marital happiness. The choices couples make about marital work are tied to the economy, the technology, and the gender role beliefs of the society in which they live. Couples living under similar societal conditions tend to make similar decisions about which type of marital work to emphasize and about how to divide the work. These "similar decisions" can be thought of as marital work patterns. When the economy, technology, or gender role beliefs change, so do marital work patterns.

To show you how past societal conditions affected the choices people made about marital work and to help you understand where present patterns came from, we will first discuss two marital work patterns more often associated with the past than with the present. The first pattern, economic partnership, characterized the colonial, preindustrial period of U.S. history. The second pattern, separate spheres, developed throughout the nineteenth century in response to changes brought about by industrialization and lasted well into the twentieth century.

Economic Partnership

Economic partnership

a pattern of dividing marital work in which husband, wife, and children jointly participate in each type of marital work, assigned to different tasks but dependent on one another.

Like many other preindustrial peoples, the early English settlers and their descendents living in the United States from the early 1600s until about 1800 followed a marital work pattern of economic partnership. In the pattern of **economic partnership**, husband, wife, and older children jointly participated in household production, people production, and money production. Each family member had different tasks, but the tasks were linked together such that each member was dependent upon the others.

Economic partnership showed up most clearly in household production work, the most time-consuming and important type of marital work in preindustrial times. Consider the household production task of breadmaking. The wife mixed and kneaded bread dough that contained grain grown and milled by her husband. To make the bread rise, she used yeast produced from beer she had made with barley grown by her husband. She built the fire needed to bake the bread with wood chopped by her husband (Cowan, 1983, p. 25). Husband and wife performed different tasks, but the tasks were linked together and, thus, so was the couple.

Breadmaking and other household chores often included people production as well. For example, while making bread, the wife may have cared for an infant and instructed her older daughter in kneading

Household production was the major type of family work in the American colonial era and all family members participated in it.

dough, while the husband taught the boys about chopping wood and growing grain. People production in the colonial household consisted mostly of caring for infants (done by the wife) and instructing and disciplining older children (done by both parents). Emotional support, affection, and friendly interaction between husband and wife might occur, but they were not considered essential to the marriage and were not associated with one partner more than the other. So perhaps husband and wife talked to one another as they made their bread, perhaps they did not. What mattered was that each did his or her work; their economic partnership was the core of the marriage (Ryan, 1979, Chapter 1). As noted in Chapter 1, these marriages were based on economic need, not on intimacy.

When these early settlers needed small amounts of cash to purchase essential supplies, such as salt and cooking pots, they simply made more of what they were already producing (for example, grain, maple syrup, woven cloth) and sold or traded it. Like household production, money production was done at or near home, was often seasonal in nature, and involved all members of the family (Cowan, 1983).

These married economic partners were not equals in terms of formal political and economic rights; legally and according to the religious doctrines of the time, wives were under their husband's patriarchal authority. However, the very apparent economic dependence of husbands on their wives may well have given the wives a degree of informal leverage (Epstein, 1982, p. 90). While husbands and wives did not view one another as equals, neither did they see one another as opposites (Ryan, 1979, Chapter 1). The development and spread of starkly contrasting masculine and feminine stereotypes came in the nineteenth century with the development of the separate spheres pattern.

Separate Spheres

The United States gradually became an industrialized, urbanized nation between about 1780 and 1920. As the economic basis and technology of the society changed, married couples adapted by developing the marital work pattern referred to as separate spheres. The pattern of **separate spheres** is one in which the husband is fully responsible for money production and the wife is fully responsible for household production and people production. Each spouse has a "separate sphere" and the two spheres, joined like two halves of a circle, combine to make up the marriage. Children participate less in the family work than they did under the pattern of economic partnership but, depending on their sex and on family circumstances, may contribute to all three types of work as they grow older.

> **Separate spheres**
> a pattern of dividing marital work in which the husband is responsible for money production work and the wife is responsible for household production and people production.

Men's Sphere

The industrialization process, with its mass production of goods that had once been home produced, made money production work much more important than it had previously been and removed it from the home. In the early days of industrialization, out-of-the-home money production involved men, unmarried women, and children. Over time, however, money production became defined as "men's work" and the world outside the home as "men's sphere." Nineteenth- and early twentieth-century novelists, poets, biologists, politicians, and advertisers described the world of work (which had come to mean *paid* work) as dangerous, exciting, competitive, and insecure. They upheld the traits believed necessary to succeed in this world—toughness, confidence, self-reliance, competitiveness—as the traits of "real men" (Filene, 1986). Not only did money production become known as "men's work," but "provider" or "breadwinner" became the husband's *major role in the family*, more significant than father, household production partner, or emotional supporter (Bernard, 1981). Under the pattern of separate spheres, men proved their love and commitment to their wives and children by being successful at money production.

Women's Sphere

The nineteenth-century married woman who fully conformed to the pattern of separate spheres played *no* part in money production. However, she assumed responsibility for both household production and people production. Industrialization changed household production as well as money production. Industrial processes *replaced* many male household production tasks (for example, coal delivered to the home replaced husband-chopped wood) but *elaborated* the traditionally female household production tasks of cleaning, cooking, and laundry. For example, nineteenth-century women's magazines urged women to use their new factory-produced ovens and finely ground flour to bake pies, cakes, cookies, muffins, and biscuits in addition to simple loaves of bread (Cowan, 1983). Cleanliness, variety, and comfort replaced simple survival as the objectives of household production.

This newly elaborated household production, referred to as "housework" beginning in 1841, began to take on a symbolic meaning. Household production was no longer simply practical work necessary for survival; it became a *symbol* of a woman's love for her husband and children. A cleaner house and more elaborate meals symbolized greater love. Increasingly, household production and people production were merged, and both became women's responsibilities. Commentators in nineteenth-century women's magazines, religious publications, and novels defined the house as "women's world" and medical authorities believed that staying at home was part of women's "nature." One well-known medical educator put it like this in a lecture to his students:

> The great administrative faculties are not hers. She plans no sublime campaigns, leads no armies to battle, nor fleets to victory.... Such is not woman's province, nature, power, or mission. She reigns in the heart; her seat and throne are by the hearthstone—The household altar is her place of worship and service.... Home is her place ... (Meigs, 1848, p. 41)

The true woman would *make* her house into a secure, calm, comfortable, and comforting *home*, providing the spousal affection and emotional support her husband needed to be a good economic provider (Welter, 1966).

Although emotional support of the husband was considered more important than it had been earlier, the woman's major people production activity was motherhood. "Motherhood" had come to mean much more than giving birth. In fact, the number of children per family dropped steadily throughout the nineteenth century. While the average woman at the beginning of the nineteenth century gave birth to seven children, her counterpart at the end of the century bore only three or four children (Coale & Zelnick, 1963, p. 36). Each generation of mothers was expected to do more for their children than their mothers had done for them. New, elaborate childrearing manuals reminded women that children needed a *mother's* special care and guidance throughout childhood, not just in infancy (Epstein, 1982, p. 96; Ryan, 1979, p. 99). With fathers out of the home in a world thought entirely inappropriate for children, mothers became responsible for shaping the character of the next generation.

An Assessment of Separate Spheres

How did the separate spheres pattern affect marital relationships? In its ideal form, as described by family experts of the time, separate spheres marriages were more intimate and more egalitarian than economic partnership marriages had been. Husbands and wives were supposed to contribute equally, but differently, to the building of intimate marriages and strong families. However, the fact that husband and wife were separated six days a week for at least 10 hours a day to pursue work in their separate, very different spheres often made it difficult for them to develop a truly intimate relationship; they had little time together and little in common. And, although commentators of the time argued that both spheres were equally important, the male sphere of work and money came to be seen as the more prestigious and the female sphere of home and children was devalued (Kahn-Hut, Daniels, & Colvard, 1982). Men's greater prestige outside the home led to increased power within the home and the marriage. Meanwhile, women, who now had no way of making financial contributions to their families, lost some of the informal marital power they had held previously (Epstein, 1982, p. 94).

The industrialization and urbanization that made the separate spheres pattern possible made life more comfortable. For about the same amount of total work time, the nineteenth-century urban family had more material possessions, a larger house, and more variety in clothing and food than their eighteenth-century farming ancestors (Cowan, 1983, Chapter 3). However, not all nineteenth-century couples were able to enjoy these comforts or to try out the separate spheres pattern. As with the broader family changes described in Chapter 1, the separate spheres pattern developed first among white, native-born, urban couples in which the husband held a managerial or professional position. Husbands in these marriages could make enough money to support an entire household. Most nineteenth- and many twentieth-century husbands could not.

For more than half the nineteenth century, most black families lived in slavery, producing money and household goods and services for their white owners in exchange for subsistence. After slavery, low wages and limited work opportunities meant that all family members had to work at either making money or at preindustrial-style household production to survive. Rural families—both black and white—could *read* about urban husbands who left home to work and urban wives who spent their lives creating a comfortable, emotionally close home, but their own lives and marital work patterns remained, in many ways, preindustrial.

Nor did city life guarantee the comforts shown in the magazines. Most factory jobs available to immigrant and native-born working-class people in the new industrial economy simply did not pay enough so that a husband alone could support a wife and children at a comfortable level. To compensate, working-class wives engaged in money-producing work, such as sewing or taking in boarders at home. A few women and a substantial number of children obtained work outside the home, and many families survived at less than adequate levels (Hood, 1986, p. 350). For rural and working-class families, the separate spheres pattern was simply not a realistic option.

According to sociologist Jane Hood (1986, p. 350), it was the middle of the *twentieth* century before working-class men received a wage sufficient for family living without help from their wives or children. For the twenty years between 1950 and 1970, the one-earner, separate spheres family prevailed in the United States. Families, especially white families, could live in moderate comfort and even improve their standard of living year by year on one male salary (Hood, 1986, p. 350). However, events that would eventually change the separate spheres pattern were already underway.

DUAL HELPERS

Today some couples continue to maintain a strict separate spheres pattern of marital work. You might personally know couples in which the husband makes all the money and the wife does all the household work, child care, and spouse-comforting. And a few families, especially those engaged in farming, continue to divide marital work along the lines of the economic partnership pattern. The economic changes of recent decades, however, led most families to reassess old marital work patterns and to develop new ones. We will discuss two such emerging patterns: the dual-helpers pattern, characteristic of the majority, and symmetrical work sharing, the alternative choice of a minority. Table 9–2 summarizes both the two historical patterns and the two emerging patterns for dividing marital work.

The most common pattern for dividing marital work in the United States today is a pattern we refer to as the dual-helper pattern; other names for the pattern are "transitional marriage" (Ross, Mirowsky, & Huber, 1983, p. 809) and "the stalled revolution" (Hochschild, 1989, p. 12). **Dual helpers** is a pattern of dividing marital work in which the husband maintains primary responsibility for money production but helps the wife with household and people production, while the wife maintains primary responsibility for household and people production but helps the husband with money production. The dual-helpers pattern is a variation of the separate spheres pattern and is still evolving. At this point in its evolution, wives contribute more to money production than husbands contribute to household and people production. Because this pattern is so prevalent in the United States today, we will examine it in detail, looking at how and why it evolved, the changes and continuities it incorporates, and at its effects on marriage.

The Evolution of the Dual-Helpers Pattern

The dual-helpers pattern developed in a series of rather uneven steps. First, large numbers of wives and mothers became involved in money production. Next, attitudes about women's roles changed. Finally, husbands and fathers became more involved in household and people production. As you will see, the steps overlapped to some extent but did not occur simultaneously. Thus, the transition from separate spheres to dual helpers was a gradual and rocky one.

Step 1: Women Become Money Production Helpers

The first step in the development of the dual-helpers pattern was that large numbers of wives and mothers began to assist their husbands with money production by obtaining paying jobs in the labor force. The proportion of married women in the labor force has been increasing steadily ever since 1940 (Oppenheimer, 1976), but most journalists and social scientists did not pay much attention to the phenomenon until the 1970s. Once they noticed, they referred to the change as "a revolution in women's behavior" (Gerson, 1987, p. 270), "a tide of enormous

---

Dual helpers

a pattern of dividing marital work in which the husband maintains primary responsibility for money production but helps the wife with household and people production while the wife maintains primary responsibility for household and people production but helps the husband with money production.

Table 9–2 Marital Work Patterns

	Economic Partnership	Separate Spheres	Dual Helpers	Symmetrical Work Sharing
Money Production				
How important?	not very important	very important	very important	moderately important
Where done?	family home	away from home	away from home	away from home
Who does it?	husband and wife	husband	husband, assisted by wife	husband and wife equally
People Production				
How important is:				
child care?	moderately important	increasingly important	very important	very important
spouse care?	not important	increasingly important	very important	very important
Who is responsible for:				
child care?	wife—infants both—training and discipline of older children	wife	wife, assisted by husband and outsiders	husband and wife equally
spouse care?	neither	wife	husband and wife	husband and wife equally
Household Production				
How important?	very important	less important—more produced outside home	less important—much more produced outside home	less important—much produced outside home
Who does what?	Husband and sons: plowing, sowing, chopping wood, large animal care, making wooden and leather goods Wife and daughters: cooking, laundry, cleaning, small animal care, making cloth goods, gardening	wife: cleaning, cooking, laundry, sewing, other inside work husband: outside work and repairs servants do heavy work, especially in wealthy families	wife, with some help from husband: cleaning, cooking, laundry, shopping, other inside work husband: outside work and repairs commercial services may do some of the above	husband and wife equally share both inside and outside tasks

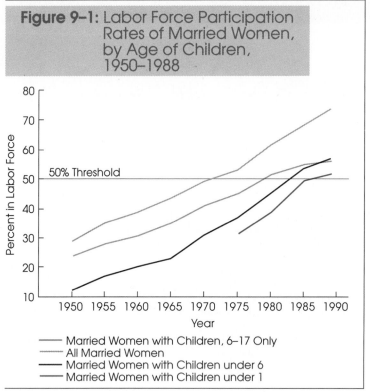

Figure 9–1: Labor Force Participation Rates of Married Women, by Age of Children, 1950–1988

Source: U.S. Bureau of the Census, 1988, 1989b, 1991a; U.S. Department of Labor, 1983, p. 123.

By 1972, wives with children aged 6–17 were more likely to be in the labor force than not to be in it; wives with children under 6 years old reached this threshold in 1984; married women with infants (children under 1 year old) crossed the 50 percent threshold in 1987.

proportions" (Lindsey, 1976, p. 1), and "one of the major social phenomena of the twentieth century" (Freudiger, 1983, p. 213). Figure 9–1 provides a closer look at this momentous change. In 1950, only one out of every four wives worked outside the home; by 1988, more than half of all married women were in the labor force. Married women whose children had grown up and left home were the first to enter the labor force in large numbers (Moen, 1985; Moore, Spain, & Bianchi, 1984). Those with school-aged children followed soon thereafter, and mothers with preschool-aged children entered the labor market somewhat later. By 1972, wives with children aged 6–17 were more likely to be in the labor force than not to be in it; wives with children under six years old reached this threshold in 1984; married women with infants (children under one year old) crossed the 50 percent threshold in 1987 (U.S. Bureau of the Census, 1989b, 1988; U.S. Department of Labor, 1983, p. 123). This chapter's Cohort Comparison and Figure 9–2 show how the birth cohorts we are following participated in these trends.

Cohort Comparison   Labor Force Participation of Women

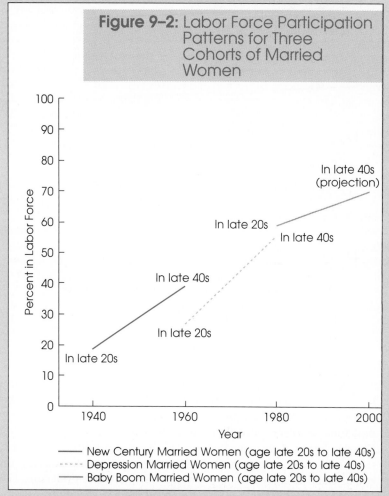

Figure 9–2: Labor Force Participation Patterns for Three Cohorts of Married Women

Source: U.S. Department of Labor, 1985, p. 120; Oppenheimer, 1970, p. 11.

Women in the New Century, Depression, Baby Boom, and Baby Bust birth cohorts have all been affected by the late twentieth-century movement of women into the labor market. Figure 9–2 summarizes the labor force participation of married women belonging to each of the three oldest cohorts. Each of the three lines in Figure 9–2 represents a birth cohort of married women. The first point on each line represents the proportion of married women in the cohort who were in the labor force during their late twenties. This is an important time of life to have information about because it is these years when women are most likely to have preschool or school-aged children at home. As you can see

(continued)

Cohort Comparison
Labour Force Participation of Women. (cont'd)

by comparing the starting points of the lines, Depression cohort women (born 1930–1934) were slightly more likely than New Century women (born 1910–1914) to be employed in their late twenties. The big change, however, came with the Baby Boom cohort (born 1950–1954), almost 60 percent of whom held jobs in their late twenties. Changes in birth patterns provide a partial explanation for the dramatic change: more Baby Boom women than Depression women put off having children until their thirties. Nonetheless, most of the Baby Boom working wives were mothers as well (O'Connell & Bloom, 1987).

The end point of each line shows the proportion (projected in the case of the Baby Boomers) of married women employed in their late forties. This, too, is an important age for women because, by then, most of them have completed or have nearly completed their childrearing duties. During their late forties, married women typically say good-bye to their youngest child (or anticipate doing so soon) and first become grandmothers. As you can see, women in the New Century and Depression cohorts were much more likely to be working in their late forties than in their late twenties. Also, Depression co- hort women were more likely to be employed in middle age than New Century women. The Baby Boom women have not yet reached their late forties; projections are, though, that their labor force participation at that age will not be much different than at earlier stages of their adulthood. In other words, their higher than ever labor force participation will continue.

The Baby Bust cohort (born 1970–1974) is too young to be represented in Figure 9–2. Unless they reverse previous trends, their work patterns will probably be similar to those of the Baby Boomers—high rates of employment throughout adulthood.

Dual-earner couple
a married couple in which both husband and wife are in the labor force.

Dual-career couple
a married couple in which both husband and wife are committed to full time, continuous involvement in their individual careers.

When a woman married to an employed man joins the paid labor force, they become a **dual-earner couple**. About one-third of all working wives are employed less than thirty-five hours a week, making them part-time workers, according to Department of Labor definitions (Jacobs, Shipp, & Brown, 1989, p. 18). Back-and-forth movement between no paid employment, part-time employment, and full-time employment is fairly common among married women (Gerson, 1987; Moen, 1985). However, nearly all married women spend at least some time in the labor force during their marriage, and increasing numbers of them work full time throughout their marriage (O'Connell & Bloom, 1987). About 5 percent of all dual-earner couples are **dual-career couples**, a special type of dual-earner family in which both husband and wife are committed to lifelong, full-time careers (Berardo, Shehan, & Leslie, 1987). Because dual-career couples are relatively rare and because their ways of dividing marital work are similar to other dual-earner couples (Berardo, Shehan, & Leslie, 1987; Benenson, 1984), we will not deal with them separately.

Why did so many married women decide to enter the labor market and become money producers during the last half of the twentieth century? They did so because their families needed the money, because the economy needed their talents, and because they were in a better position to be money producers than earlier generations of women had been.

During the 1950s and 1960s, increasing numbers of married women went to work to buy the things that families wanted but could not afford on one salary. Anthropologist Marvin Harris (1981) explains:

> The 1950s and early 1960s were a period of consumer expectations aimed at the ownership of clothing, household furnishings, automobiles, telephones, and many new or previously prohibitively expensive product lines such as washing machines, dryers, dishwashers, and color TV sets. Much of married women's initial surge toward the job market was keyed toward purchasing specific products deemed important for a decent standard of living in what was then being called the affluent society. (p. 90)

The economic changes of the 1970s and 1980s (described in Chapter 10) brought even more married women into the labor market. As the wages for many men's jobs failed to keep up with rising costs, and as the chances of unemployment increased, some families could maintain their former standard of living and feel economically secure only if both husband and wife had jobs (Gerstel & Gross, 1987; Moore, Spain, & Bianchi, 1984).

The wife's financial contribution has been and remains particularly important in racial minority families. Figure 9–3 (on page 318) demonstrates that, strictly speaking, the average white married couple could get along with only the husband's salary (Eggebeen & Hawkins, 1990). Note, however, that most Hispanic and black couples need two earners to meet or surpass a level of living most people consider adequate.

Family economic needs alone do not explain why married women entered the labor force in such large numbers. Expanding employment opportunities for women also played a part. Since 1940, the greatest rates of employment growth have been in retail trade, service, and clerical work, low wage jobs traditionally thought to be appropriate for women and therefore labeled "female" jobs (Oppenheimer, 1976). Because of the increased need for workers in such jobs, employers in the past 50 years have been seeking female employees at least as vigorously as women have been seeking jobs (Harris, 1981). In addition, especially in recent years, the Women's Movement has succeeded in breaking down some of the barriers that once excluded women from traditionally male jobs, opening up even more opportunities and gradually increasing women's wages.

Finally, because of their lower fertility rates, women of the late twentieth century are in a better position to enter and remain in the labor force than were women of earlier generations. Women in the late-twentieth-century United States, particularly those reaching adulthood

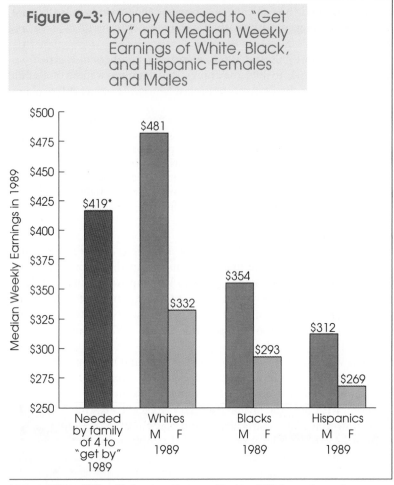

Figure 9–3: Money Needed to "Get by" and Median Weekly Earnings of White, Black, and Hispanic Females and Males

According to public opinion polls, a family of four needed $419 a week to "get by" economically in 1989. White males were the only workers with median weekly earnings this high. The figure helps explain why many families require two earners and why black and Hispanic families often remain close to poverty level despite their work in the labor force.

* Source: O'Hare, 1990, p. 38, *American Demographics*, May 1990. Source for median earnings: U.S. Department of Labor, 1990, p. 70.

since about 1965, tend to have very small, closely spaced families of two or three children. Even if they choose to withdraw from money production while their children are at home, modern married women still have many years available for money production. All these factors taken together—increased family economic need, increased employer demand for women workers, and decreased fertility—help explain why married women became involved in money production.

Step 2: Attitudes Change

Married women's increased participation in money production work can be traced back to the 1950s (look again at Figure 9–1). However, attitudes about women's involvement in money production did not begin to change until the late 1960s and early 1970s. In 1960, for example, the Michigan Survey Research Center posed this question to a cross-section of husbands: "There are many wives who have jobs these days. Do you think it is a good thing, a bad thing, or what?" About one-third (34 percent) of the husbands approved of working wives, almost half (46 percent) disapproved, and the remainder (18 percent) said it depended on the situation (Oppenheimer, 1976, p. 46). Such disapproving attitudes eventually changed, but not until many more married women worked for pay.

Between the 1960s and the 1980s, U.S. adults changed their opinions about women's proper role in the family. After analyzing the results of several large-scale surveys, sociologist Arland Thornton (1989) discovered "a very substantial and continuing transformation of sex role attitudes in the United States" (p. 875) in an egalitarian direction. By the 1980s, for example, a majority of U.S. adults approved of married women earning money, even if their husbands could support them, and disagreed with the notion that "It is more important for a wife to help her husband's career than to have one herself" (Thornton, 1989 pp. 876–877). Not everyone has abandoned separate spheres ideas completely, however. Table 9–3 presents 1989 national survey results for the questions you answered in the "What Do You Think?" section.

Table 9–3 Attitudes about Men, Women, and Work, 1989

Statement	Percent Agreeing	
	Men	Women
1. It is much better for everyone involved if the man is the achiever outside the home and the woman takes care of the home and family.	53	51
2. Women are more capable of managing a household than men.	64	68
3. Men are more capable of being successful in the business world than women.	46	40
4. Women who have successful careers end up sacrificing too much of their family and personal life.	69	69
5. Men who have successful careers end up sacrificing too much of their family and personal life.	68	64

Source: DeStefano & Colasanto, *The Gallup Poll Monthly*, February 1990, p. 32.

As you can see, adults in the United States are somewhat divided in their opinions about which division of work is best for the family and about the capabilities of men and women.

There is little doubt, however, that married women who first joined the labor force after the mid-1970s had substantially more public support than did women who worked outside the home before that time. Indeed, favorable public attitudes may have contributed to the continuing increases in female employment in very recent years. They also led people to reconsider what was going on at home.

Step 3: Men Become Household Production and People Production Helpers

Women's help with money production was well underway before men's help with household production and people production (in the form of child care) increased at all. Only after large numbers of people began to change their minds about "women's place" did husbands begin to change their customary patterns of behavior at home.

In the middle 1960s, when women's money production was increasing but still somewhat unusual, the *husbands* of employed wives did *no* more household work than the husbands of nonemployed wives (Pleck, 1985, p. 30). Employed wives of the 1960s had total work weeks (time in paid work plus time in household work) of 65 to 70 hours, while husbands and nonemployed wives averaged total work weeks of about 50 to 55 hours (Pleck, 1985). By the middle 1970s, married men with employed wives were doing a little more at home than they had in the previous decade, but still much less than their wives (Pleck, 1985, p. 34 ff., p. 143).

The situation had changed by the 1980s. By then, men spent more hours per week doing household work and child care than they had in the 1960s and 1970s (Juster, 1985, Figure 12–2) and also did a higher proportion of total household production. However, they still put in only half as many household production and child care hours per week as women. Researcher Joseph Pleck (1985) estimates that between the 1960s and the 1980s, men increased their participation in family work (housework plus childcare) from 20 percent of the total to 30 percent of the total. He summarizes as follows:

> Overall, the preponderance of evidence is that men's time in the family is increasing while women's is decreasing. Men and women are moving toward convergence in their family time, though it will clearly be a long time—if ever—before they reach parity. More of the convergence is due to women's decrease than to men's increase, though men's increase is not trivial. (p. 146)

Change and Continuity in the Dual-Helpers Pattern

The dual-helpers pattern of dividing marital work clearly represents a change from the separate-spheres pattern in some respects. In other ways, however, the dual-helper pattern simply continues the ways of thinking and patterns of work characteristic of separate spheres. Let us briefly consider the ways in which marital work under the dual-helpers pattern differs from that of the separate-spheres pattern (the changes) and also examine how separate-spheres pattern carries over into dual-helper marriages (the continuities).

Change in Marital Work Priorities

As more families become dual-earner families and as more of them adopt a dual-helpers pattern of marital work, the amount of time devoted to each type of marital work and the priority attached to it has shifted somewhat. Money production occupies many more total hours in dual-earner, dual-helper families than in single-earner, separate-spheres families. The typical working husband spends about 44 hours a week at his job; the typical working wife has a paid work week of 36 hours (U.S. Department of Labor, 1991, p. 35). This "typical couple," then, spends almost 80 hours a week in money production, nearly twice as much time as single-earner, separate-spheres couples spend (Juster, 1985; Pleck, 1985).

While spending more time earning money, dual-earner couples devote less time to household production. In the mid-1960s, couples devoted about 55 hours a week to household work; most of this work was done by the wife. By the mid-1980s, couples spent about 45 hours a week in household production, with women putting in fewer hours than previously and men and children putting in a few more hours than they had before (Robinson, 1989, 1988; White & Brinkerhoff, 1987; Juster, 1985; Pleck, 1985). Some of the reduction in household production time is due to greater use of convenience foods, no-iron clothing, microwave ovens, and other labor-saving devices. Some of it can also be explained, however, in terms of less-demanding standards; today's families, especially the younger ones, no longer feel that every meal has to be a sit-down, homecooked one or that undusted furniture and unmade beds are scandalous (Shelton, 1990; DeStefano, 1989).

While dual-earner, dual-helper couples have reduced the amount of time devoted to household production, they have made extra efforts to maintain their people production activities. Dual-earner families are slightly more likely than single-earner families to spend off-work, weekend hours as a mother-father-children family unit, engaging in activities such as sitting and talking, vacationing, participating in recreational activities, and attending concerts together (*American Demographics,* 1991; Nock & Kingston, 1988). Nonetheless, because of the greater amount of time devoted to money production, dual-earner couples spend considerably less total time with their children during the week than single-earner couples do (Nock & Kingston, 1988). Dual-earner couples often hire babysitters, child-care centers, or relatives to cover some of their people production tasks.

The demands of work schedules, household work, and children also make it difficult for dual-earner couples to find time and energy for their own intimate relationship. As a consequence, husbands and wives in dual-earner marriages spend about thirty minutes less time together each day than do husbands and wives in single-earner marriages. The researchers who discovered this call it a "modest difference" and conclude that "dual-earner couples apparently try hard to share time" (Kingston & Nock, 1987, p. 396).

Continuities in Work Responsibility

The time and effort devoted to each type of marital work changed somewhat with the transition to dual-earner, dual-helper marriages. The division of *responsibility*, however, carried over from separate-spheres marriages to dual-helpers marriages. Two continuities (or carryovers) deserve attention: money production continues to be men's major responsibility and household and people production continue to be sex-typed, female responsibilities.

Men's continuing responsibility for money production can be illustrated by considering the following list of questions:

1. (asked to a young woman) Do you plan to keep working after you get married and have children?
2. (asked to a young man) Do you plan to keep working after you get married and have children?
3. (asked to a young woman) How do you feel about your future husband working outside the home when the children are young?
4. (asked to a young man) How do feel about your future wife working outside the home when the children are young?

Do any of them sound strange to you? Which ones? Why?

Questions 1 and 4 are frequently asked both by social scientists (for example, Komarovsky, 1985, 1976) and in everyday conversation. Questions 2 and 3 are hardly ever asked. *The employment of married men (once they finish school) is not seen as a choice while the employment of married women is still seen as optional.*

One reason that most husbands lack the choice of working for money is economic. Despite recent improvements, women who work full time still earn only 74 percent of what men who work full time earn (U.S. Department of Labor, 1991, p. 73); many couples could survive on the husband's salary, most could not on the wife's (look again at Figure 9–3). When all dual-earner couples are considered, the typical husband earns about 70 percent of the total family income while his wife contributes the other 30 percent. Wives who work full time supply about 40 percent of their family's income (U.S. Department of Labor, 1991, p. 73; Spitze, 1988, p. 603).

Because most husbands continue to contribute more than half the family income and because occupational success continues to be such an important component of being a "real man" in U.S. culture (recall Chapter 2), most dual-earner couples today define the husband as the "primary" provider and the wife as a "secondary" provider or "helper" in money production (Thompson & Walker, 1989; Weiss, 1987; Hood, 1986). This description is applied not only when the wife works part time and the husband earns most of the income but also in many cases where the wife works full time, earns close to half the family income, and is essential to the couple's economic survival (Rosen, 1987, p. 103). Consider the following quotes:

> I used to think of myself as "the provider" because I was. Now I think I'm the "main provider." . . . we just use her paycheck to pay the house payments. . . . [when asked to rank his family roles] I suppose I would put provider first, companion, and then father. ("Richard James," a machinist married to a secretary who supplies 30 percent of family income, both work full time, quoted in Hood, 1986, p. 355)

> I feel that when I'm working I bring home a good pay. It helps out. I wouldn't say I'm working just to spend. Today you need to work. A woman needs to help out her husband. ("Sara Talbot," female factory worker married to blue-collar worker, quoted in Rosen, 1987, p. 104)

If the husband's paid work is defined as "primary," it only makes sense that the family adapt to and support the demands of that work. This was part of the traditional separate-spheres idea and continues to receive support today. The types of adaptation required vary with the husband's occupation. If the husband works as a policeman on the night shift and sleeps at home during the day, the wife must do the noisy housework at night or very early in the morning and keep the children quiet during the day (Piotrkowski, 1979, Chapter 7). If the husband spends six months of the year on a submarine, the wife and children must adapt to living half of each year with an adult male in the home and half of the year without one (Voydanoff, 1987, p. 67).

If the husband's work requires that the family move frequently or join certain social circles, the supportive family is expected to make these adaptations as well (Fowlkes, 1987; Gowler & Legge, 1978). You may be able to think of similar examples from your own family.

While employed married men expect their families to adapt to their jobs, employed married women, as "economic helpers" or "secondary providers," often expect to adapt their paid work to family needs. The choice a married woman makes to work only at home, to work part time outside the home, or to work full time outside the home is a complex one. The decision is typically made jointly with her husband after taking into account the family's economic needs and desires, the ages and needs of their children, and the preferences of both husband and wife (Gerson, 1987; Rosen, 1987).

Because married women often base their employment decisions on ever-changing family needs, they are more likely than men to have work histories interrupted by time out for childbearing, periods of part-time work, and job changes associated with husbands' transfers (Moen, 1985). Paying attention to family needs often places limits on women's advancement in the work world. The best-paying, traditionally male, professional, technical and executive careers are "greedy institutions" (Coser, 1974). They demand long hours at work, carrying work home at night and on weekends, and a willingness to accept transfers. Furthermore, the demands are heaviest during the early years of the career (the late twenties to early forties for most people), exactly the same years in which couples are most likely to have small children in the home.

In summary, married women have more choice than married men in deciding whether to work outside the home or not, *but* men find it easier to "have it all" (career success, marriage, and parenthood) than women. Women who decide to focus on career success must often make sacrifices in terms of marriage and parenthood; men do not. As Gerstel and Gross (1987) put it: " . . . the success of men's careers depends on incorporating their wives' labor, the success of wives' careers depends on containing their family's claims" (p. 259).

The second continuity between the separate-spheres and dual-helpers patterns is in the sex-typing of household work and in the definition of household and people production as women's responsibilities. Men do more household work than they used to do, but *household work remains heavily sex-typed.* Husbands continue to be most active in the "outside" or "masculine" aspects of household production including yard and car maintenance, home repairs, and garbage-handling. While husbands do a little more cleaning and cooking than they once did, wives continue to do the majority of this "inside" work (Hochschild, 1989).

The continued sex-typing of household work means that women and men experience such work in different ways. More of the "inside" (female) tasks must be done on a *daily* basis and according to an externally imposed timetable whereas more of the "outside" (male) tasks can be scheduled at the worker's convenience and delayed until weekends or vacation time (Hochschild, 1989, pp. 8–9).

Men and women also differ in the types of child care they do. In contrast to mothers, fathers spend more of their total child care time on weekends and more of it engaging in specific "fun" activities (Nock & Kingston, 1988). Mothers, employed or not, do more of the "maintenance" care (for example, washing and dressing) of children, are more often "available" or "on call" for children while engaged in another work activity, and do more of the child care on weekdays (Hochschild, 1989; Nock & Kingston, 1988). The fact that women do much more of the routine, tedious household production and child care adds to the greater pressure women feel about household work. It also explains why men more often categorize their household chores as "leisure," while women classify theirs as "work" (Shaw, 1988).

Women are also likely to classify household chores and child care as work because they are held responsible for them. Most men and women continue to view these tasks as the wife's responsibility (Thompson & Walker, 1989; Szinovacz, 1984) and to see women as more capable household managers (look again at Question 2 on Table 9–2). "Having responsibility for" household work means keeping track of which chores have to be done and when, making sure the materials necessary to carry out the chores are available, deciding who should do them and how they should be done, and getting that person to do them. For example, "having responsibility for meals" involves not only actual meal preparation but also planning what to eat (based on what is available, what members of the family will eat, what they had to eat on the previous day, what diets they are on, which foods "go together" and so forth) and managing the atmosphere at the dinner table so that the meal is a time of relaxation and communication (DeVault, 1987). A "helper" husband might do much of the actual meal preparation; the "responsible" wife, however, typically does the planning and managing, often while she is doing something else.

Because of the timing and nature of their household work, husbands still find it rather easy to see the home as a "separate sphere" in which they can relax, be relieved of responsibility, and make choices about how to spend their time (Weiss, 1987; Zussman, 1987). Employed wives, responsible for household production and continuing to do most of the weekday household chores, often see the home, not as a place of leisure but as a second workplace (Hochschild, 1989). Sociologist Arlie Hochschild (1989) describes how the home life of employed wives

Leisure gap
the difference between the amount of leisure time employed husbands have and the amount employed wives have.

Second shift
the household and child care duties of one who is responsible for both and who is also employed full time.

differs from that of employed husbands by introducing the concepts **leisure gap** and **second shift**:

> Over a year, they [employed wives compared to their husbands] worked an *extra month of twenty-four hour days a year*.... Just as there is a wage gap between men and women in the workplace, there is a "leisure gap" between them at home. Most women work one shift at the office or factory and a "second shift" at home. (emphasis in original) (pp. 3–4)

Marriage and the Dual-Helpers Pattern

How has this uneven combination of change and continuity affected parent-child and husband-wife relationships? Have families benefited in shifting from a separate-spheres to a dual-helpers pattern of dividing marital work or have they been hurt by it?

Most of the available research on how the dual-helpers pattern affects family life focuses on the effects of wife employment, comparing employed wives and their families to nonemployed wives and theirs. Research on the children of employed mothers concludes that they are neither positively nor negatively affected by their mother's working (Spitze, 1988; Moore, Spain & Bianchi, 1984). How children turn out is influenced by factors much more complex than whether their mother is employed or not. Chapter 12 will explain what those factors are and also deal with the critical issue of who takes care of young children when both parents are employed.

cathy®   **by Cathy Guisewite**

In this chapter, though, our focus is on marriage. There are a number of both individual and marital benefits associated with dual-helpers marriages as well as some special strains. The following discussion of benefits and strains should help you to think about whether the dual-helpers pattern is the one that best fits your situation and priorities. The Personal Application might also help you clarify your thoughts about the division of marital work.

Personal Application

Who Should Do What, and How Much?

For each of the following types of work, indicate what proportion you think should be done by the husband, what proportion by the wife, and what proportion by someone else (make sure to specify whom). Proportions for each type of work should add across to 100 percent. If you are married or plan to be, compare and discuss your answers with your partner.

Type of Work	What Proportion Should be Done by			Total
	Wife?	Husband?	Someone Else?	
1. Cooking dinner.	_____	_____	_____	100%
2. Repairing things around the house.	_____	_____	_____	100%
3. Helping small children get dressed in the morning.	_____	_____	_____	100%
4. Earning money for family through paid job.	_____	_____	_____	100%
5. Keeping the house clean and picked up.	_____	_____	_____	100%
6. Taking out the trash.	_____	_____	_____	100%
7. Caring for sick child.	_____	_____	_____	100%
8. Caring for the yard.	_____	_____	_____	100%
9. Shopping for groceries.	_____	_____	_____	100%
10. Handling auto maintenance and repair.	_____	_____	_____	100%

Benefits

All in all, employment has positive effects for both working women and for their families. The economic benefits are easiest to document. In 1991, single-earner married couples in which the husband was the earner had median weekly earnings of $521 while dual-earner married couples had median weekly earnings of $938 (U.S. Department of Labor, 1991, p. 71). Writing about New England factory worker couples, Rosen (1987) notes that the wife's income frequently made it possible for these couples to own their own home, have a savings account, and send at least some of their children to college, little of which would have been possible with only the husband's salary. Besides being able to afford more of the "extras," families with two earners are less devastated economically by one spouse's unemployment and have more financial resources available for emergencies than do single-earner families. In short, working wives add to economic security and lessen economic stress.

Working for pay changes women in certain ways and this, in turn, affects certain aspects of marriage. Numerous studies have found that, despite the burdens of the second shift, employed married women are happier and show fewer symptoms of psychological distress, depression, or physical illness than women who are full-time homemakers (Coleman, Antonucci, & Adelmann, 1987; Gove & Zeiss, 1987; Kessler & McRae, 1982). Working outside the home gives women the status of paid worker, allows them to discover and develop new skills, and gives them greater confidence in their abilities (Ferree, 1987; Rosen, 1987; Blumstein & Schwartz, 1983, p. 141). These research findings are true for women employed in unskilled factory jobs as well as for women in prestigious, professional careers. Women receive certain kinds of satisfaction from being wives and mothers but other, quite different, types of satisfaction from being employed (Ferree, 1987; Rosen, 1987). The principle at work here is simple and applies to men as well: *in general, people are better off if they are active in a multiplicity of approved adult roles than if they hold only one or two* (Coleman, Antonucci, & Adelmann, 1987).

The money they earn by working and the gains they make in self-confidence and self-esteem lead employed women to assert themselves in couple decision making more often than women who are completely dependent on their husbands for money. Husbands more often listen to employed wives and take their suggestions seriously. Like the culture in general, husbands seem to respect paid work (and the wives who do it) more than they respect household work (Blumstein & Schwartz, 1983, pp. 140–41). The end result is that dual-earner husbands and wives have more egalitarian marriages; they are more likely to share power and decision making, particularly about financial matters, than are husbands and wives in single-earner marriages (Voydanoff, 1987, p. 47; Ferber, 1982, p. 465).

Does this mean that dual earners have happier, more satisfying marriages? Research results are mixed but, overall, indicate that *marital satisfaction is affected neither positively nor negatively by the wife's employment* (Spitze, 1988). Dual-earner marriages vary so much that wife's employment is not a good predictor of marital quality. The more meaningful research question is this: Under what conditions does a wife's employment result in greater marital satisfaction and under what conditions does it lessen marital quality? We will answer this question by focusing on marital strains related to the division of work. Those who can avoid or handle such strains are in a better position to enjoy the benefits of the dual-helper pattern.

Strains

When both partners are satisfied with the marital division of labor, their marriage is less strained and more satisfying. When one or both partners are dissatisfied with how they have divided the work, however, their marriage is likely to be strained and less satisfying. For example, husbands whose wives work outside the home despite the husband's opposition show higher levels of personal depression and marital dissatisfaction than other husbands (Blumstein & Schwartz, 1983; Ross, Mirowsky, & Huber, 1983). There were many more such husbands in the 1960s and early 1970s, before widespread public acceptance of employment for wives, than there are today and, thus, more marital dissatisfaction in dual-earner marriages then than now (Spitze, 1988; Yogev, 1982). The same principle holds for wives who stay at home when they want to have a job: they too show higher levels of depression and marital dissatisfaction than those whose actual employment patterns match their desires (Blumstein & Schwartz, 1983; Ross, Mirowsky, & Huber, 1983).

In other words, *which* decision a couple makes about the wife working is not nearly as important as that they agree and that they are able to carry out their desires. Lack of agreement between the partners or lack of correspondence between what they want and what they can do adds to marital strain.

The same holds for the division of household work. A majority of both husbands and wives see their own division of household labor as "fair," despite the fact that full-time employed wives still do much more housework than their full-time employed husbands (Whyte, 1990; Spitze, 1988; Berk, 1985). Those who are dissatisfied with how household labor is divided are also more likely to be dissatisfied with the marriage (Suitor, 1991). Wives are more likely than their husbands to be dissatisfied with this aspect of their marriage. For example, one national survey found that 78 percent of the husbands but only 56 percent of the wives were satisfied with their current division of household work (Suitor, 1991, p. 224). When employed wives receive very little or no help from their husbands at home and feel that this is unfair, they often show symptoms of depression and anxiety (Rosenfield, 1989). In effect, the benefits received from the job are outweighed by the lack of control over (and lack of help with) the workload at home (Rosenfield, 1989; Ross & Mirowsky, 1988). In these cases, a redistribution of household work (husband and children do more) or a shift from full-time employment to part-time employment by the wife can relieve the overload while maintaining some of the benefits of employment (Rosenfield, 1989).

Some marriages, both dual-earner and single-earner, are under strain because both partners become so involved with their respective work that they forget about the relationship. Every couple needs at least one partner who is "relationship centered," who pays attention to the quality of the relationship, and who makes sure that the partners have time to be with one another (Blumstein & Schwartz, 1983, p. 171).

If both partners abandon the relationship for other activities, however unintentionally, it is unlikely to survive. Hochschild (1989), summarizing her interviews with dual-earner couples, writes:

> The most strained marriages I found were generally between two people more centered on career than on family, and in dispute over their roles at home. In no other kind of marriage was gratitude so scarce, the terms of its exchange so much the object of dispute, and the marital heartbeat so precariously slow. (p. 127)

A middle-aged chemical plant worker said the same thing in simpler language:

> What makes a good marriage? Well, you have to care for each other. You can't spend all your time working and drinking. You have to have time for each other. You have to appreciate her. (quoted in Halle, 1984, p. 56)

Marital Instability

Overall, people in dual-earner marriages are no more often dissatisfied with their marriages than are those in single-earner marriages. When dual helpers are dissatisfied, however, they are more likely than separate-spheres couples to consider and go through with divorce (Booth et al., 1984). Couples in which the wife started to work for pay rather recently, works more than 45 hours a week, and took the job despite her husband's wishes are especially prone to divorce (South & Spitze, 1986; Spitze & South, 1985; Booth et al., 1984, p. 581). So are couples who work different shifts—for example, the husband works from 8 A.M.–5 P.M. and the wife works from 7 P.M.–3 A.M. (White & Keith, 1990).

Separating cause and effect is difficult in these cases. Having very little time together and disagreeing about how to divide marital work can *lead* to marital dissatisfaction and ultimately divorce (Hochschild, 1989; Blumstein & Schwartz, 1983). At the same time, partners who are already dissatisfied with their marriage might work longer hours, different shifts, or against the wishes of their spouse *because* they do not like their marriage and are preparing to leave it (Spitze, 1988; Greene & Quester, 1982). The complex issues surrounding these divorces and others will be discussed further in Chapter 14. For now, we will discuss an alternative way of dividing marital work that may, ultimately, overcome some of the strains associated with the dual-helpers and separate-spheres patterns.

Alternative
Choice

**Symmetrical work
sharing**

a pattern of dividing
and balancing
marital work in
which husband
and wife are
considered economic
coproviders and in
which both are
responsible (in
approximately equal
measure) for
household work and
child care.

Symmetrical Work Sharing

A minority of dual-earner couples are now trying out a new, significantly different, marital work pattern. Work-family expert Patricia Voydanoff (1987) lays out the basic principles of this new pattern, **symmetrical work sharing**, as follows:

> A major difference between traditional families with some role sharing and symmetrical families with extensive sharing of tasks and responsibilities is one of responsibility. Wives in symmetrical families are co-providers with a responsibility to make a significant economic contribution to the family. In addition, in symmetrical families, husbands move beyond "helping" their wives with family work and assume responsibility in this area. . . . Symmetrical role allocation requires more accommodation to family needs by men and more accommodation to work demands by women than the traditional pattern. (pp. 93–94)

Several studies of dual-earner marriages have identified a number of couples who meet (or come close to meeting) the criteria of symmetrical role sharers. A large-scale study done in the 1970s identified 10 percent of the husbands as "outliers" because they did as much or more household work as the average wife in the study (although not necessarily as much as their own wives) (Berk, 1985, p. 209). In a 1985 study focusing on highly educated employees of a western university, Benin and Agostinelli (1988) found that a little more than one-third shared the work equally. Finally, nine of the fifty couples Arlie Hochschild (1989) interviewed between 1980 and 1988 divided household work and children fifty-fifty. These figures suggest that the symmetrical work-sharing pattern is chosen by a small, but possibly growing, proportion of U.S. married couples.

What distinguishes these symmetrical couples from others? How did they get to be that way? Support for the general principles of gender equality—for example, the ideals of equal earning opportunities for women and equal sharing of housework by men—is not enough to insure that the household work and child care will be shared (Thompson & Walker, 1989, p. 857). Many men and women who express support for such abstract ideals of gender equality simply do not apply these ideals in their own marriages.

Family-specific gender equality attitudes are important, though. Husbands who consider their wives "coproviders" rather than simply "helpers" are more likely to share household work equally. (Perry-Jenkins & Crouter, 1990). This coprovider attitude is most likely to develop when the wife's income is clearly needed for family survival (Hood, 1986) and when husband and wife make about the same amount of money (Hochschild, 1989). Contrast the following quotes from symmetrical work sharers to the dual helpers quoted earlier:

> It takes so much money to make this boat float a month and I don't have enough by myself and she knew that before we were ever married. One of the things that we made sure was understood was that she was definitely going to have to work when we got married if we needed the money or if we were going to be a family unit. (TV cameraman married to a day-care worker, quoted in Blumstein & Schwartz, 1983, p. 122)

> I think it's more a fifty-fifty deal. We're both providers and we're both homemakers and we're both parents. . . . I think we're sharing our responsibilities. ("James Mooney," a machinist married to a secretary, quoted in Hood, 1986, pp. 354–55)

The wife's attitude toward the husband as parent and houseworker is also important. Husbands in dual-helper marriages are often reluctant about doing household work because their wives criticize their attempts or otherwise fail to offer sufficient support. In contrast, wives in symmetrical work-sharing marriages welcome, urge, and support their husbands' help. They view their husbands as competent household workers and fathers, let them find their own ways of doing things, loosen up on standards, and do not try to "hoard" child care or household chores for themselves (Coltrane, 1990; Hochschild, 1989).

The wife's willingness to give up sole responsibility for household work and the husband's willingness to see his wife as a coprovider are more common in black couples than in white ones, and so is work sharing at home (Ross, 1987; Willie, 1985; Maret & Finlay, 1984). This may be because black couples have a much longer tradition of wives earning money than white couples do and because black men and women earn more nearly the same salaries (Willie, 1985).

There are also certain structural circumstances under which men do considerably more household work than is usual, whether or not they hold work-sharing attitudes. Couples who delay having children until they have been married for several years are more likely to be work-sharers, even after the children are born, than are couples who have their children early in the marriage (Coltrane, 1990). However, early childbearers may end up sharing work equally through other circumstances. For example, financially strapped dual-earner couples with several preschool children find that in order to get everything done, *both* spouses must work a "second shift" at home until the children get a little older (Berk, 1985, pp. 209–210). Finally, husbands who work a day shift with wives who work at night (an arrangement frequently chosen by young parents with preschool children) often do the week-day meal preparation, cleanup, and child care that other husbands leave to their wives (Presser, 1988).

What does symmetrical work-sharing do for the marriage? Both employed and nonemployed wives are more satisfied with their marriages when their husbands share equally in housework and child care, especially if the men take on some of the "feminine" routine tasks such as washing dishes, cleaning bathrooms, and diapering babies (Benin & Agostinelli, 1988; Yogev & Brett, 1985). No surprise here! The findings on husbands, however, are mixed (Thompson & Walker, 1989). Husbands who share the household work *and* who believe that all three types of marital work should be shared show high levels of satisfaction with their marriages (Perry-Jenkins & Crouter, 1990). In contrast, husband who are ambivalent about their wives' provider role or who take on additional child care and housework because of structural circumstances *may* be somewhat less satisfied with the marriage (Perry-Jenkins & Crouter, 1990; but see Staines, 1986).

Husbands and wives who choose the symmetrical-work-sharing pattern will have more in common with one another and may well spend more time together than spouses who choose the dual-helpers

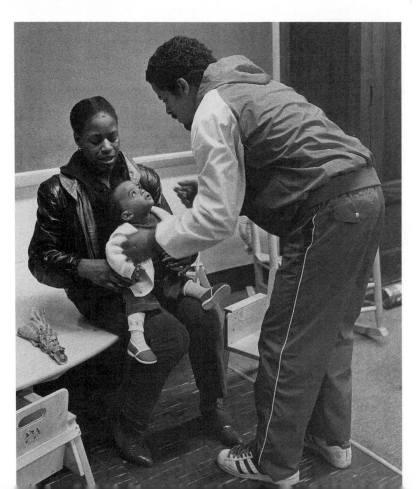

Mothers and fathers in symmetrical work-sharing marriages split child care duties equally.

or separate-spheres patterns. However, they will probably have more arguments about household work. After all, they are experimenting with something new, often with little support or advice from others. These symmetrical work sharers can take comfort in the idea that they may be initiating the next major pattern of marital work (Ross, Mirowsky, & Huber, 1983). Perhaps their (your?) grandchildren or great grandchildren will accept symmetrical work sharing as the "traditional" pattern, the way "things have always been."

Summary

Married couples make decisions about three types of marital work: 1. money production, work that involves earning money to buy family necessities, 2. people production, work having to do with the physical, psychological, and emotional care of family members, and 3. household production, work having to do with acquiring, producing, and maintaining possessions. Couples must decide on the priority and division of each type of work.

Marital work decisions vary according to the economic and technological characteristics of the societies in which couples live. Certain marital work patterns, or ways of dividing work, tend to be associated with certain historical eras. In the preindustrial, colonial United States, an economic partnership pattern prevailed: household production occupied most of the time, and husband and wife had distinct but interdependent tasks. Money production, much less important, was an extension of household production and was also shared. Child care and spousal support, much less emphasized than today, were responsibilities of both spouses.

Industrialization brought a new pattern of marital work—separate spheres—in which men left the home to work and became solely responsible for money production and women stayed at home and assumed responsibility for household and people production. All three types of work were elaborated and specialized and effectively segregated men and women into separate, and somewhat opposite, workplaces. Although it was presented as the ideal for many, only some families, especially white, middle-class, urban families, could afford to pursue this pattern prior to the mid-twentieth century.

During the late twentieth century a third major marital work pattern emerged: the dual-helpers pattern. A variation on the separate-spheres pattern, the dual-helpers pattern involves the wife helping the husband with money production by taking a paid job and the husband helping the wife with some household and child care tasks. The pattern evolved in three stages. First, married women began to enter the labor force to help their families financially, because of greater demand for their labor and because they had fewer children at home. Second, public attitudes toward wife employment changed from unfavorable to favorable. Third, husbands began to do a greater (although still much less than their wives') proportion of housework and child care than previously. In contrast with separate-spheres couples, couples using the dual-helpers pattern spend more time in money production and less time on household production, while still striving to reserve adequate time for children and for each other. Marriages with two earners are more financially secure, and employed wives tend to have less psychological distress, greater confidence, and more egalitarian marriages than nonemployed wives. Dual-helper marriages are neither more nor less satisfying than separate-sphere marriages. However, couples with a working wife are somewhat more likely to divorce. Disagreement about and dissatisfaction with the division of marital work, neglecting the marital relationship because of long work hours, and different employment shifts for husbands and wives are especially likely to create strain and dissatisfaction.

Some couples make the alternative choice of symmetrical work sharing, a marital work pattern in which both partners assume equal responsibility for money production, household production, and people production. Some couples enter into the pattern because it seems fairest to them, some because circumstances demand it. Wives, and husbands who entered the pattern voluntarily, express satisfaction with both the arrangement and their marriages. This pattern could become the prevailing marital work pattern in the future.

CHAPTER 10

THE TASKS OF MARRIAGE: MANAGING MONEY IN A CHANGING ECONOMY

In 1988, the average U.S. married couple whose oldest child was less than six years old spent $30,944, not including taxes. Where did the money go? Make your best estimates here. You will be able to find out how accurate you were by reading the chapter.

	Amount in Dollars	Percent of Total
Food (groceries, eating out, alcohol)		
Housing (rent/mortgage, utilities, furniture, appliances, supplies)		
Transportation (car payments, gas, repair, insurance, public transportation)		
Clothing and Personal Care (for example, hair cuts, hygiene needs)		
Health Care (medical care, insurance, medication)		
Pensions, Social Security		
Other Expenditures		
Total	$30,994	100%

In July, 1985, Ruth and Nate Reese and their teenage children, Darnell and Annie, took a room at the Prince George Hotel in New York City. The Reeses were not on vacation; the hotel they moved into that July was "home" for them and 458 other homeless families. For five months before moving into the hotel, the Reeses had shared overcrowded apartments with a series of friends and had spent some nights in emergency shelters. The Reeses' $325 a month apartment had burned to the ground in February, destroying all their possessions. They had known about the apartment's faulty wiring when they had moved in 10 months earlier but felt they had little choice—without warning, the rent on their previous, safer, Brooklyn apartment had doubled from $190 to $380 a month, too much for the Reeses' low-income budget (adapted from Freedman, 1990, Chapter 6).

In December, 1985, a multiple murder-suicide shocked a small farming community in Iowa. A 63-year-old farmer, depressed about his tremendous debts and fearing foreclosure of his farm, had shot and killed his 64-year-old wife, a neighbor, and the town banker, before turning his 12-gauge shotgun to his own chest (adapted from *Associated Press*, 1985).

In 1986, Mary Ann, a restaurant manager, and her husband Larry, a mechanic, invested $152,000 in a Connecticut home. Encouraged by a booming real estate market, the couple hoped to sell the home at a profit four years later and cruise the Caribbean in a sailboat. Four years later, however, the house was worth only $115,000 and the house payments had risen. Mary Ann and Larry, both reemployed at lower salaries after a period of unemployment, were making $500 a week less than when they had purchased the house and were two months behind on their house payments—"We feel trapped. . . . This house consumes every dollar we make" (adapted from Schmitt, 1990).

The three cases described above, despite their differences, all have something in common. In each case, regional or local economic changes contributed to the disruption or destruction of family stability, family lives, and family dreams. The Reeses' rent doubled and their path to homelessness began when New York City tax policies and foreign investment decisions changed to favor the development of high-priced condominiums over the maintenance of middle- and low-income rental housing. This change drove middle-income renters into surrounding boroughs like Brooklyn, raised rental prices in those areas, and left lower-income renters, like the Reeses, without safe, affordable housing. A similar high-income real estate boom in Connecticut encouraged Mary Ann and Larry to take on a tremendous debt; a subsequent real estate bust dashed their dreams. In the 1970s, high prices for crops, national economic policies, and local banks persuaded Iowa farmers to expand their dreams and borrow money; the low farm prices of the early 1980s left them with no way to repay their loans. Some of them, like the farmer described in the story, responded in a way that tragically destroyed their own families and disrupted several others.

News stories such as these do not usually detail what happens to the intimate relationships *inside* families in the face of such economic adversity. You can imagine, though, that the Reeses had a more difficult time monitoring the activities of their teenage children when they could no longer provide a permanent home, that Mary Ann and Larry had more than a few arguments about their economic woes, and that many Iowa farm wives, after reading about farm murder-suicides, began to wonder about their husbands' mental stability under stress.

Chapter 10 discusses how economic events on a national, regional, and local level can either enlarge the opportunities or limit the choices of individual couples and families when it comes to making decisions about money. It also considers how both large-scale economic forces and small-scale financial decisions affect husband-wife and parent-child relationships. To accomplish these aims, the chapter moves back and forth between the national economy and the individual family unit. Chapter 10 begins by reviewing the major economic trends affecting families since World War II, contrasting the prosperous 1947–1973 period to the less prosperous years that continue up to the present. This section should help you understand some of the economic ups and downs you have observed in your own families.

Events over which families have no control can disrupt family financial plans and dreams for the future.

Next we turn to the financial affairs of individual couples. Here we discuss why most couples find money a source of contention, the choices they make in devising a money management system, and how their choices reflect both larger social forces and their own personal histories. The section also includes a short segment on making a budget and considers two types of families in economic trouble—the poor and the unemployed. These economically distressed families illustrate most clearly the interplay between external economic forces and internal family dynamics, a major theme of the chapter.

ECONOMIC CHANGE AND
FAMILY LIFE

As other chapters and the Cohort Comparisons in this text make clear, large-scale economic forces affect many decisions related to family life—when to marry, whether to have children and how many to have, whether to stay in the community where one grew up or to move to another part of the country. That is one reason for having a short section on economic history in a text about marriages and families. The second reason relates more directly to this particular chapter. All adults, married and unmarried, homosexual and heterosexual, white, black, Hispanic, and Asian-American, make decisions about how to spend money. These decisions are tied not only to their current economic situation but also to mental images about money and lifestyle they formed while growing up. Any attempt to understand peoples' money images must begin with a knowledge of the general economic conditions of their youth.

We will consider two historical periods: the period from 1947–1973 and the period from 1974 to the present. Most readers of this text formed their first ideas and images about money during one of these two periods; all readers have lived through one or both periods. The two periods also present a clear contrast: 1947–1973 was a period of increasing family prosperity while the period since 1973 has represented economic stagnation or decline for many families.

10 The Tasks of Marriage: Managing Money in a Changing Economy

1947–1973: Increasing Family Prosperity

Between the end of World War II in 1945 and the energy crisis in 1973, families from all racial and ethnic groups saw improvements in their incomes and in their standard of living. There are many ways to document such changes, but we will focus on two of them: changes in the median income and changes in the rate of absolute poverty.

Changes in Median Income

Figure 10–1 provides a graphic illustration of changes in median family income between 1947 and 1987. The income figures are given in 1987 dollars as a way of adjusting for inflation over time; thus, a family earning at the median level in 1947 had an income equivalent to that of a 1987 family making about $15,000. Focus on that part of the graph covering 1947 to 1973. As you can see, over these years *median real family income nearly doubled* from $15,422 to $30,820 (U.S. Bureau of the Census, 1989d). The average family in the early 1970s could afford a material life twice as comfortable as the average family just after World War II. In 1947, for example, one-third of all families lived in

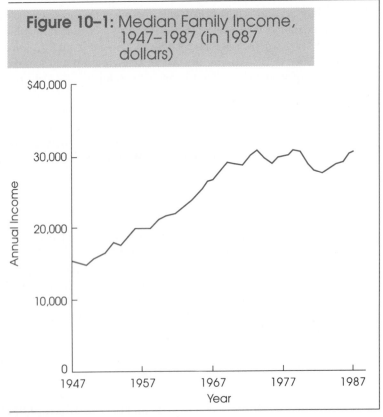

Figure 10–1: Median Family Income, 1947–1987 (in 1987 dollars)

The income figures are given in 1987 dollars as a way of adjusting for inflation over time; thus, the median income of families in 1947 was equivalent to the income of a 1987 family making about $15,000. Note that median family income nearly doubled between the late 1940s and the early 1970s but has fluctuated right around the $30,000 mark for the last two decades. This is despite the fact that most families are now two-earner families.

Source: U.S. Bureau of the Census, 1989d, p. 21.

homes without running water, 60 percent lacked central heating, and about half did not have an electric refrigerator (Levy, 1987, p. 25). By 1973, these household features, along with many others, were basics that almost all families took for granted.

Figure 10–1 lumps together data for all kinds of families—black, white, and Hispanic, married-couple and single-parent. Did all types of families actually share in these improvements? In general, the answer is "yes." Minority group families (blacks, Hispanics, and American Indians), while starting and ending the period with median incomes substantially below those of white families, all showed improvements in median family income between 1947 and 1973 (Tienda & Jensen, 1988). All of the minority groups except Puerto Ricans also improved their income position *relative* to the white population (Tienda & Jensen, 1988). To cite one example: in 1949, the median black family income was 50 percent of the median white family income; by 1973, black families at the median level made 58 percent of what white families did (Levy, 1987, pp. 47, 66). Clearly, there was still a substantial gap between black families and white families in the early 1970s, but the gap had narrowed somewhat since the late 1940s.

The picture is less encouraging when married-couple and single-mother families are compared. Families headed by women did show small improvements in real income between 1947 and 1973—from about $10,000 to about $15,000 a year—but, as illustrated by Figure 10–2 (on page 344), the *gap* between these families and married-couple families greatly widened during this period. The benefits of postwar prosperity went mostly to married-couple families.

Changes in Absolute Poverty Rates

A second way to measure the changes in family economic well-being is to look at **absolute poverty rates**—the proportion of families living below an objectively defined minimum standard. Since 1959, the federal government has set this standard (often called the "official poverty level") by deciding how much a family eating an adequate but minimum cost diet would spend on food and multiplying by three (Orshansky, 1968). Different official poverty levels are set according to family size and urban or rural residence. Official poverty levels are always substantially below the median income and also below what most citizens consider "poor." For example, in 1964, when the poverty level for a nonfarm family of four was set at $3100 (Orshansky, 1968, p. 68), the median family income was $6569 (U.S. Bureau of the Census, 1975, p. 297) and the Gallup Poll found that a cross-section of the U.S. population felt that $81 a week ($4212 a year) was the smallest amount a nonfarm family of four could "get by on" (*The Gallup Report*, 1985, p. 18).

Absolute poverty rate
the proportion of families living below an objectively defined minimum standard.

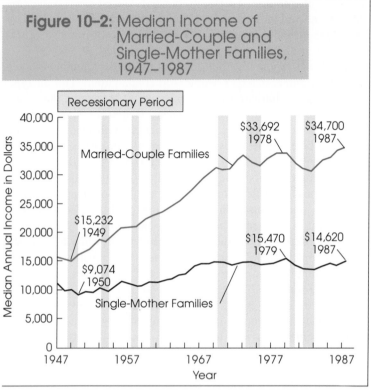

Figure 10–2: Median Income of Married-Couple and Single-Mother Families, 1947–1987

Source: McChesney, K. Y. 1990, Figure 5. "An integrated model of economic and sociological theories of family poverty 1947–1987." Dept. of Sociology, University of Missouri- St. Louis, 8001 Natural Bridge Road, St. Louis, MO 63121.

The economic plight of single-mother families in comparison with that of married-couple families has gotten progressively worse. In 1950, the median income of single-mother families was 60 percent of married couple family income; it is now only 42 percent.

Thus, the term absolute poverty means exactly what it says—living *below* a very basic minimum level.

The overall proportion of families living in absolute poverty dropped from an estimated 32 percent in 1949 to 11 percent in 1973 (Levy, 1987, pp. 47, 66). Table 10–1, focusing on the period since 1959, shows that the postwar decline in absolute poverty affected minority groups as well as the white majority. Blacks and American Indians showed especially dramatic reductions in absolute poverty during this period.

Absolute poverty rates, like median incomes, changed much more for married-couple families than for single-mother families between the late 1940s and the early 1970s. In 1950, 20 percent of intact, married-couple families were poor; by 1970, only 8 percent fell below the poverty line. In contrast, 48 percent of female-headed families were poor in 1950 and, by 1970, 39 percent were still living below the poverty level (Smith, 1988, p. 149).

Table 10-1 Changes in Absolute Poverty Rates for Minority and Nonminority Families, 1959–1984

	Percent of Families below Official Poverty Level			
	1959	1969	1979	1984
Blacks	47.8	29.8	26.3	30.6
Mexicans	37.7	28.3	21.7	24.0
Puerto Ricans	35.8	28.8	34.9	41.4
Other Hispanics	31.7	20.7	16.1	17.8
American Indians	54.2	29.5	20.5	NA
Whites	14.6	8.1	6.5	7.7

Source: Marta Tienda & Leif Jensen "Poverty and Minorities: A Quarter-Century Profile of Color and Socioeconomic Disadvantage." Gary D. Sandefur and Marta Tienda (eds.) *Divided Opportunities: Minorities, Poverty, and Social Policy.* Plenum Publishing Corporation. 1988. Table 2.

Explaining the Improvements

Why were so many U.S. families so much better off economically in 1973 than in 1947? The economic improvements in family life noted above were due mostly to the tremendous expansion of the United States economy after World War II. Three factors were important in starting and sustaining this growth:

1. Postwar U.S. factories were geared up, ready to turn the innovations in electronics, transportation, and petrochemicals developed during the war into products for consumers. More importantly, they faced *very little international competition.* While much of the industrial capacity of Europe and Japan was destroyed in World War II, the United States remained physically unscathed.
2. There was a *tremendous pent-up consumer demand* for housing, cars, appliances and other consumer products. People limited by lack of money during the Depression and by rationing during the war were anxious to begin spending. The tremendous growth in young families with their multiple Baby Boom children sustained the demand for many years.
3. *The labor force was experienced, relatively small, and growing slowly.* Birth rates had been low in the 1920s, 1930s, and early 1940s, so that the number of new workers entering the labor force each year until the middle 1960s was relatively small.

This combination of factors meant that employers could make hefty profits and still afford to pay their employees well. Employees, being in demand, felt secure in pressing for further benefits; labor unions underwent major growth during this period. The end result was an expanding economy from which families at all economic levels received some benefits (Levy, 1987).

1973 to the Present: Family Prosperity on Hold

As a result of their postwar experiences, many U.S. family wage earners came to expect year-by-year improvements in real income and in their standard of living. And just as they were much more prosperous than their parents had been, so they expected their children to make even further advancements. The millions of Baby Boom children born during the 1950s and 1960s expected these year-by-year improvements as well.

Figures 10–1 and 10–2 and Table 10–1 suggest that these optimistic expectations have not been fulfilled, at least on the aggregate level. Focus now on the right-hand side of these diagrams. During the 1970s and 1980s, real median family income stopped its steady growth and actually fell in some years; the economic gap between married-couple families and single-mother families increased, minority groups lost some of the gains of previous years, and all groups experienced greater rates of absolute poverty. In the words of economists Bennett Harrison and Barry Bluestone (1988), the U.S. economy made a "Great U-Turn."

Explaining the Changes

What factors contributed to the stagnation and reversals of the 1970s and 1980s? Essentially, the factors that created the prosperity of the earlier era no longer held.

1. *An international economy matured and offered notable competition.* By the middle 1960s, the countries that had been devastated by World War II had recovered and had entered the international market on a large scale, offering high quality products at competitive prices. By the early 1970s, the major oil-producing countries had unified and were demanding much higher prices for the petroleum they produced. Both developments cut into the profitability of U.S. corporations, which responded by closing less profitable plants, trimming their workforce, and holding steady or reducing pay and benefits for workers. The workers, meanwhile, paid higher prices for everything linked to petroleum—gasoline, utility bills, plastic goods, and food (Harrison & Bluestone, 1988).

2. *Consumer demand approached the saturation point.* Birth rates in the United States began to fall in the 1960s and plummeted in the 1970s. The ever-increasing market for consumer goods that had existed during the postwar period was no longer growing in size and, with the increased choices offered by international competitors, consumers could afford to be more selective.

3. *The size and inexperience of the labor force increased.* Beginning in the late 1960s, the Baby Boom children, both male and female, began to enter the labor force. In addition, many older women entered or reentered the labor market during these years, in part as a response to inflation. Some of the stagnation in the median income and in the rates of poverty after 1973 may be due, therefore, to the fact that more workers were young or female and such workers generally receive less pay (Johnston & Packer, 1987). The fact that there were so *many* new workers also had a depressing effect on income (Easterlin, 1987).

These changes in international competition, consumer demand for products, and the labor force may well have accelerated a change that was already underway: the shift from a medium-wage manufacturing economy to a low-wage service economy, a process known as **deindustrialization** (Bluestone & Harrison, 1982). In a **manufacturing economy**, many workers are involved in turning raw materials into finished goods; in a **service economy**, the vast majority of workers are involved with delivering goods, information, and services. The broad category "service workers" includes workers at all levels of skill, education, and income—plastic surgeons, advertising executives, college presidents, nurses, secretaries, cashiers, child-care workers, and janitors are all service workers. However, more service workers than manufacturing workers receive low wages for their work (Johnston & Packer, 1987). When a country deindustrializes, the proportion of middle-income jobs drops and the proportion of low-income jobs increases. Thus, the shift to a service economy undoubtedly contributed to the increases in poverty and stagnation in median income observed in the 1970s, 1980s, and early 1990s (Bluestone & Harrison, 1982).

Deindustrialization
the shift of a national economy from emphasis on medium-wage manufacturing jobs to emphasis on low-wage service jobs.

Manufacturing economy
an economy in which many workers are involved in turning raw materials into finished goods.

Service economy
an economy in which the vast majority of workers are involved with delivering goods, information, and personal or professional services.

The Helped and the Harmed

Families at every stage of family life, from all racial and ethnic groups, whether married couple or single parent, all benefited, at least somewhat, from the expanding economy of the 1950s and 1960s. The inflation, recession, and deindustrialization of the 1970s and 1980s did *not* affect all families in the same way. Rather, some types of families (the helped) were able to hold their own or even improve their economic standing during these years, while others (the harmed) saw their economic situation deteriorate.

Figure 10–3 indicates that, during the 1980s, people over age 65 did especially well in terms of income while people under 35 suffered in comparison to their counterparts 10 years earlier. Much the same is true if total assets are considered (Bodnar & Wilcox, 1990). One explanation for these trends is that, beginning in 1974, Social Security benefits, a major source of income for many elderly people, were tied to the cost of living. This provided elderly people some protection against inflation that younger families did not have. Furthermore, when the recessions and inflation of the 1970s and 1980s hit, this older age group had already acquired most of the major goods necessary for family life (Caplovitz, 1979).

Overall, young adults were economically harmed during these years. They were more likely than other age groups to see declines in family income and prosperity and were most vulnerable to long-term unemployment (Moen, 1983, 1979). Young people with a high school education or less were especially vulnerable. In the past, they could have obtained middle-income, secure, manufacturing jobs with benefits that increased over the years. In the 1970s and 1980s, they obtained, instead, the lower paying jobs of the service economy (Cutler, 1989).

Minority group members, especially black males, were hard hit by the deindustrialization of the 1970s and 1980s. Deindustrialization and

This graph documents how much median family incomes have increased (above the 0 percent line) or decreased (below the 0 percent line), according to the age of householder. Households headed by young adults have seen substantial declines in median income while those headed by elderly people have seen substantial increases.

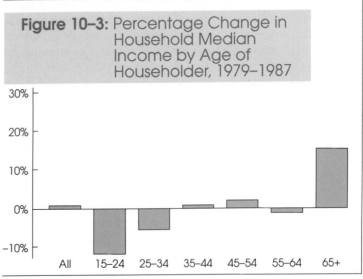

Figure 10–3: Percentage Change in Household Median Income by Age of Householder, 1979–1987

Source: Waldrop, 1989, p. 22. "Reprinted with permission © *American Demographics*, March, 1989."

the subsequent displacement of workers was most pronounced in blue-collar industries located in or near the central city regions of the oldest industrial cities—precisely the places where black males were likely to work (Bowman, 1988; Ellwood, 1988). Once laid off, blacks and Hispanics had a more difficult time obtaining another job (Horvath, 1987), in part because they lacked the extensive informal networks more readily available to whites (Ellwood, 1988). The hesitancy of young blacks to marry during the last two decades could well be related to the difficulties young males had in finding well-paying jobs (Bowman, 1988).

Married couples of all races did much better at maintaining or increasing their incomes during the 1970s and 1980s than did female-headed households (Smith, 1988; Tienda & Jensen, 1988). The reason is simple—many of them added an earner, the wife. A household with only one potential earner does not, of course, have this option. Furthermore, a disproportionate number of these single-earner, female-headed households are headed by women who are young, belong to a minority group, have small children, and lack higher education. Each of these factors reduces their chances of obtaining good-paying work and makes them more vulnerable to long-term unemployment, inflation, and recession (Caplovitz, 1979; Moen, 1979). High divorce rates and high rates of unmarried teenage pregnancy during the 1970s and 1980s meant that the proportion of these highly vulnerable families increased relative to married couple families, especially among minority groups (Smith, 1988).

In short, the economically helped of the 1970s and 1980s were middle-aged and older married couples who stayed together. The harmed were young adults, those with less education and fewer skills, never married or divorced women with children, and minority group members.

MONEY AND FAMILY RELATIONSHIPS

How do these large-scale changes affect what goes on *inside* families? In one sense, not very much. Couples at all income levels, in good economic times and bad, argue and worry about money (Shriver, 1989, p. 21; Erskine, 1973; Blood & Wolfe, 1960, p. 241). Certain financial tensions are *expected* and *predictable* parts of modern marriage. Most married couples move through different stages of family development, known as the **family life cycle**. The family life cycle begins when husband and wife marry, enters a second stage when they have their first child, and proceeds through subsequent stages as the oldest child enters school and becomes an adolescent. The final stages of the family life

Family life cycle stages of family development, beginning with marriage and ending with one spouse's death.

cycle are the period when all children have left home and the period when both spouses have retired but are still living. Whether married couples go through all the stages or not, different expected and predictable financial tensions are associated with each stage.

External economic changes that bring about booms and busts, housing shortages, high levels of inflation, unemployment, and poverty mean that many families, like those described at the beginning of the chapter, are put under *extraordinary* and *unexpected* economic stress. Such stress can have profound effects on physical and mental health, the husband-wife relationship, and the relationship between children and parents. We will discuss the expected and predictable types of financial tensions and how people deal with them first and then explore the effects of two forms of extraordinary (and often unexpected) economic stress—poverty and unemployment.

Money as an Expected Source of Family Tension

According to numerous public opinion polls, scientific surveys, family therapists, and financial advisors, couples all over the United States worry about money, argue about money, and identify money as a source of considerable stress. Although people with lower incomes definitely worry about money more frequently than those with higher incomes, some people at *every* income level have money worries (Shriver, 1989, p. 21; Rubenstein, 1981, p. 32). Marital therapists estimate that 39 percent of their clients identify "money management or finances" as a problem area in their marriage (Geiss & O'Leary, 1981). The estimates are that high or higher when couples not in therapy are asked about sources of conflict in their marriage (Blumstein & Schwartz, 1983; Blood & Wolfe, 1960). In a study of sources of stress throughout the family life cycle, couples at *every* stage of the family life cycle listed "financial strain" as a significant stress. In fact, in five out of the seven stages, financial strain was the most often mentioned source of strain (Olson *et al.*, 1983, p. 123).

Hidden Investments and the Great Taboo

Why should money be the source of so much anxiety and so many arguments within marriage? One reason people argue about money so much after marrying is that they talked so little about it before they wed. Money is, in effect, a taboo subject of conversation prior to marriage (Lobsenz, 1989; Blumstein & Schwartz, 1983), just as it is a taboo subject between many parents and their children (Kutner, 1990). Many people, especially those married for the first time, go into marriage believing that money is something "nice people just don't talk about."

Once married, couples have to make a number of choices about their financial life together: whether to pool or to keep financial resources separate, how to make major and minor financial decisions, who will implement financial decisions on a day-to-day basis, whether to make and follow a planned budget, and whether to engage in long-term financial planning. *These choices work out most satisfactorily when both partners participate in making them.* Participation here means talking to one another and listening to one another extensively. Financial advisor Sylvia Porter (1975) insists on such mutual participation in her budgeting advice:

> You must work together if you are married. Your plan must be a joint project and you must talk about a wide variety of things before trying to put down a single figure about income or outgo. (p. 10)

Conversations about money early in the marriage are likely to lead to some arguments; perhaps this is one reason so many couples

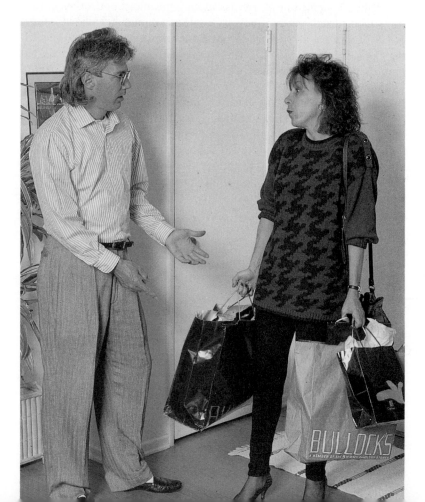

Marital arguments about money are common, especially during the early years of marriage.

Hidden investments the values, meanings, fears, and experiences regarding money that people carry with them into marriage.

avoid discussing money. However, the *failure* to discuss money means that the two partners have no way of knowing about the hidden investments of the other. **Hidden investments** is a term used by psychologist and financial advisor Victoria Felton-Collins (1990) to refer to all the values, meanings, fears, and experiences regarding money that people carry with them into marriage. These hidden investments develop as a result of childhood socialization and experiences, religion, the historical era and subculture in which one was reared, the mass media, and personal experiences as an adult (Felton-Collins, 1990; Hogan & Bauer, 1988). They influence beliefs about which family member should manage money and how it should be managed, about spending and saving, and about what material possessions families "need."

One important hidden investment is feelings about the *meaning* of money. Most people view money as more than just paper that is traded for goods and services. It has an emotional meaning; people feel that having and spending money is the way to achieve certain desirable feelings—freedom, security, power, or love (Felton-Collins, 1990). Answer the questions in the Personal Application "What Does Money Mean to You?" to find out about the meanings you attach to money.

When couples fail to discuss money meanings and other hidden investments, each partner judges the other's money behavior from his or her own (often unacknowledged) money meanings and sees the partner's behavior as "irrational," "irresponsible," or "well-intentioned but dumb." For example, a wife to whom money means security cannot figure out the free-spending ways of her husband who was brought up to believe that money was made to be spent. She sulks and nags and he cannot figure out why. Meanwhile, her husband complains that she "wastes time" clipping and sorting coupons that save, at most, a few dollars a week. What she sees as an important contribution to household economy, he sees as time taken away from more pleasurable activities. Each situation results in arguments or festering, unexpressed tension about money.

Personal Application

What Does Money Mean to You?

These questions will help you determine what meaning money has for you. Select the answer that best matches your feelings or behavior and then score yourself using the instructions that follow the quiz.

1. Money is important because it allows me to . . .
   a. do what I want to do.
   b. feel secure.
   c. get ahead in life.
   d. buy things for others.

2. I feel that money . . .
   a. frees up my time.
   b. can solve my problems.
   c. is a means to an end.
   d. helps make relationships smoother.

3. When it comes to saving money, I . . .
   a. don't have a plan and don't often save.
   b. have a plan and stick to it.
   c. don't have a plan but manage to save anyway.
   d. don't make enough money to save.

4. If someone asks about my personal finances, I . . .
   a. feel defensive.
   b. realize I need more education and information.
   c. feel comfortable and competent.
   d. would rather talk about something else.

5. When I make a major purchase, I . . .
   a. go with what my intuition tells me.
   b. research a great deal before buying.
   c. feel I'm in charge—it's my/our money.
   d. ask friends/family first.

6. If I have money left over at the end of the month, I . . .
   a. go out and have a good time.
   b. put the money into savings.
   c. look for a good investment.
   d. buy a gift for someone.

7. If I discover I paid more for something than a friend did, I . . .
   a. couldn't care less.
   b. feel it's okay because I also find bargains at times.
   c. assume he spent more time shopping, and time is money.
   d. feel upset and angry at myself.

8. When paying bills, I . . .
   a. put it off and sometimes forget.
   b. pay them when due, but no sooner.
   c. pay when I get to it, but don't want to be hassled.
   d. worry that my credit will suffer if I miss a payment.

9. When it comes to borrowing money, I . . .
   a. simply won't—don't like to feel indebted.
   b. only borrow as a last resort.
   c. tend to borrow from banks or other business sources.
   d. ask friends and family because they know I'll pay.

10. When eating out with friends I prefer to . . .
    a. divide the bill proportionately.
    b. ask for separate checks.
    c. charge the bill to my bank card and have others pay me.
    d. pay the entire bill because I like to treat my friends.

11. When it comes to tipping, I . . .
    a. sometimes do and sometimes don't.
    b. Just call me Scrooge.
    c. resent it, but always tip the right amount.
    d. tip generously because I like to be well thought of.

12. If I suddenly came into a lot of money, I . . .
   a. wouldn't have to work.
   b. wouldn't have to worry about the future.
   c. could really build up my business.
   d. would spend a lot on family and friends and enjoy time with them more.

13. When indecisive about a purchase I often tell myself . . .
   a. it's only money.
   b. it's a bargain.
   c. it's a good investment.
   d. he/she will love it.

14. In my family . . .
   a. I handle all the money and pay all the bills.
   b. my partner takes care of the finances.
   c. I pay my bills and my partner does the same.
   d. we sit down together to pay bills.

For scoring: Count the number of times you responded with an a, b, c, or d, excluding questions 3, 4, and 7 (which are for your information only). Whichever letter you chose most frequently reveals your primary money motivation: a. freedom; b. security; c. power; and d. love.

Source: From *Couples and Money* by Victoria Felton-Collins. Copyright © 1990 by Victoria Felton-Collins. Used by permission of Bantam Books, a division of Bantam Doubleday Dell Publishing Group, Inc.

   Talking openly about money feelings, money experiences, and money fears is one way that newly married couples learn to better understand one another and is a first step in developing a family culture regarding money and a viable money management plan. Once such discussions have taken place, partners with different money values and feelings can broaden one another's understandings of money and help curb one another's excesses (Felton-Collins, 1990). The discussions themselves, however, will probably engender some conflict. Such conflict may be a necessary part of making money choices early in the marriage. In their research on couples, Blumstein and Schwartz (1983) found that married couples argued about money management more often than other types of couples, but also that such arguments were more common among newly married couples than among those married ten years or more. Once couples develop standard procedures for handling money and making future money choices, they have less to argue about.

Unfulfilled Aspirations

Couples who have come to understand one another's hidden investments and who have learned to argue constructively about money may nonetheless continue to feel money frustrations. Picture the couple's financial situation as a three-legged stool. One leg is costs; one is resources; and one is aspirations. When costs, resources, and aspirations are well-balanced—when there is enough money (resources) to pay for (costs) the desired items (aspirations)—finances are not likely to be a source of frustration. If the three legs are not in balance—aspirations or costs rise faster than resources, for example—the stool totters and financial stress increases (Oppenheimer, 1982, p. 6).

Most U.S. couples, most of the time, have enough resources to cover the costs of the basic necessities, objectively defined. Many couples, however, lack the resources to fulfill their subjective aspirations. A 1980 *Psychology Today* survey of a highly educated, affluent sample found that most people had **unfulfilled aspirations** exceeding their resources; 70 percent agreed that "there always seem to be things I want that I can't have" (Rubenstein, 1981, p. 31). Such people are likely to be dissatisfied both with their financial situation and with the quality of their life in general. In fact, researchers find that it is not income that determines financial satisfaction or satisfaction with life in general, but rather one's *perception* of income adequacy and one's financial aspirations. *Those who perceive that their income is inadequate and those who hold high financial aspirations are likely to feel dissatisfied financially and with life in general regardless of how much money they have.* (Hogan & Bauer, 1988; Davis & Helmick, 1985).

> **Unfulfilled aspirations**
> the situation in which peoples' desires for material possessions exceed their economic resources.

Many money-related aspirations are part of the hidden investments discussed earlier; they arise out of individuals' own particular socialization and financial history. Lifestyle aspirations—for example, how many bathrooms a "decent" house should have, how to use vacation time, how often a family "needs" a new car—are very much influenced by reference groups outside the family, such as work groups, families of orientation, and neighbors. As noted earlier, couples who are in their thirties and early forties today grew up during a period when most families improved their economic situation year-by-year. Ever rising aspirations and expectations of upward mobility are very much a part of their hidden investments (Hogan & Bauer, 1988).

In many senses, the U.S. economic system is based on encouraging people to have ever increasing desires for material possessions. Advertising continually urges adults to acquire more fashionable clothes, newer automobiles, more advanced entertainment systems, and more elaborate bedroom furniture while reminding children that their status among their peers depends on wearing a certain brand of expensive athletic shoes or having a certain toy. The same advertising informs consumers that they can have what they want immediately by charging purchases to their credit cards.

The problem with all this emphasis on material possessions is that, given today's costs and the resources available, many people cannot afford the aspirations they are encouraged to have. Take the home-owning aspiration, for example. In the 1950s, a typical 30-year-old man could make payments on a typical home using 14 percent of his gross monthly pay; by the early 1970s, a 30-year-old had to spend 21 percent of his pay if the family wanted a typical home; by the mid-1980s, the percentage had risen to 44 percent (Levy, 1987, p. 68).

Families can and do make adjustments, of course. Some decide that owning a home is not a top priority and settle for apartment living; others add an earner and use the wife's entire salary for house payments; still others scale down their aspirations concerning the type of home they desire.

Some families, however, are not able to achieve an adequate balance between aspirations, resources, and costs. Consumer debt, personal bankruptcy, and foreclosures on home mortgages rose dramatically during the middle to late 1980s, even though the economy was growing and median family income was increasing (Godwin, 1990). These trends indicate that, in recent years, many families have been unsuccessful at scaling back their aspirations to levels compatible with their resources.

Family Life-Cycle Economic Squeezes

So far we have suggested that many couples experience tension and conflict about money, both because partners fail to communicate openly about their hidden investments and because of frequent imbalances between aspirations and resources. Such imbalances are more likely to occur at some stages of the family life-cycle than at others. Sociologist Valerie Oppenheimer (1982) identifies two family life-cycle stages as being particularly vulnerable to "economic squeeze": the period during which the couple is trying to set up a suitable childbearing household and the period when the children are adolescents. Oppenheimer (1982) predicts that, because of differences in career patterns and earnings, couples from different social classes will experience their squeezes at different times. Middle-class couples are more likely to feel the early squeeze since preparation for childbearing often occurs when they are just beginning their careers and earn fairly low incomes but hold high aspirations. Working-class couples, who often have their highest earning years early in the marriage, are more likely to be squeezed during the expensive adolescent stage.

Oppenheimer's predictions are somewhat confirmed by other research on family life cycle and financial stress: couples in the childbearing stage and in the adolescent stage are more likely to identify themselves as experiencing financial stress than couples in other stages. During both the childbearing and the adolescent stages, financial stress was mentioned more often than any other type of stressor (Olson *et al.*, 1983, p. 123). We will deal with financial stresses related to family life-cycle stages in more depth in the chapters on pregnancy and childbirth, parents and children, later life marriages, divorce, and remarriage.

Coping with Money Management

Thus far, we have focused on the problems couples with sufficient resources face as they make decisions about money. Many such couples find that, once they have established a regular system for making and implementing money choices, they feel a sense of real accomplishment. A good money management system can bring partners closer together, give them a shared source of pride and satisfaction, and help them face more serious financial stress when it arises (Blumstein & Schwartz, 1983).

But what is meant by "a good money management system"? Financial analysts and social scientists focus on somewhat different aspects of money management. As you will see in the sections that follow, financial analysts concern themselves with record-keeping and planning techniques while social scientists focus more on the human elements— who makes financial decisions and how each partner feels about the decision-making process.

Advice from Financial Analysts

Financial experts claim that budgeting and long-range financial planning are necessary for all families wishing to establish sound financial management and to prepare for periods of unexpected financial stress (Williams, 1988). Budget-making advice varies from expert to expert but almost always involves the following steps:

1. Estimate income from all sources for each of the next 12 months, using a form similar to Table 10–2 (on pages 358–359).
2. Project fixed expenses for the next 12-month period using existing records of prior expenditures on a form similar to Table 10–3 (on pages 360–361). **Fixed expenses** are those that are unavoidable, expected, and inflexible. They include items such as rent or mortgage payments, insurance premiums, installment payments on cars, loans, and credit cards, utilities, and predictable transportation expenses.
3. Subtract the monthly totals obtained in Step 2 from those estimated in Step 1. These figures represent how much is available each month for flexible expenses. Couples who come up with negative numbers (indicating that their fixed expenses exceed their incomes before any flexible expenses are taken into account) are clearly in economic trouble.
4. Decide what can be spent each month in each category of the flexible expenses, using a form similar to Table 10–4 (on pages 362–363). **Flexible expenses** are expenses desirable or necessary to family life (food, for example, is a flexible

Fixed expenses expenses that are unavoidable, expected, and inflexible. Taxes, insurance, and rent or mortgage payments are examples.

Flexible expenses expenses that are necessary or desired but are not fixed and are thus subject to more family control. Examples would be food, entertainment, and clothing.

30,994

Table 10-2 Estimating Income

Source	January	February	March	April	May	June	July	August	September	October	November	December	Yearly Totals
Net salary:*													
Household Member 1													
Household Member 2													
Household Member 3													
Household Member 4													
Social Security Payments													
Pension Payments													
Annuity Payments													
Veterans' Benefits													
Assistance Payments													
Unemployment Compensation													
Allowances													

Table 10–2 (continued)

Alimony													
Child Support													
Gifts													
Interest													
Dividends													
Rents from Real Estate													
Other													
Monthly Totals													

* Net salary is the amount that comes into the household for spending and saving after taxes, Social Security, and other deductions.

Source: Pitts, 1986.

Table 10–3 Estimating Fixed Expenses

	January			February			March			April			Subtotal
	Amount Estimated	Amount Spent	Difference	Amount Estimated	Amount Spent	Difference	Amount Estimated	Amount Spent	Difference	Amount Estimated	Amount Spent	Difference	
Rent	550			550									
Mortgage				0									
Installments:													
Credit Card 1	50			0									
Credit Card 2	50			0									
Credit Card 3				0									
Automobile Loan				0									
Personal Loan				0									
Student Loan				0									
Insurance:													
Life				0									
Health				300									
Property				0									
Automobile	60			60									
Disability				0									
Set-Asides:				0									

Table 10-3 (continued)

Category		
Emergency Fund	50	100
Major Expenses		50
Goals		
Savings and Investments		100
Allowances		0
Education:		0
Tuition		0
Books	400	100
Transportation:	50	0
Repairs	100	50
Gas and Oil		100
Parking and Tolls		20
Bus and Taxi		50
Recreation	20	150 350
Gifts		50
Other		250 50
Total Fixed Expenses for Month		1520

Source: Pitts, 1986.

Grand Total - 2250   Savings- 332

Salary - 2,582

Table 10–4 Estimating Flexible Expenses

	January			February			March			April			Subtotal
	Amount Estimated	Amount Spent	Difference	Amount Estimated	Amount Spent	Difference	Amount Estimated	Amount Spent	Difference	Amount Estimated	Amount Spent	Difference	
Food:													
At Home	400			400									
Away from Home	100			150									
Utilities:													
Gas/Fuel	60			60									
Electricity	40			40									
Telephone				40									
Water	20			0									
Household:													
Maintenance and Supplies	10			0									
Furnishings				10									
Decorating	10			10									
Clothing:													
Household Member 1	10			10									
Household Member 2				10									
Household Member 3													

Table 10-4 (continued)

Household Member 4		0											
Health Care:													
Doctors		0											
Dentist		10											
Other		10											
		0											
Medicines and Prescriptions		10											
Personal Care	5	10											
Other:													
Total Flexible Expenses for the Month		150											

Source: Pitts, 1986.

expense) but are not considered fixed since they are more subject to family control. Since most people do not realize how much they are already spending on day-to-day items, experts recommend that budget-makers keep track of all such expenditures for several weeks or months (Stauffer, 1988; Williams, 1988; Porter, 1975) before making a flexible expense budget. Table 10–4 provides a space for this.

Couples who find that they are in serious economic trouble after putting themselves through such a budgeting exercise will have to increase their resources or reduce their expenses (often by clarifying priorities and "reframing" aspirations) or both. Financial counselors can be helpful in this attempt (Williams, 1988).

Social Science Research

In contrast to financial analysts, social scientists who study family money management are most interested in who does what in dividing money management tasks, how they feel about it, and how it affects the marriage. Despite the importance of money in marriage, social scientists have done relatively little research in this area of family life (Godwin, 1990; Blumstein & Schwartz, 1983). It appears that social scientists, like courting couples, have a taboo about discussing money and marriage! In the next several paragraphs, we summarize the social science research that has been done on money management.

One fairly common marital money management pattern is for the husband to provide all or most of the economic resources and for the wife to manage them (Whyte, 1990). While the husband earns the money, the wife writes the checks, decides what to buy, and tracks expenditures. This method works well if it is mutually decided upon, if there is enough money to allow for some choices, and if the husband truly trusts his wife's judgment. When these conditions exist, both parties feel that they have some control: the husband because he has delegated the authority, the wife because she is fully aware of the family's financial situation and because she makes many of the actual decisions (Blumstein & Schwartz, 1983).

The husband-as-earner, wife-as-manager arrangement works less well if the wife feels that the job was forced upon her without her consent, if one or both partners perceive the income to be inadequate, or if the husband continually complains about the choices his wife makes. This was the case with many of the working-class couples Lillian Rubin (1976) interviewed in the early 1970s. Here is how one working class wife described her financial role in the family:

> I pay all the bills and manage the money—if you can call it managing. All it means is that I get stuck with all the scut work.

When there's a problem with the dun [demand for payment of debt]
notices, or what have you, I'm the one who faces it. (p. 107)

In cases like this one, neither partner feels in control and both are
dissatisfied.

As more couples become dual-earner couples, this pattern seems
to be undergoing some change. Wives who have their own income have
more influence in overall policy setting and in shared decisions than
do wives without an income of their own (Voydanoff, 1987; Ferber,
1982). As the gap between husband's income and wife's income decreases, so does the husband's relative power in financial decision
making (Blumstein & Schwartz, 1983). One practical result of this power
shift is that more couples are turning money management duties over
to the partner who is most interested and most skilled without automatically assuming that this person is the wife (Hogan & Bauer, 1988).

Dual-income couples face the decision of whether to pool their incomes or to keep them separate. Most married couples in the United
States prefer pooling, at least to some extent (Whyte, 1990; Blumstein
& Schwartz, 1983). Although the majority of all married people favor
pooling, husbands favor it more often than wives, people who have
been married longer favor it more than those married only a few years,
and those who believe that marriage is a permanent commitment favor
it more than those who see marriage as a voluntary arrangement
(Blumstein & Schwartz, 1983). Pooling also seems to be practiced more
often by whites than by blacks, at least according to Whyte's (1990)
survey of Detroit wives.

The vast majority of married couples in the United States pay
their bills on time, keep receipts and records of major purchases, and
establish policies for organizing tax records and important papers.
However, most of them do *not* follow the expert-recommended practices
of keeping a formal, written-down budget, carrying out reviews of their
total financial situation, saving a set amount of money each month, or
setting future-oriented financial goals (Titus, Fanslow, & Hira, 1989;
Hogan & Bauer, 1988; Pershing, 1979).

Couples who stay married and those who divorce show some differences in the *choices* they make about expenditures early in their marriage. Sociologists Schaninger and Buss (1986) traced newly married
couples for 10 years and compared the consumption patterns and finance handling of couples who stayed married to those of couples who
divorced. Those who stayed married made consumption choices that
reflected their commitment to spending time together and building for
the future—they spent more of their income on household appliances,
home purchases and down payments, and recreational vehicles, and
less on stereos, color TVs, and living room furniture than did those
who divorced within 10 years. More importantly, perhaps, the couples

who stayed married showed more equality and wife influence in financial decision making; among those who divorced, husbands more often dominated both decision making and money handling. Communicating openly about money and ensuring that both partners participate in setting the family guidelines for money handling seem to be more important for marital financial satisfaction than the use of any one particular budgeting method. Going through the budget-making process together offers one way of starting the communication and joint participation; other techniques may work equally well.

Families in Economic Trouble

Table 10–5 illustrates how the average young family spent its $30,944 income in 1988. How do these expenditure patterns compare to the estimates you made in the "What Do You Think?" exercise? Imagine for a moment that this income dropped one year to just $20,000 or that you were part of a household that had *never* had more than $15,000 with which to work. How would you change the categories and the expenditures?

Such an income loss dilemma is faced by millions of people each year who lose their jobs or have their hours cut back, become disabled,

Table 10–5 How the Average Married Couple Family with Preschool Child Spent Its Money, 1988	Amount in Dollars	% of total
Food (groceries, eating out, alcohol)	$4,350	14%
Housing (rent/mortgage, utilities, furniture, appliances, supplies)	$10,808	35%
Transportation (car payments, gas, repair, insurance, public transportation)	$6,249	20%
Clothing and Personal Care (for example, hair cuts, hygiene needs)	$1,764	6%
Health Care (medical care, insurance, medication)	$1,206	4%
Pensions, Social Security	$2,502	8%
Other Expenditures	$4,065	13%
Total	$30,944	100%

Source: U.S. Bureau of the Census, 1991a, pp. 446–47.

or get divorced. One study following families throughout the 1970s found that nearly one-third experienced an income drop of 50 percent or more at some time during the decade (Newman, 1989). Meanwhile, millions more working for low wages or living on welfare exist in a situation of continuous economic deprivation—they simply do not have enough resources to afford everything necessary for family life, even at a very low level of aspirations. In 1989, for example, 20 percent of all U.S. families had annual incomes lower than $16,003 and an additional 20 percent had incomes between $16,004 and $28,000 (U.S. Bureau of the Census, 1991a, p. 455).

How do such families cope? How do income loss and economic deprivation affect relationships within families?

The Economically Deprived

"Carol Morgan," a divorced mother with two children, provides a starting point for our discussion of economically deprived families. Carol makes $12,000 a year working as a nurse's aide at a hospital. Since she makes less than half the median family income, Carol falls into a category often called **relative poverty** (Tienda & Jensen, 1988, p. 29). The relative poor are not poor using the minimum government standard, but, when compared to most other families in the population, they are economically deprived. Because Carol and her family are not "absolutely poor" by official government standards, they do not qualify for food stamps, school lunches, government-subsidized housing, or Medicaid (government-supported health care for the poor).

Here is Carol's monthly budget when she is able to get a 40-hour work week:

Relative poverty situation of those families making less than one-half the median family income, whether or not they are absolutely poor.

Rent	$436
Taxes	198
Electricity	194
Insulin and Supplies	87
Food	73
Payments to Doctors	48
School Lunches	48
Gasoline	36
Telephone	24
Laundry	24
Personal Care	24
Pet Food	12
Household Needs	12

Total Expenses = $1216   Total Income = $1182   Difference = −$34

(Source of original budget: *Consumer Reports*, 1987, p. 439. Updated to 1991 using Consumer Price Index).

Carol's budget is clearly made up almost entirely of fixed expenses. Such a budget allows no room for choices, except possibly the choice of which bill to delay paying. Note that the family has no savings, no allowances, and that their major entertainment is their pets. A reduction in working hours, a serious illness or injury, or an unexpected rent increase could wreck the family's fragile budget.

The Working Poor   By most peoples' standards (although not by official government standards), Carol Morgan is one of the **working poor**, a category of economically deprived people who "have devoted at least half the year to labor market efforts, being either employed or in search of a job during that period, but who still lived in poor families" (Klein & Rones, 1989, p. 4). The working poor work in low wage jobs, most of them in the service sector of the economy. Throughout most of the 1960s and 1970s, a parent with two children working 40 hours a week, 50 weeks a year, for the minimum wage could just barely make it above the official poverty line. Since 1979, that has not been possible: in 1991, such a person would have made $8,500, 76 percent of the poverty level income of $11,140 for a family of three. While the poverty level goes up as the cost of living does, the minimum wage does not.

Most of the working poor, like Carol, are in families with only one earner. And most of them (83 percent as compared with 55 percent of nonpoor families), like Carol, have dependent children in the home. Because they make lower wages at every level of education, women of all races and black men are much more likely to be among the working poor than are white males (Klein & Rones, 1989).

The Welfare Poor   About half of those who qualified as "poor" by government standards worked at least part of the year in 1987 (Klein & Rones, 1989). Of those poor not working, some were retired, some were disabled or ill, some could not find work, and some were taking care of small children (Littman, 1989).

Our focus here will be on this latter group—nonworking, poor women with young children, often referred to as the **welfare poor**. Many such women qualify for and receive income from a government-sponsored program known as Aid to Families with Dependent Children (AFDC), known by most people as "welfare." AFDC began in the 1930s as part of the Social Security Act to offer financial support to widows with dependent children who did not qualify for Social Security. The program gradually expanded in the 1960s and 1970s to cover needy, never married women whose children were born out of wedlock, divorced mothers, and mother-children families whose male earner had deserted them. Half the states allow AFDC payments to two-parent families with children under certain circumstances; the other half restrict AFDC to homes without an adult male present.

Working poor
a category of economically deprived people who, although they were employed or looking for employment at least half the year, still fell below income standards for poverty.

Welfare poor
a category of economically deprived people who are not employed, usually because they are caring for young children, and who receive governmental financial aid.

Although the federal government provides some of the money for AFDC, each state decides who is eligible and how much they will receive. Eligibility requirements and payment levels vary greatly from state to state. In 1989, the average U.S. family receiving AFDC received $388 a month, but the range was from $620 (California) to $114 (Alabama) (U.S. Bureau of Census, 1991a, p. 373). Qualifying for AFDC benefits makes families eligible for government-subsidized health care (Medicaid) and public housing (in areas where they are available) and food stamps. How much these benefits are worth and how poor a family has to be to qualify vary greatly from state-to-state and from year-to-year.

Generally speaking, benefit levels and eligibility standards were at their most generous level in the early 1970s; since then, benefit levels have dropped (in terms of real income) and eligibility standards have tightened. *In no case, however, does AFDC and its accompanying benefits provide enough to lift families out of poverty.* Indeed, the welfare poor are often among the poorest of the poor (Children's Defense Fund, 1987).

The financial situation of a family receiving AFDC is similar to that of the working poor, but at an even more extreme level. The working poor parent worries constantly about how to stretch the dollars, but she does it within the confines of her own family. The welfare poor mother trying to survive must do so under the scrupulous eyes of others:

> Someone who is enmeshed in the public assistance system may have to deal with an intake worker, an emergency assistance worker, an eligibility worker, a caseworker, an employment and training worker, a food stamps eligibility worker, and others. . . . She will have to tell her life story several times to workers who are supposed to be alert to catching applicants who are committing fraud. (Ellwood, 1988, p. 140)

For at least half of all AFDC recipients, welfare is a temporary solution to an emergency situation, something to tide them over until they can find work or recover from an illness or other family crisis; their average time on welfare is two years or less (Edelman, 1987). Women who first received welfare after having an out-of-wedlock child, who did not finish high school, who are nonwhite, and who have many children (contrary to the myth, *most* "welfare mothers" have only one or two children) receive AFDC for a more prolonged period (Edelman, 1987, p. 73). Such women stay on AFDC rather than working for a number of reasons. For most of them, the types of jobs they could get would not lift them from welfare poor to nonpoor but rather from welfare poor to working poor. Because of the cost of child care (a cost they avoid by not working) and because of the subsidiary benefits (food stamps, Medicaid) they would lose if they began to work, staying on AFDC may be a rational economic choice. Their dilemma is illustrated in Table 10–6.

The Feminization of Poverty   By the 1980s, poverty had become most characteristic of families with only one potential earner; most of these families were headed by women and most included children. This tendency for poverty to be increasingly concentrated among nonmarried women and their children is known as the **feminization of poverty**. Poverty became "feminized" for two basic reasons: great increases in the rates of divorce and unmarried motherhood, and the persistence of a substantial wage gap between men and women.

When women enter poverty, they generally have their children with them. Recent statistics regarding children and poverty are particularly alarming. In 1989, 43 percent of all black children, 36 percent of all Hispanic children, and 14 percent of all white children lived in poor families (U.S. Bureau of the Census, 1991a, p. 462). One extensive study of children and poverty concluded:

> Nearly half of the children in the United States find themselves in a vulnerable economic position at least once during their childhood; about one-third actually fall below the official poverty line. Persistent

Feminization of poverty
the tendency, especially noticeable during the 1970s and 1980s, for poverty to be increasingly concentrated among nonmarried women and their children.

			Taxes and			
Level of Work and Wages	Earnings	Day Care	Earned Income Tax Credit	AFDC and Food Stamps	Disposable Income* **	Receipt of Medicaid
No work	$0	$0	$0	$6,284	$6,284	Yes
Half time at the minimum wage†	$3,350	−$1,000	+$229	$4,577	$7,156	Yes
Full time at the minimum wage†	$6,700	−$3,000	+$373	$2,744	$6,816	Yes
Full time at $4.00 per hour	$8,000	−$3,000	+$171	$1,624	$6,795	Yes
Full time at $5.00 per hour	$10,000	−$3,000	−$172	$970	$7,798	No
Full time at $6.00 per hour	$12,000	−$3,000	−$515	$538	$9,023	No

Table 10–6 Earnings, Taxes, Benefits, and Total Income for a Single Parent and Two Children, 1986

* The figures in the table were derived using the regulations of the new tax law as of January 1987.
** Earnings plus AFDC and food stamps less taxes and day care.
† The minimum wage rate is $3.35 per hour.

Source: From *Poor Support* by David Ellwood. p. 167. Copyright © 1988 by Basic Books, Inc. Reprinted by permission of Basic Books, a division of HarperCollins Publishers. Modeled after an unnumbered table from Committee on Ways and Means, U.S. House of Representatives, *Background Material and Data on Programs within the Jurisdiction of the Committee on Ways and Means* (Washington, D.C.: U.S. Government Printing Office, 1987), p. 404.

> poverty is a way of life for $2\frac{1}{2}$ million children under age 15 today, and intermittant poverty characterizes the lives of an additional $3\frac{1}{2}$ million children. (Duncan & Rodgers, 1988, p. 1018)

Black children, whether in two-parent or one-parent families, are much more likely than white children to spend a large part of their childhood living in poverty, but any child in a one-parent home is very vulnerable to spending some years being poor. Figures 10–4 (on page 372) and 10–5 (on page 373) illustrate this.

The Effects of Poverty   How does being poor affect children and the intimate relationship between parent and child? The physical effects may begin before birth. Poor mothers who lack good prenatal care and nutrition are more likely to give birth to premature or low birth weight babies (Children's Defense Fund, 1987). Such babies are more likely than others to die during the first year of life. Premature, low birth weight babies tend to cry more and are generally more difficult to care for, making them more vulnerable to physical abuse by mothers who are already under stress (Tower, 1989). Poor children are more likely than others to be malnourished or to go hungry from time to time. They cannot depend on having their illnesses treated promptly or on receiving good dental care. Although most poor mothers care

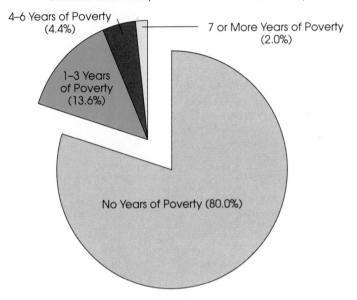

Figure 10–4: Years of Poverty for Children by Family Living Arrangement

Children Who Always Lived in a Two-Parent Family

4–6 Years of Poverty (4.4%)

7 or More Years of Poverty (2.0%)

1–3 Years of Poverty (13.6%)

No Years of Poverty (80.0%)

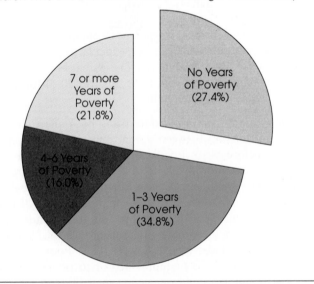

Children Who Lived for Some Period in a Single-Parent Family

7 or more Years of Poverty (21.8%)

No Years of Poverty (27.4%)

4–6 Years of Poverty (16.0%)

1–3 Years of Poverty (34.8%)

Compare the two graphs and you can see the economic advantage of growing up in a two-parent family. While eight out of ten children in two-parent families spend no time in poverty, only one in four children in single-parent families avoid poverty entirely. Data for this figure and for Figure 10-5 are from a study of children born between 1967 and 1972 and followed for 10 years. It is highly probable that the proportions of children in poverty now are even higher.

Source: From *Poor Support* by David Ellwood, p. 84. Copyright © 1988 by Basic Books, Inc. Reprinted by permission of Basic Books, a division of HarperCollins Publishers.

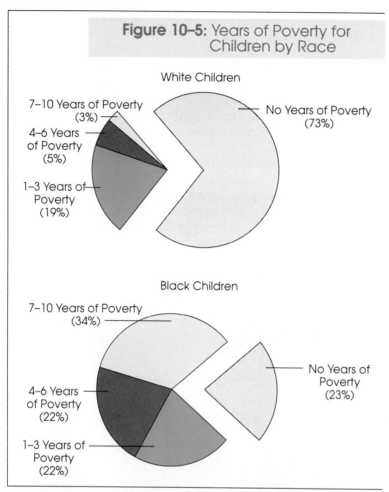

Figure 10–5: Years of Poverty for Children by Race

White Children

7–10 Years of Poverty (3%)

4–6 Years of Poverty (5%)

1–3 Years of Poverty (19%)

No Years of Poverty (73%)

Black Children

7–10 Years of Poverty (34%)

4–6 Years of Poverty (22%)

1–3 Years of Poverty (22%)

No Years of Poverty (23%)

White children have a clear advantage over black children in avoiding poverty. While only one in four white children spend any time in poverty, more than three in four black children spend at least some of their childhood in poverty.

Source: From *Poor Support* by David Ellwood, p. 201. Copyright © 1988 by Basic Books, Inc. Reprinted by permission of Basic Books, a division of Harper Collins Publishers.

for their children adequately, physical neglect of children (that is, inadequate food, shelter, medical care, and supervision) is most common in the poorest homes, particularly those in rundown, depressed neighborhoods (Tower, 1989).

Poor children grow up in an atmosphere where the adults they depend on are under a great deal of stress much of the time. Poverty "spells" for children not born into poverty often begin when their parents separate or when one parent loses a job (Bane & Ellwood, 1986). Besides the economic stress brought about by the change in income, the child's parents are often under considerable emotional and psychological stress. Parents under stress do not inevitably change the way they treat their children; indeed, parents and children with a strong relationship before the economic crisis might be drawn closer together by it. Often, however, parents under stress are not able to offer children the support, guidance, praise, and consistent discipline they did prior to the family's economic change. Parenting becomes less child-centered and more adult-centered, less nurturant and more rejecting (Lempers, Clark-Lempers, & Simons, 1989; Elder, Nguyen, & Caspi, 1985). Under such conditions, adolescents become depressed and lonely and younger children withdraw from peers (Lempers, Clark-Lempers, & Simons, 1989; McLoyd, 1989).

Children born into and remaining in poverty generally score lower on tests of cognitive development, especially if their mothers never finished school nor entered the job market (Furstenberg, Brooks-Gunn, & Morgan, 1987). Since such tests are good predictors of performance in school, it is not surprising that poor children are much more likely to drop out of school (Children's Defense Fund, 1987). Adolescents living in poor families often feel pressure to enter the job market early, limiting their schooling and skill-development, and, thus, their long-term earning potential (Bowman, 1988).

Although most single mothers care for their children adequately, dismal living conditions often add to the continual financial stress on the family.

The Unemployed

One way in which families enter into poverty is when one of the family earners loses his or her job. Thus, many of the problems and changes in parent-child relationships that economically deprived families encounter also hold for families of the unemployed. Unemployment does have some distinctive features, however.

Much of the unemployment during the last two decades has affected whole communities, not just individual families. When a large plant (or several large plants) closes down, the whole community suffers the economic and social effects. Property values go down; people who would like to move find it difficult to sell their homes; merchants and professionals lose business; the community loses much of its tax base and public services are cut (Bluestone & Harrison, 1982). In such a setting, laid-off workers are unlikely to be reemployed quickly. Communities or regions with high unemployment rates show increased suicide rates and increased rates of reported child abuse; some researchers also associate unemployment with increased admissions to mental hospitals and other psychiatric treatment facilities (Horwitz, 1984).

The effects of unemployment on the unemployed worker and the family vary according to both the circumstances of the unemployment and the characteristics of the family. Workers who lose their jobs as the result of a strike in which they were upholding an important principle (for example, the fired air traffic controllers of 1981) feel that they are part of a larger cause and have the social support of a sympathetic group (Newman, 1989). Workers who lose their jobs individually for ambiguous or unexplained reasons have a much more difficult time avoiding self-blame and the consequent feelings of low self-esteem.

When unemployment does not increase financial strain (that is, the worker receives generous severance pay or unemployment benefits or someone else in the family finds a better-paying job), the worker is much less likely to suffer the anxiety, depression, sleeplessness, and physical illness that typically increase with unemployment (Kessler, Turner, & House, 1988). Workers are better able to cope with unemployment and the financial strain it usually brings if unemployment is their only source of stress; when faced with multiple, unrelated stresses simultaneously (for example, unemployment *and* a death in the family), they more often suffer mental and physical ill health (Kessler, Turner, & House, 1988).

Characteristics of a family prior to unemployment can be important in determining its reponse to that event. Marriages characterized by openness, mutual support, and nonrigid sex roles are better able to withstand the stresses of unemployment than are marriages in which partners avoid talking about problems, blame rather than support one another, and hold rigid ideas about sex roles (Aldous & Tuttle, 1988; Wilhelm & Ridley, 1988; Larson, 1984). Both types of marriages will be stressed by unemployment, but the first has built up more resources to deal with it. Communicating, supportive spouses can work together to define the unemployment as a positive event ("This gives you a chance to try something new"), make the necessary adjustments in managing finances, and, perhaps, exchange roles for awhile. Noncommunicating, nonsupportive spouses often move further apart and their relationship may become even more unstable as a result of the unemployment. Like so many stresses, unemployment can become either a challenge that ultimately strengthens the marriage or the final stress that ends it.

Summary

Large-scale economic changes can have profound effects on the ways in which families perceive and handle their financial affairs. The years between the end of World War II and the early 1970s were years of economic prosperity for the United States and of economic improvement for U.S. families. During these years, median family incomes rose, the proportion of families living in poverty declined, and the huge economic gap between white families and minority group families narrowed.

Since 1973, some families—particularly those with two-earners and those who are older—have continued to improve their economic status, but young families, one-parent families, and minority groups have seen stagnation or decline in their economic situation. Overall, median family incomes during these years showed little change, while poverty increased and the income gap between whites and minority groups, as well as between two-parent families and one-parent families, widened.

Financial stress and money arguments are very common in families in all eras and at all income levels. The fact that partners seldom talk about money before marriage and that many couples hold aspirations far beyond their resources increases marital money tension. Money squeezes and money stress are especially likely during the childbearing and adolescent family life-cycle stages. Eventually, most couples manage to come up with a workable money management system. Egalitarian systems in which both partners feel they have some control, even though the actual money management is done by only one of them, seem to work best to relieve some of the money tension.

Some families suffer financial stress far beyond the expected, predictable family money stresses mentioned above. Both the working poor and the welfare poor are under continuous economic stress. Mother-only families are most likely to be poor today. Poverty has a number of negative effects on children and on the child-parent relationship. Unemployment, especially large-scale layoffs affecting whole communities, became more common in the 1970s and 1980s. Its consequences for communities are negative; individual and family reaction to unemployment depends on the circumstances of the unemployment, the way in which the family defines the situation, prior family resources, and how many other stresses are present.

CHAPTER 11

BECOMING A PARENT

Read each of the following statements and check those that best summarize your feelings about the *advantages* of having children. Choose no more than four statements; you may choose fewer than four.

___ 1. Having children brings love and companionship, completes the family, and benefits the couple's relationship.
___ 2. Having children brings stimulation and fun; watching them grow is a pleasurable activity.
___ 3. Having children gives a purpose to life, enhances self-learning and self-fulfillment, and carries on the family.
___ 4. Having children is something useful to do, enhances feelings of maturity and adulthood, and is natural and socially expected.
___ 5. Having children is a creative activity and a way to achieve satisfaction from doing a good job.
___ 6. Having children makes the parents better people.
___ 7. Having children brings help with household chores and security in old age.

For purposes of comparing your answers with those of the national sample represented in Figure 11–3:

Statement 1 = Primary Ties and Affection on Figure 11–3.
Statement 2 = Stimulation and Fun on Figure 11–3.
Statement 3 = Expansion of Self on Figure 11–3.
Statement 4 = Adult Status and Social Identity on Figure 11–3.
Statement 5 = Achievement, Creativity on Figure 11–3.
Statement 6 = Morality on Figure 11–3.
Statement 7 = Economic Utility on Figure 11–3.

July 19, 1992. The Green Hills High School class of 1972 is staging its twentieth high school reunion on this hot July weekend. One event of the reunion weekend is a family picnic at which the men and women of the class show off their children to their classmates. Most of the class of 1972 married and had children while they were in their twenties; thus, many of the children at the picnic are of junior high and grade school age. However, there are some older teenagers (looking *very* bored) and some toddlers at the picnic as well.

Twenty years after they graduated, the class of 1972 have children of differing ages because they made different choices about parenthood. For example, Sally and Jay married right after high school graduation because Sally was then four months pregnant. Five children later, at age 25, they decided "five was enough" and Jay had a vasectomy. Sally and Jay are now awaiting the birth of their first grandchild.

Because of differences in marriage and childbearing patterns, adults of about the same age often have children of widely varying ages.

Their classmates Kelly and Sonny, on the other hand, waited until their middle thirties to become parents for the first time and are now busy keeping up with an active three year old and looking forward to the arrival of their second child in September. Linda, another member of the class, married for the first time only last summer. She and her husband, anxious to have a child, both have infertility problems. They are undergoing treatment in hopes of having their own baby but are also considering adoption. Meanwhile, Jennifer and Ken, married for 15 years, have made the decision not to have children, a decision that is reinforced for them as they listen to their classmates complain about the problems of parenthood.

Chapter 11 deals with the decision to become first-time parents and with the short-term consequences—pregnancy and childbirth—of that decision. The chapter should help you understand why and how most members of the class of 1972 decided to become parents and why some, like Jennifer and Ken, decided against it. The chapter will also explore the variations in parenthood timing revealed in the story: Why did Jay and Sally become parents while still in their teens and Kelly and Sonny wait until they were nearly forty? In addition, the chapter will deal with the alternatives faced by infertile couples like Linda and her husband.

Chapter 11 begins with a discussion of the parenthood decision. We will consider the nature of the decision, why most people want to become parents, the factors people consider in timing their children, and why some people decide to remain child-free. Next we discuss pregnancy, with emphasis on how it affects the intimate couple relationship. Three pregnancy-related problems—miscarriage, infertility, and unequal access to prenatal care—are considered next. Then we examine the choices in childbirth available today. The chapter ends by describing adoption as an alternative route to parenthood.

PARENTHOOD DECISIONS

The decision to become a parent is a very important, life-changing, unique decision. People who choose to have a child commit themselves to the care, support, and training of another human being for years into the future. Strangely enough, they make this substantial commitment before they ever meet the other human being. And unlike other adult roles, parenthood includes no try-out period, no engagement, and no job training—only total responsibility! (Rossi, 1968). Once carried out, the parenthood decision is essentially *irrevocable*. Sociologist Alice Rossi (1968) puts it succinctly, "We can have ex-spouses and ex-jobs but not ex-children" (p. 32).

Compared to people in most other times and places, couples living in the United States today have much more choice about whether, when, how often, and even *how* to become parents. Effective contraceptive and sterilization methods make it easier for them to plan the timing of their children, to stop childbearing when they have the number of children they planned, or to remain permanently child-free. More knowledge about and new treatments for infertility give infertile couples a better chance of producing their own child than ever before.

Still, not every pregnancy in the United States is the result of a clearly thought-out, conscious decision, and not every child born is explicitly planned. Slightly over half the pregnancies occurring in the United States each year are unplanned. Unplanned pregnancy can occur at any age during a woman's reproductive years but is especially likely among teenagers. Between 1984 and 1988, for example, 81 percent of pregnancies among 15–19-year old women were unplanned (Forrest & Singh, 1990, p. 212). Some unplanned pregnancies are the

11

result of contraceptive failure: that is, the couple made an explicit decision *not* to become parents, took measures to prevent pregnancy, but ended up pregnant anyway. Other couples drifted into pregnancy. They did not decide about parenthood either way, did not use contraceptive methods or used them inconsistently, and "got caught." Researchers Neal, Groat, and Wicks (1989), writing about newly married couples, describe the "drifters" like this:

> It seems likely that rather than deciding on the number and timing of children, some couples simply experience their pregnancies as happenings, unplanned events, occurrences, or the will of God. Such fertility behavior still persists among many couples within the overall societal context of greater emphasis on rational decision making and personal choice. (p. 325)

One mother interviewed by Kathleen Gerson (1985) confirms these research observations in describing her own situation:

> You get married; you get pregnant. We were only married a month, and I got pregnant. I guess I wouldn't have thought of getting married and *not* having children; put it that way. For me, the way my family grew was natural for us. It just was not a conscious decision-making thing. (pp. 101–102)

Not all those with unplanned pregnancies become parents. As Figure 11–1 (on page 384) documents, over 40 percent of the unexpectedly pregnant in 1987 decided to end their pregnancies by abortion (that is, they made or remade the decision against parenthood *after* conception had occurred) and about 13 percent miscarried. However, over 40 percent continued with the pregnancy and had a baby. Of those who ended up giving birth, some decided during the pregnancy that they wanted to be parents after all while others decided nothing and, thus, drifted into parenthood just as they had drifted into pregnancy.

Overall, about 40 percent of those who become parents in the United States each year did not plan to do so at the time of conception (Forrest & Singh, 1990, p. 214). Nonetheless, parenthood, especially among those who are married, is more often planned, decided upon, and timed today than at any time in the past (Pratt *et al.*, 1984). In the early 1960s, for example, nearly two-thirds of the births in the United States were unplanned; by the early 1980s, almost that many were planned (Pratt *et al.*, 1984, p. 31). What goes into this planning? What factors influence people as they decide to become parents and when to do so? What factors influence those who decide to remain child-free?

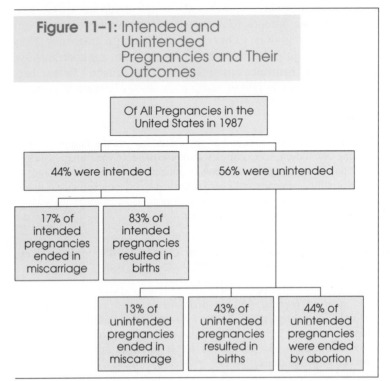

Figure 11-1: Intended and Unintended Pregnancies and Their Outcomes

Of All Pregnancies in the United States in 1987

44% were intended

56% were unintended

17% of intended pregnancies ended in miscarriage

83% of intended pregnancies resulted in births

13% of unintended pregnancies ended in miscarriage

43% of unintended pregnancies resulted in births

44% of unintended pregnancies were ended by abortion

Despite the advances in contraception information and technology, more pregnancies are unintended than intended. More than 40 percent of the unintended pregnancies result in the birth of a baby. (These statistics are from 1987.)

Source: Jacqueline D. Forrest and Susheela Singh, "The Sexual and Reproductive Behavior of American Women, 1982–1988," *Family Planning Perspectives* Volume 22: Number 5, 1990, p. 213. © The Alan Guttmacher Institute.

Why Most People Become Parents

Modern U.S. married couples have much more choice in making parenthood decisions than their parents and grandparents did and over 90 percent of them choose (or at least do not make a choice against) parenthood. One reason for this is a definite cultural bias in favor of married people becoming parents. This proparenthood bias is known as pronatalism. **Pronatalism** refers to cultural attitudes and policies favoring the birth of children. An attitude is pronatalist if it promotes the satisfactions and advantages of having children while emphasizing the disadvantages of childlessness. A policy is pronatalist if it provides incentives to people for becoming parents or if it punishes people who remain childless.

U.S. public opinion reflects a moderate pronatalism. According to the polls, U.S. adults favor having children, but not many children. As Figure 11–2 indicates, in 1990, most adults thought that the ideal family size was two children. No-child families, one-child families, and

Pronatalism
cultural attitudes and policies favoring the birth of children.

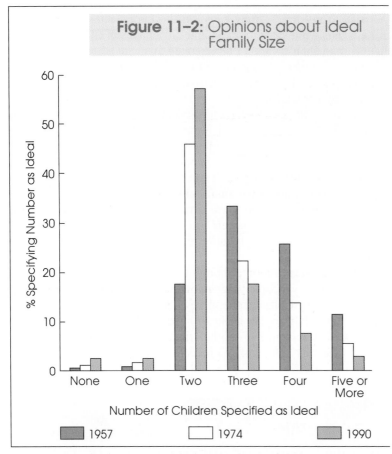

Figure 11–2: Opinions about Ideal Family Size

At the peak of the Baby Boom in 1957, there was a good deal of variation in ideas about ideal family size, with most favoring 3- or 4-child families. By 1990, there was much less variation: almost six in ten said two children are ideal.

Source: *The Gallup Report* 1983, p. 12 and Gallup & Newport, 1990, p. 17. "The Gallup Poll, March 1983 and June 1990."

families with five or more children were all unpopular choices (Gallup & Newport, 1990). Figure 11–2 also indicates that there have been some changes in ideas about ideal family size since 1957; in that year, just as the Baby Boom peaked, three or four child families were considered ideal (*The Gallup Report*, 1983).

U.S. adults see many benefits to having children (Hoffman, McManus, & Brackbill, 1987; Neal, Groat, & Wicks, 1989). Figure 11–3 (on page 387) gives the results of a survey similar to the one you answered in the "What Do You Think?" exercise. The figure reveals that parents, both black and white, valued children most for the affection and primary ties they brought ("they bring love," you're never lonely," "they bring husband and wife closer together") and for the stimulation and fun they provided. A substantial minority of parents also felt that children were valuable because they expanded the self ("they give purpose to my life," "they carry on the family name"). More black parents than white cited the economic advantages of children ("they can help with the housework," "children are financial security in old age"), but this advantage was mentioned much less often than the emotional benefits. Generally speaking, Hispanics cite the same advantages of children that blacks and whites do (Hoffman & Manis, 1979).

As you will see, lower- and working-class couples tend to have their children earlier, to have more unplanned pregnancies, and to think about pregnancy and childbirth in somewhat different ways than middle-class couples. However, people in all social classes are similar in their pronatalist attitudes: all cite similar advantages and disadvantages of children and favor small families (Seccombe, 1991; Gallup & Newport, 1990). There are *some* variations in pronatalism: those with fundamentalist religious beliefs are distinctly more pronatalist than others, and men are slightly more pronatalist than women (Seccombe, 1991).

Pronatalist attitudes, although still strong, have weakened somewhat. Specifically, people today show more *tolerance* for the choice to remain childless. Consider the survey question: "Do you feel almost all married couples who can *ought* to have children?" In the early 1960s, 85 percent of a sample of mothers in a large-scale Detroit study answered "yes." By 1985, only 43 percent of the same mothers answered

Modern parents value children partly because children add fun and stimulation to the parents' lives.

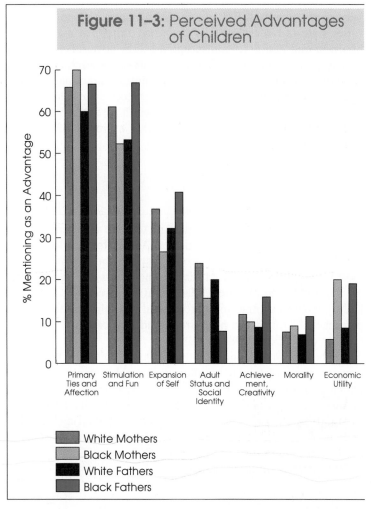

Figure 11-3: Perceived Advantages of Children

% Mentioning as an Advantage

Primary Ties and Affection | Stimulation and Fun | Expansion of Self | Adult Status and Social Identity | Achievement, Creativity | Morality | Economic Utility

White Mothers
Black Mothers
White Fathers
Black Fathers

Black and white mothers and fathers tend to perceive the same advantages to having children. Most mention strong emotional attachments and the stimulation that children bring to family life.

Source: Lois Hoffman, Karen McManus, and Yvonne Brackbill, "The Value of Children to Young Elderly Parents," *International Journal of Aging and Human Development,* Vol. 25 No. 4, 1987, pp. 309–322. Copyright © 1987, Baywood Publishing Company, Inc.

"yes" as did 33 percent of their daughters and 41 percent of their sons (Thornton, 1989, p. 882). Although a majority of people are now willing to tolerate childlessness for others, this is *not* a choice they see as ideal or favor for themselves. In one recent survey of high school seniors, only 7 percent of females and 5 percent of males viewed themselves as "fairly unlikely" or "very unlikely" to want children (Thornton, 1989, p. 882).

Pronatalist attitudes have historically been matched by pronatalist policies in the United States and, like the attitudes, the policies have weakened somewhat. For much of the nineteenth and twentieth centuries, state and federal policies encouraged childbearing by prohibiting abortion and access to contraceptives; U.S. government policy today remains pronatalist in some ways (for example, each child represents a tax deduction for the parents) but neutral or antinatalist in others (for example, parents in the United States receive much less government help in paying for prenatal and child health care than parents in most of Europe). Can you come up with other examples of pronatalist or antinatalist policies?

Timing Parenthood

Although most married couples want to have children, they vary in terms of *when* they have their children. As the story at the beginning of the chapter illustrated, some people first become parents as teenagers, most when they are in their twenties, and others not until their thirties or even forties. In the late 1980s, about 12 percent of all babies born had a teenaged mother; 62 percent had a mother in her twenties; 25 percent had a mother in her thirties; and 1 percent had a mother aged forty or over (Exter, 1988, p. 63).

What factors account for the timing of children? Using information gathered in both large-scale surveys and in-depth interviews with parents, sociologists have been able to assemble fairly extensive information on the social characteristics of people who have their first child "early" (before the age of 20), "on time" (first child during their twenties), and "late" (first child after age 30). Four factors influence the timing of children: alternative commitments, financial stability, relationship stability, and small group support.

Alternative Commitments

Individuals attempt to delay parenthood as long as they are involved in alternative activities that are important to them and that they feel would conflict with parenthood. There are numerous illustrations of this general principle. One large-scale study that followed members of the high school class of 1972 for seven years after their graduation found that college or graduate school attendance was a major factor delaying the first child for both men and women. Men and women not attending school in the seven years after high school were much more likely than college-attenders to have a first child during those years (Rindfuss, Morgan, & Swicegood, 1988). Following the same principle, women who held full-time jobs were much less likely than women who were homemakers or part-time employees to become mothers during the seven years following high school graduation (Rindfuss, Morgan, & Swicegood, 1988; Teachman & Polonko, 1985). Going to school is clearly incompatible with having a new baby and, for women, full-time work is as well.

"Having fun" is also an alternative commitment for some young couples. The planned pregnancy of rock musicians "Casey and Doug Sterling," described by Sandra Jaffe and Jack Viertel (1984), illustrates this point:

> For seven years (five of them in marriage), they had done just what they wanted to do. They had done the work and reaped the benefits. They had been to the parties, to the movies, to the concerts. They had laughed a lot and slept late. . . . They saw family expansion as a total upheaval of ther lives, but they had had seven selfish years, and sometimes it felt as if they had already done everything at least once. (p. 46)

While those who have important alternative commitments typically delay parenthood, those who *lack* such commitments are more likely to become parents as teenagers (Adams, Adams-Taylor, & Pittman, 1989; Yamaguchi & Kandel, 1987). This generalization holds on

Some women become mothers as teenagers and must quickly learn how to shop for bargains.

both the large-scale level of states and the small-scale level of individual teenagers. Thus, states that do little to provide meaningful schooling or employment for young adults have higher rates of teenage pregnancy than states that do provide such opportunities (Zimmerman, 1988). Similarly, students who do well in school and have important plans for the future (even if they attend poor schools in high unemployment states) are much less likely to become teenage parents than their less motivated classmates (Adams, Adams-Taylor, & Pittman, 1989; Yamaguchi & Kandel, 1987).

Financial Stability

Individuals also attempt to delay parenthood until they have reached what they consider to be financial stability. Most people, parents and nonparents alike, are well aware that children are expensive; in fact, economic cost is the most often cited "disadvantage" of children (Neal, Groat, & Wicks, 1989; Bulatao, 1981). Table 11–1 gives estimates of child costs for the first year of life, not including the cost of the birth itself. How much any given child will cost its parents depends, of course, on circumstances, such as where the family lives, how much help they can expect from relatives, the work schedules of the parents, the health of the child, and parental values. The Personal Application "How Much Does a Baby Really Cost?" illustrates this point.

Because potential parents vary in their personal values and family backgrounds, no one figure represents financial stability. For a pregnant teenager from a poor family, "financial stability" may mean being able to move out of her parents' home and receiving welfare benefits of $381 a month (the average *family* AFDC payment in 1989); those

Table 11–1 Cost of Baby in First Year, 1990	
Food and Feeding Equipment	$ 855
Diapers	$ 570
Clothes	$ 352
Furniture	$ 995
Bedding and Bath Supplies	$ 223
Medicine, Vitamins, and Personal Care Products	$ 396
Toys	$ 199
Child Care	$2,184
Total	$5,774

Source: Cutler, 1990, p. 37. Reprinted with permission © *American Demographics*, January 1990.

who are older or from richer backgrounds may not feel financially secure until they can afford a $200,000 home.

<table>
<tr><td>

**Personal
Application**

</td><td>

How Much Does a Baby Really Cost?

These two letters were published in *The New York Times* in response to an article on the cost estimates for a baby's first year as published in *American Demographics* magazine (the same estimates found in Table 11–1). Which letter best represents your point of view?

Baby's First-Year Costs Won't Approach $5,774

To the Editor:

   I hope no readers really believe the American Demographics maga-zine estimate of $5,774 for baby's first year's costs (Week in Review, Dec. 31). As a college teacher and mother of five children born between 1962 and 1981, I have to say, "Ridiculous!"

   Such costs might be incurred by double-income couples with no other children, no friends or family. If you have friends with children, you know babies don't need $233 worth of bedding and $995 worth of furniture. You borrow, you shop for used furniture or empty a few of your own drawers, you hem up a few sheets—you've got baby supplies.

   The greatest expenses—day care ($2,184) and paper diapers ($570)—should be linked to the cost of both parents' working. Day care centers require paper diapers; day care centers also expose the baby to lots of germs (add here the $396 in medical bills). If you take care of the baby yourself, you save—right off the top—a fast $3,000 to $3,150 (allowing a little for shots and checkups).

   And, if the mother decides to breast-feed the baby, she can chalk up another $855 saved because many experts agree that breast milk alone suffices the first year.

   And toys? Why spend $199 on toys when babies can't tell the difference between the box the toy came in and the toy itself? Babies play with spoons, cloths, pans—things parents already have. Now we've cut $4,054 from the list.

   Babies aren't expensive: ignorance is; trying to have it all is. The Amer-ican Demographics magazine's list applies only to misinformed parents who decorate their babies with expensive items before leaving them in the care of strangers. For such parents, the baby-expense list might include the cost of therapy and special schools their usually less hardy offspring will need after a few years as a status symbol.

LAURA B. KENNELLY
Denton, Tex., Jan. 8, 1990

Source: Laura B. Kennelly, Dept. of English, Univ. of North Texas, Denton, TX 76203. *New York Times,* January 30, 1990.

</td></tr>
</table>

Baby Costs Plenty

To the Editor:

In response to Laura B. Kennelly (letter, Jan. 31), who suggests that parents work to "decorate their babies with expensive items" and that children raised in such an environment will require therapy and special schools, we would like to say, "Grow up!"

Many dual-income families work out of economic necessity. For those women who choose to work, we hope Ms. Kennelly respects their decision, just as we respect her decision to be a full-time mother with her baby supplies of borrowed clothing, used furniture, and hemmed-up sheets for bedding.

Your publication of such a letter, however, was offensive and hurtful. As young working parents living in New York City, we know how difficult and expensive a task it is to raise a baby. The expense cited by American Demographics magazine for a baby's first year of $5,774 is realistic, if not low. Believe us, it is a struggle to balance family and career and to find quality child care. We are doing the best we can and do not appreciate harsh judgments.

SUSAN LIPP
MITCHELL LIPP
New York, Jan. 31, 1990

Source: Susan Lipp, Mitchell Lipp, *New York Times*, February 8, 1990.

While perceptions are important, they reflect economic realities. The Class of 1972 study found that men who were unemployed, working only part time, in school, or "just hanging out" delayed parenthood, whereas those in the military or in full-time civilian jobs did not (Rindfuss, Morgan, & Swicegood, 1988). Young people from working-class families tend to end their education, enter the labor force, and start making money earlier in life than those from upper-middle-class families and, consequently, tend to marry and have children earlier as well. As pointed out in Chapter 10, this strategy makes economic sense. Wages for working-class jobs tend to peak rather early; blue-collar workers who wait until their thirties to have children risk confronting childrearing expenses at the very time their wages have stopped increasing.

The connection between financial stability and the timing of parenthood is clear on the national level as well as on the personal level. One very extensive analysis of twentieth century U.S. birth patterns concluded that *the socioeconomic climate of the country when couples are in their twenties is extremely important in determining when they will have their first child* (Rindfuss, Morgan, & Swicegood, 1988). In a socioeconomic climate of low unemployment rates, plentiful job oppor-

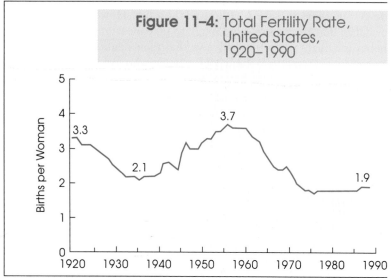

Figure 11-4: Total Fertility Rate,
United States,
1920-1990

Source: Wetzel, 1990, p. 9.

Remember that total fertility rate is the number of children the average woman will give birth to if she conforms to prevalent patterns. This figure shows the fluctuations in fertility rates since 1920. Compare fertility rates to public opinions about ideal family size in Figure 11-2.

tunities for young adults, affordable family housing, and economic expansion, more couples marry and have their first child early in their twenties. This describes the situation of young adults during the late 1940s, the 1950s, and the early 1960s. Conversely, when unemployment or inflation rates are high, job opportunities for young adults are limited, and family housing is very expensive, more couples delay marriage and wait until their late twenties or early thirties for their first child. This describes the situation of husbands and wives entering their twenties during the Great Depression years of the 1930s and the Great Inflation years of the 1970s (Rindfuss, Morgan, & Swicegood, 1988).

These same economic factors also help to explain why people have more children in some eras than in others. Figure 11-4 illustrates twentieth-century fluctuations in total fertility rate. **Total fertility rate** is a measure of how many babies an average woman would have during her lifetime if she reproduced at the rate characteristic of a given calendar year. Note that in the relatively prosperous 1950s and 1960s, total fertility rates were almost double what they had been 20 years earlier but dropped to the lowest point ever in the late 1970s.

Total fertility rate
the number of babies the average woman would have during her lifetime if she reproduced at the rate characteristic of a given calendar year.

Relationship Stability

Couples generally attempt to delay parenthood until they have achieved *what they consider to be* a stable relationship. *Some* unmarried teenagers decide to have a child even though they lack a stable relationship with a partner and *some* married couples have a child in a desperate effort to save a failing relationship. However, there is also evidence that people are more likely to take measures to prevent pregnancy (or birth) when they perceive that their relationship is unstable. Kathleen Gerson (1985) found that women who feel their relationships are faltering are often particularly anxious to avoid parenthood. One such woman said:

> By that time I was twenty-six, and I thought, "Oh, what if I never had kids?" But at the same time, it just wasn't the time. Our marriage was rocky. . . . I was ambivalent. . . . It was a survival thing to get out of that marriage. I would have gone nuts if I had stayed there. (pp. 72–73)

Many couples choose parenthood *because* they feel their relationship is solid. For example, pregnant teenagers who feel very close to their boyfriends are less likely to terminate a pregnancy (Brazzell & Acock, 1988) and those who first become parents after age thirty say they would not have considered parenthood if their marriage had not been stable (Soloway & Smith, 1987). What is true for those at the childbearing-age extremes also holds for those in their twenties. Prospective parents frequently view having a child as a symbol of their marriage's solidity. One husband interviewed by public health practitioner Elizabeth Whelan (1978) noted, "We have a feeling that a child will add more depth to our already strong relationship" (p. 27) while one of the wives interviewed by sociologist Ann Oakley (1980) explained, "I think the reason we want a baby is because it's cementing our marriage and our love. And we want to produce this thing *from* our love" (p. 34).

Small Group Support

Finally, couples attempt to delay parenthood until it is accepted and approved by those who are closest to them, those whose opinions they value and whose approval they seek. Because couples live in varying family and peer group atmospheres, they pick up different subtle and unsubtle messages about the "proper" age to have children. For example, one study of "delayers" found that those who waited until after age thirty to become parents did so because they received "family messages" not to rush parenthood—including the parental message "We do *not* want to be grandparents" (Soloway & Smith, 1987). At the other age extreme, pregnant teenagers are very dependent on their mothers and best friends in deciding what to do about an unintended pregnancy (Brazzell & Acock, 1988). Those who perceive that their mothers and best friends approve of abortion will probably choose that option, while those whose unmarried friends have given birth and kept their babies are likely to become mothers themselves (Brazzell & Acock, 1988; Hudis & Brazzell, 1981).

The spouse or intimate partner is of particular importance in deciding when to have a child. Men and women who are ambivalent or indifferent about parenthood often eventually give in to a partner with a strong prochild preference. One mother interviewed by Gerson (1985) put it like this:

> Jim was the person of primary importance, and he wanted kids. If I had married a man who didn't want children, fine. I would have gone along with that, too. I didn't think much about it. Motherhood was no big thing to me. I took it very casually. I had no great emotional interest in it. I didn't fight it or anything. [But I did it] to please my husband. (p. 101)

Why Some Choose Nonparenthood

About 3–6 percent of married couples who are biologically capable of having children make the decision not to be parents at all. These couples, known as the **voluntarily childless**, are an interesting group. Learning more about why and how the child-free minority choose not to have children can help us understand why the majority continue to do so.

The voluntarily childless share many characteristics with parenthood delayers. Both husband and wife in voluntarily childless marriages tend to be first born or only children, college-educated, engaged in high-status jobs, and not currently affiliated with a religion (Houseknecht, 1987). The wives were often raised in homes with moderate (rather than high) levels of family warmth and were encouraged to be independent achievers early in life. In their adult life, they have a less traditional view of the female role, a higher level of commitment to their jobs, and earn more money than other women (Houseknecht, 1987). About one-third of the voluntarily childless decided before marriage that they did not want to be parents (Ory, 1978; Veevers, 1973). Most, however, decided on permanent childlessness after several years of successfully "postponing" children for one reason or another; "they make their decision to remain childless after they have married and have developed a lifestyle that they do not want to give up" (Houseknecht, 1987, p. 379). The reason the voluntarily childless give most often for their choice is "freedom"—staying childless allows them greater opportunity for self-fulfillment, mobility, and career without the responsibilities of parenthood (Houseknecht, 1987). Figure 11–5 (on page 396) suggests that more couples today are deciding to remain child-free (or to postpone children).

Voluntarily childless those who are reproductively capable but decide not to have children.

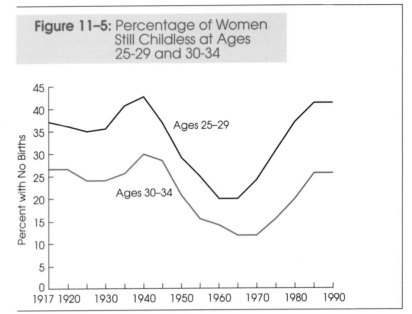

Figure 11–5: Percentage of Women Still Childless at Ages 25-29 and 30-34

Ages 25–29

Ages 30–34

Percent with No Births

1917 1920   1930   1940   1950   1960   1970   1980   1990

Sources: Heuser, 1976; U.S. Bureau of the Census, 1991 b, p. 13.

The figure shows an increase in childlessness among women in their late twenties and early thirties since 1975. Nonetheless, almost 60 percent of women are mothers by age 30 and 75 percent are mothers by age 35.

Among voluntarily childless couples, the wife most often initiates the idea of remaining child-free but the husband rarely challenges her choice. Indeed, the spouse is a major source of support for those who decide not to be parents (Houseknecht, 1987; Gerson, 1985). Although childless couples (especially wives) are aware of the pronatalist pressures exerted by both the culture in general and people they know, they do not allow such pressures to bother them (Houseknecht, 1987). The autonomy, independence, and nonconformity developed first in other areas of life apparently makes it easier for them to accept the unusual status of voluntary childlessness.

PREGNANCY

Physical pregnancy the external and internal changes that occur in a woman's body while she carries a developing fetus within her uterus.

Parenthood is generally, but not always, preceded by pregnancy. Every pregnancy is really two—the physical pregnancy and the social pregnancy (LaRossa, 1986). Both pregnancies are a preparation for parenthood, and each one affects the other. What is each pregnancy like?

Physical pregnancy refers to the external and internal changes that occur in a woman's body while she carries a developing fetus within her uterus. Physical pregnancy begins at conception, when male sperm and female ovum unite, a process described in Chapter 3. During physical pregnancy, the fertilized ovum first becomes a multicellular system of specialized parts and then grows into a human being capable of living outside the mother's body. This fetal development involves considerable physical change in the mother's body, first in terms of hormonal changes and then in terms of size and shape. Figure 11–6, illustrating uterine growth throughout pregnancy, shows some of this change. Physical pregnancy generally ends some 38 to 42 weeks after conception with the birth of a baby.

Social pregnancy refers to the pattern of social behaviors expected of prospective parents. Social pregnancy begins when someone—a woman, her partner, her mother or a doctor—decides that certain physical symptoms indicate impending parenthood. Typically, social pregnancy begins several weeks after physical pregnancy; that is, women are physically pregnant before they are socially pregnant. In fact, in cases of ambiguous symptoms, lack of awareness about the body, or denial, the physical pregnancy might be three or four months (or even more) advanced before the social pregnancy begins! On the other hand, a woman is sometimes socially pregnant (that is, she *believes* that she is pregnant, and begins behaving as an expectant mother) when, physically, she is not (LaRossa, 1986, p. 40). Social pregnancy differs from physical pregnancy in that, in most pregnancies (those in which the

Social pregnancy the pattern of social behaviors expected of prospective parents.

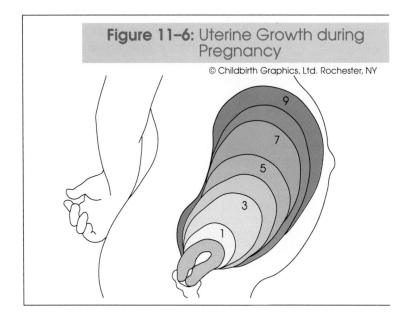

Figure 11–6: Uterine Growth during Pregnancy

© Childbirth Graphics, Ltd. Rochester, NY

As the fetus grows, it comes to occupy a large part of the mother's midsection. Its size eventually affects her ability to move around, maintain her equilibrium, produces lower back pain, causes frequent urination, interferes with sexual intercourse, and makes it hard for her to tie her shoes. (The numbers in the illustration refer to the months of pregnancy).

prospective father is known and acknowledged), *both mother and father are socially pregnant* (LaRossa, 1986). Both hold the status of expectant parent and, like people in any new status, they are expected to act and feel somewhat differently than they acted and felt before acquiring the status. Like physical pregnancy, social pregnancy ends with the birth of the child.

Pregnancy and the Intimate Relationship

Physical pregnancy subjects a woman's body to a variety of different sensations—some pleasant and some not so pleasant. Social pregnancy also involves a variety of conflicting feelings. Both socially pregnant partners experience these feelings, but not always in the same way or on the same schedule. At times, differences in the timing of feelings produce some emotional ups and downs in the partners' intimate relationship.

Early Pregnancy

Initially, most couples expecting a child for the first time have difficulty accepting the fetus as a part of themselves or visualizing themselves as parents; the fact that the pregnancy is not visible and that there is no real sign of a baby during the first three months makes the status of expectant parent seem particularly unreal (Breen, 1989; LaRossa, 1986). Even couples who planned their pregnancy and are generally pleased about it often have mixed feelings about the prospect of parenthood during the early months. This is how one couple interviewed by British sociologist Ann Oakley (1980) described their reaction to positive pregnancy test results:

> [the wife, an illustrator] ... terrified and very pleased. I would have been disappointed I think had it been negative. As to feeling absolutely jubilant and on top of the world: no. ... We've never been parents before. I mean, it's terrifying.

> [the husband, a musician] You didn't seem to me at that time to have mixed feelings any more than I did. ... I felt: what the hell are we going to be like as parents and how are we going to get through the nine months? (p. 38)

During early pregnancy, expectant parents frequently experience anxiety (sometimes manifested in upsetting dreams) about finances, the woman's work, changes in their marriage, the normality of the fetus, or the pain of childbirth (Breen, 1989; Lederman, 1984; Oakley, 1980). Because of these anxieties and because many women feel fatigued and perhaps ill during the first three months of pregnancy, most couples engage in sexual intercourse slightly less frequently than they did in the prepregnancy period (Selby & Calhoun, 1981).

Those who intended to become pregnant can begin the process of dealing with the anxieties and of adjusting to their new status early in the pregnancy. Those who did not intend to get pregnant have to make a more basic decision first: Do we (or I) want this pregnancy to continue? If they decide to end the pregnancy, they must deal with the issues of where to obtain an abortion, how to pay for it, and whom to tell. Sometimes these issues are rather easily resolved; sometimes they involve a great struggle. Unmarried, unexpectedly pregnant couples who decide to continue the pregnancy face the additional decision of whether to marry or to remain single. If they decide to marry, they will be adjusting to an unintended or early marriage while preparing to be parents. If they decide to remain single, the woman may worry about financial and social support and the man about his rights and obligations. In short, almost everyone has some anxieties about accepting prospective parenthood in the early weeks and months of pregnancy. However, those in a stable relationship who intended the pregnancy have a head start in dealing with them.

During middle pregnancy, the expectant mother and others can feel the fetus move within the mother's body. Feeling such movement can be exciting for "big-brother-to-be" as well as for the parents.

Middle Pregnancy

As the pregnancy progresses into its middle stages, the expectant mother often becomes preoccupied with her changing body and with the growing fetus. Figure 11–7 illustrates just how rapidly the fetus grows after the first 12 weeks. An important turning point during the second trimester of pregnancy, the fourth to sixth month after conception, is **quickening** or the movement of the fetus inside the mother's body (Whelan, 1978). Once quickening occurs, the pregnant woman can observe fetal wake and sleep cycles and often begins to attribute personal characteristics to the fetus (Mercer, 1986). In other words, quickening makes the growing fetus a "real person" to many pregnant women.

Expectant mothers have continuous physical reminders of upcoming parenthood. As their pregnancy begins to show, friends, relatives, and strangers give them numerous *social* reminders as well. Pregnant women find themselves in somewhat the same position as physically handicapped people—people will alternately stare, avoid them, ask them personal questions, help them with the simplest physical tasks, and pat them on the belly (LaRossa, 1986, pp. 47–48; Oakley, 1980, pp. 48–50). All this attention makes it difficult for them to forget that they will soon be mothers.

Expectant fathers, meanwhile, do *not* carry visible signs announcing to the world "Hey, I'm going to be a father!" They can experience the physical pregnancy only indirectly—by touching their partner's abdomen to feel the kicks, by listening through a special stethoscope

Quickening
the first movement of the fetus within the mother's body.

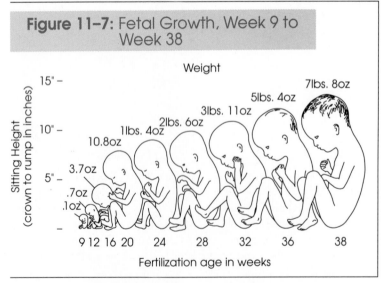

Figure 11–7: Fetal Growth, Week 9 to Week 38

Weight

15" –
Sitting Height (crown to rump in inches)

7lbs. 8oz
5lbs. 4oz
3lbs. 11oz
2lbs. 6oz
1lbs. 4oz
10.8oz
10" –
3.7oz
.7oz
.1oz
5" –

9 12 16 20   24   28   32   36   38
Fertilization age in weeks

The human fetus undergoes tremendous gains in length and weight between the ninth week after fertilization and birth at the age of about 38 weeks. At 9 weeks, the fetus "sits" less than 2 inches tall and weighs about as much as one penny. By the time of birth, it sits over 14 inches tall and weighs 7 pounds or more.

Source: K. L. Moore, *The Developing Human*, 1982. W. B. Saunders, Philadelphia.

to hear the fetal heartbeat, or by viewing an electronic sonogram image on a monitor. Men often need more time to truly accept the pregnancy and are slower in developing an emotional relationship with the growing fetus. One fairly common pattern is for expectant fathers to go into a "moratorium" during the second trimester, forgetting the pregnancy for days at a time (May, 1982).

For the couple, then, the middle part of pregnancy can mean a temporary drawing apart—the woman increasingly focused on the pregnancy and perhaps resentful that her partner is ignoring it, the man puzzled by his partner's new emotional involvement. There is an experiential gap (and perhaps a communication gap) between the future mother and father at this point, with one experiencing the pregnancy much more intensely than the other. Sexually, however, the couple may be closer than ever before. Some sex researchers believe that sexual desire, intercourse satisfaction, and intercourse frequency all peak during the second trimester of pregnancy, exceeding prepregnancy levels (Masters & Johnson, 1966). Most researchers, however, feel that sexual activity in the second trimester is similar to that in the first—slightly below prepregnancy levels (Selby & Calhoun, 1981).

For Better or For Worse®   **by Lynn Johnston**

Late Pregnancy

During the last three months of pregnancy, most couples grow closer together again. Some men become reinvolved in the pregnancy when, several weeks after quickening, they *personally* can feel fetal movement rather than just listening to their partner's description of it. When both partners finally define the fetus as a "real baby," they can talk about and to it, often by name (Whelan, 1978). This shared experience makes it easier for men to offer their partners **expressive support**, a type of much-needed social support that includes being available to talk, sharing ideas, understanding the woman's feelings, and showing affection (Liese, Snowden, & Ford, 1989).

Expressive support
a type of social support that involves being available to talk, sharing ideas, understanding feelings, and showing affection.

Husband and friends can offer important instrumental support during pregnancy.

Instrumental support
a type of social support that involves helping out with practical matters such as household chores and shopping.

Not all fathers feel comfortable establishing an emotional relationship with their child before birth or with showing expressive support (May, 1980). These men may offer another type of social support—they take over some household chores, do more errands, and make practical preparations for the new baby, such as remodeling a bedroom or buying supplies (Goldberg, Michaels, & Lamb, 1985; May, 1980). This type of social support, called **instrumental support**, is especially appreciated by wives. In one study, married women whose husbands helped them more with the household chores during pregnancy *felt* that they were receiving expressive support as well: they interpreted their husband's increased involvement in household work as a sign of love and affection (Liese, Snowden, & Ford, 1989). Unmarried "partnered" women typically received instrumental support from family members but were very dependent on their male partners for expressive support (Liese, Snowden, & Ford, 1989).

Probably as a result of the shared involvement and increased male support, expectant mothers and fathers often report that they feel closer to one another, more connected to one another, and more love for one another during the last three months of pregnancy than ever before in their relationship (Saunders & Robins, 1989; LaRossa, 1986, p. 53).

This closeness occurs in the absence of frequent sexual intercourse. Indeed, intercourse frequency typically declines rather drastically during the last trimester of pregnancy (Selby & Calhoun, 1981; Masters & Johnson, 1966).

This generally cheery picture of late pregnancy does not apply to all couples, however. Some men are indifferent or detached throughout the pregnancy and offer neither expressive nor instrumental support. If their pregnant partners are unable to get such support from other sources, they are more likely than women who do receive support to be depressed during and after pregnancy, to suffer physical complications and a hard birth, and to have generally negative feelings about pregnancy, childbirth, and motherhood (Liese, Snowden & Ford, 1989; Mercer, 1986, pp. 14–17). In other words, social support—both expressive and instrumental—during pregnancy is more than just niceness or courtesy: it can make a real difference in pregnancy outcome.

Some pregnant women not only fail to receive adequate social support during pregnancy, they also suffer actual physical abuse. According to the results of one large-scale national survey, about one in ten pregnant women is the victim of either minor or severe violence at some time during her pregnancy. One out of four pregnant women younger than 25 is a victim of domestic violence (Gelles, 1988). Such violence is slightly more likely to occur during the last half of the pregnancy, with blows often directed to the abdominal area (Gelles, 1988). Although pregnant women are no more likely than nonpregnant women of the same age to be violence victims, neither does pregnancy seem to stand in the way of abuse (Gelles, 1988).

The findings on violence during pregnancy parallel what is more generally true: pregnancy introduces some pleasures and stresses into couple relationships that would not otherwise exist but does not truly change the preexisting relationship. Researchers studying pregnancy and marital satisfaction, for example, find that marital satisfaction remains at a stable level throughout pregnancy (Saunders & Robins, 1989; Snowden et al., 1988). Satisfying marriages do not become less satisfying because of the pregnancy nor does pregnancy transform unhappy marriages into happy ones.

Pregnancy Problems

Relationship worries and conflicts are not the only problems related to pregnancy. Some pregnancies end involuntarily through miscarriage, some couples have a very difficult time conceiving a child, and some have problems securing adequate prenatal care. All three problems can cause significant social and emotional stress.

Miscarriage

Miscarriage
the termination of pregnancy and the expulsion of the fetus by natural means during the first 20 weeks of pregnancy.

Miscarriage is the termination of pregnancy and the expulsion of the fetus by natural means during the first 20 weeks of pregnancy (May & Mahlmeister, 1990, p. 494). Between 10 and 20 percent of pregnancies miscarry (May & Mahlmeister, 1990, p. 494; Day & Hooks, 1987). The vast majority of miscarriages occur in the first 12 weeks of pregnancy, sometimes before the pregnancy is even recognized, and involve genetically abnormal, fertilized eggs that never developed into fetuses (Hotchner, 1984, p. 444). These are "random mistakes of nature" and chances of a repeated miscarriage in the same woman are rare (Hotchner, 1984, p. 444). Other, less common, types of miscarriages are associated with structural problems in the uterus or cervix, hormonal imbalances, and exposure to toxic chemicals, the same kinds of factors responsible for infertility in some women (Clapp & Swenson, 1984, p. 426). Women who miscarry for these reasons are vulnerable to miscarriage in every pregnancy.

Both men and women who desired the pregnancy and had already begun thinking of themselves as parents experience high levels of stress and a sense of loss after a miscarriage. They feel the loss as the loss of a *child* and experience the miscarriage as the death of a real person. They are socially isolated in their feelings, though, because few people around them treat the miscarriage as a death. The expelled blood and tissue are often treated as hospital waste or disposed of in a public grave; there is no funeral, no burial, no sympathy cards. Hospital personnel frequently inform the couple that the miscarriage was "for the best" because the fetus (or potential fetus) was "abnormal" and that they should "go home and try again" (Day & Hooks, 1987, p. 307).

Even those who are sympathetic to the loss often do not know what to say and, consequently, say nothing or speak only about the physical aspects of the loss. One woman described her experience as follows:

> . . . People were more comfortable talking about the physical and not the emotional side of miscarriage. I needed to talk about both. It was also difficult for my husband, because people could at least ask how my body was doing. Unfortunately, he would sometimes be completely bypassed when someone called to talk with us, despite the fact that he, too, was in deep emotional pain. (quoted in Clapp & Swenson, 1984, p. 427)

As with the death of a living child, parents affected by a miscarriage carry the sadness with them for many years.

Infertility

Infertility is defined as "the inability to conceive and carry a pregnancy to viability after at least one year of regular sexual intercourse without contraception" (May & Mahlmeister, 1990, p. 137). Couples who want to become parents but are unable to do so because of the infertility of one or both partners are defined as **involuntarily childless** (Miall, 1986). Somewhere between one out of thirteen (Waldrop, 1991) and one out of five U.S. couples (May & Mahlmeister, 1990, p. 136; Link & Darling, 1986) experience temporary or permanent infertility; experts disagree about whether the proportion of infertile couples is on the increase (Waldrop, 1991).

Whether the proportion of infertile couples is increasing or decreasing, more infertile couples are seeking help and more effective help is available to them. Today, infertility specialists are able to discover the cause of infertility in about 90 percent of the cases and to correct it in about half (Clapp & Swenson, 1984, p. 420; Hotchner, 1984, p. 39). About 40 percent of infertility cases are due to a male biological

Infertility
the inability to conceive and carry a pregnancy to viability after at least one year of regular sexual intercourse without contraception.

Involuntarily childless
couples who want to have children but are unable to because of infertility problems.

Infertile couples have more sources of help available today than in the past. Doctors are able to discover the cause of infertility in about 90 percent of the cases and to correct it in about half of them.

difficulty, about 40 percent to a female biological difficulty, and about 20 percent to joint difficulties (May & Mahlmeister, 1990, p. 137).

Table 11–2 details the most usual causes of and treatments for infertility. Some couples who remain unable to conceive after undergoing these types of treatment try methods that involve nonintercourse fertilization and, in some cases, the involvement of persons other than the prospective parents as sperm or egg donors or carriers (Thom, 1988). These nonintercourse methods include:

1. **Artificial Insemination** A woman is inseminated with a man's (her partner's or a donor's) sperm without sexual intercourse.

Artificial insemination the introduction of male sperm into a woman's body without sexual intercourse.

Table 11–2 Infertility Problems, Causes, and Treatments

Problem	Possible Causes	Possible Treatments
Inadequate sperm quantity, quality, or motility	1. Past or present infections	1. Antibiotics for some infections
	2. Testes exposure to excessive heat, radiation, or other environmental hazards	2. Remove exposure to hazard
	3. Stress, smoking, poor nutrition, high alcohol use, some prescription drugs, heavy marijuana use	3. Change habits, testosterone or other hormone treatment
	4. Varicose vein in spermatic cord	4. Surgical correction
Failure to ovulate regularly, inadequate ovum production	Malfunctions in hormone-producing organs; prior use of birth control pill (esp. for women who started menstruation late or have irregular periods); age	Hormone treatment with drugs such as Clomid and Pergonal

	Table 11–2 (*continued*)	
Problem	**Possible Causes**	**Possible Treatments**
Failure of sperm and ovum to unite	1. Lack of knowledge about ovulation, or about the "best time" to get pregnant	1. Education, more awareness and observation of body changes
	2. Vaginal or cervical mucus not conducive to sperm survival and movement, sometimes because of infection	2. Estrogen treatment; alkaline douche before intercourse; treat infections; artificial insemination
	3. Blockage or scarring in penis or fallopian tubes from STD, or endometriosis (female), or Pelvic Inflammatory Disease (female) from prior IUD use	3. Microsurgery; laser surgery to remove scarring; pregnancy-simulating drugs to treat endometriosis; *in vitro* fertilization
	4. Male impotence, premature ejaculation	4. Sexual therapy; artificial insemination
Failure of egg to implant	Structural problems of cervix or uterus, congenital or caused by mother's DES use	Surgery

Sources: May & Mahlmeister, 1990; Clapp & Swenson, 1984; Hotchner, 1984.

2. **In Vitro Fertilization**   An egg is removed from the woman's ovary, fertilized with a man's sperm, and transferred to the woman's uterus.
3. **In Vivo Fertilization with Embryo Transfer**   Sperm from the partner of one woman is used to inseminate a second woman. If conception occurs, the embryo is transferred to the body of the first woman for gestation.

In vitro fertilization fertilization of a female egg by male sperm outside the woman's body with subsequent transferral into the uterus.

In vivo fertilization with embryo transfer the fertilized egg of one woman is transferred into the body of another woman (the sperm donor's partner) for gestation.

Surrogate pregnancy
a woman is inseminated, carries and bears the child of a nonpartner sperm donor, with the understanding that the sperm donor and his partner will raise the child.

4. **Surrogate Pregnancy**   A woman is inseminated, then carries and bears the child of a nonpartner sperm donor, with the understanding that the sperm donor and his partner will raise the child.

Because these ways of conceiving a child are different from the usual process and because some of them raise legal issues about who the "real" parents are, they remain controversial.

More than a physical problem, infertility represents a social and emotional crisis for those who had planned on having children (Sabatelli, Meth, & Gavazzi, 1988; Porter & Christopher, 1984). Besides having to deal with their anger, disbelief, loss of control, and sadness, couples diagnosed as infertile have to make difficult decisions about "who to tell" and about what treatment, if any, to undertake. Like others with a hidden physical handicap, infertile couples feel that telling friends and relatives about their "problem" will open their private lives to scrutiny and brand them as "failures." On the other hand, *not* telling isolates them from possible help and leaves them vulnerable to the harsh criticism directed towards the voluntarily childless (Miall, 1986).

Undergoing treatment for infertility can bring about further stress and couple conflict, particularly for those in less-than-strong marriages (Sabatelli, Meth, & Gavazzi, 1988; Link & Darling, 1986). The infertile couple who seek infertility treatment may have to make multiple trips

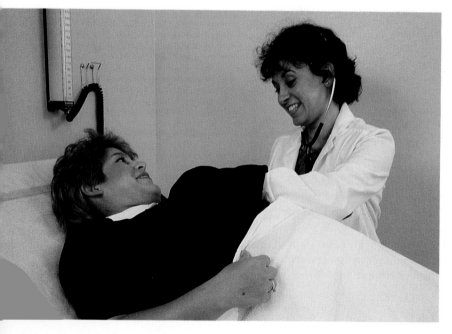

Social inequalities have a significant impact on differences in the experience of pregnancy. Overall, Hispanics are less likely than other groups to receive adequate prenatal care.

to the doctor's office at inconvenient times, subject their once private sex life to scientific scrutiny, experience a subsequent decline in sexual satisfaction, and spend a lot of money. About half the couples diagnosed as infertile are eventually able to have their own child. Many of the remainder choose to adopt a child, an option covered in the alternative choice section.

Inequality in Prenatal Care

Modern U.S. pregnancies occur in a society marked by significant economic and regional inequality. Couples with sufficient financial, educational, and time resources have the luxury of searching for the type of prenatal care or infertility treatment they desire. Those who are poor, lack medical insurance, or live in rural counties without practicing doctors, midwives, or public health clinics have many fewer choices.

About 16 percent of pregnant women in the United States receive inadequate prenatal care. Teenagers, unmarried women, blacks, Hispanics, Native Americans, and those with less than high school educations are especially likely to receive inadequate prenatal care. One result is that prematurity and infant death rates, along with the accompanying social and emotional trauma, are much higher in these groups than in others (Witwer, 1990). Table 11–3 provides further details.

Table 11–3 Prenatal Care and Prematurity by Ethnic Group, United States, 1984–1986					
	White	Black	Hispanic	Asian	Native American
Percent Receiving Inadequate* Prenatal Care	13	27	30	< 13	32
Percent Premature** Births	8.6	18.3	11.1	7.4	12.3

* inadequate prenatal care: care beginning after first four months or consisting of less than half the recommended number of visits.
** premature births: born before 37 weeks gestation.

Source: Martha Witwer, "Prenatal Care in the United States," *Family Planning Perspectives,* Volume 22: Number 1 (January/February 1990), p. 33 © The Alan Guttmacher Institute.

CHILDBIRTH

Physical childbirth
the bodily exertions and changes necessary for a child to leave its mother's body and enter the outside world.

Childbirth, like pregnancy, is both a physical and a social event. **Physical childbirth** refers to the bodily exertions and changes necessary for a child to emerge from its mother's body and enter the outside world. During the first or "labor" part of childbirth, the woman's uterine muscles alternately tighten and relax (contractions) and her cervix gradually widens (dilates) to a width of ten centimeters, about the width of ten fingers. In the "delivery" part of childbirth, contractions stop, the baby is pushed (or sometimes pulled with forceps) out of the mother's body and into the world through the widened cervix. Shortly after the baby is born, the mother's body expels the placenta, the organ that linked mother and baby throughout the pregnancy. Finally, contractions resume as the mother's body readjusts.

Models of Social Childbirth

Social childbirth
the social and cultural aspects of childbirth: how the woman and others around her think about childbirth, where the birth takes place, who is present during childbirth and what they do, and what kinds of interventions are made.

Social childbirth has to do with how the woman and others around her think about childbirth, where the birth takes place, who is present during childbirth and what they do, and what kinds of interventions are made. Barbara Rothman (1986; 1982), a sociologist who has attempted to discover regular patterns in the history of social childbirth in the United States, defines three models of social childbirth: the mutual participation model, the active-passive model, and the guidance-cooperation model. While Rothman (1986; 1982) treats the models historically, we will focus on how each of them exists today in the United States. This chapter's Cohort Comparison offers an historical perspective.

The Mutual Participation Model

Mutual participation model
a type of social childbirth in which the childbearing woman and her attendant are equals working together toward a common goal.

The **mutual participation model** emphasizes that the childbearing woman and her attendant are equal partners working together toward a common goal (Rothman, 1986, p. 114). Most often, the attendant is a midwife, an experienced woman with a wealth of practical knowledge about childbirth, who defines her job as *making it easier for the pregnant woman to deliver her own baby*. Midwife-attended, mutual participation births typically occur at home, allowing the birthgiving woman maximum freedom to move around, eat, change clothes, and talk with family and friends while in labor. In the past, mutual participation births were "women only" events. However, in most mutual participation

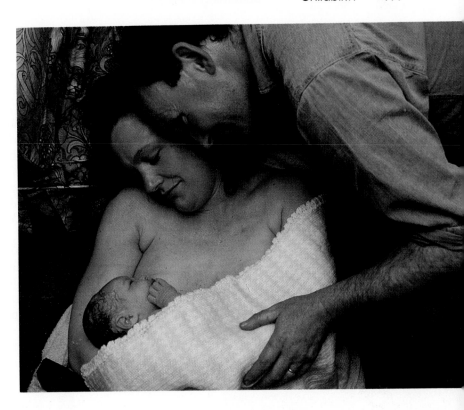

Mutual participation births typically occur at home, with the father sometimes acting as midwife.

home births today, the father actively assists in the birth, in some cases playing the midwife role. Siblings of the new baby often attend the birth as well.

People who plan home births are a diverse lot. Sometimes home birth with a midwife is part of an ethnic or religious tradition that the couple wishes to maintain. A few women give birth at home not out of choice but from necessity—they lack the private insurance, Medicaid coverage, or income to cover the cost of a hospital birth or cannot get to a hospital in time (Hinds, Bergeisen, & Allen, 1985; Anderson & Bauwens, 1982). Often, however, the desire for this kind of birth grows out of the individual's personal belief system. One woman giving birth at home cited religious reasons " . . . it was God's will that our baby be born at home. . . . I would only consider a maternity facility if it was Christ-centered and gave all glory and credit to God" (Anderson & Bauwens, 1982, pp. 301–302). Others choose home birth because they see birth as a natural and normal process, best left under individual control: " . . . my body and what happened to it was my responsibility. . . . pregnancy and birth were natural processes that probably did best with little interference" (Anderson & Bauwens, 1982, pp. 299–300).

The Active-Passive Model

Active-passive model
a type of social childbirth in which the childbearing woman hands control over the birth to a physician.

The active-passive model of social childbirth is, in many ways, the direct opposite of the mutual participation model. In the **active-passive model**, an attendant, typically a doctor, "delivers" the baby from an unconscious or partially conscious woman using forceps or surgery (Rothman, 1986, p. 113). This model of childbirth maximizes doctor participation and decision making and minimizes parent participation. The doctor defines his or her role as one of *using the most modern technological interventions to assure the delivery of a healthy baby.* Other medical personnel are also present and, today, husbands (or, much less frequently, unmarried male partners) are often allowed to attend the birth as well.

Active-passive births occur in hospitals. Hospital attendants treat the woman as a surgical patient, often shaving her pubic hair, giving her an enema, hooking her up to an I.V. (intravenous feeding) device, monitoring the condition of the fetus electronically, and administering pain-blocking medication (Eakins, 1986, p. 5). Cesarean sections rep-

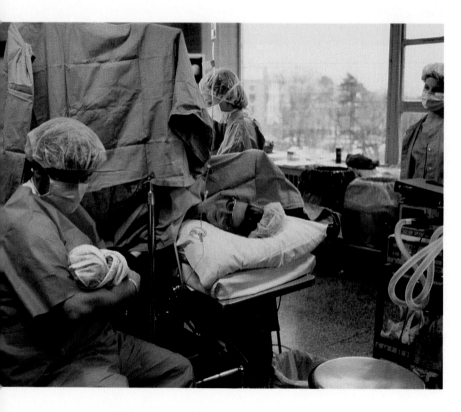

Active-passive births occur in hospital settings, amidst medical personnel and specialized monitoring equipment.

resent the ultimate in active-passive births. In a **Cesarean section**, the doctor removes the baby through an incision made in the woman's abdominal wall while the woman is under general or regional anesthesia. Although some practices associated with active-passive births have declined in the past twenty years (Kozak, 1989; Ahmed & Kolker, 1981), the incidence of Cesarean sections greatly increased during the 1970s and 1980s. In 1970, only 5 percent of all births were Cesarean sections (Ryan, 1988); by the late 1980s, about 25 percent were (Kozak, 1989).

Women who prefer active-passive hospital births believe them to be the safest, shortest, and least painful way to give birth. They like the idea of being taken care of and worry more than other women about possible complications (Sacks & Donnenfeld, 1984). In a study of new mothers in a Vermont hospital, Nelson (1986, 1983) found that working-class mothers were more likely than middle-class mothers to favor the interventions associated with active-passive births. These women wanted their husbands to be present and wanted to be with their babies soon after birth, but preferred that the birth itself be speedy, painless, and medically supervised. They perceived the birth process as something they had to go through to have the baby, not as a particularly significant event in and of itself (Nelson, 1986, 1983). An ethnographic study of pregnant black teenagers in rural Florida found much the same thing: these teenagers saw birth as something that happened to them and welcomed medical intervention (Dougherty, 1978).

The Guidance-Cooperation Model

The **guidance-cooperation model** of childbirth involves direction by a medically trained team (childbirth educators, nurse-midwives, and doctors) and cooperation by the pregnant woman (Rothman, 1986, p. 114). The role of the team is one of *urging the cooperation of the expectant mother by educating and supporting her throughout pregnancy and childbirth*. The guidance-cooperation model lies between the other two: the woman giving birth is more informed, aware, and in control than in the active-passive model and the attendants are more directive and authoritative than in the mutual participation model.

Women undergoing "prepared childbirth" in a hospital or alternative birth center illustrate the guidance-cooperation model. **Prepared childbirth** means that the pregnant woman learns about the physical aspects of childbirth and practices for it before the event takes place. Today the preparation is typically done in classes sponsored by hospitals or community centers. Classes involve learning about the physiology of childbirth, practicing breathing and other relaxation techniques to control pain, exercising, and discussing common problems (Pincus,

---

Cesarean Section
a procedure in which the doctor removes the baby through an incision made in the woman's abdominal wall while the woman is under general or regional anesthesia.

Guidance-cooperation model
a type of social childbirth in which a medical team and the partner of the childbearing woman guide and support a prepared woman through childbirth.

Prepared childbirth
learning about the physical aspects of childbirth and practicing for it before the event takes place.

Many women choosing the guidance-cooperation model of childbirth give birth in an alternative birth center under the guidance of a doctor or midwife.

Swenson, & Poor, 1984). A partner, usually the father, attends the classes with the pregnant woman and learns how to be a "labor coach." In addition to these types of preparation, the prospective parent(s) makes regular prenatal visits to a physician and reads about pregnancy and childbirth.

After several months of preparation, the woman gives birth in a hospital or alternative birth center under the direction of a physician or nurse-midwife and a team of medical helpers, with her "labor coach" partner helping her implement the breathing and concentration exercises they learned in class. The woman is conscious throughout the procedure and both partners see the baby being born.

Guidance-cooperation births are particularly attractive to educated, middle-class couples (Nelson, 1986, 1983). These couples often plan their pregnancies and are generally older than working-class couples when their first child is born. They believe that pregnancy and childbirth are special peak physical and emotional experiences that intimate couples should plan, control, and share (Wertz & Wertz, 1989; Ahmed & Kolker, 1981). Going to classes, reading books, and searching out alternative birthing places are easier for them than for younger, less educated, or poorer couples since these tasks correspond well with their prior adult experiences (Mercer, 1986; Block *et al*, 1981). In contrast to those choosing passive-active births, those choosing the guidance-cooperation model are most concerned with maintaining control and with avoiding excessive obstetrical intervention (Sacks & Donnenfeld, 1984). Childbirth itself is an important event to them and they want to experience it fully (Nelson, 1986, 1983).

Choices and Outcomes

Theoretically at least, modern couples can choose a childbirth that is based on any one of the three models or on some combination of the three. Does choosing one model over the others make a difference in how parents and baby emerge from the experience?

Regardless of the type of childbirth chosen, preparation makes a difference. Women who prepare for birth by learning about and considering their options ahead of time are less anxious and depressed during and after the pregnancy. Lessened anxiety reduces the length and painfulness of labor (May & Mahlmeister, 1990; Mercer, 1986; Lederman, 1984). However, the particular choices a woman makes in terms of who has control, who is present at the birth, and how conscious she is during labor are less important than that *she is able to get what she chooses* (May & Mahlmeister, 1990; Mercer, 1986; Lederman, 1984). Since many hospitals tend to apply the same procedures to everyone, regardless of personal choice, getting what one chooses may be problematic. Nelson (1986) found that *neither* the working-class mothers who favored active-passive procedures nor the middle-class mothers who favored guidance-cooperation procedures were completely satisfied with their Vermont hospital experience but that the latter group got what they wanted more often than the former did.

Being present at the birth seems to be the critical factor for men. Fathers who witness their child's birth, regardless of whether they attended prenatal preparation classes, have closer contact with their baby and show more infant-father interaction than fathers absent during the birth (Miller & Bowen, 1982; Peterson, Mehl, & Leiderman, 1979). As noted earlier, however, father participation in preparation and planning is one way men give much needed social support to their partners.

How do the three models of childbirth compare in terms of safety for mother and child? The prepregnancy condition of the mother and the level of prenatal care are the critical safety factors. For women in good health who have received good prenatal care, mutual participation home births and guidance-cooperation births in alternative birth centers are as safe for mother and baby as hospital births (*Family Planning Perspectives*, 1990; Rooks *et al.*, 1989; Hinds, Bergeisen, & Allen, 1985).

Cohort Comparison   Changes in Models of Childbirth

One way to learn more about the three models of childbirth is to see how they developed and changed historically. In this Cohort Comparison, we focus on twentieth-century changes involving our four cohort groups.

Almost all members of the New Century cohort (born 1910–1914) were born at home. In the early years of the twentieth century, all but the very poorest urban women (who went to charity hospitals) gave birth in their own homes. In the home, expectant mothers ready to deliver surrounded themselves with the people they felt could best help with the birth. For rural women and recent immigrants, female friends, neighbors, and a midwife were the most common choices, and the birth followed the guidelines of the mutual participation model. Middle-class women, particularly those in urban areas, frequently invited a physician into their homes to help with the birth, although friends and relatives might be present as well. Some physicians brought forceps and ether, tools characteristic of active-passive births with them, but the woman had considerable choice about whether they were used. The physician-attended birth might be mutual participation, active-passive, or guidance-cooperation, depending on the physician-

mother relationship and circumstances of the particular birth. Some fathers stayed around and assisted with the birth, others waited elsewhere; the choice was up to the parents. These women had considerable control over the social circumstances of the birth but felt considerable anxiety over the physical aspects. Both maternal and child deaths were common, and birth was often seen as a scary and treacherous event.

By the time the New Century women had their babies in the 1930s and 1940s, hospital births were much more common, especially in urban areas. By 1938, about half of all babies were born in hospitals. Hospital births increased because automobiles made hospitals more accessible, because many couples no longer lived close to relatives who could help with home births, and because hospital births came to be seen as fashionable, safe, and painless. In reality, hospital births were not particularly safe until after about 1940, but hospitals did fulfill the promise of less painful childbirth. In response to earlier, women-led campaigns, many hospitals routinely used drugs that both anesthetized women and made them forget everything about the birth.

When women decided to give birth in hospitals, they gave up most of their control

over social childbirth and submitted themselves to increasingly elaborate hospital routines. By the 1950s and 1960s when members of the Depression cohort were having their children, virtually all urban births and more than 80 percent of the rural births were hospital births. Most involved the extensive intervention typical of the active-passive model; the use of drugs, the practice of strapping the woman into position with her legs up, and the presence of monitoring and feeding machines became common. Authors of one book on the history of childbirth describe the expectant woman of the 1940s, the 1950s, and the 1960s like this:

> She was isolated during birth from family and friends, and even from other women having the same experiences. She had to think of herself instrumentally, not as a woman feeling love and fear or sharing in a creative event, but as a body-machine being manipulated by others for her ultimate welfare. (Wertz & Wertz, 1989, p. 173)

Fathers, meanwhile, were relegated to hospital waiting rooms, not allowed to be present at nor to participate in the birth of their child.

Some women in the 1950s and 1960s protested

these practices and promoted the preparation and relaxation techniques of European doctors such as Grantly Dick-Read, author of *Childbirth without Fear*, and Ferdinand Lamaze, developer of breathing and coaching techniques. Hospitals did not change their practices very much, however, until the 1970s and 1980s when the Baby Boomers started having their babies. During these decades, many hospitals began to incorporate childbirth practices more compatible with the guidance-cooperation model. In contrast to their own fathers, men of the Baby Boom cohort could stay with their wives during labor and delivery and hold their new son or daughter within minutes of birth. Unlike their own mothers, female Baby Boomers could remain "awake" for the birth of their babies, use the breathing techniques learned in prenatal classes, and make some decisions about drug administration.

If the past is any guide, members of the Baby Bust cohort will also face their share of controversy and fads as they begin their childbearing years. Will birthing centers managed by nurse-midwives become routine? Will obstetricians be driven out of their practices by high insurance rates? What new forms of technology will enter the delivery room and what effect will they have on the birth experience? Will this cohort campaign for more home births? more painkillers? more decision-making power? These are just a few of questions that might arise.

Sources: Wertz & Wertz, 1989; Leavitt, 1986; Rothman, 1982.

Alternative Choice

Parenthood through Adoption

Pregnancy and childbirth are one route to parenthood; adoption is another. Adoption is an alternative choice for two of the groups discussed in this chapter. A small proportion of unmarried women with unplanned pregnancies bypass both abortion and parenthood by choosing to put their babies up for adoption. And many involuntarily childless couples fulfill their dreams of parenthood by adopting a child.

In this alternative choice section, we focus on **nonrelative adoptions**, adoptions in which the adopted child and the adoptive parents have no prior biological or family ties. Keep in mind, though, that about half of all adoptions are "relative adoptions," adoptions in which the adopted child and adoptive parent have some kind of preexisting family tie. The most usual type of relative adoption occurs when a stepfather adopts the biological children of his wife in a remarriage situation; this type of adoption will be dealt with in Chapter 15.

Nonrelative adoption
a legal procedure through which adults with no prior biological or family ties to a child become the parents of that child.

Sources of Adoptive Children

For a nonrelated adoption to take place, prospective parents have to locate a child to adopt. They have four major routes to adoption: a public agency; a private, nonprofit agency; a private, for-profit agency; or an independent entrepreneur.

Public adoption agencies are funded by the state and staffed by social workers who are state employees. Most of the children available for adoption through public agencies today are children whose biological parents abandoned, neglected, or abused them. When such parental mistreatment cannot be stopped through long-term social work intervention, the parental rights of the biological parents are terminated and their children become eligible for adoption by other families. Some of these children are adopted by relatives; some are adopted by the foster parents with whom they have been living. Many, however, remain in the foster care system as children of the state awaiting adoption (Kadushin & Martin, 1988, Chapter 9).

Potential adoptive parents who want to adopt an older child, a sibling group, or a child with special physical and emotional needs are well-served by public adoption agencies. Couples who enjoy the challenge of a large family made up of children from different backgrounds with different needs, older couples whose children (if any) are grown, and single people are frequent adopters of such children.

Most infertile married couples, however, prefer to start their parenthood experience with a single, healthy, newborn child. Discouraged by the long waiting period (three to five years) for the type of child they want and the elaborate screening procedures of public agencies, they

Adoption is an alternative way of beginning parenthood. About half of all adoptions are nonrelative adoptions in which the child and adoptive parents have no biological or family ties.

often turn to private agencies. Private adoption agencies and independent entrepreneurs are more likely to specialize in infant adoption. Some private adoption agencies are nonprofit, charitable organizations associated with a particular religion or ethnic group. Others specialize in children from a particular country (for example, Korea or Romania). Adoptable babies are obtained from pregnant teenagers staying in group homes run by the organization or from overseas sources. Except for their specialization, nonprofit, private adoption agencies operate in much the same way as public agencies. Adopting parents are subject to screening and pay a small fee for agency services but have no financial or personal contact with the biological mother.

The two other major routes to adoption—for-profit, private agencies and independent entrepreneurs (typically lawyers or doctors who arrange adoptions occasionally but not as a full-time business)— are more aggressive than other agencies in seeking out adoptable babies. Both typically expect the adoptive parents to pay at least some of the expenses of the biological mother during pregnancy and childbirth.

For-profit, private agencies and independent entrepreneurs encourage pregnant teenagers to choose adoption over abortions or single motherhood by promising them financial support during the pregnancy, by giving them some choice in selecting adoptive parents, and by appealing to them to consider "what's best for your baby." They promise adoptive parents a shorter waiting period than the traditional agencies do and offer a chance to select and sometimes meet the biological mother. These for-profit adoption alternatives may provide the types of counseling and screening done by traditional adoption agencies, but they do not always do so. Some operate strictly in accordance with state law, but others engage in practices that are on the borderline legally or that are clearly illegal (Kadushin & Martin, 1988, p. 608). In short, adoptions done through independent entrepreneurs or for-profit agencies are frequently faster, more open (in the sense of biological and adoptive parents knowing about one another), and involve less scrutiny than traditional agency adoptions. However, they are also more expensive and riskier, sometimes failing to protect the rights of either the biological mother or the adoptive parents.

Adoption Outcomes

Most adoptions, regardless of how they are arranged, are successful in terms of parents and children remaining together and adapting satisfactorily as a family. A summary of all adoption outcome studies done between 1924 and 1977 found that 66 percent of the adoptions were "unequivocally successful," 18 percent were of "intermediate success," and 16 percent were "unsuccessful" (Kadushin & Martin, 1988, Table 9.5). Adoptions arranged by traditional agencies had a somewhat lower failure rate (15 percent) than independent adoptions (25 percent) (Kadushin & Martin, 1988, p. 619).

Adoptions that work out satisfactorily benefit adoptive parents, adopted children, and birth mothers. In a nationwide interview study, Christine Bachrach (1983) found that *almost half* the married women over 30 who had never borne a child of their own because of sterility had become parents through adoption. A smaller scale study of similar women found that, despite the public stigma associated with adoption, the adoptive mothers were personally very pleased with their decision to adopt (Miall, 1987). Children who are adopted are economically better off than children raised by never-married mothers, a fact that presumably affects their educational and long-term future (Bachrach, 1986). Compared with teenagers who keep their babies, those who put their babies up for adoption are more likely to finish high school and less likely to be poor in later years (Bachrach, 1986). In short, adoption has a profound and beneficial impact on those it touches.

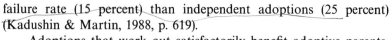

Summary

Encouraged by a pronatalist culture and by expectations about the emotional satisfaction children can bring, most adults in the United States decide to become parents. Although an increasing proportion of pregnancies and births are planned, about 40 percent of all births each year are to parents who did not intend the birth at the time of conception. In deciding when and if to have a child, couples generally consider alternative commitments, their financial stability, their relationship stability, and the attitudes of the friends and relatives closest to them. A small number of couples, after considering their other commitments and after postponing parenthood for a number of years, go against the tide and decide to remain voluntarily childless.

Pregnancy is both physical (for the prospective mother) and social (for both parents). During physical pregnancy, the woman's body changes to nurture and carry a developing fetus. The couple relationship is vulnerable to ups and downs during pregnancy: mixed feelings and anxieties during early pregnancy, differential experiences and often a communications gap in middle pregnancy, and special closeness in late pregnancy. Expressive and instrumental support of the expectant mother by the expectant father generally increases in late pregnancy and has important effects on her well-being. Pregnancy has no significant effect on overall marital satisfaction, however: it neither improves weak marriages nor weakens strong ones.

Ten to 20 percent of pregnancies end in miscarriages and bring significant emotional trauma to parents who have become attached to the fetus. Infertility causes significant emotional trauma. However, its causes are now discoverable in about 90 percent of the cases and are treatable in about half. Inadequate prenatal care, with subsequent prematurity or infant death, remains a problem for teenagers, the less educated, the unmarried, and certain racial minorities.

Childbirth is also both physical and social. There are three major models of social childbirth: mutual participation, active-passive, and guidance-cooperation. The guidance-cooperation model, emphasizing preparation for childbirth and a relationship between a cooperative birthgiving woman, her helping partner, and a guiding hospital team, seems to be the most popular today, particularly among middle-class women. However, the increasing use of Cesarean sections indicates that the active-passive model is still strong as well. A small minority favors home births and the mutual participation model. Preparing for childbirth and being able to have the kind of childbirth one wants are important for women's wellbeing before and after childbirth. The father's relationship with the infant is enhanced if he is present at the birth.

Adoption is an alternative route to parenthood. Public adoption agencies, non-profit private agencies, for-profit private agencies, and individual entrepreneurs are the major routes to adoptive parenthood. The type of child available, the cost, the amount of screening, and the openness of the adoption varies according to which route is used. Most adoptions work out well for adoptive parents, adoptive children, and biological mothers.

CHAPTER 12

PARENTS AND CHILDREN

1. Has good manners.
2. Tries hard to succeed.
3. Is honest.
4. Is neat and clean.
5. Has good sense and sound judgement.
6. Has self-control.
7. Acts like a boy (if male) or like a girl (if female) should.
8. Gets along well with other children.
9. Obeys parents well.
10. Is responsible.
11. Is considerate of others.
12. Is interested in how and why things happen.
13. Is a good student.

A. All of the qualities listed may be important to you but which *three* of them do you consider to be the *most* desirable for an 8-year-old child to have? _____ _____ _____

B. Of these three, which *one* do you consider the most desirable of all? _____

C. Which *three* of the qualities listed do you consider to be the *least* important for an 8-year-old child to have? _____ _____ _____

D. Of these three, which do you consider the *least* important? _____

Scoring: Give a 5 to the quality you selected in Question B.
Give a 4 to the two other qualities selected in Question A.
Give a 3 to the 7 qualities not used as answers to any of the questions.
Give a 2 to the two qualities selected in Question C which were not selected for Question D.
Give a 1 to the quality selected in Question D.

Compare your personal answers for good manners, obedience, good judgment, and responsibility (or, better yet, class answers averaged together) to the national results for different parent groups found on Table 12–1.

How far we all come. How far we all come away from our-selves. So far, so much between, you can never go home again. You can go home, it's good to go home, but you never really get all the way home again in your life. . . . Just one way you do get back home. You have a boy or girl of your own and now and then you remember, and you know how they feel, and it's almost the same as if you were your own self again, as young as you could remember. (Writer James Agee in his novel *A Death in the Family*, 1957, pp. 93–94)

My children cause me the most exquisite suffering of which I have any experience. It is the suffering of ambivalence: the murderous alternation between bitter resentment and raw-edged nerves, and blissful gratification and tenderness. (Jour-nal entry by poet Adrienne Rich, 1976, p. 21, at a time when she was the mother of three boys under the age of seven.)

The novelist and the poet quoted above use more elegant lan-guage about parenthood than most social scientists (or most parents!) might. But the high expectations and profound ambivalence these writers express about parent-child relationships correspond well with what social scientists have discovered. Parenthood is both highly frus-trating and highly satisfying; the parent-child relationship, one of the most intense intimate relationships, has the potential for both great closeness and great bitterness and resentment.

Chapter 12 deals with what social scientists know about parent-child relationships. Although there will be occasional references to sin-gle, never-married parents in this chapter, the focus will be on married couples and their children. The special concerns of divorced parents and of stepparents will be dealt with in the chapters on divorce and remarriage.

The chapter begins with a short discussion of the broad social con-text of modern, Western parenthood and how what parents expect from children and what society expects of parents have changed over time. Next, we discuss how parenthood complicates the parents' lives by describing the changes in the division of family work, changes in the marital relationship, and the problems of balancing multiple roles that occur when husbands and wives become mothers and fathers. The last major section of the chapter concerns how parental choices about child care and child treatment affect children. In addition to discussing the several typical patterns of childrearing and their outcomes, the sec-tion includes a discussion of parents who abuse their children. Finally, an Alternative Situation section describes the special challenges facing parents with disabled children.

PARENTHOOD IN A CHANGING WORLD

Bringing up children is, in many ways, a very private activity in which parents have many choices. Like other activities of family life, however, parenthood is shaped by the social context in which it occurs. What parents expect their children to be like, what parents expect of themselves and what others expect of parents are all influenced by factors outside the family. These factors change over time and vary from society to society.

What Parents Expect from Children

As noted in Chapter 11, adults in modern societies expect children to be cute, sweet, and loving, and feel that childrearing will bring emotional satisfaction, stimulation, and fun into their lives (LeMasters & DeFrain, 1983; Hoffman & Manis, 1979). Potential parents envision children both as symbols of marital love and as givers and recipients of a different, but equally special, kind of affection (Hoffman & Manis, 1979). At the same time, most people in the United States today realize that children are both expensive and economically dependent for many years (Neal, Groat, & Wicks, 1989; Bulatao, 1981).

These expectations about children are somewhat different from those prevalent one hundred years ago. Then, parents expected their daughters to care for younger children, help with housework, or get a paid job outside the home in a mill or another household as soon as they were able. They expected their sons to work on the farm, in the family business, or for another adult. Children were economic burdens

12 Parents and Children

Enduring cultural image of motherhood
an image of motherhood that emphasizes that motherhood is a full-time occupation and that mothers sacrifice all for their children.

Enduring cultural image of fatherhood
an image of fatherhood that emphasizes the breadwinning role and the non-involvement of the father in day-to-day nurturance of children.

Emerging cultural image of motherhood
an image of motherhood emphasizing that the ideal mother is very dedicated to her children but also very involved in a full-time occupation.

Emerging cultural image of fatherhood
an image of fatherhood emphasizing that fathers should be actively involved in the day-to-day care and nurturance of children as well as dedicated to a full-time occupation.

for the first few years of their lives but were expected to "pay off" by the time they were young teenagers (Zelizer, 1985). Although children might also provide emotional satisfaction for their parents, *their major value was economic*—they helped the family survive.

As we have noted, parents have very different ideas today. One way to succinctly summarize the changes in parental expectations is to consider the "ideal adoptive child" in the 1890s and the 1990s. In the 1890s, a strong teenage boy capable of doing physical labor for the family was the adoptive child most in demand. Today, the "ideal adoptive child" is an infant girl, the type of child felt to have maximum potential for emotional satisfaction and affection (Zelizer, 1985, Chapter 6).

What Society Expects from Parents

Modern parents expect a lot from their children but even more from themselves. Their expectations about themselves as parents are shaped by strong cultural images of motherhood, of fatherhood, and of the absolute importance of early childhood experiences.

Parents today are influenced by both enduring and emerging cultural images of motherhood and fatherhood (Thompson & Walker, 1989). These cultural images are descriptions of ideal mothers and fathers presented in magazines, books, television programs, and advertising that help shape the standards parents use to judge themselves. The enduring images became prominent in the United States during the nineteenth century and were described in the "Separate Spheres" section of Chapter 9: the **enduring cultural image of motherhood** features a full-time mother who cheerfully and naturally sacrifices all for her children; the **enduring cultural image of fatherhood** pictures a man uninvolved in the day-to-day nurturance of children who provides the income necessary for mother and children to have a comfortable life. The newer **emerging cultural image of motherhood** portrays the ideal modern mother as a "superwoman" who has added full-time employment to her household and child care responsibilities. The **emerging cultural image of fatherhood** features a "new" father who is intimately and actively involved with his children on a day-to-day basis, while maintaining his chief breadwinner role (Thompson & Walker, 1989; LaRossa, 1988).

In actuality, both the enduring and the emerging cultural images of parenthood are historically recent and restricted only to certain cultures (Kagan, 1986; Epstein, 1982). The images are closely tied to a firmly held belief about the importance of parental behavior during the child's early years. This belief asserts that "the experiences of the infant in the family set the course of the child's development, and once these original qualities are established they are difficult to change" (Kagan, 1986, p. 394). With increasing emphasis on the importance of early childhood, the scope of parental responsibility has broadened as well. From colonial times until into the nineteenth century, parents were held responsible only for the moral and vocational development of their children (Geboy, 1981); there was little concern for the psychological and emotional aspects of child development. Twentieth-century images and beliefs about parenthood continue to emphasize the moral guidance role of parents but also hold parents responsible for the psychological, emotional, and social well-being of their children. The Cohort Comparison "Bedtime according to Childrearing Experts" illustrates some of these trends by focusing on advice given by the authors of four twentieth-century childrearing manuals about handling bedtime for small children.

Cohort Comparison   Bedtime according to Childrearing Experts

Infant care and childrearing manuals have existed in the United States since at least the 1820s (Sunley, 1955). In the early years, advice books were usually written by clergymen; later, pediatricians, psychologists, and writers for women's magazines began to contribute their advice as well. Until about the 1940s, well-educated, urban, middle-class mothers were the major consumers of such books; today, a majority of all mothers read at least one book on how to care for children, although the well-educated continue to consult such books most often (Clarke-Stewart, 1978).

In this cohort comparison, we look at the advice experts have given parents about children and bedtime throughout the twentieth century. Of course, such books are not necessarily an accurate measure of what parents actually did. They do, how-

ever, reflect changing ways of viewing both childhood and parenthood.

Childrearing and infant care manuals written early in the twentieth century emphasized the importance of controlling the child's impulsive nature and of establishing good habits very early in life (Wolfenstein, 1955). Some mothers of New Century cohort children, for example, might have read this advice from *The Mother's Book* about putting their children to bed:

At night it [the child] should be undressed early, not later than half past five, bathed, rubbed, dressed in light, warm night-clothing, made perfectly comfortable, and then fed and put down in a darkened room to go to sleep by itself.

If this habit is begun at the very beginning of the

baby's life, it will never rebel because it will never know any other way of going to sleep; but if it is kept up till it is overtired, and played with till it is wakeful, and then put down alone, a hard cry will undoubtedly result, and perhaps a struggle begin which it will take years to settle. It is a temptation to a mother to rock her baby to sleep and sing to it, and the baby enjoys it quite as much as the mother. Yet, if she is truly unselfish she will deny herself and the baby, and by starting it right she will lay foundations for after life which will be invaluable. (Burrell, 1909, p. 165)

By the time the Depression cohort was born in the 1930s, some of the new ideas of psychologists had begun to enter childrearing advice

Cohort Comparison
Bedtime according to Childrearing Experts (cont'd)

books. Ideas about bedtime, though, remained much the same. This selection is from a 1935 book entitled *Growing Superior Children*.

Sleep reproduces the conditions of intrauterine life, its warmth, protection, and darkness. In fact, sleep becomes a refuge, a sort of return to the fetal situation, whenever the baby is disturbed. . . . The baby must be educated to sleep and be taught not to cry. . . . From the outset he should be accustomed to being put into his crib while awake and falling asleep of his own accord. Rocking and other means of soothing the baby to sleep are harmful. Training him to sleep amidst the customary sounds of the household cultivates independence of any special environment for sleep. (Kugelmass, 1935, pp. 72–73)

Parents of the Baby Boom cohort, as well as the parents who followed them, read the advice of pediatrician Dr. Benjamin Spock more often than any other source of information. By the time Dr. Spock wrote his famous childrearing manuals, parenthood had come to be seen as a "fun" activity (Wolfenstein,

1955). Note that Spock (1957) still stresses the importance of parents setting the rules and the value of a regular routine, but he also sees bedtime as an occasion for parents and children to spend time together:

Remember that [bedtime] is delicious and inviting to the tired child if you don't turn it into an unpleasant duty. Have an air of cheerful certainty about it. Expect him to turn in at the hour you decide as surely as you expect him to breathe. . . . Small children are comforted by having a certain amount of ritual about going to bed. For example, the dolly is put in her bed and tucked in. Then the teddy bear is put in the child's bed. Then the child is tucked in and kissed. Then the mother pulls down the shade or puts out the light. Try not to rush going to bed, no matter how much of a hurry you are in. (On the other hand, it isn't wise to let the child keep lengthening the rituals). (pp. 316–317)

While Dr. Spock continued to influence parents of the Baby Bust children, there were many other advice-givers as well. One of the best known is Dr. T. Berry Brazelton, who began writing articles on child care for *Redbook* magazine in the early 1970s

and who frequently appears on television programs about child care. Note how Brazelton (1987) acknowledges individual differences in children and also the special needs of parents:

QUESTION: My two-year-old wakes at six, naps in the afternoon for one hour and doesn't fall asleep until ten, even when I put her to bed at eight. What can I do?

DR. BRAZELTON: Grab all the sleep you can whenever she does. Many active children don't seem to need sleep. But their parents and sitters do. I'd urge you to set up very firm bedtime limits. Insist on a naptime routine, as a break for you. If she doesn't want to sleep, that's her problem, but she has to be away from stimulation. At night, I'd institute a very definite soothing routine before eight o'clock. Then, expect her to go to her room and crib. Whether she sleeps or not isn't the question. Both of you need space from each other. (pp. 42–43)

Like the cultural images of parenthood, this belief about the importance of early childhood and the crucial role of parents is promoted through the mass media. How often have you read a newspaper article attributing some social problem (for example, drugs, illiteracy, or crime) to "inadequate parenting" or heard a television talk show expert trace adult feelings and behavior back to early childhood experiences? This strong belief in the power of parents is also a guiding premise for much psychological research on child development (Kagan, 1986, 1984). Like the images of parenthood, this assumption about the importance of parental behavior in early childhood is a rather recent one, is not widely held cross-culturally, and has only limited scientific support (Kagan, 1986; Skolnick, 1983).

The Social Context of Modern Parenthood

Industrialized Western societies generally, but especially the United States, set high standards for parents but offer mothers and fathers little help or reinforcement. Several commentators (Greer, 1984; Pogrebrin, 1983; Benedict, 1938) have pointed out how modern societies segregate children (and, thus, those adults who care for them) from the flow of community life. For example, Germaine Greer (1984) writes:

> The scale and speed of our world is all anti-child; children cannot be allowed to roam the streets, but must run a terrifying gauntlet to get to the prime locus of their segregation, school. They cannot open doors or windows, cannot see on top of counters, are stifled and trampled in crowds, hushed when they speak or cry before strangers, apologized for by harassed mothers condemned to share their ostracized condition. (pp. 3–4)

Even those who do not share the opinion that the United States is fundamentally "anti-child" point to the difficulties modern parents have in acquiring, coordinating, and supervising the resources needed to rear their children successfully and lament the small amount of support they receive from national policies and programs (Grubb & Lazerson, 1988; Sidel, 1986; Keniston, 1977). For example, U.S. parents do not routinely have access to child-rearing allowances, national health insurance, parental leave, or government-subsidized child care, benefits common in most European countries (Grubb & Lazerson, 1988; Sidel, 1986; Keniston, 1977).

The specialized nature of modern society, combined with high expectations about parents and children, means that parents today depend on many other people—teachers, pediatricians, coaches, babysitters— to help them with their children. All these people have a "piece" of their child, but only parents are likely to know the whole child and only parents will be held responsible for how the child turns out. Sociologist Kenneth Keniston (1977) sees the modern parental role as one of a "weakened executive" coordinating the services of many experts but lacking true authority over them. Keniston (1977) explains:

> ... as an executive, the parent labors under enormous restrictions. Ideally, an executive has firm authority and power to influence or determine the decisions of those whose work needs coordination. Today's parents have little authority over those others with whom they share the task of raising their children. ... As a result, the parent today is usually a coordinator without voice or authority, a maestro trying to conduct an orchestra of players who have never met and who play from a multitude of different scores, each in a notation the conductor cannot read. (p. 18)

In short, modern parents operate in a social context that, when compared to other times and other places, encourages them to expect great emotional satisfaction from their children and to accept great responsibilities for their children. These parents live in a society that encourages childbirth but offers little support for children or parents. They must depend on others to help them rear their children but often have little control over these others. How do they cope? Do the high expectations lead to high satisfaction or to bitter disappointment? In such a social context, how do children change their parents and how do parents affect their children?

HOW CHILDREN CHANGE THEIR PARENTS

Compared to nonparents and to parents whose children no longer live at home, *parents with children in the home are less happy and satisfied with life, more often worried and stressed, and less satisfied with their marriages* (Umberson & Gove, 1989; White, Booth, & Edwards, 1986; Glenn & McLanahan, 1982; Houseknecht, 1979). At the same time, *parents feel that their lives have more meaning than nonparents do, are glad they became parents and would do it over again, and derive great satisfaction and fulfillment from their parental role* (Umberson & Gove, 1989; Goetting, 1986). Couples looking back over 50 years of marriage say that the childbearing years were both the most satisfying *and* the least satisfying (Sporakowski & Hughston, 1978). Children clearly affect their parents in a variety of seemingly contradictory ways. Let us look at this more closely by observing how peoples' lives change when they become parents.

Changes in Family Work

Think back to our discussion of types of family work in Chapter 9. Children add two new categories of people production work (child care and socialization); create much more household production work (more laundry, more shopping, more cleanup, more things to maintain); and necessitate either more money production work or adjustment to a somewhat lower economic standard of living. Couples have to rethink the division of labor within their household after they have their first child. Who does all the additional work that a child requires? How is the remaining work reallocated? How do these changes affect parents?

Studies comparing couples' division of labor before and after they have their first child show that most couples move in the direction of **traditionalization**—the division of family work becomes more gender-specialized and more in line with traditional patterns (Cowan *et al.*, 1985; Goldberg, Michaels, & Lamb, 1985; LaRossa & LaRossa, 1981). New mothers assume almost all of the at-home child care, do even more of the household work than they did before the baby was born, and often temporarily cut back on labor force participation. New fathers continue or add to their labor force work, perform a few of the added child care tasks, and cut back on the proportion of household work they do (Cowan *et al.*, 1985). New parents end up with a division of labor that is more gender-separate than what they had before the child was born, more gender-separate than what nonparents have, and more gender-separate than they expected it to be (Cowan *et al.*, 1985). Although some of the details of this division of labor change as the children grow older, the basic "dual-helpers" (women responsible for majority of home and child care tasks with some help from men; men responsible for bringing in money with some help from women) pattern set in the first months of parenthood persists in most families until the children leave home.

The increase in, and traditionalization of, family work that begins when the first child is born results in longer work weeks for both parents, but especially for the mother. Figure 12–1 (on page 432) illustrates how the presence of children in the home affects the parents' work weeks. Note especially the long work week associated with caring for preschool children and the differences between the husband's and wife's work weeks.

Most couples report that they argue more after they have children than they did before and that many of the arguments are about "who

Traditionalization
the tendency for the family division of labor to become more gender-specialized and more traditional after the birth of the first child.

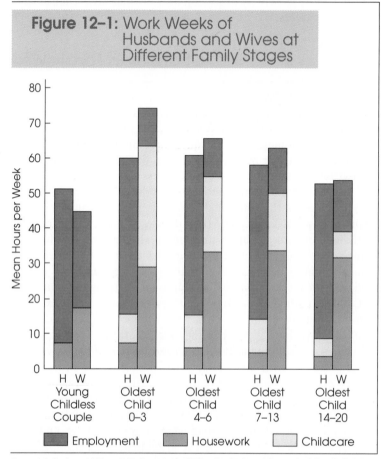

Figure 12–1: Work Weeks of Husbands and Wives at Different Family Stages

Notice how much more time wives spend on housework and child care during the years when they have children at home and the especially dramatic increase in time spent from no children to first child (oldest child, 0–3). Data are from a 1976 study.

Rexroat & Shehan 1987, p. 745. Copyright 1987 by the National Council on Family Relations, 3989 Central Ave. N.E., Suite #550, Minneapolis, MN 55421. Reprinted by permission.

does what" (Belsky & Rovine, 1990; Cowan *et al.*, 1985). Wives are particularly sensitive to increases in the amount of conflict. Their perception of increased conflict, when combined with their longer work week, makes wives in the "traditionalized" work arrangements less satisfied with their marriages (White, Booth, & Edwards, 1986; Cowan *et al.*, 1985). Meanwhile, traditionalization tends to *increase* the marital happiness of men (White, Booth, & Edwards, 1986). Fathers are more dissatisfied with their marriages and more stressed when their family division of labor does *not* "traditionalize," when they have to do more child care and household work than their counterparts in other families (Hawkins & Belsky, 1989; Crouter *et al.*, 1987). Like the mothers in traditionalized households, fathers in nontraditionalized households feel unduly burdened and less satisfied with their marriage as a result.

Changes in Time and Privacy

Traditionalization does not fully explain why parents are less satisfied with their marital relationships and with their lives than nonparents. A second factor is how parenthood changes the availability of time and privacy. New parents often express their frustrations about their increased work demands and the post-child division of labor by referring to "time disruptions," "time pressures," or the "scarcity of time" (Worthington & Buston, 1986; LaRossa & LaRossa, 1981). What they mean is that fulfilling their multiple roles adequately requires much more time after they became parents than it did before—they have less unobligated time, leaving them with the feeling that time itself is in short supply (LaRossa, 1983).

In fact, parents caring for a very young child may have no "off-duty" time at all. Sociologist Ralph LaRossa (1986) explains that, like a hospital, a home with a new baby becomes a **continuous coverage system**, offering round-the-clock care:

> ... the parents of a newborn must care for their child regardless of the time of the day, the day of the week, or the time of the year. They must, in other words, *always* be accessible to their baby. Even if they hire a baby-sitter they are still "on call," as evidenced by the fact that they will leave a phone number where they can be reached. If the baby is sleeping, they might be able to attend temporarily to their own needs—get in some private time—but when the baby signals for help (typically by crying), they or their representative—again the baby-sitter—must respond in much the same way as the nurses who are on duty, but perhaps resting, must respond to a patient whose emergency light is blinking. (pp. 90–91)

Continuous coverage system
a situation, such as a hospital or a home with small children, in which someone must be "on call" at all times.

The fact that one parent must continually be "on-call" clearly cuts into and changes the time that parents spend with one another.

Romantic, intimate time together is especially affected. Not unexpectedly, parents are sexually intimate less often than they were before becoming parents (Reamy & White, 1987). Although husbands and wives continue to spend time with one another after becoming parents, most of their shared time is spent in practical, child-oriented tasks (MacDermid, Huston, & McHale, 1990). Because of these rather predictable, parenthood-precipitated changes away from romance and towards partnership, those who entered marriage with the highest romantic expectations experience the most severe decline in marital satisfaction after children are born (Belsky & Rovine, 1990).

Becoming a parent also means giving up both couple and personal privacy. The privacy issue affects mothers more than fathers and becomes especially acute when a nonemployed mother stays at home with several preschool children. Such mothers, feeling that they can never be alone, are more likely than other parents to report that their children are "burdensome" to them and cause them difficulty (Goldsteen & Ross, 1989; Pittman, Wright, & Lloyd, 1989).

As children get older, they require fewer "on-call" hours from their parents and learn to respect the needs of their parents for personal space and privacy (and, indeed, demand such space for themselves). Nonetheless, a household with children will never offer as much free time or privacy as a household without them. This is yet another reason that parents often feel more stress than nonparents.

Changes in Roles

First-time parenthood requires new mothers and fathers to learn an entirely new adult role and to balance this new role with the other adult roles of marriage partner and worker. The fact that modern parenthood is an especially demanding role makes these learning and balancing tasks difficult and stressful. At the same time, successful balancing of several difficult roles provides a source of great satisfaction.

Learning the Parenthood Role

Parenthood is an unusually difficult adult role that differs from other roles in a number of ways. While most adult roles have a training or engagement period, people are thrust into parenthood roles all at once on a twenty-four hour basis without training (Rossi, 1968). Born into small families of closely spaced children, most of the new parents of the 1990s lacked the opportunity to "practice" infant care skills on younger brothers and sisters. Of course, many new parents receive help and instruction from relatives and friends during the first weeks of parenthood (Belsky & Rovine, 1984). Furthermore, modern parents have much more written information about infant care and childrearing available to them than their predecessors did (Geboy, 1981; Clarke-Stewart, 1978). Still, anxieties about incompetence and worries about "doing the right thing" are very common in parents (McKim, 1987; Ventura, 1987).

New parents can expect many ups and downs in self-esteem and feelings of competence as their children develop. For example, mothers caring for their first newborn give themselves rather low self-evaluations when the infant is one month old—they worry that they lack the skills to care for their child properly and are frustrated by the baby's crying, feeding, and sleeping problems. By the end of the child's first year, however, these same mothers have recovered their self-esteem and evaluate themselves highly (Reilly, Entwisle, & Doering, 1987). The mother quoted here reflects the subtle change that occurs as a new parent becomes an experienced parent:

> . . . on the whole I suppose I'm fairly confident. I just feel as though I've been looking after him for years now. Strange. And I feel I know him very well, I know his habits. (quoted in Oakley, 1980, p. 246)

Parents are likely to experience these lows and highs over and over again because children at different developmental stages present different challenges. A parent who has successfully learned how to calm a screaming infant will not necessarily know how to handle a two-year-old's temper tantrum, negotiate an eight-year-old's bedtime, or deal with a teenager bored with school. This up and down nature of parenthood might well explain how parents can say that parenthood is both very stressful and very satisfying. The stress comes from continually being placed in new situations with inadequate skills; the satisfaction comes from learning new skills and seeing their good results.

Adults who become parents do not give up their other adult roles; they continue to be marriage partners, lovers, and workers. How does parenthood affect their self-perceptions and their other adult roles? One common research technique for assessing self-perceptions is to instruct a person to divide a circle or "pie," representing the self, into parts with the size of each part corresponding to the perceived importance of each role. In research using this technique, men increase the "worker" part of the pie as they move from being expectant fathers to being fathers of a six-month-old child to being fathers of an eighteen-month-old child. Women, meanwhile, decrease the "worker" part of the pie. Both parents enlarge the "parent" part of the pie after a child is born, but mothers enlarge it much more than fathers do. Both husbands and wives, but especially wives, reduce the size of the pie portions labeled "partner" and "lover" after they have a child (Cowan et al., 1985).

Because most new parents continue to be marital partners and employees as well as mothers and fathers, they face potential role conflict and its accompanying stresses. **Role conflict** refers to situations in which fulfilling the demands of one role keeps one from fulfilling the demands of a second role. For example, if Frank's boss requests him to work overtime on the same night Frank has promised to attend his daughter's school play, Frank faces a role conflict: he cannot be both a perfect employee and a perfect father. In the sections that follow, we look first at parent-employee conflict and then at parent-spouse conflict.

Role conflict
a situation in which fulfilling the demands of one role keeps one from fulfilling the demands of a second role.

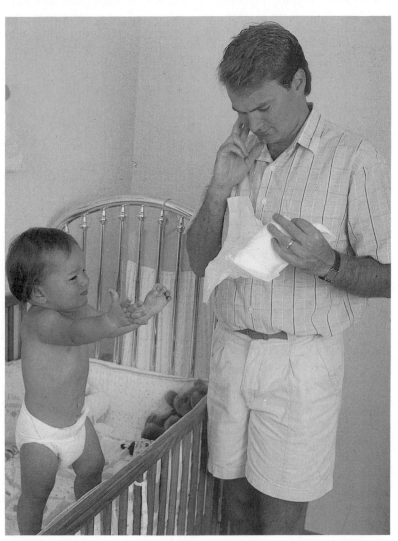

Parenthood is a continual learning experience.

Parent-Employee Conflicts

More than new parents in earlier generations, modern parents, especially mothers, face potential conflicts in trying to balance employment roles with parental roles. A very large proportion of mothers believe that parental care (preferably by the mother or by the father if she is not available) is best for preschool children (Mason & Kuhlthau, 1989; Hock, Gnezda, & McBride, 1984). Yet 56 percent of all mothers of preschoolers (including 51 percent of mothers of children under one year of age) and virtually all fathers of preschoolers are employed, typically full time. Are not conflict and stress inevitable when belief and behavior seem to contradict one another so directly?

Mothers (or fathers) who withdraw from employment to stay home and care for their infant are not immune from potential stress either. Remember that the emerging cultural images of motherhood and fatherhood described earlier in the chapter picture both fathers and mothers as fully involved parents *and* as full-time workers. Stay-at-home mothers are fulfilling the enduring cultural image of motherhood very well. However, since they are not employed, they fail to live up to the emerging cultural image of motherhood. Torn between two different cultural images of motherhood, they may suffer role strain. **Role strain** occurs when different people expect different behaviors within the same role. For example, a new mother whose friends accept the emerging cultural image of motherhood (care for children *and* be employed full time) and whose husband believes strongly in the enduring cultural image of motherhood (stay home with children full time) is likely to be affected by role strain. Consider the conflicting feelings of this mother who believes strongly that "good mothers" should stay at home but who receives different messages from others:

> Our fathers and mothers (who underwrote our higher education) remind us that *our* "careers won't wait forever" and we "didn't go to college for nothing." Our employers give us explicit policy on maternity leave .... Our husbands let us know that the mortgage is due and our bank balances are dropping ... some of our career-oriented, childless female friends see us as total and unredeemable idiots. (Triedman, 1989, p. 60)

Does this mean that new parents, and especially new mothers, inevitably suffer guilt, ambiguity, and stress regardless of the choices they make about employment and child care? Numerous articles in the popular press (for example, Berg, 1987; Davitz, 1984) with titles such as "The Guilt That Drives Working Mothers Crazy" maintain that guilt about both work and motherhood is extremely common today.

Role strain
a situation in which different people expect different behaviors within the same role.

In addition, some social science research shows that the "worry levels" of both working and nonworking mothers have increased with the growing number of mothers in the work force (McLanahan & Adams, 1989).

Systematic studies, however, show a good deal of *variation* in the amount of stress that employed mothers of preschoolers feel: some experience very little, some quite a lot (Tiedje *et al.*, 1990). Generally speaking, mothers who are able to arrange part-time employment experience less stress than those who work full time (Avioli, 1985; Pistrang, 1984; Thomson, 1980). For one thing, part-time workers find it easier to arrange acceptable substitute care for their children (often by the father) than do full-time workers. For white working wives, the amount of internal conflict is also influenced by their husbands' attitude toward their work—a supportive husband means less conflict (Avioli, 1985).

A number of studies find that the highest stress levels are found, not among employed mothers, but rather among *certain categories* of the nonemployed. Sociologists Karen Goldsteen and Catherine Ross (1989) found that nonemployed mothers of preschool children perceived their children to be more "burdensome" than did mothers who were employed—in large part because the nonemployed had a more difficult time being alone when they wanted to be. Stay-at-home mothers who were highly committed to their jobs before motherhood show more irritability and depression than other mothers, even though they feel they are doing what is best for their infant (Pistrang, 1984). Racial differences show up as well—black married mothers who stay home with their infants are more stressed than black working mothers and also more stressed than either employed or nonemployed white mothers (Avioli, 1985). These nonemployed black mothers, unable to find work, desire employment because of financial need and strong beliefs (stronger among blacks than among whites) that adult women should have a job.

Some fathers also experience work-parent conflicts and stress. Most often, their stresses are work-related—the pressure to work longer and harder because of the increased financial responsibility of parenthood (Ventura, 1987).

Parent-Spouse Conflict

Given the high expectations regarding both marital and parental roles in the United States, some conflict seems almost inevitable when spouses become parents. In *both* roles, people are expected to be emotionally supportive, interact frequently in meaningful ways, and provide practical help and companionship. Yet time and energy are limited. Further, the traditionalization accompanying new parenthood separates husband and wife into somewhat "different worlds"—the husband becomes more involved in the world of work outside the family and the wife becomes more involved in the day-to-day details of motherhood. Both move away from the world of their own intimate relationship.

Most couples handle the parent-spouse conflict by emphasizing the parent-child relationship and by downplaying certain aspects of the marital relationship during the years when children are at home. Married couples with children at home interact less often with one another (White, Booth, & Edwards, 1986) and offer one another less positive emotional support (Belsky, Lang, & Rovine, 1985) than do nonparents or parents without children at home. The orientation of the marital relationship also changes. When asked to characterize their relationship in terms of "romance," "friendship," and "partnership," couples put more emphasis on the "romance" aspect before they have children but on the "partnership" aspect afterwards (Belsky, Lang, & Rovine, 1985; Belsky, Spanier, & Rovine, 1983). The marital relationship does not disappear with parenthood but it does change in nature.

Changes in Parental Social Networks

While children weaken the marital relationship somewhat, they gradually tie their parents into larger social networks of relatives, neighbors, and friends. Parents with preschool children are especially likely to interact with and receive help from relatives, although support from neighbors and close friends is rather low at this stage. By the time children are school-age, their parents have more interactions and connections with neighbors, close friends, *and* relatives than do nonparents of the same age (Ishii-Kuntz & Seccombe, 1989).

Like so many things about parenthood, increased social ties to those outside the immediate nuclear family are mixed blessings. Sociologist Lucy Fischer (1983) found that the mother-daughter relationship became less strained and less ambiguous with the birth of a child but that ties between mother-in-law and daughter-in-law became more strained. Daughters (new mothers) regard advice from their mothers as "helpful," but deemed similar advice from mothers-in-law "interference." The availability of nearby relatives and helpful neighbors eases child-care dilemmas, but it sometimes creates more stress because parents often feel obligated to those who help (Goldsteen & Ross, 1989).

Research Limitations

The traditionalization of family work, the time pressures, the role conflicts, and the changes in outside-the-family relationships all help to explain the decline in marital satisfaction and the increase in stress that often accompany parenthood. Some of the differences between parents and nonparents reported in research findings, however, may show up because of the ways in which researchers design their studies and report their results. Here are some things to keep in mind if the findings discussed previously have concerned you:

1. Research summaries average all cases together. For example, a research finding that "marital conflict increases after couples become parents" is a general finding and masks the fact that some couples argue much more after the birth of a child, some argue a little more, some argue the same amount, and some argue less (Belsky & Rovine, 1990; Lewis, 1988).

2. Husbands and (especially) wives in the United States start off with such a high degree of marital satisfaction that, if their satisfaction level changes at all, downward is the only possible direction. Many of the changes that occur when couples become parents also occur, though at a somewhat slower rate, in couples who remain childless. Some researchers, in fact, argue that virtually *all* the changes attributed to parenthood—the reduced emphasis on romance, the increase in conflict, the decrease in affectionate, positive interaction— are common to all marriages over time (McHale & Huston, 1985; White & Booth, 1985a). For example, an overall decline in the frequency of sexual activity occurs in virtually all marriages over the first several years (Frank & Anderson, 1985; Greenblat, 1983).

3. The best predictor of how satisfying and strong a marriage will be after the birth of a baby is how strong and satisfying it was before the baby was born (Wallace & Gotlib, 1990; Belsky, 1985). That is, *in the usual case*, having a baby will not ruin a strong, satisfying marriage nor improve a weak, dissatisfying one.

4. Some of the differences between parents and nonparents emerge because parents, especially parents of very young children, stay in unhappy, stressful marriages longer than nonparents do. Childless parents who find themselves in an unsatisfactory marriage usually divorce rather quickly; parents with young children in a similar marriage will probably eventually divorce but delay it for several years. Thus, when large numbers of parents are compared to large numbers of nonparents, there are more unsatisfactory marriages among the parents, pulling down the average marital satisfaction of all parents (White, Booth, & Edwards, 1986).

5. Overall, social scientists have emphasized the stresses and problems of parenthood more than they have examined its

satisfactions and rewards. As we have noted above, parents do gain certain satisfactions from parenthood. But the satisfactions do not come automatically by simply having a child. Rather, the satisfactions of parenthood and the meaning that children add to life come as the result of successfully coping with the stresses and challenges that children bring.

HOW PARENTS AFFECT CHILDREN

Rearing children in the United States today, in contrast with many other times and places, is a highly private, parental responsibility, not a state, community, or extended family function. U.S. parents have a considerable amount of choice about which qualities to encourage in their children and about how to do so. At the same time, many factors that influence what children might become as adults are not under direct parental control. Parents do not choose a child's genetic characteristics, temperament, nor birth order in the family; neither do they determine their children's experiences in late adolescence and early adulthood. As noted earlier, parents have only limited control over the other adults who help them bring up their children. Neither can parents choose

Parents cannot control everything that might affect their children during their growing up years. This mother and her teenage daughter probably did not expect to be separated by a military conflict in the Persian Gulf.

what happens in the larger world—wars, economic changes, or natural disasters—during the years when their children are growing up. Finally, parents have only limited control over their own economic and social circumstances.

In short, the whole issue of how much impact parents have on children is highly complex. Here we will focus on aspects of child-rearing about which parents have some choice. We will look first at the qualities U.S. parents choose to instill in their children and why different parents make different choices in this regard. Then we will discuss variations in parent-child relationships along three dimensions known to be associated with socialization outcomes: attachment, support, and control.

Parental Choices about Child Qualities

U.S. children grow up in an industrially developed, changing, mobile, culturally diverse society. To fit into such a culture, children need to develop qualities of both conformity and self-direction. Because they will spend much of their lives as members of groups and organizations, they must learn how to get along well with many types of people and to be reasonably compliant with the desires and demands of superiors. Because they will be leaving their families and entering new situations for which few clear guidelines exist, they must also learn to make their own independent decisions based on their own private consciences. And, because the U.S. economy emphasizes intellectual skills more than simple physical strength, they must master the kinds of skills taught in school (Kagan, 1984).

Although there is general agreement that all these qualities are important, parents differ in which qualities they emphasize for their own children. One of the methods used to measure which qualities parents value most highly is the survey featured in the What Do You Think? questions for this chapter. The survey results show that parents who belong to the less dominant groups in society (for example, parents with less education, parents in highly supervised occupations, and racial minority group parents) generally emphasize qualities having to do with compliance and conformity such as obedience and good manners. Life experiences have taught them that success—or, at least, avoiding problems—comes from complying with authority and obeying the rules. Parents with more education and parents who work in jobs without very much supervision more often see the beneficial results of exercising their own judgment. Thus, they are more likely to emphasize qualities having to do with self-direction (for example, honesty and responsibility) in rearing their children (Alwin, 1989; Luster, Rhoades, & Haas, 1989).

Table 12–1 Ratings of Child Qualities by Parents with Differing Characteristics, 1980–1984

Parent Characteristics	Child Qualities*			
	Compliance Values		Self-Direction Values	
	Good Manners	Obedience	Good Judgment	Responsibility
Less than High School	3.30	3.54	3.26	3.16
High School Graduate	3.04	3.47	3.45	3.33
Some College	2.87	3.34	3.58	3.39
College Graduate	2.86	3.16	3.65	3.67
Black Protestant	3.40	3.76	3.20	3.05
Jewish	2.83	3.09	4.09	3.78

* The higher the score, the more valued the quality.

Source: Alwin, 1989, Tables A4 and A8.

Table 12–1 illustrates the general findings described above by showing some of the differences between parents with differing amounts of education. Black Protestant parents and Jewish parents are also featured on the table because each is distinctive: blacks in their emphasis on conformity and Jews (who overall are more highly educated and in higher status occupations) in their emphasis on self-direction (Alwin, 1989).

Attachment

Regardless of which qualities parents decide to instill in their child, they will be more successful at doing so if the child has developed a secure attachment to them (Kagan, 1984). **Attachment** is a special type of emotional bond between the infant and his or her primary caretakers. A baby who is attached to a caregiver chooses that person over others when distressed, is comforted more readily by that person than by others, and is less upset by strange objects or events when that person is nearby (Bretherton, 1985; Kagan, 1984).

Attachment normally develops over the first year of life. Babies are likely to develop the most secure attachments to caregivers who respond to their distress cries promptly, engage them in interaction and respond warmly to their smiles and cooing, and present them with a variety of sights and sounds (Belsky, 1990). As these caregivers feed,

Attachment
a special type of emotional bond between the infant and his or her primary caretakers such that the infant prefers these caretakers when distressed.

bathe, smile at, play with, and comfort the infant, he or she comes to associate pleasure and relief from discomfort with particular people and comes to prefer them in future distressful situations. Insecure attachment in the infant results when caregivers ignore or respond inconsistently to distress cries, when they are indifferent or nonresponsive to the infant's attempts at interaction, or when they are insensitive to the amount of visual and auditory stimulation the infant desires (Belsky, 1990).

How is attachment associated with socialization? Simply put, *a child who has established a secure attachment to a caregiver will be especially receptive to that person's attempts at socialization because the child wants approval and the continued security of the attachment relationship* (Kagan, 1984). Thus, for example, when the mother of a securely attached two-year-old boy consistently and persistently expresses her disapproval of the loud noises he makes while his baby sister is sleeping, he will make efforts to curb the disapproved behavior so as not to threaten the attachment. The expressed wishes of those to whom this little boy is not attached will have less of an impact—displeasing them does not threaten a valued relationship.

The securely attached child, having been more responsive to socialization efforts, fits in better with peers, suffers less rejection from them, and is thus more trusting and less anxious in future relationships. When compared to less securely attached children, those with secure attachments are more empathetic, more sociable, more compliant and more confident (Belsky, 1990; Bretherton, 1985).

Nonparental Care, Attachment, and Early Socialization

Are attachment and subsequent socialization threatened when young children are cared for by people other than their mothers? Do children cared for by nonparents many hours a day differ from those cared for at home by parents?

These questions have become increasingly important as more and more mothers of infants and preschoolers enter the labor force. Before addressing them, we need to learn a little bit about child-care arrangements available to parents in the United States today. Table 12–2 describes the major types of child-care arrangements, indicates how extensively each is utilized by parents with preschool children of different ages, and notes the advantages and disadvantages of each. Although the table hints at the variety of child-care arrangements available, it understates the actual diversity. State regulations regarding child-care facilities vary greatly within the United States, but generally fall below what child-care experts recommend, and do not apply to all child-care arrangements (Young & Zigler, 1986). Thus, there are great variations in quality.

The best child-care arrangements feature very low child to adult ratios, frequent adult-child interaction, age-appropriate activities, and staff stability. The worst arrangements crowd many children and a few untrained, overworked, high turnover caregivers into a small amount of space, provide few activities and little adult direction (Vandell,

Table 12–2 Child-Care Alternatives for Preschool Children of Working Mothers

Child Care Arrangement	Description	Who and How Many Use?	Advantages	Disadvantages
Care in Child's Own Home	Child stays at home. Relative or nonrelative cares for child and siblings. Father is caregiver in half the cases.	Most often used by: —married mothers —moderate income families —parents with less than H.S. education —part-time workers Children cared for this way: 31% under 1 yr. 33% 1–2 yr. olds 27% 3–4 yr. olds	Least disruptive for child and parent. Low caregiver to child ratio allowing for personal attention. Siblings can stay together. Adaptable to odd hours, sick child.	Social isolation of caregiver and child. No peer interaction unless siblings present. Caregiver often untrained or inexperienced. Shift work (in cases where father is caregiver) may cause marital stress.
Care in Another Home	Child is taken to and cared for in home of a relative or nonrelative. Other children often present. If 2–6 children, it is called a *family day care home*. If 7–12 children, a *group day care home*.	Widely used, especially for children under 3 and by full-time workers. Children cared for in this way: 38% under 1 yr. 41% of 1–2 yr. olds 29% of 3–4 yr. olds	Homelike atmosphere, personal attention possible. Flexible—often has drop-off service, kids of all ages, flexible hours, care for infants and sick children. Less structured than center care, but group activities are possible.	Caregiver often untrained. Regulation often haphazard, wide variations in quality. Less parental scrutiny possible than in other arrangements.

(*continued*)

Table 12-2 (continued)

Child Care Arrangement	Description	Who and How Many Use?	Advantages	Disadvantages
Care in a Group Center	Child taken to special facility where 13 to several hundred children are grouped in classes by age. May be nonprofit or for-profit. Emphasis may be on custodial care, socio-emotional development, school preparation or a combination.	More heavily used by parents with more than high school education and higher incomes and for 3–4 year olds. Children cared for in this way: 14% under 1 yr. 18% 1–2 yr. olds 34% 3–4 yr. olds	Children grouped by age, exposed to age-appropriate activities and peer interaction directed by child-care professionals. Greater variety of toys, equipment, and activities possible. More subject to public scrutiny and regulation than others.	Least flexible because of fixed hours and eligibility (infants, sick and handicapped children often not accepted). Child may get less personal attention because of size of group, high turnover of caregivers. Actual caretakers often untrained and poorly paid. Highly structured, less room for spontaneity. Higher illness rates
Mother Cares for Child While Working	Child is taken to mother's workplace or mother is employed at home.	More often used by those with more than high school education and by those in service occupations. Children cared for in this way: 16% under 1 yr. 8% 1–2 yr. olds 7% 3–4 yr. olds	Child receives mother's attention and care at no cost while mother earns money. Continuity and stability of caregiver.	Difficult to arrange and manage.

Sources: Descriptions, advantages, and disadvantages: Clarke-Stewart, 1982; Data on who and how many use each: O'Connell and Bachu, 1990; O'Connell and Bloom, 1987.

Henderson, & Wilson, 1988). This chapter's Personal Application gives some hints on what to look for in selecting a child-care arrangement.

Personal Application

Selecting a Child-Care Arrangement

The best way to check out a child-care arrangement is to visit it and make your own observations. The following list of questions, compiled from the ideas of various child-care experts, is particularly relevant to child-care centers, but could be applied to other child-care settings as well.

1. Are child-care policies and emergency procedures clear and in written form? Do they conform to what you want for your child?

2. Are parents welcome to visit at any time? Are staff members willing to answer questions about their program?

3. Do staff members have some training in child care and child development? Is the adult to child ratio low enough to assure that each child gets individual attention? (recommended: one adult per six children for children three years old and older, one adult per three or four children for children younger than three).

4. Do staff members look busy and involved, rather than bored? Do they kneel down or bend over to a child's eye level when speaking to a child? Do they pay attention to all children rather than spending time with only one or two?

5. Are there different kinds of spaces for different kinds of activities—a dark, quiet space for napping, open space for active play indoors and outdoors, individual storage space for each child's things, indoor areas for quiet play stocked with toys and books? Are the spaces designed with children in mind—for example, windows placed so children can see out and toilets that children can use easily?

6. Are both planned learning activities (for example, story time, crafts, group games) and free play time part of the schedule? If there is a TV, how much time do children spend watching it and what do they watch?

7. Is the facility clean and free of safety hazards? Are furniture and toys sturdy and in good condition? Are the snacks and meals nutritionally balanced?

Source: Ideas drawn from Greene and McMath, n.d.; "How to Choose Day Care," 1989; Miller & Norris, 1985: 58; Scarr, 1985, p. 97.

Now to our questions. *The overwhelming evidence is that receiving care from others in itself does not prevent young children from establishing close attachments to their parents.* Infants are capable of forming multiple attachments of varying strengths; they can be attached to nonparental caregivers as well as to their parents (Clarke-Stewart, 1989;

Peterson & Rollins, 1987). This general conclusion should not surprise you. After all, attachments grow from interaction and involvement and even parents (especially mothers) who work full time spend considerable time interacting with and caring for their children during nonwork hours.

At the same time, some recent research suggests that, *under certain conditions*, nonparental care can have a negative effect on infant-parent attachment. Compiling the results of several different studies, researchers Belsky and Rovine (1988) concluded that *when children under one year of age* receive nonmaternal care for *more than twenty hours a week*, they are 1.6 times more likely than other children to be insecurely attached to their mothers. Even in this "high risk" group, however, two-thirds of the children established a secure relationship with at least one parent (Belsky & Rovine, 1988). Boys, babies who were fussy and irritable, and babies who had a stressful home environment were more vulnerable than others to insecure attachments (Belsky & Rovine, 1988; Gamble & Zigler, 1986). Infants in nonmaternal care for less than twenty hours a week and those cared for by their fathers at home or in a nonrelative's home—the two child-care alternatives most often chosen for children under one year of age—did not run the increased risk of insecure attachment (Belsky & Rovine, 1988). These findings are somewhat controversial because they have not been confirmed in every study and because of questions about the methods used to measure insecure attachment (Clarke-Stewart, 1989; King & MacKinnon, 1988).

The findings are significant enough so that several prominent child experts have urged the adoption of a national policy of paid maternal leave for at least three or four months (Brazelton, 1986; Gamble & Zigler, 1986). As these experts point out, the United States is the only industrialized society without such a policy. Leave policies, pediatricians point out, are good for parents as well as children—they give parents time to get to know their baby and become confident in their own infant care skills before having to separate from the child (Brazelton, 1986).

What about other effects of nonparental care on socialization? Preschool children receiving nonparental care differ in several ways from those cared for exclusively at home by parents. Most studies on this topic compare children reared at home by mothers to children cared for in group ("day care") centers. By the time they enter school, daycare children are friendlier, more socially confident and competent, and more intellectually advanced than children who spent their preschool years at home, although at-home children catch up quickly. The daycare children are also more aggressive towards their peers, less patient and persistent in problem-solving situations, and less compliant to the wishes of adults (Clarke-Stewart, 1989; King & MacKinnon, 1988).

Not all day care is the same and neither are all daycare children. The particular combination of qualities daycare children develop are related to when they first enter nonparental care and to the quality of care they receive. As Figure 12–2 indicates, at age 5, children who

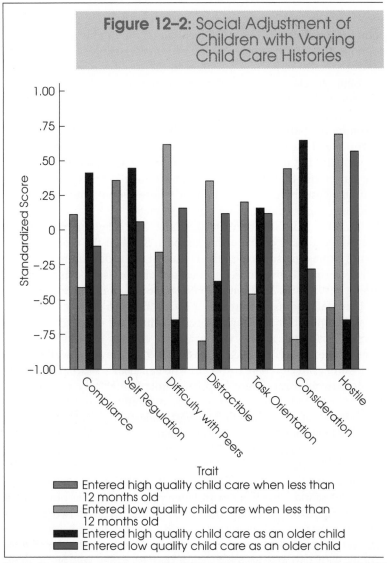

Figure 12–2: Social Adjustment of Children with Varying Child Care Histories

To read this graph, select one category of children and see which traits they score higher on (a tall bar) and which they are lacking (a short bar).

Entered high quality child care when less than 12 months old
Entered low quality child care when less than 12 months old
Entered high quality child care as an older child
Entered low quality child care as an older child

entered high quality care after their first year of life are best off and children who entered low quality care during their first year are the worst off in terms of traits necessary for later school success, such as compliance, consideration, and lack of hostility (Howes, 1990).

Support, Control, and Parental Patterns

Secure attachment between parent and child is an important starting point for socialization, but attachment alone will not insure that a child develops the qualities parents desire. Parental support and parental control are also important variables in the socialization process.

Support refers to parental behavior towards a child "that makes the child feel comfortable in the presence of the parent and confirms in the child's mind that he is basically accepted and approved as a person by the parent" (Rollins & Thomas, 1979, p. 320). "Acceptance," "nurturance," "warmth," and "love" are everyday words which help convey what the term "support" encompasses. Children who feel that they *matter* and that they are important to their parents are supported children (Rosenberg, 1985). Children whose parents make them feel irrelevant, bad, or rejected are not supported.

Families from different racial, ethnic, and religious backgrounds have different ways of expressing support. Some of the more common ways of expressing support in the United States today are hugging and kissing, verbal "I love yous," encouragement, praise, listening to, and helping out (Rollins & Thomas, 1979). Although counting up such positive parental actions can provide a rough measure of whether parents are high support or low support parents, how the child *perceives* and *interprets* parental actions within a total context is what matters in terms of outcomes (Felson & Zielinski, 1989; Gecas & Schwalbe, 1986). For example, an eleven-year-old girl who can clearly see that the chores she does around the house help her whole family may well feel that she *matters* whether or not her parents offer effusive praise.

Control refers to parental behavior undertaken "with the intent of directing the behavior of the child in a manner desirable to the parents" (Rollins & Thomas, 1979, p. 321). Control is what most parents call "discipline." Parents attempt to control their children's behavior when they give directions or suggestions, lay down rules, give explanations for the rules, and administer or threaten physical or other punishment. Most research on parental control designates at least two types of control—coercive and inductive. **Coercive control** depends on *external* force to get the child to conform to parental desires—that is, children comply with parental wishes because they fear they will be punished

Support
parental behavior that makes a child feel accepted and approved as a person.

Control
parental actions intended to direct the behavior of a child in a manner desirable to the parents.

Coercive control
directs behavior through the use of external force or threat of force.

physically or through withdrawal of privileges if they do not. **Inductive control** depends on convincing the child *internally* that complying with the parent's desires is the right thing to do through reasoning and explanation (Rollins & Thomas, 1979). A parent who washes out a child's mouth or who refuses to speak to the child after finding out that the child has lied is using coercive control; a parent who explains to a lying child how much lying can hurt other people is using inductive control.

The child-parent relationship is so complex, so long-lasting, and so subject to change that most parents, sometime during their parental careers, show many possible variations of support and control. That is, they can identify times when they were very supportive of their child—saying exactly the right, comforting words—and times when they rejected their child with harsh, cutting comments. They can remember times when they used physical punishment, times when they used the explanation approach, and times when they despaired of exercising any control at all.

Nonetheless, parents tend to develop certain identifiable patterns of support and control in dealing with their children. Three such patterns are common in the United States today; each represents a different combination of support and control and each has reasonably reliable outcomes for children.

The **authoritarian** pattern combines high coercive control with low inductive control and low to moderate support (Baumrind, 1978). Authoritarian parents see children as clearly subordinate to parents; they set standards without consulting children and often without paying attention to the child's capabilities, tell their children what their standards are and what the consequences will be for noncompliance, and follow through with punishment if the children do not obey. Parents who place a high value on obedience and conformity and who feel that affectionate behavior "spoils" children frequently choose an authoritarian pattern (Luster, Rhoades, & Haas, 1989).

The **permissive** pattern combines moderate to high support with low coercive and inductive control (Baumrind, 1978). Permissive parents believe that children should be free to act as they please. According to parents using this pattern, parental control interferes with children's self-discovery of appropriate behavior. Permissive parents frequently support their children, listen to their views, and are available as a resource but do not attempt to explicitly direct or set standards for their children.

The **authoritative** pattern combines high support with high inductive control (Baumrind, 1978). Authoritative parents attempt to direct children without coercing them. Like authoritarian parents, authoritative parents set high standards for their children and make these standards very clear. Unlike authoritarian parents, they pay attention

---

Inductive control
directs behavior through the use of reason and explanation

Authoritarian
a pattern of parental behavior that combines high coercive control with low to moderate support and low inductive control.

Permissive
a pattern of parental behavior that combines moderate to high support with low coercive and inductive control.

Authoritative
a pattern of parental behavior that combines high support with high inductive control.

to the child's age, capabilities, and input in setting the standards and offer generous praise and support when the child complies.

Generally speaking, the authoritative combination of high support and high inductive control is best at promoting those qualities most often favored by U.S. parents—cognitive development, compliance, self-control, and social competence (Gecas & Seff, 1990; Peterson & Rollins, 1987; Clark, 1983; Baumrind, 1978). Reginald Clark's (1983) study of successful and unsuccessful high school students living in poor, black, urban neighborhoods provides one good example. Clark found that parental behavior separated successful from unsuccessful students. Parents of successful students expected their children to contribute to the family by doing specific chores, established clear, strict rules about studying and social life, and encouraged their children's intellectual abilities by involving themselves in homework, reading, and games. Their children could see that they mattered to their parents; they responded by doing well in school and avoiding most of the dangers of the neighborhoods in which they lived (Clark, 1983). Parents of the unsuccessful students did not expect their children to help out at home, made few rules, and did not interact with their children about school activities (Clark, 1983).

Generally speaking, children of authoritarian parents are less socially competent than children of authoritative parents—as young children, they tend to be somewhat discontented, withdrawn, and distrustful (Baumrind, 1978); by late childhood and adolescence, they are frequently rebellious and aggressive (Gecas & Seff, 1990; Baumrind, 1978).

Permissively-reared children, receiving praise regardless of what they do and without clear standards by which to measure themselves, turn out lacking in self-direction and self-control. In early childhood, they are the *least* socially competent, self-directed, and responsible children (Berns, 1985; Baumrind, 1978); in adolescence, they are at increased risk for delinquent behavior (Gecas & Seff, 1990).

What practical advice for parents emerges from all this research? Jerome Kagan (1984), a developmental psychologist writing specifically about childrearing in the contemporary United States, provides a very good summary of our points:

> ... the best advice for parents is to establish an affectionate relation with the child, to decide on the particular behavior to be socialized, and to communicate disapproval of undesirable behavior when it occurs, along with the reasons for punishment. If this strategy does not work, deprivation of privileges the child enjoys can be used to accomplish the socialization goal. Harsh physical punishment and excessive threat of withdrawal of love are probably unwise and, I may add, unnecessary if the first two conditions are met. (p. 264)

Child Maltreatment

Parental treatment of children takes place behind closed doors and is not normally subject to public scrutiny. In recent years, however, some extreme types of parental behavior have attracted legal, medical, and media attention. These types of behavior—neglect, physical abuse, emotional abuse, and child sexual abuse—are often categorized together as "child maltreatment." In 1990, slightly more than 1200 U.S. children died as a result of abuse and neglect and many more suffered the consequences (*Associated Press*, 1991).

All these types of child maltreatment fall outside the limits of what U.S. adults of all ethnic groups and economic classes consider acceptable parental behavior (Giovannoni & Becerra, 1979) and are dealt with by the same social service and law enforcement agencies. All occur more frequently in families that are socially isolated from others, have an alcoholic parent, and have more discord and less interaction than other families (Martin & Walters, 1982). Beyond these similarities, the forms of maltreatment are distinct from one another.

Neglect

Neglect can be defined as parental failure to provide what children need. Most public attention is focused on physical neglect—failure to provide adequate food, shelter, clothing, hygiene, or medical care—but some parents also fail to provide adequate emotional support, supervision, and guidance. Parents who neglect their children emotionally and psychologically seldom come to public attention; thus, most of our comments pertain to physical neglect. Although physical abuse receives much more publicity, physical neglect is more common. Recent estimates based on official reports indicate that while 5.7 per 1000 U.S. children are physically abused each year, 9.1 per 1000 are physically neglected (U.S. Department of Health and Human Services, 1988).

The number of children physically neglected by their parents rose throughout the late 1980s and early 1990s. Most experts attribute the increase to the "crack epidemic" (Besharov, 1990; Hinds, 1990). Parents addicted to crack cocaine spend their money on drugs rather than on food for their children and frequently leave very young children completely unattended. Parental drug and alcohol abuse have always been tied to child maltreatment, but the connection became much more pronounced during the late 1980s. Previously, 30 to 40 percent of child maltreatment cases involved parental substance abuse (most of it alcohol); today, substance abuse (much of it crack cocaine) is implicated in 50 to 90 percent of child maltreatment cases (Hinds, 1990).

> **Neglect**
> parental failure to provide what children need.

Certain parental characteristics are clearly associated with physical and emotional neglect. Parents (typically mothers) who are physically neglectful are much more likely than other parents to be extremely poor, low in intelligence, socially isolated, and to have a large number of children (Tower, 1989; Zuravin, 1988; Martin & Walters, 1982). Poverty is an important component of child neglect, but poverty alone is not decisive: many poor parents make great efforts to provide for their children's physical needs. Rather, it is the *combination* of extreme poverty, isolation, low intelligence, and numerous children that results in persistent physical neglect.

In a typical case of physical neglect, *all* the children in the family suffer the consequences. Parents who are too overwhelmed or withdrawn to provide minimal physical care are also unlikely to provide adequate support and control; their children not only suffer physically but are also likely to suffer the consequences of low support and low control mentioned previously.

Physical Abuse

Physical abuse intentional physical injury of a child by a parent or caregiver.

Physical abuse can be defined as "intentional physical injury of a child by a parent or caregiver" (Martin & Walters, 1982, p. 269). Some, but not all, physical abuse is discipline-related and is associated with more extreme versions of the authoritarian parental pattern.

Physical abuse rates are measured in two different ways: surveys of the general population and cases reported to officials. Rates are much higher when measured by survey research (basically, parents are asked about which particular acts of violence they have used on their children) than when they are measured by official records (acts of abuse reported to and *confirmed by* social service and law enforcement agencies). Survey reports of physical abuse show a *decline* in recent years from 36 incidents per 1000 children in 1975 to 19 incidents per 1000 children in 1985 (Straus & Gelles, 1986, p. 469). Official reports show an *increase* from 3.1 per 1000 in 1980 to 5.7 per 1000 in 1986 (U.S. Department of Health and Human Services, 1988). The increase in official rates is almost certainly due to increased publicity and concern about abuse; the decrease shown in the survey data may indicate that parents are less likely to report their own violent behavior than they were in the past. In short, it is simply not possible to say whether physical abuse is increasing or decreasing (Gelles & Conte, 1990).

A recent review of research on physical abuse concluded that "there is no typical abusive parent" (Starr, 1988, p. 138). Although some parents who abuse their children are undoubtedly psychologically disturbed, *as a group* abusive parents do not differ from nonabusive parents in terms of personality or psychological traits (Starr, 1988). Parents who were themselves abused as children are more likely to be abusive than parents who were not, but even here the connection is far from perfect. Only about 30 percent of parents who were abused as children repeat the pattern (Gelles & Conte, 1990); the other 70 percent are able to escape the pattern by receiving support from non-abusive adults, participating in therapy, or establishing a supportive, stable, satisfying marital relationship (Egeland, Jacobvitz, & Sroufe, 1988).

Physical abuse is often child-specific—the parent abuses one child, typically one perceived as being different or difficult, while leaving others in the family alone (Tower, 1989). It also occurs more often in families under economic, employment-related, and family-related stress (Starr, 1988). Still, most parents with different, difficult children and most parents under stress do not abuse (Starr, 1988). Physically abusive parents tend to be more isolated from neighbors, relatives, and friends than nonabusive parents and more likely to use violence in other family relationships as well (Straus & Smith, 1990; Starr, 1988). Finally, cross-cultural evidence indicates that cultures, such as the United States, that approve of physical punishment and glorify adult-adult violence have much higher rates of parent-child violence and injury (Korbin, 1981).

Every year, over 1000 children, most of them infants, die as a result of parental violence. For the majority who survive, there is no single set of consequences (Starr, 1988), but withdrawal, passiveness, hypervigilance (being very watchful of everyone around them), and the ability to quickly adapt to a changing situation are commonly observed traits in abused children (Tower, 1989). The most common long-term result of parental violence seems to be a greater tendency for abused children to be verbally and physically aggressive (Starr, 1988). Beyond that, how the child turns out seems to depend on factors that affect all children: the amount of support they receive from others, their own temperament, how they interpret the abuse, and future experiences.

Emotional Abuse

Emotional abuse is belittling, rejecting, denigrating, or excessively criticizing a child using words, threats, or humiliating punishments. Emotionally abusive parents use words rather than belts and whips to express their dissatisfaction with their children. Emotionally abused children receive very little support from their parents; instead, they are

Emotional abuse belittling, rejecting, denigrating, or excessively criticizing a child using words, threats, or humiliating punishments.

reminded over and over again that they *do not matter* to their parents, that nothing they do is praiseworthy. Here is one example:

> [Sally] looked as if she had just been beaten, but her father never touched her. Instead, he berated her: "How did I ever deserve a girl? Girls are lesser beings." He had her hair cut in an unbecoming style, saying there was no point in trying to make an ugly girl look any better. He demanded complete obedience and subservience, including having her stand beside him as he ate to cut and salt his food. He rationalized this activity saying that her only hope in life was to be of use to a husband, if in fact anyone would want her. Even when Sally scored 160 on an IQ test, her father assured her the teachers were wrong—she was only a girl. (Tower, 1984, p. 39)

Because emotional abuse is difficult to see and because it has only recently been recognized as harmful, there is little research on how often it occurs and what types of parents use it. However, emotionally abusive parents seem to have some things in common with physically abusive parents: both hold very high, unrealistic expectations for their children and both tend to exert rigid control. In fact, the two types of abuse often occur together or consecutively—parents who used beatings to punish young children often use harsh criticism when the children reach adolescence and are too large to beat (Mayhall & Norgard, 1983). Emotionally abused children frequently believe what their parents tell them and often enter adulthood with very poor self-images and with the feeling that they can do nothing right.

Intrafamilial Sexual Abuse

Sexual abuse (as applied to children) forced, tricked, or coerced sexual behavior between a young person and an older person.

Intrafamilial sexual abuse or incest sexual abuse directed toward a family member.

Sexual abuse, as applied to children, is "forced, tricked, or coerced sexual behavior between a young person and an older person" (Gelles & Conte, 1990, p. 1050). When this type of behavior is directed toward a family member, it is known as **intrafamilial sexual abuse** or **incest**. Reliable statistics about the incidence of incest are difficult to obtain, but several recent surveys indicate that somewhere between *16 percent and 28 percent of all adults* experienced some type of sexual contact with a relative before the age of 18 (Becker & Coleman, 1988). Perpetrators of intrafamilial sexual abuse are almost always male, victims are most often, but not always, female. When adults are surveyed about childhood sexual abuse, they most often identify brothers, uncles, or grandfathers as the perpetrators of sexual abuse (Wolfe, Wolfe, & Best, 1988). However, most of the research on incest focuses on father-daughter or stepfather-stepdaughter incest.

There is, as yet, no complete definitive profile of incestuous fathers, but there is evidence showing that they have "deviant sexual arousal" patterns which first emerged during adolescence (Becker & Coleman, 1988). Certain family characteristics—lack of a strong marital bond, a physically or psychologically distant wife-mother, a daughter who takes over parts of the mother's role, unequally distributed marital power, confused communication, and social isolation—are often associated with incestuous families (Berns, 1985). However, these factors may be the result rather than the cause of incestuous behavior (Becker & Coleman, 1988).

Intrafamilial sexual abuse has a range of consequences. As with other forms of maltreatment, some children seem to escape this inappropriate parental behavior unscathed while others suffer emotional and psychological trauma the rest of their lives. How a child responds to intrafamilial sexual abuse is dependent on the form of the molestation and on the response of other family members. One study of lower-income Hispanic, black, and white adolescent female incest victims found that those who suffered the most severe forms of abuse and those whose mothers responded in a negative way to the reported abuse suffered the most severe consequences. Victims with these two characteristics were the most depressed, had the lowest self-esteem, and were the most likely to exhibit negative behaviors, such as running away from home, attempting suicide, or engaging in illegal activities (Morrow & Sorell, 1989). Younger victims more often experienced lowered self-esteem; older victims, especially the nonwhites, more often became depressed and acted out their frustrations in negative ways (Morrow & Sorell, 1989).

The sad cases of child maltreatment remind us that parents have the capacity to cut short their children's full potential. The consequences of child maltreatment by parents are especially devastating if the children are unable to get support from other adults.

Alternative Situation

Rearing a Disabled Child

Some 10 percent–20 percent of people under 20 years old in the United States are chronically ill or disabled to some extent and their numbers are increasing (Brody, 1989). Children with cancer, asthma, heart problems, AIDS, spina bifida, learning disabilities, mental retardation, impairments in speech, hearing, sight, or mobility (to name but a few examples) are included in these figures. Medical technology is keeping more of these children alive than in the past and has helped many of them to live relatively normal lives. Achieving such normality, though, requires the aggressive involvement of caring parents. Even more than healthy children, disabled children are dependent upon their parents.

A few parents—those who adopt a handicapped youngster and those who decide to give birth rather than abort when disability is diagnosed prenatally—*choose* to rear disabled children. Most parents of disabled children, however, did not choose the situation but simply found themselves in it. In some cases, the parents know about the disability as soon as the child is born; in others, they discover it only gradually; in still others, their previously normal child becomes disabled as a result of an accident or severe illness. To a large extent, the type and severity of the child's disability influences just what it is parents must adapt to. Parents whose child is deaf or blind, for example, will have to learn special techniques but can expect to see their children reach adulthood and live relatively independent lives. The parents of some chronically ill children, on the other hand, cannot realistically expect their offspring to survive until adulthood. And parents

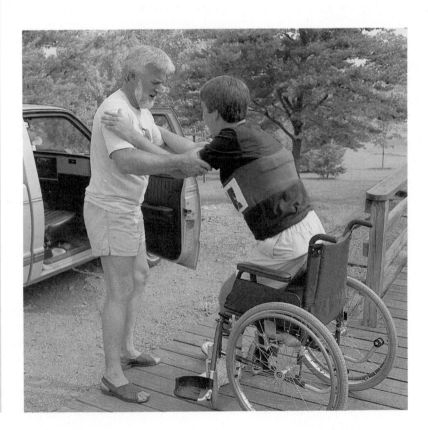

Even more than healthy children, disabled children are dependent upon their parents.

of severely mentally or physically handicapped children face the prospect of lifetime care of a child who can never "grow up" in the usual sense.

The problems faced by parents with healthy, normally developing children are greatly intensified for parents rearing children with chronic illnesses or disabilities. Parents whose children spend their first weeks or months in a hospital incubator have a more difficult time doing those things which contribute to secure attachment. The skills they must learn in order to provide good care are more complicated and less agreed upon than the skills other parents must learn, and the sheer physical work involved is more extensive and tiring (Mullins, 1987; LaRossa, 1986). The conflicting emotions felt by all new parents are greatly intensified among the parents of disabled children; they have more guilt, more loneliness, and more self-doubt (LaRossa, 1986). Parents of disabled children also typically have greater financial burdens than parents of nondisabled children (Mullins, 1987).

Some studies of these parents show that they experience significantly more depression, have less effective family functioning, and report lower marital adjustment than parents without disabled children (Shapiro & Tittle, 1990; Bristol, Gallagher, & Schopler, 1988). However, there is also extensive evidence that many families with disabled children overcome substantial odds and find great rewards in learning about and dealing with their child's disability (Mullins, 1987; Darling, 1979).

Both systematic studies and personal memoirs of these families indicate that their major difficulties often come from outside the nuclear family rather than from within it. Parents can spend many frustrating years simply obtaining a correct diagnosis of their child's condition and prospects. Then they must locate, evaluate, and pay people who are willing to babysit, educate, play with, and provide routine medical care to their special children. These tasks are taxing and time-consuming enough for parents who come from the same socioeconomic class as the doctors, teachers, and experts with whom they must deal. The process of seeking out care is even more intimidating and less often rewarding for those with less education and income (Shapiro & Tittle, 1990; Darling, 1979).

While parents of disabled children see themselves as doing what any parent should do—seeking out the best for their child—friends, relatives, and often professionals see such extraordinary actions as inappropriate for a handicapped child and accuse the parents of "being on a guilt trip" (Darling, 1979). This feeling, plus the fact that those outside the family are uncertain about how to treat either the disabled child or the parents, often isolates and stresses the families of disabled children even more (Zarling, Hirsch, & Landry, 1988). The mother of a profoundly mentally retarded girl put it like this:

The fact of life for parents of handicapped children which is least understood by others is this: It is difficult and exhausting to live normally, and yet we must. To decide on the other route, to admit that having a disabled child makes us disabled persons, to say no to the ordinary requirements of daily living is to meet the second enemy—loneliness. It means drifting slowly out of the mainstream of adult life. In a very real sense, we are damned if we do make the extraordinary effort required to live normally, and damned if we don't . . . . (Quoted in Berns, 1985, p. 471)

Many parents who share this mother's feelings find that their best support comes from other parents whose children have similar disabilities. To an extent unimaginable to other parents, their lives come to be organized and structured around advocacy and support of their special children.

Summary

Both parents and children today are expected to live up to rather high standards. Children are expected to be socially competent, achieve independence, do well in school, and bring great emotional satisfaction to their parents. Parents are held responsible for how their children turn out and are increasingly expected to be totally involved employees as well as totally involved parents. Although U.S. culture glorifies children and childhood, many of its policies—especially those regarding parental leave and child care—make childrearing a difficult, isolating, and stressful task.

Children create work and stress for their parents and limit parental privacy, self-fulfillment, and couple time. Most couples assume more traditional patterns of family work after children are born and this traditionalization adds to conflict and dissatisfaction with marriage. However, parenthood also offers great satisfactions, and more parents than nonparents believe that their lives have meaning and purpose.

In the United States today, parents are the major socializers of their children. Effective socialization is best achieved by parents who form a close attachment to their child early in life, provide generous emotional support, and set clear standards that are fully explained to their children. Parents who fail to support their children, do not set clear guidelines for behavior, or depend on coercive punishment are less successful in producing well-socialized children. Some parents put their children's futures in even greater danger by maltreating them through neglect, physical abuse, emotional abuse, or sexual abuse.

Parents of disabled children face the problems of other parents but at a much more intense level and with even less outside support. To get their children what they need, these parents must work harder and longer, often risking contempt and isolation from others.

CHAPTER 13

MARRIAGES AND FAMILIES IN THE MIDDLE AND LATER YEARS

Answer the following true-false questions based on your knowledge of middle-aged and elderly people. Correct answers can be found in Chapter 13.

T F 1. Most mothers feel relief rather than depression when their young adult children move out of the home.

T F 2. More than half of all divorces take place in middle-age, usually at about the time the children leave home.

T F 3. Most retired people left the labor force involuntarily and have a difficult time adjusting to retirement.

T F 4. Couples in their seventies and eighties are no longer capable of nor interested in sexual intercourse.

T F 5. Less than 10 percent of people over the age of 65 live in nursing homes.

"My parents really seem to have gone to pieces since I left home," 19-year-old Daniel commented to some of his college friends. "My mom seemed to take my sister's marriage and my brother's going into the military OK but now that 'Daniel her youngest' is gone, she's really depressed and doesn't know what to do with herself. Then there's my Dad. He's always threatening my mother with divorce and mom's afraid he has a young girlfriend on the side." Melissa, another 19-year-old, said "That doesn't sound like my parents at all. I'm the youngest, too, but my parents seem kind of relieved to have the house to themselves again. They're acting like a couple of honeymooners!" "Yeah, my parents had a few years like that," said Tina, a 28-year-old returning student, "But that was before my grandmother had a stroke and had to move in with them. My mom feels overwhelmed trying to take care of grandma and do all the things dad and she wanted to do with this part of their lives. In fact, I'm on my way over there now to take over so mom can spend a few hours by herself." After a few seconds, Henry, a 63-year-old college returnee, chimed in "Well, I guess I have the opposite problem! Our *children* have started to come back home. First, my daughter got laid off and moved back in with us and now it looks like my divorced son will too! I retired early and my wife expects to retire in a few years. We weren't expecting to spend our retirement years with our children!"

In their discussion, Daniel, Melissa, Tina, and Henry illustrate a few of the many diverse paths couples can take after their children leave home. As the students indicate, the middle and later years of life can be filled with self-questioning and lifestyle changes, with increased freedom and contentment, or with new obligations to older and younger generations.

Chapter 13 details the continuities and changes typically associated with marriage and parenthood in the middle and later years of life. For most married couples, these years are marked by several turning points: departure of children from the home, retirement from the labor force, and death of a spouse. These turning points represent changes in three major adult social roles: the role of parent, the role of worker, and the role of spouse. Chapter 13 covers the first two turning points; Chapter 14 (in the sections on marital dissolution through death) will cover the third.

Chapter 13 consists of two major sections. The first deals with the **empty nest stage**, the period of marriage between the departure of the last child from home and the retirement of both spouses from the labor force. In discussing this stage, we emphasize issues introduced in earlier chapters—adjustment to a new stage of parenthood, marital satisfaction, sexuality, work, money, gender roles, relationships with people outside the immediate family, and intergenerational relationships with children, grandchildren, and parents. In addition, we consider the physical and psychological changes that often accompany the empty nest stage.

The second section focuses on the same issues with respect to the **retirement stage**, the stage of family life beginning when both spouses have retired and ending when one spouse dies. In addition, we discuss

---

Empty nest stage
the period of the marriage lasting from the departure of the last child from home to the retirement of both spouses from the labor force.

Retirement stage
the stage of family life beginning when both spouses retire and ending when one spouse dies.

adjustment to retirement and health care of the elderly. The empty nest and retirement stage sections assume that middle-aged and elderly couples have children. Clearly, not all do. The Alternative Choice section considers the lives of middle-aged and elderly, childless, married couples.

Although Chapter 13 focuses on husbands and wives who stay with their original partner "till death do us part," some of the material in the chapter applies to middle-aged and elderly divorced individuals and to remarried couples as well. These two groups will receive additional attention in Chapters 14 and 15. For now, let us take a look at the changes and choices long-term married couples confront in the last half of marriage.

WHAT HAPPENS WHEN THE KIDS LEAVE HOME? CONTINUITY AND CHANGE IN THE EMPTY NEST STAGE

The empty nest stage begins when the last child moves away from home. It derives its name from the fact that a home without children is somewhat emptier and quieter than a home with children. During this stage, mothers and fathers decrease their involvement as active parents. Of course, they do not stop being parents simply because their children no longer live at home. They continue to worry, give advice, send money, and make subtle or not-so-subtle demands on their children. However, the parental role definitely changes since their children are now adults. Parents go from being live-in, day-to-day maintainers, supporters, and supervisors of their children to being long-distance advice givers, increasingly less aware of and less responsible for the day-to-day activities of their adult children.

Assessing the Empty Nest Syndrome

Empty nest syndrome a condition of deep depression, physical illness, and loss of purpose some parents, especially mothers, show in middle age after the departure of their children.

How does the departure of children from the home affect parents and their marriage? Some years ago, clinical psychiatrists developed the term **empty nest syndrome** to describe the deep depression, physical illness, and loss of purpose that some parents, especially mothers, showed in middle age after their children left home. The syndrome made sense to psychiatrists, as well as to much of the public: motherhood was a major focus of life for many women in the United States, and losing the mother role would seemingly represent a major crisis.

At one time, experts assumed that the empty nest syndrome affected large numbers of middle-aged women. Today we know it does not (Harris, Ellicott & Holmes, 1986; Lowenthal & Chiriboga, 1972). Most parents, especially mothers, adapt quickly and often joyfully to an emptier nest. Sociologist Lillian Rubin (1979) confirmed the findings of many other studies when she interviewed middle-aged women about life after children. Here is what two mothers reported:

> I can't tell you what a relief it was to find myself with an empty nest. Oh sure, when the last child went away to school, for the first day or so there was a kind of a throb, but believe me, it was only a day or two. (p. 15)

> I think when my son left—he was the first to go—we suddenly realized that this family unit wasn't going to go on forever, and that things were going to be different from then on; you know, I mean that eventually everybody would go off and lead their own lives. So the first month or so after he left was hard, but no big problems since then. And there won't be big problems when the girls' turns come. I'm ready now—maybe more than ready. (p. 16)

What about fathers? Some writers suggest that, because they have been less involved in preparing their children for independence, fathers are less willing to let go and suffer more from their children's departure than do mothers (Rubin, 1979; Back, 1971). A few fathers (somewhere between 10 and 20 percent, depending on the study) do see the empty nest stage as an unhappy one, and, for *some* of these unhappy fathers, the departure of children is the critical factor (Lewis, Frenau, & Roberts, 1979; Lowenthal & Chiriboga, 1972).

More often, however, the small proportion of fathers and mothers who experience the symptoms of the empty nest syndrome do so because their *marriages* are disappointing to them (Bart, 1979; Lewis, Frenau, & Roberts, 1979). When children leave, disappointed marriage partners lose much of their day-to-day, in-home support, affection, and activity and become depressed. Partners in satisfying marriages, on the other hand, can depend on each other for support, affection, and activity.

In fact, single parents may be the most frequent victims of the empty nest syndrome. Such parents frequently develop "best friend" relationships with their children and lack other intimate ties (Brozan, 1986). When all the children leave, they may find it difficult to find substitute sources of affection and support.

Marital Satisfaction in the Empty Nest Stage

Rather than leading to depression and a less satisfying marriage, the departure of children from the home generally has beneficial effects on the parents' marriage. Most studies of marital satisfaction are **cross-sectional studies**, studies comparing couples at different stages of the

Cross-sectional studies studies comparing couples at different stages of the family life cycle.

family life cycle. These studies find that empty nest couples score higher on marital satisfaction than do couples in earlier, child-rearing stages of marriage (Anderson, Russell, & Schumm, 1983; Olson *et al.*, 1983; Rollins & Cannon, 1974). Rollins and Galligan (1978) summarize these findings by noting:

> In general, the research seems to support the idea that general marital satisfaction decreases during marriage simultaneously with the arrival and development of the oldest child in the family until about adolescence, and then as children mature and leave home, it increases. (p. 81)

Why? There are many possible explanations for why empty nest stage marriages are more satisfying. Three stand out as most promising: more resources, age-related changes, and survivorship.

More Resources

The first explanation suggests that marriages improve after the kids leave home because the departure of children typically restores or increases the resources associated with marital satisfaction at any stage. These resources include money, time, and privacy.

Money   In general, people in their mid-forties to mid-sixties (the most common empty nest stage years) are better off financially than other adults. Table 13–1 documents this, especially in terms of net worth (the value of all their property and possessions minus what they owe).

Table 13–1 Median Monthly Income and Net Worth of Households by Age of Household Head		
Age of Household Head	**Median Monthly Income, 1988**	**Median Net Worth, 1988**
under 35	$2,000	$ 6,078
35–44	$2,500	$33,183
45–54	$2,604	$57,466
55–64	$2,071	$80,032
65–69	$1,497	$83,478
70–74	$1,330	$82,111
75 and over	$ 977	$61,491

Source: Eargle, 1990, Table E.

Empty nest stage couples often have higher incomes than younger couples because both partners are able to work full time and because one or both may be in their peak-earning years. In contrast to younger couples, more of the older couple's income is likely to be uncommitted—their house is paid for or requires only relatively small monthly payments (especially if they were able to buy it during a period of low interest rates) and is already filled with furniture and appliances. Empty nest couples often continue to help their children financially, but this help is not obligatory and is likely to diminish over time.

Thus, for many couples, the empty nest stage is one of lessened economic strain and increased choice about how to spend money. Some couples buy luxuries or take vacations they could not afford previously, others spend it on children and grandchildren, still others invest it in hopes of living comfortably during the retirement years.

Time   Empty nest couples, on average, have shorter total work weeks than do couples with children in the home (Rexroat & Shehan, 1987). Since both husband and wife typically hold full-time jobs in the labor force during the empty nest stage, the difference is not primarily attributable to changes in the amount of time spent working in a paying job. Rather, empty nest couples have *no* time devoted to child care on a day-to-day basis *and* they also do less housework. The elimination of child-care responsibilities and the reduction in the total amount of housework gives wives about fifteen more hours of nonwork time per week than they had when their children were adolescents at home (Rexroat & Shehan, 1987). They are likely to have considerable control over this extra time and might choose to spend it sleeping more, going back to school, or talking with their husbands.

The total work weeks of husbands and of wives are more nearly equal during the empty nest stage than at any time since early marriage. Rexroat and Shehan (1987) found that wives employed full time worked about 16.5 hours more per week than their husbands during the years when their children were teenagers living at home but only nine hours a week more after the family teenagers moved out. Not surprisingly, both husband and wife perceive more fairness in the division of family work at this stage than during earlier ones (Suitor, 1991; Menaghan, 1983). Once again, the empty nest years bring some relief in an area which is often a source of strain and conflict earlier in the marriage.

Privacy   Empty nest couples are also likely to have more privacy. For the first time since they became parents, they have the home to themselves and can reasonably expect to have uninterrupted time alone or with one another. This new privacy can give the empty nest couple freedom to do things they could not do when they were responsible for children. For example, they might turn a child's bedroom into a den or hobby room, eat meals wherever and whenever they want, or tell jokes and use language they censored when the children were at home.

Increased privacy also gives married couples the freedom to make love whenever and wherever they want within their own home without fear of interruption by the children. In her study of middle-aged women, Rubin (1979) entitled the chapter on sex "Sex? It's Gotten Better and Better" to reflect the feelings of the women whom she interviewed. These women, born between about 1920 and 1940, had been sexually repressed and ignorant during their honeymoons and physically overwhelmed and fatigued during their childrearing years. The improvement in their sex lives in middle age came about partly because they were more experienced with their husbands, partly because they had more time and privacy, and partly because of the new sexual openness of the culture. The woman quoted below indicates the importance of privacy:

> We're a lot freer sexually now than we ever were before. And now that it's just the two of us in the house, you can do it when you feel like it, and you can take your time—you know, just lie there together for an hour or two, or even more. It makes all the difference when you don't have to worry who's listening in one of the other bedrooms. (Rubin, 1979, pp. 93–94)

Not all empty nest couples can depend on having more money, more time, and more privacy. And, of course, simply having more resources does not necessarily mean that couples will use them to improve their relationship. However, more than at other stages of their marriage, empty nest couples *do* have the choice and the opportunity to do so. Findings of the marital satisfaction studies, as well as of interview studies like Rubin's, indicate that many couples seize that opportunity.

Age-Related Changes

The second explanation of higher marital satisfaction during the empty nest stage suggests that marriages improve at about the time the children leave home because of changes the *adults* are going through. This explanation asserts that empty nest marriages are more satisfying marriages because both partners have undergone age-related changes and have matured in ways that make high marital quality more likely.

Physical Changes   For most married couples, the empty nest years fall sometime between the ages of 45 and 65. During these years, most adults begin to recognize the first signs of aging. Wrinkles, gray hairs, and pot bellies appear. Visual acuity, hearing, energy level, and physical strength decrease slightly, and recovery from injury takes longer. (The male author of this text was forced to accept the fact he was deteriorating rapidly when he snapped an Achilles tendon playing tennis!) Both men and women experience hormonal changes. Men have lower testosterone levels; women produce less estrogen and progesterone (Croft, 1982).

These physical changes generally do not make any major differences in day-to-day life. They may, however, make middle-aged people more conscious of their own mortality. So might the death of their parents (a common experience during the empty nest stage) or of someone close to their own age. Death rates per 1000 rise steadily after the age of 50. As Figure 13–1 indicates, middle-aged death rates are higher for

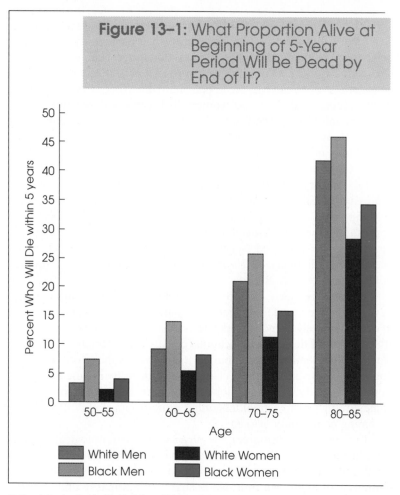

Figure 13–1: What Proportion Alive at Beginning of 5-Year Period Will Be Dead by End of It?

White Men   White Women
Black Men   Black Women

The figure shows that the chances of dying within a five-year period increase dramatically with advancing age. Note also that the probability of dying is greater for blacks and for males at every age.

National Center for Health Statistics, 1988, pp. 7, 9.

males than for females, higher for blacks than for whites, and increase with age in every category.

People respond in different ways when faced with their own aging and eventual death. One fairly common reaction seems to be a greater appreciation of a still-living partner and a desire to make the best of the remaining years. One woman put it like this:

> It was a shock when a friend of ours, a middle-aged man, died suddenly. It got me thinking that I don't know how many years Dan and I have left together. I've been working hard and had some successes. Work is still very important to me, but I no longer want it to absorb my whole life. Now that we're in our forties, I want to spend time together and have fun. (Doress *et al.*, 1984, p. 440)

Personality and Gender Role Changes   Most adults do not undergo a traumatic mid-life crisis that transforms their personality, values, and behavior. **Longitudinal studies**, studies that trace change or lack of change by following the same people over a period of years, indicate considerable *continuity* in basic personal traits (Bee, 1987). However, many middle-aged men and women do become somewhat less rigid in their conformity to culturally defined gender roles, becoming more androgynous as they age (Zube, 1982).

Men in middle age tend to become less competitive and more nurturing (Goleman, 1990; Moreland, 1989). They are less concerned with control, mastery, and the future and more concerned with emotional expression, companionship, and the present. Work becomes somewhat less important and people, both inside and outside the family, more important. One middle-aged man reviewed his adulthood like this, " . . . in my 20s I learned to get along with my wife, in my 30s to get ahead in my job. In my 40s I worried about other people's lives" (quoted in Goleman, 1990, p. B8).

Women, like men, often recognize and develop new sides of themselves in middle age. They become less passive and docile, more willing to assert themselves and to make decisions (Harris, Ellicott, & Holmes, 1986). Years of dealing with schools, pediatricians, teenagers, and employers while their husbands buried themselves in their own work undoubtedly contribute to these changes in women. By middle age, many women are ready to make major commitments to activities outside the home—returning to school, assuming more responsibility at work, or becoming community leaders.

Like increased resources, the physical and psychological changes of middle age can work in subtle ways to improve marriage. For example, changes in gender role orientation and recognition of the common symptoms of aging can improve husband-wife empathy and communication. This is especially likely to occur if both marriage partners

Longitudinal studies
studies that trace change or lack of change by following the same people over a period of years.

change at the same time, recognize the changes in themselves and in one another, and are able to talk to their spouse about the changes.

Increased empathy can contribute to better sexual relationships in the empty nest stage. When accompanied by a willingness to redefine what "good sex" is, empathy can help couples deal with the delayed sexual arousal time and erectile delay sometimes associated with male middle age. Under these circumstances, sexual intercourse can become more pleasurable, if somewhat less frequent, for both partners. The following quotes, the first by a male, the second by a female, illustrate these points.

> Well, Lila makes me feel like a real lover. I'll be honest. Believe me, as you get older, sometimes you get impotent, and sometimes it's a matter of concentration—you've brought a million things home from the office and you just can't function. Then you begin to question your own abilities. You need a woman who is compassionate about that. . . . You need a woman who is able to say, "Don't worry, that was today. There's always tomorrow." (quoted in Klagsburn, 1985, p. 111)

> When Jay used to lose his erection I would think that I had failed as a woman because I couldn't keep him aroused. But now I see that it can mean more time to play around and a chance to start over again so that lovemaking lasts longer. (quoted in Doress *et al.*, 1984, p. 452)

Thus, the physical and psychological changes associated with middle age have the potential for making empty nest marriages better. Whether or not they do so seems to depend on the partners' ability to adapt to change and to communicate well with one another, abilities developed earlier in the marriage.

Survivorship

A third explanation for the higher proportion of satisfied marriages in the empty nest stage suggests that those in dissatisfying marriages divorced before reaching this stage. This explanation differs from the others because it assumes that marriages do not really *improve* as a result of children leaving home or of couples experiencing middle age together. Rather, satisfied marriages dominate during the empty nest stage because only satisfied marriages survive that long. Consider a hypothetical neighborhood made up of 100 couples of about the same age who married at about the same time. Pretend that people do not leave the neighborhood as long as they are married to their original partner and that no one moves in to replace those who have left the neighborhood because of divorce. If all the couples are interviewed about their marriages after being married for three years, some (say about 25) will say that their marriages are dissatisfying. Five years later, many who were dissatisfied previously will have divorced and will not be around for the second round of questioning. Of course, a few more will have become dissatisfied in the meantime and most of them will eventually divorce. With each passing year, however, the *proportion* of satisfied marriages in the neighborhood is likely to increase since *most people who divorce do so within the first ten years of marriage* (Sweet & Bumpass, 1987). By the time the remaining couples have been married 20 or 30 years, the neighborhood will be one of mostly happy marriages.

The Nature of Empty Nest Marriages

The conclusion that all marriages lasting until the empty nest stage are happy, high quality marriages should not be carried too far, however. There are unhappy empty nest marriages. In fact, about 20 percent of all divorces take place in the middle and later years of marriage (Lloyd & Zick, 1986).

In addition, the *nature* of marital satisfaction in the empty nest stage is somewhat different than in the earliest stages of marriage. Marriage in the middle years is much less passionate, intense, and up-and-down than early marriage. Empty nest couples express their love for one another less often and spend less time in "positive interaction" (for example, discussing things calmly, working on a joint project, laughing together) than couples in earlier stages of marriage (Swensen, Eskew, & Kohlhepp, 1981; Gilford & Bengtson, 1979). At the same time, however, they identify fewer problems in their marriage and express fewer negative sentiments, such as sarcasm, belittlement, or anger, toward their partner (Swensen, Eskew, & Kohlhepp, 1981; Gilford & Bengtson, 1979). Thus, while many empty nest partners choose not to take advantage of their increased time and privacy to learn more about one another, neither do they do spend much time being mean to one another.

Couples who have been married for 20 or 30 years differ from newlyweds in other ways as well. Partners involved in a long-term marriage have an enormous investment in one another. They share a family culture, a collection of memories and material assets, and their children. They are tied to at least one other generation and often to two or even three others. Furthermore, they are recognized by the law, by major financial institutions, by their relatives, and by the community as an ongoing, established social unit. All these factors can contribute to marital satisfaction and to the commitment to stay together. Ongoing ties to other generations and to their communities present continuing challenges to empty nest couples, and their stable (if somewhat boring) marriage can help them to deal with these challenges. The next section emphasizes these outside-the-marriage commitments and challenges.

Continuity and Change in Nonfamily and Family Roles

As a general rule, couples in the empty nest stage of marriage are active participants in their neighborhoods, communities, and workplaces. Most continue to live in the same community, work in the same jobs, and participate in the same church, community, and recreational activities as they did before their children left home. These activities offer them high levels of social support as well as continuity. Empty nest couples are more involved in neighborhood, friendship, and marital networks of support than either parents with younger children or childless middle-aged couples (Ishii-Kuntz & Seccombe, 1989). Couples in the empty nest stage can call upon their many social ties to help them through times of change and trouble (Olson *et al.*, 1983). As one researcher put it, "Like placing one's eggs in many baskets, investing in several roles is likely to mean having several sources of stimulation, gratification, and social validation" (Baruch, 1984, p. 178).

While nonfamily roles, such as employee, church member, and neighbor, offer continuity in the middle years, empty nest couples can expect to see substantial changes, as well as some continuity, in their family roles. Some family changes involve loss—a parent dies or a child becomes increasingly independent—but more involve adjustments in the balance of generational obligations. More and more middle-aged people in the United States today are truly a **sandwich generation**, a term used to describe the unique position of adults who have one or more living parents and one or more adult children. When daughters- and sons-in-law, grandchildren, ex-daughters- and ex-sons-in-law, and stepchildren are added to the mix, the "sandwich" becomes especially complex. Giordano (1988) describes the family ties of those in their middle and later years as a submarine sandwich:

> A submarine sandwich is longer, bigger, and more complex as will be the network and kinship relations for this new generation of young-old. When one begins to contemplate the complexity of relationships resulting from the divorce and remarriage patterns over the past 20 to 25 years, it becomes mind boggling. (p. 413)

The next section describes how empty nest couples adjust to their new roles as parents of adult children, grandparents, and aging children of elderly parents.

Sandwich generation adults who have one or more living parents and one or more adult children.

Relationships with Adult Children

Whether parents rejoice in or regret the departure of children from the home, the departure changes parent-child relationships. Parents of young *adults* have neither legally defined financial obligations to their children nor legal authority over them. Both parents and children have to find new ways of interacting with one another. Although U.S. culture holds vague, informal norms such as "family members should remain in contact with one another and help one another out," it provides few specific guidelines about the nature or extent of the contact or of the help to be provided. Both parents and their young adult children are likely to have competing commitments—to their spouses, work, and communities—demanding their day-to-day attention. They typically live in different households and often in different cities or states. Taken together, these facts mean that contemporary U.S. parent-adult child relationships are largely *voluntaristic* in nature. The parties involved have a good deal of choice regarding the amount and nature of their contact; the contact is likely to take place during leisure time and there is likely to be variation from family to family, child to child, and over time (Thompson & Walker, 1984; Hess & Waring, 1978).

"Thank you all for coming. Starting next year, Mother's Days will find me at the Desert Palm Spa."

Source: *New Yorker,* May 14, 1990.

Although norms about intergenerational support obligations are rather vague, research on parent-young adult child relationships shows that, during the empty nest years, parents tend to assist their young adult children in terms of services, money, and gifts much more often than young adult children help out their parents (Thompson & Walker, 1984; Cheal, 1983). If financially able, parents frequently supply their children with the down payment for a house or the deposit on an apartment, continue allowances at least through the college years, and support children going through job changes or divorce (Aldous, 1987). The giving of such aid does not necessarily reflect or bring about close emotional ties since the help is often given in troubled, conflictive situations (Aldous, 1987). In fact, long-term *nonreciprocal* (children mostly receiving, parents mostly giving) patterns may get in the way of close, lasting ties on an equal basis (Aldous, 1987; Thompson & Walker, 1984). Both the adult child (who may feel under pressure to conform to parental wishes in exchange for parental aid) and the parent (who worries whether the child will ever be self-supporting) are likely to be uncomfortable with such nonreciprocal arrangements. As in any voluntary relationship, parents seem to have their highest quality, most enjoyable relationships with adult offspring who share their values, reciprocate emotional support, and do not require financial assistance (Aldous, 1987; Thompson & Walker, 1984).

Some parents aid their adult children by continuing to share their home with them. Throughout much of U.S. history, many children remained in the parental home until they married. During the 1960s and 1970s, unmarried young adults diverged somewhat from this pattern and lived independently from their parents in the years before marriage. The 1980s saw a slight turn back toward the historic pattern. In 1970, 54 percent of all men and 41 percent of all women aged 18 to 24 were living with one or both parents; by 1988, 61 percent of all men and 48 percent of all women, 18 to 24, were residing in the parental home (Saluter, 1989, Table G). The reasons for the increase included an older age at marriage, more difficulty in finding jobs, higher rates of unwed pregnancy, separation and divorce, and higher attendance at community colleges (Riche, 1987; Glick & Lin, 1986b).

For some young adults, staying at home is merely a temporary delay in leaving home. Most of those 18 to 20 years old who continue to live with their parents do so because they are attending a nearby school. Since many parents with college-aged children also have younger children in the home and since college attendance typically follows right after high school, this situation delays but does not interrupt the empty nest stage. More stressful are situations in which children continue to live in the household after the age of 22 (Clemens & Axelson, 1985) or in which they move back home after having lived independently for some years. In these cases, the parents have probably already spent some time alone as a couple and have grown to like it; moreover, they *expected* their children to be on their own by this time.

Family therapists such as Clemens and Axelson (1985) suggest that such living arrangements may delay the development of *both* the young adult *and* his or her middle-aged parents. In respect to the parents, they write:

> As individuals, these parents are often prevented from experiencing the freedom necessary to develop further interests without the burdens of children at home. As a couple, they may be prevented from evaluating their marital relationship and resolving issues which may have been "on the back burner" while there were still children at home. (p. 262)

Other researchers find that couples with children still in the home have lower marital satisfaction than those of the same age without children at home (Lee, 1988; Pittman & Lloyd, 1988). At the very least, the situation often leads to a prolongation or resumption of conflicts that first emerged when the children were adolescents—How should the young adults dress? When should they come home at night? Who can they bring home with them and for how long? What family expenses should they share? What household chores will they be responsible for?

Although there may be continuing problems between adult children and their parents after children leave home, the relationship tends to improve as children take on the adult roles of worker, spouse, and parent. During the empty nest years, parents see their children go through a number of important transitions. The transitions affect the views of both child and parent. Fischer's (1981) study of mothers and their daughters found the transition to motherhood by the daugther (and to grandmotherhood by the mother) to be of special significance. The first quote is from a new grandmother; the second from a new mother:

> She's an excellent mother. You know I was surprised. You see your children as teenagers. She was extremely attractive and she was very interested in clothes. She wouldn't mind spending $100 on an outfit but wouldn't care if she went without food. But I'm pleased that she's turned out to be a marvelous mother. (quoted in Fischer, 1981, p. 617)

> I understand how hard it was for her—like, to cook a meal and not have everybody like the meal. And have them complaining. "Oh, this again," or "I don't like this," but you can't satisfy everyone. You know—things like that. You understand what they went through more. (quoted in Fischer, 1981, p. 618)

Grandparents today can choose in what ways and how often to be involved with their grandchildren.

Relationships with Grandchildren

Because of increased life expectancy, more people than ever before live long enough to become grandparents and to know their grandchildren as both children and adults (Hagestad & Burton, 1986). Most parents first make the transition to grandparenthood some time between their fortieth and sixty-fifth birthdays. Grandparents show tremendous diversity in their relationships with grandchildren—ranging from "remote" to "very involved and influential" (Cherlin & Furstenberg, 1985). A remote relationship is one in which the grandparents seldom see their grandchild and never share activities, offer services, or discuss serious concerns. At the opposite extreme are grandparent-grandchild relationships in which the grandparent is an everyday presence in the life of the grandchild, giving advice and comfort and sharing a variety of activities. The grandfather quoted below, reviewing his years with a grandson now in college, shows this pattern:

> ... if he has some problem, he'll come over to see me. . . . And if I need some help, like getting some screens down for putting screens in for the summer, I'll get him to help me bring those down. . . . You know, we used to take tremendous numbers of trips together and things. I've had him up to Canada, I've had him down in Florida, I've had him out at the lake. (quoted in Cherlin & Furstenberg, 1985, pp. 108–109)

What factors influence whether the grandparent-grandchild relationship is remote, involved, or somewhere in between? Geographic proximity is one important factor: the most involved grandparents are those who share a home with the grandchild. Geographic closeness does not guarantee a close relationship, however. Parents have considerable influence over how often grandparents see their grandchildren and what they do together. When grandparents and parents are in conflict with one another, grandparents' contact with their grandchildren may be extremely limited, even if they live close to one another (Cherlin & Furstenberg, 1985). Divorce also influences grandparent-grandchild relationships. A common pattern is for grandparents to become closer to a daughter's children following her divorce, but to see much less of a son's children after his divorce (Furstenberg *et al.*, 1983). In addition, the age of both the grandparents and the grandchildren influences the relationship. The combination of young grandparents and young grandchildren generally brings about the most involvement.

Beyond all these factors, the grandparents have considerable choice about which grandchild (or grandchildren) to be involved with and how involved to be. Cherlin and Furstenberg (1985) call this "selective investment." A grandfather or grandmother frequently selects a special favorite from among his or her grandchildren and develops an intimate bond with that grandchild while maintaining more remote relationships with other grandchildren.

Most grandparents say they are happy being grandparents and find grandparenthood easier than parenthood. In one study of grandmothers, for example, 40 percent said they enjoyed grandparenting more than parenting and an additional 25 percent enjoyed it just as much (Robertson, 1977, p. 170).

Relationships with Elderly Parents

In addition to adapting to ever-changing adult children and developing relationships with new grandchildren, the "sandwich generation" must also learn how to relate to aging, sometimes frail, but still living parents. This is a challenge that most empty nest couples have not previously

	Table 13–2 Actual and Projected Growth of Population Aged 85 and Older, United States, 1910–2050	
Year	Number of People Aged 85 and Older	Percent of Total U.S. Population
1910	167,000	.2
1930	272,000	.2
1950	577,000	.4
1970	1,409,000	.7
1990	3,313,000	1.3
2010	6,551,000	2.3
2030	8,612,000	2.8
2050	16,034,000	5.2

Source: U.S. Senate Special Committee on Aging, 1986, p. 12.

faced during their own marriage. Furthermore, the current empty nest generation is the first to have to deal with very elderly parents to any great extent. Of course, many people still lose their parents early in middle age or even before, but in 1980, 40 percent of those in their late fifties and 20 percent of those in their early sixties had at least one surviving parent (Brody, 1985, p. 20). These proportions are certain to increase in the future.

Many of the interaction patterns elderly parents and adult children follow are of the voluntaristic, parent-as-friend, reciprocal model discussed earlier with each generation living independently and taking care of most of its own needs. However, as people become very old, they often become more dependent on younger people to help them with daily activities. People over the age of 85 are especially likely to need such assistance. This 85 and over age group is the fastest growing segment of U.S. population. Table 13–2 illustrates the extent of its proportional growth; the Personal Application "How to Calculate Your Life Expectancy" can help you estimate if you are likely to live this long.

Most aid received by the very old is given by family members—by the spouse until she or he is no longer alive or able and then by children. Although adults of all ages are involved in aiding elderly relatives, people in their forties, fifties, and sixties are the most usual helpers. Women are more frequent helpers than men, and unmarried children supply more help than married children (Stoller, 1983).

What form does the aid take? Most often, the aid is practical and emotional rather than financial. Parents over 65 continue to *give more*

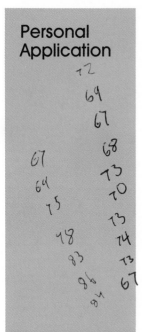

Personal Application

72
69
67
67   68
64   73
15   70
          73
48   74
  83   73
   86   67
     84

How to Calculate Your Life Expectancy

While there is no sure way to calculate your life expectancy even with computer systems, there are certain guidelines, such as this test, that can give you rough estimates. If you are age 20 to 65 and reasonably healthy, this test provides a life insurance company's statistical view of your life expectancy.

Start with the number 72.

Personal data:

If you are male, subtract three.

If female, add four.

If you live in an urban area with a population over two million, subtract two.

If you live in a town under 10,000 or on a farm, add two.

If a grandparent lived to 85, add two.

If all four grandparents lived to 80, add six.

If either parent died of a stroke or heart attack before the age of 50, subtract four.

If any parent, brother, or sister under 50 has (or had) cancer or a heart condition, or has had diabetes since childhood, subtract three.

Do you earn over $50,000 a year? Subtract two.

If you finished college, add one. If you have a graduate or professional degree, add two more.

If you are 65 or over and still working, add three.

If you live with a spouse or friend, add five. If not, subtract one for every 10 years alone since age 25.

Health style facts:

If you work behind a desk, subtract three.

If your work requires regular, heavy physical labor, add three.

If you exercise strenuously (tennis, running, swimming, etc.) five times a week for at least a half-hour, add four. Two or three times a week, add two.

Do you sleep more than 10 hours each night? Subtract four.

Are you intense, aggressive, easily angered? Subtract three.

Are you easygoing and relaxed? Add three.

Are you happy? Add one. Unhappy? Subtract two.

Have you had a speeding ticket in the last year? Subtract one.

Do you smoke more than two packs a day? Subtract eight. One to two packs? Subtract six. One-half to one? Subtract three.

Are you overweight by 50 pounds or more? Subtract eight. By 30 to 50 pounds? Subtract four. By 10 to 30 pounds? Subtract two.

If you are a man over 40 and have annual checkups, add two.

If you are a woman and see a gynecologist once a year, add two.

Age adjustment:
If you are between 30 and 40, add two.

If you are between 40 and 50, add three.

If you are between 50 and 70, add four.

If you are over 70, add five.

Add up your score to get your life expectancy at this time. Now compare it to the national average for various ages:

CHECKING YOUR PERSONAL AND CULTURAL HEALTH STATUS

AGE NOW	MALE	FEMALE
0–10	69.8	77.2
11–19	70.3	77.5
20–29	71.2	77.8
30–39	71.3	77.9
40–49	73.5	79.4
50–59	76.1	79.0
60–69	80.2	83.6
70–79	85.9	87.7
80–90	90.0	91.1

If you would like your life expectancy to come out at a later age, look back over the questions relating to health practices and find those in which you subtracted years. Change those to positive health practices and you can add many years to your life expectancy.

Source: Allen with Linde, 1981, pp. 19–21. Further information concerning this quiz may be obtained from Human Resources Institute, Inc., 115 Dunder Road, Burlington, VT 05401.

financial aid within the family than they receive. However, they *receive more services* from family members than they give (Cheal, 1983). Adult children most often assist their elderly parents in the areas of shopping and transportation, emotional support, managing money and services, housework, and laundry. Assistance with meal preparation, personal care, and using the telephone is less common (Brody & Schoonover, 1986).

The decisions about when an elderly parent needs help and what types of help to give are often difficult ones. When mother consistently fails to take her prescribed medicine, is this a dangerous sign of memory loss or is she just choosing not to take the medicine? Should dad be allowed to keep living in a house to which he is very attached if it is filled with fire hazards? One in-depth study of how families make decisions about such questions found that, after considerable consultation among themselves, adult siblings typically opted for "an unstated principle of least involvement" in the lives of frail, elderly parents (Matthews & Rosner, 1988, p. 187). That is, they chose the alternative that would interfere with the parents' lives the least, while still protecting their frail parents from harm. For example, children chose to indirectly monitor parental well-being by telephoning several times a day instead of removing the parent from the home or making drastic changes in parental routine. In this way, the children helped preserve the independence of both generations.

In cases where the parent becomes mentally incompetent or severely physically incapacitated, children must make choices about **eldercare**, care provided to mentally or physically incapacitated elderly people by relatives or nonrelatives. One choice in such cases is for the incapacitated parent to move into the home of an adult child. Nationally, 10 percent of people aged 65–74 and 17 percent of those over the age of 75 share a home with a relative (Saluter, 1989), and one longitudinal survey of middle-aged couples estimated that 16 percent of these couples had taken in an elderly relative at some time (Beck & Beck, 1984).

The strain of parent care is especially wearing because it is unexpected, because it reverses dependency relationships, and because it is likely to become more taxing as time goes on. Daughters and daughters-in-law who provide most eldercare frequently report feeling depressed, anxious, frustrated, and exhausted (Brody, 1985). Providing eldercare often means that the caregivers must reduce their involvement in other activities. Nationwide, 12 percent of women who care for elderly relatives give up paid jobs to do so; an additional 14 percent shift from full-time to part-time work (Beck et al., 1990).

In a small percentage of cases (3 to 4 percent according to several estimates), the frustrations of eldercare lead to **elder abuse**—neglect, the use of physical violence, or the use of verbal aggression against the elderly person (Pillemer & Finkelhor, 1988). Elder abuse is more likely if a household contains both an elderly married couple *and* an adult child and if one of the elderly spouses is in poor health (Pillemer & Finkelhor, 1988).

The strain of eldercare can also affect the relationship between the caregiving daughter or daughter-in-law and her husband. In the worst case, care of an elderly relative can become a point of couple conflict

Eldercare care provided to mentally or physically incapacitated elderly people by relatives or nonrelatives.

Elder abuse neglect, the use of physical violence, or the use of verbal aggression against an elderly person.

(Kleban *et al.*, 1989; Matthews & Rosner, 1988). Even if the husband is helpful and sympathetic, taking care of an elderly person in the home often means that a couple cannot take vacations, spend private time together, or carry through on career or educational plans (Kleban *et al.*, 1989).

In short, caring for an elderly parent can adversely affect the privacy, time, and money resources of empty nest couples. There is no definitive information that such care arrangements adversely affect the marriage itself (Kleban *et al.*, 1989), but eldercare in the child's home certainly presents yet another challenge to empty nest couples.

Such family strains sometimes lead adult children to place their ailing parent in a nursing home. Coming to this decision is often a painful experience, preceded by months or years of trying other alternatives. Once accomplished, it can free adult children to focus on the emotional and social aspects of their relationship with their parent, leaving physical care to others (Smith & Bengtson, 1979). Only a small proportion of the elderly—about 5 percent of all those over age 65—live in a nursing home. Even elderly over the age of 85 are more likely to live alone or with a relative (usually a child) than in a nursing home: nearly 30 percent of them live alone, 27 percent live with relatives, and 23 percent reside in an institution, with the remainder living with a spouse or a nonrelative (Bould, Sanborn, & Reif, 1989, p. 34).

CONTINUITY AND CHANGE IN THE RETIREMENT STAGE

The second turning point in the later years of long-term marriages is marked by the giving up of another major adult role—that of wage-earning worker. Paid work in the labor force is a major source of identity for adults (especially men) and a major way of structuring family time. Thus, the voluntary or involuntary relinquishment of the active worker role involves a number of personal and family adjustments. At one time, these adjustments centered around only the husband's retirement—no longer. Today, since many wives also undergo a retirement transition, the number of potential family adjustments has been compounded.

Perhaps more than any other stage of marriage, the retirement stage is highly variable from couple to couple. Couples vary in terms of when they retire, how long the retirement stage lasts, and where (and how well) they live in retirement. Some couples, especially those who had a child in their late thirties or forties and who retired before age 65, may leave their work before or at about the same time they retire from active parenting. Others work well into their eighties and do not "retire" from work until they die. Some couples have 25 or 30 years of retirement together; others have less than a month. (For example, one professor friend of ours graded the final exams for the last course he taught before retirement while in the hospital where he died less than a month later.) A minority of couples in the retirement stage move far from the community where they spent their middle age. Most, however, continue to live in the same house in which they raised their children. Some couples in retirement are plagued by income and health problems; others are among the most affluent and healthiest married couples in the United States.

The Retirement Transition

The retirement stage begins when both spouses cease working in their regular jobs. Sixty-five is often assumed to be the start of retirement in the United States and, since many of the studies we refer to use 65 as a breaking point, we will assume that couples in which the husband is older than 65 are retired couples and couples in which the husband is younger than 65 are not. In fact, however, at least in recent years, most men and women retire *before* reaching age 65. A recent nationwide 15 year longitudinal study of men retiring during the late 1960s and the 1970s found that about 70 percent retired before the age of 65 (Parnes & Less, 1985c, p. 75). On the other hand, 17 percent of all men and about 8 percent of all women remain in the labor force after age 65 (U.S. Bureau of the Census, 1991a, p. 384).

Involuntary Retirement

Involuntary retirement permanent withdrawal from the labor force for reasons not under the worker's control.

People retire for a variety of reasons. According to the longitudinal study mentioned previously, about 40 percent of men experienced **involuntary retirement,** withdrawal from the labor force for reasons not under the worker's control (Parnes & Less, 1985c, p. 71). The most common reason for involuntary retirement (accounting for one-third of *all* retirements) was poor health; many health-related retirements occurred before the age of 62. Men and women in especially physically demanding or hazardous occupations who started their working lives at an early age and who had limited schooling were most vulnerable to health problems and, consequently, to early, involuntary retirement. Others (about 5 percent of the retirees in the study) retired involuntarily after losing their jobs in late middle age because of layoffs, bankruptcy, or mergers. Finally, a small proportion (about 3 percent of all retirees) retired before they wanted to because of mandatory retirement rules (Parnes & Less, 1985c, p. 70).

Voluntary Retirement

The majority of retirees today choose to give up their paid work roles while still in good health and without being under organizational pressure to do so. They experience **voluntary retirement**. Voluntary retirees choose when to retire by assessing their potential retirement benefits, their level of dissatisfaction with work, and their personal preference for leisure over work (Parnes, 1985). When both husband and wife are in the labor force, they often coordinate their dates of retirement so as to receive maximum benefits and to retire at about the same time. Thus, some husbands delay their own retirement if their (usually younger) wives are due to receive an especially attractive benefits package at a certain age, and some wives (especially those whose own benefits are rather meager) retire early so that they can be at home when their husband retires.

Voluntary retirement permanent withdrawal from the labor force while still in good health and without being under organizational pressure to do so.

Adjusting to Retirement

Retirement represents many potential losses. Work is a major source of adult identity, status, and income. Work hours structure daily, weekly, and seasonal time for individuals and for families. Most people find many of their friends and engage in much of their social interaction in the workplace. For these reasons, the first sociologists and psychologists to study retirement predicted that individuals would experience retirement as a devastating loss and have substantial difficulty adjusting to it.

More than 30 years of research have largely eliminated these fears. Most retirees seem to adapt quickly and well to retirement. Retirement, by itself, does not substantially affect one's satisfaction with life or one's morale (Atchley, 1991; Hooyman & Kiyak, 1991). Parnes (1985) makes the following generalization based on his research and that of others: "If one is compelled to make a single generalization about retirement, perhaps the most valid would be that it is generally entered into voluntarily, found to be pleasant, and not regretted even after many years" (p. 218). In other words, the picture of the retired man as miserable and depressed, like the picture of the depressed empty nest mother, seems largely mythical.

There are many possible reasons why retirement is a less devastating event than was once predicted. Chapter 9 indicated that work in an industrial economy, while very necessary for most families, is, in many ways, incompatible with good family relationships. Retirement eliminates many of the tensions and conflicts between family and work. Men who shift toward a more androgynous gender role orientation in middle age may find their work less and less meaningful as they

Retirement often gives couples more relaxed time together, as it eliminates many work-family tensions present earlier in marriage.

enter their fifties and sixties and welcome more time at home. The fact that recent generations of workers, particularly those who worked for large organizations or who belonged to labor unions with generous pension programs, can retire without substantial changes in their standard of living makes retirement even more attractive. Quite a number of adults express a preference for family and leisure over work throughout their adult years; for them, the "loss" of work is a welcome loss.

Some people continue to be truly commited to work and know that they would find themselves bored and unhappy if they retired. Such people often stay in the labor market past the age of 65. For most of them, work fills a psychological, not an economic, need (Parnes & Less, 1985b). These elderly workers tend to be healthy, well-educated people in professional, managerial or self-employed occupations. Even if they retire from their previous job, these individuals are able to take advantage of opportunities to work part time or even to start new businesses (Croft, 1986).

There are, of course, some dissatisfied retirees. Men and women who retired involuntarily for health or labor market adversity reasons are particularly prone to dissatisfaction in retirement (Crowley, 1985). These involuntary retirees started the retirement stage before they wanted or expected to and, in many cases, are out-of-sync with their agemates. Retiring involuntarily, especially at an earlier-than-normal age, often has negative economic consequences as well. For these dissatisfied retirees, poor health and inadequate income rather than retirement *per se* probably explain much of their negative reaction.

Marriage in the Retirement Years

In some ways, retirement stage marriages are simply continuations of empty nest stage marriages. The newly retired couple is part of a family network of adult children, grandchildren, occasionally parents and great-grandchildren, and siblings. They maintain many of the ties to their neighborhood, community, and church established much earlier in their marriage. The physical and psychological changes that began in middle age continue into the retirement years. Most retirement couples continue to engage in the same leisure activities that they did prior to retirement. And, of course, husband and wife continue to have one another.

Whatever the continuity, there are also differences between the empty nest and retirement stages of marriages. Couples in the retirement stage, on average, have less money, more free time, greater health problems and higher probability of death, and greater marital satisfaction than couples in the empty nest stage.

Less Money

The income of married couples typically declines after retirement. Look back at Table 13–1 and you will see that the median monthly income of elderly people is far less than the median monthly income of middle-aged people. Table 13–1 also indicates, however, that those currently in their late sixties and early seventies have a median net worth slightly higher than those in late middle age and much higher than that of younger people.

Despite the fact that they have much less monthly income than the middle aged, most retired married couples claim to be satisfied with their financial status and do not see themselves as having money problems (Parnes and Less, 1985a; Crystal, 1982). There are probably several reasons for this. First, some expenses—transportation and clothing, in particular—decline when one is no longer working. Secondly, the current generation of **young-old** (those 60–75 years of age) are much better off economically than their surviving parents and grandparents were in old age and probably better off than they themselves expected to be.

Young-old people 60 to 75 years of age.

One measure of the improvement in elderly income over time is the proportion of elderly falling below the official poverty line. In 1959, 35 percent of the elderly were poor by official standards (Hooyman & Kiyak, 1991); by 1989, the proportion had dropped to 11 percent (U.S. Bureau of the Census, 1991a, p. 463). Much of this improvement is due

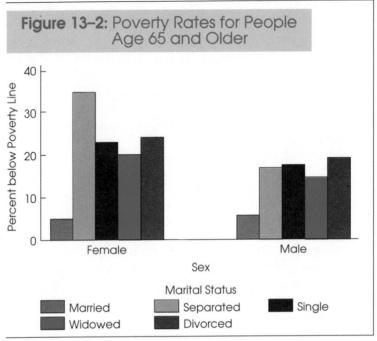

Figure 13–2: Poverty Rates for People Age 65 and Older

The figure shows the financial advantages of having a spouse in the later years of life. Being nonmarried is associated with high rates of poverty, especially for women.

Source: Madonna Harrington Meyer © 1990 by the Society for the Study of Social Problems. Reprinted from *Social Problems*, Vol. 37, No. 4, p. 552 by permission.

to increases in Social Security benefits; part of it is because the current generation of young elderly is better educated and held better paying occupational positions during more favorable economic times than previous generations. Among the elderly, married couples are the least likely to be poor, a fact illustrated by Figure 13–2. Their relative prosperity makes them generally pleased with their economic situation.

More Time

Unlike empty nest couples who still have major commitments to work, retired couples have much more unstructured time. The "loss" of work results in a gain in choices about how to spend time. For the most part, retired couples spend their time doing many of the same things they did earlier in life—individual or shared leisure activities, visiting with friends and relatives, and maintaining and improving the house and yard. The difference is that they have more time to do so.

Retirement with its abundance of unstructured time opens up the *possibility* of doing things that were impossible during the working years. For example, some retired couples leave home and travel for months or even years. Others choose to change getting-up times, bedtimes, and mealtimes to a pattern that better conforms to their personal preferences. Still others structure their time by putting together a busy schedule of leisure activities, club meetings, and volunteer work.

Retirees express some ambivalence about the availability of large amounts of unstructured time. Men in one national survey cited "the amount of time available for one's choice of activity" second most often when asked to list the best things about retirement (not working was mentioned most often), but 35 percent of them also cited "boredom" as a negative aspect of retirement (Crowley, 1985, p. 158). A much smaller scale study of the wives of retirees found much the same ambivalence: wives mentioned "time available to do what you want" most often when asked about positive aspects of their husbands' retirements, but 31 percent also felt that their husbands did not have enough to do (Hill & Dorfman, 1982).

Setting up a new routine that allows some time for joint projects and some time for individual privacy is an important adjustment task for couples in the early years of retirement. One change that many couples make is to move toward a less rigid division of household labor along gender lines. Rexroat and Shehan (1987) found that retired couples spend about four more hours a week doing housework than empty nest couples. This study and others conclude that retired husbands put in more hours doing housework and do a somewhat greater proportion of the total than in earlier stages of marriage (Dorfman & Heckert, 1988; Rexroat & Shehan, 1987; Albrecht, Bahr, & Chadwick, 1979).

Health and Death

Changes in health and the increasing probability of death are minor issues for most middle-aged people. They take on increasing importance as people age, often shaping how retirement stage couples spend their days and their money.

Health Status of the Elderly   For many, although not all elderly, the retirement years coincide with an increase in health problems. Health is important because it influences how much control retired people have over their day-to-day lives and how they can use their ample free time. Elderly in good health and with few impairments in hearing, sight, or mobility can travel, continue to visit old friends and make new ones, help out family members, and maintain their financial independence. Those in poor health or with significant impairments may be confined to their home (or even to one room), unable to interact with friends, incapable of offering services to their family, dependent on their spouse or other people, or forced to spend much of their income on medication and health care. Studies consistently identify good health and physical mobility as major determinants of life satisfaction (McGhee, 1985; Hill & Dorfman, 1982), retirement satisfaction (Seccombe & Lee, 1986), financial satisfaction (Hennon & Burton, 1986), and psychological well-being (Quinn, 1983) in old age.

The elderly are more likely than younger people to have one or more activity-limiting chronic conditions such as heart problems, arthritis, hypertension, or back problems. While fewer than 10 percent of those under 45 have health-related activity limitations, the proportion rises to almost 25 percent for those 45 to 65 and to nearly 40 percent for those over 65 (U.S. Bureau of the Census, 1991a, p. 121). In most cases, these chronic conditions do not interfere with such basic activities as walking, dressing, bathing, and household work. Chronic conditions develop gradually and people adapt to them by adopting a more relaxed pace and by giving up their most strenuous activities. The longer a person lives, however, the greater the probability that the most basic activities of daily life will be affected by chronic health problems. Consider, for example, the basic activity of being able to "get around outside." Six percent of those 65 to 74 have difficulty with this activity; the proportion rises to 15 percent of those 75 to 84 and to 38 percent of those over 85 (U.S. Bureau of the Census, 1991a, p. 121).

Many of the chronic impairments associated with old age are not inevitable; some are even reversible. Certain heart problems, circulatory problems, and cancers are directly related to eating patterns, smoking, drinking, and a sedentary lifestyle (instead of exercising) throughout adulthood (Rowe & Kahn, 1987; Chapman, LaPlante, & Wilensky, 1986). These behaviors are under individual control. Younger people can make choices now which will make a difference in later life. Elderly people who watch their diets and engage in moderate exercise can avoid certain further health impairments.

Death   The possibility of losing a spouse through death exists at all stages of marriage but becomes much more probable with age (review Figure 13–1). Couples in the retirement stage are likely to see more and more of their agemates cease being "couples" and becoming widows or widowers. They also live with the reality that their years together are coming to an end.

Since the average life expectancy of women in the United States exceeds that of men by about seven years (look back to Figure 1–2) and since most women marry older men, wives experience the death of a spouse much more often than husbands do. These same facts make it much more likely that women (especially older women) who are widowed will remain widowed while widowed men have more chances for remarriage. Figure 13–3 depicts the marital statuses of all men and women over the age of 65. As you can see, elderly women as a whole are slightly more likely to be widowed than married, whereas elderly men are much more likely to be married than widowed. The discrep-

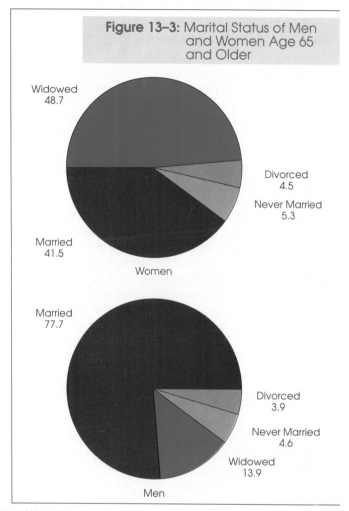

Figure 13–3: Marital Status of Men and Women Age 65 and Older

Widowed
48.7

Divorced
4.5

Never Married
5.3

Married
41.5

Women

Married
77.7

Divorced
3.9

Never Married
4.6

Widowed
13.9

Men

Continuation of the role of marriage partner is much more common for elderly men than for elderly women. When all people over age 65 are taken into account, women are somewhat more likely to be widowed than married and men are much more likely to be married than widowed.

Source: Saluter, 1989, p. 9.

ancy between men and women increases with age: two-thirds of all women over the age of 75 are widows, while almost 70 percent of men over the age of 75 are married (U.S. Bureau of the Census, 1991a, p. 42). *Most men die married; most women die after living without a spouse for some years.*

Marital Satisfaction in Retirement Couples

Retirement couples, in general, seem as fully satisfied with their marriages as empty nest couples. In fact, in most studies of marital satisfaction, retirement stage couples have higher satisfaction scores than empty nest couples (Gilford & Bengtson, 1979; Sporakowski & Hughston, 1978; Spanier, Lewis, & Cole, 1975; Rollins & Cannon, 1974). The finding holds for both cross-sectional and longitudinal studies of marital satisfaction (Weishaus & Field, 1988; Ferraro & Wan, 1986).

Like empty nest couples who stay together, retirement stage couples are satisfied survivors—most agemates who were strongly dissatisfied with their marriages probably divorced long ago. Retirement couples have even more time together than empty nest couples do and there is less chance that they will have a child or elderly parent sharing the home with them and interfering with their privacy. Even more than the empty nest couples, retirement couples can look around at the family they have created and back at the joyful and sad times they have shared together.

The gender role orientation changes begun in middle age continue. Elderly couples share more household work and decision making than do empty nest couples (Dorfman & Heckert, 1988; Albrecht, Bahr, & Chadwick, 1979) and perceive the division of marital tasks to be more equitable (Schafer & Keith, 1981). Like those couples slightly younger than themselves, retirement stage couples are rather low on love expression (Swensen, Eskew, & Kohlhepp, 1981). They have intermediate levels of positive interaction and very low levels of both negative interaction (Gilford & Bengtson, 1979) and marital problems (Swensen, Eskew, & Kohlhepp, 1981).

The benefits of marriage discussed in Chapter 6 still apply in old age. Elderly married people have higher survival rates, higher incomes (remember Figure 13–2), a better chance of remaining noninstitutionalized, and better health than elderly people who are widowed, divorced, or permanently single (Johnson, 1985). The sections that follow detail two additional benefits of marriage in old age: ready access to a sexual partner and ready access to a caregiver.

Sexual Activity in Elderly Couples   Old age by itself eliminates neither interest in sex nor the capacity for an active sex life. Elderly people who are married have ready access to a very familiar sexual partner and often want to remain sexually active. The Duke Longitudinal Studies, one of the best known longitudinal studies of middle age and aging, found that the most common pattern in terms of sexual intercourse in the last half of life was stability. Most of those in the Duke sample (ranging in age from 46 to 71 at the beginning of the study) had sexual intercourse once or twice a week during both the first year they were surveyed and also six years later. Of the couples not following this pattern of stability, more decreased than increased their sexual activity (George & Weiler, 1985). Both husbands and wives agreed that health impairments of the husband were the major contributor to reduced sexual activity.

The health changes associated with old age require some elderly married couples to make adjustments in the sexual aspects of marriage. Generally, this adjustment entails slowing down the love-making process, more emphasis on oral sex and manual stimulation, and more fondling and cuddling (Brecher, 1984). Sexual intercourse does not, in the usual case, end; it simply becomes less of a focus. Given reasonably good health, most elderly couples can remain sexually active until the end of marriage. As with many physical and mental activities, those couples who "stay in practice" with sex throughout their marriage are the most sexually active in old age. Luria and Mead (1984) summed up the issue when they wrote: "The sexual rule for men is: Stay well. For women, it is: Stay married. For both, the implicit rule is: Stay sexually active" (p. 375).

As the quote implies, elderly individuals who are not currently married have a difficult time finding a sexual partner even though they may continue to have sexual interests and needs. The problem is especially acute for unmarried elderly women. Many such women were socialized to believe that sex should occur only within marriage; they enter a dating world in which such values are no longer as strongly held. In addition to this values barrier, they also face a competition barrier. There are many more elderly women without partners than elderly men without partners and some of the available men prefer younger women.

Elderly unmarried men have less difficulty with respect to the number of potential partners. However, initiating new sexual relationships may be difficult and frightening for older men. Their former wives were often aware of and understanding about sexual limitations; the men fear that new partners may not show such understanding.

Once elderly people break through the obstacles to dating, they behave much like younger daters. Elderly daters experience the same " . . . perspiring hands, a feeling of awkwardness, inability to concentrate, anxiety when away from the loved one and heart palpitations" that younger daters do (Bulcroft & O'Conner-Roden, 1986a, p. 68). The small amount of available research on elderly daters further suggests that their dating relationships progress into sexual ones very quickly and very openly (Bulcroft & O'Conner-Roden, 1986a).

The Spouse as Caregiver   Being married is one of the best ways for disabled and sick elderly people to avoid both institutionalization and heavy dependence on adult children. Despite all the recent attention to middle-aged caretakers, eldercare is done by the spouse first. Ailing elderly prefer care by a spouse rather than dependence on adult children for a number of reasons. For one thing, elderly receiving care from a spouse generally stay in their own home, whereas those cared for by children sometimes have to move in with or closer to the child.

Care given by a spouse is more reciprocal, more between equals, and less a reversal of a previous relationship than care given by children. Spouse care maintains the independence between generations—an important value for most U.S. families—and allows younger generations to take care of their own family and personal needs.

Although care by a spouse is usually preferable to other alternatives, it can be stressful for both partners. Among the most stressful of caregiving situations is care of a person with **dementia**, a condition involving memory loss, wandering, incontinence (lack of bladder control), paranoia, and repetitive behaviors. (Alzheimer's Disease is one form of dementia that has received much publicity in recent years). Zarit, Todd, and Zarit (1986), in a study of dementia patients and their spousal caregivers, found that some spouses adapted to the caregiving role much better than others. In fact, the subjective feelings of the caregiver—for example, frustration, guilt, depression—rather than the actual symptoms of the patient best predicted which patients entered nursing homes. The researchers also discovered that even those severely stressed in the early stages of their spouse's disease learned to tolerate the disease symptoms over time. Caregiving husbands reported less stress than caregiving wives in both this study of dementia and Johnson's (1985) study of spousal caregiving after hospitalization. Researchers do not fully understand the reasons for the differences. Perhaps husbands have a higher tolerance level than wives, perhaps they are more reluctant to admit that they are stressed, or perhaps caregiving husbands report less stress than caregiving wives because they typically receive more help from adult children (Zarit, Todd, and Zarit, 1986; Johnson, 1985).

Despite the possible stress involved, spousal caregiving has few effects on the quality of the marriage or on the couple's satisfaction with it. Couples continue to share activities and interests and turn to one another for help with problems despite the health limitations of one partner (Johnson, 1985). Illness of one partner and caregiving by the other has the potential for bringing a couple closer together; some caregiving spouses feel important and strongly needed by their partner for the first time in the marriage (Weishaus & Field, 1988). Finally, although poor health is a very good predictor of dissatisfaction in other areas of life, poor health on the part of one partner in a retirement stage marriage does not seem to affect the *marital* satisfaction of either partner (Weishaus & Field, 1988; Johnson, 1985).

Johnson (1985) summarized her interview study of elderly couples in which one spouse had been recently hospitalized with the following words that probably hold true for many marriages at this stage:

> . . . old age is a time when being married provides a significant dyadic relationship for which there are few substitutes. . . . the criteria for a successful marriage in old age is neither a romantic relation-

Dementia
a condition involving memory loss, wandering, incontinence, paranoia, and repetitive behaviors.

ship or one laden with positive or negative emotions. Instead, there is a muted quality . . . where the fact of the marriage's mere survival connotes success. The many years of shared experiences, of hardships as well as successes, are usually viewed as a source of cohesion. (p. 171)

The Later Years of Childless Couples

When people in the United States think about middle-aged and older couples, they often imagine a white-haired couple surrounded by middle-aged children, in-laws, grandchildren, and perhaps great-grandchildren. Not all middle-aged and older married couples have children, however. Does having children make a difference? Are married couples without children lonelier and unhappier in their later years than married couples with children? Are the people who say "Have children now or you'll be sorry in your old age" correct?

There has been little sociological research focused specifically on childless married couples in their middle and later years. Furthermore, available research frequently fails to distinguish between various subcategories of childless couples—couples who chose not to have children, couples who wanted to have children but could not, and couples whose children died early in life. Some of the research does not even specify marital status—"the childless" (childless couples, childless widows and widowers, childless divorced people and childless, never married people) are contrasted, as a group, to "the parents," people of all marital statuses with surviving children.

The existing research suggests that "the parents" and "the childless" are different in some important ways. Older couples who have had children have more contact with neighbors and a greater number of friends than do childless older couples (Ishii-Kuntz & Seccombe, 1989; Rempel, 1985). Childless elderly people who live alone interact less with other people during an average day than do parents of the same age living alone (Bachrach, 1980). Finally, childless people in poor health and of low occupational status are more likely to be socially isolated than parents in the same situation (Bachrach, 1980).

Remaining childless seems to bring one closer to one's spouse (Ishii-Kuntz & Seccombe, 1989). Childless couples probably never experienced the traditionalization of sex roles and the stresses of balancing child care, work, and marriage—things that tend to draw parents apart. The childless have had a lot of time to work on their relationship with one another; those still together in middle and late life undoubtedly stayed together because they liked one another and not because of obligations to the children. Because the partners in childless marriages are so close to one another and because they often lack the networks of friends and neighbors that those with children develop, the death of a spouse is particularly difficult for them.

Although having children seems to make a difference in patterns of day-to-day interaction, middle-aged and elderly parents are no happier or more satisfied with life than their childless contemporaries. Glenn and McLanahan (1981) found that parents were not happier with life in general nor more satisfied with the various dimensions of life (for example, community, health, friendships and so forth) than nonparents. In fact, two categories of parents—black males and highly educated white males—were somewhat more dissatisfied than their childless equivalents. Only one type of parent—the unmarried (presumably divorced or widowed) woman—was any more satisfied with any area of life than her childless equivalent. Other studies of personal satisfaction have shown much the same thing: overall, whether one has children or not has little to do with satisfaction with the last half of life (Rempel, 1985; Keith, 1983).

Adult children may bring married couples a great deal of joy, satisfaction, and support but they might also be major sources of worry, conflict, and dissatisfaction. There are no guarantees. As Glenn and McLanahan (1981) put it:

> ... the best evidence now available indicates that the present young adults should not decide to have children on the basis of expectations that parenthood will lead to psychological rewards in the later years of life. The prospects for such rewards seem rather dim, at best. (p. 419)

The husband and wife in childless couples are often especially close to and dependent upon one another.

Summary

Modern married couples who remain married can expect to spend between one-third and one-half of their marriage without children in the home. The last half of long-term marriages can be divided into two stages: an empty nest stage, beginning when the last child leaves home and ending with retirement, and a retirement stage, beginning when both spouses have withdrawn from the labor force and ending when the first of them dies.

Married couples in the empty nest stage tend to be more satisfied with their marriage and happier with life in general than are couples with children still in the home. Empty nest couples tend to have more time, more discretionary income, and more privacy than couples with children at home. The changes brought about by middle age and the first signs of aging make both men and women cling less firmly to rigid gender roles and remind spouses of their similarities. Furthermore, couples who stay together this long are survivors with a shared history and family culture. Their marriages are less passionate but more stable than those of newlyweds.

Parents in the empty nest stage have to learn new ways of interacting with their now-adult children, decide what kind of grandparents they want to be, and sometimes begin caring for elderly parents. The movement of young adult children back into the parental home and increasing responsibilities for eldercare sometimes make the "nests" of empty nest couples full again and can add to marital strain.

Most people today live at least a few years beyond the time they stop working. The decision to retire is usually voluntary and most people adapt to it easily. Retired couples typically have less income and more free time than empty nest couples. Their satisfaction with life is closely tied to having enough income and remaining in good health; overall, they tend to be somewhat more satisfied in their marriages than empty nest couples. Being married in old age has several advantages: the married are in better health, better off economically, less likely to be institutionalized, and have easier access to sex and more help with disabilities than the unmarried elderly.

When compared to married parents, married people who reach middle or old age without children are typically more dependent on one another and less dependent on neighbors, friends, and relatives for social interaction. Thus, the death of a spouse tends to socially isolate the childless more than it does those with children. Having children does not, however, make parents more satisfied than nonparents with life in old age since children often bring worry and anxiety as well as satisfaction.

CHAPTER 14

THE END OF A MARRIAGE

Divorce rates vary from group to group. Answer each of the following questions about variations in divorce rates. Check your answers by reading the chapter.

1. Of the countries listed, which has the highest divorce rate? the lowest?
   Canada   Italy   Sweden   United States   Japan
2. Of the states listed, which has the highest divorce rate? the lowest?
   Arizona   California   Massachusetts   New York   Iowa
3. Who has the higher divorce rate?
   childless married couples   married couples with children
4. Who has the higher divorce rate?
   couples of high socioeconomic status   couples of low socioeconomic status
5. Who has a higher probability of divorce?
   couples married for five years   couples married for twenty-five years

Lynn, a widow in her early forties, whose husband died of cancer at age 50:

> I knew Martin was dead, but somehow it took a long time for the reality to seep in, become part of me. I would go to the supermarket and think, "Oh, they have endive today. I'd better get some. Martin likes it so much." I would pick out an avocado for him, a fruit I've never really liked. Then I would realize, "My God! He is dead!" and put the avocado back as if it were burning me. (Caine, 1974, p. 101)

David, divorced 15 years ago at age 51, his wife had sole custody of their only child:

> I'm sort of a loner. I don't think I'll ever remarry. . . . What I miss most is watching my daughter grow up. She'd come over but it's not like living with her. . . . It's gone. It will never come back. That's what I regret the most. It's like a death, only worse. In a death, a person is gone and fades away. But not in a divorce. (quoted in Wallerstein & Blakeslee, 1990, p. 44)

A divorced woman, age 40, who we will call "Ann":

> I don't always have to be ready to make good conversation and listen to him if I don't want to or I'm tired. I don't have to be on display, and there's all kinds of freedom now. I realize now, at forty, that I've been a child all my adult life. I've been a doll and a child—taken care of while being the perfect hostess and wife. My husband shaped me in the ways he wanted, and I never even questioned it. Now I can be my own person with the right to feel, the right to have an opinion, the right to be. This [divorce] has given me the opportunity to grow up, even when I didn't really want to! (quoted in Arendell, 1986, p. 147)

Denise, age 6 when parents divorced, now 21:

> There's another chapter in this that I might as well tell you. I stopped eating and my weight dropped to ninety-seven pounds. Then, one day in the dorm, a friend made me look in the mirror and I got real scared. I realized how depressed I was and what I was doing to myself. I began to get real angry. I'm still very angry. I'm angry at my parents for not helping me face up to these feelings of mine. They never asked about or acknowledged my pain . . . I try. . . . I really try. But I have a hard time forgiving them. (quoted in Wallerstein & Blakeslee, 1990, p. 59)

Each of the people quoted above has experienced the end of a marriage. As the quotes indicate, the end of a marriage affects not only those directly involved in the marriage like widow Lynn, ex-husband David, and ex-wife Ann, but also people who were not partners in the marriage like Denise, the daughter of divorced parents. Lynn, David, Ann, and Denise all illustrate, though in different ways, that past marriages continue to be important long after they end.

Chapter 14 focuses on **marital dissolution**, the end of marriage. We begin the chapter by briefly defining the types of marital dissolution and considering major historical trends in death and divorce, the most common types of marital dissolution. Then we describe which marriages are most likely to end by the death of a spouse and which are most likely to end in divorce. The next section seeks to explain the trends and patterns, relying on an attractions-barriers-alternatives theory. In the second half of the chapter, we focus on the emotional, psychological, physical, and economic consequences of marital dissolution for both former spouses and for their children.

Marital dissolution
the end of a marriage through death, divorce, desertion, annulment or permanent separation.

TRENDS AND PATTERNS IN MARITAL DISSOLUTION

In 1989, an article in a scholarly journal predicted that two out of every three recent marriages will ultimately end by permanent separation or divorce, rather than through death (Martin & Bumpass, 1989). Whether this estimate—or the more conservative estimate of one out of two recent marriages—is correct (Norton & Moorman, 1987; Thornton & Freedman, 1983; Cherlin, 1981), there is little doubt that marital dissolution is a major part of marriage for many people today. Those marriages and remarriages that avoid divorce or separation will ultimately end in death, another fairly common marital experience, especially for the elderly.

In this section of the chapter, we ask many "what" and "who" questions: What are the types of marital dissolution? What are the major historical trends in death and divorce? Who is most likely to experience the end of a marriage through death? Who divorces? Our strategy will be to describe the broad patterns before tackling the "why" questions in the section following this one.

Types of Marital Dissolution

The End of
a Marriage
14

All marriages end, but they end in different ways. Death brings an involuntary end to a large number of marriages each year. Currently, even more marriages end because the partners made a choice to divorce and asked the state to dissolve their marriage. Death and divorce are the two most common types of marital dissolution; therefore they provide the major focus of this chapter. Some marriages also come to an end through permanent separation, desertion, or annulment, however.

Permanent separation is just what the term indicates: a married couple decides to end their marriage by permanently living apart but chooses not to divorce, perhaps because they cannot afford it, perhaps because they belong to a religion opposed to divorce, or perhaps simply because they do not want to go through the legal process. Some permanent separations are legally recorded as such, but others are simply informal agreements between the spouses (Sweet & Bumpass, 1987). Either way, permanently separated spouses cannot legally remarry without first divorcing. Experts estimate that no more than five percent of currently existing marriages will end through permanent separation (Martin & Bumpass, 1989, p. 40).

Desertion is similar to permanent separation in that the married partners live permanently apart without divorcing; it is different in that desertion is usually the choice of only one spouse, the one who departs from the couple's home and their marriage. Desertion is grounds for divorce in many states but does not, in itself, bring a legal end to the marriage. Although accurate figures are difficult to obtain, desertion was almost certainly a more common way of ending a marriage 100 years ago than it is today (Hareven, 1988).

A small proportion of marriages end through **annulment**, a legal declaration that a marriage never existed. For a marriage to be annulled, one of the partners must file a petition requesting that the marriage be voided. The legal grounds for annulment are fairly specific. States typically grant an annulment if one of the partners was under the age of consent at the time of the marriage, if either partner consented to the marriage through fraud or duress, or if one partner had another spouse at the time of the marriage. Since an annulled marriage never legally existed, partners are legally free to marry again.

> **Permanent separation**
> marriage partners agree to live apart from one another on a permanent basis, without divorcing.

> **Desertion**
> one spouse leaves the other on a permanent basis, without divorcing.

> **Annulment**
> a legal action that declares the marriage was never a legal marriage.

Historical Changes in Marital Dissolution Rates

One hundred years ago, most marriages in the United States ended when one spouse died or when one spouse deserted the other; divorce was a very uncommon way to end a marriage. Today, slightly more marriages end through divorce than through death each year. Figure 14–1 (on page 506) illustrates the changes in death and divorce rates in detail. Look first at the death line. The death rate of married people has clearly fluctuated from year to year, due in part to the impact of war and disease epidemics. Overall, however, the trend has been downward. Out of every 1000 marriages that existed at the beginning of 1880, for example, 26 had dissolved by the end of the year because of the death of a spouse. By 1980, the comparable figure was about 18.

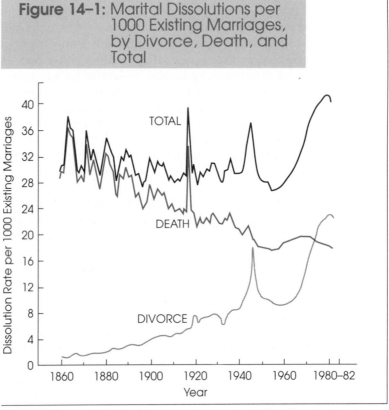

Figure 14–1: Marital Dissolutions per 1000 Existing Marriages, by Divorce, Death, and Total

This figure shows how many marriages out of every 1000 in existence at the beginning of a given year ended in death or divorce during that year. Until 1970, more marriages each year ended through death than divorce; since then, more end through divorce.

Source: Taken from Arland Thornton and Deborah Freedman, "The Changing American Family," *Population Bulletin,* October, 1983, p. 7.

While the death rate dropped, the divorce rate rose steadily. As you can see by looking at the divorce line, the rate climbed steadily but rather slowly from 1860 to 1960 (with some fluctuations) and then experienced an especially steep rise between 1965 and 1980. Only about 2 of every 1000 existing marriages ended through divorce in the year 1880. During 1980, 23 out of every 1000 marriages ended in divorce. Since 1980, the divorce rate has remained high but has dropped somewhat from its late 1970s-early 1980s peak (Martin & Bumpass, 1989). In 1986, for example, the rate was 21.2 (National Center for Health Statistics, 1990).

Which Marriages End through Death?

Throughout this chapter, we will be pointing out the differences and similarities between marriages that end through divorce and those that end with death. We begin this process by asking which types of marriages are most likely to end through death and which are most likely to end with divorce.

In the late twentieth-century United States, death comes most often to the elderly. Thus, marriages in which one or both partners are elderly are much more likely to be ended by death than are marriages composed of young or middle-aged partners. Most marriages with elderly partners are of long duration and have completed the childbearing, childrearing, and empty nest stages of the family life cycle. Since most women marry slightly older men and since women have longer life expectancy than men, the surviving partner in marriages broken by death is most often the wife.

To illustrate some of these points, let us imagine 1000 couples in which the partners are aged 40–44, 1000 couples in which they are aged 60–64, and 1000 couples in which they are aged 80–84. The year is 1980. By the end of that year, three of the 40–44-year-old women and two of the 40–44-year-old men were widowed; 25 of the 60–64-year-old women and 10 men of that age were widowed; and 156 of the 80–84-year-old women and 56 of the 80–84-year-old men had experienced the death of a spouse (Sweet & Bumpass, 1987, p. 202).

Although widowhood is fairly unusual among the young and middle aged today, some categories of people are more vulnerable to experiencing a premature end to their marriage through death than others. At every age, blacks have a higher probability of losing their spouse than whites, reflecting higher death rates among blacks and also a greater average age difference between partners in black marriages (Sweet & Bumpass, 1987, p. 202). Mortality rates are also very closely tied to educational level. College graduates are less likely to be widowed before old age than are those with a high school diploma, and high school graduates are less likely to be widowed before old age than nongraduates (Sweet & Bumpass, 1987, pp. 202–203).

Who Divorces?

Trying to answer the question "Who Divorces?" is one of the most popular pastimes in divorce research. In reviewing the vast research on this topic, we will start with broad, geographic factors and then move to individual-level factors such as age at marriage, length of marriage, race, socioeconomic status, religion, and the presence of children. Cohort variations in divorce rates are discussed in this chapter's Cohort Comparison.

Cohort Comparison   Divorce in Three Cohorts

The time period in which people are born and reared influences how they think about marriage and what they expect of it. The social conditions around the time of early marriage influence the special pressures that can affect young marriages in their most vulnerable years. These generalizations show up very clearly for the New Century (born 1910–1914), Depression (born 1930–1934), and Baby Boom (born 1950–1954) birth cohorts. Ninety to 95 percent of each of these birth cohorts married, but their rates

of divorce are quite different: less than 20 percent of the New Century cohort women ended their first marriage by divorce; about a third of the Depression-era women did so or will do so; but about half of the first marriages undertaken by the Baby Boom cohort ended or are projected to end in divorce (Norton & Moorman, 1987, p. 12; Kitson, Babri, & Roach, 1985; Thornton & Freedman, 1983, p. 4; Cherlin, 1981).

Both New Century women (most of whom married in the 1930s and 1940s) and

Baby Boom women (most of whom married in the 1970s and 1980s) had divorce rates higher than the historical trend would predict, but Depression cohort women (most of whom married in the 1950s or early 1960s) divorced at a rate *lower* than expected, given historical trends (Cherlin, 1981). This difference is illustrated in Figure 14–2.

Within this chapter, we try to explain why divorce rates are high. But, as Cherlin (1981) points out, the lower than expected divorce rates of the Depression cohort provide a

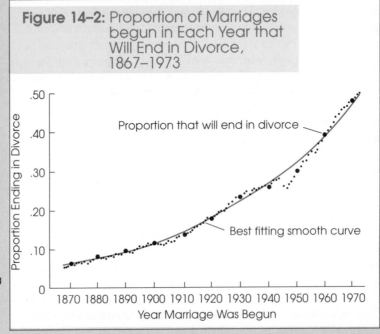

Figure 14–2: Proportion of Marriages begun in Each Year that Will End in Divorce, 1867–1973

The figure documents the proportion of marriages begun each year that ended in divorce; for the more recent years, the proportion is a prediction based on prevailing rates. Estimates for those marrying in the late 1970s and early 1980s were slightly higher than for the 1973 group (Martin & Bumpass, 1989).

Proportion that will end in divorce

Best fitting smooth curve

Proportion Ending in Divorce

Year Marriage Was Begun

Source: Cherlin, 1981, p. 23. "Reprinted by Permission of the publishers from *Marriage, Divorce, and Remarriage* by Andrew Cherlin, Cambridge, MA, Harvard University Press, Copyright © 1981 by the President and Fellows of Harvard College."

tantalizing mystery. The Depression cohort grew up in an era of deprivation when families frequently had to pull up roots, move, or split up in order to survive economically. This, perhaps, made them value family security and stability and to use economic well-being as a major criterion by which to judge the quality of their marriages (Cherlin, 1981). The fact that they began their marriages in a period of economic prosperity, were a small cohort (meaning more opportunities and less competition), and were accustomed to living on a low budget probably helped keep their marriages together during the crucial early years (Easterlin, 1987; Cherlin, 1981).

Geographic Factors

*Industrial/
Urban
Western*

Married people living in some locations are more likely to divorce than those living in others. To begin with, divorce is much more common in highly industrialized societies than in less industrialized ones (Trent & South, 1989). But as Figure 14–3 (on page 510) indicates, some industrialized societies have much higher divorce rates than others. Note that the divorce rates shown in Figure 14–3 are **crude divorce rates**, based on divorces *per 1000 population*, rather than divorces per 1000 marriages as in Figure 14–1.

> **Crude divorce rate**
> the number of divorces per 1000 population.

Divorce, as a way of dealing with an unsatisfactory marriage, began to take hold in the United States in the latter part of the nineteenth century. By 1889, the United States had the world's highest divorce rate, a record it has held ever since (Mintz & Kellogg, 1988, p. 109). Today, however, some other countries may be "catching up" with the United States in this respect. From 1965 to 1980, a period in which the U.S. divorce rate increased 208 percent, divorce rates were increasing even more dramatically in Canada (520 percent), the United Kingdom (375 percent), Australia (325 percent), the Netherlands (320 percent), and the USSR (218 percent) (Kitson, Babri, & Roach, 1985, p. 257).

Within the United States, married people living in Western states are more likely to divorce than people living in other regions of the country, with the Northeastern states having especially low divorce rates (U.S. Bureau of the Census, 1990a, p. 89). This regional pattern first appeared in the nineteenth century and has held since that time (Phillips, 1988). State-by-state differences in crude divorce rates diminished somewhat in the 1970s and 1980s but, as Table 14–1 (on page 511) reveals, a great deal of variation persists.

Finally, those living in urban areas have long been more divorce-prone than rural inhabitants (Breault & Kposowa, 1987; Shelton, 1987). In fact, the size of a community is a very good predictor of divorce rates. For example, in 1980, cities with populations over 250,000 had a crude divorce rate of 5.4; cities with populations between 10,000 and

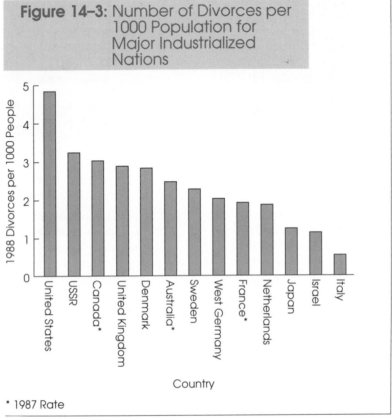

Figure 14-3: Number of Divorces per 1000 Population for Major Industrialized Nations

The divorce rates of all industrialized countries are fairly high and increasing, but the United States continues to have the highest rates. Industrialized countries with a Catholic religious tradition (like Italy and France) or with a lack of ethnic diversity (like Japan) tend to have lower rates.

* 1987 Rate

Source: United Nations, 1991, pp. 513–15.

50,000 had a rate of 4.7; and towns with fewer than 3,000 people posted a rate of 3.0 (Shelton, 1987, p. 829).

Individual Factors

The broad geographical factors discussed thus far give only a partial answer to the question "Who Divorces?". In this section, we consider the individual-level factors of age at marriage, length of marriage, age, race, socioeconomic status, religion, and children.

Age at First Marriage   In general, the younger people are when they marry for the first time, the higher the probability they will divorce (White, 1990; Price & McKenry, 1988; Kitson, Babri, & Roach, 1985). As Figure 14–4 clearly shows, marriages among teenagers are espec-

| Table 14–1 | Divorce Rate per 1000 Population, by U.S. States, 1988 (arranged from highest rate to lowest rate) | | |

State	Divorce Rate per 1000 population	State	Divorce Rate per 1000 population
Nevada	14.1	Missouri	4.8
Arizona	7.1	Mississippi	4.7
Oklahoma	7.1	Hawaii	4.6
Arkansas	7.0	Ohio	4.6
Alaska	6.9	Utah	4.6
Wyoming	6.9	Delaware	4.5
Tennessee	6.5	New Hampshire	4.4
Florida	6.3	Michigan	4.3
Kansas	6.2	Virginia	4.3
Idaho	6.0	South Carolina	4.2
District of Columbia	5.9	Illinois	4.0
Alabama	5.7	Nebraska	4.0
Colorado	5.7	Iowa	3.8
Washington	5.7	Rhode Island	3.8
Georgia	5.6	South Dakota	3.7
Texas	5.6	Maryland	3.6
Kentucky	5.5	New York	3.6
Oregon	5.4	North Dakota	3.6
New Mexico	5.3	Minnesota	3.5
Montana	5.1	New Jersey	3.5
North Carolina	5.0	Wisconsin	3.5
Vermont	4.9	Pennsylvania	3.3
West Virginia	4.9	Connecticut	3.2
California	4.8	Massachusetts	2.9
Maine	4.8		

Note: 1988 figures not available for Indiana (6.4 in 1985) or Louisiana (4.3 in 1980).

Source: Data from U.S. Bureau of the Census, 1990a, p. 89.

ially prone to divorce, with divorce rates two to three times higher than those characteristic of nonteenage marriages (Price & McKenry, 1988; Kitson, Babri, & Roach, 1985).

The negative impact of being married at a very young age does not disappear with time. Even after 20 years of marriage, couples who first married as teenagers are at higher risk for divorce than couples who

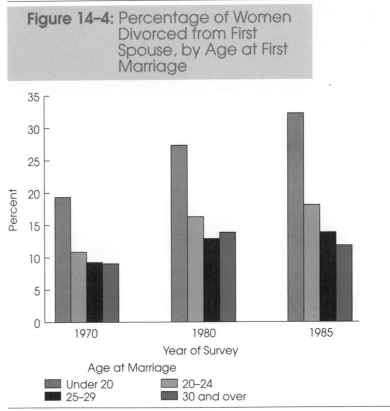

Figure 14–4: Percentage of Women Divorced from First Spouse, by Age at First Marriage

Year of Survey

Age at Marriage
■ Under 20   ■ 20–24
■ 25–29   ■ 30 and over

Source: Norton & Moorman, 1987, p. 9. Copyrighted (1987) by the National Council on Family Relations, 3989 Central Ave. N.E., Suite #550, Minneapolis, MN 55421. Reprinted by permission.

Regardless of the time period, the basic relationship between age and the risk of divorce remains the same: the younger the age at marriage, the greater the likelihood of divorce.

married after their teenage years (Martin & Bumpass, 1989). Furthermore, the effects of early first marriage carry over into subsequent marriages: those who married as teenagers, divorced, and then remarried are at a higher risk of a second divorce than are those who first married at a later age, divorced, and remarried (Martin & Bumpass, 1989).

Age of Couple and Length of Marriage   Most divorces occur when both the couple and the marriage are relatively young. The older the husband and wife are, the lower their chance of divorce (Thornton & Rodgers, 1987). Divorce is relatively rare among those over age 40. Only 13 percent of all first-marriage divorces involve women 40 or older (Glick & Lin, 1986a, p. 740). When divorces from second and subsequent marriages are added, the percentage rises to 20 percent (Canter, 1990). Table 14–2 illustrates that the chances of divorce are highest in the early years of marriage, dropping to 30 percent by the tenth anniversary.

Table 14–2 Duration and Divorce in U.S. Marriages		
Years of Marriage	Average Years Remaining	Percent Expected to Divorce
0	24.8	51.6
1	24.4	50.9
2	24.5	49.1
3	24.8	46.7
4	25.2	44.0
5	25.4	41.9
6	25.8	39.0
7	26.0	36.5
8	26.2	34.1
9	26.1	32.2
10	26.1	30.0
11	26.0	28.0
12	25.9	26.2
13	25.6	24.6
14	25.5	22.6
15–19	25.2	21.0
20–24	23.4	13.8
25–29	·21.3	7.8
30–34	18.6	3.8
35–39	15.8	1.9
40–44	13.1	0.9
45–49	10.9	0.4
50–54	8.9	0.2
55–59	7.7	0.1
60+	7.4	0.1

Source: Reprinted with permission © *American Demographics*, February 1989, page 12.

Socioeconomic Status   Generally speaking, people with more education, higher incomes, and higher-status occupations are less likely to divorce than those who have less education, lower incomes, and lower-status occupations (White, 1990; Raschke, 1987). Stability and dependability of husband's income is an especially important factor. As one researcher put it:

> . . . a lower but dependable income promotes marital stability more than a higher but erratic income, . . . a higher dependable income promotes marital stability even more, . . . for whites, not being in debt and/or having a certain level of assets increases marital stability. (Raschke, 1987, p. 604)

Marriages in which the wife earns money are less prone to divorce if her income is only a fraction of her husband's than if it equals or exceeds his (Raschke, 1987). Although higher socioeconomic status still means less chance of divorce, there are fewer differences between the social classes in terms of divorce rate than there once were and, among whites, socioeconomic status is no longer a strong predictor of divorce (Glenn & Supancic, 1984, p. 572).

Race   Socioeconomic status, and particularly income, continues to be a very important factor in the stability of black marriages. Since most black couples have lower incomes than most white couples and since income is very important to the stability of black marriages, it is not surprising to find that blacks overall have separation and divorce rates 50 to more than 100 percent higher than those of whites (Martin & Bumpass, 1989; Saluter, 1989; Teachman, 1986). As noted, many of the black-white differences in divorce rates can be attributed to income; blacks in higher income categories have divorce rates similar to those of whites in the same income brackets (Price & McKenry, 1988; Raschke, 1987).

Religion   The effect of religious affiliation on divorce is difficult to study since neither divorce records nor the Census Bureau collects information on religion. The existing research indicates that Catholics have lower divorce rates but higher separation rates than Protestants, that religiously mixed marriages (Jewish-Gentile, Protestant-Catholic) are less stable than religiously homogamous marriages, and that fundamentalist Protestants (for example, Baptists and Nazarenes) divorce more frequently than Protestants from mainstream denominations (for example, Methodists and Presbyterians) (Raschke, 1987). Regardless of denominational affiliation, those who are involved in the organizational activities of their religion divorce less often than others. One study found, for example, that white males who never attended religious services had divorce rates *three times as high* as those who attended them two or three times a month (Glenn & Supancic, 1984).

The Presence of Children   Do children help keep marriages together as the old adage "staying together for the sake of the children" suggests? Yes, at least up to a point. One national longitudinal study compared young adults who married and then had children to those who married but remained childless and came up with unequivocal results: the presence of children reduced the chance of divorce (Waite, Haggstrom, & Kanouse, 1985). By the time the first child reached its second birthday, the odds of parents being divorced or separated were only 5 to 8 percent, compared to more than 20 percent for the childless couples (Waite, Haggstrom, & Kanouse, 1985).

The circumstances of a child's birth also affect marital stability. Children conceived and born before marriage increase rather than decrease the chances of parental divorce, those conceived before marriage but born during it have no effect either way, and those conceived and born during marriage decrease the chance of divorce (Martin & Bumpass, 1989; Morgan & Rindfuss, 1985).

If having one child helps prevent or delay divorce, does having more than one insure even greater marital stability? The findings are contradictory. Spanier and Glick (1981) found that the larger the number of children, the less the probability of divorce. In contrast, Thornton (1977) found that families with five or more children had higher rates of divorce than those with one, two, three, or four children and concluded: "... women with no children had the highest odds of experiencing disruption while the next highest odds were for those with large families" (p. 538).

EXPLAINING THE TRENDS AND PATTERNS

Thus far, we have presented a great deal of information about changes in the way marriages end, about geographic variations in the divorce rate, and about who is most and least likely to divorce. How can these trends and patterns be explained? Specifically, why do more marriages in industrial societies end by divorce now than in the past? Why do some countries, states, and communities have higher divorce rates than others? And, why are some people in unsatisfactory marriages less willing than others to end their marriages by divorce?

One prominent explanation of why some marriage partners stay together while others go their separate ways is elaborated by social psychologist George Levinger (1965). His explanation suggests that the decision to divorce or to stay together results from considering and balancing three factors—attractions, barriers, and alternative attractions. **Attractions** are those elements of the marriage that draw people toward one another; **barriers** are obstacles that discourage them from leaving the marriage; and **alternative attractions** are the rewarding possibilities existing outside of the marriage. In its simplest form, the explanation says that people stay together when either the attractions of marriage or the barriers to leaving marriage (or both) are high. Marriages break up when both attractions and barriers are low, and especially if more attractive alternatives are available (Levinger, 1965). In short: Attractions + Barriers − Alternative Attractions = Likelihood of Staying Married (Adams, 1986, p. 331).

Attractions
those elements of a marital relationship that draw people toward one another.

Barriers
obstacles that discourage people from leaving a marriage.

Alternative attractions
attractions existing outside of marriage.

The attraction-barrier-alternative attractions explanation can also be used to understand why modern, industrialized, urbanized societies have more divorce than traditional, nonindustrialized, rural societies. In comparing industrialized societies to nonindustrialized ones, three things are apparent: 1. As societies become more modern, the attractions of marriage do not necessarily decrease, but people do come to hold higher expectations about marriage; 2. The social and legal barriers to ending the marriage are typically lower in industrialized societies; and 3. The alternative attractions outside of marriage are greater in industrialized societies.

Changes in Attractions

Marriage offers different attractions in different types of societies and to different types of people. As noted throughout this book, the major attractions of traditional marriage were practical attractions: economic survival and the production of legitimate offspring. These continue to be the most attractive features of marriage for some people, but in general they have become less important. Instead, the emotional benefits of marriage—close companionship, intimate conversation, frequent affection, emotional support, and sexual pleasure—attract most modern individuals to marriage and to their particular partner. When modern husbands and wives evaluate the attractions of their marriage, they are likely to ask: How well is this marriage meeting my needs for intimacy? How close do I feel to my partner? How compatible are we? How happy am I? In contrast, husbands and wives in more traditional societies, on the rare occasions when they evaluated their marriages at all, might have asked: Does my spouse give me economic security? Has (s)he provided me with healthy children? Do my parents and siblings benefit from being tied to my spouse's family? In short, people expect different things of marriage than they once did.

Historians cite "rising expectations" about marriage as one reason for the increased divorce rate over the past century (Phillips, 1988). These rising expectations are reflected in the reasons divorced people give for their own divorces. When asked "Why did you divorce?", respondents most often give answers that have to do with lack of intimacy and self-satisfaction. In a 1989 Gallup poll, over half the respondents listed "incompatibility" as the principal reason for their divorce (Colasanto & Shriver, 1989). In a study of people divorcing in Wisconsin, both husbands and wives ranked communication, basic unhappiness, and incompatibility as the top three reasons for divorcing (Cleek & Pearson, 1985). Other studies show similar results; people divorcing in the 1970s and 1980s accounted for their own divorces primarily in terms of the failure of intimacy (Burns, 1984; Kitson & Sussman, 1982).

These answers stand in sharp contrast to the answers given by previous generations of divorcing people: nonsupport, physical violence, husband staying "out with the boys" and away from home, and excessive drinking (Kitson & Sussman, 1982; Levinger, 1965). Money conflicts, disputes about children, drug and alcohol problems, and physical abuse are still cited as contributing to divorce by a minority of divorcing people (Colasanto & Shriver, 1989), but most, by their own accounts, divorce because the emotional attractions of their marriage declined. Marriages based on emotion, shared interests, and personal traits (as modern marriages are) are particularly fragile because all these are subject to change.

The emotional and compatibility expectations attached to marriage today may offer a partial explanation for why so many teenage marriages end in divorce. Teenagers who marry generally have less practice in communication, are less settled (and thus, more likely to change) in their interests and emotional development, and more often marry with very high expectations about the power of love than people who marry at older ages (Raschke, 1987). Given these facts, there is a very good chance that their satisfaction with the marriage will fade over time as partners mature and grow apart.

Changes in Social and Legal Barriers

The barriers to divorce are generally higher in traditional societies than in modern ones and are higher among some groups in modern societies than among others. Remember that barriers are factors that make it difficult to break up a marriage—as Levinger (1965) notes, " . . . marital strength is a function of bars as well as bonds" (p. 20). Possible barriers to divorce include religion, children, legal restrictions concerning divorce, economic dependence, the feelings of the family, and community stigma. Here we consider two barriers—social integration and the law—and how changes in them affect divorce.

Social Integration

The geographic mobility and large community size characteristic of industrialized societies generally mean a lessening of **social integration**, the sense of cohesion and belonging found in stable social groupings holding shared values and beliefs. In highly socially integrated groups, such as ethnic neighborhoods, close-knit extended families, or local religious congregations, every member knows and cares about what every other member is doing. Individuals are often identified by their connection to their spouse or family ("He's married to one of the O'Neill girls"; "She's the pharmacist's wife"), and married couples are

Social integration the sense of cohesion and belonging characteristic of stable social groupings holding shared values and beliefs.

treated as a single unit. Membership in such groups presents a barrier to divorce because other group members care that marriages stay together, exert pressure on them to do so, and constantly reinforce the individual's identity as half of a married couple. Some people to whom such groups are important might like to divorce because they are miserable in their marriages but risk losing their identity and the respect of the group if they do so. Thus, they may stay married and tolerate some marital unhappiness because they value their place in the group.

In modern societies, fewer people are part of such highly integrated groups for their entire life; they have the freedom (and are sometimes required) to move to places where few people know them very well and where their marriage is considered their own private business. In breaking their ties with socially integrated groups, they gain freedom and privacy but lose one of the barriers to divorce.

The social integration factor helps to explain not only why modern societies have higher divorce rates than traditional societies, but it also explains why some people in modern society are more prone to divorce than others. Two separate studies seeking to explain why rural areas have lower divorce rates than urban areas found that the higher social

Children sometimes serve as a barrier to divorce. However, if the parents divorce, strengthening the children's relationship with their grandparents can provide an avenue to emotional support.

integration of rural areas was the key factor (Breault & Kposowa, 1987; Shelton, 1987). Those who attend religious services are also part of a group with high social integration and this integration acts as a barrier to divorce (Glenn & Supancic, 1984).

As noted, children also tend to act as a barrier to divorce. They are a barrier in part because children typically tie their parents into a number of different social groups—other families in the neighborhood, schools, recreational groups, and relatives. Many of these ties continue long after the children have left home, particularly if the parents continue to live in the same community. All in all, married couples with children have more contact with neighbors, relatives, and friends than childless couples do (Ishii-Kuntz & Seccombe, 1989) and each of these ties presents a potential barrier to divorce.

Legal Barriers

The laws of a nation or of a state can make it fairly simple, very difficult, or impossible to end a marriage through divorce. The law, then, can be a barrier urging people to stay married by making it difficult for them to dissolve their marriage legally. For example, between 1878 and 1949, South Carolina had no legal provisions for divorce; those wishing to divorce had to travel to another state (Blake, 1962, p. 235). In Europe, Italy and Spain did not legalize divorce until 1970 (Phillips, 1988, p. 572).

Beginning about 1965, most Western countries changed their laws to make divorce a less time-consuming, less expensive process (Phillips, 1988; Weitzman, 1985). Our focus will be on the United States; however, similar changes occurred elsewhere.

Prior to the 1960s, married couples could obtain a divorce only if they could show they had specific "grounds" for doing so. The underlying principle of these divorces was that one of the spouses was guilty of wrongdoing. In other words, these **fault divorce laws** (sometimes labeled absolute divorce laws) assumed one person was at fault for the collapse of the marriage. The legal grounds (or reasons) for divorce varied from state to state, but the most commonly accepted grounds were adultery and desertion. No state recognized incompatibility of the partners or dissatisfaction with the marriage as acceptable grounds for divorce. The divorce proceedings were adversarial in nature, designed to ferret out and punish the guilty party and to compensate the innocent victim. In many cases, however, neither partner was at fault on the grounds recognized by the state; the marriage simply did not work. In such cases, marriage partners sometimes conspired, often with the knowledge of both lawyers and the judge, to manufacture fake evidence proving fault so that a divorce could be granted (Jacob, 1988).

Fault divorce laws also known as **absolute divorce laws;** laws that allow for divorce only on specific grounds that find one partner guilty.

No-fault divorce laws
laws that allow
divorce without
specifying
responsibility or fault.

Concerned about the expense, the lengthy time in court, and the hostility created by fault-based divorce laws and faced with processing an increasing number of divorces, states searched for different ways of handling divorce. By the late 1980s, all had chosen some form of "no-fault" divorce. **No-fault divorce laws** allow divorce without specifying responsibility for the collapse of the marriage. Their guiding principle is that marriages can end without either partner being at fault. Some states kept their old fault-based grounds for divorce and added one or more no-fault grounds, such as "incompatibility," "separation for one (or two) years," or "irretrievable breakdown." Others eliminated all fault-based grounds for divorce. As of 1989, 18 states had only no-fault divorces and the remainder had both fault and no-fault grounds for divorce. Table 14–3 summarizes the current divorce laws for each state.

Did the change in divorce laws contribute to the rising divorce rate of the 1970s and early 1980s? Would divorce be less common today if the laws were stricter?

Variations in divorce rates do reflect, at least to some extent, variations in divorce law. For example, a glance back at Table 14–1 will remind you that Nevada has a divorce rate twice as high as the state with the next highest rate. A look at Table 14–3 will show you that Nevada also has fairly lenient rules about divorce. Many of the divorces granted in Nevada are granted to residents of other states who came to Nevada for the express purpose of obtaining a divorce. This example makes an important point: when laws make it difficult to obtain a

Table 14–3 Grounds for Divorce by State

	Residence	Adultery	Cruelty	Desertion	Alcoholism	Impotency	Non-support	Insanity	Pregnancy at marriage	Bigamy	Separation	Felony conviction or imprisonment	Drug addiction	Fraud, force, duress
							Some grounds for absolute divorce							
PR	1 yr.	Yes	Yes	1 yr.	Yes	Yes	No	Yes	No	A	2 yrs.	Yes*	Yes	No
AL	6 mos.*	Yes	Phys. only	1 yr.	Yes	Yes*	2 yrs.	5 yrs.	Yes	A	2 yrs.*	2 yrs.*	Yes	A
AK	*	Yes	Yes	1 yr	1 yr.	Yes	No	18 mos.	No	A	No	Yes	Yes	A
AZ	90 da.	No	No	No	No	No	No	No	No	A	No	No	No	No
AR	60 da.	Yes	Yes	1 yr.	1 yr.	Yes	Yes	3 yrs.	No	No	3 yrs.	Yes	No	A
CA	6 mos.	No	No	No	No	A	No	Yes, A	No	A	No	No	No	A
CO	90 da.	No	No	No	No	No	No	No	No	A	No	No	No	A
CT	1 yr*	Yes	Yes	1 yr.	Yes	A	No	5 yrs.	Yes*	A	18 mos.*	life*	No	Yes
DE	6 mos.	Yes	Yes	Yes	Yes	A	No	A	No	Yes	6 mos.	Yes	No	No
FL	6 mos.	No	No	No	No	No	No	3 yrs.	No	No	No	No	No	No
GA	6 mos.	Yes	Yes	1 yr.	Yes	Yes	No	2 yrs.	No	A	No	Yes*	Yes	Yes

Table 14–3 (continued)

Some grounds for absolute divorce

	Residence	Adultery	Cruelty	Desertion	Alcoholism	Impotency	Non-support	Insanity	Pregnancy at marriage	Bigamy	Separation	Felony conviction or imprisonment	Drug addiction	Fraud, force, duress
HI	6 mos.*	No	No	No	No	No	No	A	No	A	2 yrs.*	No	No	A
ID	6 wks.	Yes	Yes	Yes	Yes	A	Yes	3 yrs.	Yes	A	5 yrs.	Yes	No	A
IL	90 da.	Yes	Yes	1 yr.	2 yrs.	Yes	No	No	No	Yes	2 yrs.*	Yes	2 yrs.	No
IN	6 mos.*	No	No	No	No	Yes	No	2 yrs.	Yes	A	No	Yes	No	A
IA	1 yr.*	No	No	No	No	A	No	A	No	A	No	No	No	No
KS	60 da.	No	No	No	No	No	Yes	2 yrs.	A	A	No	No	No	A
KY	180 da.	No	No	No	No	A	No	No	No	No	No	No	No	A
LA	1 yr.*	Yes	Yes	Yes	Yes	No	Yes	No	No	A	6 mos.	Yes*	No	A
ME	6 mos.*	Yes	Yes	3 yrs.	Yes	Yes	Yes	No	No	No	No	No	Yes	No
MD	1 yr.	Yes	No	1 yr.*	No	No	No	3 yrs.	No	A	1 yr.*	1 yr.*	No	No
MA	1 yr.*	Yes	Yes	1 yr.	Yes	Yes	Yes	No	No	A	No	5 yrs.	Yes	No
MI	180 da.	No	No	No	No	No	No	No	No	A	No	No	No	A
MN	180 da.	No	No	No	No	No	No	No	No	No	No	No	No	A
MS	6 mos.	Yes	Yes	1 yr.	Yes	Yes	No	3 yrs.	Yes	Yes	No	Yes*	Yes	A
MO	90 da.	No	No	No	No	No	No	No	No	No	No	No	No	A
MT	90 da.	No	No	No	No	A	No	No	No	No	180 da.*	No	No	A
NE	1 yr.*	No	No	No	No	A	No	No	No	A	No	No	No	A
NV	6 wks.	No	No	No	No	No	No	2 yrs.	No	A	1 yr.	No	No	A
NH	1 yr.*	Yes	Yes	2 yrs.	2 yrs.	Yes	2 yrs.	No	No	No	No	1 yr.*	No	No
NJ	1 yr.*	Yes	Yes	1 yr.	1 yr.	A	No	2 yrs.	No	A	18 mos.	18 mos.	1 yr.	A
NM	6 mos.	Yes	Yes	Yes*	No	No	No	No	No	No	No	No	No	No
NY	1 yr.*	Yes	Yes	1 yr.	No	No	No	No	No	A	1 yr.	3 yrs.	No	No
NC	6 mos.	No	No	No	No	A	No	3 yrs.	No	A	1 yr.	No	No	No
ND	6 mos.	Yes	Yes	1 yr.	1 yr.	A	1 yr.	5 yrs.*	No	A	No	Yes	1 yr.	A
OH	6 mos.	Yes	Yes	1 yr.	Yes	Yes	Yes	No	No	Yes, A	1 yr.	Yes	No	Yes
OK	6 mos.	Yes	Yes	1 yr.	Yes	Yes	Yes	5 yrs.	Yes	Yes	No	Yes	No	Yes
OR	6 mos.*	No	No	No	No	No	No	No	No	No	No	No	No	A
PA	6 mos.	Yes	Yes	1 yr.	No	No	No	18 mos.*	No	Yes	2 yrs.*	Yes	No	No
RI	1 yr.	Yes	Yes	5 yrs.*	Yes	Yes	1 yr.	No	Yes	Yes	3 yrs.	No	Yes	No
SC	1 yr.*	Yes	Phys. only	1 yr.	Yes	No	No	No	No	No	1 yr.	No	Yes	No
SD	none*	Yes	Yes	1 yr.	1 yr.	A	1 yr.	5 yrs.	No	A	No	Yes	No	A*
TN	6 mos.	Yes	Yes	2 yrs.	Yes	Yes	Yes	No	Yes	Yes	2 yrs.	Yes	Yes	A
TX	6 mos.*	Yes	Yes	1 yr.	*	A	No	3 yrs.	No	A	3 yrs.	1 yr.	No	No
UT	3 mos.	Yes	Yes	1 yr.	Yes	Yes	Yes	Yes	No	A	3 yrs.*	Yes	No	A
VT	6 mos.*	Yes	Yes	7 yrs.*	No	No	Yes	5 yrs.	No	No	6 mos.	3 yrs.	No	A
VA	6 mos.*	Yes	Yes*	1 yr.	No	A	No	No	A	A	1 yr.*	1 yr.*	No	No
WA	bona fide res.	No	No	No	No	No	No	No	No	No	No	No	No	No
WV	1 yr.	Yes	Yes	6 mos.	Yes	A	A	3 yrs.	A	A	1 yr.	Yes	Yes	No
WI	6 mos.	No	No	No	No	A	No	No	No	A	1 yr.	No	No	A
WY	60 da.*	No	No	No	No	No	No	2 yrs.	No	A	No	No	No	No
DC	6 mos	No	No	No	No	A	No	A*	No	A	6 mos. 1 yr.	No	No	A

* indicates qualification-check local statutes: (A) indicates grounds for annulment.

Source: *The World Almanac and Book of Facts,* 1991 edition, Copyright Pharos Books 1990, New York, NY 10166.

divorce, people find other ways to escape from failed marriages. Historically, societies that have tried to solve the "problem" of divorce by outlawing or restricting it sometimes end up with solutions that are just as bad or worse: "In societies where divorce is difficult to obtain, there is a tendency toward dishonest annulment, fabrication of legally accepted offenses, migratory divorce, and legal separations . . . " (Price & McKenry, 1988, p. 9). Other "solutions" to the problem of failed marriage include tolerance of extramarital affairs, murder of the spouse, and suicide (Phillips, 1988).

No-fault divorce laws removed a barrier to divorce in the sense that they made divorce easier. Although some states had a one year "spurt" in divorces right after the no-fault laws were enacted, *there is little evidence that these laws contributed to the long-term rise in divorce rates* (Dixon & Weitzman, 1982; Wright & Stetson, 1978; Schoen, Greenblatt, & Mielke, 1975). Indeed, divorce rates were rising *before* such legislation passed; states like California went to no-fault divorce, in large part, *because* of increasing demand for divorces.

Changes in Alternative Attractions

Even people who feel that their marriage does not meet their expectations and who perceive few barriers to divorce may stay married if they perceive no more attractive alternatives outside of marriage. As Levinger's theory suggests, the presence of desirable alternatives outside of marriage may be even more important than marital satisfaction when it comes to predicting divorce (Udry, 1981). Attractive alternatives might include a new partner who better meets one's needs, a fulfilling and financially rewarding career, or freedom from financial obligations. Generally speaking, there are more such alternatives *and* greater awareness of them in modern, urban societies than in traditional, rural ones. For example, working outside the home exposes both men and women to more potential eligible partners than either could have met in the days when both worked at home. Expanding employment opportunities for women make it possible for them to survive economically without a husband; modern household technology plus the expansion of personal service businesses makes it possible for men to get through day-to-day life without the services of a wife. The changing attitudes that accompanied the Sexual Revolution, the cohabitation revolution, and the Women's Movement have made both men and women aware of attractive alternatives outside of marriage and have made such alternatives more acceptable.

Employment can provide attractive alternatives to wives. As noted in Chapter 9, there is little evidence that employment of the wife leads to greater marital problems in most marriages, and, in fact, the wife's employment can strengthen already strong marriages in a number of ways. At the same time, wives who already have a job, especially a full-time, well-paid job with possibilities for future advancement, have an attractive alternative to marriage. Should their marriages become dissatisfying to them, they would be able to support themselves. Wives who have devoted their lives solely to husband and children, who lack employment experience, and who are totally economically dependent on their spouse lack this alternative. If such a wife becomes unhappy in her marriage, she is less likely than the employed wife to seek divorce because the prospect of being poor (though possibly happier) outside of marriage seems less attractive than the prospect of remaining in a somewhat unhappy, economically secure marriage (Udry, 1981).

The factor of alternative attractions can also help explain why young people seek divorce more often than older ones. Younger people, and particularly younger women, are in a better position to find an alternative mate than are middle-aged and older people. Not only are younger people likely to have had more recent dating experience, they are also more physically attractive by societal standards and have more unattached people of the same age available to them. If there are no barriers (such as children or economic dependence) holding them back, young people who are unhappy in their current marriage might conclude that they should "get out while the getting is good."

CONSEQUENCES OF MARITAL DISSOLUTION

The end of any marriage, regardless of how it occurs, means the end of a unique, emotional, psychological, social, and economic unit that bound partners together in a very intimate way. Both widowed people and divorced partners have to learn to live without someone to whom they had grown accustomed and to establish an emotional, psychological, social, and economic life separate from their former spouse. Doing so is not an easy task, even for people whose marriages were full of conflict and not particularly happy. In fact, researchers classify the death of a spouse and divorce as among the five most stressful life events (Dohrenwend et al., 1978).

In this section, we will consider the emotional, psychological, health, social, and economic consequences of marital dissolution. We will deal with effects of marital dissolution on former spouses first, considering divorced people and widowed people separately. Then we will discuss the consequences of marital dissolution on children.

Consequences for Divorced Spouses

In all but a few cases, divorce is an emotionally traumatic event for both spouses (Price & McKenry, 1988; Weiss, 1981). The trauma begins, in most cases, before the divorce takes place. In fact, some couples who eventually divorce legally are emotionally and socially divorced from one another while still legally married and physically living together. The loss of intimate connection between them is, as you have learned, a major factor in the decision to divorce. How does this separation occur?

Emotional Uncoupling

Uncoupling
the process of ending an intimate relationship; in many ways, a reversal of the process through which relationships develop.

Sociologist Diane Vaughan (1986) studied the process of ending an intimate relationship—what she calls **uncoupling**—by interviewing cohabitors, homosexual couples, and married couples who had ended their relationship. She also talked with professionals who deal with couples contemplating a breakup. According to Vaughan (1986), the process of ending an intimate relationship is almost a mirror image of the process of developing one. In developing a relationship, partners focus on the positive characteristics of one another and of the relationship; in dissolving a relationship, partners recall and emphasize the negative characteristics. Instead of spending more time with each other, partners in collapsing relationships spend less time together. In a developing relationship, partners increasingly base their self-identity on the relationship; in a dissolving one, one or both partners move toward identifying with something or someone outside of the relationship. Finally, instead of assuming that the relationship will endure forever, the partners in a collapsing relationship come to believe that the relationship will end.

Initiator
the first person in a relationship to become dissatisfied and to take steps to end it.

Both partners go through the same steps in exiting the relationship, but they experience them on different schedules. The person, called the **initiator**, who becomes unhappy or dissatisfied with the relationship first, tries to deal with the unhappiness by attempting to change the situation. This might mean trying to change the partner's appearance or behavior, expressing small complaints, or renegotiating the rules of the relationship. If such attempts fail to resolve the dissatisfaction and if both attractions and barriers seem low and the alternatives attractive, the initiator decides that the relationship cannot be saved and begins to leave the relationship emotionally, socially, and psychologically. Now the initiator's goal is to convince the partner that the end of the relationship would serve the best interests of all involved. In doing so, the initiator makes considerable (though often unsuccessful) efforts to protect the partner from hurt. The whole process of recognizing dissatisfaction, deciding how to deal with it, and trying to protect the partner (while also desperately manuevering an escape) involves considerable external and internal conflict and emotional trauma.

The "partner left behind," still committed to the relationship, may at first be oblivious to or deny the hints that the initiator makes. Once confronted with the information that the initiator wants to end the relationship, the partner left behind must go through the same uncoupling process: recognizing dissatisfaction, trying desperately to change things, withdrawing emotionally and psychologically from the other person, and establishing a new self-identity. In many cases, the partner left behind goes through the stressful uncoupling process only after the separation or divorce has occurred (Vaughan, 1986).

According to public opinion polls of divorced people and to social science research, wives initiate the divorce process more often than husbands; somewhere between 55 percent and 66 percent of divorces are wife-initiated (Colasanto & Shriver, 1989; Thompson & Spanier, 1983). Husbands, more often the "partner left behind," may find their marriage over without ever knowing what happened. In one study, 18 percent of divorced or separated husbands (but less than 2 percent of the wives) said that they were "not sure what happened" when asked the reason for their divorce (Kitson & Sussman, 1982).

Despite the fact that a kind of emotional divorce may occur long before a couple actually separates, many former spouses continue to feel a strong emotional and physical attachment to one another. This continued attachment is a source of confusion and ambivalence. One divorced woman, exasperated at her continued yearning for her ex-husband, stated: "It is like the battered child syndrome. You never find a battered child that does not want to be back with its parents, because they are the only parents it has. I just have very much the same feeling" (quoted in Weiss, 1981, p. 71). Some ex-spouses, even those whose divorces were bitter and confrontational, feel the attachment so strongly that they continue to have occasional sexual intercourse with one another (Price & McKenry, 1988; Weiss, 1981). Ex-spouses might also continue their sexual relationship for some time because finding a new sexual partner may be time-consuming, unsatisfying, and, in an era of sexually transmitted diseases, risky. The former partner provides a known, comfortable, sexual alternative.

Physical and Mental Health Consequences

The effects of the stress and confusion of breaking up, separating, and divorcing are reflected in the mental and physical health of separated and divorced people. When compared to the married, the separated and divorced display markedly poorer psychological well-being, with older divorced people being somewhat better off psychologically than younger ones (Gove & Shin, 1989; Kitson *et al.*, 1989). The divorced and separated are also less psychologically healthy than the never-married, suggesting that the lowered state of their psychological well-being is due not to their single status but to their being "formerly married" (Gove & Shin, 1989). Suicide is frequently interpreted as a sign of extreme mental distress; here again the divorced are exceptional. Divorced men have suicide rates five times higher than married men, and divorced women have suicide rates three and one half times those of married women (Price & McKenry, 1988).

The divorced and separated have higher motor vehicle accident rates, higher rates of alcoholism, higher physical and mental illness rates, and higher death rates than do married, never-married, or widowed people (Gove, Style, & Hughes, 1990; Kitson & Morgan, 1990; Raschke, 1987). Alcoholism and illness, of course, may have preceded and perhaps precipitated the divorce so the direction of causality is not always clear. There is evidence, however, that the stress of dissolving a marriage actually interferes with the normal biological functioning of the body. Individuals undergoing stress-generating marital problems are at increased risk for suppressed immunological functioning, making them more vulnerable to disease (Kitson & Morgan, 1990).

How long do such effects last? Most studies find that the majority of divorced individuals arrive at a more-or-less successful adjustment within two to five years after their divorce, often through dating and remarrying (Price & McKenry, 1988), a process covered in more detail in the next chapter. But divorce does not inevitably make life better. Those who want to be married again but cannot find an intimate partner, like David quoted at the beginning of the chapter, often become lonely and bitter (Wallerstein & Blakeslee, 1990; Weiss, 1981). In one of the few longitudinal studies focusing on psychological responses to divorce, Wallerstein and Blakeslee (1990) found that half the women and two-thirds of the men in their small, middle-class sample were no better off ten years after the divorce than they had been in their original marriages.

Social Consequences

Divorced and separated people have to learn to live alone, adopt new work roles, decide what kind of relationship to have with their ex-spouse, and construct a new social network. Getting married is the transformation of two individuals into a single social unit. With divorce, the single unit is gone. In its place are two single individuals, or one parent-child unit and one single person, or two parent-child units. Whatever the situation, the end of the marriage means the end of the marital division of labor. Money production, household production, and people production tasks are no longer shared as they were during marriage. In the typical divorce, the woman assumes more money production work—often shifting from part-time to full-time work or taking second or third jobs—and both spouses become responsible for the maintenance of their own separate households. Typically, this means that women have to learn more about home repairs and auto care and that men have to learn more about laundry, shopping, and meal-preparation. If one partner managed all the money during the marriage, the other partner must also acquire this skill after the divorce. Child-care falls to the person with custody of the children; this person is "on call" all or most of the time, with little "down time" and often no readily available back-up. The challenge of adapting to these new roles while coping with significant stress explains why newly single males eat out a lot or skip meals entirely and why the households of newly divorced women sometimes seem chaotic and unorganized (Price & McKenry, 1988).

Some divorced people are able to completely end the relationship with their former spouse, but quite a few struggle to construct a new kind of relationship with the ex-spouse. The reasons for continued contact between former spouses are numerous: an intense emotional attachment, a continuing business partnership, or children. As Wallerstein and Blakeslee (1990) point out, the parenthood tie is especially likely to bind ex-spouses into a relationship of indefinite duration as they negotiate visitation or joint custody, consult about their children's problems, attend important events in their children's lives such as graduations and weddings, or meet in court to amend the original divorce decree.

Married partners develop their own social network of friends, parents, and other relatives. When they divorce, neither partner "fits" into the social network in the same way as before. Married friends may be uncomfortable with them now that they are single or may feel torn between loyalties to the ex-husband and to the ex-wife. Relatives are often disappointed, angry, or even bitter that they could not hold their marriage together. Even if their former networks continue to welcome them, the former spouses may have to reduce social contacts because they feel overwhelmed with new responsibilities or because they move away.

One study found that divorced people dropped or were excluded from about 40 percent of their social network ties soon after their divorce (Milardo, 1987). In the years that followed, both men and women rebuilt their network, but in very different ways. Men's new networks consisted mainly of friends and included few relatives (Thompson & Spanier, 1983), reflecting the fact that many of the "friends of the marriage" started out as husband's friends (Milardo, 1987). Women, with few easy links to the friends of the marriage and often with increased work and parental responsibilities, built new networks consisting mainly of parents, siblings, and other relatives (Milardo, 1987; Thompson & Spanier, 1983).

Economic Consequences

One of the most consistent findings in the research on divorce is that women, and especially women with custody of children, frequently suffer severe economic consequences when the marriage breaks up (Furstenberg, 1990; Kitson & Morgan, 1990; Morgan, 1989; Arendell, 1986; Weitzman, 1985). Current laws regarding property division, alimony, and child support, the place of women in the U.S. economy, and custody patterns all help explain women's poor economic position following divorce.

Economic Winners and Losers in Divorce   Perhaps the best known investigation into the economic consequences of divorce is Weitzman's (1985) 10 year study of the effects of California's no-fault divorce laws. Using divorce court records and interviews with divorce lawyers, judges, and recently divorced men and women, Weitzman found that men were most often economic "winners" and women and children most often economic "losers" in divorce. During the first year after the divorce, men's economic status (income compared to needs) *improved* by an average of 42 percent. Meanwhile, the economic status of women and their dependent children during the first year after divorce *declined* by an average of 73 percent (Weitzman, 1985). Another study, focusing on middle-aged divorcées, found that 25 percent of them were pushed below the poverty line sometime during the first five years after divorce (Morgan, 1989).

Sociologist Terry Arendell (1986) did a smaller scale but more detailed study of 60 divorced middle-class mothers. All but two experienced a substantial loss of family income; 56 of the 60 were pushed into poverty or near poverty. The adverse economic consequences did not end after just a few years but, in most cases, were long term (Arendell, 1986). The mothers' economic misfortunes were a major source of stress and they worried especially about the effects of the economic hardship on their children. One mother, accustomed to an income of $4,000 a month during the marriage, dropped to having $950 a month—$760 of it committed to the house payment—after her divorce. Here she describes one effect on her son:

> My son is real tall and growing, I really didn't have any money to buy him clothes, and attorneys don't think school clothes are essential. So he was wearing these sweatshirts that were too small for him. Then one day he didn't want to go to school because the kids had been calling him Frankenstein because his arms and legs were hanging out of his clothes—they were too short. (Arendell, 1986, p. 49)

The women in Arendell's study were very aware that their former husbands were maintaining a higher standard of living and expressed bitterness about it. One woman stated:

> I know my ex-husband goes somewhere almost every weekend, and he usually takes a friend along. I wonder how he can do that. How can he go somewhere every weekend? The only way I could do that is find a rich man! I couldn't possibly work enough hours to pay for that much stuff. I'd be doing well to finance a (twenty-mile) trip to San Francisco. (Arendell, 1986, p. 44)

Property Division, Alimony, and Child Support   Unless you have been involved in a divorce as a partner or child of partners, these economic findings may surprise you. What about equal property division? Alimony? Child support? Working women? Should not all these provisions make the financial aspects of life easy for divorced women and difficult for their ex-husbands?

When it comes to the division of property in divorce, both community property states and separate property states recognize that every marriage has some community property—property acquired after the marriage that belongs to both partners—and follow one of two rules in distributing it (Jacob, 1988). Five states abide by the **rule of equal division**, a rule requiring that husband and wife each get one-half of all marital property in case of divorce. Most of the rest of the states specify that the property be divided according to the **rule of equitable division** in which husband and wife each receive a fair, but not necessarily equal, portion of the marital property, based on their respective needs. The court might decide, for example, that the spouse with custody of the children needs the family home and a greater proportion of the wealth, resulting in an uneven division (Jacob, 1988).

Although the equal or equitable division of marital property at the time of divorce seems fair, it usually does not allow all family members to live an equal style of life after the divorce. One reason it does not is the failure of the courts to recognize intangible property as community property. **Intangible property** includes assets which are not "touchable" in the way that money, cars, land, houses, stocks and bonds

Rule of equal division
a rule of property distribution requiring that in cases of divorce husband and wife each get one-half of all marital property.

Rule of equitable division
a rule of property division requiring that in cases of divorce husband and wife each receive a fair but not necessarily equal portion of the marital property.

Intangible property
"untouchable" assets that represent future potential economic benefits, such as health insurance or an advanced professional degree.

are. Rather, intangible property represents potential future economic benefits. Work-related pensions, health insurance, and advanced educational degrees are examples of intangible property. Such intangible assets are often acquired through joint efforts (for example, one partner works while the other goes to school to get an advanced degree) but are frequently concentrated in one spouse.

Since more husbands than wives hold such intangible property, property divisions that disregard intangibles most often favor husbands and hurt wives. As one divorced woman explained it:

> ... we merely did the modern thing: we split everything down the middle. Everything, that is, except what could be the single most lucrative asset of our marriage—his newly earned postprofessional degree. *I'd put him through school, yet he would keep an earning power that had doubled while mine stood still.* (Takas, 1986, p. 48, emphasis added)

A few divorce courts have begun to accept intangible assets as community property subject to division. A 1987 Massachusetts court, for example, awarded a woman who had put her ex-husband through medical school a percentage of his earnings because of her financial contribution to his degree. The Massachusetts Supreme Court ratified the award and stated that divorce settlements need no longer be restricted to current earnings but could be based on the future earnings resulting from a professional degree (Associated Press, 1987a).

Contrary to much public opinion, plaintive country music lyrics, and articles on celebrity divorces, most divorced women do not receive alimony from their ex-husbands. **Alimony** was originally established as a means by which former husbands financially supported their ex-wives until the wives died or remarried. In the days of fault divorce, judges awarded alimony to reward the faithful wives of guilty husbands and withheld it to punish guilty wives (Jacob, 1988; Price & McKenry, 1988; Oster, 1987). However, even during the era of fault divorce, only a small minority of divorcing women were awarded alimony (Weitzman, 1985).

Alimony
court-ordered payments that a spouse makes to a former spouse.

What was once called alimony is now called **spousal support**. Spousal support is sex-neutral, either spouse can receive it or be obligated to pay it. Although a few states have recently reinstated permanent spousal support as an option for older women with little chance of becoming self-supporting (Associated Press, 1987b), spousal support is usually temporary and rehabilitative, awarded only when necessary to allow one spouse time to recover from the divorce and become self-sufficient (Jacob, 1988; Oster, 1987). Legally, judges are supposed to award spousal support only on the basis of ability to be self-supporting. In actual cases, some judges still consider the behavior of each party, the number of children involved, and whether or not the divorce was

Spousal support
new term for alimony; usually temporary.

contested and by whom when awarding spousal support (Oster, 1987). In most cases, however, there is no awarding of spousal support at all. In 1985, U.S. judges awarded spousal support in only 15 percent of the cases and only 43 percent of the payments were met in full (Kitson & Morgan, 1990, p. 914; Price & McKenry, 1988, p. 113).

Neither can most divorced women depend on child-support payments to balance their budget after divorce. Mothers are awarded sole custody in about 90 percent of the divorces involving children (Teachman & Polonko, 1990). But the court orders child support to be paid to only about 80 percent of these mothers (Price & McKenry, 1988, p. 113). Fathers only fully comply with the child support decrees in about half the cases and only partially comply in another one-quarter of the cases (Price & McKenry, 1988, p. 116).

Even when the court orders child support and the fathers pay, the amount is generally far less than that needed to raise a child (Price & McKenry, 1988). During the 1980s, the federal government enacted legislation to address the problem of delinquent or nonexistent child support payments (Lewin, 1988; Price & McKenry, 1988; Weitzman, 1985). As a result, custodial parents, who take the initiative and invest the necessary time, can now arrange for the interception of the tax refunds or garnishment of the wages of noncompliant ex-spouses delinquent in child support payments. In addition, the legislation required states to establish specific, nonbinding guidelines for child support payments. The South Dakota Child Support Guidelines reproduced as Table 14–4 (on pages 532–533) are fairly typical in this respect.

The failure to include intangible property in most property distribution settlements, the limited and temporary nature of spousal support, and the inadequacy of child support would not be so devastating to the economic situation of divorced women and their children if women were able to earn salaries equal to those of men. As noted in Chapter 10, the average full-time working woman makes about 74 percent of what the average working man makes and, as a working wife, contributes about 30–40 percent of the family's income (U.S. Department of Labor, 1991, p. 73; Spitze, 1988, p. 603). After the divorce, she makes the same 30–40 percent but, if she has custody of children, probably has two-thirds or more of the expenses. Her ex-husband continues to receive the same salary as before the divorce, and even if he makes regular child support payments, has many fewer expenses.

Consequences for Widowed Spouses

In many ways, the death of a spouse affects the surviving spouse in much the same way as divorce. Here we will comment on some of the differences.

Table 14–4 South Dakota Child Support Guidelines

Support obligation schedule. The child support obligation shall be established in accordance with the combined monthly net income of both parents as provided in the following schedule subject to such revisions or deviations as may be permitted pursuant to §§ 25-7-6.1 to 25-7-6.17, inclusive.

Combined Monthly Net Income	One Child	Two Children	Three Children	Four Children	Five Children	Six or More Children
0–800	43	47	50	54	57	60
850	68	77	82	88	93	98
900	91	103	112	120	128	135
950	111	132	144	154	162	171
1,000	130	156	173	184	196	208
1,050	146	184	204	218	231	244
1,100	161	209	232	249	265	280
1,150	173	237	263	282	300	315
1,200	183	260	291	313	333	350
1,250	198	287	321	346	367	384
1,300	212	309	349	377	400	418
1,350	227	337	379	409	434	454
1,400	242	358	406	439	468	485
1,450	257	384	437	471	494	519
1,500	274	404	463	500	526	553
1,550	282	429	493	532	558	585
1,600	291	448	519	560	590	620
1,650	299	465	548	592	622	651
1,700	308	479	574	620	653	686
1,750	316	492	604	651	684	717
1,800	325	506	632	678	715	751
1,850	333	519	649	710	748	785
1,900	342	532	666	741	781	816
1,950	351	546	683	769	813	849
2,000	360	559	700	788	842	881
2,050	368	573	717	808	870	915
2,100	377	587	734	826	902	944
2,150	385	600	751	845	922	978
2,200	394	613	767	864	943	1,006
2,250	402	626	784	883	963	1,031
2,300	411	640	801	902	984	1,053
2,350	419	654	818	921	1,005	1,075
2,400	427	665	831	937	1,022	1,093
2,450	434	676	845	953	1,040	1,112

Table 14–4 *(continued)*						
Combined Monthly Net Income	One Child	Two Children	Three Children	Four Children	Five Children	Six or More Children
2,500	441	687	859	968	1,057	1,130
2,550	449	698	873	984	1,074	1,148
2,600	456	710	887	1,000	1,091	1,166
2,650	463	721	901	1,016	1,108	1,185
2,700	471	732	915	1,032	1,125	1,204
2,750	478	743	929	1,047	1,143	1,221
2,800	485	754	943	1,063	1,160	1,240
2,850	493	766	957	1,079	1,177	1,258
2,900	500	777	971	1,095	1,194	1,277
2,950	507	788	985	1,111	1,212	1,295
3,000	514	799	999	1,126	1,229	1,313
3,050	522	810	1,013	1,142	1,246	1,332
3,100	529	820	1,025	1,157	1,262	1,349
3,150	534	829	1,036	1,169	1,276	1,363
3,200	540	837	1,047	1,182	1,289	1,377
3,250	546	846	1,058	1,193	1,302	1,391
3,300	552	855	1,069	1,206	1,316	1,406
3,350	557	864	1,080	1,218	1,329	1,420
3,400	563	872	1,091	1,230	1,343	1,435
3,450	569	881	1,102	1,243	1,356	1,449
3,500	574	889	1,113	1,255	1,369	1,464
3,550	580	898	1,124	1,267	1,383	1,477
3,600	586	907	1,135	1,279	1,397	1,492
3,650	591	915	1,146	1,291	1,410	1,506
3,700	598	924	1,157	1,305	1,424	1,522
3,750	604	935	1,170	1,319	1,440	1,539
3,800	610	945	1,183	1,334	1,456	1,556
3,850	617	955	1,196	1,348	1,472	1,573
3,900	624	966	1,210	1,363	1,488	1,590
3,950	631	977	1,222	1,378	1,505	1,607
4,000	637	987	1,236	1,392	1,520	1,624

The child support obligation from the schedule shall be divided proportionately between the parents, based upon their respective net incomes. The share of the custodial parent is presumed to be spent directly for the benefit of the child. The share of the noncustodial parent establishes the amount of the child support order.

Source: *South Dakota Codified Laws,* Annotated, Vol. 9A, 1991 Pocket Supplement, 1991, pp. 39–40. © State of South Dakota, 1991.

The widowed, like the divorced, must separate physically, emotionally, and psychologically from their former spouse and begin to build a new social identity for themselves. A long period of illness preceding death allows the opportunity for married partners to begin their separation and for the surviving partner to prepare for life alone. For the survivor, the post-death grieving period may be shortened somewhat. But many of the widowed begin their separation only after the marriage ends. In contrast to the divorced, the widowed are physically separated completely and irretrievably from their spouse. Once a marriage has ended through death, there are no last chances to settle arguments, to express appreciation and thanks for the good things about the marriage, to consult about the children, or to have sexual intercourse—all things that the divorced can do. Death produces a final and unambiguous separation, creating some problems but eliminating others.

Emotional and psychological separation from a deceased spouse takes place in three bereavement stages: a period of numbness, disbelief, and denial lasting several weeks; a longer period of emotional confusion marked by varying combinations of immobilizing grief, anger, depression, guilt, and relief and accompanied by physical symptoms, such as sleep and eating disturbances; and a period of sadness and loneliness, typically, although not always, followed by a recovery period (Hiltz, 1981).

Overall, the physical and psychological well-being of the widowed is considerably worse than that of the married although slightly better than that of the divorced (Kitson et al., 1989). Wives and husbands widowed at a young age suffer more than those who are older, in part because they have less preparation time and leave much more "unfinished business" (Gove & Shin, 1989). Research results are mixed as to whether men or women suffer more physically and psychologically from the death of a spouse (Farnsworth, Pett, & Lund, 1989; Kitson et al., 1989). Widowed men have higher rates of serious illness and death (including suicide) than widowed women, but widowed women may have more overall health problems (Kitson, et al., 1989). While one study showed that widowed women are significantly happier and satisfied with life than widowed men (Gove & Shin, 1989), another found that widows reported more grief and depression than widowers and that they were less successfully adjusted overall (Farnsworth, Pett, & Lund, 1989). Time is apparently a more dependable healer among the widowed than among the divorced; most widowed people adjust well to their loss with the passage of time (Farnsworth, Pett, & Lund, 1989).

At least in the short run, death brings social networks together rather than splitting them apart. In the period immediately following the death, friends and relatives gather to emphasize the good things about the deceased and to offer support to the surviving spouse. This is in marked contrast to the lack of ritual and the splitting up of social networks at the time of divorce. After the first weeks, the widowed person faces some of the same social adjustment problems that the divorced person does—fitting into a "couples" world, deciding which of the former friends to keep and which to let go, and choosing whether to attempt future intimate relationships. As you will learn in Chapter 15, many widowers rebuild their social network and alleviate loneliness by remarrying. This solution is less available to widows, especially elderly ones. Some reconstruct social networks based on friends, children, or interests, discover they like being unmarried, and actively choose not to remarry (Gentry, Rosenman, & Shulman, 1987). Others, especially those who want to remarry but are not able to, cite loneliness as their greatest problem (Gentry, Rosenman, & Shulman, 1987; Hiltz, 1981).

Widowed women are generally less well off economically after the death of their husband than they were while married; widowed men's economic circumstances either stay about the same or decline somewhat. In addition to adjusting emotionally, psychologically, and socially to their husbands' deaths, many widows face the problem of how to live on a much lower income. After loneliness, the problems most often mentioned by widows are, in fact, related to finances and housing (Gentry, Rosenman, & Shulman, 1987, p. 166).

A widow's economic situation depends on her age, her employment status, whether or not she has children, the benefits attached to her husband's job, how much financial planning was done prior to the death, and the debts her husband left behind. The widow who suffers the most economically as a result of her husband's death is one who is in her late forties to early sixties, has been out of the labor market for years, has no dependent children, and whose husband had little or no savings or life insurance and many debts. If this woman were a little older, she would qualify for Social Security benefits (a fairly low but very dependable source of income) and perhaps for her husband's pension benefits as well. If she had children living at home, she would receive a small Social Security payment for them but would also have greater expenses (Morgan, 1989).

One study comparing the financial status of divorced and widowed women aged 45–59 found that, at least in this age group, more widowed women than divorced women were hurt economically when their marriage ended (Morgan, 1989). Forty percent of the widowed (as compared with 25 percent of the divorced) lived in poverty or near-poverty at some time during the five years after their marriage ended. Widowed women and divorced women both tended to move in and out of poverty as their circumstances changed, but widowed women generally had longer "spells" of poverty (Morgan, 1989).

Consequences of Marital Dissolution for Children

The end of a marriage through divorce or death affects not only the former partners but also their children. Today, in the United States, almost half of all children experience the end of their parents' marriage before reaching adulthood. Estimates are that 40–45 percent of U.S. children born during the 1980s will experience one parental divorce and that 20 percent will experience a second (Cherlin *et al.*, 1991; Tennant, 1988). In addition, some 5–8 percent of U.S. minor children will experience parental death (Tennant, 1988; Uhlenberg, 1980). These children must adjust to new living arrangements, adapt to the partial or total loss of a parent, observe the emotional turmoil of the adults around them, and still deal with the usual challenges of growing up. How do they do so?

Living Arrangements

Most children who experience the death of a parent continue to live with their surviving parent. Their situation is more stable than that of comparable children who lived prior to the second half of the twentieth century. In past eras, children whose parent (especially the father) died were frequently sent to live with relatives, adopted by nonrelatives, or placed in orphanages (Bane, 1976).

The living arrangements for children of divorced parents also have undergone some changes over time. Until the middle of the nineteenth century, the law required that children remain with their father in the event of divorce. From about 1850 until about 1940, an era emphasizing

When parents divorce and one moves away, the children endure many of the consequences. They sometimes must travel a great deal to be with their parents.

the importance of the mother-child tie, the courts routinely left children of divorcing parents with their mother. By the middle 1940s, the "**best interests of the child**," a legal principle that required divorce courts to weigh all pertinent factors and award custody based on what was best for the child, prevailed. As the divorce laws changed in the 1960s and 1970s and as experts worried that many children of divorce were being financially and socially abandoned by their fathers, custody provisions changed again. Today a majority of states allow or favor either **joint legal custody**, in which parents share legal jurisdiction over the child and have an equal say in health, education, and financial decisions, or joint legal custody combined with joint physical custody. In **joint physical custody**, the child is a regular part of two parental households, spending approximately equal amounts of time with father and with mother (Wallerstein & Blakeslee, 1990; Nyberg, 1989; Coysh *et al.*, 1989; Jacob, 1988).

Despite changes in the laws, most children of divorced parents today, as in the past, live with only one parent—typically the mother—and are not part of a joint physical custody arrangement (Price & McKenry, 1988). Using data on a national sample of divorces, Teachman and Polonko (1990) found that 91 percent of custody settlements resulted in sole custody, and that the mother was awarded the children in more than 97 percent of those cases. However, part of the reason so few fathers are awarded sole custody is that many do not seek it. When fathers do challenge for the custody of their children, they obtain it in about 50 percent of the cases (McCubbin & Dahl, 1985).

Besides changing the number of adults in the household on a day-to-day basis, marital dissolution frequently means a decline in the child's standard of living and sometimes a move to a different home as well. Table 14-5 documents the income differences between one-

Best interests of the child

legal principle stating that courts should determine the most beneficial situation for the child in making custody decisions.

Joint legal custody

both divorced parents share legal jurisdiction over, and have equal say in, decisions affecting their child's life.

Joint physical custody

child of divorced parents lives approximately half the time in one parent's household and half the time in the other's.

Table 14–5 Mean Income of Families of Children under 18, by Number of Parents and Race			
Number of Parents	Yearly Income by Race		
	Black	Hispanic	White
Both Parents	$31,423	$27,159	$40,833
Mother Only	$8929	$9507	$13,754
Father Only	$15,525	$18,750	$25,418

Source: Rawlings, 1989, p. 24.

parent and two-parent families with children. Note that minority group children and children living with the mother only (as most children living with one parent do) are especially vulnerable to being poor. Look back to Chapter 10 for information about how poverty can affect children.

Psychological and Behavioral Consequences

Children often have intense and frequently dramatic short-term responses to parental death or divorce. For younger children, both death and divorce are experienced as separations—an emotionally crucial adult has disappeared from their lives, often suddenly and without explanation. As a result, children might feel afraid of being abandoned by the remaining parent or of dying themselves, angry, lonely, powerless, rejected, profoundly sad, or guilty (Wallerstein & Kelly, 1980; Furman, 1974). These are the internal feelings; behaviorally, the feelings might be manifested in the form of bad dreams, increased aggressive behavior toward other children or the remaining parent, regression into babyish behavior such as thumb-sucking or clinging, withdrawal, frenetic activity, or extreme concern for the parent or parents (Wallerstein & Kelly, 1980; Furman, 1974). Older children, better able to understand what happened and with somewhat more social and emotional resources, undergo a period of emotional turmoil and mourning closer to that of bereaved adults and are less likely to "act out" their reactions than younger children (Wallerstein & Kelly, 1980; Furman, 1974).

In Chapter 12, we noted that children need both support and control from their parents or other adults. Children involved in the dissolution of the parents' marriage are in special need of support and adult interaction. Children whose parent has died, for example, are much less likely to become permanently "stuck" in their short-term emotional reactions if an adult explains to them the finality of death and encourages them to mourn openly (Murphy, 1986–87; Furman, 1974). Similarly, it should be explained to the children of divorcing parents why one parent no longer lives at home, and the children should be assured that they will still receive good parental care (Wallerstein & Kelly, 1980).

Getting enough emotional support while also receiving appropriate amounts of parental control may be especially problematic for children in the first weeks and months after marital dissolution. In the case of death, there is only one parent left and that one parent may well be overwhelmed with grief, emotional turmoil, and the challenge of learning new roles and making a living. Children of divorce still have two parents available, but contact with the noncustodial parent varies greatly—they may see or talk to their noncustodial parent every day, several times a month, very occasionally, or not at all. For example, a state-wide survey in Wisconsin found that about one-third of noncustodial fathers saw their children at least once a week but that over 40 percent saw their children less than once a month or never (Seltzer, Schaeffer, & Charng, 1989).

Many children whose families are disrupted by parental death or divorce go through a short period of "diminished parenting" by their residential parent. During this time, the parent is preoccupied with grief or worry, unable to keep up normal household routines, and less available to the child (Wallerstein & Blakeslee, 1990). In most cases, however, the residential parent is able to reestablish a stable household routine and resume parental duties within several months or a year (Wallerstein & Blakeslee, 1990).

One study comparing parental support and control in mother-only (because of divorce) families and in two parent families found that children in both types of families received similar (usually high) levels of support from their mothers. However, children in the mother-only families received less support from their fathers than those in intact homes (Amato, 1987). Grade-school aged children in the study received similar amounts of parental control regardless of family structure, with divorced mothers increasing their control to compensate for the absence of the father (Amato, 1987). Adolescents in one-parent families, however, had less parental control than did adolescents living with both parents (Amato, 1987). Adolescents in one-parent households might receive less parental control in part because they need less. More than their peers in two-parent families, they have already assumed some adult responsibilities and taken an active role in making decisions that affect the household. Some studies have discovered that adolescents living in single-parent homes feel more competent, mature, and in control of their own lives and that they feel especially close to their custodial parent (Black, 1982; Demo & Acock, 1988).

With the resumption of a stable (though different) family life, sufficient amounts of parental support and control, and the passage of time, most children of marital dissolution are able to adapt and resume the tasks of growing up in a way comparable to children in intact families (Furstenberg, 1990; Demo & Acock, 1988; Tennant, 1988). For example, most studies find that children from one-parent homes do just as well in school and on standardized tests of academic achievement as those from two-parent homes, especially when socioeconomic status is taken into account (Krantz, 1989; Blum, Boyle, & Offord, 1988; Black, 1982). Nor do they differ significantly in terms of emotional and social well-being (Krantz, 1989). However, children of divorce are behaviorally different from other children in a few respects: they more often exhibit anti-social and aggressive behavior and are more often negative and more pessimistic about the world (Krantz, 1989). On a more positive note, they also develop more household skills and competencies at an earlier age (Demo & Acock, 1988).

Experiencing parental death or parental divorce as a child may have some effects on the formation of intimate relationships later in life. One study found that college students who had experienced an earlier parental death tended either to avoid intimate relationships or to accelerate their courtship activities more often than students from intact marriages. The avoidance pattern was the somewhat more common reaction (Hepworth, Ryder, & Dreyer, 1984). One female student in the study explained her ambivalence about forming relationships:

> One effect it [her father's death] had on me at first was that I don't ever want to be that close to someone that it hurts that much. I saw what my mother went through. They were in love . . . to have something that close and have it taken away. But then, my mother's talked about her feelings . . . she lives on her memories and their good times. So then I came around and I really want to have someone like that to share things with because it's worth it, to have it as long as you can. (quoted in Hepworth, Ryder, & Dreyer, 1984, p. 80)

When they marry, children who have lost a parent through death show greater marital closeness, more protectiveness toward children, and less separation and divorce than others their age who have not lost a parent (Tennant, 1988).

Children of divorced parents more often show accelerated courtship behaviors (Hepworth, Ryder, & Dreyer, 1984) and have higher rates of marital dissolution as adults (Amato & Keith, 1991). In addition, adults who experienced parental divorce as children have somewhat greater psychological adjustment and social relationship problems and somewhat lower educational and occupational attainment than adults who grew up in intact families (Amato & Keith, 1991).

These greater problems do not seem to be the result of the loss occasioned by the divorce itself. Rather, parental conflict seems to be the key to explaining the long-term negative effects of parental divorce on children (Amato & Booth, 1991; Demo & Acock, 1988). On the whole, children whose parents divorce are more likely than other children to have observed parental discord and conflict—before and during the separation period, sometimes for years after the divorce, and sometimes within a second failed marriage. Sustained parental conflict not only confuses children, but it often means that they receive less dependable support and control from their preoccupied parents.

However, not all divorces involve sustained parental conflict and not all parents who stay married have happy, conflict-free marriages. Children of divorce have somewhat more psychological, social, and marital difficulties as adults than children from very happy marriages (including happy marriages ended by death), but they have fewer difficulties than adults who spent their childhood in unhappy, conflicted, intact marriages (Amato & Booth, 1991). In short, *what happens after divorce is more important than the fact of the divorce itself*. Summarizing the results of a national study, Amato and Booth (1991) write:

> If parental divorce does not lead to a decline in children's relationships with parents, and if there are no subsequent divorces, relatively little risk is involved. Indeed, respondents in the *"low-stress" divorce group were similar to those who grew up in the very happy intact families* and better off than those from unhappily intact families. (pp. 912–13, emphasis added)

The Personal Application on helping children through divorce gives some suggestions on how to reduce the stress children experience when their parents divorce.

Personal Application

Helping Children through Divorce

Divorce has few, if any, intrinsic advantages for children; it is a solution for the problems of parents, not those of children. While children are often strongly and immediately affected by divorce, they have virtually no say in whether the divorce will take place, when it will take place, or under what conditions it will take place. Parents need to be especially sensitive to the needs of their children during this trying time. Research on the effects of divorce on children provides a few simple guidelines for helping children adapt to the divorce of their parents.

1. Minimize the disruption in the lives of the children. If possible, keep the children in the same house, the same school, and the same neighborhood.
2. Work diligently to maintain the relationship the children have with each parent. The loss of contact with either parent often has both short-term and long-term negative effects for the children.
3. Encourage close relationships with other adult relatives (for example, aunts, uncles, and grandparents). Such kin are often the only adults the children can lean on when their parents are caught up in the divorce and its aftermath. Help relatives understand what kind of role you would like them to play for the children. Do you want them to be "back-up" parents? good friends?
4. Provide for the economic security of the children.
5. Work to develop and sustain a low-stress and low-conflict divorce. Children care about both parents and do not want to see either hurt.
6. Maintain a well-organized life for the children. Parents should work to establish the common rules and standards applying to issues such as curfews, doing chores, dating, driving, school work, and wearing make-up that are similar to those the children had before the divorce.

Alternative Choice

Marital enrichment programs
programs designed to strengthen healthy marriages.

Behavioral marital therapy
under the supervision of a therapist, married couples work to solve their marital problems by changing their behavior patterns.

Programs to Preserve Marriages

Divorce is one solution to the problem of a troubled marriage. But, as demonstrated throughout the chapter, dissolving a marriage through divorce is a stressful, traumatic process with no guarantee of uniformly successful outcomes. Are there ways of avoiding the marital problems that lead to divorce or of preserving already troubled marriages? In this alternative choice section, we deal with three alternatives: marriage enrichment programs, marital therapy, and temporary separation.

Marital enrichment programs, such as Marriage Encounter, the Minnesota Couple Communication Program, Relationship Enhancement, Training in Marriage Enrichment, and the Association of Couples for Marriage Enrichment, are designed to strengthen healthy marriages by teaching couples skills related to better marital relations. Enrichment programs vary in their format, length, and effectiveness. One comprehensive review of these programs found that longer-lasting programs led by a trained leader were generally more effective than short-term discussion group type programs. Relationship Enhancement, a 10-week program that teaches listening and communication skills, gives homework assignments so couples can practice what they learn in class, and administers positive reinforcements (Kersten & Kersten, 1988, p. 287) was judged particularly effective (Giblin, Sprenkle, & Sheehan, 1985). But marital enrichment programs, particularly if they focus on only one skill area, can also have detrimental effects (Kersten & Kersten, 1988, p. 288). One study of the National Marriage Encounter program, for example, estimated that about 6 percent of the participants experienced highly positive effects on their marriage, 87 percent experienced mildly positive effects or no effects at all, and 7 percent experienced *distinctly negative effects* (Doherty, Lester, & Leigh, 1986).

Behavioral marital therapy (BMT) is an alternative some couples turn to when they feel that their marriage is in trouble, but has not ended. **Behavioral marital therapy** involves meetings between a therapist and the troubled couple during which the therapist helps the couple address their specific marital problems by changing the partners' behavior, interaction, and communication patterns, and problem-solving skills (Jacobson, 1984). One critical review of the effectiveness of BMT indicated that about half the couples experienced improvement, slightly less than 10 percent experienced deterioration, and the rest remained unchanged. Six months later, about 60 percent of the couples maintained the gains made during therapy (Jacobson *et al.*, 1984).

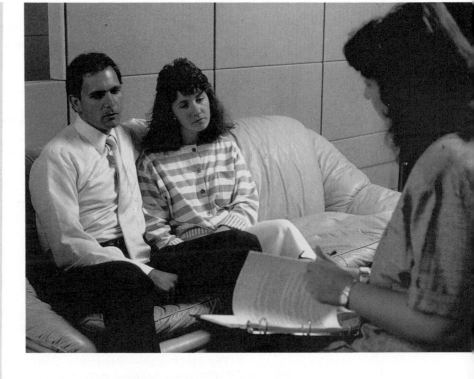

Many couples who believe their marriage is troubled, but not ended, turn to marital therapy as an alternative to divorce.

Temporary separation

partners with severe marital difficulties live apart while attempting to solve their problems.

Structured marital separation

partners with severe difficulties live apart under conditions specified by a mutually agreed upon contract and undergo marital therapy.

The third alternative, temporary separation, is often employed by couples in serious marital distress (Granvold 1983; Granvold & Tarrant, 1983). In a **temporary separation**, the partners live apart while they attempt to solve their marital problems. Unlike permanent separation, it does not indicate that the marriage has ended. However, most couples who get to the point of temporary separation are not able to save their marriages. A longitudinal study of a national sample of women aged 30–44 found that four years after the separation, 40 percent had divorced, 22 percent had reconciled and were again living as husband and wife, and 38 percent were still separated (Morgan, 1988). In other words, only about one couple in five managed to rebuild their marriage after temporary separation.

However, when combined with marital therapy temporary separation may be capable of preserving substantially more marriages than separation alone. Therapists working with separated couples have developed a distinct therapy strategy—the **structured marital separation** (Granvold, 1983; Granvold & Tarrant, 1983). Structured marital separation combines a contract between the husband and wife specifying the conditions of the separation (for example, details on the length of the separation and a promise to delay any decisions about whether to reunite or divorce) with an agreement to undergo marital therapy

(Granvold & Tarrant, 1983). Granvold and Tarrant (1983) report that slightly more than half of the couples in their structured separation program chose to reconcile, while the other half chose divorce.

Summary

Marriages can end through permanent separation, annulment, desertion, death, or divorce. Most marital dissolution today comes through death or divorce, with somewhat more marriages ending through divorce than through death. This trend reflects a reversal of earlier historical patterns. Death most often ends marriages of long duration or marriages in which at least one partner is elderly. Blacks and those with less education more frequently suffer the premature end to a marriage through death. Industrialized countries have higher divorce rates than nonindustrialized countries, with the United States leading the world in divorce. Within the United States, divorce rates are higher in Western states and in urban areas. On an individual level, those who married as teenagers, young adults, those in marriages of short duration, blacks, the childless, those of lower socioeconomic status, and mixed religion or no-religion marriages are more vulnerable to divorce.

The Attractions + Barriers − Alternative Attractions = Likelihood of Staying Married theory helps explain many observed divorce patterns. Generally speaking, people are attracted to the emotional benefits of modern marriage; if these fade, divorce is more likely since the other attractions have less power to hold the marriage together. Barriers to divorce are generally lower today than previously. Fewer people are part of strongly integrated social groups that pressure people to stay married. And the shift to no-fault divorce, though not responsible for increased divorce, did make it easier to obtain. In addition, both men and women are aware of more alternative attractions to marriage and such alternatives have become more acceptable. Individuals who find their marriage meets their expectations, who find the barriers to divorce too steep, or who perceive that their current marriage is preferable to the available alternatives tend to stay married; many others divorce.

Both death and divorce require the spouses to adjust to the stress of being physically, emotionally, economically, and socially separated from one another. Divorced and widowed people are less often physically and psychologically well-off when compared to the married and never-married, with the divorced being particularly affected. Because intangible property is often not divided in divorce settlements, because of limited spousal support and inadequate levels of child support, because they usually receive sole custody of the children, and because of lower salaries for employed women, women usually suffer economic loss as a result of divorce while their husbands enjoy some economic benefit. Both widows and widowers lose economically, but widows lose much more. In the long run, not all husbands and wives are better off socially and emotionally than they were in their marriage, but some make a satisfactory adjustment. Time seems to be a more dependable healer for those who lost a spouse through death than for those who lost one through divorce.

Children experiencing parental death and children experiencing parental divorce have similar, age-related reactions to their loss in the short run. They are emotionally devastated by the loss or absence of an emotionally crucial figure in their lives and often are faced with a change in living conditions and with diminished parenting as well. After the short-term emotional trauma, most receive sufficient emotional support and physical control from their residential parent and adjust fairly well, although children of divorced parents continue to engage in more anti-social behavior and are more pessimistic than others. Provided that parental conflict is limited, that they receive good parental care, are adequately provided for economically, and that they do not go through additional marital dissolutions, children of marital dissolution are as well off as children who spent their whole childhood in intact families. In fact, they are better off than those who lived in intact, but tense and conflict-ridden homes. Children experiencing parental death more often match these conditions than children of divorce and, consequently, less often carry scars into adulthood.

Marital enrichment programs, behavioral marital therapy, and temporary separation are three alternatives to divorce. All seek to preserve marriages—the first by helping untroubled marriages develop skills to become even stronger, the second by intervention in already troubled but not dissolved marriages, and the third by giving partners in severely troubled marriages a chance to live apart and resolve their problems. Each alternative has varying rates of success in keeping marriages together.

REMARRIAGE AND STEPFAMILIES

What do you think about relationships between ex-spouses? For each question, select one of the following answers:

1. Absolutely must.
2. Preferably should.
3. I don't think it should matter one way or the other.
4. Preferably should not.
5. Absolutely must not.

A. Should a woman discuss current marital problems with her former husband?
B. Should a man visit his former wife in the hospital?
C. Should a divorced and remarried woman give her small children a Father's Day card to give to their father?
D. Should a divorced and remarried woman stop allowing her children to watch "scary" movies at the request of their father?
E. Should a divorced and remarried man take his children to church on the Sundays they are visiting him at the request of their mother?

Source: Ann Goetting, "The Normative Integration of the Former Spouse Relationship," *Journal of Divorce*, Vol 2(4). Copyright 1979 by The Hawthorne Press, Inc., 10 Alice Street, Binghamton, NY 13904.

1972. John and Marsha marry, each for the first time.

1974. John and Marsha have their first child, Jeff.

1976. John and Marsha have their second child, Jessica.

1978. John and Marsha separate. John moves out and Marsha stays in their home with Jeff and Jessica.

1979. John and Marsha divorce. Marsha receives physical custody of the children and moves to a smaller house. The children visit John on weekends.

1980. John's girlfriend Tina moves in with him. Marsha continues to live with the children, who visit John and Tina on weekends.

1982. John and Tina marry. It is John's second marriage and Tina's first. Tina becomes a stepmother to Jeff and Jessica, who continue to live with their mother and visit their father on weekends.

1984. Marsha meets and marries Tim, a divorced man with no children. Tim moves into Marsha's home and becomes a stepfather to Jeff and Jessica.

1985. John and Tina have a child, Tessie. Jeff and Jessica, who continue to visit their father and stepmother on weekends, now have a baby half-sister.

1987. Jeff, now 13 years old, moves in with John, Tina, and Tessie. Jessica continues to live with her mother and stepfather and visits her father, stepmother, brother, and half-sister.

1990. Marsha and Tim divorce. Tim moves out and Marsha and Jessica continue to share a home. Jeff continues to live with John, Tina, and Tessie.

In the nineteen years covered by this vignette, John has been a husband in a first and second marriage, has lived alone, first separated and then divorced, has cohabited, and has been both a custodial and noncustodial father. Marsha has experienced life as a wife in a first and second marriage, as a single, divorced parent, and as a single, redivorced parent. Jeff and Jessica have lived in a two-parent family with their biological parents, in a single-parent family, and in two different stepfamilies. Tina has been both a residential and nonresidential stepmother as well as a residential mother, and Tim had a brief experience as a stepfather.

The scenario outlined above is not particularly unusual today. Some experts predict that as many as 40 percent of married couple families with children will become stepfamilies before the youngest child reaches adulthood (Glick, 1989, p. 26). This chapter deals with the formation and functioning of remarriages and stepfamilies. We will look briefly at historical trends regarding remarriage and at current statistics on remarriages and stepfamilies. Then we will examine how people move into remarriage, who is most likely to remarry, and why they do so. A major part of the chapter focuses on the remarried couple and seeks to answer the question: Are remarried couples different from first-married couples in their patterns of intimacy, work, money, adjustment, and satisfaction? Finally, we turn to parent-child relationships within stepfamilies and examine how remarriage affects children, their custodial and noncustodial parents, and their stepparents.

REMARRIAGE AND STEPFAMILIES: PAST AND PRESENT

Remarriage
any marriage in which at least one of the partners has been previously married.

Any old cemetery will reveal that **remarriage**, any marriage in which at least one of the partners has been previously married, is not a new phenomenon. Visit such a cemetery and you will see numerous family plots where a husband's headstone is flanked by the headstones of two or three wives who preceded him in death or where a long-lived wife's grave is surrounded by the graves of multiple former husbands. High death rates during the eighteenth and early nineteenth centuries meant that death disrupted many marriages while spouses were still young. The economic-partners marital work pattern prevalent at the time made remarriage a desirable and common option (Ihinger-Tallman & Pasley, 1987; Cherlin, 1981).

Trends in Remarriage

Remarriage and Stepfamilies **15**

Virtually all remarriages occurring in the seventeenth, eighteenth, and nineteenth centuries in the United States followed the death of the original spouse. As death rates dropped over these centuries, so did remarriage rates. Divorce rates increased during the late twentieth century, and remarriage became more common. *Today 40 to 50 percent of all new marriages are remarriages* (Bumpass, Sweet, & Martin, 1990; Coleman & Ganong, 1990). Ninety percent of current remarriages follow the divorce of one or both partners; the remaining ten percent involve widows or widowers (Glick, 1989).

During most of the twentieth century in the United States, remarriage rates paralleled divorce rates: when divorce rates were low (the 1930s and the 1950s), so were remarriage rates; when divorce rates rose

In previous centuries, remarriage following the death of a spouse was a common phenomenon.

(1945–1947 and again in the early 1960s), so did rates of remarriage (Glick & Lin, 1986a). Since 1966, however, the remarriage rate has declined, even in periods when the divorce rate was increasing rapidly (Bumpass, Sweet, & Martin, 1990; Glick & Lin, 1986a). Figure 15–1 (on page 552) illustrates these trends. Most experts attribute this decrease in remarriage rates to the acceptance of cohabitation as an option. Divorced people continue to form new relationships, just as in the past, but they are less likely to enter into remarriage (Bumpass, Sweet, & Martin, 1990; Glick & Lin, 1986a).

Despite these downward trends, remarried couples are far from rare. In 1987, the eleven million remarried couple families in the United States made up 21 percent of all married couple families (Glick, 1989, p. 25). The number and proportion of remarried couple families remained fairly stable throughout the 1980s and similar stability is expected for the 1990s (Giles-Sims & Crosbie-Burnett, 1989b). In short, remarried couples are a persistent, although no longer increasing, component of the total family picture in the United States.

Trends in Stepfamily Formation

A **stepfamily** is "a remarried family with a child under 18 years of age who is the biological child of one of the parents and was born before

Stepfamily
a remarried family with a residential child under 18 years of age who is the biological child of one of the parents and was born before the remarriage occurred.

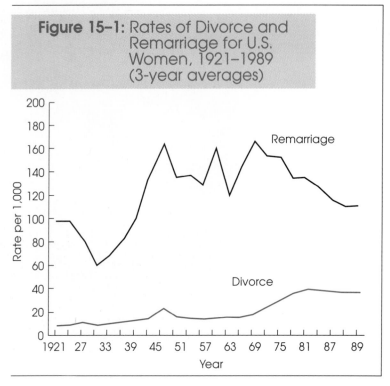

Figure 15–1: Rates of Divorce and Remarriage for U.S. Women, 1921–1989 (3-year averages)

The divorce rates in Figure 15-1 are rates per 1000 married women, aged 14-44 (the major potential group for divorces); the remarriage rates are rates per 1000 widowed and divorced women, aged 14-54 (the major potential group for remarriages). Since the chances of a widowed or divorced woman remarrying in a given year are much greater than the chances of a married woman divorcing in that year, the remarriage rates are higher and changes appear more dramatic. Since 1970, remarriage rates have fallen while divorce rates have increased.

Source: Norton & Moorman, 1987, p. 5. Copyright 1987 by the National Council on Family Relations, 3989 Central Ave. N.E., Suite #550, Minneapolis. MN 55421. Reprinted by permission.

the remarriage occurred" (Glick, 1989, p. 24). In counting stepfamilies for research purposes, only those with a *resident* child are included. Thus, a household consisting of a woman, her child from a previous marriage, and her new husband is counted as a stepfamily. A household consisting of a previously married woman and her husband, with her child from a previous marriage visiting on weekends, is a remarried family but not a stepfamily. If this definition is used, 4.3 million of the 11 million remarried families in the United States are stepfamilies (Glick, 1989, p. 24).

Children in many past historical periods, like children today, had a fairly high probability of seeing their families disrupted and then reconstituted through parental remarriage at sometime during their childhoods. This was particularly true for colonial-era children (Ihinger-Tallman & Pasley, 1987; Demos, 1981), but many children continued to experience family disruption because of parental death until fairly recent times. For example, black children born in 1900 had a 33 percent probability of losing a parent to death before age 15; the comparable probability for white children was 22 percent (Kain, 1990). Some became children in a single-parent household, some eventually became step-

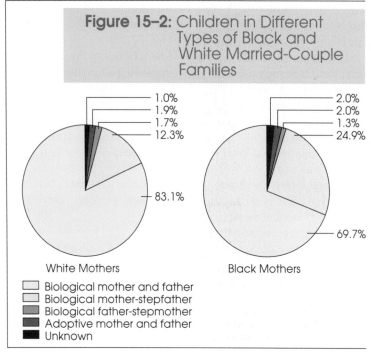

Figure 15–2: Children in Different Types of Black and White Married-Couple Families

White Mothers
- 1.0%
- 1.9%
- 1.7%
- 12.3%
- 83.1%

Black Mothers
- 2.0%
- 2.0%
- 1.3%
- 24.9%
- 69.7%

- ☐ Biological mother and father
- ☐ Biological mother-stepfather
- ▨ Biological father-stepmother
- ▨ Adoptive mother and father
- ■ Unknown

Source: Miller & Moorman, 1989, p. 30.

Most children in married-couple families live with their biological parents. However, black children are twice as likely as white children to live with a stepfather.

children in a remarried family, and some left home. In short, their family living situations were at least as diverse as those of children today.

Figure 15–2 presents a snapshot of the living arrangements of U.S. black children and white children living in two-parent families in 1985. At any given point in time, most children in two-parent households are living with their biological parents, although this pattern is more common for white children than for black children. The most common stepfamily pattern features children living with their biological mother and a stepfather; other possible combinations are much less common (Miller & Moorman, 1989).

REMARRYING

For widowed and divorced people in some societies, whether to remarry and whom to remarry have not been matters of choice but have been governed by formal rules and informal customs. For example, the ancient Hebrews specified that childless widows should marry their deceased husband's brother and that the preferred mate of a widower was his deceased wife's sister; early Christian rules saw any remarriage as evil; and the traditional Chinese allowed remarriage for men but not for women (Spanier & Furstenberg, 1987).

Most potential remarriers in the United States today, particularly the divorced, lack such clear guidelines regarding courtship and remarriage (Rodgers & Conrad, 1986; Cherlin, 1978). There are few formal or informal rules regarding whether to remarry, how soon to establish a new relationship, how to select a remarriage partner, or whose approval is necessary. Current norms regarding sexuality are also confusing, particularly to divorced or widowed people whose first dating experience was many years ago.

Lacking clear guidelines, potential remarriers have maximum choice and minimum guidance. They are new pioneers, carving out new norms where few existed before.

Courtship for Remarriage

Although sociologists know a great deal about premarital dating and courtship, they have only begun to study dating and courtship that occur after a first marriage dissolves. Some differences between premarital and postmarital daters stand out clearly. Most premarital daters

Mothers have long helped their daughters prepare for dates. In an era of between-marriage dating, daughters sometimes help their mothers get ready to go out.

are young, and many of them are still living with or financially dependent upon their parents; typical postmarital daters are residentially and financially independent adults. Most premarital daters are sexually inexperienced when they begin dating, while postmarital daters typically have years of sexual experience. While premarital daters may have parents and, occasionally, ex-boyfriends or ex-girlfriends who are interested in their current dating activities, many postmarital daters date under the watchful eyes of parents, ex-in-laws, ex-spouses, and their own children. Finally, while premarital courtship affects mostly the lives of the two partners, postmarital courtship may potentially affect a large number of kin and ex-kin (Rodgers & Conrad, 1986).

Postmarital courtship is often an accelerated version of premarital courtship. One study comparing courtships for first and subsequent marriages found that the median first marriage courtship (first date to marriage) lasted 17 months, while the median remarriage courtship lasted only nine months. Men had shorter postmarital courtships than women (O'Flaherty & Eells, 1988).

Postmarital daters also seem to proceed more quickly to sexual intimacy than do premarital daters. For example, a study of elderly dating couples (some widowed and some divorced) found that they dispensed with the "game-playing" common in premarital dating and proceeded quickly and openly into sexual intimacy (Bulcroft & O'Conner-Roden, 1986a).

As noted in Chapter 5, cohabitation precedes remarriage more often than it precedes first marriage. You may recall that, during the 1980s, two-thirds of the remarriers but only 44 percent of the first marriers cohabited (Bumpass & Sweet, 1989). Remarried people, when asked to recall how they prepared for remarriage, listed "cohabitation" much more often than they mentioned advice from friends, reading, counseling, support groups, or education programs (Ganong & Coleman, 1989). Cohabitation before remarriage may be one of the few emerging norms of postmarital courtship.

Who Remarries?

Although some previously married people remain single and some become long-term cohabitors, the majority chose marriage again. Three out of four women with disrupted first marriages enter into a second marriage (Bumpass, Sweet, & Martin, 1990, p. 753). Remarriage typically occurs within five years of the initial separation and, as noted above, often follows a period of cohabitation (Bumpass, Sweet, & Martin, 1990). Most of those who remarry, then, move rather quickly from one intimate relationship to another.

Certain categories of people are much more likely to remarry than others. Men remarry at a higher rate than women and divorced people remarry at a much higher rate than the widowed (U.S. Bureau of the Census, 1991a, p. 87). In fact, divorced people are more likely to remarry than never-married people of the same age are to marry for the first time. Racial minority groups have remarriage rates far below those of the white majority: black remarriage rates are one quarter those of whites; Hispanics remarry only half as often as whites (Bumpass, Sweet, & Martin, 1990).

Women who remarry and men who remarry have somewhat different characteristics. The woman most likely to remarry is a white woman who married young, had a short first marriage, separated before age 25, and had no children (Bumpass, Sweet & Martin, 1990). These women have a wide selection of potential remarriage partners. Besides large numbers of never-married men their own age, divorced men their own age and older are available. Having children from a previous marriage inhibits remarriage for women, especially if the woman is young and the children are numerous (Teachman & Heckert, 1985). However, the presence of children certainly does not preclude remarriage; indeed, 73 percent of women with one or two children and 57 percent of those with three or more eventually remarry (Bumpass, Sweet, & Martin, 1990, p. 754).

Women who are over 30, belong to a racial minority, or earn a high income are much less likely to remarry and take longer to do so when and if they do (Bumpass, Sweet, & Martin, 1990; O'Flaherty & Eells, 1988). Once again, availability of suitable partners seems to be the key. In remarriage, even more than in first marriage, men seem to prefer a younger (often a much younger) partner (Spanier & Furstenberg, 1987). When combined with the lower life expectancy of men, this male preference for younger women means fewer available partners for older women. Women seem to look for economic security more in second marriages than in first ones (Coleman & Ganong, 1990). Women who earn high incomes can obtain such security without remarrying. Therefore, they are likely to be more cautious about remarriage.

Men are more likely to remarry than women regardless of other factors. Some men remarry more quickly than others, however. Older divorced men with high incomes are the most likely to remarry quickly (O'Flaherty & Eells, 1988). Younger divorced men, who more often have lower incomes and longer-lasting child support obligations, must "compete" in the remarriage market with both never-married, unencumbered men their own age and with better-off, older divorcees and widowers.

A first marriage, by definition, comes in only one form: a never-married man marries a never-married woman. In contrast, remarriages come in eight possible combinations:

Husband	Wife
Never Married	Divorced
Never Married	Widowed
Divorced	Never Married
Widowed	Never Married
Divorced	Divorced
Divorced	Widowed
Widowed	Divorced
Widowed	Widowed

ZIGGY®
© 1992 Ziggy and Friends, Inc.

Of these possible combinations, some are more likely than others. For example, because most widowed people are middle-aged or older and most divorced people are young, the widowed-divorced combinations are probably relatively rare. A little more than half of all remarriages involve two previously married partners; the rest involve one partner who has never been married before (U.S. Bureau of the Census, 1991a, p. 87).

Why Remarry?

Given the trauma associated with divorce or death of a spouse, why do most people (especially the divorced) remarry quickly? Although there may be no formal rules or explicit informal customs about remarriage, there may be subtle social pressures for men and women, especially if they are young, to remarry and to do so within a specified amount of time. Consider, for example, a survey of remarried persons done by family studies specialists Ganong and Coleman (1989). When asked why they remarried, 56 percent of the men and 50 percent of the women answered simply "It was time." Other frequently stated reasons, given in descending order, were "convenience," "social pressure," "love," and "wanted help raising the children" (Ganong & Coleman, 1989, p. 30). Note that pragmatic rather than romantic reasons prevailed.

Although not usually stated openly, financial security may be a primary consideration for women who remarry. Higher income women are less likely to remarry at all and take longer when they do so when compared with lower income women. One woman, married, mother of two, and divorced before the age of 25, gave this mixture of romantic and financial security reasons for remarrying:

> . . . I thought I'd never meet a guy I could love, live with, and still want to marry. It's not only good for me, it's great for my kids. . . . He owns a tree nursery that's doing real good. At last I'm going to have some financial security. We won't be affluent but I've sure joined another world when it comes to money. That end of the month freakout won't happen. (quoted in Wallerstein & Blakeslee, 1990, p. 209)

Although remarriers appear to engage in very little specific preparation for remarriage (Ganong & Coleman, 1989), they do choose second spouses based in part on their perceptions of their previous marriages. Within their small sample of divorced Californians, researchers Wallerstein and Blakeslee (1990) found that women, in selecting a second husband, looked for stability, economic dependability, affection, and sex. Men openly acknowledged the importance of sex as a consideration in their remarriage choices and also looked for second wives who were more flexible and accommodating than their first wives had been.

HOW IS REMARRIAGE DIFFERENT?

First marriages and remarriages have many similarities. In fact, many of the points we have made about marriage throughout this text apply equally well to both first and subsequent marriages. First-time marriers and remarriers have to meet identical legal requirements in order to marry. Once married, husbands and wives in remarriages have the same legal obligations in respect to one another as husbands and wives in first marriages. In each of these types of marriage, the two partners must learn to communicate effectively with one another, divide family work, decide how to make and spend money, adjust to one another sexually, and build a family culture. Keep in mind also that about half of all remarriages *are* first marriages for one of the partners (Spanier & Furstenberg, 1987).

Nonetheless, remarriages are different from first marriages in at least four ways:

1. At least one of the partners in every remarriage is *experienced* at marriage. In first marriages, both partners are inexperienced.
2. The norms for remarriage are more *ambiguous* than the norms for first marriage.
3. Members of remarried families are typically involved in more *complex kin networks* than people in first marriages.
4. Remarried people are more subject to *negative stereotyping* than people marrying for the first time.

Remarriages vary a great deal, of course, and not all of these differences are relevant to every type of remarriage. A divorced woman and a widowed man, each with dependent children, who marry can expect to confront all of these differences. Two childless divorced people, each of whom had a first marriage lasting less than a year, are much less likely to be strongly affected by the differences.

Experience

A first-married man and a first-married woman are like apprentices learning a new occupation. They are unpracticed in many of the skills of marriage, have only a vague idea about what the "jobs" of husband

and wife involve, and may hold unrealistic expectations about the rewards of their new positions. In a remarriage, at least one of the partners knows about marriage through experience. The remarried partner knows something about how much it costs to be married, something about how passion and sexual intensity fade over time, and something about the conflicts that arise in even the most perfect of marriages. Furthermore, people remarrying after their first marriage dissolved have typically spent some time alone and have had time to contemplate what worked and what did not in their first marriage. Such prior preparation and contemplation would seem to benefit remarriages and to help them avoid some of the pitfalls of first marriages.

There is another side to this prior experience, of course. In every marriage, both partners carry at least one prior marriage (their parents') around in their heads and, consciously or unconsciously, use it as a baseline for comparison. In remarriage, the remarried partner or partners have additional, more recent, and more direct marital experience to use in assessing the current marriage. Remarried people, when questioned by researchers, draw clear distinctions between their first and their subsequent marriages. They note, in particular, that they try to avoid behavior—for example, nagging, drinking excessively, or sloppiness—which they perceive was harmful in their first marriage (Spanier & Furstenberg, 1987; Kalmuss & Seltzer, 1986).

If their perceptions are accurate, if they are relevant to the new marriage, and if the remarried persons are successful in changing negative behaviors, then using lessons from prior marriage(s) as a guide may have positive results. However, another possibility is that old negative patterns will be carried, intentionally or not, into the new marriage. The "lingering effects" (Spanier & Furstenberg, 1987) of prior marriages can affect both people in the remarriage, even if it is a first marriage for one of them. Consider the situation of the woman quoted here:

> Ours is a situation where my husband's wife left him for another man. It left him with bitter feelings that sometimes inadvertently carry over into our marriage. I also know that he still and always will love his ex-wife very much. And even though he loves me, I feel sometimes that if she would have him, he would be happier married to her. . . . I compete with his first wife in things I do in everyday living—for instance, wondering if I keep house as well as she or cook as well . . . . (quoted in Ihinger-Tallman & Pasley, 1987, p. 73)

In the remarriage described above, the ex-spouse is clearly a very significant psychological presence. In some remarriages, especially those in which a remarried partner continues to communicate with an ex-spouse about their mutual children, the ex-spouse can be a *physical* presence as well.

Ambiguous Norms

In a classic article on the subject, sociologist Andrew Cherlin (1978) referred to remarriage, especially remarriage after divorce, as an "incomplete institution." Remarriage, in contrast to first marriage, is an "incomplete institution" according to Cherlin because the norms governing remarriage and stepfamily life are ambiguous. In the absence of clear standard guidelines, each remarried family has to make up its own rules about what types of contact to have with ex-spouses, how much authority stepparents should have over stepchildren, the economic responsibilities of parents and stepparents, and even what family members should call one another (Cherlin, 1978).

To get a more concrete understanding of these matters, consider again the family described at the beginning of the chapter. Their 1990 situation is diagrammed in Figure 15–3.

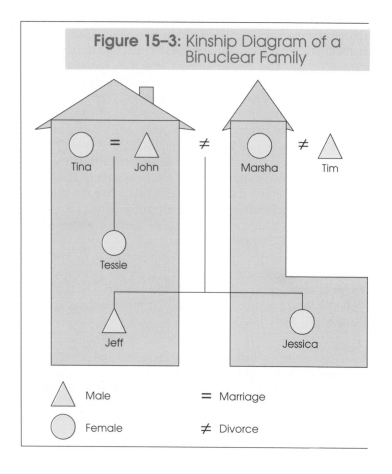

Figure 15–3: Kinship Diagram of a Binuclear Family

Tina = John ≠ Marsha ≠ Tim

Tessie

Jeff   Jessica

△ Male   = Marriage

○ Female   ≠ Divorce

This drawing shows a kinship diagram for the family described at the beginning of the chapter. A triangle indicates a male, a circle indicates a female, = means marriage, ≠ means divorce, vertical lines indicate a parent-child relationship and horizontal lines indicate a sibling relationship. Those enclosed within the same "house" live together most of the time.

Binuclear family
a group of parents and children who used to live together but now live separately after divorce or death followed by remarriage.

Sociologically speaking, Figure 15–3 pictures a **binuclear family**, "a group of parents and children . . . who used to live together but now live separately after divorce or the death of a spouse was followed by remarriage" (Glick, 1989, p. 26; Ahrons, 1980). Binuclear family members have to make a number of choices that nuclear family members never face. For example, should Jeff and Jessica call Tina "mom"? "step-mom"? "Tina"? Should Tina treat Jeff, the stepson who lives with her, differently than stepdaughter Jessica who only visits? Should she exercise as much authority over them as she does over her own daughter, Tessie? Should Marsha call John at home when she wants to discuss their children? Can she request that John and Tina maintain the same bedtime and household rules with Jessica and Jeff that she does? If money is tight, should John give first priority to Tina and Tessie or to Jeff and Jessica?

Binuclear families face these types of questions everyday. Are there any emerging norms to give them guidance? Is there any kind of consensus about how to best handle these issues? Sociologist Ann Goetting (1979) found that remarried adults agreed rather consistently about *some* aspects of the ex-spouse relationship but held widely varying opinions about others. You answered some of Goetting's questionnaire items in the What Do You Think? section; refer back to your answers now. Goetting found that her respondents were strongly *against* discussing the current marriage with the former spouse (Question A) and that they *favored* the idea of a mother providing small children with a Father's Day card for her ex-husband (Question C). The questions about visiting a former spouse in the hospital (Question B) and about how much influence the custodial parent should have over the non-custodial parent on childrearing issues (Questions D and E) elicited no such consensus. Goetting (1979) concluded that, while the situation of remarried families was not as normatively ambiguous as some observers make it out to be, there are still many areas of remarried life not adequately covered by existing norms.

The ambiguity regarding informal norms extends to formal legal norms as well. As noted earlier, legally a remarriage is treated as a first marriage in terms of the husband-wife relationship. The confusion comes with the legal relationship between stepparent and stepchild. Psychologist Mark Fine (1989) notes:

> In contrast to the biological parent-child relationship, there is an absence of clearly defined legal rights and duties for the step-parent-stepchild relationship. Rather, in attempting to extend the legal aspects of the biological parent-child relationship to the step-family context, lawmakers and judicial officials have done so in an "ad hoc fashion with inconsistent results." (p. 53)

Fourteen states require stepparents to support stepchildren who are living with them and some others may require support if the stepparent is otherwise acting *in loco parentis* (Fine, 1989). However, such obligations do not extend beyond the life of the marriage. In contrast to biological parents, stepparents typically do not have child support obligations, visitation rights, or the opportunity to be custodial parent if their marriage is disrupted by divorce or death unless they have formally adopted their stepchildren (Fine, 1989; Kargman, 1983). Consider the position of Tim in Figure 15–3. He was married to Marsha for six years. Quite possibly he developed a close, "fatherlike" relationship with one or both of her children and helped to support them financially. But his relationship with Jeff and Jessica ended with the marriage; it is very unlikely that he was required by the court to provide child support or that he was granted the right to visit the children.

Some family experts (Fine, 1989; Giles-Sims and Crosbie-Burnett, 1989b; Cherlin, 1978) believe that this ambiguity about both informal norms and legal obligations puts stepfamilies under special pressures.

Complex Kin Networks

Remarriage, particularly when it includes two previously married partners and their children, often involves people in fairly complex relationships with a variety of current and ex-in-laws. This collection of people can be called a remarriage kin network. A **remarriage kin network** is "the group of persons sharing kinship ties as a result of the *current and prior* marriage relationships of a remarried couple, who exert some degree of influence in the affairs of that family" (Hobart, 1988, p. 649). For example, John (in our beginning of the chapter example) has both ex-in-laws (Marsha's relatives) and current in-laws (Tina's relatives), and Jeff and Jessica might have as many as eight people acting as grandparents (John's parents, Marsha's parents, Tina's parents, and Tim's parents). The situation can become even more complex if one or more of the grandparents have divorced and remarried or if there are multiple remarriages.

> **Remarriage kin network**
> the group of persons sharing kinship ties as a result of the current and prior marriage relationships of a remarried couple, who exert some degree of influence in the affairs of that family.

All of the people tied together in a remarriage kin network might well have reasons to be involved with one another, at least occasionally (for example, to arrange who will be where and when during the Christmas holidays). The involvements will not necessarily be pleasant ones "because the network links together people who have various reasons to compete with, mistrust, dislike, or even hate each other" (Hobart, 1988, p. 651).

Some other cultures have rather elaborate rules for dealing with complex kin networks and have norms that allow and encourage the involvement of kin in nuclear family life. The United States, however, has family norms that emphasize the privacy and independence of the nuclear family unit. Remarried families, and especially stepfamilies, may have a difficult time conforming to these nuclear family norms. After all, they may receive part of their family income from outside the immediate family in the form of child support payments. At the same time, part of *their* income may go to help pay the expenses of another nuclear family unit (again in the form of child support payments). Step-families involved in a remarried kin network exchange not only money but also members. While first-married nuclear families generally have the same members present 7 days a week and 12 months a year, the composition of a stepfamily household might be different on weekends than on weekdays and different in the summer than in the winter.

All this stepfamily complexity can lead to a situation known as boundary ambiguity. **Boundary ambiguity** is "the uncertainty of family members regarding . . . who is in or out of the family and who is per-forming what roles and tasks within the family system" (Pasley & Ihinger-Tallman, 1989, p. 46). First marriage nuclear family households have rather clear boundaries about which all members of the family agree. Stepfamily households, for reasons mentioned above, often have fuzzy boundaries and different members of the household might have different perceptions of who belongs to "my family."

Let us return once more to John and Marsha's binuclear family as an illustration. John may well consider Tina, Tessie, Jeff, and Jessica as his family while Tina considers John, Tessie, and perhaps residential stepson Tim (but not Jessica) as hers. Jeff and Jessica may well envision their family as the original nuclear family (John, Marsha, Jeff, Jessica) into which they were born, or they might each have a separate and distinct conception of "my family." The points here are two familiar ones:

Boundary ambiguity the uncertainty of family members in remarriage kin networks regarding who belongs to the family and who does not, and about who should fulfill which family roles.

1. There are *few norms or guidelines* for stepfamily members to use in deciding who is in their family and whose family they belong to.
2. Such ambiguity may lead to increased stress within the re-married family.

Negative Stereotypes

Finally, remarried family members, particularly stepfamily members, confront negative stereotypes. Many people grew up hearing fairy tales about "evil stepmothers" and "selfish stepsisters." Numerous stud-ies confirm that negative stereotyping of "steps" is not limited to fairy tales. When people are asked to judge hypothetical others knowing only their family position (for example, mother, stepmother, brother, grandmother), the "steps," particularly "stepmothers" and "stepchildren," end up with the least positive evaluations (Ganong, Coleman, & Mapes, 1990; Bryan *et al.*, 1986; Fine, 1986). For example, in one study, stepmothers were judged to be unhappier, crueler, less likeable, less loving, and more hateful than mothers (Fine, 1986). People with the least experience with stepfamilies hold the most negative views of them; in the study described above, members of stepfamilies judged the "steps" slightly less harshly but still gave the "nonsteps" the most positive evaluations (Fine, 1986).

Such negative stereotypes of stepfamilies, especially when contrasted with the extremely positive stereotypes of first-married families, might place additional stress on stepfamily members (Ganong, Coleman, & Mapes, 1990). Like other negatively stereotyped groups, some (perhaps many) remarried families hide their remarried family status, attempting to "pass" as first-married, biologically connected, nuclear families (Ganong & Coleman, 1989).

HUSBAND-WIFE RELATIONSHIPS IN REMARRIAGE

How, if at all, do these differences between first marriages and remarriages actually affect the husband-wife relationship? Are remarried husbands and wives different from first-married husbands and wives in their intimate behavior? their division of family labor? their methods of handling finances? How satisfied are remarried couples with their remarriage? How likely are they to divorce?

Good empirical research on most of these topics is in its early stages (Coleman & Ganong, 1990; Spanier and Furstenberg, 1987; Ganong and Coleman, 1986). Thus, the findings discussed below are tentative and suggestive rather than definitive.

Intimacy, Work, and Money in Remarriage

In many ways, the day-to-day lives of first-married couples and remarried couples are similar. Remarried partners are just as likely to be affectionate, close, expressive, and sexually satisfied as partners in a first marriage (Larson & Allgood, 1987). Like first-married partners, remarried partners tend to adopt a rather traditional division of household labor: men do the outside work, women the inside work and most of the child care (Guisinger, Cowan, & Schuldberg, 1989). Although money issues may be even more important in remarriages than in first marriages, remarrying people, like those marrying for the first time, seldom discuss money before they marry (Ganong & Coleman, 1989; Lown, McFadden, & Crossman, 1989).

A few differences in day-to-day functioning do show up when first marriages as a whole are compared to remarriages as a whole. Several studies (Whyte, 1990; Larson & Allgood, 1987; Kalmuss & Seltzer, 1986) show that remarried couples are more likely to use unproductive strategies (shouting, violence, opening old wounds) to deal with conflicts. This might be because their problems are greater, or it might be a matter of carrying over bad habits from the previous marriage (Larson & Allgood, 1987; Kalmuss & Seltzer, 1986).

Division of labor arguments are common in all marriages but the peculiar position of the stepmother makes them particularly likely in remarriages involving nonresidential stepchildren (Guisinger, Cowan, & Schuldberg, 1989). The new husbands of such stepmothers often expect them to provide meals, laundry, and child-care for visiting stepchildren, tasks that the stepmothers feel husbands should share (Guisinger, Cowan, & Schuldberg, 1989).

Although remarriage often greatly improves the economic situation of single-parent mothers (Buehler *et al.*, 1986), money is more likely to be problematic in remarriage than in first marriage. For one thing, some remarried families experience *both* the new baby financial squeeze and the adolescent child financial squeeze simultaneously (Ihinger-Tallman & Pasley, 1987). The issue of whether to pool funds is more of an issue in remarriages, especially those involving children. Remarried families in which ex-spouses are still financially tied to their prior families and that have higher overall income tend to adopt a **Two Pot Economy**. Under this arrangement, the remarried wife handles her expenses and those of her biological children (typically with help from her ex-husband) and the remarried husband handles his expenses as well as continuing to support his biological children (who typically live in another household) (Fishman, 1983). Stepfamilies in which financial support from ex-spouses is sporadic or nonexistent and in which overall income is low tend to adopt the **One Pot Economy**, more typical of first marriages, in which spouses pool their incomes and share expenses. (Fishman, 1983). Money-handling strategies are, thus, more diverse in remarriages than in first marriages and so are potential money problems.

Two Pot Economy
a financial arrangement of stepfamilies in which the remarried wife handles her expenses and those of her biological children and the remarried husband handles his expenses as well as continuing to support his biological children.

One Pot Economy
a financial arrangement of stepfamilies in which spouses pool their incomes and share expenses.

Remarital Quality

Overall marital quality scores are similar for first marriages and remarriages. A research project that summarized 34 studies of marital satisfaction in first marriage and remarriage concluded that first marriages were slightly more satisfied than remarriages, but that the difference was "miniscule" (Vemer et al., 1989). Other studies and summaries surmise that marital satisfaction and happiness are very much the same in first marriage and in remarriage (Whyte, 1990; Kurdek, 1989; Ihinger-Taller & Pasley, 1987; White and Booth, 1985b).

Researchers have just begun to look at differences in satisfaction and happiness *among* remarriages—that is, to determine why some remarriages are more satisfying than others. Some factors that might be expected to affect remarital satisfaction apparently do not. For example, high boundary ambiguity remarriages and low boundary ambiguity remarriages have similar marital satisfaction scores (Pasley & Ihinger-Tallman, 1989). The presence of stepchildren, residential or nonresidential, does not lower remarital satisfaction (Vemer et al., 1989; White & Booth, 1985b), nor does having a new child within the remarriage improve it (Ganong & Coleman, 1988). While remarried men are slightly more likely to be satisfied in remarriage than remarried women, stepmothers and stepfathers are similar in terms of remarital satisfaction (Vemer et al., 1989).

Some of the factors that influence remarital quality are factors that have to do with how remarried couples handle decision-making, household work, and relationships with ex-spouses. As in first marriages, when remarried spouses perceive that they are each getting a "fair deal" in terms of household work, they are more likely to be satisfied with the remarriage. In remarriages involving the husband's nonresidential children, this means that a more *nontraditional* division of labor (especially when it comes to caring for nonresidential children) yields higher satisfaction (Guisinger, Cowan, & Schuldberg, 1989). In stepfather families (husband, wife, and the wife's biological children), satisfying interaction with stepchildren is not necessary for the husband's marital satisfaction, but being involved in household decision-making and agreement with his wife is (Orleans, Palisi, & Caddell, 1989). Feelings about the ex-spouse can affect satisfaction with the current marriage. Many of the remarried couples interviewed by psychologists Guisinger, Cowan, and Schuldberg (1989) felt that the husband's ex-wife created many more marital problems than the husband's children did. Remarried husbands and wives who could not overcome their negative feelings about the husband's ex-wife were more dissatisfied with their own current marriage (Guisinger, Cowan, & Schuldberg, 1989).

Prior cohabitation may have beneficial effects on remarriages. One study, comparing remarried couples who had cohabited prior to remarriage to those who had remarried without cohabiting, found that the former cohabitors showed higher scores on four of eight measures of family strength. Former cohabitors also judged their marital adjustment to be better than did the noncohabitors (Hanna & Knaub, 1981).

Although cohabitation does not improve the quality of first marriages, it does seem to help in remarriages.

Remarital Stability

Overall, remarriages are slightly more likely to be disrupted by divorce than are first marriages (Spanier & Furstenberg, 1987, p. 424; White & Booth, 1985b). This general pattern holds for whites but not for blacks. One study of black women and white women married during the 1950s, 1960s, and early 1970s found a first marriage divorce rate of 19 percent for white women and 40 percent for black women; redivorce rates (divorce from a remarriage) were 22 percent for whites and 37 percent for blacks (Teachman, 1986, Table 2). Figure 15–4 illustrates this in graphic form: black divorce rates are higher than white divorce rates in both first marriage and remarriage, but blacks are *less* likely

This graph shows the *cumulative* proportion of marriages and remarriages ending in divorce for the first 10 years of marriage. That is, the proportion dissolved by year 5 represents marriages ending in years 1, 2, 3, 4, and 5 added together. By the tenth year, about 4 out of 10 black first marriages and 2 out of 10 white first marriages have dissolved. White second marriages are more prone to dissolution than white first marriages but black second marriages are less prone to dissolution than black first marriages.

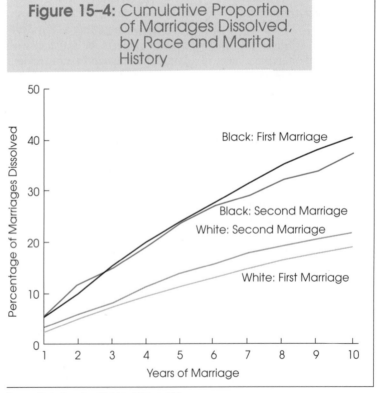

Figure 15–4: Cumulative Proportion of Marriages Dissolved, by Race and Marital History

Source: Data from Teachman, 1986, p. 578.

to divorce after remarriage than after first marriage and whites are *more* likely to do so. The reasons for the racial differences in redivorce patterns are unclear (Teachman, 1986). You might recall, though, that blacks take longer to remarry than whites do; this might contribute to their relatively lower divorce rates in remarriage.

Cohabitation before remarriage seems not only to improve the quality of remarriages, but also to increase the chances that they will last. A four-year study of the consequences of cohabitation in the United States found that individuals who married, divorced, cohabited, and remarried had a much *lower* chance of divorcing a second time than those who married, divorced, and then remarried without cohabiting (Newcomb & Bentler, 1980b). In other words, *cohabitation aids in the survival of second marriages*, perhaps because the formerly married are better equipped to take advantage of the "testing ground" aspects of cohabitation (Newcomb & Bentler, 1980b).

As we have noted previously, remarried people are no more likely than first married people to be unhappy or dissatisfied with their marital relationship. Why, then, are they more likely to divorce? One possible explanation is that most remarried people are experienced in divorce as well as in marriage (Spanier & Furstenberg, 1987). People who enter remarriage after divorce know what divorce is like and have survived it once. To first-married people, on the other hand, divorce is a great unknown and some of them are probably unwilling to consider it an option regardless how dissatisfying their marriage (Spanier & Furstenberg, 1987).

An alternative explanation is that the ambiguities and complexities associated with remarriage put even strong, satisfying remarriages under special stress (Cherlin, 1978). This explanation states that, given the same quality of marriage, remarriages are more likely to dissolve than first marriages because of the unusual external pressures of ex-spouses, ex-in-laws, and stepchildren sometimes associated with remarriage. Some research supports this explanation, at least indirectly. The most ambiguity-ridden, complex remarriages are those in which both remarried partners were previously married (a double remarriage) and those in which one or both partners have children from the prior marriages. These are also the remarriages most likely to break up (Teachman, 1986; White & Booth, 1985b). Figure 15–5 summarizes the findings of one study conducted over a three-year period during the early 1980s. Note that, during this interval, remarriages involving only one remarried partner and no stepchildren had divorce rates very nearly identical to first marriages. Meanwhile, double remarriages with stepchildren had divorce rates nearly *triple* those of first marriages.

In the study described above, the quality of *family* life, not the quality of the *marriage*, determined which remarriages survived and which did not (White & Booth, 1985b). The remarried couples who

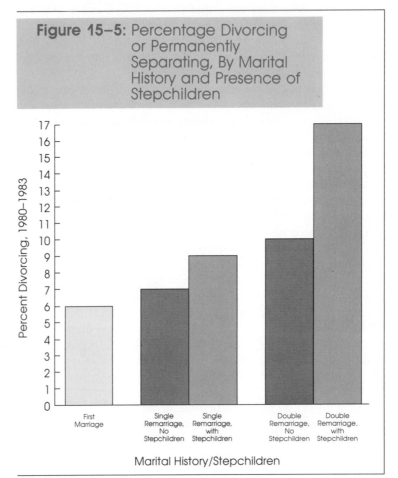

Figure 15–5: Percentage Divorcing or Permanently Separating, By Marital History and Presence of Stepchildren

This figure compares divorce rates for various types of remarriages and for first marriages for the period 1980–1983. Double remarriages (both partners had been previously married) were more prone to redivorce than single remarriages (only one partner had been previously married). The presence of stepchildren increases the probability of divorce, especially in double remarriages. Note that a single remarriage with no stepchildren involved is only slightly more likely to end in divorce than a first marriage.

Source: Data from White & Booth, 1985b, p. 693.

divorced saw divorce as one possible solution to extreme family—not marital—stress. Apparently, the presence of children in unsatisfactory first marriages tends to delay divorce, but the presence of stepchildren in remarriages tends to speed it up.

Although remarriages have slightly higher rates of disruption by divorce than first marriages, many remarriages are highly successful and satisfying, continuing until one of the partners dies. Such remarriages have the effect of bolstering the confidence and self-esteem of the partners and of reassuring them that their earlier choice to divorce was a wise one. For those in successful remarriages, the remarriage marks the end of the divorce chapter of their lives and the beginning of a new and better life (Wallerstein & Blakeslee, 1990; Spanier & Furstenberg, 1982).

But remarriage, like divorce, has losers as well as winners. Divorced people who experience a remarriage followed by a redivorce are likely to see the failed remarriage as one more defeat in a downward spiral. Interviews with the twice-divorced husbands and wives in their longitudinal study led Wallerstein and Blakeslee (1990) to this conclusion:

> The consequences of two divorces are inevitably traumatic. But when men and women—especially later in life—are twice rejected, the emotional blow is enough to make them feel as if their lives are over. They feel that life holds no more chances. (p. 228)

STEPFAMILY RELATIONSHIPS

As noted earlier in the chapter, about 4.3 million of the 11 million remarried families in the United States are residential stepfamilies. Stepfather families, consisting of husband, wife, and wife's child(ren) from a previous marriage, are far more common than stepmother families, those consisting of husband, wife, and husband's child(ren) from a previous marriage. For every one child residing in a stepmother family, eight live in stepfather families (Miller & Moorman, 1989). Thus, most of the research about stepfamilies is about stepfather families. Of course, stepfamily *relationships* cross household boundaries—a fairly common situation is for a child to have some kind of relationship with a biological, residential mother, a residential stepfather, a biological, nonresidential father, and a nonresidential stepmother.

Consequences of Remarriage for Children

Remarriage can have varied consequences for children as well as for adults. One fairly reliable consequence of remarriage for many children is decreased contact with the noncustodial parent (typically the father). Father-child contact typically decreases somewhat at the time of the divorce, declines even more if the noncustodial father remarries, and decreases even further if the mother remarries (Ihinger-Tallman & Pasley, 1987). This loss of contact can be devastating to children or it can make very little difference at all, depending upon both child and stepfamily circumstances (Wallerstein & Blakeslee, 1990).

In Chapter 12, we noted that children do best when they receive generous psychological support and firm, noncoercive control from adults. How do children in stepfamilies fare in this regard? Children living in intact families and those living in stepfather families receive similar levels of support from their mothers, and these levels of support are generally high (Amato, 1987). In other words, remarriage generally does not seem to change maternal support for children. However, children in intact families receive more support from fathers than do children who live in stepfather families. Generally speaking, stepfathers do not replace the support that children lose from their noncustodial biological fathers, unless the children are young (Amato, 1987). Thus, *the typical stepchild receives high levels of support from its mother and low to moderate levels of support from father and stepfather.*

Grade-school-aged children living with both biological parents and children of the same age in stepfather families are subjected to approximately equal amounts of control (Amato, 1987). The story is different for adolescents. Adolescents in intact families and in stepfather families receive about equal levels of maternal control, but neither noncustodial fathers nor stepfathers exercise much day-to-day control (Amato, 1987). However, stepfathers who provide financial support have more authoritative control over stepchildren of all ages than those who do not (Giles-Sims & Crosbie-Burnett, 1989a).

Most studies comparing the psychological health of children in intact families and in stepfamilies find few differences. Children in stepfamilies have about the same self-esteem, self-confidence, and self-image as children living with both biological parents (Coleman & Ganong, 1990; Ihinger-Tallman & Pasley, 1987). While children often experience negative emotional changes (for example, confusion, tenseness, and unhappiness) at the time of remarriage, these are generally short-lived (Baydar, 1988).

Stepchildren have slightly more behavior problems—for example, fighting, school-related problems, and drug and alcohol use—than children in intact families (Coleman & Ganong, 1990). This might be related to the lower levels of control noted above, especially where adolescents are concerned. It might also help to explain why stepchildren leave home earlier in life than children in intact families (Mitchell, Wister, & Burch, 1989; White & Booth, 1985b).

Stepfamily Stresses

Many observers and experts hold the opinion that, because stepfamilies are structurally complex, negatively stereotyped, and normatively ambiguous, they will experience higher levels of stress than first-marriage nuclear families. Research on actual stepfamilies shows that, in general, predictions about much higher levels of stress in stepfamilies are not accurate (Buehler *et al.*, 1986; Lutz, 1983). There are two areas, however, in which stepfamily stress is rather high: divided loyalties (or loyalty conflicts) and discipline (Giles-Sims & Crosbie-Burnett, 1989a; Lutz, 1983).

Divided Loyalties

Members of stepfamilies are frequently torn between their former and their current nuclear families. The term **divided loyalty** refers to feelings of disloyalty to one person because of positive feelings for another (Lutz, 1983). In one survey of adolescent stepchildren, "divided loyalty" emerged as the issue which brought the most stress (Lutz, 1983). Adolescents felt divided between their natural parents when one spoke negatively about the other and divided between natural father and stepfather when they began to like their stepfather as much or more than their natural father (Lutz, 1983). Other stepfamily members can also experience divided loyalties (Hobart, 1987). For example, newly remarried women want and need to spend time alone with their new husbands but also know that their children may need extra amounts of support in making the transition to stepfamily life. And remarried husbands may feel torn between providing financially for their first family children and for their new stepchildren.

One way of relieving such divided loyalty stress for adolescents is to exhibit negative feelings towards the stepparent (Lutz, 1983). Adults sometimes "solve" their divided loyalty dilemmas by redivorcing (essentially choosing the old family over the new) or by encouraging children to live with the other parent or on their own (choosing their new family over the old) (White & Booth, 1985b). This chapter's Personal Application gives some suggestions about how to deal with the divided loyalty problem and with other possible stresses of stepfamily life.

> **Divided loyalty**
> feelings of disloyalty to one person because of positive feelings for another, a common source of stress in stepfamilies.

Personal Application

Building a Strong Stepfamily

Stepfamilies are different from first-marriage families in a number of ways and, therefore, face additional challenges. Here is a list of suggestions, based on the recommendations of several experts, for building a strong stepfamily.

1. Try to avoid carrying too much of the old family history into the new stepfamily. If possible, move to a residence new to both partners. Allow all members of the stepfamily to participate in negotiating new family routines, traditions, and values.
2. Arrange family time so that all family members can maintain old ties but also work on developing new bonds by arranging subgroup activities. The new husband and wife need some time to themselves, without the children, in order to form a primary bond. Each also needs special, separate time with the children. For example, the new stepfather might take his stepchildren fishing one day a week and, on another day, their mother takes them (without the stepfather) out for a special meal.

3. Avoid hostility with the former spouse(s). Do not allow children to become message-carriers between two households; rather, arrange for direct contact between the adults. Do not withhold children's visitation with noncustodial parent as a punishment. Expect children to have loyalty conflicts and urge them to accept the fact that they can have positive feelings for more than two parental adults.

4. Stepparents are usually more successful if they carve out a new role for themselves rather than trying to replicate or compete with the natural parents. What seems like rejection on the part of a stepchild may reflect a loyalty conflict; the stepparent should avoid taking it personally and strive to maintain contact, even at a minimal level.

5. Visiting stepchildren will feel more comfortable and connected if they have a special place—even just a shelf or drawer—of their own, if they can bring a friend with them, and if they have some special family activity to anticipate.

6. Do not expect instant love or "living happily ever after." On the other hand, do not give up too early on the possibility of successful stepfamily life. Time and maturity can bring changes.

Based on suggestions in Ihinger-Tallman & Pasley, 1987, and in Visher & Visher, 1979.

Discipline

A second area of stress for stepfamilies is discipline of the children. Stepfamily adults frequently identify "discipline" as a major stress of stepfamily life; children, particularly adolescents, agree (Ihinger-Tallman & Pasley, 1987; Lutz, 1983). Stepfathers often enter remarriage without any prior experience with children. Even when they do have experience with children, they do not have experience with (or extensive knowledge of) the *particular* children with whom they are now living. Since the ability to discipline effectively is tied to adult-child attachments built up over time, stepfathers are at an initial disadvantage.

Stepchildren, meanwhile, may well resent stepparent attempts to control their behavior or to punish them. During the post-divorce, single-parent family stage, adolescents frequently have greater autonomy and less parental control than their peers in intact families. The abrupt change to a stepfamily situation in which both mother and stepfather seem anxious to exercise control brings about stress.

Most stepfather families seem to deal with the discipline issue by giving disciplinary authority to the mother. This "laid-back" attitude on the part of stepfathers is especially prevalent when the stepchildren are teenagers (Giles-Sims & Crosbie-Burnett, 1989a; Amato, 1987). Stepfathers who enter the stepfamily early in the child's life, who provide most of the child's support, and who establish a new home rather than moving into the child's old one are the most like true fathers in terms of exercising discipline, making decisions about the children, and administering punishment (Giles-Sims & Crosbie-Burnett, 1989a; Amato, 1987). Not all stepfamilies are able to resolve disputes about discipline, however, and the conflict that ensues may well contribute to both the high redivorce rate and to the early leaving home rates of stepfamily teenagers.

STEPFAMILY ALTERNATIVES

The findings that we have discussed refer to stepfamilies in general. They mask the incredible diversity of adaptations that stepfamily members make to a world where few guidelines are laid out in advance. The three alternatives that follow, each described from the child's point of view and based on compilations of research findings, suggest just a few of the possible outcomes of stepfamily formation.

No Family

In the saddest cases, stepfamily formation leaves children feeling that their family has contracted or that they have no family at all. Typically, several different contingencies must merge to produce such an outcome. The child loses meaningful contact with the noncustodial parent, and usually with the relatives on that side of the family as well, either because the parents are hostile to one another or because the noncustodial parent withdraws into a new remarriage. Although the noncustodial parent is physically absent and offers little support, he or she remains very important psychologically to the child. Meanwhile, the custodial parent remarries and turns attention to the new marriage. The child resents the stepparents, sees them as intruders, and acts out rebelliously. This behavior distances the child even more from the custodial family, who begins to suggest in subtle and not-so-subtle ways that the child is ruining their family life. The child feels abandoned by both parents and part of no one's family. Such an outcome is much more common for children who are adolescents when their parent(s) remarry. Children whose parent has died might also be especially vulnerable to such an outcome (Wallerstein & Blakeslee, 1990; Whiteside, 1989; Lutz, 1983).

Substitute Family

For other children, the stepfamily becomes a substitute nuclear family and the children think of their stepfamily as their only family. Such an outcome is most likely when the disruption of the original marriage occurred very early in the child's life, the noncustodial parent and his or her extended family disappeared from the child's life almost immediately, and the remarriage of the custodial parent took place soon thereafter. Under such circumstances, stepparent and stepchild can more easily establish a close relationship and the stepchild more readily accepts the authority and support of the stepparent. Indeed, in many such cases, the stepparent formally adopts the child and becomes legal parent as well as functioning parent. If the stepparent's extended family is equally accepting of the "new family," the child has both a nuclear and an extended family very equivalent to those of children whose parents stayed together (Whiteside, 1989).

Expanded Family

For some children, remarriage means family expansion. They feel accepted by many adults who care about them and support them and belong to a huge network of relatives all of whom have some remote connection to one another. For such an adaptation to come about, the parents must remain on good terms with one another and with their ex-in-laws. The new spouses and their extended families must be able to accept continuing involvement with "old" family ties. Such tolerance and coordination is not always easy to achieve but some families do so. Consider this description of the remarriage ceremony of bride "Pam" and groom "Al":

> Serving as the official wedding photographer was Pam's ex-husband, Don Franklin, who was accompanied by Shirley Moskowitz, his live-in lover and would-be third wife. All of the wedding attendants were stepkin and step-in-laws to the groom. Pam's two daughters from her first marriage, Lanny and Katie, were her bride matrons, and Melissa, Lanny's young daughter from her own first marriage, was her grandma's proud flower girl. Joining Katie's husband Eric as Al's ushers were Lanny's second husband, Ken, and Pam and her ex-husband's son, Jimmy.... the home-baked, three-tiered cake [was] generously contributed by the divorced single mother of Lanny's second husband. (Stacey, 1990, pp. 64–65)

Children belonging to such an extended kin network have more potential role models, more adults to go to for support, and probably more financial security than children growing up in conventional nuclear families (Whiteside, 1989). One author (Stacey, 1990) refers to "divorce-extended" families, such as the one described above, as "postmodern" families and perhaps a prediction of things to come. What do you think?

Summary

Remarriage and stepfamilies are not new phenomena in the United States. Historically, remarriage rates have been highest when death rates or divorce rates are high. Forty to fifty percent of the marriages in the United States are remarriages.

Most remarriages involve divorced people who marry after a short, sexually active courtship and often a period of cohabitation. Men are more likely to remarry than women, and whites are more likely to remarry than blacks or Hispanics. Women who remarry most quickly are young and childless; men who remarry quickly are older and have high incomes. Although there are few clearly stated norms about remarrying, many remarriers seem to feel time pressures or social pressures to do so.

Remarriages can be expected to be somewhat different from first marriages because at least one partner is experienced in marriage, because the norms are more ambiguous and the kin network more complex, and because of negative stereotypes.

In most respects, the day-to-day functioning of remarriages is similar to that of first marriages. Remarried couples tend to be just as intimate and satisfied with their marriages as first married couples and they divide family work in similar ways. Remarried couples do use nonproductive conflict resolution strategies more often and more often keep their money separated into two "pots." Divorce rates are slightly higher for remarriages than for first marriages. The presence of stepchildren increases the probability of redivorce and double remarriages have higher redivorce rates than single remarriages.

In general, children in stepfamilies are similar to children in intact two-parent families in psychological traits and functioning but show somewhat more negative behaviors. They receive the same amount of maternal support as other children do but generally less support from the male adults in their lives. Young children in both stepfamilies and intact families receive similar amounts of parental control. Adolescents in stepfamilies are less controlled by adults than adolescents in intact families and leave home earlier in life.

The major stresses in stepfamilies are divided loyalties and discipline. These stresses are more apt to arise when the children are old enough to have known their biological father well.

Remarriage has a variety of effects on both children and adults. For both, remarriage can mean the contraction and even disappearance of a family or life in a happy, highly satisfactory substitute family, or membership in a large, close kin network of relatives related by prior and current marriage.

Abbey, A. (1987). Misperceptions of friendly behavior as sexual interest: A survey of naturally occurring incidents. *Psychology of Women Quarterly, 11,* 173–194.

Abrams, B. M. (1986). Nonmarital cohabitation: Its perils and its pleasures. *Florida Bar Journal, 60*(9), 47–50.

Adams, B. N. (1988). Fifty years of family research: What does it mean? *Journal of Marriage and the Family, 50,* 5–17.

Adams, B. N. (1986). *The family: A sociological interpretation.* (4th ed.). San Diego: Harcourt Brace Jovanovich.

Adams, G., Adams-Taylor, S., and Pittman, K. (1989). Adolescent pregnancy and parenthood: A review of the problem, solutions, and resources. *Family Relations, 38,* 223–229.

Agee, J. (1957). *A death in the family.* New York: Bantam.

Ahmed, P., and Kolker, A. (1981). Pregnancy in modern society. In P. Ahmed (Ed.), *Pregnancy, childbirth, and parenthood* (pp. 3–18) New York: Elsevier.

Ahrons, C. R. (1980). Redefining the divorced family: A conceptual framework. *Social Work, 25,* 437–441.

Alagna, S. W. (1982). Sex role identity, peer evaluation of competition, and the responses of women and men in a competitive situation. *Journal of Personality and Social Psychology, 43,* 546–554.

Albiston, C. R., Maccoby, E. E., and Mnookin, R. R. (1990). Does joint legal custody matter? *Stanford Law and Policy Review, 2,* 167–179.

Albrecht, S. L., Bahr, H. M., and Chadwick, B. A. (1979). Changing family and sex roles: An assessment of age differences. *Journal of Marriage and the Family, 41,* 41–50.

Aldous, J. (1987). New views on the family life of the elderly and the near-elderly. *Journal of Marriage and the Family, 49,* 227–234.

Aldous, J. and Tuttle, R. C. (1988). Unemployment and the family. In C. S. Chilman, F. M. Cox, and E. W. Nunnally (Eds.), *Employment and economic problems* (pp. 17–41) Families in Trouble Series, Volume 1. Newbury Park, CA: Sage.

Alexander, J., and Eiduson, B. T. (1980). Alternative families and children: Implications for education. *Educational Horizons, 59,* 40–46.

Allee, S. D. (1988). Sexually transmitted diseases and some possible methods for their control. in A. R. Cavaliere and J. M. Riggs (Eds.), *Selected Topics in Human Sexuality* (pp. 121–133) Lanham, MD: University Press of America.

Allen, R. F., with Linde, S. (1981). *Lifegain: The exciting new program that will change your health & your life.* Morristown, NJ: Human Resources Institute.

Allgeier, E. R. (1985). Are you ready for sex: Informed consent for sexual intimacy. *SIECUS Report, 8*(6), 8–9.

Alwin, D. F. (1989). Changes in qualities valued in children in the United States, 1964 to 1984. *Social Science Research, 8,* 195–236.

Amato, P. R. (1987). Family processes in one-parent, stepparent, and intact families: The child's point of view. *Journal of Marriage and the Family, 49,* 327–337.

Amato, P. R., and Booth, A. (1991). Consequences of parental divorce and marital unhappiness for adult well-being. *Social Forces, 69,* 895–914.

Amato, P. R., and Keith, B. (1991). Parental divorce and adult well-being: A meta-analysis. *Journal of Marriage and the Family, 53,* 43–58.

Ambry, M. (1990). The age of spending. *American Demographics, 12,* November, pp. 16–23, 52.

American Association of Retired Persons. (1989). *A profile of older Americans: 1989* (brochure). Washington, DC: American Association of Retired Persons.

American Demographics. (1989a). 1990 census questionnaire. April, 24–31.

American Demographics. (1989b). The life of a marriage. February, 12.

American Demographics. (1991). Work, money, children. February, 11.

American Demographics. (1990). What the 1990 census will show. January, 20–30.

American Jurisprudence. (1962). Volume 2. (2nd ed.). San Francisco, CA: Bancroft-Whitney Company.

Ammons, P., and Stinnett, N. (1980). The vital marriage: A closer look. *Family Relations, 29,* 37–42.

Anderson, L. (1987–1988). Property rights of same-sex couples: Toward a new definition of family. *Journal of Family Law, 26,* 357–372.

Anderson, M. L. (1988). *Thinking about women: Sociological perspectives on sex and gender.* (2nd ed.) New York: Macmillan.

Anderson, S. V. and Bauwens, E. E. (1982). An ethnography of home birth. In M. A. Kay (Ed.), *Anthropology of Human Birth* (pp. 289–303) Philadelphia: F.A. Davis Company.

Anderson, S. A., Russell, C. S., and Schumm, W. R. (1983). Perceived marital quality and family life-cycle categories: A further analysis. *Journal of Marriage and the Family, 45,* 127–139.

Antonovsky, A., and Sourani, T. (1988). Family sense of coherence and family adaptation. *Journal of Marriage and the Family, 50,* 79–92.

Arafat, I., and Yorburg, B. (1963). On living together without marriage. *The Journal of Sex Research, 9,* 97–106.

Aral, S. O., and Holmes, K. K. (1991, February). Sexually transmitted diseases in the AIDS era. *Scientific American,* pp. 62–69.

Archer, J., and Lloyd, B. (1985). *Sex and gender.* Cambridge: Cambridge University Press.

Ard, B. N., Jr. (1977). Sex in lasting marriages: A longitudinal study. *The Journal of Sex Research, 13,* 274–285.

Arendell, T. (1989). Mothers and divorce: Downward mobility. In A. S. Skolnick and J. H. Skolnick (Eds.), *Family in Transition,* (6th ed.) (pps. 328–340) Glenview, IL: Scott, Foresman and Company.

Arendell, T. (1986). *Mothers and divorce: Legal, economic, and social dilemmas.* Berkeley: University of California Press.

Associated Press. (1991, April 17). Child abuse cases up 4% in '90. *The News and Courier* (Charleston, SC), p. 3A.

Associated Press. (1990, August 31). Law against adultery surfaces in Conn.; 4 charged this summer. *Brookings Daily Register,* p. 12.

Associated Press. (1992, January 17). Number of AIDS cases rising more rapidly, U.S. reports. *The Post and Courier* (Charleston, SC), p. 5A.

Associated Press. (1989, July 7). Court expands family. *The News and Courier* (Charleston, SC), p. 4A.

Associated Press. (1988, May 26). Cervical cap wins approval from FDA. *Brooking Daily Register,* p. 10.

Associated Press. (1987b, April 20). Experts say court shifting back to permanent alimony awards. *Brookings Daily Register,* p. 9.

Associated Press. (1987a, February 18). Future earnings held part of divorce accord. New York Times, p. A18.

Associated Press. (1985, December 11). Killer was distraught over debt. *The News and Courier* (Charleston, S.C.), p. 20C.

Astin, A. W., Green, K. C., and Korn, W. S. (1987). *The American freshman twenty year trends, 1966–1985.* Higher Education Research Institute, Graduate School of Education, University of California, Los Angeles.

Atchley, R. C. (1991). *Social forces and aging: An introduction to social gerontology.* (6th ed.). Belmont, CA: Wadsworth.

Atkinson, J. (1987). Gender roles in marriage and the family: A critique and some proposals. *Journal of family issues, 8,* 5–41.

Atwater, L. (1982). *The extramarital connection: Sex, intimacy, and identity.* New York: Irvington Publishers.

Avioli, P. S. (1985). The labor-force participation of married mothers of infants. *Journal of Marriage and the Family, 47,* 739–745.

Bachrach, C. A. (1987). Cohabitation and reproductive behavior in the U.S. *Demography, 24,* 623–637.

Bachrach, C. A. (1986). Adoption plans, adopted children, and adoptive mothers. *Journal of marriage and the family, 48,* 243–253.

Bachrach, C. A. (1983). Adoption as a means of family formation: Data from the national survey of family growth. *Journal of Marriage and the Family, 45,* 859–865.

Bachrach, C. A. (1980). Childlessness and social isolation among the elderly. *Journal of marriage and the family, 42,* 627–637.

Back, K. W. (1971). Transition to aging and the self-image. *Aging and human development, 2,* 296–304.

Bailey, B. L. (1988). *From the front porch to back seat: Courtship in twentieth-century America.* Baltimore: The Johns Hopkins Press.

Balakrishnan, T. R., Rao, K. V., Lapierre-Adamcyk, E., and Krotki, K. J. (1987). A hazard model analysis of the covariates of marriage dissolution in Canada. *Demography, 24,* 395–406.

Baldwin, W. H., and Nord, C. W. (1984). Delayed childbearing in the U.S.: Facts and fiction. *Population Bulletin, 39*(4). Washington, DC: Population Reference Bureau, Inc.

Bane, M. J. (1976). *Here to stay: American families in the twentieth century.* New York: Basic Books.

Bane, M. J., and Ellwood, D. T. (1986). Slipping into and out of poverty: The dynamics of spells. *Journal of Human Resources, 21,* 1–23.

Barnard, J., and Fain, M. (June 1980). Why living together was not enough. *Redbook Magazine,* p. 31+.

Barrow, G. (1989). *Aging, the individual, and society.* (4th ed.). St. Paul: West Publishing Company.

Bart, P. (1979). The loneliness of the long-distance mother. in J. Freeman (Ed.), *Women: A Feminist Perspective,* (2nd ed.). (pp. 245–261) Palo Alto: Mayfield.

Baruch, G. K. (1984). The psychological well-being of women in the middle years. in G. Baruch and J. Brooks-Gunn (Eds.), *Women in Midlife.* (pp. 161–180) New York: Plenum.

Basic legal forms with commentary, (2nd ed.). (1991). New York: Warren, Gorham & Lamont, Inc.

Baumgartner, A. (1983). My daddy might have loved me: Student perceptions of differences between being male and being female. Denver: Institute for Equality in Education.

Baumrind, D. (1982). Are androgynous individuals more effective persons and parents? *Child Development, 53,* 44–75.

Baumrind, D. (1978). Parental disciplinary patterns and social competence in children. *Youth and Society, 9,* 239–276.

Baydar, N. (1988). Effects of parental separation and re-entry into union on the emotional well-being of children. *Journal of Marriage and the Family, 50,* 967–981.

Bean, F. D., and Tienda, M. (1987). *The Hispanic population of the United States.* New York: Russell Sage.

Becerra, R. M. (1988). The Mexican American family. in C. H. Mindel, R. W. Habenstein, and R. Wright, Jr. (Eds.), *Ethnic Families in America,* (3rd ed.). (pp. 141–159) New York: Elsevier.

Beck, M., with Kantrowitz, B., Beachy, L., Hager, M., Gordon, J., Roberts, E., and Hammill, R. (1990, July 16). Trading places. *Newsweek,* pp. 48–54.

Beck, S. H., and Beck, R. W. (1984). The formation of extended households during middle age. *Journal of Marriage and the Family, 46,* 277–287.

Becker, G. S. (1981). *A treatise on the family.* Cambridge, MA: Harvard University Press.

Becker, G. S. (1976). *An economic approach to human behavior.* Chicago: University of Chicago Press.

Becker, J. V., and Coleman, E. M. (1988). Incest. in V. B. Van Hasselt, R. L. Morrison, A. S. Bellack, and M. Hersen (Eds.), *Handbook of Family Violence.* (pp. 187–205) New York: Plenum Press.

Bee, H. L. (1987). *The journey of adulthood.* New York: Macmillan.

Beeghley, L., and Sellers, C. (1986). Adolescents and sex: A structural theory of premarital sex in the United States. *Deviant Behavior, 7,* 313–336.

Bell, D. C., Chafetz, J. A., and Horn, L. H. (1982). Marital conflict resolution: A study of strategies and outcomes. *Journal of Family Issues, 3,* 111–132.

Bell, S. (1984). Birth control. In The Boston Women's Health Book Collective (Eds.), *The New Our Bodies, Ourselves.* (pp. 220–262) New York: Simon and Schuster.

Bell, R. R., and Coughey, K. (1980). Premarital sexual experience among college females, 1958, 1968, 1978. *Family Relations, 29,* 353–357.

Bell, A. P., and Weinberg, M. S. (1978). *Homosexualities: A study of diversity among men and women.* New York: Simon and Schuster.

Bellah, R. N., Madsen, R., Sullivan, W. M., and Tipton, S. M. (1985). *Habits of the heart: Individualism and commitment in American life.* Berkeley: University of California Press.

Belsky, J. (1990). Parental and nonparental child care and children's socioemotional development: A decade in review. *Journal of Marriage and the Family, 52,* 885–903.

Belsky, J. (1985). Exploring individual differences in marital change across the transition to parenthood: The role of violated expectations. *Journal of Marriage and the Family, 47,* 1037–1044.

Belsky, J., Lang, M. E., and Rovine, M. (1985). Stability and change in marriage across the transition to parenthood: A second study. *Journal of Marriage and the Family, 47,* 855–865.

Belsky, J., and Rovine, M. (1990). Patterns of marital change across the transition to parenthood: Pregnancy to three years postpartum. *Journal of Marriage and the Family, 52,* 5–19.

Belsky, J., and Rovine, M. (1988). Nonmaternal care in the first year of life and the security of infant-parent attachment. *Child Development, 59,* 157–167.

Belsky, J., and Rovine, M. (1984). Social-network contact, family support, and the transition to parenthood. *Journal of Marriage and the Family, 46,* 455–462.

Belsky, J., Spanier, G. B., and Rovine, M. (1983). Stability and change in marriage across the transition to parenthood. *Journal of Marriage and the Family, 45,* 567–577.

Bem, S. L. (1977). On the utility of alternative procedures for assessing psychological androgyny. *Journal of Consulting and Clinical Psychology, 45,* 196–205.

Bem, S. L. (1975). Sex role adaptability: One consequence of psychological androgyny. *Journal of Personality and Social Psychology, 31,* 634–643.

Bem, S. L. (1974). The measurement of psychological androgyny. *Journal of Consulting and Clinical Psychology, 42,* 155–162.

Bem, S. L., and Lenney, E. (1976). Sex typing and the avoidance of cross-sex behavior. *Journal of Personality and Social Psychology, 33,* 48–54.

Benedict, R. (1938, 1955). Continuities and discontinuities in cultural conditioning. In M. Mead and M. Wolfenstein (Eds.), *Childhood in Contemporary Cultures.* (pp. 21–31) Chicago: University of Chicago Press.

Benenson, H. (1984). Women's occupational and family achievement in the U.S. class system: A critique of the dual-career family analysis. *British Journal of Sociology, 35,* 19–41.

Benin, M. H., and Agostinelli, J. (1988). Husbands' and wives' satisfaction with the division of labor. *Journal of Marriage and the Family, 50,* 349–361.

Bennett, N. G., Blanc, A. K., and Bloom, D. E. (1988). Commitment and the modern union: Assessing the link between premarital cohabitation and subsequent marital stability. *American Sociological Review, 53,* 127–138.

Bennett, N. G., Bloom, D. E., and Craig, P. H. (1989). The divergence of black and white marriage patterns. *American Journal of Sociology, 95,* 692–722.

Berardo, D. H., Shehan, C. L., and Leslie, G. R. (1987). A residue of tradition: Jobs, careers, and spouses' time in housework. *Journal of Marriage and the Family, 49,* 381–390.

Berardo, F. M., and Vera, H. (1981). The groomal shower: A variation of the American bridal shower. *Family Relations, 30,* 395–401.

Berg, B. (1987, May). The guilt that drives working mothers crazy. *Ms* pp. 56–59, 73–74.

Bergen, D. J., and Williams, J. E. (1991). Sex stereotypes in the United States revisited: 1972–1988. *Sex Roles, 24,* 413–423.

Berk, R. A., and Newton, P. J. (1985). Does arrest really deter wife battery? An effort to replicate the findings of the Minneapolis Spouse Abuse Experiment. *American Sociological Review, 50,* 253–262.

Berk, S. F. (1985). *The gender factory: The apportionment of work in American households.* New York: Plenum.

Berns, R. M. (1985). *Child, family, community.* New York: Holt, Rinehart and Winston.

Bernard, J. (1981). The good-provider role: Its rise and fall. *American Psychologist, 36,* 1–12.

Bernard, J. (1972). *The future of marriage.* New York: World Publishing.

Besharov, D. J. (1990, July–August). Crack children in foster care. *Children Today,* pp. 21–25, 35.

Beutler, I. F., Burr, W. R., Bahr, K. S., and Herrin, D. A. (1989). The family realm: Theoretical contributions for understanding its uniqueness. *Journal of Marriage and the Family, 51,* 805–816.

Bishop, K. (1991, February 15). Not quite a wedding, but quite a day for couples by the bay. *New York Times,* p. A20.

Bishop, M. W. H. (1970). Aging and reproduction in the male. *Journal of Reproduction and Fertility, 12* (Supplement), 65–87.

Black, K. N. (1982). Consequences for offspring of single-parent families. *Academic Psychology Bulletin, 4,* 527–534.

Blake, N. M. (1962). *The road to Reno: A history of divorce in the United States.* New York: Macmillan.

Blanc, A. K. (1987). The formation and dissolution of second unions: Marriage and cohabitation in Sweden and Norway. *Journal of Marriage and the Family, 49,* 391–400.

Blanc, A. K. (1984). Nonmarital cohabitation and fertility in the United States and Western Europe. *Population Research and Policy Review, 3,* 181–193.

Block, C. R., Norr, K. L., Meyering, S., Norr, J. L., and Charles, A. G. (1981). Husband gatekeeping in childbirth. *Family Relations, 30,* 197–204.

Blood, R. O., Jr., and Wolfe, D. M. (1960). *Husbands and wives: The dynamics of married living.* New York: Free Press.

Bloom, D. E. (1982). What's happening to the age at first birth in the United States? A study of recent cohorts. *Demography, 19,* 351–370.

Bluestone, B., and Harrison, B. (1982). *The deindustrialization of America: Plant closings, community abandonment, and the dismantling of basic industry.* New York: Basic Books.

Blum, H. M., Boyle, M. H., and Offord, D. R. (1988). Single-parent families: Child psychiatric disorder and school performance. *Journal of the American Academy of Child and Adolescent Psychiatry, 27,* 214–219.

Blumstein, P., and Schwartz, P. (1983). *American couples: Money, work, sex.* New York: William Morrow.

Bodnar, J., and Wilcox, M. D. (1990, March). Status report on the American dream. *Changing Times* pp. 40–49.

Booth, A., and Johnson, D. (1988). Premarital cohabitation and marital success. *Journal of Family Issues, 9,* 255–272.

Booth, A., Johnson, D. R., White, L., and Edwards, J. N. (1984). Women, outside employment, and marital instability. *American Journal of Sociology, 90,* 567–583.

Botwin, C. (1985). *Is there sex after marriage?* Boston: Little, Brown and Company.

Bould, S., Sanborn, B., and Reif, L. (1989). *Eighty-five plus: The oldest old.* Belmont, CA: Wadsworth.

Bowen, G. L., and Orthner, D. K. (1983). Sex-role congruency and marital quality. *Journal of Marriage and the Family, 45,* 223–230.

Bower, D. W., and Christopherson, V. A. (1977). University student cohabitation: A regional comparison of selected attitudes and behavior. *Journal of Marriage and the Family, 39,* 447–452.

Bowman, M. L. (1990). Coping efforts and marital satisfaction: Measuring marital coping and its correlates. *Journal of Marriage and the Family, 52,* 463–474.

Bowman, P. J. (1988). Postindustrial displacement and family role strains: Challenges to the black family. In P. Voydanoff and L. C. Majka (Eds.), *Families and Economic Distress: Coping strategies and social policy.* (pp. 75–96) Newbury Park, CA: Sage.

Brannon, R. (1976). The male sex role: Our culture's blueprint of manhood, and what it's done for us lately. In D. S. David and R. Brannon (Eds.), *The Forty-nine Percent Majority: The male sex role* (pp. 1–35) Reading, MA: Addison-Wesley.

Brazelton, T. B. (1987). *What every baby knows.* Reading, MA: Addison-Wesley.

Brazelton, T. B. (1986, January). Issues for working parents. *American Journal of Orthopsychiatry,* pp. 14–25.

Brazzell, J. F., and Acock, A. C. (1988). Influence of attitudes, significant others, and aspirations on how adolescents intend to resolve a premarital pregnancy. *Journal of Marriage and the Family, 50,* 413–425.

Breault, K. D., and Kposowa, A. J. (1987). Explaining divorce in the United States: A study of 3,111 counties, 1980. *Journal of Marriage and the Family, 49,* 549–558.

Brecher, E. M., and the Editors of Consumer Reports Books, Inc. (1984). *Love, sex, and aging: A consumers union report.* Boston: Little, Brown and Company.

Breen, D. (1989). *Talking with mothers.* London: Free Association Books.

Brehony, K. A., and Geller, E. S. (1981). Relationships between psychological androgyny, social conformity, and perceived locus of control. *Psychology of Women Quarterly, 6,* 204–217.

Bretherton, I. (1985). Attachment theory: Retrospect and prospect. In I. Bretherton and E. Waters (Eds.), *Growing Points of Attachment Theory and Research.* (pp. 3–35) Monographs of the Society for Research in Child Development 50 (1–2, Serial No. 209).

Brinkerhoff, D. B., and White, L. K. (1978). Marital satisfaction in an economically marginal population. *Journal of Marriage and the Family, 40,* 259–267.

Bristol, M. M., Gallagher, J. J., and Schopler, E. (1988). Mothers and fathers of young developmentally disabled and nondisabled boys: Adaptation and spousal support. *Developmental Psychology, 24,* 441–451.

Broderick, C. B. (1988). *Marriage and the family.* (3rd ed.). Englewood Cliffs, NJ: Prentice Hall.

Brody, E. M. (1985). Parent care as a normative family stress. *The Gerontologist, 25,* 19–29.

Brody, E. M., and Schoonover, C. B. (1986). Patterns of parent-care when adult daughters work and when they do not. *The Gerontologist, 26*(4), 372–381.

Brody, J. E., (1989, November 2). Personal health: For millions of sick children, a lifetime of pain, support and understanding. *New York Times,* p. 20.

Brozan, N. (1986, September 29). When a child goes away. *New York Times,* p. 813.

Bryan, L. R., Coleman, M., Ganong, L. H., and Bryan, S. H. (1986). Person perception: Family structure as a cue for stereotyping. *Journal of Marriage and the Family, 48,* 169–174.

Buehler, C., Hogan, M. G., Robinson, B., and Levy, R. J. (1986). Remarriage following divorce: Stressors and well-being of custodial and noncustodial parents. *Journal of Family Issues, 7,* 405–420.

Bulatao, R. A. (1981). Values and disvalues of children in successive childbearing decisions. *Demography, 18,* 1–25.

Bulcroft, K., and O'Connor-Roden, M. (1986, June). Never too late. *Psychology Today, 20,* pp. 66–69.

Bumpass, L. L., and Sweet, J. A. (1989). National estimates of cohabitation. *Demography, 26,* 615–625.

Bumpass, L. L., Sweet, J. A., and Martin, T. C. (1990). Changing patterns of remarriage. *Journal of Marriage and the Family, 52,* 747–756.

Burns, A. (1984). Perceived causes of marriage breakdown and conditions of life. *Journal of Marriage and the Family, 46,* 551–562.

Burrell, C. B. (Ed.) (1909). *The mothers' book.* New York: The University Society Inc.

Buss, D. M. (1985, January–February). Human mate selection. *American Scientist, 73,* pp. 47–51.

Butler, R. N., and Lewis, M. I. (1986). *Love and sex after 40.* New York: Harper & Row.

Byer, C. O., Shainberg, L. W., and Jones, K. L. (1988). *Dimensions of human sexuality.* (2nd ed.). Dubuque, IA: Wm. C. Brown Publishers.

Caine, L. (1974). *Widow.* New York: William Morrow.

Cancian, F. M. (1987). *Love in America: Gender and self-development.* Cambridge: Cambridge University Press.

Cancian, F. M. (1986). The feminization of love. *Signs: Journal of Women in Culture and Society, 11,* 692–709.

Canter, C. (1990, July 4). More women over 40 getting divorces on L.I. *The New York Times,* pp. 6–7.

Caplovitz, D. (1979). *Making ends meet: How families cope with inflation and recession.* Sage Library of Social Research, Volume 86. Beverly Hills: Sage.

Caplow, T., Bahr, H. M., Chadwick, B. A., Hill, R., and Williamson, M. H. (1985). Sexual Revolution, sexual evolution—Or just more of the same? In J. M. Henslin (Ed.), *Marriage and Family in a Changing Society,* (2nd ed.). (pp. 210–215) New York: The Free Press.

Carlson, E., and Stinson, K. (1982). Motherhood, marriage timing, and marital stability: A research note. *Social Forces, 61,* 258–267.

Carns, D. E. (1973). Talking about sex: Notes on first coitus and the double sexual standard. *Journal of Marriage and the Family, 35,* 677–688.

Caron, S. L., and Bertran, R. M. (1988, April). What college students want to know about sex. *Medical Aspects of Human Sexuality* pp. 18–25.

Carr, D. (1989, July/August). Birth control goes skin deep. *Ms.*, p. 77.

Carrol, L. (1988). Concern with AIDS and the sexual behavior of college students. *Journal of Marriage and the Family, 50*, 405–411.

Cerhan, J. U. (1990). The Hmong in the United States: An overview for mental health professionals. *Journal of Counseling & Development, 69*, 88–92.

Chapman, S. H., LaPlante, M. P., and Wilensky, G. (1986). Life expectancy and health status of the aged. *Social Security Bulletin, 49*(10), 24–48.

Chase, M. (1990, April 2). Recent progress against the spread of AIDS is threatened by relapse in safe-sex practices. *Wall Street Journal*, pp. B1, B4.

Cheal, D. J. (1983). Intergenerational family transfers. *Journal of Marriage and the Family, 45*, 805–813.

Cherlin, A. J. (1981). *Marriage, divorce, remarriage.* Cambridge, MA: Harvard University Press.

Cherlin, A. J. (1978). Remarriage as an incomplete institution. *American Journal of Sociology, 84*, 634–650.

Cherlin, A. J., and Furstenberg, F. F. (1985). Styles and strategies of grandparenting. In V. L. Bengtson and J. F. Robertson (Eds.), *Grandparenthood.* (pp. 97–116) Beverly Hills: Sage.

Cherlin, A. J., Furstenberg, F. F., Jr., Chase-Lansdale, P. L., Kiernan, K. E., Robins, P. K., Morrison, D. R., and Teitler, J. O. (1991). Longitudinal studies of effects of divorce on children in Great Britain and the United States. *Science, 252*, 1386–1389.

Cherlin, A. J., and McCarthy, J. (1985). Remarried couple households: Data from the June 1980 current population survey. *Journal of Marriage and the Family, 47*, 23–30.

Cherlin, A. J., and Walters, P. B. (1981). Trends in United States men's and women's sex-role attitudes: 1972 to 1978. *American Sociological Review, 46*, 453–460.

Children's Defense Fund. (1987). *A children's defense budget FY 1988.* Washington, DC: Children's Defense Fund.

Christopher, F. S., and Cate, R. M. (1988). Premarital sexual involvement: A developmental investigation of relationship correlates. *Adolescence, 23*, 793–803.

Chronicle of Higher Education, The. (1990, March 21). College students put sex partners at risk of AIDS by lying about past experiences. p. A15.

Chronicle of Higher Education, The. (1991, January 30). This year's college freshmen: Attitudes and characteristics. pp. A30–31.

Chudacoff, H. P., and Hareven, T. K. (1979). From the empty nest to family dissolution: Life course transitions into old age. *Journal of Family History, 4*, 69–83.

Clapp, D., with Swenson, N. (1984). Infertility and pregnancy loss. In The Boston Women's Health Book Collective (Eds.). *The New Our Bodies, Ourselves* (pp. 419–431) New York: Simon and Schuster.

Clark, R. (1983). *Family life and school achievement: Why poor black children succeed or fail.* Chicago: University of Chicago Press.

Clarke-Stewart, K. A. (1989). Infant day care: Maligned or malignant? *American Psychologist, 44*, 266–273.

Clarke-Stewart, K. A. (1982). *Daycare.* Cambridge, MA: Harvard University Press.

Clarke-Stewart, K. A. (1978). Popular primers for parents. *American Psychologist, 33*, 359–369.

Clatworthy, N. M. (1985). Morals and the ever-changing college student: 1968–1982. *Free Inquiry in Creative Sociology, 13*, 83–86.

Cleek, M. G., and Pearson, T. A. (1985). Perceived causes of divorce: An analysis of interrelationships. *Journal of Marriage and the Family, 47*, 179–183.

Clemens, A. W., and Axelson, L. J. (1985). The not-so-empty-nest: The return of the fledgling adult. *Family Relations, 34*, 259–264.

Coale, A. J., and Zelnick, M. (1963). *New estimates of fertility and population in the United States.* Princeton: Princeton University Press.

Cockrum, J., and White, P. (1985). Influences on the life satisfaction of never-married men and women. *Family Relations, 34*, 551–556.

Cohen, W., Schwartz, M., and Sobul, D. A. (1968). *The bill of rights: A source book.* New York: Benziger Brothers.

Colasanto, D., and Shriver, J. (1989, May). Middle-aged face marital crisis. *The Gallup Report* No. *284*, 34–38.

Coleman, L. M., Antonucci, T. C., and Adelmann, P. K. (1987). Role involvement, gender, and well-being. In F. J. Crosby (Ed.), *Spouse, parent, worker: On gender and multiple roles.* (pp. 138–153) New Haven: Yale University Press.

Coleman, M., and Ganong, L. H. (1990). Remarriage and step-family research in the 1980s: Increased interest in an old family form. *Journal of Marriage and the Family, 52*, 925–940.

Coltrane, S. (1990). Birth timing and the division of labor in dual-earner families: Exploratory findings and suggestions for future research. *Journal of Family Issues, 11*, 157–181.

Condry, J., and Condry, S. (1976). Sex differences: A study of the eye of the beholder. *Child Development, 47*, 812–819.

Constantine, L. L. (1983). Dysfunction and failure in open family systems, I: Application of a unified theory. *Journal of Marriage and the family, 45*, 725–738.

Consumer Reports. (1987, July). Life at the edge. *52*, pp. 436–439.

Cooney, T. M., and Uhlenberg, P. (1990). The role of divorce in men's relations with their adult children after mid-life. *Journal of Marriage and the Family, 52*, 677–688.

Coser, L. A. (1974). *Greedy institutions: Patterns of undivided commitment.* New York: Free Press.

Cowan, P., and Cowan, R. (1987). *Mixed blessings: Marriage between Jews and Christians.* New York: Doubleday.

Cowan, C. P., Cowan, P. A., Heming, G., Garrett, E., Coysh, W. S., Curtis-Boles, H., and Boles A. J., III. (1985). Transitions to parenthood: His, hers, and theirs. *Journal of Family Issues, 6,* 451–481.

Cowan, R. S. (1983). *More work for mother: The ironies of household technology from the open hearth to the microwave.* New York: Basic Books.

Cox, F. D. (1990). *Human intimacy: Marriage, the family, and its meaning.* (5th ed.). St. Paul, MN: West Publishing Company.

Coysh, W. S., Johnston, J. R., Tschann, J. M., Wallerstein, J. S., and Kline, M. (1989). Parental postdivorce adjustment in joint and sole physical custody families. *Journal of Family Issues, 10,* 52–71.

Croft, N. L. (1986, September). It's never too late. *Nation's Business.* Reprinted in H. Cox (Ed.), *Annual Editions: Aging,* (6th ed.) (pp. 99–103) Guilford: Dushkin.

Croft, L. H. (1982). *Sexuality in later life: A counseling guide for physicians.* Boston: Wright–PSG.

Crohan, S. E., and Veroff, J. (1989). Dimensions of marital well-being among white and black newlyweds. *Journal of Marriage and the Family, 51,* 373–383.

Crouter, A. C., Perry-Jenkins, M., Huston, T. L., and McHale, S. M. (1987). Processes underlying father involvement in dual-earner and single-earner families. *Developmental Psychology, 23,* 431–440.

Crowe, M., with Norsigian, J. (1984). Sexually transmitted diseases. In The Boston Women's Health Book Collective (Eds.), *The New Our Bodies, Ourselves.* (pp. 263–283) New York: Simon and Schuster.

Crowley, J. E. (1985). Longitudinal effects of retirement on men's psychological and physical well-being. In H. S. Parnes, J. E. Crowley, R. J. Haurin, L. J. Less, W. R. Morgan, F. L. Mott, and G. Nestel, *Retirement among American Men.* (pp. 147–173) Lexington: D.C. Heath.

Crystal, S. (1982). *America's old age crisis: Public policy and the two worlds of aging.* New York: Basic Books.

Cutler, B. (1989, April). Up the down staircase. *American Demographics, 11,* pp. 32–36, 41.

Cutler, B. (1990, January). Rock-a-buy baby. *American Demographics, 12,* pp. 35–39.

D'Emilio, J., and Freedman, E. B. (1988). *Intimate matters: A history of sexuality in America.* New York: Harper and Row.

Darling, J. (1981). Late marrying bachelors. in J. Stein (Ed.), *Single Life: Unmarried Adults in Social Context.* (pp. 34–40) New York: St. Martin's Press.

Darling, C. A., Kallen, D. J., and VanDusen, J. E., (1984). Sex in transition, 1900–1980. *Journal of Youth and Adolescence, 13,* 385–399.

Darling, R. B. (1979). *Families against society: A study of reactions to children with birth defects.* Sage Library of Social Research, Volume 88. Beverly Hills: Sage.

Davidson, B., Balswick, J., and Halverson, C. (1983). Affective self-disclosure and marital adjustment: A test of equity theory. *Journal of Marriage and the Family, 45,* 93–102.

Davidson, J. K., Sr., and Darling, C. A. (1988). The stereotype of single women revisited: Sexual practices and sexual satisfaction among professional women. *Health Care for Women International, 9,* 317–336.

Davis, A. J. (1984). Sex-differentiated behaviors in nonsexist picture books. *Sex Roles, 11,* 1–16.

Davis, E. P., and Helmick, S. A. (1985). Family financial satisfaction: The impact of reference points. *Home Economics Research Journal, 14,* 123–131.

Davitz, L. L. (1984, July). Are you a better mother than your mother? *McCall's* vol. III, pp. 83, 126–127.

Day, R. D., and Hooks, D. (1987). Miscarriage: A special type of family crisis. *Family Relations, 36,* 305–310.

DeLucia, J. L. (1987). Gender role identity and dating behavior: What is the relationship? *Sex Roles, 17,* 153–161.

DeMaris, A., and Leslie, G. R. (1984). Cohabitation with the future spouse: Its influence upon marital satisfaction and communication. *Journal of Marriage and the Family, 46,* 77–84.

Demo, D. H., and Acock, A. C. (1988). The impact of divorce on children. *Journal of Marriage and the Family, 50,* 619–648.

Demos, J. (1981). Family membership in Plymouth Colony. In M. Albin and D. Cavallo (Eds.), *Family Life in America, 1620–2000.* (pp. 3–13) St. James, NY: Revisionary Press.

DeStefano, L. (1989, November). Mirror of America: New lifestyles are changing the way we dine. *The Gallup Report* No. 290, pp. 25–35.

DeStefano, L., and Colasanto, D. (1990, February). Unlike 1975, today most Americans think men have it better. *The Gallup Report Monthly,* pp. 25–36.

DeVault, M. L. (1987). Doing housework: Feeding and family life. In N. Gerstel and H. Gross (Eds.), *Families and Work.* (pp. 178–191) Philadelphia: Temple University Press.

Diamond, J. (1986, November). I want a girl just like the girl . . . *Discover,* pp. 65–68.

Discover. (1991, January). The First Case. p. 74.

Discover. (1988, February). A Little whoopee with LY163502. pp. 10, 12.

Dixon, R. B., and Weitzman, L. J. (1982). When husbands file for divorce. *Journal of Marriage and the Family, 44,* 103–115.

Doddridge, R., Schumm, W. R., and Bergen, M. B. (1987). Factors related to decline in preferred frequency of sexual intercourse among young couples. *Psychological Reports, 60,* 391–395.

Doherty, W. J., Lester, M. E., and Leigh, G. (1986). Marriage encounter weekends: Couples who win and couples who lose. *Journal of Marital and Family Therapy, 12*(1), 49–61.

Dohrenwend, B. S., Krasnoff, L., Askenasy, A. R., and Dohrenwend, B. P. (1978). Exemplification of a method for scaling life events: The PERI life events scale. *Journal of Health and Social Behavior, 19*, 205–229.

Doress, P. B., with Swenson, N. M., Cohen, R., Friedman, M., Harris, E., and MacPherson, K. (1984). Women growing older. In The Boston Womens' Health Book Collective (Eds.), *The New Our Bodies, Ourselves,* pp. 435–472. New York: Simon and Schuster.

Dorfman, L. T., and Heckert, D. A. (1988). Egalitarianism in retired rural couples: Household tasks, decision making, and leisure activities. *Family Relations, 37*, 73–78.

Doudna, C., and McBride, F. (1981). Where are the men for the women at the top? in P. J. Stein (Ed.), *Single Life: Unmarried Adults in Social Context.* (pp. 21–34) New York: St. Martin's Press.

Dougherty, M. C. (1978). *Becoming a woman in rural black culture.* New York: Holt, Rinehart and Winston.

Douthwaite, G. (1979). *Unmarried couples and the law.* Indianapolis, IN: The Allen Smith Company.

Duncan, G. J., and Rodgers, W. L. (1988). Longitudinal aspects of childhood poverty. *Journal of Marriage and the Family, 50*, 1007–1021.

Duncan, M. J. (1987). Doe v. Duling: Is Virginia for lovers? *Journal of Contemporary Law, 12*(2), 271–287.

Dunn, M. E., and Trost, J. E. (1989). Male multiple orgasms: A descriptive study. *Archives of Sexual Behavior, 18*, 377–387.

Eakins, P. S. (1986). The American way of birth. in P. S. Eakins (Ed.), *The American Way of Birth.* (pp. 3–15) Philadelphia: Temple University Press.

Eargle, J. (1990). Household wealth and asset ownership: 1988. U.S. Bureau of the Census, Current Population Reports, Series P-70, No. 22. Washington, DC: Government Printing Office.

Earle, J. R., and Perricone, P. J. (1986). Premarital sexuality: A ten-year study of attitudes and behavior on a small university campus. *The Journal of Sex Research, 22*, 304–310.

Easterlin, R. A. (1987). *Birth and fortune: The impact of numbers on personal welfare.* (2nd ed.). Chicago: University of Chicago Press.

Eckland, B. K. (1985). Theories of mate selection. In J. M. Henslin (Ed.), *Marriage and Family in a Changing Society,* (2nd ed.). (pp. 232–241) New York: The Free Press.

Edelman, M. W. (1987). *Families in peril: An agenda for social change.* Cambridge, MA: Harvard University Press.

Edgerton, C. (1985). *Raney.* Chapel Hill, NC: Algonquin Books.

Egeland, B., Jacobvitz, D., and Sroufe, L. A. (1988). Breaking the cycle of abuse. *Child Development, 59*, 1080–1088.

Eggebeen, D. J., and Hawkins, A. J. (1990). Economic need and wives' employment. *Journal of Family Issues, 11*, 48–66.

Ehrenreich, B. (1983). *The hearts of men: American dreams and the flight from commitment.* Garden City, NY: Anchor Press.

Eiduson, B. T., and Alexander, J. W. (1978). The role of children in alternative family styles. *Journal of Social Issues, 34*, 149–167.

Elder, G. H., Van Nguyen, T., and Caspi, A. (1985). Linking family hardship to children's lives. *Child Development, 56*, 361–375.

Ellwood, D. T. (1988). *Poor support: Poverty in the American family.* New York: Basic Books.

England, P., and Swoboda, D. (1988). The asymmetry of contemporary gender role change. *Free Inquiry in Creative Sociology, 16*, 157–161.

Epstein, B. (1982). Industrialization and feminity: A case study of nineteenth-century New England. In R. Kahn-Hut, A. K. Daniels, and R. Colvard (Eds.), *Women and Work: Problems and Perspectives.* (pp. 88–100) New York: Oxford University Press.

Erskine, H. (1973). The polls: Hopes, fears, and regrets. *Public Opinion Quarterly, 37*, 132–145.

Espenshade, T. J. (1985). Marriage trends in America: Estimates, implications, and underlying causes. *Population and Development Review, 11*(2), 193–245.

Exter, T. (1988, December). Demographic forecasts: Peak-a-boo. *American Demographics, 10*, 63.

Fagot, B. I., and Leinbach, M. D. (1989). The young child's gender schema: Environmental input, internal organization. *Child Development, 60*, 663–672.

Family Planning Perspectives. (1990). For low-risk deliveries, birth centers offer care comparable to hospitals. *22*, 141–142.

Family Planning Perspectives. (1988). STD worries on the wane. *20*, 111.

Farley, R., and Allen, W. R. (1987). *The color line and the quality of life in America.* New York: Russell Sage.

Farnsworth, J., Pett, M. A. and Lund, D. A. (1989). Predictors of loss management and well-being in later life widowhood and divorce. *Journal of Family Issues, 10*, 102–121.

Felson, R. B., and Zielinski, M. A. (1989). Children's self-esteem and parental support. *Journal of Marriage and the Family, 15*, 727–735.

Felton-Collins, V. (1990). *Couples and money: Why money interferes with love and what to do about it.* New York: Bantam.

Ferber, M. A. (1982). Labor market participation of young married women: Causes and effects. *Journal of Marriage and the Family, 44*, 457–468.

Ferraro, K. F., and Wan, T. T. H. (1986). Marital contributions to well-being in later life. *American Behavioral Scientist, 29,* 423–437.

Ferree, M. M. (1987). Family and job for working-class women: Gender and class systems seen from below. In N. Gerstel and H. Gross (Eds.), *Families and Work* (pp. 289–301) Philadelphia: Temple University Press.

Filene, P. G. (1986). *Him/her/self: Sex roles in modern America.* (2nd ed.). Baltimore: Johns Hopkins University Press.

Findlay, S. (1990, December 24). Birth control. *U.S. News & World Report,* pp. 58–64.

Findlay, S., and Silberner, J. (1990, January 29). The worsening spread of the AIDS crisis. *U.S. News & World Report,* p. 28.

Fine, M. A. (1986). Perceptions of stepparents: Variation in stereotypes as a function of current family structure. *Journal of Marriage and the Family, 48,* 537–543.

Fine, M. A. (1989). A social science perspective on stepfamily law: Suggestions for legal reform. *Family Relations, 38,* 53–58.

Fischer, L. R. (1983). Mothers and mothers-in-law. *Journal of Marriage and the Family, 45,* 187–192.

Fischer, L. R. (1981). Transitions in the mother-daughter relationship. *Journal of Marriage and the Family, 43,* 613–622.

Fischer, C. S. (1988). Gender and the residential telephone: 1890–1940. *Sociological Forum, 3,* 211–233.

Fisher, H. E. (1983). *The sex contract: The evolution of human behavior.* New York: Quill.

Fishman, B. (1983). The economic behavior of stepfamilies. *Family Relations, 32,* 359–366.

Fishman, P. M. (1978). Interaction: The work women do. *Social Problems, 25,* 397–406.

Fitzpatrick, M. A., Fallis, S., and Vance, L. (1982). Multifunctional coding of conflict resolution strategies in marital dyads. *Family Relations, 31,* 61–70.

Forrest, J. D., and Fordyce, R. R. (1988). U.S. women's contraceptive attitudes and practice: How have they changed in the 1980s? *Family Planning Perspectives, 20,* 112–118.

Forrest, J. D., and Singh, S. (1990). The sexual and reproductive behavior of American women, 1982–1988. *Family Planning Perspectives, 22,* 206–214.

Fowlkes, M. R. (1987). The myth of merit and male professional careers: The roles of wives. In N. Gerstel and H. Gross (Eds.), *Families and Work* (pp. 347–360) Philadelphia: Temple University Press.

Frank, E. and Anderson, C. (1985). The sexual stages of marriage. In J. M. Henslin (Ed.), *Marriage and Family in a Changing Society,* (2nd ed.). (pp. 368–373) New York: The Free Press.

Frank, E., Anderson, C., and Rubinstein, D. (1978). Frequency of sexual dysfunction in 'normal' couples. *New England Journal of Medicine, 229* (3), 111–115.

Freed, D. J., and Walker, T. B. (1987). Family law in the fifty states: An overview. *Family Law Quarterly, 20,* 439–587.

Freedenthal, S. (1992, January 11). Jewish leaders worry about interfaith marriages. *The Post and Courier* (Charleston, SC), p. 4D.

Freedman, S. G. (1990). *Small victories: The real world of a teacher, her students and their high school.* New York: Harper and Row.

Freudiger, P. (1983). Life satisfaction among three categories and married women. *Journal of Marriage and the Family, 45,* 213–219.

From the Centers for Disease Control: HIV prevalence, projected AIDS case estimates: Workshop. October 31–November 1, 1989. (1990). *Journal of the American Medical Association, 263(11),* 1477, 1480.

Fulton, G. B. (1988). Sexuality in later life. In C. S. Kart, E. K. Metress, and S. P. Metress (Ed.), *Aging, Health, and Society* (pp. 273–284) Boston: Jones and Bartlett Publishers.

Furman, E. (1974). *A child's parent dies: Studies in childhood bereavement.* New Haven: Yale University Press.

Furstenberg, F. F., Jr. (1990). Divorce and the American family. *Annual Review of Sociology, 16,* 379–403.

Furstenberg, F. F., Brooks-Gunn, J., and Morgan, S. P. (1987). *Adolescent mothers in later life.* New York: Cambridge University Press.

Furstenberg, F. F. Jr., Morgan, S. P., Moore, K. A., and Peterson, J. L. (1987). Race differences in the timing of adolescent intercourse. *American Sociological Review, 52,* 511–518.

Furstenberg, F. F., Jr., Nord, C. W., Peterson, J. L., and Zill, N. (1983). The life course of children of divorce: Marital disruption and parental contact. *American Sociological Review, 48,* 656–668.

Gaelick, L., Bodenhausen, G. V., and Wyer, R. S., Jr. (1985). Emotional communication in close relationships. *Journal of Personality and Social Psychology, 49,* 1246–1265.

Gagnon, J. H. (1977). *Human sexualities.* Glenview, IL: Scott, Foresman and Company.

Gagnon, J. H., and Henderson, B. (1975). *Human sexuality: An age of ambiguity.* Boston: Little, Brown and Company.

Gagnon, J. H., and Henderson, B. (1980). The social psychology of sexual development. In J. M. Henslin (Ed.), *Marriage and Family in a Changing Society* (pp. 49–55) New York: Free Press.

Gagnon, J. H., and W. Simon. (1987). The scripting of oral genital contacts. *Archives of Sexual Behavior, 16,* 1–25.

Gallup, G. H., Jr., and Newport, F. (1990, June). Virtually all adults want children, but many of the reasons are intangible. *The Gallup Poll Monthly* No. 297, pp. 8–22.

Gallup Report, The. (1987, March). Sex education in grades 4–8 soars in public acceptance. Report No. 258, p. 19.

Gallup Report, The. (1985, March). Family of four needs $302 per week to get by. Report No. 234, pp. 17–18.

Gallup Report, The. (1983, March). Ideal number of children. Report No. 210, pp. 10–12.

Gamble, T. J., and Zigler, E. (1986, January). Effects of infant day care: Another look at the evidence. *American Journal of Orthopsychiatry, 56,* 26–42.

Ganong, L. H., and Coleman, M. (1986). A comparison of clinical and empirical literature on children in stepfamilies. *Journal of Marriage and the Family, 48,* 309–318.

Ganong, L. H., and Coleman, M. (1988). Do mutual children cement bonds in stepfamilies? *Journal of Marriage and the Family, 50,* 687–698.

Ganong, L. H., and Coleman, M. (1989). Preparing for remarriage: Anticipating the issues, seeking solutions. *Family Relations, 38,* 28–33.

Ganong, L. H., Coleman, M., and Mapes, D. (1990). A meta-analytic review of family structure stereotypes. *Journal of Marriage and the Family, 52,* 287–297.

Garcia, J. M., and Montgomery, P. A. (1991). The Hispanic population of the United States. Current Population Reports, Series P-20, No. 449. Washington, DC: Government Printing Office.

Gayle, H. D., Keeling, R. P., Garcia-Tunon, M., Kilbourne, B. W., Narkunas, J. P., Ingram, F. R., Rogers, M. F., and Curran, J. W. (1990). Prevalence of the human immunodeficiency virus among university students. *The New England Journal of Medicine, 323,* 1538–1541.

Geboy, M. J. (1981). Who is listening to the 'Experts'? The use of child care materials by parents. *Family Relations, 30,* 205–210.

Gecas, V., and Schwalbe, M. L. (1986). Parental behavior and adolescent self-esteem. *Journal of Marriage and the Family, 48,* 37–46.

Gecas, V., and Seff, M. A. (1990). Families and adolescents: A review of the 1980s. *Journal of Marriage and the Family, 52,* 941–958.

Geiss, S. K., and O'Leary, D. (1981). Therapist ratings of frequency and severity of marital problems: Implications for research. *Journal of Marital and Family Therapy, 7,* 515–520.

Gelles, R. J. (1988). Violence and pregnancy: Are pregnant women at greater risk of abuse? *Journal of Marriage and the Family, 50,* 841–847.

Gelles, R. J. (1980). Violence in the family: A review of research in the seventies. *Journal of Marriage and the Family, 42,* 873–885.

Gelles, R. J., and Conte, J. R. (1990). Domestic violence and sexual abuse of children: A review of research in the eighties. *Journal of Marriage and the Family, 52,* 1045–1058.

Gelles, R. J., and Cornell, C. P. (1985). *Intimate violence in families.* Newbury Park, CA: Sage Publications.

Gelles, R. J., and Straus, M. A. (1988). *Intimate violence.* New York: Simon and Schuster.

Gelles, R. J., and Straus, M. A. (1979). Determinants of violence in the family: Toward a theoretical integration. In W. A. Burr, R. Hill, F. I. Nye, and I. Reiss (Eds.), *Contemporary theories about the family,* (Vol. 1) (pp. 549–581) New York: Free Press.

Gelman, D., Doherty, S., Murr, A., Drew, L., and Gordon, J. (1987, October 26). Not tonight, dear. *Newsweek,* pp. 64–66.

Gentry, M., Rosenman, L., and Shulman, A. D. (1987). Comparison of the needs and support systems of remarried and nonremarried widows. in H. Z. Lopata (Ed.), *Widows,* Volume II: North America. (pp. 158–170) Durham: Duke University Press.

George, L. K., and Weiler, S. J. (1985). Sexuality in middle and late life. In E. Palmore, E. W. Busse, G. L. Maddox, J. B. Nowlin, and I. C. Siegler (Eds.), *Normal Aging III* (pp. 12–19) Durham: Duke University Press.

Gerson, K. (1987). How women choose between employment and family: A developmental perspective. In N. Gerstel and H. Gross (Eds.), *Families and Work.* (pp. 270–288) Philadelphia: Temple University Press.

Gerson, K. (1985). *Hard choices: How women decide about work, career, and motherhood.* Berkeley: University of California Press.

Gerstel, N., and Gross, H. (Eds.). (1987). *Families and Work.* Philadelphia: Temple University Press.

Gettys, L. D., and Cann, A. (1981). Children's perceptions of occupational sex stereotypes. *Sex Roles, 7,* 301–308.

Giblin, P., Sprenkle, D. H., and Sheehan, R. (1985). Enrichment outcome research: A meta-analysis of premarital, marital and family interventions. *Journal of Marital and Family Therapy, 11,* 257–271.

Giele, J. Z. (1988). Gender and sex roles. In N. J. Smelser (Ed.), *Handbook of Sociology* (pp. 291–323) Newbury Park, CA: Sage.

Giles-Sims, J., and Crosbie-Burnett, M. (1989a). Adolescent power in stepfather families: A test of normative-resource theory. *Journal of Marriage and the Family, 51,* 1065–1078.

Giles-Sims, J., and Crosbie-Burnett, M. (1989b). Stepfamily research: Implications for policy, clinical interventions, and further research. *Family Relations, 38,* 19–23.

Gilford, R., and Bengtson, V. (1979). Measuring marital satisfaction in three generations: Positive and negative dimensions. *Journal of Marriage and the Family, 41,* 387–398.

Gillespie, M. A. (1991, January/February). HIV: The global crisis. *Ms., 1,* pp. 17–22.

Giordano, J. A. (1988). Parents of the baby boomers: A new generation of young-old. *Family Relations, 37,* 411–414.

Giovannoni, J. M., and Becerra, R. M. (1979). *Defining child abuse.* New York: Free Press.

Glaberson, W. (1989, July 8). Ruling stretches legal concept of family. *New York Times,* pp. 25, 28.

Glenn, N. D. (1990). Quantitative research on marital quality in the 1980s: A critical review. *Journal of Marriage and the Family, 52,* 818–831.

Glenn, N. D. (1989). Duration of marriage, family composition, and marital happiness. *National Journal of Sociology, 3,* 3–24.

Glenn, N. D. (1975). The contribution of marriage to the psychological well-being of males and females. *Journal of Marriage and the Family, 37,* 594–601.

Glenn, N. D., and McLanahan, S. (1982). Children and marital happiness: A further specification of the relationship. *Journal of Marriage and the Family, 44,* 63–72.

Glenn, N. D., and McLanahan, S. (1981). The effects of offspring on the psychological well-being of older adults. *Journal of Marriage and the Family, 43,* 409–421.

Glenn, N. D., and Supancic, M. (1984). The social and demographic correlates of divorce and separation in the United States: An update and reconsideration. *Journal of Marriage and the Family, 46,* 563–575.

Glick, P. C. (1989). Remarried families, stepfamilies, and stepchildren: A brief demographic profile. *Family Relations, 38,* 24–27.

Glick, P. C., and Lin, S. (1986a). Recent changes in divorce and remarriage. *Journal of Marriage and the Family, 48,* 737–747.

Glick, P. C., and Lin, S. (1986b). More young adults are living with their parents: Who are they? *Journal of Marriage and the Family, 48,* 107–112.

Glick, P. C., and Spanier, G. B. (1980). Married and unmarried cohabitation in the United States. *Journal of Marriage and the Family, 42,* 19–30.

Godwin, D. D. (1990). Family financial management. *Family Relations, 39,* 221–228.

Goetting, A. (1986). Parental satisfaction: A review of research. *Journal of Family Issues, 7,* 83–109.

Goetting, A. (1979). The normative integration of the former spouse relationship. *Journal of Divorce, 2,* 395–414.

Goldberg, W. A., Michaels, G. Y., and Lamb, M. E. (1985). Husbands' and wives' adjustment to pregnancy and first parenthood. *Journal of Family Issues, 6,* 483–503.

Goldscheider, C., and Goldscheider, F. K. (1987). Moving out and marriage: What do young adults expect? *American Sociological Review, 52,* 278–285.

Goldsteen, K., and Ross, C. E. (1989). The perceived burden of children. *Journal of Family Issues, 10,* 504–526.

Goleman, D. (1990, February 6). Compassion and comfort in middle age. *New York Times,* pp. C1, C14.

Goode, W. J. (1959). The theoretical importance of love. *American Sociological Review, 24,* 38–47.

Goodrich, T. L. (1990, September 1). What's love got to do with it? Plenty, according to women. *The News and Courier/The Evening Post* (Charleston, SC), p. 10–C.

Goodwin, J. S., Hunt, W. C., Key, C. R., and Samet, J. M. (1987). The effect of marital status on stage, treatment, and survival of cancer patients. *Journal of the American Medical Association, 258,* 3125–3130.

Gordon, L. (1988). *Heroes of their own lives: The politics and history of family violence, Boston 1880–1960.* New York: Viking.

Gottman, J. M., and Krokoff, L. J. (1989). Marital interaction and satisfaction: A longitudinal view. *Journal of Consulting and Clinical Psychology, 57,* 47–52.

Gottman, J. M., and Porterfield, A. L. (1981). Communicative competence in the nonverbal behavior of married couples. *Journal of Marriage and the Family, 43,* 817–824.

Gove, W. R., and Shin, H. (1989). The psychological well-being of divorced and widowed men and women: An empirical analysis. *Journal of Family Issues, 10,* 122–144.

Gove, W. R., Style, C. B., and Hughes, M. (1990). The effect of marriage on the well-being of adults: A theoretical analysis. *Journal of Family Issues, 11,* 4–35.

Gove, W. R., and Zeiss, C. (1987). Multiple roles and happiness. In F. J. Crosby (Ed.), *Spouse, Parent, Worker: On Gender and Multiple Roles* (pp. 125–137) New Haven: Yale University Press.

Gowler, D., and Legge, K. (1978). Hidden and open contracts in marriage. In R. and R. Rapoport (Eds.), *Working Couples* (pp. 47–61) New York: Harper Colophon.

Granvold, D. K. (1983). Structured separation for marital treatment and decision-making. *Journal of Marital and Family Therapy, 9,* 403–412.

Granvold, D. K., and Tarrant, R. (1983). Structured marital separation as a marital treatment method. *Journal of Marital and Family Therapy, 9,* 189–198.

Greeley, A. M. (1978, September). To increase the enjoyment of sex in marriage. *The Reader's Digest,* pp. 111–114.

Greenberg, D. F. (1988). *The construction of homosexuality.* Chicago: University of Chicago Press.

Greenblatt, C. S. (1983). The salience of sexuality in the early years of marriage. *Journal of Marriage and the Family, 45,* 289–299.

Greene, L. E., and McMath, J. S. (No Date). A guide to choosing a child care center. Charleston, SC: College of Charleston.

Greene, W. H., and Quester, A. O. (1982). Divorce risk and wives' labor supply behavior. *Social Science Quarterly, 63,* 16–27.

Greer, G. (1984). *Sex and destiny: The politics of human fertility.* New York: Harper and Row.

Grubb, N., and Lazerson, M. (1988). *Broken promises: How Americans fail their children.* Chicago: University of Chicago Press.

Guisinger, S., Cowan, P. A., and Schuldberg, D. (1989). Changing parent and spouse relations in the first years of remarriage of divorced fathers. *Journal of Marriage and the Family, 51,* 445–456.

Gutis, P. S. (1989, November 9). New York housing officials redefine family to block evictions. *New York Times,* pp. B1, B7.

Guttentag, M., and Secord, P. F. (1983). Too many women?: The sex ratio question. Beverly Hill: Sage.

Gwartney-Gibbs, P. A. (1986). The institutionalization of premarital cohabitation: Estimates from marriage license applications, 1970 and 1980. *The Journal of Marriage and the Family, 48,* 423–434.

Hagestad, G. O, and Burton, L. M. (1986). Grandparenthood, life context, and family development. *American Behavioral Scientist, 29,* 471–484.

Halle, D. (1984). *America's working man: Work, home, and politics among blue-collar property owners.* Chicago: University of Chicago Press.

Hampton, R. L., Gelles, R. J., and Harrop, J. W. (1989). Is violence in black families increasing? A comparison of 1975 and 1985 national survey rates. *Journal of Marriage and the Family, 51,* 969–980.

Hanna, S. L., and Knaub, P. K. (1981). Cohabitation before remarriage: Its relationship to family strengths. *Alternative Lifestyles, 4,* 507–522.

Hareven, T. K. (1988). American families in transition: Historical perspectives on change. In A. S. Skolnick and J. H. Skolnick (Eds.), *Family in Transition,* (6th ed.) (pp. 39–57) Glenview, IL: Scott, Foresman and Company.

Harris, F. (1937, September). The sexual relationship in marriage. *The Reader's Digest* pp. 23–26.

Harris, M. (1981). *America now: The anthropology of a changing culture.* New York: Simon and Schuster.

Harris, R. L., Ellicott, A. M., and Holmes, D. S. (1986). The timing of psychosocial transitions and changes in women's lives: An examination of women aged 45 to 60. *Journal of Personality and Social Psychology, 51,* 409–416.

Harrison, B., and Bluestone, B. (1988). *The great U-turn: Corporate restructuring and the polarizing of America.* New York: Basic Books.

Hartley, R. E. (1959). Sex-role pressures and the socialization of the male child. *Psychological Reports 5,* 457–468.

Hastings, P. K., and Hoge, D. R. (1981). Religious trends among college students, 1948–79. *Social Forces, 60,* 517–531.

Hastings, P. K., and Hoge, D. R. (1986). Religious and moral attitude trends among college students, 1948–84. *Social Forces, 65,* 370–377.

Hatcher, R. A., Stewart, F., Trussell, J., Kowal, D., Guest, F., Stewart, G. K., and Cates, W. (1990). *Contraceptive technology, 1990–1992,* (15th rev. ed.). New York: Irvington Publishers.

Haugh, S. S., Hoffman, C. D., and Cowan, G. (1980). The eye of the very young beholder: Sex typing of infants by young children. *Child Development, 51,* 598–600.

Hawkins, A. J., and Belsky, J. (1989). The role of father involvement in personality change in men across the transition to parenthood. *Family Relations, 38,* 378–384.

Healey, M. (1986, December 17). 57% of teens have sex at 17. *USA Today,* Section D:1.

Heaton, T. B., Lichter, D. T., and Amoateng, A. (1989). The timing of family formation: Rural-urban differentials in first intercourse, childbirth, and marriage. *Rural Sociology, 54,* 1–16.

Heiman, J. R. (1975). The physiology of erotica: Women's sexual arousal. *Psychology Today, 8*(11), 90–94.

Heiman, J. R., LoPiccolo, L., and LoPiccolo, J. (1976). *Becoming orgasmic: A sexual growth program for women.* Englewood Cliffs, NJ: Prentice-Hall.

Hendrick, S. S. (1981). Self-disclosure and marital satisfaction. *Journal of Personality and Social Psychology, 40,* 1150–1159.

Hendrick, C., Hendrick, S., Foote, F. H., and Slapion-Foote, M. J. (1984). Do men and women love differently? *Journal of Social and Personal Relationship 1*(2), 177–195.

Hennon, C. B., and Burton, J. R. (1986). Financial satisfaction as a developmental task among the elderly. *American Behavioral Scientist, 29,* 439–452.

Hepworth, J., Ryder, R. G., and Dreyer, A. S. (1984). The effects of parental loss on the formation of intimate relationships. *Journal of Marital and Family Therapy, 10,* 73–82.

Herold, E. S., and Goodwin, M. S. (1981). Adamant virgins, potential nonvirgins and virgins. *Journal of Sex Research, 17,* 97–113.

Hershey, M. R. (1978). Racial differences in sex-role identities and sex stereotyping: Evidence against a common assumption. *Social Science Quarterly, 58,* 583–596.

Hess, B. B., and Markson, E. W. (1980). *Aging and old age: An introduction to social gerontology.* New York: Macmillan.

Hess, B. B., and Waring, J. M. (1978). Parent and child in later life: Rethinking the relationship. In R. M. Lerner and G. B. Spanier (Eds.), *Child Influences on Marital and Family Interaction: A Life Span Perspective* (pp. 241–273) New York: Academic Press.

Heuser, R. L. (1976). Fertility tables for birth cohorts by color: United States, 1917–73. Rockville, MD: U.S. Department of Health, Education, and Welfare, Public Health Service, Health Resources Administration, National Center for Health Statistics.

Higginbotham, E. (1981). Is marriage a priority? Class differences in marital options of educated black women. In P. J. Stein (Ed.), *Single life: Unmarried Adults in Social Context.* (pp. 259–267) New York: St. Martin's Press.

Hill, E. A., and Dorfman, L. T. (1982). Reaction of housewives to the retirement of their husbands. *Family Relations, 31,* 195–200.

Hill, R. (1949). *Families under stress: Adjustment to the crises of war separation and reunion.* New York: Harper and Row.

Hilliard, M. (1957, June) The act of love: Woman's greatest challenge. *The Reader's Digest* pp. 43–46.

Hiltz, S. R. (1981). Widowhood: A roleless role. In P. J. Stein (Ed.), *Single Life: Unmarried Adults in Social Context* (pp. 79–97) New York: St. Martin's Press.

Hinds, M. (1990, March 17). Addiction to crack can kill parental instinct. *New York Times*, pp. 1A, 8A.

Hinds, M. W., Bergeisen, G. H., and Allen, D. T. (1985). Neonatal outcome in planned v. unplanned out-of-hospital births in Kentucky. *Journal of the American Medical Association, 253*(11), 1578–1582.

Hirschorn, M. W. (1987a, April 29). AIDS is not seen as a major threat by many heterosexuals on campuses. *The Chronicle of Higher Education,* pp. 1, 32–34.

Hirschorn, M. W. (1987b, June 10). Persuading students to use safer sex practices proves difficult, even with the danger of AIDS. *The Chronicle of Higher Education,* p. 30, 32.

Hirschorn, M. W. (1988, January 20). Freshman interest in business careers hits new level, and money remains a top priority, study finds. *The Chronicle of Higher Education,* pp. A31, A34.

Hobart, C. (1987). Parent-child relations in remarried families. *Journal of Family Issues, 8,* 259–277.

Hobart, C. (1988). The family system in remarriage: An exploratory study. *Journal of Marriage and the Family, 50,* 649–661.

Hochschild, A. R., with Machung, A. (1989). *The second shift: Working parents and the revolution at home.* New York: Viking.

Hock, E., Gnezda, M. T., and McBride, S. L. (1984). Mothers of infants: Attitudes toward employment and motherhood following birth of the first child. *Journal of Marriage and the Family, 46,* 425–431.

Hoffman, L. W., and Manis, J. D. (1979). The value of children in the United States: A new approach to the study of fertility. *Journal of Marriage and the Family, 41,* 583–596.

Hoffman, L. W., McManus, K. A., and Brackbill, Y. (1987). The value of children to young and elderly parents. *International Journal of Aging and Human Development, 25*(4), 309–322.

Hofsess, D. (1988, January 27). Michigan bill lets cousins marry. *Argus Leader,* (Sioux Falls, SD), p. 7A.

Hogan, M. J., and Bauer, J. W. (1988). Problems in family financial management. In C. S. Chilman, F. M. Cox, and E. W. Nunnally (Eds.), *Employment and Economic Problems* (pp. 137–153). Families in Trouble Series, Volume 1. Newbury Park, CA: Sage.

Hood, J. C. (1986). The provider role: Its meaning and measurement. *Journal of Marriage and the Family, 48,* 349–359.

Hooyman, N., and Kiyak, H. A. (1991). *Social Gerontology: A Multidisciplinary Perspective.* (2nd ed.). Boston: Allyn and Bacon.

Horowitz, R. (1983). *Honor and the American dream: Culture and identity in a Chicago neighborhood.* New Brunswick, NJ: Rutgers University Press.

Horowitz, H. L. (1987). *Campus life: Undergraduate cultures from the end of the eighteenth century to the present.* Chicago: University of Chicago Press.

Horvath, F. W. (1987, June). The pulse of economic change: Displaced workers of 1981–85. *Monthly Labor Review, 110,* pp. 3–12.

Horwitz, A. V. (1984). The economy and social pathology. In R. H. Turner and J. F. Short, Jr. (Eds.), *Annual Review of Sociology,* Volume 10. (pp. 95–119) Palo Alto: Annual Reviews Inc.

Hotchner, T. (1984). *Pregnancy and childbirth: The complete guide for a new life.* New York: Avon.

Houseknecht, S. K. (1987). Voluntary childlessness. In M. B. Sussman and S. K. Steinmetz (Eds.), *Handbook of Marriage and the Family* (pp. 369–395). New York: Plenum.

Houseknecht, S. K. (1979). Childlessness and marital adjustment. *Journal of Marriage and the Family, 41,* 259–265.

Houseknecht, S. K., Vaughan, S., and Macke, A. S. (1984). Marital disruption among professional women: The timing of career and family events. *Social Problems, 31,* 273–284.

Houseknecht, S. K., Vaughan, S., and Statham, A. (1987). The impact of singlehood on the career patterns of professional women. *Journal of Marriage and the Family, 49,* 353–366.

"How To Choose Day Care." (1989, April 30). *The News and Courier / The Evening Post* (Charleston, SC), pp. 2D.

Howard, J. (1978). *Families.* New York: Simon and Schuster.

Howes, C. (1990). Can the age of entry into child care and the quality of child care predict adjustment in kindergarten? *Developmental Psychology, 26,* 292–303.

Hudis, P. M., and Brazzell, J. F. (1981). Significant others, adult-role expectations, and the resolutions of teenage pregnancies. In P. Ahmed (Ed.), *Pregnancy, Childbirth, and Parenthood* (pp. 167–187) New York: Elsevier.

Huey, C. J., Kline-Graber, G., and Graber, B. (1981). Time factors and orgasmic response. *Archives of Sexual Behavior, 10,* 111–118.

Hunt, J. G., and Hunt, L. L. (1977). Dilemmas and contradictions of status: The case of the dual-career family. *Social Problems, 24,* 407–416.

Hunt, M. (1974). *Sexual behavior in the 1970s.* Chicago: Playboy Press.

Hunt, M. (1983). Marital sex. In A. Skolnick and J. H. Skolnick (Eds.), *Family in Transition* (4th ed.) (pp. 219–234) Boston: Little, Brown and Company.

Hutter, M. (1988). *The changing family: Comparative perspectives,* (2nd ed.). New York: Macmillan.

Hyde, J. S. (1990). *Understanding human sexuality,* (4th ed.). New York: McGraw-Hill.

Hyman, M. (1991). *Basic legal forms, with commentary.* Boston, MA: Warren, Gorham and Lamont, Inc.

Ihinger-Tallman, M. and Pasley, K. (1987). *Remarriage.* Family Studies Text Series 7. Newbury Park, CA: Sage.

Information Please Almanac, Atlas, and Yearbook 1992. (1991). (45th ed.). Boston: Houghton Mifflin Company.

Ishii-Kuntz, M., and Seccombe, K. (1989). The impact of children upon social support networks throughout the life course. *Journal of Marriage and the Family, 51,* 777–790.

Jackson, P. G. (1985). On living together unmarried. In J. M. Henslin (Ed.), *Marriage and Family in a Changing Society,* (2nd ed.) (pp. 252–260) New York: The Free Press.

Jacob, H. (1988). *Silent revolution: The transformation of divorce law in the United States.* Chicago: The University of Chicago Press.

Jacobs, E., Shipp, S., and Brown, G. (1989). Families of working wives spending more on services and nondurables. *Monthly Labor Review, 112*(February), 15–23.

Jacobson, N. S. (1984). A component analysis of behavioral marital therapy: The relative effectiveness of behavior exchange and communication/problem-solving training. *Journal of Consulting and Clinical Psychology, 52,* 295–305.

Jacobson, N. S., Follette, W. C., Revenstorf, D., Baucom, D. H., Hahlweg, K. and Margolin, G. (1984). Variability in outcome and clinical significance of behavioral marital therapy: A reanalysis of outcome data. *Journal of Consulting and Clinical Psychology, 52,* 497–504.

Jaffe, S. S., and Viertel, J. (1984). The Sterling family. In R. LaRossa (Ed.), *Family Case Studies: A Sociological Perspective* (pp. 45–60) New York: The Free Press.

James, W. H. (1974). Marital coital rates, spouses' ages, family size and social class. *The Journal of Sex Research, 10,* 205–218.

James, W. H. (1981). The honeymoon effect on marital coitus. *The Journal of Sex Research, 17,* 114–123.

Jessor, S. L., and Jessor, R. (1975). Transition from virginity to nonvirginity among youth: A social-psychological study over time. *Developmental Psychology, 11,* 473–484.

John, R. (1988). The Native American family. In C. H. Mindel, R. W. Habenstein, and R. Wright, Jr. (Eds.), *Ethnic Families in America,* (3rd ed.) (pp. 325–363) New York: Elsevier.

Johnson, C. L. (1985). The impact of illness on late-life marriages. *Journal of Marriage and the Family, 47,* 165–172.

Johnson, D. R., White, L. K., Edwards, J. N., and Booth, A. (1986). Dimensions of marital quality: Toward methodological and conceptual refinement. *Journal of Family Issues, 7,* 31–49.

Johnson, W. B., and Packer, A. H. (1987). *Workforce 2000: Work and workers for the twenty-first century.* Indianapolis: Hudson Institute.

Jones, E. F., Forrest, J. D., Henshaw, S. K., Silverman, J., and Torres, A. (1989). *Pregnancy, contraception, and family planning services in industrialized countries.* New Haven: Yale University Press.

Juster, F. T. (1985). A note on recent changes in time use. In F. T. Juster and F. P. Stafford (Eds.), *Time, Goods, and Well-being* (pp. 313–332) Ann Arbor: Survey Research Center, Institute for Social Research, University of Michigan.

Kadushin, A., and Martin, J. A. (1988). *Child welfare services.* (4th ed.). New York: Macmillan.

Kagan, J. (1984). *The nature of the child.* New York: Basic Books.

Kagan, J. (1986, 1988). The power and limitations of parents. In N. D. Glenn and M. T. Coleman (Eds.), *Family Relations: A Reader.* (pp. 393–405) Chicago: Dorsey.

Kahn-Hut, R., Daniels, A. K., and Colvard, R. (Eds.) (1982). *Women and Work: Problems and Perspectives.* New York: Oxford University Press.

Kain, E. L. (1990). *The myth of family decline.* Lexington, MA: Lexington Books.

Kalmuss, D. (1984). The intergenerational transmission of marital aggression. *Journal of Marriage and the Family, 46,* 11–19.

Kalmuss, D., and Seltzer, J. A. (1986). Continuity of marital behavior in remarriage: The case of spouse abuse. *Journal of Marriage and the Family, 48,* 113–120.

Kargman, M. W. (1983). Stepchild support obligations of stepparents. *Family Relations, 32,* 231–238.

Keith, P. M. (1983). A comparison of the resources of parents and childless men and women in very old age. *Family Relations, 32,* 403–409.

Keith, P. M., and Schafer, R. B. (1986). Housework, disagreement, and depression among younger and older couples. *American Behavioral Scientist, 29,* 405–422.

Keniston, K., and the Carnegie Council on Children. (1977). *All our children: The American family under pressure.* New York: Harcourt Brace Jovanovich.

Kersten, K. K. and Kersten, L. K. (1988). *Marriage and family: Studying close relationships.* New York: Harper and Row.

Kessler, R. C., and McRae, J. A., Jr. (1982). The effect of wives' employment on mental health of married men and women. *American Sociological Review, 47,* 216–227.

Kessler, R. C., Turner, J. B., and House, J. S. (1988). Effects of unemployment on health in a community survey:

Main, modifying, and mediating effects. *Journal of Social Issues, 44*(4), 69–85.

Kimmel, M. S. (1989). Judaism, masculinity and feminism. In M. S. Kimmel and M. A. Messner (Eds.), *Men's Lives* (pp. 98–100) New York: Macmillan.

Kinch, J. W. (1963). A formalized theory of the self-concept. *American Journal of Sociology, 68,* 481–486.

King, D., and MacKinnon, C. E. (1988). Making difficult choices easier: A review of research on day care and children's development. *Family Relations, 37,* 392–398.

King, K., Balswick, J. D., and Robinson, I. E. (1977). The continuing premarital sexual revolution among college females. *Journal of Marriage and the Family, 39,* 455–459.

Kingston, P. W., and Nock, S. L. (1987). Time together among dual-earner couples. *American Sociological Review, 52,* 391–400.

Kinkade, S. (1989, January–February). 12 nations approve norplant. *Popline,* p. 3.

Kinsey, A. C., Pomeroy, W. B., and Martin, C. E. (1948). *Sexual behavior in the human male.* Philadelphia: W. B. Saunders Company.

Kinsey, A. C., Pomeroy, W. B., Martin, C. E., and Gebhard, P. H. (1953). *Sexual behavior in the human female.* Philadelphia: W. B. Saunders Company.

Kirby, D., Waszak, C., and Ziegler, J. (1991). Six school-based clinics: Their reproductive health services and impact on social behavior. *Family Planning Perspectives, 23,* 6–16.

Kitano, H. H. L. (1988). The Japanese American family. In C. H. Mindel, R. W. Habenstein, and R. Wright, Jr. (Eds.), *Ethnic Families in America,* Third Edition (pp. 258–275) New York: Elsevier.

Kitson, G. C., Babri, K. B., and Roach, M. J. (1985). Who divorces and why: A review. *Journal of Family Issues, 6,* 255–293.

Kitson, G. C., and Sussman, M. B. (1982). Marital complaints, demographic characteristics, and symptoms of mental distress in divorce. *Journal of Marriage and the Family, 44,* 87–101.

Kitson, G. C., Babri, K. B., Roach, M. J., and Placidi, K. S. (1989). Adjustment to widowhood and divorce: A review. *Journal of Family Issues, 10,* 5–32.

Kitson, G. C., and Morgan, L. A. (1990). The multiple consequences of divorce: A decade review. *Journal of Marriage and the Family, 52,* 913–924.

Klagsburn, F. (1985). *Married people: Staying together in the age of divorce.* New York: Bantam.

Kleban, M. H., Brody, E. M., Schoonover, C. B., and Hoffman, C. (1989). Family help to the elderly: Perceptions of sons-in-law regarding parent care. *Journal of Marriage and the Family, 51,* 303–312.

Klein, B. W., and Rones, P. L. (1989, October). A profile of the working poor. *Monthly Labor Review, 112,* 3–13.

Kleinke, C. L., Meeker, F. B., and Staneski, R. A. (1986). Preference for opening lines: Comparing ratings by men and women. *Sex Roles, 15,* 585–600.

Knauerhose, E. (1989). The sexually active custodial parent: A contradiction in terms?: Parrillo v. Parrillo. *Cooley Law Review, 6,* 545–563.

Knox, D., and Wilson, K. (1981). Dating behaviors of university students. *Family Relations, 30,* 255–258.

Kohlberg, L. (1966). A cognitive-developmental analysis of children's sex-role concepts and attitudes. In E. E. Maccoby (Ed.), *The Development of Sex Differences,* (pp. 82–172). Stanford: Stanford University Press.

Kohn, M. (1977). *Class and conformity: A study of values.* (2nd ed.). Chicago: University of Chicago Press.

Kolbe, R., and LaVoie, J. C. (1981). Sex-role stereotyping in preschool children's picture books. *Social Psychology Quarterly, 44,* 369–374.

Kolbert, K., and Mertus, J. (1991, January/February). Pro-choice: Keeping the pressure on. *Ms., 1,* p. 92.

Kollock, P., Blumstein, P. and Schwartz, P. (1985). Sex and power in interaction: Conversational privileges and duties. *American Sociological Review, 50,* 34–46.

Komarovsky, M. (1985). *Women in college: Shaping new feminine identities.* New York: Basic Books.

Komarovsky, M. (1976). *Dilemmas of masculinity: A study of youth.* New York: Norton.

Komarovsky, M. (1946). Cultural contradictions and sex roles. *American Journal of Sociology, 52,* 184–189.

Korbin, J. E. (Ed.). (1981). *Child abuse and neglect: Cross-cultural perspectives.* Berkeley: University of California Press.

Korman, S. K. (1983). Nontraditional dating behavior: Date-initiation and date expense-sharing among feminists and nonfeminists. *Family Relations, 32,* 575–581.

Kozak, L. J. (1989). Surgical and nonsurgical procedures associated with hospital delivery in the United States: 1980–1987. *Birth, 16,* 209–213.

Krantz, S. E. (1989). The impact of divorce on children. In A. S. Skolnick and J. H. Skolnick (Eds.), *Family in Transition,* (6th ed.) (pp. 341–362) Glenview, IL: Scott, Foresman and Company.

Krause, E. A. (1971). *The sociology of occupations.* Boston: Little, Brown.

Krokoff, L. J., Gottman, J. M., and Roy, A. K. (1988). Blue-collar and white-collar marital interaction and communication orientation. *Journal of Social and Personal Relationships, 5,* 201–221.

Kugelmass, I. N. (1935). *Growing superior children.* New York: D. Appleton-Century Company.

Kurdek, L. A. (1989). Relationship quality for newly married husbands and wives: Marital history, stepchildren, and individual-difference predictors. *Journal of Marriage and the Family, 51,* 1053–1064.

Kutner, L. (1990, January 11). Parent & child: Money is often a stressful subject. *New York Times,* p. C8.

Lakoff, R. (1979). Talking like a lady. In B. J. Wishart and L. C. Reichman (Eds.), *Modern Sociological Issues*, (2nd ed.) (pp. 81–90) New York: Macmillan.

Lamanna, M. A., and Riedmann, A. (1988). *Marriages and families: Making choices and facing change*, (3rd ed.). Belmont, CA: Wadsworth.

Landers, A. (1985, July 13). She was smart in school but dumb about sex. *Argus Leader* (Sioux Falls, SD), p. 3B.

Landers, A. (1989, December 24) Superwomen: How do they do it all? *The News and Courier/The Evening Post* (Charleston, SC), p. 2E.

Langbein, E. J. (1988). Post-dissolution cohabitation of alimony recipients: A legal fact of life. *Nova Law Review, 12,* 787–795.

LaRossa, R. (1983). The transition to parenthood and the social reality of time. *Journal of Marriage and the Family, 45,* 579–589.

LaRossa, R. (1988). Fatherhood and social change. *Family Relations, 37,* 451–457.

LaRossa, R. (1986). *Becoming a parent.* Family Studies Text Series 3. Beverly Hills, CA: Sage.

LaRossa, R. (1983). The transition to parenthood and the social reality of time. *Journal of Marriage and the Family, 45,* 579–589.

LaRossa R. and LaRossa M. M. (1981). *Transition to parenthood: How infants change families.* Beverly Hills, CA: Sage.

Larson, J. H. (1984). The effect of husband's unemployment on marital and family relations in blue-collar families. *Family Relations, 33,* 503–511.

Larson, J. H., and Allgood, S. M. (1987). A comparison of intimacy in first-married and remarried couples. *Journal of Family Issues, 8,* 319–331.

Larson, J. and Edmondson, B. (1991, March). Should unmarried partners get married benefits? *American Demographics, 13,* p.47

Laslett, B. (1978). Family membership, past and present. *Social Problems, 25,* 476–490.

Lauer, R. H. and Lauer, J. C. (1991). *Marriage and family: Quest for intimacy.* Dubuque, IA: William C. Brown.

Leavitt, J. W. (1986). *Brought to bed: Childbearing in America 1750 to 1950.* New York: Oxford University Press.

Lederman, R. P. (1984). *Psychosocial adaptation in pregnancy: Assessment of seven dimensions of maternal development.* Englewood Cliffs, NJ: Prentice-Hall.

Lee, G. R. (1988). Marital satisfaction in later life: The effects of nonmarital roles. *Journal of Marriage and the Family, 50,* 775–783.

LeMasters, E. E., and DeFrain, J. (1983). *Parents in contemporary America: A sympathetic view* (4th ed.). Homewood, IL: Dorsey Press.

Lempers, J., Clark-Lempers, D., and Simons, R. L. (1989). Economic hardship, parenting, and distress in adolescence. *Child Development, 60,* 25–39.

Leppel, K. (1987). Income effects on living arrangements: Differences between male and female householders. *Social Science Research, 16,* 138–153.

Lester, J. (1973, July). Being a boy. *Ms.*, pp. 112–113.

Levin, R. J., and Levin, A. (1975, September). Sexual pleasure: The surprising preferences of 100,000 women. *Redbook,* pp. 51–58.

Levinger, G. (1965). Marital cohesiveness and dissolution: An integrative review. *Journal of Marriage and the Family, 27,* 19–28.

Levy, F. (1987). *Dollars and dreams: The changing American income distribution.* New York: Russell Sage Foundation.

Lewin, T. (1988, November 25). New law compels sweeping changes in child support. *New York Times,* pp. A1, A20.

Lewin, T. (1990, September 21), Suit over death benefits asks, what is a family? *New York Times,* pp. B7.

Lewin, M., and Tragos, L. M. (1987). Has the feminist movement influenced adolescent sex role attitudes? A reassessment after a quarter century. *Sex Roles, 16,* 125–135.

Lewis, J. M. (1988). The Transition to parenthood: II. Stability and change in marital structure. *Family Process, 27,* 273–283.

Lewis, R. A., Freneau, P. J., and Roberts, C. L. (1979). Fathers and the postparental transition. *The Family Coordinator, 28,* 514–520.

Lewis, R. A., Spainer, G. B., Atkinson, V. L. S., and Lehecka, C. F. (1977). Commitment in married and unmarried cohabitation. *Sociological Focus, 10,* 367–374.

Li, J. T., and Caldwell, R. A. (1987). Magnitude and directional effects of marital sex-role incongruence on marital adjustment. *Journal of Family Issues, 8,* 97–110.

Lichter, D. T., LeClere, F. B., and McLaughlin, D. K. (1991). Local marriage markets and the marital behavior of black and white women. *American Journal of Sociology, 96,* 843–867.

Liese, L. H., Snowden, L. R., and Ford, L. K. (1989). Partner status, social support, and psychological adjustment during pregnancy. *Family Relations, 38,* 311–316.

Lindsey, R. (1976, September 12). Women entering job market at an "extraordinary" pace. *New York Times,* pp. 1, 49.

Link, P. W., and Darling, C. A. (1986). Couples undergoing treatment for infertility: Dimensions of life satisfaction. *Journal of Sex and Marital Therapy, 12,* 46–59.

Littman M. S. (1989, August). Reasons for not working: Poor and nonpoor householders. *Monthly Labor Review, 112,* pp. 16–21.

Lloyd, S. A. (1991). The darkside of courtship: Violence and sexual exploitation. *Family Relations, 40,* 14–20.

Lloyd, S. A., and Zick, C. D. (1986). Divorce at mid and later life: Does the empirical evidence support the theory? *Journal of Divorce, 9,* 89–102.

Lobsenz, N. (1989, June/July). Why it's okay to disagree about money. *Modern Bride,* pp. 70, 162.

Loewenstein, S. F., Bloch, N. E., Campion, J., Epstein. J. S., Gale, P., and Salvatore, M. (1981). A study of satisfactions and stresses of single women in midlife, *Sex Roles*, *7*, 1127–1141.

Long, B. H. (1983). Evaluations and intentions concerning marriage among unmarried female undergraduates. *The Journal of Social Psychology*, *119*, 235–242.

Longino, C. F., Jr. (1988, June). The comfortably retired and the pension elite. *American Demographics*, *10*, pp. 22–24.

Lord, L. (1991, August 19). The captain's call. *U.S. News and World Report*, p. 11.

Lowe, G. D., and Smith, R. R. (1987). Gender, marital status, and mental well-being: A retest of Bernard's his and her marriages. *Sociological Spectrum*, *7*, 301–307.

Lowenthal, M. F., and Chiriboga, D. (1972). Transition to the empty nest: Crisis, challenge, or relief? *Archives of General Psychiatry*, *26*, 8–14.

Lown, J. M., McFadden, J. R., and Crossman, S. M., (1989). Family life education for remarriage focus on financial management. *Family Relations*, *38*, 40–45.

Lueptow, L. B., Guss, M. B., and Hyden, C. (1989). Sex role ideology, marital status, and happiness. *Journal of Family Issues*, *10*, 383–400.

Luria, Z., and Meade, R. G. (1984). Sexuality and the middle-aged woman. in G. Baruch and J. Brooks-Gunn (Eds.), *Women in Midlife*, pp. 371–397 New York: Plenum.

Luster, T., Rhoades, K., and Haas, B. (1989). The relation between parental values and parenting behavior: A test of the Kohn hypothesis. *Journal of Marriage and the Family*, *51*, 139–147.

Lutz, P. (1983). The stepfamily: An adolescent perspective. *Family Relations*, *32*, 367–375.

Maccoby, E. E. (Ed.). (1966). *The Development of sex differences*. Stanford: Stanford University Press.

Maccoby, E. E., and Jacklin, C. N. (1974). *The psychology of sex differences*. Stanford: Stanford University Press.

MacDermid, S. M., Huston, T. L. and McHale, S. M. (1990). Changes in marriage associated with the transition to parenthood: Individual differences as a function of sex-role attitudes and changes in the division of household labor. *Journal of Marriage and the Family*, *52*, 475–486.

Mace, D., and Mace, V., (1959). *Marriage: East and west*. Garden City, NY: Dolphin Books.

Macklin, E. D. (1988). Cohabitation in the United States. In J. G. Wells (Ed.), *Current Issues in Marriage and the Family*, (4th ed.), pp. 61–76 New York: Macmillan.

Macklin, E. D. (1986). Nonmarital heterosexual cohabitation. In A. S. Skolnick and J. H. Skolnick (Eds.), *Family in Transition*, (5th ed.) pp. 210–231 Boston: Little, Brown and Company.

Macklin, E. D. (1980). Nontraditional family forms: A decade of research. *Journal of Marriage and the Family*, *42*, 905–922.

Macklin, E. D. (1974, November). Cohabitation in college: Going very steady. *Psychology Today*, pp. 53–59.

Mahoney, E. R. (1978). Gender and social class differences in changes in attitudes toward premarital coitus. *Sociology and Social Research*, *62*, 279–286.

Mangan, K. S. (1988, September 28). Sexually active students found failing to take precautions against AIDS. *The Chronicle of Higher Education*, *1*, pp. 32–33.

March of Dimes Birth Defects Foundation. (1990). STDs . . . How not to get them. (pamphlet).

Maret, E., and Finlay, B. (1984). The distribution of household labor among women in dual-earner families. *Journal of Marriage and the Family*, *46*, 357–364.

Margolin, L., and White, L. (1987). The continuing role of physical attractiveness in marriage. *Journal of Marriage and the Family*, *49*, 21–27.

Marino, V. (1990, April 14). Experts say role of women in family finance is still small. *The News and Courier/Evenig Post* (Charleston, SC), pp. 1C, 5C.

Martin, D. (1989, March 22). Singles bars: Not really gone, just forgotten. *The New York Times*, Section II, p. 1.

Martin, M. J., and Walters, J. (1982). Familial correlates of selected types of child abuse and neglect. *Journal of Marriage and the Family*, *44*, 267–276.

Martin, T. C., and Bumpass, L. L. (1989). Recent Trends in marital disruption. *Demography*, *26*, 37–51.

Mason, K. O., and Kuhlthau, K. (1989). Determinants of child care ideals among mothers of preschool-aged children. *Journal of Marriage and the Family*, *51*, 593–603.

Masters, W. H., and Johnson, V. E. (1966). *Human sexual response*. Boston: Little, Brown and Company.

Matthews, S. H., and Rosner, T. T. (1988). Shared filial responsibility. *Journal of Marriage and the Family*, *50*, 185–195.

May, K. A. (1982). Three phases of father involvement in pregnancy. *Nursing Research*, *31*, 337–342.

May, K. A. (1980). A typology of detachment/involvement styles adopted during pregnancy by first-time expectant fathers. *Western Journal of Nursing Research*, *2*, 445–453.

May, K. A., and Mahlmeister, L. R. (1990). *Comprehensive maternity nursing*. (2nd ed.). Philadelphia: Lippincott.

Mayhall, P. D., and Norgard, K. E. (1983). *Child Abuse and neglect: Sharing responsibility*. New York: John Wiley and Sons.

Mayseless, O. (1991). Adult attachment patterns and courtship violence. *Family Relations*, *40*, 21–28.

McBroom, W. H. (1987). Longitudinal change in sex role orientations: Differences between men and women. *Sex Roles*, *16*, 439–451.

McChesney, K. Y. (1990). An integrated model of economic and sociological theories of family poverty, 1947–1987. Department of Sociology, University of Missouri-St. Louis, St. Louis, Mo. 63121.

McCubbin, H. I., Joy, C. B., Cauble, A. E., Comeau, J. K., Patterson, J. M., Needle, R. H. (1980). Family stress and coping: A decade review. *Journal of Marriage and the Family, 42;* 855–871.

McCubbin, H. I., and Dahl, B. B. 1985. *Marriage and family: Individuals and life cycles.* New York: John Wiley and Sons.

McFalls, J. A., Jr. (1990). The risks of reproductive impairment in the later years of childbearing. *Annual Review of Sociology, 16,* 491–519.

McFalls, J. A., Jr. (1979). *Psychopathology and subfecundity.* New York: Academic Press.

McGhee, J. L. (1985). The effects of siblings on life satisfaction of the rural elderly. *Journal of Marriage and the Family, 47,* 85–91.

McHale, S. M., and Huston, T. L., (1985). The effect of the transition to parenthood on the marriage relationship: A longitudinal study. *Journal of Family Issues, 6,* 409–433.

McKim, M. K. (1987). Transition to what? New parents' problems in the first year. *Family Relations, 36,* 22–25.

McLanahan, S., and Adams, J. (1989). The effects of children on adults' psychological well-being: 1957–1976. *Social Forces, 68,* 124–146.

McLoyd, V. C. (1989). Socialization and development in a changing economy: The effects of paternal job and income loss on children. *American Psychologist, 44,* 293–302.

Meigs, C. D. (1848). *Females and their diseases; A series of letters to his class.* Philadelphia: Lea and Blanchard.

Menaghan, E. G. (1983). Marital stress and family transitions: A panel analysis. *Journal of Marriage and the Family, 45,* 371–386.

Menaghan, E. G. (1982). Measuring coping effectiveness: A panel analysis of marital problems and coping efforts. *Journal of Health and Social Behavior, 23,* 220–234.

Menaghan, E. G., and Parcel, T. L., (1990). Parental employment and family life: Research in the 1980s. *Journal of Marriage and the Family, 52,* 1079–1098.

Mennell, R. L., and Boykoff, T. M., (1988). *Community property in a nutshell.* (2nd ed.). St. Paul: West Publishing Co.

Mercer, R. T. (1986). *First-time motherhood: Experiences from teens to forties.* New York: Springer Publishing Co.

Meyer, M. H. (1990). Family status and poverty among older women: The gendered distribution of retirement income in the United States. *Social Problems, 37,* 551–563.

Miall, C. E. (1986). The stigma of involuntary childlessness. *Social Problems, 33,* 268–282.

Miall, C. E. (1987). The stigma of adoptive parent status: perceptions of community attitudes toward adoption and the experience of informal social sanctioning. *Family Relations, 36,* 34–39.

Mika, K., and Bloom, B. L. (1980). Adjustment to separation among former cohabitors. *Journal of Divorce, 4,* 45–66.

Milardo, R. M. (1987). Changes in social networks of women and men following divorce: A review. *Journal of Family Issues, 8,* 78–96.

Miller, B. C., and Bowen, S. L. (1982). Father-to-newborn attachment behavior in relation to prenatal classes and presence at delivery. *Family Relations, 31,* 71–78.

Miller, B. C., and Olson, T. D. (1988). Sexual attitudes and behavior of high school students in relation to background and contextual factors. *The Journal of Sex Research, 24,* 194–200.

Miller, J. A., and Norris, G., (1985, March). Who's minding our kids? *Redbook,* pp. 55–58.

Miller, L. F., and Moorman, J. E. (1989). Married-couple families with children. U.S. Bureau of the Census, Current Population Reports, Series P-23, No. 162, *Studies in Marriage and the Family,* pp. 27–36 Washington, DC: Government Printing Office.

Miller, R. S., and Lefcourt, H. M. (1982). The assessment of social intimacy. *Journal of Personality Assessment, 46,* 514–518.

Mintz, S., and Kellogg, S. (1988). *Domestic revolutions: A social history of American family life.* New York: The Free Press.

Mischel, W. (1966). A social learning view of sex differences in behavior. In E. E. Maccoby (Ed.), *The Development of Sex Differences.* (pp. 56–81) Stanford: Stanford University Press.

Mitchell, B. A., Wister, A. V., and Burch, T. K. (1989). The family environment and leaving the parental home. *Journal of Marriage and the Family, 51,* 605–613.

Modell, J. (1989). *Into one's own: From youth to adulthood in the United States, 1920–1975.* Berkeley: University of California Press.

Moeller, I., and Sherlock, B. J. (1981). Making it legal: A comparison of previously cohabiting and engaged newlyweds. *Journal of Sociology and Social Welfare, 8,* 97–110.

Moen P. (1985). Continuities and discontinuities in women's labor force activity. In G. H. Elder, Jr. (Ed.), *Life Course Dynamics.* (pp. 113–155) Ithaca: Cornell University Press.

Moen, P. (1983). Unemployment, Public Policy, and Families: Forecasts for the 1980s. *Journal of Marriage and the Family, 45,* 751–760.

Moen, P. (1979). Family impacts of the 1975 recession: Duration of unemployment. *Journal of Marriage and the Family, 41,* 561–572.

Moffatt, M. (1989). *Coming of age in New Jersey: College and American culture.* New Brunswick: Rutgers University Press.

Money, J. and Ehrhardt, A. A. (1975). Rearing of a sex-reassigned normal male infant after traumatic loss of the penis. In J. W. Petras (Ed.), *Sex: Male/Gender: Masculine: Selected Readings in Male Sexuality* (pp. 46–51) Port Washington, NY: Alfred Publishing Co., Inc.

Moore, K. A., Peterson, J. L., and Furstenberg, F. F. (1986). Parental attitudes and the occurrence of early sexual activity. *Journal of Marriage and the Family, 48,* 777–782.

Moore, K., Spain, D., and Bianchi, S. (1984). Working wives and mothers. In B. B. Hess and M. B. Sussman (Eds.), *Women and the Family: Two Decades of Change* (pp. 77–98) New York: Haworth.

Moreland, J. (1989). Age and change in the adult male sex role. In M. S. Kimmel and M. A. Messner (Eds.), *Men's Lives* (pp. 115–124) New York: Macmillan.

Morgan, E. S. (1966). *The Puritan family: Religion & domestic relations in seventeenth century New England*. New York: Harper & Row, Publishers.

Morgan, L. A. (1989). Economic well-being following marital termination: A comparison of widowed and divorced women. *Journal of Family Issues, 10,* 86–101.

Morgan, L. A. (1988). Outcomes of marital separation: A longitudinal test of predictors. *Journal of Marriage and the Family, 50,* 493–498.

Morgan, S. P., and Rindfuss, R. R. (1985). Marital disruption: Structural and temporal dimensions. *American Journal of Sociology, 90,* 1055–1077.

Morrow, K. B., and Sorell, G. T. (1989). Factors affecting self-esteem, depression, and negative behaviors in sexually abused female adolescents. *Journal of Marriage and the Family, 51,* 677–686.

Mortensen, C. D. (1972). *Communication: The study of human interaction*. New York: McGraw-Hill.

Muehlenhard, C. L., and Scardino, T. J. (1985). What will he think? Men's impressions of women who initiate dates and achieve academically. *Journal of Counseling Psychology, 32,* 560–569.

Muller, T., and Espenshade, T. J. (1985). *The fourth wave: California's newest immigrants*. Washington, DC: The Urban Institute Press.

Mullins, J. B. (1987). Authentic voices from parents of exceptional children. *Family Relations, 36,* 30–33.

Murgatroyd, L. (1985). The production of people and domestic labour revisited. In P. Close and R. Collins (Eds.), *Family and Economy in Modern Society* (pp. 49–62) London: Macmillan.

Murphy, P. A. (1986–87). Parental death in childhood and loneliness in young adults. *Omega, 17,* 219–228.

Murstein, B. I. (1986). *Paths to marriage*. Newbury Park, CA: Sage Publications.

Murstein, B. I., Chalpin, M. J., Heard, K. V., and Vyse, S. A. (1989). Sexual behavior, drugs, and relationship patterns on a college campus over thirteen years. *Adolescence, 24,* 125–139.

Nanda, S. (1990). *Neither man nor woman; The hijras of India*. Belmont, CA: Wadsworth.

National Center for Health Statistics. (1988). *Vital statistics of the United States, 1986,* Vol. II, Mortality, Part A. DHHS Pub. No. (PHS) 88-1122. Public Health Service, Washington. U.S. Government Printing Office.

National Center for Health Statistics. (1990). *Vital statistics of the United States, 1986,* Vol. III, Marriage and Divorce. DHHS Pub. No. (PHS) 90-1103. Public Health Service, Washington. U.S. Government Printing Office.

Neal, A. G., Groat, H. T., and Wicks, J. W. (1989). Attitudes about having children: A study of 600 couples in the early years of marriage. *Journal of Marriage and the Family, 51,* 313–328.

Neale, A. V., Tilley, B. C., and Vernon, S. W. (1980). Marital status, delay in seeking treatment and survival from breast cancer. *Social Science and Medicine, 23,* 305–312.

Nelson, M. K. (1983). Working-class women, middle-class women, and models of childbirth. *Social Problems, 30,* 284–297.

Nelson, M. K. (1986). Birth and social class. In P. S. Eakins (Ed.), *The American Way of Birth* (pp. 142–174) Philadelphia: Temple University Press.

New York Times, The. (1990a, January 30). Baby's first-year costs won't approach $5,774. p. A22.

New York Times, The. (1990b, February 8). Baby costs plenty. p. A28.

Newcomb, M. D. (1986). Sexual behavior of cohabitors: A comparison of three independent samples. *The Journal of Sex Research, 22,* 492–513.

Newcomb, M. D. (1983). Relationship qualities of those who live together. *Alternative Lifestyles, 6,* 78–102.

Newcomb, M. D., and Bentler, P. M. (1980a). Cohabitation before marriage: A comparison of married couples who did and did not cohabit. *Alternative Lifestyles, 3,* 65–85.

Newcomb, M. D., and Bentler, P. M. (1980b). Assessment of personality and demographic aspects of cohabitation and marital success. *Journal of Personality Assessment, 44,* 11–24.

Newcomb, P. R. (1979). Cohabitation in America: An assessment of Consequences. *Journal of Marriage and the Family, 41,* 597–603.

Newcomer, S., and Udry, J. R. (1985). Parent-child communication and adolescent sexual behavior. *Family Planning Perspectives, 17,* 169–174.

Newman, K. S. (1988). *Falling from grace: The experience of downward mobility in the American middle class*. New York: Vintage.

Newsweek. (1987, October 26). Not tonight, dear. pp. 64–66.

Nichols, M. P. (1988). *The power of the family*. New York: Simon and Schuster.

Nicholas, S. C., Price, A. M., and Rubin, R. (1979). *Rights and wrongs: Women's struggle for legal equality*. Old Westbury, NY: The Feminist Press.

Nock, S. L., and Kingston, P. W. (1988). Time with children: The impact of couples' work-time commitments. *Social Forces, 67,* 59–85.

Noller, P. (1982). Channel consistency and inconsistency in the communications of married couples. *Journal of Personality and Social Psychology, 43,* 732–741.

Noller, P., and Fitzpatrick, M. A. (1990). Marital communication in the eighties. *Journal of Marriage and the Family, 52,* 832–843.

Norton, A. J., and Glick, P. C. 1981 (1979). Marital instability in America: Past, present, and future. In P. J. Stein

(Ed.), *Single Life: Unmarried Adults in Social Context* (pp. 57–69) New York: St. Martin's Press.

Norton, A. J., and Miller, L. F. (1991). Marriage, divorce and remarriage in the 1990s. Presented at the Annual Meetings of the American Public Health Association, Atlanta, GA, November.

Norton, A. J., and Moorman, J. E. (1987). Current trends in marriage and divorce among American women. *Journal of Marriage and the Family, 49*, 3–14.

Norton, R. (1983). Measuring marital quality: A critical look at the dependent variable. *Journal of Marriage and the Family, 45*, 141–151.

NOW Legal Defense and Education Fund, and Cherow-O'Leary, R. (1987). *The state-by-state guide to women's legal rights*. New York: McGraw-Hill.

Nyberg, C. R. (1989). *Subject compilation of state laws 1985–1988: An annotated bibliography*. Copyright Cheryl R. Nyberg. Urbana, Illinois.

O'Connell, M., and Bachu, A. (1990). *Who's minding the kids? Child care arrangements: Winter 1986–87*. Current Population Reports, Series P-70, No. 20. Washington, DC: Government Printing Office.

O'Connell, M., and Bloom, D. E. (1987). Juggling jobs and babies: America's child care challenge. *Population Trends and Public Policy*, No. 12. Washington, DC: Population Reference Bureau.

O'Flaherty, K. M., and Eells, L. W. (1988). Courtship behavior of the remarried. *Journal of Marriage and the Family, 50*, 499–506.

O'Hare, W. (1990, May). What does it take to get along? *American Demographics, 12* pp. 36–39.

Oakley, A. (1980). *Becoming a mother*. New York: Schocken Books.

Oboler, R. S. (1980). Is the female husband a man? Woman/woman marriage among the Nandi of Kenya. *Ethonology, 19*, 69–88.

Olson, D. H., McCubbin, H. I., Barnes, H. L., Larsen, A. S., Muxen, M J., and Wilson, M. A. (1983). *Families: What makes them work*. Beverly Hills, CA: Sage Publishing Company.

Olson, D. H., Russell, C. S., and Sprenkle, D. H. (1983). Circumplex model of marital and family systems: VI. Theoretical update. *Family Process, 22*, 69–83.

Oppenheimer, V. K. (1976). *The female labor force in the United States*. Westport, CT: Greenwood Press.

Oppenheimer, V. K. (1982). *Work and the family: A study in social demography*. New York: Academic Press.

Oppenheimer, V. K. (1988). A theory of marriage timing. *American Journal of Sociology, 94*, 563–591.

Orleans, M., Palisi, B. J., and Caddell, D. (1989). Marriage adjustment and satisfaction of stepfathers: Their feelings and perceptions of decision making and stepchildren relations. *Family Relations, 38*, 371–377.

Orshansky, M. (1968). Counting the poor: Another look at the poverty profile and author's note: Who was poor in 1966. In L. A. Ferman, J. L. Kornbluh, and A. Haber (Eds.), *Poverty in America: A Book of Readings* (pp. 67–115) Ann Arbor: University of Michigan.

Ory, M. G. (1978). The decision to parent or not: Normative and structural components. *Journal of Marriage and the Family, 40*, 531–539.

Oster, S. M. (1987). A note on the determinants of alimony. *Journal of Marriage and the Family, 49*, 81–86.

Parke, R., Jr., and Glick, P. C. (1967). Prospective changes in marriage and the family. *Journal of Marriage and the Family, 29*, 249–256.

Parnes, H. S. (1985). Conclusion. In H. S. Parnes, J. E. Crowley, R. J. Haurin, L. J. Less, W. R. Morgan, F. L. Mott, and G. Nestel, *Retirement among American men* (pp. 290–224) Lexington: D.C. Heath.

Parnes, H. S., and L. J. Less. (1985c). The volume and pattern of retirements, 1966–1981. In H. S. Parnes, J. E. Crowley, R. J. Haurin, L. J. Less, W. R. Morgan, F. L. Mott, and G. Nestel, *Retirement among American men*. (pp. 57–77) Lexington: D.C. Heath.

Parnes, H. S., and Less, L. J. (1985b). Shunning retirement: The experience of full-time workers. In H. S. Parnes, J. E. Crowley, R. J. Haurin, L. J. Less, W. R. Morgan, F. L. Mott, and G. Nestel, *Retirement among American men* (pp. 175–208) Lexington: D.C. Heath.

Parnes, H. S., and Less, L. J. (1985a). Economic well-being in retirement. In H. S. Parnes, J. E. Crowley, R. J. Haurin, L. J. Less, W. R. Morgan, F. L. Mott, and G. Nestel, *Retirement among American men*. pp. 91–118. Lexington: D.C. Heath.

Pasley, B. K. and Ihinger-Tallman, M. (1989). Boundary ambiguity in remarriage: Does ambiguity differentiate degree of marital adjustment and integration? *Family Relations, 38*, 46–52.

Peck, K. (1988, September). When 'Family' is not a household word. *The Progressive*, pp. 16–17.

Perlman, D., and Fehr, B. (1987). The development of intimate relationships. In D. Perlman and S. Duck (Eds.), *Intimate Relationships: Development, Dynamics, and Deterioration* (pp. 13–42). Newbury Park, CA: Sage.

Perry-Jenkins, M., and Crouter, A. C. (1990). Men's provider-role attitudes: Implications for household work and marital satisfaction. *Journal of Family Issues, 11*, 136–156.

Pershing, B. (1979). Family policies: A component of management in the home and family setting. *Journal of Marriage and the Family, 41*, 573–581.

Peterman, D. J., Ridley, C. A., and Anderson, S. M. (1974). A comparison of cohabiting and noncohabiting college students. *Journal of Marriage and the Family, 36*, 344–354.

Peterson, G. H., Mehl, L. E., and Leiderman, P. H. (1979).

The role of some birth-related variables in father attachment. *American Journal of Orthopsychiatry, 49,* 330–338.

Peterson, G. W., and Rollins, B. C. (1987). Parent-child socialization. In M. B. Sussman and S. K. Steinmetz (Eds.), *Handbook of Marriage and the Family* (pp. 471–507) New York: Plenum.

Peterson, K. S. (1989, June 6). Sex survey: Many too tired to tango. *Argus Leader* (Sioux Falls, SD) p. 9A.

Peterson, N. L. (1982). *The ever single woman.* New York: Quill.

Phillips, R. (1988). *Putting asunder: A history of divorce in western society.* Cambridge: Cambridge University Press.

Pillemer, K., and Finkelhor, D. (1988). The prevalence of elder abuse: A random sample survey. *The Gerontologist, 28,* 51–57.

Pincus, J., with Swenson, N. and Poor, B. (1984). Pregnancy. In The Boston Women's Health Book Collective (Eds.). *The New Our Bodies, Ourselves* (pp. 329–360) New York: Simon and Schuster.

Piotrkowski, C. S. (1979). *Work and the family system.* New York: The Free Press.

Pistrang, N. (1984). Women's work involvement and experience of new motherhood. *Journal of Marriage and the Family, 46,* 433–447.

Pittman, J. F., and Lloyd, S. A. (1988). Quality of family life, social support, and stress. *Journal of Marriage and the Family, 50,* 53–67.

Pittman, J. F., Wright, C. A., and Lloyd, S. A. (1989). Predicting parenting difficulty. *Journal of Family Issues, 10,* 267–286.

Pitts, J. M. (1986). *Managing your personal finances: The principles of managing your finances.* United States Department of Agriculture, Extension Service, Agricultural Research Service. Home and Garden Bulletin No. HG-245-1. Washington, DC: Government Printing Office.

Pleck, J. H. (1985). *Working wives/working husbands.* Beverly Hills, CA: Sage.

Pogrebin, L. C. (1983). *Family politics: Love and power on an intimate frontier.* New York: McGraw-Hill.

Pogrebin, L. C. (1981). *Growing up free.* New York: Bantam.

Pollitt, K. (1991, April 7). Hers: The smurfette principle. *New York Times Magazine* pp. 22, 24.

Porter, N. L., and Christopher, F. S. (1984). Infertility: Towards an awareness of a need among family life practitioners. *Family Relations, 33,* 309–315.

Porter, S. (1975). *Sylvia Porter's money book.* New York: Doubleday.

Porterfield, E. (1978). *Black and white mixed marriages: An ethnographic study of black-white families.* Chicago: Nelson-Hall.

Postel, J. P. (1990). Housing discrimination: Cohabitation. *Chicago Daily Law Bulletin, 136,* (190), 1, 14.

Pratt, W. F., Mosher, W. D., Bachrach, C. A., and Horn, M.

C. (1984). *Understanding U.S. fertility: Findings from the national survey of family growth, cycle III.* Vol. 39(5). Washington, DC: Population Reference Bureau, Inc.

Presser, H. B. (1988). Shift work and child care among young dual-earner American parents. *Journal of Marriage and the Family, 50,* 133–148.

Preston, S. H., and Richards, A. T. (1975). The influence of women's work opportunities on marriage rates. *Demography, 12,* 209–222.

Price, S. J., and McKenry, P. C. (1988). *Divorce.* Newbury Park, CA: Sage Publications.

Pritchard, J. A., and MacDonald, P. C. (1976). *Williams obstetrics,* (15th ed.). New York: Appleton-Century-Crofts.

Purcell, P., and Stewart, L. (1990). Dick and Jane in 1989. *Sex Roles, 22,* 177–185.

Questions about AIDS. (1989, March). *Consumer Reports,* p. 142.

Quinn, W. H. (1983). Personal and family adjustment in later life. *Journal of Marriage and the Family, 45,* 57–73.

Rainwater, L. (1965). *Family design: Marital sexuality, family size, and contraception.* Chicago: Aldine Publishing Company.

Rape and marriage. (1990, February). *New Statesman & Society,* p. 5.

Raschke, H. J. 1987. Divorce. In M. B. Sussman and S. K. Steinmetz (Eds.), *Handbook of Marriage and the Family* (pp. 597–624). New York: Plenum.

Rawlings, S. W. (1989). Single parents and their children. In *Studies in marriage and the family,* U.S. Bureau of the Census, Current Population Reports, Series P-23, No. 162. (pp. 13–25) Washington, DC: Government Printing Office.

Reamy, K. J., and White, S. E. (1987). Sexuality in the puerperium: A review. *Archives of Sexual Behavior, 16,* 165–186.

Reilly, T. W., Entwisle, D. R., and Doering, S. G. (1987). Socialization into parenthood: A longitudinal study of the development of self-evaluations. *Journal of Marriage and the Family, 49,* 295–308.

Reiss, I. L. (1986). A sociological journey into sexuality. *Journal of Marriage and the Family, 48,* 233–242.

Reiss, I. L. (1970). Premarital sex as deviant behavior: An application of current approaches to deviance. *American Sociological Review, 35,* 78–87.

Reiss, I. L., and Miller, B. C. (1979). Heterosexual permissiveness: A theortical analysis. In W. R. Burr, R. Hill, F. I. Nye, and I. L. Reiss (Eds.), *Contemporary theories about the family: Research based theories,* Volume 1 (pps. 57–100) New York: The Free Press.

Rempel, J. (1985). Childless Elderly: What Are They Missing? *Journal of Marriage and the Family, 47,* 343–348.

Rexroat, C., and Shehan, C. (1987). The family life cycle and spouses' time in housework. *Journal of Marriage and the Family, 49,* 737–750.

Rice, F. P. (1983). *Contemporary marriage.* Boston: Allyn and Bacon.

Rich, A. (1976). *Of woman born: Motherhood as experience and institution.* New York: Norton.

Riche, M. F. (1987, February). Mysterious young adults. *American Demographics, 9.* pp. 38–43.

Riche, M. F. (1988, November). The postmarital society. *American Demographics, 10,* pp. 22–26, 60.

Richmond-Abbott, M. (1983). Heredity, environment, or both? Similarities and differences between the sexes. In M. Richmond-Abbott (Ed.), *Masculine and Feminine: Sex Roles over the Life Cycle* (pp. 41–87) Reading, MA.: Addison-Wesley.

Rindfuss, R. R., Morgan, S. P., and Swicegood, G. (1988). *First births in America: Changes in the timing of parenthood.* Berkeley: University of California Press.

Risman, B. J., Hill, C. T., Rubin, Z., and Peplau, L. A. (1981). Living together in college: Implications for courtship. *Journal of Marriage and the Family, 43,* 77–83.

Robertson, I. (1987). *Sociology.* New York: Worth Publishers, Inc.

Robertson, J. F. (1977). Grandmotherhood: A study of role conceptions. *Journal of Marriage and the Family, 39,* 165–174.

Robinson, I. E., and Jedlicka, D. (1982). Change in sexual attitudes and behavior of college students from 1965 to 1980: A research note. *Journal of Marriage and the Family, 44,* 237–240.

Robinson, I. E., King, K. and Balswick, J. O. (1972). The premarital sexual revolution among college females. *Family Coordinator, 21,* 189–194.

Robinson, I. E., King, K., Dudley, C. J., and Clune, F. J. (1968). Change in sexual behavior and attitudes of college students. *The Family Coordinator, 17,* 119–123.

Robinson, I., Ziss, K., Ganza, B., Katz, S., and Robinson, E. (1991). Twenty years of the sexual revolution, 1965–1985: An update. *Journal of Marriage and the Family, 53,* 216–220.

Robinson, J. (1978). *An American legal almanac; Law in all states: Summary and update.* Dobbs Ferry, NY: Oceana Publications.

Robinson, J. P. (1988, December). Who's doing the housework? *American Demographics, 10* pp. 24–28, 63.

Robinson. J. P. (1989, February). When the going gets tough. *American Demographics, 11,* p. 50.

Rodgers, R. H. and Conrad, L. M. (1986). Courtship for remarriage: Influences on family reorganization after divorce. *Journal of Marriage and the Family, 48,* 767–775.

Rodgers, W. L., and Thornton, A. (1985). Changing patterns of first marriage in the United States. *Demography, 22,* 265–279.

Rodin, M. (1985). The world of singles. In J. M. Henslin (Ed.), *Marriage and Family in a Changing Society,* Second Edition (pp. 261–269) New York: The Free Press.

Roff, L., and Atherton C. R. (1989). *Promoting successful aging.* Chicago: Nelson-Hall.

Rollins, B. C., and Cannon K. L. (1974). Marital satisfaction over the family life cycle: A reevaluation. *Journal of Marriage and the Family, 36,* 271–282.

Rollins, B. C., and Galligan, R. (1978). The developing child and marital satisfaction of parents. In R. M. Lerner and G. B. Spainer (Eds.), *Child Influences on Marital and Family Interactions: A Life-span Perspective* (pp. 71–105) New York: Academic Press.

Rollins, B. C., and Thomas, D. L. (1979). Parental support, power, and control techniques in the socialization of children. In W. R. Burr, R. Hill, F. I. Nye, and I. L. Reiss (Eds.), *Contemporary Theories about the Family: Research-based Theories,* Vol. 1, (pp. 317–364) New York: The Free Press.

Rome, E. (1984). Anatomy and physiology of sexuality and reproduction. In The Boston Women's Health Book Collective, *The New Our Bodies, Ourselves,* (pp. 203–219) New York: Simon and Schuster.

Rooks, J. P., Weatherby, N. L., Ernst, E. K. M., Stapleton, S., Rosen, D., and Rosenfield, A. (1989). Outcomes of care in birth centers. *The New England Journal of Medicine, 321*(26), 1804–1811.

Roscoe, B., and Kruger, T. L. (1990). AIDS: Late adolescents' knowledge and its influence on sexual behavior. *Adolescence, 25,* 39–48.

Rosen, E. I. (1987). *Bitter choices: Blue-collar women in and out of work.* Chicago: University of Chicago Press.

Rosenberg, M. (1985). Self-concept and psychological well-being in adolescence. In R. L. Leahy (Ed.), *The Development of the Self* (pp. 205–246) Orlando: Academic Press.

Rosenfield, S. (1989.) The effects of women's employment: Personal control and sex differences in mental health. *Journal of Health and Social Behavior, 30,* 77–91.

Ross, C. E. (1987). The division of labor at home. *Social Forces, 65,* 816–833.

Ross, C. E., and Mirowsky, J. (1988). Child care and emotional adjustment to wives' employment. *Journal of Health and Social Behavior, 29,* 127–138.

Ross, C. E., Mirowsky, J., and Huber, J. (1983). Dividing work, sharing work, and in-between: Marriage patterns and depression. *American Sociological Review, 48,* 809–823.

Ross, J. A. (1989). Contraception: Short-term vs. long-term failure rates. *Family Planning Perspectives, 21,* 275–277.

Rossi, A. S. (1968). Transition to parenthood. *Journal of Marriage and the Family, 30,* 26–39.

Rothman, B. K. (1982). *In labor: Women and power in the birthplace.* New York: Norton.

Rothman, B. K. (1984). Women, health, and medicine. In J.

Freeman (Ed.), *Women: A Feminist Perspective,* (3rd ed.). (pp. 70–80) Palo Alto, CA: Mayfield.

Rothman, B. K. (1986). The social construction of birth. In P. S. Eakins (Ed.), *The American Way of Birth* (pp. 104–118) Philadelphia: Temple University Press.

Rowe, J. W., and Kahn, R. L. (1987). Human aging: Usual and successful. *Science, 237,* 143–149.

Rowe, D. C., Rodgers, J. L., and Meseck-Bushey, S. (1989). An "epidemic" model of sexual intercourse prevalences for black and white adolescents. *Social Biology, 36,* 127–145.

Rubenstein, C. (1988, March). Is there sex after baby? *Parenting Magazine,* pp. 76, 78, 80, 82, 84.

Rubenstein, C. (1981, May). Money & self-esteem, relationships, secrecy, envy, satisfaction. *Psychology Today, 15,* pp. 29–44.

Rubenstein, C., and Tavris, C. (1987, September). Special survey results: 26,000 women reveal the secrets of intimacy. *Redbook,* pp. 147–149, 214, 216.

Rubin, A. M., and Adams, J. R. (1986). Outcomes of sexually open marriages. *The Journal of Sex Research, 22,* 311–319.

Rubin, J. Z., Provenzano, F. J., and Luria, Z. (1974). The eye of the beholder: Parents' views on sex of newborns. *American Journal of Orthopsychiatry, 44,* 512–519.

Rubin, L. B. (1989). Blue-collar marriage and the sexual revolution. In A. S. Skolnick and J. H. Skolnick (Eds.), *Family in Transition,* (6th ed.) (pps. 203–218) Glenview, IL: Scott, Foresman and Company.

Rubin, L. B. (1983). *Intimate strangers: Men and women together.* New York: Harper and Row.

Rubin, L. B. (1979). *Women of a certain age: The midlife search for self.* New York: Harper and Row.

Rubin, L. B. (1976). *Worlds of pain: Life in the working-class family.* New York: Basic Books.

Ryan, K. J. (1988). Giving birth in America, 1988. *Family Planning Perspectives, 20,* 298–301.

Ryan, M. P. (1979). *Womanhood in America.* (2nd Ed.). New York: New Viewpoints.

Ryder, N. B. (1965). The cohort as a concept in the study of social change. *American Sociological Review, 30,* 843–861.

Sabatelli, R. M., Meth, R. L., and Gavazzi, S. M. (1988). Factors mediating the adjustment to involuntary childlessness. *Family Relations, 37,* 338–343.

Sacks, S. R., and Donnenfeld, P. B. (1984). Parental choice of alternative birth environments and attitudes toward childrearing philosophy. *Journal of Marriage and the Family, 46,* 469–475.

Saluter, A. F. (1989). Singleness in America. U. S. Bureau of the Census, Current Population Reports, Series P-23, No. 162, *Studies in Marriage and the Family,* pp. 1–12. Washington, DC: Government Printing Office.

Sánchez-Ayéndez, M. (1988). The Puerto Rican American family. In C. H. Mindel, R. W. Habenstein, and R. Wright, Jr. (Eds.), *Ethnic Families in America,* (3rd ed.). (pp. 173–195) New York: Elsevier.

Sandefur, G. D., and McKinnell, T., (1986). American Indian intermarriage. *Social Science Research, 15(4),* 347–371.

Sanford, W., with Hawley, N. P., and McGee, E. (1984). Sexuality. In The Boston Women's Health Book Collective, *The New Our Bodies, Ourselves* (pp. 164–197) New York: Simon and Schuster.

Saunders, R. B., and Robins, E., (1989). Changes in the marital relationship during the first pregnancy. In P. N. Stern (Ed.), *Pregnancy and Parenting* (pp. 13–29) New York: Hemisphere.

Scarr, S. (1985, January). A child-care checklist: Choosing an affordable, safe, and happy environment. *Ms.,* pp. 95–98.

Schafer, R. B., and Keith, P. M. (1981). Equity in marital roles across the family life cycle. *Journal of Marriage and the Family 43,* 359–367.

Schaninger, C. M., and Buss, W. C. (1986). A longitudinal comparison of consumption and finance handling between happily married and divorced couples. *Journal of Marriage and the Family, 48,* 129–136.

Schmitt, E. (1990, April 13). Collapse in region's housing market is taking a toll on owner's emotions. *New York Times* p. B1, B4.

Schoen, R., Urton, W., Woodrow, K., and Baj, J. (1985). Marriage and divorce in twentieth century American cohorts. *Demography, 22,* 101–114.

Schoen, R., Greenblatt, H. N., and Mielke, R. B. (1975). California's experience with non-adversary divorce. *Demography, 12,* 223–243.

Schoen, R., and Kluegel, J. R. (1988). The widening gap in black and white marriage rates: The impact of population composition and differential marriage propensities. *American Sociological Review, 53,* 895–907.

Schroeder, L. O. (1986). A rose by any other name: Postmarital right to use maiden name: 1934–1982. *Sociology and Social Research, 70(4),* 290–293.

Schröter, M. (Translated by J. Bleicher). (1987). Marriage. *Theory, Culture, & Society, 4(2–3),* 317–322.

Schumm, W. R., Barnes, H. L., Bollman, S. R., Jurich, A. P., and Bugaighis, M. A. (1986). Self-disclosure and marital satisfaction revisited. *Family Relations, 35,* 241–247.

Schumm, W. R., and Bugaighis, M. A. (1986). Marital quality over the marital career: Alternative explanations. *Journal of Marriage and the Family, 48,* 165–168.

Science Impact. (1988a). A sex drug. 2(2), 2.

Science Impact. (1988b). The other epidemic. 2(2), 8.

Seccombe, K. (1991). Assessing the costs and benefits of children: Gender comparisons among childfree husbands and wives. *Journal of Marriage and the Family, 53,* 191–202.

Seccombe, K., and Lee, G. R. (1986). Gender differences in retirement satisfaction and its antecedents. *Research on Aging, 8,* 426–440.

Selby, J. W., and Calhoun, L. G. (1981). Sexuality during pregnancy. In P. Ahmed (Ed.), *Pregnancy, Childbirth, and Parenthood.* (pp. 55–77) New York: Elsevier.

Seligman, J. (1992, February 10). A condom for women moves one step closer to reality. *Newsweek,* p. 45.

Seligman, J. (1990, winter/spring). Variations on a theme. *Newsweek: The 21st Century Family.* (special ed.). pp. 38–46.

Seltzer, J. A., and Kalmuss, D. (1988). Socialization and stress explanations for spouse abuse. *Social Forces, 67,* 473–491.

Seltzer, J. A., Schaeffer, N. C., and Charng, H. (1989). Family ties after divorce: The relationship between visiting and paying child support. *Journal of Marriage and the Family, 51,* 1013–1032.

Shannon, G. W., Pyle, G. F., and Bashur, R. L. (1990). *The geography of AIDS: Origins and course of an epidemic.* New York: The Guilford Press.

Shapiro, J., and Tittle, K. (1990). Maternal adaptation to child disability in a Hispanic population. *Family Relations, 39,* 179–185.

Shaw, S. M. (1988). Gender differences in the definition and perception of household labor. *Family Relations, 37,* 333–337.

Shelton, B. A. (1990). The distribution of household tasks: Does wife's employment status make a difference? *Journal of Family Issues, 11,* 115–135.

Shelton, B. A. (1987). Variations in divorce rates by community size: A test of the social integration explanation. *Journal of Marriage and the Family, 49,* 827–832.

Sherman, L. W., and Berk, R. A. (1984). The specific deterrent effects of arrest for domestic assault. *American Sociological Review, 49,* 261–272.

Shorter, E. (1975). *The making of the modern family.* New York: Basic Books, Inc.

Shostak, M. (1981). *Nisa—The life and words of a !Kung woman.* Cambridge, MA: Harvard University Press.

Shostak, A. B. (1987). Singlehood. In M. B. Sussman and S. K. Steinmetz (Eds.), *Handbook of Marriage and the Family* (pp. 355–367) New York: Plenum.

Shriver, J. (1989, June). Financial hardship affects one-fourth of American families. *The Gallup Report,* No. 285, pp. 19–22.

Sidel, R. (1986). *Women and children last: The plight of poor women in affluent America.* New York: Viking.

Simon, A. (1989). Promiscuity as sex difference. *Psychological Reports, 64,* 802.

Simon, B. L. (1987). *Never married women.* Philadelphia: Temple University Press.

Singh, B. K. (1980). Trends in attitudes toward premarital sexual relations. *Journal of Marriage and the Family, 42,* 387–393.

Skolnick, A. S. (1983). *The intimate environment: Exploring marriage and the family.* (3rd ed.). Boston: Little, Brown.

Smith, J. P. (1988). Poverty and the family. In G. D. Sandefur and M. Tienda (Eds.), *Divided Opportunities: Minorities, Poverty, and Social Policy* (pp. 141–172) New York: Plenum.

Smith, K. F., and Bengtson, V. L. (1979). Positive consequences of institutionalization: Solidarity between elderly parents and their middle-aged children. *The Gerontologist, 19,* 438–447.

Smith, T. (1991). Personal communication. Data for marital intercourse, from General Social Surveys of National Opinion Research Center. Pool data from 1989, 1990, 1991.

Snowden, L. R., Schott, T. L., Awalt, S. J., and Gillis-Knox, J. (1988). Marital satisfaction in pregnancy: Stability and change. *Journal of Marriage and the Family, 50,* 325–333.

Society. (1973). Humanizing the meat market. *11*(1), 11.

Soloway, N. M., and Smith, R. M. (1987). Antecedents of late birthtiming decisions of men and women in dual-career marriages. *Family Relations, 36,* 258–262.

Sonenstein, F. L., Pleck, J. H., and Ku, L. C. (1989). Sexual activity, condom use and AIDS awareness among adolescent males. *Family Planning Perspectives, 21,* 152–158.

Sorrentino, C. (1990, March). The changing family in international perspective. *Monthly Labor Review,* pp. 41–58.

South Dakota Codified Laws, Annotated, vol. 9A, 1991 Pocket Supplement. (1991). State of South Dakota.

South, S. J., and Spitze, G. (1986). Determinants of divorce over the marital life course. *American Sociological Review, 51,* 583–590.

Spanier, G. B. (1983). Married and unmarried cohabitation in the United States: 1980. *Journal of Marriage and the Family, 45,* 277–288.

Spanier, G. B. (1976). Measuring dyadic adjustment: New scales for assessing the quality of marriage and similar dyads. *Journal of Marriage and the Family, 38,* 15–28.

Spanier, G. B. (1975). Sexualization and premarital sexual behavior. *The Family Coordinator, 24,* 33–41.

Spanier, G. B. and Furstenberg, F. F., Jr. (1987). Remarriage and reconstituted families. In M. B. Sussman and S. K. Steinmetz (Eds.), *Handbook of Marriage and the Family* (pp. 419–434) New York: Plenum.

Spanier, G. B. and Furstenberg, F. F., Jr. (1982). Remarriage after divorce: A longitudinal analysis of well-being. *Journal of Marriage and the Family, 44,* 709–720.

Spanier, G. B., and Glick, P. C. (1981). Marital instability in the United States: Some correlates and recent changes. *Family Relations, 30,* 329–338.

Spanier, G. B., Lewis, R. A., and Cole, C. L. (1975). Marital adjustment over the family life cycle: The issue of curvilinearity. *Journal of Marriage and the Family, 37,* 263–275.

Spanier, G. B., and Margolis, R. L. (1983). Marital separation and extramarital sexual behavior. *The Journal of Sex Research, 19*(1), 23–48.

Spector, I. P., and Carey, M. P. (1990). Incidence and prevalence of the sexual dysfunctions: A critical review of the empirical literature. *Archives of Sexual Behavior, 19,* 389–408.

Spitze, G. (1988). Women's employment and family relations: A review. *Journal of Marriage and the Family, 50,* 595–618.

Spitze, G., and South, S. J. (1985). Women's employment, time expenditure, and divorce. *Journal of Family Issues, 6,* 307–329.

Spock, B. M. (1957). *The common sense book of baby and child care.* New York: Duell, Sloan and Pearce.

Sporakowski, M. J., and Hughston, G. A. (1978). Prescriptions for happy marriage: Adjustments and satisfactions of couples married for 50 or more years. *Family Coordinator, 27,* 321–327.

Spreitzer, E., and Riley, L. E. (1974). Factors associated with singlehood. *Journal of Marriage and the Family, 36,* 533–542.

Stacey, J. (1990). *Brave new families: Stories of domestic upheaval in late twentieth century America.* New York: Basic Books.

Stack, S. (1980). The effects of marital dissolution on suicide. *Journal of Marriage and the Family, 42,* 83–92.

Stafford, R., Backman, E., and Dibona, P. (1977). The division of labor among cohabiting and married couples. *Journal of Marriage and the Family, 39,* 43–57.

Staines, G. L. (1986). Men's work schedules and family life. In R. A. Lewis and M. B. Sussman (Eds.), *Men's Changing Roles in the Family* (pp. 43–65) New York: Haworth.

Staples, R. (1988). The black American family. In C. H. Mindel, R. W. Habenstein, and R. Wright, Jr. (Eds.), *Ethnic Families in America,* (3rd ed.). (pp. 303–324) New York: Elsevier.

Starr, R. H. (1988). Physical abuse of children. In V. B. Van Hasselt, R. L. Morrison, A. S. Bellack, and M. Hersen (Eds.), *Handbook of Family Violence* (pp. 119–155) New York: Plenum Press.

Stauffer, B. (1988, January). Getting a grip on your spending. *Changing Times,* pp. 45–48.

Stein, P. J. (1981). Understanding single adulthood. In P. J. Stein (Ed.), *Single Life: Unmarried Adults in Social Context* (pp. 9–21) New York: St. Martin's Press.

Stein, P. J. (1976). *Single.* Englewood Cliffs, NJ: Prentice-Hall.

Stelzer, C., Desmond, S. M., and Price, J. H. (1987). Physical attractiveness and sexual activity of college students. *Psychological Reports, 60,* 567–573.

Stets, J. E. (1990). Verbal and physical aggression in marriage.

Journal of Marriage and the Family, 52, 501–514.

Stets, J. E., and Henderson, D. A. (1991). Contextual factors surrounding conflict resolution while dating: Results from a national study. *Family Relations, 40,* 29–36.

Stets, J. E., and Straus, M. (1990). Gender differences in reporting marital violence and its medical and psychological consequences. In M. A. Straus and R. J. Gelles (Eds.), *Physical Violence in American Families: Risk Factors and Adaptations to Violence in 8,145 Families* (pp. 151–165) New Brunswick, NJ: Transaction Press.

Stinnett, N., and DeFrain, J. (1985). *Secrets of strong families.* Boston: Little, Brown and Company.

Stoller, E. P. (1983). Parental caregiving by adult children. *Journal of Marriage and the Family, 45,* 851–858.

Straus, M. A. (1979). Measuring intrafamily conflict and violence: The conflict tactics (CT) scales. *Journal of Marriage and the Family, 41,* 75–88.

Straus, M. A., and Gelles, R. J. (1986). Societal change and change in family violence from 1975 to 1985 as revealed by two national surveys. *Journal of Marriage and the Family, 48,* 465–479.

Straus, M. A., Gelles, R. J., and Steinmetz, S. (1989). The marriage license as a hitting license. In A. S. Skolnick and J. H. Skolnick (Eds.), *Family in Transition,* (6th ed.). (pp. 301–314) Glenview, IL: Scott, Foresman and Company.

Straus, M. A., and Smith, C. (1990). Family patterns and child abuse. In M. A. Straus and R. J. Gelles (Eds.), *Physical Violence in American Families: Risk Factors and Adaptations to Violence in 8,145 Families* (pp. 245–261) New Brunswick, NJ: Transaction Publishers.

Strobino, D. M., and Sirageldin, I. (1981). Racial differences in early marriage in the United States. *Social Science Quarterly, 62,* 758–766.

Stuart, F. M., Hammond, D. C., and Pett, M. A. (1987). Inhibited sexual desire in women. *Archives of Sexual Behavior, 16*(2), 91–106.

Suitor, J. J. (1991). Marital quality and satisfaction with the division of household labor across the family life cycle. *Journal of Marriage and the Family, 53,* 221–230.

Sullivan, J. F. (1990, February 1). Top New Jersey court widens meaning of 'family' to students. *New York Times* p. B6.

Sunley, R. (1955). Early nineteenth century American literature on child rearing. In M. Mead and M. Wolfenstein (Eds.), *Childhood in Contemporary Cultures* (pp. 150–167) Chicago: University of Chicago Press.

Sweet, J. A., and Bumpass, L. L. (1987). *American families and households.* New York: Russell Sage Foundation.

Swensen, C. H., Eskew, R. W., and Kohlhepp, K. A. (1981). Stage of family life cycle, ego development, and the marriage relationship. *Journal of Marriage and the Family, 43,* 841–853.

Szinovacz, M. E. (1984). Changing family roles and interactions. *Journal of Family Issues, 5,* 163–201.

Takas, M. (1986, February). Divorce: Who gets the blame in "no fault"? *Ms.*, pp. 48–50, 52, 82–83.

Tanfer, K. (1987). Patterns of premarital cohabitation among never-married women in the United States. *Journal of Marriage and the Family, 49,* 483–497.

Tanfer, K., and Horn, M. C. (1985). Contraceptive use, pregnancy and fertility patterns among single American women in their 20s. *Family Planning Perspectives, 17,* 10–19.

Tannen, D. (1990). *You just don't understand: women and men in conversation.* New York: William Morrow.

Taylor, R. J., Chatters, L. M., Tucker, M. B., and Lewis, E. (1990). Developments in research on black families: A decade review. *Journal of Marriage and the Family, 52,* 993–1014.

Teachman, J. D. (1986). First and second marital dissolution: A decomposition exercise for whites and blacks. *The Sociological Quarterly, 27,* 571–590.

Teachman, J. D., and Heckert, A. (1985). The impact of age and children on remarriage: Further evidence. *Journal of Family Issues, 6,* 185–203.

Teachman, J. D., and Polonko, K. A. (1985). Timing of the transition to parenthood: A multidimensional birth-interval approach. *Journal of Marriage and the Family, 47,* 867–879.

Teachman, J. D., and Polonko, K. A. (1990). Negotiating divorce outcomes: Can we identify patterns in divorce settlements? *Journal of Marriage and the Family, 52,* 129–139.

Tennant, C. (1988). Parental loss in childhood. *Archives of General Psychiatry, 45,* 1045–1050.

This years' college freshmen: Attitudes and characteristics. (1991, January 30) *The Chronicle of Higher Education,* pp. A30–31.

Thom, M. (1988, May). The brave new world of technically assisted reproduction *Ms.*, p. 72.

Thompson, A. P. (1983). Extramarital sex: A review of the research literature. *The Journal of Sex Research, 19,* 1–22.

Thompson, L., and Spanier, G. B. (1983). The end of marriage and acceptance of marital termination. *Journal of Marriage and the Family, 45,* 103–113.

Thompson, L., and Walker, A. J. (1989). Gender in families: Women and men in marriage, work, and parenthood. *Journal of Marriage and the Family, 51,* 845–871.

Thompson, L., and Walker, A. J. (1984). Mothers and daughters: Aid patterns and attachments. *Journal of Marriage and the Family, 46,* 313–322.

Thomson, E. (1980). The value of employment to mothers of young children. *Journal of Marriage and the Family, 42,* 551–556.

Thornton, A. (1989). Changing attitudes toward family issues in the United States. *Journal of Marriage and the Family, 51,* 873–893.

Thornton, A. (1988). Cohabitation and marriage in the 1980s. *Demography, 25,* 497–508.

Thornton, A. (1977). Children and marital stability. *Journal of Marriage and the Family, 39,* 531–540.

Thornton, A., Alwin, D. F., and Camburn, D. (1983). Causes and consequences of sex-role attitudes and attitude change. *American Sociological Review, 48,* 211–227.

Thornton, A., and Camburn, D. (1987). The influence of the family on premarital sexual attitudes and behavior. *Demography, 24,* 323–340.

Thornton, A., and Freedman, D. S. (1983). The changing American family. *Population Bulletin, 38* (4), 2–37.

Thornton, A., and Freedman, D. S. (1982). Changing attitudes toward marriage and single life. *Family Planning Perspectives, 14,* 297–303.

Thornton, A., and Rodgers, W. L. (1987). The influence of individual and historical time on marital dissolution. *Demography, 24,* 1–22.

Thurman, Q. C., and Franklin, K. M. (1990). AIDS and college health: Knowledge, threat, and prevention at a northeastern university. *Journal of American College Health, 38,* 179–184.

Tiedje, L. B., Wortman, C. B., Downey, G., Emmons, C., Biernat, M., and Lang, E. (1990). Women with multiple roles: Role-compatibility perceptions, satisfaction, and mental health. *Journal of Marriage and the Family, 52,* 63–72.

Tienda, M., and Jensen, L. (1988). Poverty and minorities: A quarter-century profile of color and socioeconomic disadvantage. in G. D. Sandefur and M. Tienda (Eds.), *Divided Opportunities: Minorities, Poverty, and Social Policy* (pp. 23–62) New York: Plenum.

Ting-Toomey, S. (1983). An analysis of verbal communication patterns in high and low marital adjustment groups. *Human Communication Research, 9,* 306–319.

Titus, P. M., Fanslow, A. M., and Hira, T. K. (1989). Net worth and financial satisfaction as a function of household money managers' competencies. *Home Economics Research Journal, 17,* 309–318.

Tower, C. C. (1989). *Understanding child abuse and neglect.* Boston: Allyn and Bacon.

Tower, C. C. (1984). *Child abuse and neglect: A teacher's handbook for detection, reporting, and classroom management.* Washington, DC: National Education Association.

Tran, T. V. (1988). The Vietnamese American family. In C. H. Mindel, R. W. Habenstein, and R. Wright, Jr. (Eds.), *Ethnic Families in America,* (3rd ed.) (pp. 276–299) New York: Elsevier.

Trent, K., and South, S. J. (1989). Structural determinants of the divorce rate: A cross-societal analysis. *Journal of Marriage and the Family, 51,* 391–404.

Triedman, K. (1989, July/August). A mother's dilemma. *Ms.*, pp. 59–63.

Trost, J. E. (1986). What holds marriages together? *Acta Sociologica, 29,* 303–310.

Trost, J. E. (1975). Married and unmarried cohabitation: The case of Sweden, with some comparisons. *Journal of*

Marriage and the Family, 37, 677–682.

Trussell, J. (1988). Teenage pregnancy in the United States. *Family Planning Perspectives, 20,* 262–272.

Trussell, J., Hatcher, R. A., Cates, W., Jr., Stewart, F. H., and Kost, K. (1990). Contraceptive failure in the United States: An update. *Studies in Family Planning, 21,* 51–54.

Trussell, J., and Kost, K. (1987). Contraceptive failure in the United States: A critical review of the literature. *Studies in Family Planning, 18,* 237–283.

Trussell, J., and Westoff, C. F. (1980). Contraceptive practice and trends in coital frequency. *Family Planning Perspectives, 12,* 246–249.

Tucker, M. B., and Taylor, R. J. (1989). Demographic correlates of relationship status among black Americans. *Journal of Marriage and the Family, 51,* 655–665.

U. S. Bureau of the Census. (1991a). *Statistical abstract of the United States, 1991.* (111th ed.). Washington, DC: Government Printing Office.

U. S. Bureau of the Census. (1991b). *Fertility of American women: June 1990.* Current Population Reports, Series P-20, No. 454. Washington, DC: Government Printing Office.

U. S. Bureau of the Census, (1990b). *Measuring the effect of benefits and taxes on income and poverty: 1989.* Current Population Reports, Series P-60, No. 169-RD. Washington, DC: Government Printing Office.

U. S. Bureau of the Census. (1990a). *Statistical abstract of the United States, 1990.* (110th ed.). Washington, DC: Government Printing Office.

U. S. Bureau of the Census, (1989d). *Changes in American family life.* Current Population Reports, Series P-23, No. 163. Washington, DC: Government Printing Office.

U. S. Bureau of the Census. (1989c). Marital status and living arrangements: March, 1988. Current Population Reports, Series P-20, No. 433. Washington, DC: Government Printing Office.

U. S. Bureau of the Census. (1989b). *Statistical abstract of the United States: 1989.* (109th ed.). Washington, DC: Government Printing Office.

U. S. Bureau of the Census. (1989a). Households, families, marital status, and living arrangements: March, 1989. Current Population Reports, Population Characteristics, Series P-20, No. 441. Washington, DC: Government Printing Office.

U. S. Bureau of the Census. (1988). *Statistical abstract of the United States: 1988.* (108th ed.). Washington, DC: Government Printing Office.

U. S. Bureau of the Census. (1988). Households, families, marital status and living arrangements: March 1988 (advance report). Current Population Reports, Population Characteristics, Series P-20, No. 432. Washington, DC: Government Printing Office.

U. S. Bureau of the Census. (1987). Male-female differences in work experience, occupation, and earnings: 1984. Current Population Reports, Series P-70, No. 10. Washington, DC: Government Printing Office.

U. S. Bureau of the Census, (1980). *Statistical abstract of the United States: 1980.* (101st ed.). Washington, DC: Government Printing Office.

U. S. Bureau of the Census. (1975). *Historical statistics of the United States, colonial times to 1970, part 1.* Washington, DC: Government Printing Office.

U. S. Department of Health, Education, and Welfare. (1973). *Work in America.* Cambridge, MA: MIT.

U. S. Department of Health and Human Services, National Center on Child Abuse and Neglect. (1988). *Study findings, study of national incidence and prevalence of child abuse and neglect.* Washington, DC: Government Printing Office.

U. S. Department of Labor, Bureau of Labor Statistics. (1991). *Employment and Earnings,* 38 (October). Washington, DC: Government Printing Office.

U. S. Department of Labor, Bureau of Labor Statistics. (1990). *Employment and earnings,* 37 (April). Washington, DC: Government Printing Office.

U. S. Department of Labor, Bureau of Labor Statistics. (1985). *Handbook of labor statistics.* Bulletin 2217. Washington, DC: Government Printing Office.

U. S. Department of Labor, Bureau of Labor Statistics. (1983). *Handbook of labor statistics.* Bulletin 2175. Washington, DC: Government Printing Office.

U. S. News & World Report. (1990, January 15). A fresh shot at full equality. p. 12.

U. S. News & World Report. (1989, August 21). Breaking barriers in the barracks. pp. 26–27.

U. S. Senate Special Committee on Aging. (1986). *Aging America, trends and projections.* 1985–86 edition. Washington, DC: Government Printing Office.

Udry, J. R. (1981). Marital alternatives and marital disruption. *Journal of Marriage and the Family, 43,* 889–897.

Udry, J. R. (1980). Changes in the frequency of marital intercourse from panel data. *Archives of Sexual Behavior, 9,* 319–325.

Udry, J. R., and Billy, J. O. G. (1987). Initiation of coitus in early adolescence. *American Sociological Review, 52,* 841–855.

Udry, J. R., Billy, J. O. G., Morris, N. M., Groff, T. R. and Raj, M. H. (1985). Serum androgenic hormones motivate sexual behavior in adolescent boys. *Fertility and Sterility, 43,* 90–94.

Udry, J. R., Deven, F. R., and Coleman, S. J. (1982). A cross-national comparison of the relative influence of male and female age on the frequency of marital intercourse. *Journal of Biosocial Science, 14,* 1–6.

Udry, J. R., and Morris, N. M. (1978). Relative contribution of male and female age to the frequency of marital intercourse. *Social Biology, 25,* 128–134.

Udry, J. R., Talbert, L. M., and Morris, N. M., (1986). Biosocial foundations for adolescent female sexuality. *Demography, 23,* 217–227.

Uhlenberg, P. (1980). Death and the family, *Journal of Family History, 5,* 313–320.

Umberson, D., and Hughes, M., (1987). The impact of physical attractiveness on achievement and psychological well-being. *Social Psychology Quarterly, 50,* 227–236.

Umberson, D. and Gove, W. R. (1989). Parenthood and psychological well-being: Theory, measurement, and stage in the family life cycle. *Journal of Family Issues, 10,* 440–462.

United Nations. (1991). *1989 demographic yearbook.* 41st Issue. New York: United Nations.

UPI, (1986, August 28). Marriage bed not a boon to pair's sex life, study says. *The Denver Post* p. 19A.

Urban, M. (1990, January 28). The price of a wedding. *The Argus Leader* p. 26.

Valentine, B. (1978). *Hustling and other hard work: Lifestyles in the ghetto.* New York: Macmillan.

van de Kaa, D. J. (1987). Europe's second demographic transition. *Population Bulletin, 42* (1), 1–57.

Vanagel, G. W. (1987). Alimony terminated for unmarried cohabitation. *South Carolina Law Review, 39* (1), 76–80.

Vance, E. B., and Wagner, N. N. (1976). Written descriptions of orgasm: A study of sex differences. *Archives of Sexual Behavior, 5,* 87–98.

Vandell, D. L., Henderson, V. K., and Wilson, K. S. (1988). A longitudinal study of children with day-care experiences of varying quality. *Child Development, 59,* 1286–1292.

Vanek, J. (1974). Time spent in housework. *Scientific American, 231* (5), 116–121.

Vaughan, D. (1986). *Uncoupling: How relationships come apart.* New York: Vintage Books.

Veevers, J. D. (1973). Voluntarily childless wives: An exploratory study. *Sociology and Social Research, 57,* 356–366.

Vega, W. A. (1990). Hispanic families in the 1980s: A decade of research. *Journal of Marriage and the Family, 52,* 1015–1024.

Vemer, E., Coleman, M., Ganong, L. H., and Cooper, H. (1989). Marital satisfaction in remarriage: A Meta-analysis. *Journal of Marriage and the Family, 51,* 713–725.

Ventura, J. N. (1987). The stresses of parenthood reexamined. *Family Relations, 36,* 26–29.

Verbrugge, L. M. (1979). Marital status and health. *Journal of Marriage and the Family, 41,* 267–285.

Veroff, J., Douvan, E., and Kulka, R. A. (1981). *The inner American: A self-portrait from 1957 to 1976.* New York: Basic Books, Inc.

Very, D. L. (1982). *The legal guide for the family.* Garden City, NY: Doubleday.

Visher, E. B., and Visher, J. S. (1979). *Stepfamilies: A guide to working with stepparents and stepchildren.* New York: Brunner/Mazel.

Voydanoff, P. (1987). *Work and family life.* Family Studies Text Series 6. Newbury Park, CA: Sage.

Waite, L. J., Haggstrom, G. W., and Kanouse, D. E. (1985). The consequences of parenthood for the marital stability of young adults. *American Sociological Review, 50,* 850–857.

Waldrop, J. (1991, April). Stalking the stork: Infertility in America. *American Demographics, 13,* p. 20.

Waldrop, J. (1989, March). Inside America's households. *American Demographics, 11,* pp. 20–27.

Waldrop, J., and Exter, T. (1990, January). What the 1990 census will show. *American Demographics, 12,* pp. 20–30.

Wallace, P. M., and Gotlib, I. H. (1990). Marital adjustment during the transition to parenthood: Stability and predictors of change. *Journal of Marriage and the Family, 52,* 21–29.

Waller, W. (1937). The rating dating complex. *American Sociological Review, 2,* 727–734.

Wallerstein, J. S., and Blakeslee, S. (1990). *Second chances: Men, women, and children a decade after divorce.* New York: Ticknor & Fields.

Wallerstein, J. S., and Kelly, J. B. (1980). *Surviving the breakup: How children and parents cope with divorce.* New York: Basic Books.

Walsh, A., and Balazs, G. J. (1990). Love, sex, and self-esteem. *Free Inquiry, 18,* 37–41.

Walster, E., Aronson, V., Abrahams, D., and Rottmann, L. (1966). The importance of physical attractiveness in dating behavior. *Journal of Personality and Social Psychology, 4,* 508–516.

Ward, M. C. (1989). *Nest in the wind: Adventures in anthropology on a tropical island.* Prospect Heights, IL: Waveland Press.

Ward, S. K., Chapman, K., Cohn, E., White, S., and Williams, K. (1991). Acquaintance rape and the college social scene. *Family Relations, 40,* 65–71.

Watson, R. E. L. (1983). Premarital cohabitation vs. traditional courtship: Their effects on subsequent marital adjustment. *Family Relations, 32,* 139–147.

Watson, R. E. L., and DeMeo, P. W. (1987). Premarital cohabitation vs. traditional courtship and subsequent marital adjustment: A replication and follow-up. *Family Relations, 36,* 193–197.

Webster, M., Jr., and Driskell, J. E., Jr. (1983). Beauty as status. *American Journal of Sociology, 89,* 140–165.

Weinberg, M. S., and Williams, C. J. (1980). Sexual embourgeoisment? Social class and sexual activity: 1938–1970. *American Sociological Review, 45,* 33–48.

Weishaus, S. and Field, D. (1988). A half century of marriage: Continuity or change? *Journal of Marriage and the Family, 50,* 763–774.

Weiss, R. S. (1987). Men and their wives' work. In F. J. Crosby (Ed.), *Spouse, parent, worker: On gender and multiple roles* (pp. 109–121) New Haven: Yale University Press.

Weiss, R. S. (1981). The emotional impact of marital separation. In P. J. Stein (Ed.), *Single life: Unmarried adults in social context* (pp. 69–79) New York: St. Martin's Press.

Weitzman, L. J. (1985). *The divorce revolution: The unexpected social and economic consequences for women and children in America.* New York: The Free Press.

Weitzman, L. J. (1984). Sex-role socialization: A focus on women. in J. Freeman (Ed.), *Women: A feminist perspective,* (3rd ed.) (pp. 157–237) Palo Alto, CA: Mayfield.

Weitzman, L. J. (1977). Legal equality in marriage. In N. Glazer and H. Y. Waehrer (Eds.), *Woman in a Manmade World,* (2nd ed.). (pp. 287–301) Chicago: Rand McNally.

Weitzman, L. J., Eifler, D., Hokada, E., and Ross, C. (1972). Sex-role socialization in picture books for preschool children. *American Journal of Sociology, 77,* 1125–1150.

Wells, R. V. (1985). Demographic change and family life in American history: Some reflections. In *Uncle Sam's family: Issues and perspectives on American demographic history* (pp. 145–167) Albany: State University of New York Press.

Welter, B. (1966). The cult of true womanhood: 1820–1860. *American Quarterly, 18,* 151–174.

Wertz, R. W., and Wertz, D. C. (1989). *Lying in: A history of childbirth in America.* (expanded ed). New Haven: Yale University Press.

Westermeyer, J. (1987). Prevention of mental disorder among Hmong refugees in the U. S.: Lessons from the period 1976–1986. *Social Science and Medicine, 25,* 941–947.

Wetzel, J. R. (1990, March). American families: 75 years of change. *Monthly Labor Review, 113,* pp. 4–13.

Wheeler, D. L. (1990, March 21). College students put sex partner at risk of AIDS by lying about past experiences. *The Chronicle of Higher Education,* p. A15.

Whelan, E. M. (1978). *The pregnancy experience: The psychology of expectant parenthood.* New York: Norton.

White, G. L. (1980). Physical attractiveness and courtship progress. *Journal of Personality and Social Psychology, 39,* 660–668.

White, L. K. (1990). Determinants of divorce: A review of research in the eighties. *Journal of Marriage and the Family, 52,* 904–912.

White, L. K. (1983). Determinants of spousal interaction: Marital structure or marital happiness. *Journal of Marriage and the Family, 45,* 511–519.

White, L. K., and Booth, A. (1985a). The transition to parenthood and marital quality. *Journal of Family Issues, 6,* 435–449.

White, L. K., and Booth, A. (1985b). The quality and stability of remarriages: The role of stepchildren. *American Sociological Review, 50,* 689–698.

White, L. K., Booth, A., and Edwards, J. N. (1986). Children and marital happiness: Why the negative correlation? *Journal of Family Issues, 7,* 131–147.

White, L. K., and Brinkerhoff, D. B. (1987). Children's work in the family: Its significance and meaning. In N. Gerstel and H. Gross (Eds.), *Families and Work* (pp. 204–218) Philadelphia: Temple University Press.

White, L., and Keith, B. (1990). The effect of shift work on the quality and stability of marital relations. *Journal of Marriage and the Family, 52,* 453–462.

Whiteside, M. F. (1989). Family rituals as a key to kinship connections in remarried families. *Family Relations, 38,* 34–39.

Whyte, M. K. (1990). *Dating, mating, and marriage.* New York: Aldine de Gruyter.

Wilhelm, M. S., and Ridley, C. A. (1988). Stress and unemployment in rural nonfarm couples: A study of hardships and coping resources. *Family Relations, 37,* 50–54.

Williams, F. L. (1988). Helping families with financial management problems. In C. S. Chilman, F. M. Cox, and E. W. Nunnally (Eds.), *Employment and Economic Problems* (pp. 155–172) Families in Trouble Series, Volume 1. Newbury Park, CA: Sage.

Willie, C. V. (1985). *Black and white families.* Bayside, NY: General Hall.

Winnick, A. J. (1988). The changing distribution of income and wealth in the United States, 1960–1985: An examination of the movement toward two societies, separate and unequal. In P. Voydanoff and L. C. Majka (Eds.), *Families and Economic Distress: Coping Strategies and Social Policy* (pp. 232–260) Newbury Park, CA: Sage.

Witwer, M. B. (1990). Prenatal care in the United States: Reports call for improvements in quality and accessibility. *Family Planning Perspectives, 22,* 31–35.

Wolfe, D. A., Wolfe, V. V., and Best, C. L. (1988). Child victims of sexual abuse. In V. B. Van Hasselt, R. L. Morrison, A. S. Bellack, and M. Hersen (Eds.), *Handbook of Family Violence* (pp. 157–185) New York: Plenum Press.

Wolfenstein, M. (1955). Fun morality: An analysis of recent American child-training literature. In M. Mead and M. Wolfenstein (Eds.), *Childhood in Contemporary Cultures* (pp. 168–178) Chicago: University of Chicago Press.

World almanac and book of facts: 1991, The. (1990). New York: Pharos Books.

Worthington, E. L., Jr., and Buston, B. G. (1986). The marriage relationship during the transition to parenthood: A review and a model. *Journal of Family Issues, 7,* 443–473.

Wright, G. C., Jr., and Stetson, D. M. (1978). The impact of no-fault divorce law reform on divorce in American states. *Journal of Marriage and the Family, 40,* 575–580.

Wyatt, G. E. (1989). Reexamining factors predicting Afro-American and white American women's age at first coitus. *Archives of Sexual Behavior, 18,* 271–298.

Wyatt, G. E., Peters, S. D., and Guthrie, D. (1988a). Kinsey revisited, part I: Comparisons of the sexual socialization and sexual behavior of white women over 33 years. *Archives of Sexual Behavior, 17,* 201–239.

Wyatt, G. E., Peters, S. D., and Guthrie, D. (1988b). Kinsey revisited, part II: Comparisons of the sexual socialization and sexual behavior of black women over 33 years. *Archives of Sexual Behavior, 17,* 289–332.

Yamaguchi, K., and Kandel, D. (1987). Drug use and other determinants of premarital pregnancy and its outcome: A dynamic analysis of competing life events. *Journal of Marriage and the Family, 49,* 257–270.

Yogev, S. (1982). Happiness in dual-career couples: Changing research, changing values. *Sex Roles, 8,* 593–605.

Yogev, S., and Brett, J. (1985). Perceptions of the division of housework and child care and marital satisfaction. *Journal of Marriage and the Family, 47,* 609–617.

Young, K. T., and Zigler, E. (1986). Infant and toddler day care: Regulations and policy implications. *American Journal of Orthopsychiatry, 56,* 43–55.

Zarit, S. H., Todd, P. A., and Zarit, J. M. (1986). Subjective burden of husbands and wives as caregivers: A longitudinal study. *The Gerontologist, 26,* 260–266.

Zarling, C. L., Hirsch, B. J., and Landry, S. (1988). Maternal social networks and mother-infant interactions in full-term and very low birthweight, preterm infants. *Child Development, 59,* 178–185.

Zelizer, V. A. (1985). *Pricing the priceless child: The changing social value of children.* New York: Basic Books.

Zelnick, M., and Kanter, J. F. (1980). Sexual activity, contraceptive use and pregnancy among metropolitan-area teenagers: 1971–1979. *Family Planning Perspectives, 12,* 230, 231, 233–237.

Zimmerman, S. L. (1988). State level public policy choices as predictors of state teen birth rates. *Family Relations, 37,* 315–321.

Zube, M. (1982). Changing behavior and outlook of aging men and women: Implications for marriage in the middle and later years. *Family Relations, 31,* 147–156.

Zuravin, S. J. (1988). Fertility patterns: Their relationship to child abuse and child neglect. *Journal of Marriage and the Family, 50,* 983–993.

Zussman, R. (1987). Work and family in the new middle class. In N. Gerstel and H. Gross (Eds.), *Families and Work* (pp. 338–346) Philadelphia: Temple University Press.

PHOTO CREDITS

NAME INDEX

SUBJECT INDEX